THE THIRD SPRING

THE THIRD SPRING

G. K. Chesterton, Graham Greene,
Christopher Dawson, and David Jones

ADAM SCHWARTZ

The Catholic University of America Press
Washington, D.C.

Copyright © 2005
Reprinted in paperback, 2012
The Catholic University of America Press
All rights reserved
The paper used in this publication meets the minimum requirements of
American National Standards for Information Science—Permanence of
Paper for Printed Library Materials, ANSI Z39.48-1984.

∞

Library of Congress Cataloging-in-Publication Data
Schwartz, Adam, 1965–
The third spring : G.K. Chesterton, Graham Greene, Christopher Dawson, and David Jones / Adam Schwartz.
p. cm.
Includes bibliographical references and index.
ISBN 978-0-8132-1387-3 (cloth: alk. paper)
ISBN 978-0-8132-1982-0 (pbk: alk. paper)
1. Catholic converts—Great Britain—History—20th century. 2. Intellectuals—Religious life—Great Britain—History—20th century. 3. Chesterton, G. K. (Gilbert Keith), 1874–1936—Religion. 4. Greene, Graham, 1904— Religion. 5. Dawson, Christopher, 1889–1970—Religion.
6. Jones, David Michael, 1895–1974—Religion.   I. Title.

BX4668.A1S39 2005
248.2'42'092241—dc22
2004002318

For Pam, my beloved and my friend

CONTENTS

Acknowledgments		ix
Abbreviations of Frequently Cited Works		xiii
Introduction		1
1.	The Thing: Where All Roads Led G. K. Chesterton	30
2.	The Heart of the Matter: Mapping Graham Greene's Religious Journey	110
3.	Christopher Dawson's Progress in Religion: Tradition, Inheritance, and the Dynamics of World History	202
4.	Finding Harbor with a Remnant: David Jones's Religious Voyage	286
	Conclusion: "I Make Each Day My Revolution"	375
	Select Bibliography	387
	Index	411

ACKNOWLEDGMENTS

Thanks, said Chesterton, are the highest form of thought. My own thoughts are both heightened and humbled by contemplating the many debts I have incurred in composing this book. First thanks are owed to my parents, Joan Schwartz and the late Joseph Schwartz, and my late grandmother, Marie Jackson. Without their encouragement and multifarious support throughout my life, nothing I have accomplished would have been possible. I have also been blessed with caring and interested in-laws in Kay and Bob Shade, whose thoughtfulness and prayers have sustained me during difficult moments.

My thesis adviser and friend, Bill Heyck, was (and is) an ideal mentor who supplied indispensable guidance during this book's long gestation. The other members of my dissertation committee, Harold Perkin and Garry Wills, provided much useful advice and were models of scholarly excellence for their apprentice historian.

Fellow scholars of the British Catholic revival, especially Patrick Allitt, Joseph Pearce, and Ian Ker, have taught me by their writings and encouraged me by their friendly interest. I regret that Father Ker's *The Catholic Revival in English Literature* was published only after the completion of this book, as was Keith Alldritt's biography of David Jones. Several other scholars have been generous with their time and encouragement, and I thus thank David Mills, Mark Noll, Gleaves Whitney, Gregory Wolfe, and, especially, Ralph Wood for their support. Stratford Caldecott brought the eyes of both a scholar and a publisher to bear on an earlier edition of this manuscript and gave me much wise counsel about its merits and prospects. I also extend special thanks to Ian Boyd for his personal encouragement, his publication of my work in *The Chesterton Review*, and the kindness he and his fellow Basillians showed me during the month I spent with them at St. Thomas More College while I was studying Dawson's papers and library before those materials were transferred to the University of St. Thomas. Aidan Mackey was a similarly generous host when I stayed at his home in Bedford to peruse the materials held by the Chesterton Study Center.

My friends in the American Chesterton Society and the (now sadly defunct) Midwest Chesterton Society welcomed a callow scholar into their ranks and have offered much stimulating fellowship. I am grateful to all the members of those bodies, but especially to Dale Ahlquist, Sara Bowen, John Peterson, and Frank and Ann Petta.

My colleagues and students at Christendom College have been supportive of this project since my arrival in 2000. In particular, I thank Christopher Blum, John Cuddeback, William Fahey, Jay Reyes, and Trey Stanford, plus all the pupils in my courses on the Catholic Literary Revival.

The Marguerite Eyer Wilbur Foundation favored me with a fellowship in the fall of 1997 that enabled me to work on this book in the pleasant confines of the Russell Kirk Center for Cultural Renewal. I am grateful to both institutions for their support and, especially, to Annette Kirk for her continued interest and friendship.

In working in several archives in three countries, one pleasant commonalty was the helpfulness and enthusiasm of the librarians who assisted me. I hence warmly thank the staffs of the following institutions: the British Library, the National Library of Wales, the Weiner Library (London), the Marion E. Wade Center (Wheaton College), Georgetown University, the John J. Burns Library (Boston College), and St. Thomas More College (Saskatoon). The interlibrary loan departments of Northwestern University, Wheaton College, and Christendom College also provided prompt assistance in helping me obtain the resources I needed to research this project fully.

I am deeply grateful to the past and present editors of the following journals for opening their pages to a tyro as I worked on this volume: *Renascence, The Catholic Historical Review, The Chesterton Review, Logos, Faith & Reason, Thematica, Seven, Christianity & Literature, Religion and Literature, The University Bookman, Christian History,* and *Touchstone.*

I also thank the following copyright holders for allowing me to quote from material under their control: Permission to quote from the works of G. K. Chesterton was granted by A. P. Watt Ltd. on behalf of The Royal Literary Fund. Quotations from *A Historian and His World: A Life of Christopher Dawson,* by Christina Scott are © 1992 by Transaction Publishers and are reprinted by permission of the publisher. Excerpts from *The Other Man: Conversations with Graham Greene,* by Marie-Francoise Allain (trans. Guido Waldman) © 1983 by The Bodley Head, Ltd. and Simon & Schuster, Inc. are reprinted by permission of Simon & Schuster Adult Publishing Group and The Random House Group Ltd. Mrs. Catherine Trippett of Random House UK provided especially prompt and gracious assistance. Mr. Anthony Hyne, on behalf of the Trustees of the David Jones Estate, generously agreed to my use of previously unpublished Jones material.

The Catholic University of America Press has been a model of professionalism. Its director, David McGonagle, showed exemplary patience, encouragement, and integrity during the many stages of this book's journey to print. Managing editor Susan Needham offered several useful suggestions for making the manuscript more lucid and attractive. Marketing manager Beth Benevides was always full of good counsel and good cheer. Ellen Coughlin edited the manuscript lightly, yet expertly. The press's referees—Don J. Briel and Dermot Quinn—also gave very helpful advice, particularly for sharpening the Introduction.

Michael Foster and Meredith Rusoff have been stalwart, soulful friends since graduate school days. So has Gerald Russello, who also performed the yeoman task of commenting on a much longer version of this book and offered sound advice at a particularly crucial stage of this project. Their love and friendship is salutary and joyous. The Marion E. Wade Center at Wheaton College has offered not only a remarkable trove of resources and a welcome haven, but also some of the most important friendships of my life. I am thus incomparably indebted to its director, Christopher Mitchell, its associate director, Marjorie Lamp Mead, and its staff, especially Marie Benware and Alicia Pearson.

It is another (now former) Wade Center staff member, though, to whom I am most grateful. Pam Schwartz has shared all the joys and hardships entailed in composing this book, has sacrificed much to support it and its author, and has filled my life and that of our sons, Ian and James, with immeasurable love and joy. The dedication of this tome to her is a heartfelt, if entirely inadequate, attempt at repayment.

ABBREVIATIONS OF FREQUENTLY CITED WORKS

Chapter 1. G. K. Chesterton

ILN	*Illustrated London News*

Chapter 2. Graham Greene

BR	*Brighton Rock*
CE	*Collected Essays*
HC	*The Honorary Consul*
HOM	*The Heart of the Matter*
LR	*The Lawless Roads*
P&G	*The Power and the Glory*
SOL	*A Sort of Life*
WOE	*Ways of Escape*
YE	*Yours Etc.: Letters to the Press*

Chapter 3. Christopher Dawson

MOE	*The Making of Europe*
P&R	*Progress and Religion*
RMS	*Religion and the Modern State*

Chapter 4. David Jones

DG	*The Dying Gaul and Other Writings*
DGC	*Dai Greatcoat: A Self-Portrait of David Jones in his Letters*
E&A	*Epoch and Artist*
IP	*In Parenthesis*
RQ	*The Roman Quarry and Other Sequences*
SL	*The Sleeping Lord and Other Fragments*

THE THIRD SPRING

"I wish I liked Catholics more."

"They seem just like other people."

"My dear Charles, that's exactly what they're not—particularly in this country, where they're so few . . . they've got an entirely different outlook on life; everything they think is important is different from other people."

—Evelyn Waugh, *Brideshead Revisited*

"The Catholic Church! Do you consider that an alternative?"

"Well, it's a standing temptation to the intelligentsia, isn't it?"

"Not what *I* should call the intelligentsia. Though there was Eliot, of course," Ravelston admitted.

"And there'll be plenty more, you bet. I dare say it's fairly cosy under Mother Church's wing. A bit unsanitary, of course—but you'd feel safe there, anyway."

—George Orwell, *Keep The Aspidistra Flying*

"The new years walk, restoring
Through a bright cloud of tears, the years, restoring
With a new verse the ancient rhyme. Redeem
The time. Redeem
The unread vision in the higher dream."

—T. S. Eliot, "Ash Wednesday"

INTRODUCTION

UPON LEARNING in 1928 of T. S. Eliot's conversion to Christianity, Virginia Woolf wrote to her sister:

> I have had a most shameful and distressing interview with poor dear Tom Eliot, who may be called dead to us all from this day forward. He has become an Anglo-Catholic, believes in God and immortality, and goes to church. I was really shocked. A corpse would seem to me more credible than he is. I mean, there's something obscene in a living person sitting by the fire and believing in God.[1]

Woolf's dismissal of belief in traditional Christianity as a distressing obscenity was typical of British intellectuals' attitudes during her era. From Arnold Bennett to Bertrand Russell, from G. B. Shaw to H. G. Wells, the day's cultural leaders tended to see dogmatic religion as so much shameful hidebound superstition that people must be liberated from for the sake of their own well-being and society's progress. As Adrian Hastings notes,

> the principal intellectual (as distinct from social) orthodoxy of England in the 1920s was no longer Protestantism, nor was it catholicism or any other form of Christianity. It was a confident agnosticism.... To believe meant standing out against every single one of the giants of modernity, the prophets who had established the framework of understanding wherein which intellectual discourse, the whole modern civilization of the mind, seemed now established.... The 1920s, as a consequence, were the first decade in which the overturning of Chris-

---

1. Virginia Woolf to Vanessa Bell, 11 February 1928; *The Letters of Virginia Woolf*, ed. Nigel Nicholson and Joanne Trautmann (New York: Harcourt Brace Jovanovich, 1977), 457–58.

tianity effectively achieved by the previous generation could be, and was, openly accepted as a fact of modern life.

In short, "Modernity had simply no place for religion in general or Christianity in particular."[2]

Yet Eliot's action was not as anomalous as it may seem initially. Despite this hostile cultural atmosphere, a substantial number of prominent thinkers reared in the late-Victorian and Edwardian eras still chose to become Christians (and Catholic Christians) as adults, especially during the century's unpropitious early decades. As John Wolffe explains, twentieth-century British culture is marked by the paradox that "at a time when official churches were numerically in retreat and culturally insecure, a significant number of writers and artists still found considerable inspiration in the Christian tradition . . . the shoreline of the continent of faith had now retreated to form a large island."[3] Even more apparently paradoxical is the fact that a disproportionate number of these voyagers migrated to the Roman Catholic Church's section of that atoll: those eventually so drawn included Evelyn Waugh, Eric Gill, Ronald Knox, Edith Sitwell, Malcolm Muggeridge, Frederick Copelston, and E. F. Schumacher. After all, in modern times this church has never contained more than 10 percent of the British population, was the target of popular riots as late as 1868, and was increasingly at odds with its age's governing assumptions and attitudes. Its ability to attract such a large portion of these generations' leading minds into its ranks at a time when contrary convictions were at their apex is thus a cultural phenomenon that requires more adequate explanation than it has hitherto received.

Certainly there had been previous notable British Roman Catholic converts in the modern era. The "Second Spring" proclaimed by John Henry Newman (1801–1890), for instance, featured the receptions of eminent Victorian writers, such as Coventry Patmore, Alice Meynell, William Ward, even Aubrey Beardsley and Oscar Wilde, despite the fre-

---

2. Adrian Hastings, *A History of English Christianity, 1920–1985* (London: Collins, 1986), 221–22, 224.

3. John Wolffe, *God and Greater Britain: Religion and National Life in Britain and Ireland, 1843–1945* (London: Routledge, 1994), 211.

quent familial and social ostracism their choices occasioned. Newman's was the most prominent conversion, and it was driven by concern that what he called "liberalism" was ascendant: "the anti-dogmatic principle and its developments," like disregard for "authority and precedent,"[4] plus what he deemed a naive "dream" of "our race's progress and perfectibility."[5] Newman felt that Protestantism had become possessed of this liberal zeitgeist in its denial of a definitive center of doctrinal authority, and he thus moved from an early evangelicalism to believing that orthodox Catholic theology alone could uphold effectively the dogmatic principle and what he saw as its developments of respect for authority, tradition, and a tragic view of life. After years of study and spiritual struggle, he concluded reluctantly that only the Roman form of Catholicism had an authenticating historical link to Christ and His apostles; he was received into that church in 1845.

Judging the Church not only a source of personal salvation, but also "a working instrument in the course of human affairs, for smiting hard and throwing back" liberal thinking, Newman asserted clearly the contrast between his new faith's principles and those apparently dominant in his time.[6] But, despite what he saw as his age's irreligious bent, Newman posited that since "Catholicity is the only divine form of religion," it could eventually redeem the modern epoch without compromising orthodoxy.[7] Being a unique body of permanent truth, he felt, Catholicism could adjust its focus to meet each era's exigencies without sacrificing its doctrinal integrity. To him, then, the modern Church must simultaneously staunchly rebut norms contrary to orthodoxy while not despairing of its ability to resacralize an increasingly non-Christian society through persistent, resonant presentation of its ever-ancient, ever-new beliefs. To that end, Newman not only adopted this persona of a rebel against modernity's preeminent values, but he also used prophetic

---

4. John Henry Newman, *Apologia Pro Vita Sua*, ed. A. Dwight Culler (Boston: Houghton Mifflin, 1956), 65–66, 357.

5. Newman quoted in M. D. Aeschliman, "The Prudence of John Henry Newman," *First Things* no. 45 (August–September 1994): 37.

6. Newman, *Apologia*, 233.

7. Newman quoted in Robert Pattison, *The Great Dissent: John Henry Newman and the Liberal Heresy* (Oxford: Oxford University Press, 1991), 185.

tropes both to condemn continued cultural adherence to liberalism and to proclaim Roman Catholicism the best foundation for reconstituting a traditional, Christian culture.[8]

As the nineteenth century ended and the twentieth began, however, not only did the general dissatisfaction with modern society that Newman had expressed become more widespread in Britain, but so did rejection of the traditional Christianity that he had embraced as an alternative to it. After a century of almost constant growth, Britain's economy began to undergo a domestic and a relative international decline around 1870. Due primarily to competitors' tariffs, an unprotected home market, and a complacency toward technical innovation and education, British manufacturing grew at a rate of only 1.8 percent between 1875 and 1913, compared with its peak performance of 3.5 percent in 1813–17 and 1845–49.[9] Making matters worse was the contemporaneous rise of Germany and the United States, who posted growth rates of 3.9 percent and 4.8 percent respectively during this period. Britons understood the implications of this downturn and related their growing disquiet to it. They "knew that something was amiss and had reason to believe that their discontents, political as well as social and economic, had something to do with contemporary economic trends."[10] Their discontents were cultural too, as these economic developments undercut the material conditions that had abetted the rise of an optimistic, progressive mentality in the mid-Victorian era, and thus helped foster rethinkings of that outlook.

Evolutionary theory, for instance, began to take on a more pessimistic cast to many. Whereas science and evolution had once been equated with progress, numerous late-Victorians and Edwardians, seeing decline in other areas, explored Darwinism's dark side. As Michael Ruse notes, "Throughout the popular and not-so-popular literature of the time we

---

8. The best narratives of Newman's life and beliefs are Ian Ker, *John Henry Newman: A Biography* (Oxford: Oxford University Press, 1988); and Sheridan Gilley, *Newman and His Age* (London: Darnton, Longman & Todd, 1990). Pattison, *Great Dissent*, offers the most complete account of his rebuttal of liberalism and modernity.

9. Harold Perkin, *Origins of Modern English Society* (1969; reprint, London: Ark, 1985), 411–13.

10. Harold Perkin, *The Rise of Professional Society: England Since 1880* (London: Routledge, 1989), 37–38.

find constant reflections of the strife, fear, and failure that were the lot of so many."[11] The religious implications of these altered attitudes were especially unsettling. Evolutionism had already destroyed the idea of providential design for many; and the newly heightened stress on struggle and randomness in nature weakened further any vestigial belief in nature's ultimate benevolence. Moreover, biblical higher criticism simultaneously posed a radical challenge to traditional understandings of Christianity and the authorities behind them, even as scholarship in comparative religions questioned customary conceptions of Christian uniqueness. Finally, certain traditional Christian teachings—particularly the Atonement and Hell—were increasingly judged immoral. Hence, many Britons in the late nineteenth and early twentieth centuries faced what seemed to be a much more insecure life than had been assumed previously; but they did so without credible ancestral religious explanations or sources of certainty.

Although orthodox Christianity was ebbing less quickly at the popular level, most intellectuals joined the likes of Woolf in continuing to see it as on the wane when confronting their day's changed cultural conditions. Some mandarins, like Shaw, Wells, and Russell, remained proponents of a progressive worldview, particularly belief in scientific enlightenment and socialism. At the other extreme were frank pessimists like Thomas Hardy, or the self-styled Last Romantics, who sought to preserve art for a better day in the indeterminate future. Other romantics, like William Morris and G. D. H. Cole, turned to the past and hoped to reestablish medieval institutions like guilds, but with a socialist rather than a religious base. Still other thinkers desired detachment from the temporal itself and adopted fresh spiritualistic, theosophical, and vitalistic views, while T. H. Green inspired some Idealists to recast religion as a sense of civic duty and a devotion to social reform, a chord echoed by movements such as the Labor Churches that were animated by a commitment to political relevance. Some similar orienting principles, like George Orwell's democratic socialism, lamented the effects of traditional Christianity's putatively permanent decay, and aimed to conserve salu-

---

11. Michael Ruse, *The Darwinian Revolution* (Chicago: University of Chicago Press, 1979), 205.

tary aspects of its moral code in a credible, secular guise. The likes of Kipling and Cecil Rhodes looked abroad for meaning, confessing faith in taking up Britain's new imperial burden. Even among Christians, the rising force in most Protestant denominations were those (like the New Theologians) who advocated some form of liberal Christianity that tried to reconcile their faith with the this-worldly and demythologizing bents that held sway in the sciences and scholarship. Underlying all these responses, though, was a common renunciation of traditional, dogmatic Christianity. As Jung put it in 1933, "the passionate interest in these movements arises undoubtedly from the psychic energy which can no longer be invested in obsolete forms of religion. . . . The modern man abhors dogmatic postulates taken on faith and the religions based upon them."[12]

Yet the more such attitudes were accepted by many of the modern literati, the more radically were they rejected by a conspicuous minority of cultured Britons. Such thinkers were convinced that orthodox Christianity best accounted for their civilization's growing disenchantment, and provided a superior alternative way of life and thought. They were hence alarmed by the apparently prevalent a priori exclusion of customary religious categories from intellectual discourse, fearing that it augured an unprecedentedly secularized culture: like T. S. Eliot, they felt that twentieth-century men had left God for no god, and that this had never happened before. And as traditional Christianity and the principles associated with it seemed increasingly embattled, a growing segment of those so attracted to its ideals were drawn to what seemed the most authoritative, adamant defender of them: Roman Catholicism.

Sensing that dogmatic Christianity's cultural prestige had declined precipitously, even since Newman's day, a considerable number of intellectuals concluded in the new century's first decades that any compromise with ascendant unbelief would be tantamount to capitulation to it. They thus deduced (unlike Eliot) that the survival and revival of ancestral convictions and values required embracing the only version of Christianity that they thought oppugned modern irreligion at its foundations, and was strong enough to withstand its challenge. As James

---

12. C. G. Jung, *Modern Man in Search of a Soul*, trans. W. S. Dell and Cary F. Baynes (1933; New York: Harcourt, Brace & World, 1966), 206–7.

Hitchcock observes, "what most of these converts appear to have seen in Catholicism . . . is precisely some reality or vision which is not modern. They have made the judgment that modern culture, in its secularity, is radically truncated, lacking in some awareness of reality which most societies of the past possessed" but that this church alone upheld unequivocally in their day.[13] From apparently barren ground for cultivating Roman Catholics, then, came a fresh blooming of the Church's seed, one fertilized, to some extent, by those who sought to exterminate it. Out of a winter of discontent, a Third Spring was born.

It was precisely Roman Catholicism's perceived willingness to swim against what these converts considered their day's prevailing cultural currents that made this "rejected minority" so compelling to them.[14] Conversion scholar Karl Morrison maintains that all conversions are shaped by "the particular environment in which the experience and the understanding took place;"[15] and William James suggested that the kind of environment these authors discerned when they made their decisions would have made resistance to modernity seem the only way to preserve any religious sensibility. According to James, acceptance of "pessimistic and materialistic beliefs," which appeared dominant when the converts were growing up, inhibits development of the psyche's religious faculty, to the point where, with persistent accommodation of such ideas, "personal energy never gets to its religious center, and the latter remains inactive in perpetuity."[16] Whether this analysis is entirely correct or not, it does capture the converts' sense that they could not reconcile their age's governing secularity with beliefs they found expressed most fully in traditional Christianity. It explains as well the rationale behind their subsequent searches for a form of that faith that would endure, and would allow them to channel their personal energy in religious directions without the sensed blockage of attempted placations of unbelief.

---

13. James Hitchcock, *The Recovery of the Sacred* (New York: The Seabury Press, 1974), 26–27.

14. Edward Norman, *Roman Catholicism in England* (Oxford: Oxford University Press, 1985), 1.

15. Karl Morrison, *Understanding Conversion* (Charlottesville: University Press of Virginia, 1992), xxii.

16. William James, *The Varieties of Religious Experience* (1902; reprint, New York: Mentor, 1958), 168.

Although bearing many affinities to the Second Spring, then, the early-twentieth-century converts were not simply its successors. They all knew of Newman's work, and some were swayed strongly by it. But each man also responded to his day's specific circumstances, especially the discerned consolidation of culturally regnant confident agnosticism. While Newman's fears about liberalism foresaw this development to some degree, some other notable nineteenth-century converts, like George Tyrrell, had hoped to harmonize Roman Catholicism and such worldly philosophies. By contrast, irreligion's apparent pervasiveness in the early-twentieth-century climate of opinion convinced nearly all of that period's prospective Catholic converts that both individuals and British culture as a whole must now opt conclusively for either modern secularity or Roman Catholic orthodoxy. Thinkers drawn to the Church in the twentieth century's dawning decades were therefore almost exclusively those enticed by its own increasingly radical rebuttal of prevalent norms, as epitomized by Pius X's 1907 decrees *Lamentabili Sane Exitu* and *Pascendi Dominici Gregis*. Thus, while surely part of a heritage that reaches back to Newman and his age, these converts also felt that they confronted a more all-encompassing kind of secularism than any of the Victorians had envisioned, and hence an even deeper, more starkly polarized, cultural crisis than their predecessors had faced. Their decisions thus illustrate Hugh McLeod's hypothesis that "the most decisive secularization may cause dissatisfactions that prepare the way for ultimate revival."[17]

Among this cluster, four particularly illustrate how certain prominent writers from disparate backgrounds and genres followed the common early-twentieth-century pattern of dismay with modern secularity, search for an affirmative alternative, and ultimate acceptance of Roman Catholicism as the culmination of countercultural convictions: journal-

---

17. Hugh McLeod, "Secular Cities? Berlin, London, and New York in the Later Nineteenth and Early Twentieth Centuries," in *Religion and Modernization: Sociologists and Historians Debate the Secularization Thesis*, ed. Steve Bruce (Oxford: Clarendon Press, 1992), 86.

Sheridan Gilley comments cogently that "militant secularism" of the sort that became common in the twentieth century was "a tiny movement on the fringes" of even late-Victorian intellectual and religious life ("William Morris and the Mid-Victorian Crisis of Faith," *Chesterton Review* 25 [August 1999]: 326).

ist and man of letters G. K. Chesterton (1874–1936), novelist Graham Greene (1904–1991), historian and cultural analyst Christopher Dawson (1889–1970), and poet David Jones (1895–1974). These men's trainings and temperaments were as varied as the fields in which they worked: from the Oxford-educated Greene and Dawson to the autodidacts Chesterton and Jones, from the gregarious jolly journalist to the hermetic poet. Moreover, their mutual discontent with modern culture had diverse roots, as each author focused primarily on different—even conflicting— aspects of the modern temper that were nonetheless common departures from traditional Christian orthodoxy.

Chesterton, for instance, fought chiefly against the pessimistic spiritualism that he first detected in, and in reaction to, *fin-de-siècle* aestheticism, decadence, and impressionism, and that he later discerned in theological and literary Modernism. In response, he sought a proper understanding of the balance between the spiritual and the secular in both the psyche and the culture, plus the best expression of his childlike gratitude for the bare fact of existence. Greene saw his youth's progressive rationalism as insensitive to the human malevolence that he experienced early and remained acutely conscious of, and as hostile to mystical realities. He thus pursued a compelling explanation of evil's existence and persistence, along with a due regard for suprarational mysteries. Dawson became dissatisfied with his inherited religion when it appeared to be accepting his age's growing antipathy to dogma and the past. His goal, then, was an authoritative, centripetal theology and tradition that affirmed the importance of history and culture and religion's role in them. Finally, Jones found the faith of his father to be insufficiently sacramental and hence ill-equipped to combat ascendant mechanistic utilitarianism. He therefore searched for a sacral system that stressed a vital, integrated continuity between Heaven and earth, past and present, and myth and fact, and the consequent centrality of artistic craftsmanship. Uniting these converts' heterogeneous journeys, however, was a shared sense that the day's dominant cultural trends were imperiling cherished beliefs that were grounded in decisive personal, frequently youthful, episodes; that orthodox Christianity offered an intellectual and spiritual framework for upholding these ostensibly threatened ideals; and that Roman Catholicism was the kind of Christianity most committed corporately and constitutionally in their epoch to resisting modern movements resolutely, and to conserving ancient norms. All four, then, considered Roman Catholicism a foremost source of cultural rejuvenation.[18]

Yet their decisions were not simply tactical maneuvers in a culture war. All of them believed in Roman Catholicism's truth claims sincerely. In particular, its incarnational, sacramental perspective shaped their worldviews decisively, as they sought to engage their age without being conformed to it. Regarding their era's ruling secularist norms as antithetical to this faith they considered true, the converts' religious and cultural judgments were hence inextricable: "They took doctrine seriously and identified the Catholic Church as doctrinally right. . . . They also became convinced that Catholicism, the traditional faith of their civilization, was its binding force. A dogmatic church would protect them—first spiritually, and by extension, politically—from the chaotic forces loose in the twentieth-century world."[19] Roman Catholicism was thus for each man what Peter Berger calls a "nomos": a meaningful order that comprehends and integrates the whole of a person's experiences and beliefs, both spiritual and material.[20] Their decisions to convert reflected their faiths' multifaceted nature. Each author's choice was a result of both studying Catholic teachings intently and being moved by the personal examples of Catholics whom he knew prior to his reception. Though all of them tended to stress intellectual motives, both these aspects were essential; for, as conversion theorist Emilie Griffin remarks, "authentic conversion involves both the mind and the heart . . . it is not one element of the person but the whole person—mind, heart, and will" that is transformed.[21]

---

18. In large measure, then, these authors all exemplified T. S. Eliot's idea of "the Christian thinker": "He finds the world to be so and so; he finds its character inexplicable by any non-religious theory: among religions he finds Christianity, and Catholic Christianity, to account most satisfactorily for the world and especially for the moral world within. . . ." Eliot, *Essays: Ancient & Modern* (London: Faber & Faber, 1936), 146.

19. Patrick Allitt, *Catholic Converts: British and American Intellectuals Turn to Rome* (Ithaca, N.Y.: Cornell University Press, 1997), 162–63.

20. Peter Berger, *The Sacred Canopy: Elements of a Sociological Theory of Religion* (Garden City, N.Y.: Anchor Books, 1969), 19, 54.

21. Emilie Griffin, *Turning: Reflections on the Experience of Conversion* (New York: Doubleday, 1980), 51.

Among the converts' peers, even some who did not adopt, and in some cases harshly criticized, their particular vision, acknowledged its impact on their age's thought. Hannah Arendt, for instance, argued in 1945 that "as far as polemics go these Catholic converts or neo-Catholics have come out as victors."[22] Even more strikingly, despite his 1940 contention that the atmosphere of orthodoxy is "completely ruinous to the novel,"[23] Orwell nevertheless concluded eight years later that

> a fairly large proportion of the distinguished novels of the last few decades have been written by Catholics and have even been describable as Catholic novels ... the conflict not only between this world and the next world but between sanctity and goodness is a fruitful theme of which the ordinary, unbelieving writer cannot make use.[24]

As such testimony suggests, Roman Catholic rebellion against modern unbelief was a persistent presence in twentieth-century British culture; and if that era's intellectual milieu is to be understood fully, then this portion of it must be explored more thoroughly than has been done thus far. Tracing these four converts' intellectual biographies will reveal their work's common themes, even as each man's specific contribution is also clarified. These descriptions of how their religious views and cultural criticism developed will hence not only demonstrate how this single faith united people of various origins and interests, but will also enrich comprehension of each author's thought and the contexts in which he worked by seeing him as part of a broader dissenting community of discourse.

Few scholars, however, have shared Arendt's and Orwell's strong sense of the converts' presence in Britain's cultural landscape. Indeed, Tom Buchanan could claim as late as 1996 that "British twentieth-century Catholicism has been strangely neglected by historians."[25] Moreover,

---

22. Hannah Arendt, "Christianity and Revolution," *The Nation*, 22 September 1945; in *Essays in Understanding*, ed. Jerome Kohn (New York: Harcourt Brace & Co., 1994), 152.

23. George Orwell, "Inside the Whale," in *The Collected Essays, Journalism and Letters of George Orwell*, ed. Sonia Orwell and Ian Angus (New York: Harcourt, Brace & World, 1968), 1: 518.

24. Orwell, "The Sanctified Sinner," in *Collected Essays*, 4: 439.

25. Tom Buchanan, "Great Britain," in *Political Catholicism in Europe, 1918–1965*, ed. Tom Buchanan and Martin Conway (Oxford: Clarendon Press, 1996), 249.

most studies of twentieth-century British Roman Catholicism that do exist are sociological or synthetic examinations that offer glances at the convert-dominated literary revival, but provide no extensive investigation of it as a cultural phenomenon.[26] Those works that do focus more on the intellectual and cultural aspect of the Church's modern British renascence usually treat individual authors and/or genres in isolation, not as part of Catholic or counter-modern communities of discourse in Britain.[27] What collective treatments do exist are marred by various deficiencies: they are either dated irredeemably;[28] so schematic as to prevent detailed analysis of any specific thinker;[29] written to edify (or debunk) rather than foster

26. See, e.g., Norman, *Roman Catholicism*; Michael Hornsby-Smith, *Roman Catholics in England* (Cambridge: Cambridge University Press, 1987), and *Roman Catholic Beliefs in England* (Cambridge: Cambridge University Press, 1991); *Catholicism in Britain and France Since 1789*, ed. Frank Tallett and Nicholas Atkin (London: Hambledon Press, 1996); Kenneth Hylson-Smith, *The Churches in England from Elizabeth I to Elizabeth II*, vol. 3, *1833–1998* (London: SCM Press, 1998); *Catholics in England, 1950–2000*, ed. Michael Hornsby-Smith (London: Cassell, 1999); *From Without The Flaminian Gate: 150 Years of Roman Catholicism in England and Wales, 1850–2000*, ed. V. A. McClelland and M. Hodgetts (London: Darnton, Longman & Todd, 1999); David Mathew, *Catholicism in England: The Portrait of a Minority: Its Culture and Tradition* (London: Eyre & Spottiswoode, 1936, 1948); E. I. Watkin, *Roman Catholicism in England from the Reformation to 1950* (Oxford: Oxford University Press, 1957). The latter two volumes are of interest more as examples of relatively minor members of the twentieth-century revival discussing its antecedents and prospects *in media res*.

27. See, e.g., Conor Cruise O'Brien, *Maria Cross: Imaginative Patterns in a Group of Catholic Writers* (London: Burns & Oates, 1963); Gene Kellogg, *The Vital Tradition: The Catholic Novel in a Period of Convergence* (Chicago: Loyola University Press, 1970); Richard Johnstone, *The Will to Believe* (Oxford: Oxford University Press, 1982); Thomas Woodman, *Faithful Fictions: The Catholic Novel in British Literature* (Philadelphia: Open University Press, 1991); Theodore Fraser, *The Modern Catholic Novel in Europe* (New York: Twayne, 1994).

28. Chief among these is Calvert Alexander, *The Catholic Literary Revival* (Milwaukee: Bruce Publishing Co., 1935). The pioneering work in this field, it still deserves attention for its attempt to see these modern converts as part of a single movement. But an analysis with no mention of Greene's work that was written two years before Jones published his first poem is obviously inadequate as an assessment for readers nearly seventy years later.

29. The best surveys of this topic are Allitt, *Catholic Converts*, and Joseph Pearce, *Literary Converts* (London: HarperCollins, 1999); but their decisions to prioritize breadth over depth by supplying a series of sketches of convert thinkers precludes thorough discussion of any particular writer's life and views.

Maurice Cowling's work also suffers deeply from this flaw. His appraisals tend to be glib, resulting from a breezy portrayal of authors' work that he admits "ignores subtleties" and "puts a straitjacket on literature and refuses to linger over its complications." This highly impressionistic approach produces curious, and insufficiently substantiated, assertions, such

critical understanding of these figures or the movement they helped constitute;[30] or contain some combination of all these shortcomings. They are also generally inattentive to the extensive theoretical research done on the theology and psychology of conversion, while often being detached from these very public intellectuals' historical, cultural, and intellectual settings.

The work of Chesterton, Greene, Dawson, and Jones is particularly amenable to a collective, in-depth, interdisciplinary understanding of the renewal of orthodox Roman Catholicism in early-twentieth-century Britain as a form of rebellion against modern secularism that shaped both the spiritual and cultural views of those who chose to profess it as adults. While all four were public intellectuals, Chesterton cultivated this role most deliberately, and his ensuing contributions to every literary genre make him an inescapable presence in modern British letters, be it as a novelist, literary critic, poet, dramatist, biographer, historian, or social critic. Moreover, Greene, Dawson, Jones, and nearly all other leading Catholic and Christian writers (as well as many non-Christians) from this period expressed an explicit debt to Chesterton's work. Finally, Chesterton is a generational bridge from the Newman era to the thinkers born slightly later than he was (even if Dawson and Jones did formally precede him into the Church). As William Blissett puts it, "Chesterton marks the end of the Oxford Movement"; but he was also among the first shoots of the Third Spring.[31]

In the fields of history and poetry, no Roman Catholic seedlings grew so tall as Dawson or Jones. No other Catholic historian in twentieth-century Britain had Dawson's range of interest and competence, or the level and scope of respect that he earned across the ideological spectrum. Some in a later generation have tried to accord Paul Johnson like

---

as that the contributions of Chesterton, Greene, and Dawson are "ultimately insubstantial" (Cowling, *Religion and Public Doctrine in Modern England* [Cambridge: Cambridge University Press, 1985], 2: xvi, 308).

30. See, e.g., Patrick Braybrooke, *Some Catholic Novelists: Their Art and Outlook* (Milwaukee: Bruce Publishing Co., 1931); Mariella Gable, *This Is Catholic Fiction* (New York: Sheed & Ward, 1948); Joseph Foster, *Contemporary Christian Writers* (New York: Hawthorn Books, 1963); Kathleen Nott, *The Emperor's Clothes* (Bloomington: Indiana University Press, 1954).

31. William Blissett, "David Jones and the Chesterbelloc," *Chesterton Review* 23 (February–May 1997): 32.

stature, but Dawson's work was more capacious and less partisan. His true peers are Tawney and Toynbee, as the latter acknowledged. Similarly, no Roman Catholic poet in this period wrote verse as textured as Jones's nor gained a comparable amount of acclaim from notable contemporaries. If less famous than Eliot or Auden, his poetry's quality matches theirs, as they recognized. Among fiction writers, it might be argued that Waugh reproached modernity even more thoroughly than Greene did. Yet, as Patrick Allitt argues cogently, Greene's rebellion was actually more radical than Waugh's: whereas Waugh's laments tended to focus more on the outward eclipse of historical Christendom's rites and institutions, Greene probed more deeply and wrote "in a mood of estrangement from a civilization that, as he drew it, had always been inimical to Christian truth and in which the man or woman of genuine faith had always been an alien."[32] In addition, Greene's Catholicism was the heart of the matter of most of his novels, whereas Waugh's faith was as central to only two.[33]

What about other fields of humane letters?[34] Ironically, no significant theologian or philosopher sprouted during the Third Spring. Ronald Knox was a graceful apologist and a prodigious Biblical translator, yet even he did not undertake systematic theology. Sheridan Gilley suggests that this surprising lack of original theological speculation stemmed from theologians having been "generally marginal to English culture";[35] whatever its cause, the absence of a British counterpart to continental thinkers like Yves Congar, Karl Rahner, and Hans Urs von Balthasar con-

---

32. Allitt, *Catholic Converts*, 280. Greene's inclusion also fills a scholarly gap noted by Allitt, that he has not yet been studied as a figure in "British or Atlantic Catholic history or . . . the history of conversion" (ibid.).

33. Evelyn Waugh, *Brideshead Revisited* (London: Chapman & Hall, 1945); and *Unconditional Surrender* (London: Chapman & Hall, 1961).

34. Besides literary intellectuals, there were, of course, plastic artists (like Gill) who were also converts and cultural critics. A complementary assessment of their responses to modern civilization, however, demands the more specific methodology of the art historian and is a potentially fertile, if currently fallow, field of inquiry. For a prolegomenon to such a study, see Edward Yarnold, "The Catholic Cultural Contribution: Architecture, Art, Liturgy and Music," in McClelland and Hodgetts, *Flaminian*, 320–45.

35. Sheridan Gilley, "The Roman Catholic Church in England, 1780–1940," in *A History of Religion in Britain*, ed. Sheridan Gilley and W. J. Sheils (Oxford: Blackwell, 1994), 356. Cf. Allitt, *Catholic Converts*, 11, 161.

firms Edward Norman's judgment that twentieth-century British Roman Catholicism saw a "paucity of inventive theological writing."[36] Likewise, Copelston's exhaustive history of philosophy is a monumental synthesis, yet it, like most of his other works, was more a descriptive commentary than an original treatise.[37] Future ages may rank G. E. M. Anscombe and John Finnis among the twentieth century's premiere British philosophers, but they are of a different generation (as is theologian Aidan Nichols). While Schumacher's seminal efforts in the alternative economics movement make him a noteworthy contributor to the Roman Catholic rebellion against irreligious mores during this era, his Catholicism was much more eclectic, syncretistic, and seemingly tactical than the more customary version other converts subscribed to.[38] Finally, Muggeridge's high media profile, especially in broadcasting, gave his apologetics and cultural commentary wide exposure, but most of these utterances came before his relatively late reception into the Church (in 1982); his thought is also imbued with a dualism at odds with traditional Catholic orthodoxy.[39]

Evaluating these four intellectuals' individual and collective contributions to British culture seems especially appropriate now that some historical perspective on their whole careers is possible, and also because of a growing acceptance of, and interest in, such topics. Anthony Grafton argues that, until lately, there has been hostility to studying modern Roman Catholic thought:

---

36. Norman, *Roman Catholicism*, 124.

37. Frederick Copelston, *A History of Philosophy*, 9 vols. (Westminster, Md.: Newman Press, 1946–75). For a critical analysis of his work, see E. B. F. Midgley, "Concerning the Philosophy of Father Copelston," parts 1 and 2, *Chesterton Review* 10 (November 1984): 438–43; 11 (February 1985): 87–91. An overview of Roman Catholic philosophy during this period is found in Michael Hodgetts, "The Iron Form: Catholics and Philosophy Between the Councils," in McClelland and Hodgetts, *Flaminian*, 84–107.

38. According to Meredith Veldman, "Schumacher joined the Roman Catholic church for the sake of his wife and for the sake of his work. He believed fewer people would dismiss him as a 'crank' if he spoke as a Roman Catholic rather than a Buddhist," though the Buddhist element of his thought remained strong, for "he believed that religious truth was not confined to Christianity alone" (Veldman, *Fantasy, the Bomb, and the Greening of Britain: Romantic Protest, 1945–1980* [Cambridge: Cambridge University Press, 1994], 278).

39. See Adam Schwartz, "The Muggeridge Conundrum," *Touchstone* 11 (March–April 1998): 37–40.

modern Catholic culture—like most Catholics—was usually disdained, as the province of lesser breeds fit only for the legendary parochial schools where nuns told their charges never to order ravioli on a date, lest their boyfriends be reminded of pillows. Stereotypes and prejudices of this kind, as nasty as anything fastened upon Jews, persisted in American universities until an uncomfortably recent date.[40]

If he is correct in suggesting that greater academic receptiveness to investigating modern Catholicism now exists, it appears at an especially propitious moment for historians of Britain; for, as T. W. Heyck has noted, "the history of religion in Britain—as distinct from church or ecclesiastical history—is making an impressive comeback in the consciousness of historians, with important implications for British cultural and social history. Not least affected is the history of Britain in the twentieth century."[41]

In particular, analysis of this twentieth-century intellectual and cultural flowering of Roman Catholicism impinges on the burgeoning scholarly debate concerning whether or not modern Britain has been, or is, a "post-Christian" society. In a now landmark volume, Alan Gilbert posited in 1980 that modern Britain has undergone a process of progressive secularization. He held that congruity existed between Christian theology and prepotent cultural norms in the Middle Ages, but that the Reformation eliminated the defined center of authority on which this integration depended. With sacred and profane now distinct spheres, he argued, the scientific revolution and the Enlightenment facilitated secularization further by filling in "gaps" in human understanding with natural and rational explanations of phenomena previously accounted for in supernatural terms. For Gilbert, industrialization abetted this process of "modernization," as it fostered a mechanical mindset while attendant developments like urbanization and specialization broke down traditional community ties, including religious ones, and made religion only another, optional compartment of life. The end result, to him, was an ostensibly unique kind of culture, one in which some sort of secular hu-

---

40. Anthony Grafton, "The Soul's Entrepreneurs," *New York Review of Books* 41 (3 March 1994): 34.

41. T. W. Heyck, "The Decline of Christianity in Twentieth-Century Britain," *Albion* 28 (Fall 1996): 437.

Introduction 17

manism had become the dominant outlook. He thus dubbed the Britain of his day a "post-Christian" society:

> a post-Christian society is not one from which Christianity has departed, but one in which it has become marginal. It is a society where to be irreligious is to be normal, where to think and act in secular terms is to be conventional, where neither status nor respectability depends upon the practice or profession of religious faith.[42]

Gilbert contended that churches had two choices when facing this phenomenon. They could, as most mainline Protestant denominations did, "accommodate" it. Such liberal churches "avoid fundamental opposition to the conventional morals, values, and proprieties of the age." He felt that accommodation by the churches to a world grown more secular was "the dominant trend in modern British religious history;" but his conviction that "'modernity' is . . . emphatically secular" led him to conclude that accommodating it had vitiated the beliefs and behaviors that people had historically considered religious, thereby undermining these churches' once-distinctive cultural role:

> the secularization of theology passed the point beyond which there is simply no powerful ideological reason for calling people out of the "world" into a denominational "Church" . . . today denominational religion is little more than one of a growing number of equally legitimate leisure time pursuits, one of a range of recreational cultures in a situation of cultural pluralism.[43]

Yet Gilbert also thought that churches could choose the path of "resistance." Unlike a denomination, whose raison d'être disappears with accommodation, "when a Church accepts that its environment really has become post-Christian, the radical course of thorough-going sectarianism may indeed be the best way to maximize its residual cultural influence." Gilbert claimed that such a sect will be composed of those already alienated from the mainstream culture, or at least amenable to its censure; he concluded that the modern Church must adopt this model to remain viable: it must "accept a prophetic relationship with the dom-

---

42. Alan Gilbert, *The Making of Post-Christian Britain* (London: Longman, 1980), 19, 26–27, 24, 34–37, 45, 83–84, 65, 38–39, xii, 38, ix.

43. Ibid., 103, 105, 36–37, 123, 113.

inant culture.... It must be as much counter-cultural as it is, inescapably, sub-cultural," even if "the world may never be greatly influenced" by its dissent. Among rebellious, prophetic faiths, Gilbert singled out Roman Catholicism as one that "generally has stood firm against the temptation to compromise with the emerging post-Christian culture," even as it had not forsaken hope of transforming that milieu eventually.[44]

Other analysts of British religion have challenged Gilbert's thesis, disputing both his equation of the admitted decline of traditional Christianity with secularization, and his preference for resistance to this development.[45] Yet, whether he or his detractors are more precise, his paradigm—in which the modern mentality based on the decay of definitive dogmatic standards, unaided reason, material progress, and a mechanistic metaphysic is deemed inherently irreligious and dominant in his day; in which accommodation of it is the inclination and the fatal flaw of mainline Protestantism; and in which Roman Catholics resist it radically to uphold traditional Christianity—is an uncanny echo of the early-twentieth-century Catholic converts' outlook. However sound as sociology, Gilbert's theory resonates historically with the cultural gestalt configured by those modern British protesters who chose to become Roman Catholics as adults.[46] His unconscious participation in this heritage implies that scholars of the "post-Christian" question will profit from greater study of the intellectual and cultural history of twentieth-

---

44. Ibid., 134, 152, 66, 138. More recently, Linda Woodhead and Paul Heelas have crafted a model akin to Gilbert's. To them, "religions of humanity," including liberal Christianity, have a bent toward accommodating modern secular humanism, whereas "religions of difference," like orthodox Roman Catholicism, tend to be "differentiated from [the] wider society" (Linda Woodhead, "Convergences between Christianity and the New Age," *Chesterton Review* 26 [February & May 2000]: 76).

45. See, e.g., Grace Davie, *Religion in Britain Since 1945: Believing Without Belonging* (Oxford: Blackwell, 1994); Wolffe, *God and Greater Britain*, 255–58; Paul Badham, "Religious Pluralism in Modern Britain," in Gilley and Sheils, *History of Religion*, 488–502. See also Gilbert's reply to some of the criticism of his thesis in "Secularization and the Future," in Gilley and Sheils, *History of Religion*, 503–21. For a helpful sampling of the broader scholarship on this general topic, see Bruce, *Religion and Modernization*, passim.

46. It should be noted that Gilbert has expressed alarm at hopes for "desecularization," a goal that the orthodox Roman Catholic converts supported implicitly and explicitly: "the kind of demodernization which would radically reverse the process of secularization might prove catastrophic for civilization as a whole" ("Secularization and the Future," 520).

century British religion (particularly its Roman Catholic facet) than has been displayed thus far by such critics, most of whom have focused on statistical and sociological data.

Given this perception that their society was—or was fast becoming—post-Christian, it is crucial to stress that these converts selected a specific kind of Roman Catholicism, one especially suited to their radical resistance of this sensed secularization. Numerous scholars have echoed independently Gilbert's judgment that most mainline Protestant denominations, including Anglicanism, sought to accommodate worldliness in twentieth-century Britain, but that Roman Catholicism generally resisted it.[47] Yet insufficient notice has been taken of the fact that the species of Catholicism that bloomed during the Third Spring was a transplant. The man most responsible for the institutional replanting of Catholicism in Britain was Nicholas Wiseman (1802–1886). Though raised in Britain, he was educated in Rome and lived there for twenty-two years. Through frequent trips to Britain, he was instrumental in building support for a revitalized church and, when the hierarchy was restored in 1850, Wiseman was named its head. His long experience and love of Italian Catholicism, though, led him to use it as a model for the Church's reconstituted British branch. Whereas British Roman Catholicism since the Reformation had been generally pragmatic, not especially concerned with ecclesiastical matters, cool to papal primacy, and favorable to a modus vivendi with the larger culture, Wiseman imported and attempted to make normative a vastly different sensibility: his vision of the church under his stewardship was hierarchical, focused on the papacy, and acutely conscious of its separation from the British mainstream.[48]

---

47. See, e.g., Alexander, *Catholic Revival*, 4; Horton Davies, *Worship and Theology in England* (Princeton, N.J.: Princeton University Press, 1965), 5: 261; George Scott, *The R.C.s.* (London: Hutchison & Co., 1973), 13; John Stevenson, *British Society 1914–45* (Harmondsworth: Penguin, 1984), 369; Hastings, *English Christianity*, 227, 279; Jonathan Rose, *The Edwardian Temperament, 1895–1919* (Athens: Ohio University Press, 1986), 30; Hugh Kenner, *A Sinking Island: The Modern English Writers* (Baltimore: Johns Hopkins University Press, 1987), 224; Wilfrid Sheed, "Portrait of the Artist as a Self-Made Man," *New York Review of Books* 40 (16 December 1993): 28; Fraser, *Modern Catholic Novel*, 68.

48. Although these traits were not exclusive to Italian Catholicism, their predominance in that nation's ecclesiastical style was Wiseman's proximate inspiration for the renascent British Church.

This outlook displeased the cisalpine Old Catholics, like Lord Acton, and it failed to foster a substantial pragmatic infrastructure.[49] But it captivated converts, who were "anxious to luxuriate in everything which differentiated themselves from the English religion they had abandoned."[50] Given that, as conversion theorist Walter Conn puts it, "the conversion decision constitutes the personal subject with a particular standpoint and direction" that establishes his horizon on the world, this sort of Catholicism held a special appeal for the early-twentieth-century converts, who sought a standpoint as at odds with their understanding of modern culture as possible.[51] In eschewing not only Protestantism and secularism, but also the kind of Catholicism long prevalent in their native land, these authors were defining themselves as, in some crucial way, fundamentally unlike all their British contemporaries. As Arendt described their view, "their task [was] to become true revolutionaries, that is, more radical than the radicals. . . . The great advantage of these neo-Catholic writers was that when they went back to Christianity they broke with the standards of their surroundings more radically than any other sect or party."[52]

The Italianate model of the Church's stress on definitive authority was especially crucial for the early-twentieth-century converts. Though he was not similarly inclined, Orwell recognized the attraction a tightly structured institution promising certainty and clarity could have for those disturbed by the decline of ancestral sources of meaning:

> But what do you achieve, after all, by getting rid of such primal things as patriotism and religion? You have not necessarily got rid of the need for *something to believe in*. . . . It is significant that these people went almost invariably to the Roman Church, and not, for instance, to the C of

---

49. Adrian Hastings, "Some Reflections on the English Catholicism of the Late 1930s," in *Bishops and Writers: Aspects of the Evolution of Modern English Catholicism*, ed. Adrian Hastings (Wheathampsted-Hertfordshire: Anthony Clarke, 1977), 115.

50. Norman, *Roman Catholicism*, 84. See also Bernard Bergonzi, "The English Catholics," *Encounter* 24 (January 1965): 20–21.

51. Walter Conn, *Christian Conversion* (New York: Paulist Press, 1986), 192. Walter Brueggemann offers further theoretical insight on this point: "accepting identity as an exile . . . is an act of polemical theological imagination that guards against cultural assimilation." *Hopeful Imagination: Prophetic Voices in Exile* (Philadelphia: Fortress Press, 1986), 110–11.

52. Arendt, "Christianity and Revolution," 153–54.

E, the Greek Church or the Protestant sects. They went, that is, to the Church with a world-wide organization, the one with a rigid discipline, the one with power and prestige behind it.[53]

To Orwell's convert contemporaries, this staunch form of Roman Catholicism was a sharp contrast with what seemed their day's centrifugal intellectual pluralism and the Protestant churches (and even some secular protesters, like Orwell) they thought had accepted it, plus Protestant latitudinarianism generally. But embracing this type of religion also differentiated their approach from the British Old Catholic "commonsense adjustment" to other sensibilities: the converts saw such a strategy as inappropriate for secularism's heyday, deeming it a lax form of accommodation with inherently incompatible ideals that required the restraining hand of a firm, centralized dogmatic leadership.[54] In their minds, then, the Italianate style was the current expression of traditional Christianity best suited to twentieth-century Britain's cultural condition. Although this identification with a foreign model of church government helped spur "No Popery" riots when it was first established and made British Roman Catholics consistently susceptible to the charge of dual loyalty, the converts, at least, considered its distinctiveness from modern Britain's reigning principles its great virtue. For them, this kind of Roman Catholicism accented those elements of its ancient body of beliefs that their age lacked but needed most, especially a strong sense of authority. As Hastings concludes, "Its very authoritativeness was what appealed. They found in it a sure framework for spiritual progress, literary creativity and political stability, but also for an ordered and coherent view of the world to replace the increasing intellectual and ideological confusion evident outside the walls."[55]

Yet it was not the only belief system offering intellectual and ideological certitude during the century's disconcerting first decades. Some secularist ideologies also promised surety in the form of immanentized political and scientific eschatologies. These worldviews were especially alluring to many of the converts' peers who were equally dismayed by

---

53. Orwell, "Inside the Whale," 515. Emphasis in original.
54. Norman, *Roman Catholicism*, 84.
55. Hastings, *English Christianity*, 279–80.

the demise of established standards of belief and behavior, but considered their traditional Christian expression impatient of resurrection. More accommodationist churches were hesitant in dealing with these rivals due to their lack of firm countervailing doctrines. But the Roman Catholics' own sense of certainty made them confident in characterizing, and combating, such movements as fanciful, facile counterfeit faiths. As Gilley summarizes,

> The whole significance of conversion subtly changed in the 1920s, when there were strong new intellectual currents, Fascist and Communist. . . . Roman Catholicism [had] the polemical advantage of knowing its own mind with a degree of intellectual sophistication at a time when other churches seemed increasingly a prey either to fundamentalism or doubt . . . in a Protestant nation, so much of the responsibility of defending orthodox Christian doctrine now rested upon Roman Catholics.[56]

The converts thought these new secularist dogmas had some of the same developments as liberal anti-dogmatism, and they deemed their creed a superior authoritative, integrating teleology to either mindset on two key counts. First, they held that Catholicism is more sensitive to the human capacity for evil than its adversaries' bent toward belief in the temporal perfectibility of mankind. As Arendt put it, "The insistence of the Christian doctrine on man's limited condition was somehow enough of a philosophy to allow its adherents . . . [to] realize that a pursuit of happiness which actually means to wipe away all tears will pretty quickly end by wiping out all laughter."[57] Besides being more aware of the tragic nature of life, they felt, their religion also defied the modern denigration of tradition that liberal and synoptic ideologies participated in. Whereas the secular modernist thought that the past must be superseded for genuine advance to occur, the Catholic convert contended, with Eliot, that the way forward is the way back. As Eliot noted, this stress on tradition was a chief attraction of Catholicism to thinkers who chose it, in either Anglo or Roman form, as adults. Despite disagreeing about the

---

56. Sheridan Gilley, "The Years of Equipoise, 1892–1943," in McClelland and Hodgetts, *Flaminian*, 41–43.

57. Arendt, "Christianity and Revolution," 154.

ultimate temporal provenance of Catholic authority, both groups saw Catholic Christianity as the best conservator of Christendom's religious and cultural heritage:

> It is always the main religious body which is the guardian of more of the remains of the higher developments of culture preserved from a past time before the division took place.... Hence it is that the convert ... of the intellectual or sensitive type is drawn towards the more Catholic type of worship and doctrine.[58]

Thus, even as some early-twentieth-century intellectuals saw Caesar or science as sources of certainty and hope, those skeptical of materialism, progress, and the human potential for earthly perfection often found orthodox Catholicism a more satisfactory center of surety. To them, the secular certain trumpet blew a siren's song.[59]

The Roman converts' rejection of alternate secularist teleologies reveals further how utter their repudiation of modern ideals was. Yet they were not simply naysayers. Edward Said has remarked that an intellectual must be a rebel against prevailing ideas;[60] these four authors' attempted subversion of regnant irreligious beliefs exemplifies a specific conception of what a rebel is. Albert Camus defined a rebel as "a man who says no, but whose refusal does not imply a renunciation. He is also a man who says yes, from the moment he makes his first gesture of rebellion." A nihilist also says no to his time, but renounces any hope of redeeming it; the rebel's "preoccupation is to transform" his era. Hence, when negating his age's ascendant mores, the rebel is simultaneously affirming an alternative set of norms by which he has judged contemporary standards wanting, and that ground his envisioned cultural transformation:

---

58. T. S. Eliot, *Christianity and Culture* (New York: Harcourt Brace Jovanovich, 1988), 155. See also O'Brien, *Maria Cross*, 225; and James Hitchcock, "Post-Mortem on a Rebirth," *American Scholar* (Spring 1980): 213, 225.

59. A companion volume to this history will treat the four converts' social criticism, and thus analyze their more specific critiques of systems like Fascism, Communism, and political and economic liberalism.

60. Edward Said, *Peace and Its Discontents* (New York: Vintage, 1996), 184. Historian Tony Judt agrees: "for a long time, the notion of dissidence was built into the idea of being an intellectual." Judt quoted in Alan Riding, "Where Writers Leave Their Imprint on Events," *New York Times* (24 January 1998), A17.

"from the moment that the rebel finds his voice . . . he begins to desire and to judge . . . every act of rebellion tacitly invokes a value . . . [which is] the affirmation implicit in every act of rebellion."[61]

Although (at least when he penned these words) Camus did not believe that Christianity could be a source of rebellion, and while none of the converts appear to have been influenced directly by his paradigm, his theory nonetheless describes precisely Chesterton's, Greene's, Dawson's, and Jones's attitude toward their epoch. Their "no" to modern unbelief was a "yes" to traditional notions of human nature and ways of life and thought, values that they invoked to judge the post-Christian world deficient and that they found voiced best by a particular form of Roman Catholicism: it was this faith that seemed the best hope for promoting their desired transformation of their culture. Though they vowed not to compromise its tenets in pursuing that goal, they did not consider even their confidently agnostic age incapable of eventual conversion and hence asserted their alternative affirmations persistently. These writers, then, believed more in *rinnovamento* than *aggiornamento*, thinking that the twentieth-century Church existed in living continuity with its past and hence could be sensitive to current conditions without forsaking its ancestral teachings.[62] They were thus simultaneously conservative and radical: each did uphold traditional Roman Catholicism, yet not because it was hoary, but because he saw this ancient creed as a truer view of God and man than that offered by reigning irreligion, one that hence confronted secularism at its philosophical roots, and thereby provided a comprehensive alternative intellectual framework and ethical code.

Thus, unlike some of the pessimistic ideologies they opposed, the converts' condemnations of modern mores were always intertwined with overt or tacit commendation of traditional options. As Catholicism is an everlastingly valid vision of reality, they felt, it not only preserves the wisdom of the past, but is dynamic enough to translate inherited

---

61. Albert Camus, *The Rebel: An Essay on Man in Revolt*, trans. Anthony Bower (New York: Vintage, 1956), 13, 10, 14, 16.

62. This distinction between renewal and bringing up to date was made originally, in a different context, in Philip Daniel, "Have We Seen the Death of Dialogue?" in Hornsby-Smith, *Catholics in England*, 95.

truths into each time's unique idiom, and thus could transform even an epoch currently under the sway of secular skepticism. Already as an Anglican, Newman had held that "mere negatives" were insufficient, but that "it was necessary for us to have a positive Church theory erected on a definite basis," a traditional fundament that some "might call a revolution, while I thought it a restoration."[63] Yet, as Garry Wills explains, to Newman and the later converts alike, these terms were synonymous: for them, "every rebellion is a conservation: one preserves being by perfecting its vessels, not by simply destroying them. . . . The deepest radicalism is a *return* to roots, not simple deracination."[64]

While, as Morrison has shown, "even in its scriptural origins, the paradigm or morphology of Christian conversion was also subversive . . . [it has] consistently set the righteousness of the saving remnant against the wickedness of the many," Calvert Alexander argued in 1935 that this persona had particular resonance for early-twentieth-century converts.[65]

> [T]he attitude of the rebel and the heretic, always popular since the fall of man, has in our own century reached its apogee; the impression prevails that the heretic, the man in revolt, is always right. . . . What the Catholic must do is to erect the supposedly heretical doctrine of the moderns into the most intolerant species of dogma[,] . . . insist on his position as a rebel against the rule of the pontiffs,

and thereby hope to gain a sympathetic hearing for what he sees as genuine orthodoxy.[66] Moreover, Morrison maintains further that in the Old Testament model of conversion adopted by Christianity, "the heroic ideal was the prophet," a rhetorical role that all these converts assumed at points and on which some of them reflected often.[67] Indeed, Walter Breuggemann's analysis of the prophetic imagination suggests crucial affinities between the rebel and prophet roles. In Breuggemann's view, prophets too try to subvert prevalent norms on behalf of a contrary outlook grounded in tradition: "The task of prophetic ministry is to nur-

---

63. Newman, *Apologia*, 113, 167.
64. Garry Wills, *Chesterton: Man and Mask* (New York: Sheed & Ward, 1961), 95, 102. Emphasis in original.
65. Morrison, *Understanding Conversion*, 6, 22.
66. Alexander, *Catholic Revival*, 285.
67. Morrison, *Understanding Conversion*, 19.

ture, nourish and evoke a consciousness and perception alternative to the consciousness and perception of the dominant culture," attitudes that simultaneously radically criticize that governing order and radically galvanize people to realize a replacement rooted in the society's "deepest memories." Furthermore, the prophet, also like the rebel, does not despair of his audience: he activates the ancestral symbols "that have always been the basis for contradicting the regnant consciousness" by "rearticulating the old story"[68] in a current idiom, so that "the speaking and hearing are done with fresh imagination, with new power, and with authorizing energy that takes us by surprise."[69]

Attention to these roles and other metaphors and motifs that the converts used frequently is essential, despite whatever demurrals from them the writers offered. As Morrison concludes, the actual experience of a person's conversion is inaccessible to its students. Careful concentration on the language used in its presentation is hence crucial to grasping how authors understood (and wanted others to understand) their decision, its motivation, and its effects on them: "[being] detached from the event of conversion, scholars could never know what happened but only what they found in the texts before them, which, however accurate in statement, were always poetic fictions, always works of narrative composed by inclusion, omission, and deployment."[70] As Hayden White observes, the tropes a writer uses in crafting such accounts often help explain why these inclusions and omissions have occurred and been deployed in certain ways: they "exploit a certain perspective on the world that does not pretend to exhaust description or analysis of all the data in the entire phenomenal field but rather offers itself as *one way among many* of disclosing certain aspects of the field."[71] This heightened sensitivity to a thinker's rhetoric thus helps reveal his distinct standpoint by highlighting the core beliefs and experiences common to a convert's writings on dis-

---

68. Walter Brueggemann, *The Prophetic Imagination* (Philadelphia: Fortress Press, 1978), 13, 66, 77.

69. Walter Brueggemann, *Finally Comes the Poet: Daring Speech for Proclamation* (Minneapolis: Fortress Press, 1989), 138.

70. Morrison, *Understanding Conversion*, 4.

71. Hayden White, *Tropics of Discourse* (Baltimore: Johns Hopkins University Press, 1978), 46. Emphasis in original.

parate topics, plus the assumptions he made about his age when addressing it.

Although many individual twentieth-century Anglicans—like Eliot, Auden, C. S. Lewis, Dorothy L. Sayers, and Charles Williams—also found their faith amenable to the assumption of roles like rebel and prophet as they disclosed aspects of their own protests against post-Christianity, their Catholic counterparts felt that only in Rome was there a company dedicated to counter-modern action. To them, Roman Catholicism, especially its Italianate version, was the form of Christianity best structured constitutionally to guard its traditional beliefs against the encroachment of noxious notions, due to its stress on a single, central determiner of dogmas. In contrast, they sensed that the Anglican church was finding it increasingly difficult to establish definitive doctrines at a time when they considered such certainty imperative; they hence deemed their day's Anglicanism more vulnerable to predominant ideas that they judged inimical to historical orthodoxy. Radical, corporate resistance to secularizing mores was thus a constituent element of Roman Catholic identity in the century's young years, but was not a necessary facet of the Anglican outlook. From this perspective, then, the converts' Anglican allies in cultural subversion were a collection of loosely linked partisans, whereas the Roman Catholics belonged to a highly organized guerrilla force with a clear center and chain of command.

The Roman converts' fealty to this specific type of their adopted faith, though, made them wary of different models of the Church that eventually started to supplant it. Commencing in the 1950s and accelerating with the aftermath of the Second Vatican Council in the 1960s, the Catholic Church, both in Britain and globally, began to move away from the Italianate paradigm into which the converts had been received. Although Greene, Dawson, and Jones did not oppose change as such, each was distressed when the Church altered some disciplinary and liturgical practices in ways they considered imprudent accommodations of increasingly pervasive secularist biases, like disregard for tradition and promotion of a less numinous, more utilitarian aesthetic. What had been a certainty for them, that the Roman Catholic Church would defend traditional Christianity steadfastly against such profane pressures, now seemed less sure, and their consequent frustration was great. Wills summarized their reaction to these developments as they were unfolding: "This church seemed to offer men some obscure pledge of the relevance of older things. What, then, is the world to make of Rome calling herself irrelevant? The North Star has not only dimmed, but wandered."[72]

Knox identified the root of his fellow converts' dismay presciently and acutely in 1950:

> In one way or another, they are in reaction from the world about them, and the Church attracts them, partly at least, because she takes a more intelligible, a more acceptable line.... But almost always they exaggerate the extent of her protest, and when they get to know her better, they find her less intransigent than they thought.[73]

Yet the protest against a world grown more irreligious and insensitive to its patrimony that Greene, Dawson, and Jones had found ratified by Roman Catholicism in the century's first years remained a powerful shaping presence in their religious imaginations. Their rebuttals of secularism had become so intermixed with their religious beliefs that they judged their persistent rebellion a sounder Catholic approach to post-Christian culture than the more conciliatory attitude that some Church leaders and laity favored increasingly in later decades, even though preserving this position often precipitated feelings of disappointment and isolation. Although Chesterton did not live to see these changes, his successors' disquiet at alleged accommodations of modern mistakes within a chosen church was substantially akin to his rationale for leaving Anglicanism in the 1920s (though none of the other three went so far as to depart from Rome over this issue).

Understanding why a Third Spring blossomed unexpectedly in early-twentieth-century Britain requires attention to each discrete flower and to their common roots. These four authors did not agree in all areas, and telling their tales does not cancel the need to chronicle those of other Roman Catholic converts from this period. But a detailed, collective comprehension of why these four diverse thinkers each chose the same

---

72. Garry Wills, "Catholic Faith and Fiction," *New York Times Book Review*, 16 January 1972, 1.

73. Ronald Knox, *A Spiritual Aeneid* (1950; reprint, London: Sheed & Ward, 1958), xix.

unpopular religion as the framework for his contributions to twentieth-century British culture will not only deepen understanding of their individual efforts, but will also begin the process of seeing them—and their like-minded peers—as members of an interconnected movement of rebellion against modern secularism. In embracing a form of Roman Catholicism radically unlike the ideologies and British religions of their day, Chesterton, Greene, Dawson, and Jones found what they considered an authoritative source of both personal religious meaning and moral imagination; and this faith also provided a transcendent, tragic, traditional teleology that they proposed when opposing their epoch's regnant norms, a vision they voiced in the hope of revitalizing their culture without vitiating what they deemed its subversive vitality. Though fellow dissidents preferred other kinds of Christianity or nonreligious convictions when articulating a similar protest and strategy of rebellious prophecy, these four were persuaded fully only by a specific sort of Roman Catholicism. The Italianate model of the Church that they encountered when seeking a satisfying expression of their mingled fears and hopes about their ostensibly post-Christian era became and remained their standard for judging both religion and culture, despite eventual changes in each. Believing (with Yeats) that their days were dragon-ridden, these self-styled guerrillas of grace sharpened the swords of the spirit and of imagination on the rock of Peter, hoping that what they considered their contemporary crusades would make them swords of honor.

CHAPTER I

THE THING

Where All Roads Led G. K. Chesterton

ONE OF Chesterton's many complaints about modern society was that its journalism told people that a man had died before they knew that he had lived. Yet in his own case, his end is the best beginning for understanding his life and work. On 27 June 1936, thirteen days after his death, a stately memorial service was held at Westminster Cathedral. Ronald Knox (one of the two people whom Chesterton credited most for his reception into the Catholic Church) preached a panegyric that attempted to assess Chesterton's significance to his culture. Against frequent dismissals of Chesterton as a "master of paradox," or "the wit of Beaconsfield," Knox contended that he was primarily a metaphysical and religious thinker. To Knox, his greatest gift was "illuminating the ordinary, of finding in something trivial a type of the eternal.... If you look at a thing nine hundred and ninety-nine times, you are perfectly safe; if you look at it the thousandth time, you are in frightful danger of seeing it for the first time." Knox asserted that when Chesterton saw the Catholic Church with this child's-eye view, he became officially what he always was at heart: "He looked for the thousandth time at the Catholic faith and for the first time he saw it . . . it took him fourteen years after the publication of his book *Orthodoxy* to find out that he ought to be in Rome." Yet at all points on that long journey, "he saw his religion everywhere; it mattered furiously to him" and grounded all he did. Anchored in the sane balance of orthodoxy, Knox argued, Chesterton could rebel against current commonplaces like Progress, industrialism, and imperialism, making him "a prophet in an age of false prophets."[1] Chesterton, by this reading then, was an apostle of wonder at the joy of Being who found this metaphysical insight deepened by Roman Catholic theology; and these beliefs were his chief weapons in a rebellion against modernity to which he summoned his fellow Britons through his voluminous writings.

Even allowing for the hyperbole common to eulogies, Knox's tribute helps establish a framework for reconsidering Chesterton's conversion(s) and discovering how this process of spiritual unfolding manifested itself in his cultural criticism, even as many of the rhetorical modes and roles he adopted remained constant. Chesterton's philosophical and religious development went through distinct stages that need to be defined more accurately than has been done hitherto, as his spiritual story has yet to be described systematically, and earlier accounts are often marred by interpretive missteps. As James Thompson argues, "Chesterton's spiritual biography . . . has yet to be written."[2] Doing so will not only show his growth into Roman Catholicism, but will also illuminate how his religious voyage and views shaped his intellectual vision, intersected with

---

1. Ronald Knox, *Captive Flames* (London: Burns Oates, 1940), 147, 148, 144–45.
2. James Thompson, introduction to *The Collected Works of G. K. Chesterton*, vol. 3 (San Francisco: Ignatius Press, 1990), 16. Among the major critical studies of Chesterton's work, none make the history of his religious opinions central to its discussion. Although his biographers, necessarily, deal with this topic, each account has significant flaws, whether of chronology, inattention to detail, or misreading of crucial events, as this analysis will address more specifically when treating his spiritual development's particular stages.

his appraisal of his climate of opinion and molded his approach to the broad range of genres in which he expressed that worldview. Yet at all stages of these investigations, and in whatever medium he was working, Chesterton used the metaphors of sanity, rebellion, and prophecy to articulate his disquiet with modern secularism. He thus became a key link in the chain of modern British Catholic cultural dissent.

The road to Rome that he traversed began in his childhood liberal Christianity. This set of beliefs, though, was destroyed by an intellectual and spiritual crisis he underwent while at the Slade School of Art, an episode that was the pivotal event of Chesterton's life. In his recovery from this trauma, he formulated his philosophy of gratitude that eventually led him to theism and then to orthodox Christianity. His journey's final stages were his search for the truest expression of orthodoxy, which he found in Catholicism, first in its Anglo style and ultimately in its Roman form.

"Agnosticism Was an Established Church": A Post-Christian Childhood

Chesterton admitted to a "dim subconscious sympathy with any sort of religion" from childhood on, but described the cultural atmosphere of his youth as distinctly post-Christian. He held that there was "nothing new or odd about not having a religion.... We might almost say that agnosticism was an established church."[3] His upper-middle-class parents, Edward and Marie Chesterton, tended toward Unitarianism and what his brother, Cecil, called "a vague but noble theo-philanthropy."[4] Yet young Gilbert's notebooks display a strong interest in more traditional religious subjects and symbols, ranging from Francis of Assisi to chalices and the Crown of Thorns, and he had at least some curiosity about orthodox Christianity. He commented in his youthful diary on attending a High Church communion service (even if he was rather hostile to Roman Catholicism as a boy), and he voiced some early misgivings about

---

3. *The Collected Works of G. K. Chesterton*, vol. 16, *The Autobiography of G. K. Chesterton* (San Francisco: Ignatius Press, 1988), 188, 140. See also G. K. Chesterton, *Illustrated London News*, 18 September 1920 *(ILN)*.

4. Cecil Chesterton, *G. K. Chesterton: A Criticism* (London: Alston Rivers, 1908), xii. This volume was originally published anonymously.

liberal Christianity. He satirically depicted "the Church of the Future," whose services will be based on Victorian poetry "or some of our own words," and which will attract all right-minded progressives for, "of course all the New Church people will join a newer church."[5] This juvenilia thus presents hints of Chesterton's later distaste for the anthropocentrism and lack of defined doctrine that he would associate with liberal Christianity and theological Modernism. Additionally, although his attraction to scripture at this time appears to have been largely aesthetic—it is the "beauty" of the verses that entice him—he was intrigued by the prophetic, rebellious strains of religion: "the vision of Ezekiel, the valley of dry bones. I thought about what a marvelous allegory it was, and what a splendid text it would have been for a preacher in a fallen and corrupt society just before a general Revolution."[6]

While important to note, these embryonic beliefs were not dominant in the young Chesterton's mind. Most of his early writings expressed the liberalism of the French Revolution—an event that would always inspire him (although for different reasons later)—and hence condemned dogma and preached the apotheosis of humans. In the name of Progress, he advocated then-daring notions that he would renounce as an adult, including compulsory state education, a scientific curriculum, and feminism.[7] Chesterton had not yet confronted the growing pessimism of late-Victorian British culture, and any interest in orthodoxy or rebellious prophecy appears to have been largely a matter of intellectual inquisitiveness. It was religion as an emotionally tinged morality and a source of beauty that he found most sympathetic at this time. Whatever qualms he had about this outlook were suspended while he remained in the cocoon of his loving family and friends from the Junior Debating Club at

---

5. Chesterton's extant notebooks are held in the G. K. Chesterton Archives, Manuscripts Department, The British Library. See Leo Hetzler, "Chesterton's Childhood: The Golden Key 1874–1886," *Chesterton Review* 21 (August 1995): 312; and Joseph Pearce, *Wisdom and Innocence: A Life of G. K. Chesterton* (San Francisco: Ignatius Press, 1997), 12, 22, 34, for evidence of his youthful distaste for the Church of Rome.

6. G. K. Chesterton diary, 11 January 1891. Chesterton Archives, The British Library. For other early references to prophets and rebels, including his self-description as a rebel, see Garry Wills, *Chesterton: Man and Mask* (New York: Sheed & Ward, 1961), 15, 217, n. 16; and Hetzler, "Chesterton's Childhood," 309–11.

7. Hetzler, "Chesterton's Childhood," 310–11; Wills, *Man and Mask*, 15–16.

St. Paul's School, for there the ideals he had imbibed from his parents and social background went unchallenged. All this would change, however, at the Slade School of Art.

"My Period of Madness": Chesterton at the Slade School

Unlike most young men of his class, Chesterton did not follow most of his St. Paul's classmates to Oxbridge. A precocious visual artist, he began studying at a St. John's Wood art school in the fall of 1892; but by the end of the year, he had transferred to the Slade School and would remain there until 1895. The Slade School of Art, a department of University College, had opened in 1871. Its founder, Felix Slade, wanted it to be at the forefront of artistic developments, and by the time of Chesterton's matriculation "the tone of the whole college was modernity . . . change and progress come what may."[8] It was here that Chesterton first met artistic theories like impressionism and the cultural movements of aestheticism and decadence. The consequent collision with the values of his upbringing during late 1892 and 1893 was catastrophic and established the central themes and rhetoric of the rest of his life.

Numerous Chesterton scholars, however, have minimized, and thus misunderstood, this incident's importance. Both Alzina Stone Dale and Michael Coren, for instance, reduce this episode to a case of adolescent angst, and they speculate sentimentally about whether or not Chesterton contemplated suicide.[9] Both authors also underestimate the crisis's duration and thus its significance, as exemplified by Coren's patronizing comment that "Gilbert probably worried about his 'lunatic' years more than was strictly necessary."[10] Some of this misunderstanding may have

---

8. Michael Coren, *Gilbert: The Man Who Was G. K. Chesterton* (London: Jonathan Cape, 1989), 52–53.

9. Dale's most useful service on this issue is to correct its chronology. She shows that Chesterton's main circle of friends did not leave London for university until at least 1894, thereby rebutting the notion that loneliness for his boyhood chums was the chief cause of his collapse (Alzina Stone Dale, *The Outline of Sanity: A Biography of G. K. Chesterton* [Grand Rapids, Mich.: William B. Eerdmans Publishing Co., 1982], 32). Yet Coren still makes this error—despite having Dale's book in his bibliography (Coren, *Gilbert*, 43–46), as Joseph Pearce also seems to (*Wisdom and Innocence*, 23–24). On suicide, see Dale, *Outline*, 33; and Coren, *Gilbert*, 57–58.

10. Coren, *Gilbert*, 46; and Dale, *Outline*, 39. Pearce follows in this vein, comparing Chesterton's mental struggles at this time to a bout of influenza (*Wisdom and Innocence*, 24).

arisen from a letter Chesterton wrote to his closest friend at the time, E. C. Bentley, in which he spoke of a "meaningless fit of depression" that had concluded, and Bentley's subsequent reiteration of this dismissal.[11] But Chesterton was usually dismissive when writing about himself; and his culture discouraged men from discussing their inner lives, especially with each other, so he should not be expected to be found baring his soul, even to his best friend.[12]

What, then, was the nature and significance of this crisis? Chesterton himself claimed that this incident "brought my boyhood to an end," and he was not speaking merely of chronology.[13] Rather, as Garry Wills points out, the whole progressive cosmology of Chesterton's youth was destroyed by its contact with cynical pessimism: "he went from one point of high concentration direct to its opposite pole, passing from Victorian content to the *fin-de-siècle* gloom.... It was his devotion to the first set of ideals that caused his sad bewilderment among the aesthetes ... the clash of these two shallow things drove Chesterton into depths." Chesterton, who always had a "need for precise balance," saw the scales of his mental equilibrium tipping—and tipping over.[14] He called this time "my period of madness" and titled the chapter of his autobiography treating it "How to be a Lunatic."[15] His use of madness and sanity as one of his signature tropes has its origins in this crisis and arose from his

---

Despite portraying Chesterton's crisis as in part the product of being lonely in London, Dudley Barker does emphasize this breakdown's seriousness and its enduring effects more than most other Chesterton biographers, though not in sufficient detail (*G. K. Chesterton: A Biography* [New York: Stein & Day, 1973], 47–66).

11. Chesterton to E. C. Bentley, quoted in Maisie Ward, *Gilbert Keith Chesterton* (New York: Sheed & Ward, 1943), 49. Ward dates this letter to 1894. Bentley's recollection is quoted in William A. S. Sarjeant, "G. K. Chesterton at St. Paul's School," *Chesterton Review* 21 (August 1995): 320–21.

12. Seeing Chesterton's outer insouciance as a sign of inner harmony also contradicts his later, telling assertion that "youth is a period when the wildest external carelessness often runs parallel to the most gloomy and concentrated internal cares" (*Come to Think of It* [London: Methuen, 1930], 48).

13. Chesterton, *Autobiography*, 78.

14. Wills, *Man and Mask*, 19, 12. Wills is the only scholar to deal with this incident accurately at length; but William Oddie supplies some useful commentary and context in "Chesterton at the *Fin de Siècle*," *Chesterton Review* 25 (August 1999): 329–43.

15. Chesterton, *Autobiography*, 86, 105.

fear at the time that he was going insane, one his friends shared.[16] Not only this rhetoric, but also many of the issues Chesterton confronted during his crisis, would become persistent elements of his later work.

While Chesterton claimed retrospectively that he could have gone mad earlier, his actual breakdown had quite specific causes. Like Greene, Chesterton, after a very happy childhood, encountered what he deemed "the objective solidity of Sin" for the first time. This kind of evil was not the absence of positive goodness, but "positive badness,"[17] both mental and moral "morbidities that seemed as dark as diabolical possession."[18] The first such maddening evil Chesterton discussed meeting was Spiritualism. Spiritualism was one response to the collapse of mid-Victorian Progressivism, and it was highly popular amongst the middle and upper classes in late-Victorian and Edwardian Britain.[19] Chesterton's exposure to it is hence not surprising, especially since his family had no religious scruples against such dabblings in the occult. While he explored Spiritualism at the time in a spirit of play, with hindsight he came to believe that "we were playing with fire; or even with hell-fire." He acknowledged that it was a "considerable religious movement," but he judged it a demonic one, which sundered the mystical from the material, was unnatural, and lied. While he could make this analytical assessment in retrospect, his immediate reaction was one of greater confusion, for he had not yet found a new sure standard for evaluating his experiences to replace the crumbling certainties of youth. He was hungering for a fresh principle of integration and balance, but the food offered seemed insubstantial or worse:

---

16. Ward, *Chesterton*, 44.

17. Chesterton, *Autobiography*, 73–74, 78, 85, 86. He remarked further that "even in the earliest days and even for the worst reasons, I already knew too much to pretend to get rid of evil" (ibid., 104). The clarity of this evidence makes it hard to understand the usually reliable Maisie Ward's comment that at this time "we shall find Gilbert dismissing belief in any positive existence of evil" (*Chesterton*, 50).

18. G. K. Chesterton, "Immortality and Mr. Shaw" (1928); in *Chesterton Review* 26 (November 2000): 444.

19. See Samuel Hynes, *The Edwardian Turn of Mind* (Princeton, N.J.: Princeton University Press, 1968), 132–71; and Alex Owen, *The Darkened Room* (Philadelphia: University of Pennsylvania Press, 1990).

the very fact that I indulged in it [Spiritualism] without reason and without result, that I did not come to any conclusion, or really even try to come to any conclusion, illustrates the fact that this is a period of life in which the mind is dreaming and drifting; and often drifting onto very dangerous rocks.[20]

Spiritualism's siren song began to lead him away from the temporal, and boredom with his art studies drew him even further into his own mind. Unfortunately for Chesterton, the predominant philosophy in artistic circles at this time was nihilistic pessimism, which he came to associate with impressionism. Far from grounding him in something concrete, this train of thought only reinforced the skepticism about the reality of nature, and of Being itself, that he had encountered in Spiritualism:

> there was a spiritual significance in Impressionism, in connection with this age as the age of scepticism. I mean that it illustrated scepticism in the sense of subjectivism. . . . It naturally lends itself to the metaphysical suggestion that things only exist as we perceive them, or that things do not exist at all. The philosophy of Impressionism is necessarily close to the philosophy of Illusion. And this atmosphere also tended to contribute, however indirectly, to a certain mood of unreality and sterile isolation that settled at this time upon me.

Such intellectual isolation was deadly, though, for it put Chesterton within the vicious circle of withdrawing more and more into a mind whose very operations he was increasingly questioning. The balance between mind and matter had tipped so far in favor of the former that Chesterton began to think that "there is nothing but thought," that "everything might be a dream."[21] This struggle with solipsism, then, is the personal genesis of his connection of modern cultural trends with insanity.

Yet this "madness" was not merely mental. Morally too, Chesterton imagined the "maddest, when I had never committed the mildest[,] crime." As the locus of all his activity began to reside in his mind, his al-

---

20. Chesterton, *Autobiography*, 86, 90, 87, 93. See a similar, earlier view in *ILN*, 30 October 1909.
21. Chesterton, *Autobiography*, 94–95.

ready weakened resources were strained further, making it unsurprising to find his notebooks from this period filled with violent drawings, for these became the only outlet for his internal turmoil. Chesterton saw a synergy between the moral decay underlying this impulse to record awful images and his spiritual madness, with an ensuing sense that he was "plunging in deeper and deeper as in a blind spiritual suicide." He had made himself the center of everything and yet had come to doubt whether there really was anything. A creature had tried to become the creator and he could not bear the burden: "it was as if I had myself projected the universe from within, with its trees and stars; and that is so near to the notion of being God that it is manifestly even nearer to going mad."[22]

Chesterton continued to associate impressionism with this mental and moral breakdown for most of his life. He deemed impressionism a "typically modern thing," and referred to "that philosophical impressionism which means being half-witted," whose end is a "maddening horror of unreality."[23] However, as John Coates has argued persuasively, the impressionism taught at the Slade was a "perversely misinterpreted" version propounded by George Moore, one premised on separating "the visionary moment of aesthetic delight from any kind of moral or emotional framework."[24] This view was hostile to the customary Victorian conviction, as Chesterton later recalled it, "that art could not exist apart from, still less in opposition to, life; especially the life of the soul."[25] Moore's aesthetic also appears to be a species of the subjectivism Chesterton condemned, in so far as it substitutes the personal percep-

22. Ibid., 95–96. More contemporaneously with his crisis, Chesterton linked self-divinization and madness in an 1896 story (see *Chesterton Review* 27 [February & May 2001]: 189–90). In a 1926 essay, he suggested that he thought his breakdown's moral aspects were even worse than its mental dimension. See *G.K.C. as M.C.* (London: Methuen, 1929), 205.

23. G. K. Chesterton, "The Grave-digger," in *Lunacy and Letters*, ed. Dorothy Collins (London: Sheed & Ward, 1958), 114, 117; and Chesterton (c. 1900) quoted in Lynette Hunter, *G. K. Chesterton: Explorations in Allegory* (London: Macmillan, 1979), 14.

24. John Coates, *Chesterton and the Edwardian Cultural Crisis* (Hull, England: Hull University Press, 1984), 196–97.

25. G. K. Chesterton, "Milton and Merry England," in *Fancies versus Fads* (New York: Dodd, Mead & Co., 1923), 255. See also Leo Hetzler, "Chesterton's Writings in his Teenage Years," in *G. K. Chesterton: A Half Century of Views*, ed. D. J. Conlon (Oxford: Oxford University Press, 1987), 293.

tion of the artist for an external standard of sublimity or virtue. Coates's opinion gains credence from Chesterton's own early adult writings about Moore, to whom he attributed the solipsism and delusions of omnipotence ending in near-despair that he had only recovered from recently himself:

> his real quarrel with life is that it is not a dream that can be molded by the dreamer.... Mr. Moore's egoism is not merely a moral weakness, it is a very constant and influential aesthetic weakness as well.... Thinking about himself will lead to trying to be the universe; trying to be the universe will lead to ceasing to be anything.[26]

Hence it was not so much impressionism itself that helped unhinge Chesterton's mental framework, but rather a version of it that fostered detachment from concrete concerns and contravened his received assumptions about the moral and material unity of art.

Disconcerting as this may have been, it hardly suggests positive badness. The source of Chesterton's sense of moral evil at this time was less his studies than his fellow students. If the amoral view of art was the blow fashionable impressionism struck to his inherited ethic, the reversal of its conventional moral norms by aesthetes and decadents was tony pessimism's contribution to his morbidity. In an early essay, he described "by far the most terrible thing that has ever happened to me," a Slade School conversation with a classmate whom Chesterton revealingly dubbed "the Diabolist." This interlocutor agreed that following customary morality's precepts would produce what had been traditionally regarded as happiness. His goal was more radical, though, being an inversion of how the basic categories of virtue and vice are understood: "what you call evil I call good."[27] Chesterton's received liberalism, with its denial of original sin, lacked the categories to comprehend and rebut fully such an outlook, thus deepening his adolescent disquiet. Even if this pupil was not typical of all his colleagues, his extreme position be-

---

26. *The Collected Works of G. K. Chesterton*, vol. 1, *Heretics* (San Francisco: Ignatius Press, 1986), 106–8.

27. G. K. Chesterton, "The Diabolist," in *Tremendous Trifles* (New York: Dodd, Mead & Co., 1909), 275. For the continuity of this incident and perception in shaping Chesterton's outlook, see, e.g., *Weekly Dispatch*, 22 November 1925; reprinted in *Chesterton Review* 24 (August 1998): 278.

came emblematic to Chesterton of his own inadequate innocence in the face of such beliefs, and the ensuing temptations to violence that he confronted. The fact that he encountered this upending of his boyhood moral verities in the same setting whose ethos and doctrines contradicted his youthful sense of the synergy between art's matter and meaning, then, helps explain his persistent leaguing of impressionism with evil. Both artistically and personally, he sensed a steady de-moralization ushering in seemingly unanswerable, yet maddening and demonic, forces, "the unmorality of the 'nineties."[28]

How, then, did Chesterton regain his balance? The outline of his return to sanity must remain a bit sketchy, for it is difficult to pinpoint the exact origin of his recovery, though it appears to have been underway by late 1893 or early 1894.[29] His conversation with the "diabolist" seems to have been a watershed, and other specific influences on him are also evident. Chesterton credited those "few of the fashionable writers who were not pessimists" for helping him reclaim a more hopeful outlook on Being, especially Browning, Stevenson, and Whitman.[30] He believed that Browning affirmed the concrete and particular against overratiocination, was "in love with existence,"[31] and was a model metaphysical rebel who "did not explain evil, far less explain it away: he enjoyed defying it."[32] In Stevenson, he found someone with a similar biographical background, and who also came to champion Being's brightness and sharpness against decadent gloominess. Indeed he claimed that he "would hardly have been able to fight against . . . the decadent darkness of the

---

28. Chesterton, "Milton and Merry England," 273. In a record of articles planned for 1926–36, though, he did outline a series on "The religious character of Impressionism" presenting a more favorable view than he held customarily. He was thus, perhaps, able to distance the experiences he associated with his exposure to the particular form impressionism had taken at the Slade from the artistic doctrine itself as he grew older.

29. This dating is premised on Denis Conlon's judgment that *Basil Howe* was written at the end of 1893 or the beginning of 1894, as this novel is saturated with allusions to Chesterton's breakdown and his recovery from it. See G. K. Chesterton, *Basil Howe*, ed. Denis Conlon (London: New City, 2001), 12–13; and Adam Schwartz, "The Grateful Heart of G. K. Chesterton," *Faith & Reason* 28 (Spring 2003): 123–33.

30. Chesterton, *Autobiography*, 97. See also *Basil Howe*, 102.

31. Chesterton quoted in Pearce, *Wisdom and Innocence*, 85.

32. G. K. Chesterton, *The Victorian Age in Literature* (1913; reprint, Oxford: Oxford University Press, 1946), 107.

'nineties . . . or even live through it, but for the spirit and the genius of Robert Louis Stevenson."[33] But Whitman's impact seems to have been the greatest at the time of his recovery. Chesterton later expressly credited this poet with his "deliverance from the decadent cynicism that was corrupting most of the young men of my generation."[34] He was very taken with *Leaves of Grass* when he and a friend read it aloud in 1894. Whitman's robust soul and his religious attitude toward nature and humanity affected both the content and style of Chesterton's own verse at this time, making him "drunken with skies and grass."[35] As he put it in 1901, Whitman defined "the point of view of unfathomable wonder at the energy of Being, the power of God."[36]

Taking nothing away from these writers' influence, it was not solely responsible for Chesterton's restoration. He himself said that he took whatever they gave him "in a way of my own." That unique way was both an important watershed in his spiritual journey as well as a tributary that would flow into later streams of his thought. Initially, Chesterton became convinced that modern culture was a maddening "nightmare"[37] that must be resisted: "my first impulse to write, and almost my first impulse to think, was a revolt of disgust with the Decadents and the aesthetic pessimism of the 'nineties."[38] Yet if he said "no" to the current climate of opinion, what could he affirm instead? That "yes" is the root of Chestertonian thought, the kernel that would flower in Roman Catholicism and Thomism, but would not change essentially: the princi-

---

33. Chesterton, *ILN*, 22 September 1923. This connection takes on added significance in light of the fact that Chesterton wrote the section of his autobiography concerning his breakdown and recovery at the same time he was composing his study of Stevenson, which some consider his "real" autobiography (Wills, *Man and Mask*, 22). For unmistakable resonances in Chesterton's analysis of Stevenson's life with his own crisis and its effects, see *The Collected Works of G. K. Chesterton*, vol. 18, *Robert Louis Stevenson* (San Francisco: Ignatius Press, 1991), 64–65, 69–70, 72–84, 86, 91, 102, 107, 113, 121–24, 130–38, 142–43.

34. Chesterton, *ILN*, 21 April 1928. Sooner after his recovery, he called Whitman his "sole spiritual support." "Conventions and the Hero" (1904), in *Lunacy and Letters*, 63.

35. Chesterton notebook, Chesterton Archives, The British Library. See also Dale, *Outline*, 35.

36. G. K. Chesterton, "What We All Mean," *The Speaker*, 16 February 1901.

37. Chesterton, *Autobiography*, 97, 96.

38. Chesterton, "Milton and Merry England," 253. See also *Basil Howe*, 128; and *ILN*, 18 February 1933.

ple of gratitude. Following predominant pessimism had precipitated the madness of doubting the objective validity of everything. Sanity, then, was grounded in the presence, and hence goodness, of anything:

> even mere existence, reduced to its most primary elements, was extraordinary enough to be exciting. Anything was magnificent as compared with nothing... a sort of mystical minimum of gratitude.... At the back of our brains, so to speak, there was a forgotten blaze or burst of astonishment at our own existence... this submerged sunrise of wonder.[39]

As Knox's eulogy stressed, Chesterton strove to make this fundamental astonishment at, and thankfulness for, the very fact of Being central to cultural consciousness thenceforth. He judged that "gratitude, or the theory of thanks" had "fallen into great neglect in our time,"[40] yet "I always rebelled against... the spirit of taking things for granted."[41]

Chesterton claimed that this "makeshift mystical theory of my own" came to him originally with "no real help from religion."[42] He had concluded that his class's liberal Christianity saw religion as only a "vague, beautiful, correct thing, to be recognized as a matter of course."[43] It thus could not match the spiritual depth of his newfound belief in primal thankfulness, and Chesterton as yet knew too little of other theologies to measure them fairly against this fresh core conviction. Indeed, as Wills notes, "the insight is metaphysical as was the problem, and arises from the mind's encounter with evil."[44] Chesterton had not yet translated this philosophical realism into an orthodox Christian ontology. He admitted as much when he remarked that, at this time, "I hung on to the remains of religion by one thin thread of thanks" by adopting a position akin to his Puritan grandfather's, who said that he would thank God for

---

39. Chesterton, *Autobiography*, 96–97. As he put it in an 1896 story, "it is but a superficial philosophy which is founded on the existence of everything. The deeper philosophy is founded on the existence of anything." "A Picture of Tuesday," in *Daylight and Nightmare*, ed. Marie Smith (London: Xanadau, 1986), 30.

40. *The Collected Works of G. K. Chesterton*, vol. 18, *Chaucer* (San Francisco: Ignatius Press, 1991), 169.

41. G. K. Chesterton, "Strikes and the Spirit of Wonder," in *Fancies versus Fads*, 207.

42. Chesterton, *Autobiography*, 96.   43. Chesterton, *Basil Howe*, 96.

44. Wills, *Man and Mask*, 31.

creating him even if he "were a lost soul."[45] Even when his notebook poetry from this period expresses the principle of gratitude through religious imagery, it has no specifically theological content.[46] This, then, was the distinctly philosophical stage of his development. Yet his discontent with modern thought and the connection of that protest to the tropes of sanity and rebellion were present already. Moreover, Wills points out that this period was also the dawn of Chesterton's serious focus on prophecy, as the rhetoric of Isaiah and Job and Christ's apocalyptic and prophetic style imbued his imagination during his despondency, coloring it ever after: "his own style is not paradoxical but prophetic."[47] Once again, the appeal is not distinctly religious, but the role's roots are evident.

This episode was thus the crucible in which Chesterton's worldview and his means of expressing it were shaped: "We shall see the marks of this period on everything he wrote and find that the influence is of the sort he describes, involving an intellectual struggle between realism and solipsism."[48] Near the end of his career, Chesterton acknowledged the centrality of this affair: "to a boy his first hatred is almost as immortal as his first love.... I can still be stirred, as men always can be by memories

---

45. Chesterton, *Autobiography*, 97. A notebook poem written during this period confirms this statement:

>Bless thee for our creation. Say we will
>Who are called and chosen. Yet I will
>While that grass grows, I would thank God for this
>If I were damned eternally in Hell.
>(Chesterton Archives, British Library)

46. Men say that the sun was darkened. Yet I had
Thought it beat brightly even on Calvary
And he that hung upon the torturing tree
Heard all the crickets singing and was glad.
(Chesterton Archives, British Library)

47. Wills, *Man and Mask*, 33.

48. Ibid., 22. Perplexingly, Stephen Medcalf has analyzed Chesterton's fear of solipsism and consequent stress on objectivity and externality, in often insightful terms, without a single reference to its origins in the Slade crisis. In fact he dismisses what he deems attempts to "over-emphasize the possibility in him of real madness." Medcalf, "The Achievement of G. K. Chesterton," in *G. K. Chesterton: A Centenary Appraisal*, ed. John Sullivan (London: Paul Elek, 1974), 81–121.

of their first excitements or ambitions, by anything that shows" signs of the views he grappled with at the Slade.[49] Yet the crisis's effect was apparent immediately, in both his private notebooks and his first published works. Chesterton himself referred to his early poem "By The Babe Unborn," in which he imagines how precious the fact of existence itself would seem to one still in the womb, as a product of this experience.[50]

This poem also introduced the rhetorical device of using a child's perspective. Chesterton employed this motif frequently as a means of inducing wonder and gratitude in his readers, for he believed, as Aidan Nichols elucidates, that

> childhood remains the proper criterion for adult sensibility. The child's response to existence as sheer gift, through wondering joy, is the key to ontology, and by a supreme irony, far from being a piece of knowledge acquired through the ratiocination of the mature man or woman, it is a gift received with the dawn of consciousness itself.[51]

As Chesterton put it tellingly in the early 1900s, "to be childish is to be sane."[52] Moreover, he held eventually that "the most childlike thing about a child . . . his power of wonder at the world" is something "which the modern world does not understand," making his adoption of this attitude, like his related belief in gratitude, a central element of his rebellion against modernity.[53] Although this insight's full significance awaited his incorporation of it into an orthodox Christian cosmology, then, it is nonetheless another key facet of Chestertonian thought that originated in the Slade School crisis and recovery.

---

49. Chesterton, "Milton and Merry England," 254–55. See also *ILN*, 26 March 1932.

50. See *Autobiography*, 97; and G. K. Chesterton, "By The Babe Unborn," in *The Collected Works of G. K. Chesterton*, vol. 10, *Collected Poetry: Part I* (San Francisco: Ignatius Press, 1994), 194–95, 197–98.

51. Aidan Nichols, *A Grammar of Consent* (Notre Dame, Ind.: University of Notre Dame Press, 1991), 167–68.

52. *The Collected Works of G. K. Chesterton*, vol. 11, "Time's Abstract and Brief Chronicle" (San Francisco: Ignatius Press, 1989), 78.

53. *The Collected Works of G. K. Chesterton*, vol. 21, *What I Saw in America* (San Francisco: Ignatius Press, 1990), 241–42. This passage also includes a contention that "the childlike spirit is not entirely concerned about what is inside. It is the first mark of possessing it that one is interested in what is outside," thereby revealing both the antithesis Chesterton established between a childlike outlook and the self-immurement he thought it an antidote to, as well as his breakdown's lingering effects on his worldview.

Another poem written shortly after his breakdown reveals Chesterton's belief that appreciating the goodness of Being means being grateful for all beings, including those the world's elite often despise. In "The Pessimist," Chesterton sets himself against the "sages" who have "snarled through the ages," and offers his gratitude for Being as "the word of a common man."[54] It was by following the newest notions of the Slade School smart set that Chesterton had courted madness. In response, he saw the common people as touchstones of sanity, for he felt they modeled thanks for, and wonder at, all facets of reality. As one of his first essays put it, "to common and simple people this world is a work of art . . . any detail of it has a value . . . [to] the babyish and indiscriminate curiosity of a people still young and entering history for the first time."[55] Thus the populism and hostility to intellectuals that would be a hallmark of his social criticism also originated in the Slade School crisis and its aftermath. There are numerous other examples of this incident's immediate impact on his thought, all of which help to certify that the gravity he and commentators like Wills attributed to this period is not a retrospective judgment.[56]

Yet neither was it just a phase Chesterton went through. His bout with madness became the driving force not only of his spiritual journey, but also of his cultural analysis. He had tied his trauma to larger cultural trends and saw his experience as microcosmic of a greater social collapse. This breakdown so affected him that, be it consciously or not, it became his paradigm for understanding the apparent unhinging of a whole way of life. While he did not yet offer an explicitly religious prescription for this modern malady, his diagnosis was one that would be fully compatible with his later embrace of orthodoxy.

---

54. *The Collected Poems of G. K. Chesterton* (London: Methuen, 1933), 353.
55. Chesterton, "A Defense of Useful Information," in *The Defendant* (London: J. M. Dent, 1901), 97–101.
56. See, e.g., Chesterton's poems "The Wild Knight" and the revealingly titled "The Mirror of Madmen," plus early prose pieces like "The Diabolist," and *Basil Howe*. See also the tellingly titled "A Crazy Tale," a thinly veiled allegory of his experience of sensed madness being redeemed by gratitude, which appeared in the Slade School's own literary magazine (Reprinted in *Daylight and Nightmare*, 17–22).

Nightmare and Awakening:
The Man Who Was Thursday

The use of his personal wreckage and recovery as cultural allegory is the key to *The Man Who Was Thursday* (1908). While written after his adoption of orthodox Christianity (and even perhaps Catholicism), this novel is not meant to indicate religious answers to the problems his crisis raised. Rather, it is designed to be a descriptive rehearsal of his breakdown not "as a private fancy of his own adolescence, but as an historic mood shared by many."[57] It was Chesterton's way of both comprehending his experience while also portraying the cultural trends that he felt had sent him into the abyss. He also fictionalized his crisis in a later tale, showing its lasting effect on him, but *Thursday* provides more extended and richer commentary on its perceived lessons.[58]

The book's surface plot concerns the daydream occasioned by an argument between police officer Gabriel Syme and anarchist Lucian Gregory. Syme imagines an anarchist cabal, its members each code-named for a day of the week, who openly plot their subversive schemes under the direction of Sunday, a literally larger-than-life figure who seems omniscient and omnipotent. Syme penetrates this group as a replacement for the agent Thursday and soon discovers that all its other members are likewise undercover officers. After a series of misadventures, the six policemen eventually confront Sunday, who ends the daydream with an ambiguous Jobean speech. Snapping out of this trance, Syme finds himself amiably chatting with Gregory and thinking about courting his sister.

Thursday thus has the materials for a thriller, but it is not a conven-

---

57. Wills, *Man and Mask*, 40. Wills suggests insightfully that fictionalizing his experiences was Chesterton's best way of dealing with them because of his hatred of abstractions engendered by his crisis (ibid., 47). See also David Leigh's belief that Chesterton may have felt too insecure at this time to discuss his breakdown directly, but felt its effects so intensely that he had to write about it. Leigh, "The Psychology of Conversion in Chesterton's and Lewis's Autobiographies," in *G. K. Chesterton and C. S. Lewis: The Riddle of Joy*, ed. Michael Macdonald and Andrew Tadie (Grand Rapids, Mich.: William B. Eerdmans Publishing Co., 1989), 292.

58. G. K. Chesterton, *The Poet and the Lunatics* (New York: Dodd, Mead & Co., 1929), 101–35.

tional one. The first hint of Chesterton's message is the novel's subtitle, "A Nightmare," which immediately recalls his description of his breakdown, as well as being an ironic reminder of his sensation during it that everything might be a dream. Indeed, he had anticipated both the form and themes of this story in one of his first journalistic essays: "now it is this horrible fairy tale of a man constantly changing into other men that is the soul of the decadence . . . [it] may seem a nightmare; but to that nightmare we give the name of modern culture."[59] Chesterton's fictional nightmare begins in Saffron Park, based on the suburb of Bedford Park that he frequented when courting his future wife. Saffron Park is an "insane village" awash in "attractive unreality," a description that recalls many themes from his breakdown. It is a center of insanity because it is inhabited by the kinds of artists who "never in any definable way produced any art."[60] It was precisely such idlers, of whom Chesterton was one at the Slade School, whom he judged most susceptible to madness: "philosophy is generally left to the idle; and it is generally a very idle philosophy. In the time of which I write it was also a very negative and even nihilistic philosophy."[61] Yet this insanity is not simply personal; such crazy thinkers form an "intellectual conspiracy [that] would soon threaten the very existence of civilization . . . the scientific and artistic worlds are silently bound in a crusade against the Family and the State."[62] Referring to this period later, Chesterton blamed these sorts of idle intellectuals attracted to unreal abstractions for the crisis he thought he and his culture confronted:

> the main truth about all this sceptical revolt and all the rest of it, is that it . . . came from the Intelligentsia, who were perpetually discussing novels and plays and pictures instead of people. . . . But when the artists became anarchists and began to exhibit the community and the cosmos

---

59. Chesterton, "A Defense of Rash Vows," in *The Defendant*, 33–34.
 One of his notebooks contains an unfinished story that appears to be a prototype for *Thursday*. A slightly different version of it appears as "The Appalling Five," in *The Collected Works of G. K. Chesterton*, vol. 14 (San Francisco: Ignatius Press, 1993), 695–709.
60. G. K. Chesterton, *The Man Who Was Thursday* (1908; reprint, New York: Dover, 1986), 1. For a similar description of Bedford Park, see *Autobiography*, 136.
61. Chesterton, *Autobiography*, 94.
62. Chesterton, *Thursday*, 24.

by these flashes of lightning, the result was not realism but simply nightmare.[63]

The equation of anarchists with artists is central to one of *Thursday*'s major themes. The villainous anarchy of the novel is not primarily political, but is rather the loss of traditional mental and moral standards that Chesterton associated with modern culture. Speaking for modern intellectuals, Gregory claims that "an artist is identical with an anarchist.... An artist disregards all governments, abolishes all conventions. The poet delights in disorder only." Syme, though, deems order truly poetic, because it is so difficult to achieve: "The rare, strange thing is to hit the mark.... I say that one might do a thousand things instead, and that whenever I really come there I have the sense of hair-breadth escape." Chesterton recalls part of the personal experience on which this insight is based shortly after this exchange, as he invokes the Spiritualism from which he narrowly escaped by referring to "an insane seance." During the debate between Syme and Gregory, Chesterton also asserts a crucial distinction between a nihilist and a rebel. Whereas the nihilist has no desire to reroot the culture once it has been uprooted, a rebel is always affirming an alternate order when he rejects the status quo. For Gregory, "the poet is always in revolt"; but Syme declares that "revolt in the abstract is—revolting. It's mere vomiting." Syme is described later as being in "rebellion against rebellion.... Being surrounded with every conceivable kind of revolt from infancy, Gabriel had to revolt into something, so he revolted into the only thing left—sanity."[64] This portrait is remarkably similar to the one Chesterton later sketched of Stevenson, as well as one critic's picture of Chesterton himself.[65] Chesterton's struggle to maintain equilibrium in the modern mental climate, his own hair-breadth es-

---

63. *The Collected Works of G. K. Chesterton*, vol. 3, *The Thing* (San Francisco: Ignatius Press, 1990), 176.

64. Chesterton, *Thursday*, 3–4, 9, 22. See also Syme's remark that a common criminal "is a reformer, but not an anarchist. He wishes to cleanse the edifice, but not to destroy it. But the evil philosopher is not trying to alter things, but to annihilate them" (ibid., 25). For the continuity of these views in Chesterton's thought, see, e.g., "The Anarchist," in *Alarms and Discursions* (London: Methuen, 1910), 121–27; *ILN*, 13 August 1932.

65. See Chesterton, *Stevenson*, 74–75; and Andres Maurois, *Points of View* (New York: Frederick Ungar, 1968), 145.

cape from persistent madness, and his sense of his role as a cultural rebel championing sanity are hence all displayed clearly here.

Thursday itself has numerous narrow escapes from foes both real and imagined. One occurs when Syme challenges a fellow faux anarchist to a duel. Chesterton uses the interlude before the scheduled combat to present the principle of gratitude in a new way. Syme contemplates death, and realizing that he may be seeing things for the last time makes him see them as for the first time. He suddenly notices "a strange and vivid value in all the earth around him, in the grass under his feet; he felt the love of life in all living things." Chesterton then asserts that this gift of gratitude entails duties to the culture. Syme soon thinks that maybe "he had been chosen as a champion of all these fresh and kindly things to cross swords with the enemy of all creation. . . . 'I can do the one thing which Satan himself cannot do—I can die.'"[66] Chesterton had already defined himself as a rebel, and this passage reveals that he felt his rebellion was to be on behalf of the goodness of Being. His gratitude for it, and for his appreciation of it following his breakdown, made him willing (at least rhetorically) to make the ultimate human sacrifice for his ultimate principles.

Syme, though, does not have to pay this price. The duel ends abruptly with the discovery that he and his opponent are confederates. While mounting a subsequent escape from Sunday's agents in a dense French wood, Syme faces "the last and worst of his fancies," the seeming unreality of impressionism that had maddened Chesterton:

> The fancy tinted Syme's overwhelming sense of wonder. . . . For Gabriel Syme had found in the heart of that sun-splashed wood what many modern painters had found there. He had found the thing which the modern people call Impressionism, which is another name for that final scepticism which can find no floor to the universe.

Syme feels his good sense return when he sees in the forest clearing a figure "that might well stand for that common sense in an almost awful actuality . . . a heavy French peasant." As in "The Pessimist," sanity is identified with a common person. Although the detectives' faith in the

---

66. Chesterton, *Thursday*, 73–75. See also "A Defense of Rash Vows," 34.

peasantry is sorely tested when they appear to join the pursuit of the policemen, their near-despair abates when the peasants and officers discover they are really allies: "Vulgar people are never mad."[67]

Once this misunderstanding with the peasants is cleared up, the detectives return to England in pursuit of Sunday, whom they chase across London. After he escapes, the six officers engage in a colloquy about him that contains many of the elements of Chesterton's crisis and recovery, as the fundamental goodness of Being and the dangers of impressionism and Spiritualism are reiterated. They are next interrupted by emissaries from Sunday, who escort the tired detectives to their master's lodgings, where they confront their ultimate temptation, the life of "comfort." The dangers they face are what Chesterton considered the intertwined perils of servility and optimism. Everything the detectives need or want is provided by some vague agency associated with Sunday. Syme and his compatriots soon join Sunday at a vast party in a garden, as they preside together over the festivities from seven thrones. Each appears completely content, as though they are back in the original Garden. In fact, one officer is "the picture of an optimist in his element." Yet one detective is not satisfied. When Sunday finally claims to be "The Peace of God," the Secretary exclaims, "and it is exactly that that I cannot forgive you. I know that you are contentment, optimism, what do they call the thing, an ultimate reconciliation. Well, I am not reconciled . . . I cannot forgive Him His peace."[68]

To Chesterton, Sunday's peace is unforgivable because it is peace as the world gives peace. Sunday is "a blasphemous version of the Creator," and his cosmos is the supreme Impressionistic nightmare, in which illusions become realities through the acquiescence of weak wills. Reconciliation becomes fatalism and is also fatal, for it ultimately destroys the mainsprings of rebellion by dulling perception of evil. Sunday and his lieutenants have crossed the very thin line of sanity by leading the detectives to think that the presence of good things means that everything is good. In accepting his largesse, the detectives surrender their independence and cease questioning or caring about others' fate, so long as they are content. This seduction by luxury makes Sunday's

67. Chesterton, *Thursday*, 81, 82, 97.
68. Ibid., 112, 113–14, 116, 117.

universe the Servile State in miniature. Chesterton admitted to struggling with this temptation to optimism soon after his breakdown:

> I was still oppressed with the metaphysical nightmare of negations about mind and matter, with the morbid imagery of evil, with the burden of my own mysterious brain and body; but by this time I was in revolt against them; and trying to construct a healthier conception of cosmic life, even if it were one that should err on the side of health. I even called myself an optimist, because I was so horribly near to being a pessimist.[69]

Yet he did not succumb fully to this temptation, nor do his characters in *Thursday*.[70] The Secretary's outburst is followed by the entrance of Gregory. The sole sincere anarchist in the book, he chides Sunday and his minions for their capitulation to comfort and their consequent ignorance of, and inattention to, the sufferings of the weak. At this point, Syme supplies the antidote to servility's siren song: pain.

> Why does each thing on the earth war against each other thing? . . . So that the real lie of Satan may be flung back in the face of this blasphemer, so that by tears and torture we may earn the right to say to this man, "You lie." . . . We have been broken upon the wheel. . . . We have descended into hell.[71]

Like Camus in *The Plague*, Chesterton contends here that taking the victim's side produces empathetic solidarity with the sufferings of others. Pain awakens people from the nightmare of continual comfort, and enables distinction between the ultimate goodness of Being and the flaws of a fallen world, a differentiation Panglossian optimists do not acknowledge. In short, Chesterton concludes that remembering personal pain and sharing in others'—while simultaneously recalling Being's basic beneficence—prevents facile acceptance of the status quo, and also preserves the freedom that fosters rebellion with, and on behalf of, the pow-

---

69. Chesterton, *Autobiography*, 103. See also *Thursday*, 118; *Collected Works of G. K. Chesterton*, vol. 3, *Where All Roads Lead* (San Francisco: Ignatius Press, 1990), 44–49; and "Milton and Merry England," 254.

70. Commenting on this novel in 1926, Chesterton contended that "I should not wish it supposed, as some I think have supposed, that in resisting the heresy of pessimism I implied the equally morbid and diseased insanity of optimism." *G.K.C. as M.C.*, 205.

71. Chesterton, *Thursday*, 119.

erless. He elaborated this notion more fully in his later thought, but it originated in Chesterton's response to his own suffering.[72]

His position on optimism in the novel is further clarified by the influence of the Book of Job, a text Wills considers the "favorite book" of Chesterton's young creative years.[73] When Gregory emerges, a spectator quotes Job 2:1, and Gregory assumes the role of accuser from the biblical poem. The detectives are like Job's comforters, whom Chesterton called in 1907 "the official optimists," who really believe "not that God is good but that God is so strong that it is much more judicious to call Him good." It is Gregory, like Job, who is the true optimist, because "he is an outraged and insulted optimist. He wishes the universe to justify itself, not because he wishes it to be caught out, but because he really wishes it to be justified." Gregory's genuine belief in anarchism makes him outraged and insulted by what he regards as its cynical perversion by the powerful. Syme's answer of pain and Sunday's abrupt, fantastic disappearance may seem unsatisfactory to Gregory's complaint, but the problem of pain he raises is one that finally has no rationally fulfilling answer. Like Job, he must be content with the "positive and palpable unreason of things," and the promise of solidarity from fellow sufferers.[74] To Chesterton, such is the price of the freedom needed to rebel and aid those in pain. The lesson for Job, Gregory, and Syme is the same: "he must live with the mysteries of free will, suffering and evil, not resorting to his friends' refuge of optimism. . . . A single-textured optimism can only lead to a single-textured world—to pantheism, which all the fighters resent as a denial of their struggle."[75] The true peace of God is Eliot's *shantih*, that which passeth understanding.

Besides promoting vigilance, rebellion, and freedom, Chesterton also

---

72. See, e.g., Chesterton, *What I Saw in America*, 231; and *William Cobbett* (London: Hodder & Stoughton, 1925), 253. Wills also identifies Syme's speech as an expression of Chesterton's experiences (*Man and Mask*, 43–44).

73. Garry Wills, introduction to *The Man Who Was Thursday*, by G. K. Chesterton (New York: Sheed & Ward, 1975), xxi.

74. "The Book of Job," in *Selected Essays of G. K. Chesterton* (London: Methuen, 1949), 98, 97, 101. Chesterton had anticipated many of these points in a *Speaker* column of 9 September 1905 (Wills, introduction to *Thursday*, xxv–xxvi). See also C. S. Lewis, *The Problem of Pain* (New York: Collier Books, 1962), 24.

75. Wills, *Man and Mask*, 43.

portrayed pain in his later work as the best antidote to proud, solipsistic delusions of omnipotence.[76] He similarly emphasizes humility at the end of *Thursday*. As Sunday disappears, his last words are Christ's: "Can ye drink of the cup that I drink of?" Chesterton's invocation of this text has not been fully understood. The conventional interpretation—that Syme's treatise on pain is fulfilled in the example of Christ—is accurate, but insufficient.[77] The scripture referred to is the request of Zebedee's sons to sit at Jesus's left and right in Heaven, just as Syme and the Secretary are situated in Sunday's false paradise. Christ replies with the words Chesterton quotes and, after assuring Him that they can drink of His cup, He tells them that they will share His fate, but that it is the Father who will assign places of honor in Heaven. Upon hearing of James's and John's request, the other apostles grow indignant, and Jesus responds with a discourse on humility: "You know that those who are recognized as rulers over the Gentiles lord it over them, and their great ones make their authority over them felt. But it shall not be so among you. Rather, whoever wishes to be first among you will be the slave of all."[78] It is Sunday and his cohorts who have lorded their power over those beneath them, as Gregory charges. It is the detectives who have assumed the earth's thrones and powers, arrogating positions not rightfully theirs.[79] They have ceased to serve and have accepted a life of isolated comfort. Gregory's rebuke of this pride breaks the spell of servility, and with the enchantment of ease shattered, Syme realizes that he must leave his wicked throne and return to the service and shared suffering of others; only then can he hope to earn a place in the real paradise. This rebellion destroys Sunday because he cannot control someone who prefers a life

---

76. "I also dreamed that I had dreamed of the whole creation. . . . I had been behind and at the beginning of all things; and without me nothing was made that was made. Anyone who has been in that center of the cosmos knows that it is to be in hell. . . . There is no cure for that nightmare of omnipotence except pain; because that is the thing a man *knows* he would not tolerate if he could really control it. A man must be in some place from which he would certainly escape if he could, if he is really to realize that all things do not come from within." Chesterton, *Poet and Lunatics*, 125. Emphasis in original.

77. See, e.g., Coates, *Crisis*, 216; Ian Boyd, *The Novels of G. K. Chesterton* (London: Paul Elek, 1975), 46.

78. Chesterton, *Thursday*, 116; and Mark 10:42–44. Matthew 20:20–28 is an immaterially different account.

79. See Matthew 19:28.

of free and humble service to one of what seems proud dominance, but is actually deterministic dependence. Syme did not love Big Brother.

As Syme breaks free from this greatest temptation, symbolized by his snapping out of his daydream, he relearns a lesson he had posited previously but had forgotten temporarily during his seduction. It is one of the chief insights that Chesterton felt he had gained from his own crisis: "He knew simultaneously that he was a fool and a free man. For with any recovery from morbidity there must go a certain healthy humiliation." This recognition of freedom and limited power allows Syme to resume his proper place in the order of creation; and his awareness that he is an actor in, not the author of, an ultimately good drama is the "good news" that makes "every other thing a triviality, but an adorable triviality."[80] In the dawn, he sees things as for the first time, and reacts to them with a wonder and gratitude arising from humble acceptance of his creaturely status.

In addition to being considered his best novel, then, *The Man Who Was Thursday* is also Chesterton's most extended discussion of his Slade School crisis as he experienced it. Much of the Chestertonian worldview is present, showing its roots in his collapse and recovery. Some aspects are already highly developed, including the link between modernity and insanity, the need for a rebellious attitude, and the virtues of gratitude, humility, and freedom. Other elements are more embryonic, but a basic sympathy for the common people and peasants—the perceived victims of modern abuses of power—is evident, along with the more fully substantiated ethic of serving and siding with those in pain generally. What is absent is a distinctly religious foundation for these beliefs, as even scriptural references are used to make ethical or metaphysical points. Chesterton the author had a thorough theology by 1908, but this tale was meant to render his immediate post-breakdown outlook as accurately as he could: "the whole story is a nightmare of things, not as they are, but as they seemed to the young half-pessimist of the '90s . . . whose pantheism is struggling out of pessimism."[81]

---

80. Chesterton, *Thursday*, 50, 120. See also Chesterton, *Poet and Lunatics*, 127.

81. Chesterton, *Autobiography*, 103. For a perceptive review of the novel along these lines, see *G. K. Chesterton: The Critical Judgments*, ed. D. J. Conlon (Antwerp: Universitaire Faculteiten Sint-Ignatius, 1976), 145.

Marriage and a Creed: Chesterton and the Romance of Orthodoxy

As he recovered, Chesterton threw off both these ideas quickly. He rejected pantheism because he knew, with great relief, that he was not God; he was a creature, not the Creator. He deemed pessimism invalid because he saw the bare fact of existence itself as a cause for celebration; one should be grateful to be at all since there is no reason why one, or anything, should exist. He took these insights with him as he left the Slade School in 1895 and began a career in publishing, which lasted until he became a full-time journalist in 1901. These were busy years, but his spiritual journey also continued apace.

Having abandoned pantheism, Chesterton faced the choice of atheism or theism: If God was not Everyone, He must be No One or Someone. The former seemed irreconcilable with the principle of gratitude, as a gift implied a giver. Similarly to Greene's Fowler in *The Quiet American*, who wishes there were someone he could say "I'm sorry" to, Chesterton came to believe that there must be someone to whom he could say "Thank you": "There should be an eternal necessity for religion if it were only in order to explain a blessing. . . . One thing is certain; let any emotion, art, music, language, piety, admiration or affection rise to a certain point of intensity and it will get into the religious atmosphere [and] demand religious images to apprehend it."[82] Chesterton concluded that secular images and ideologies are insufficient to express full thankfulness for the wonder of Being, because there must be a Being, distinct and set apart, Who is the source of all these goods. This position flowed logically from the negations and affirmations of his crisis, as Christopher Derrick summarizes: "Chesterton went through his period of nihilism and black despair and discovered that gratitude was necessary for sanity; and gratitude implied God."[83] Conversion theorist Walter

---

82. Undated fragment, Chesterton Archives, British Library. See also his *Daily News* columns of 24 March 1903 and 20 June 1903. This contemporary evidence substantiates his reflections in his *Autobiography* (148) that "I was all groping and groaning and travailing with an inchoate and half-baked philosophy of my own. . . . The truth presented itself to me, rather, in the form that where there is anything there is God."

83. Christopher Derrick, "Some Personal Angles on Chesterton and Lewis," in Macdon-

Conn suggests that such a discovery is central to the conversion process: "Perhaps the notion of gift captures the essential reality of religious conversion best. One is able to surrender one's self, make a *gift* not only of one's illusion of absolute autonomy but of one's whole life only insofar as one can recognize one's very existence as a gift of love."[84] Chesterton had already been happily disillusioned about his fancies of omnipotence; now he was ready to give himself in service to the One who he believed had created him out of love.

Love of another kind, though, shaped that commitment's form. In 1896, he met Frances Blogg, an officer of one of Bedford Park's debating salons, and he soon became enamored. One of her chief attractions to him was her firm religious faith and her devout practice of it. Chesterton had been struggling his way into theism with no apparent assistance from his friends or culture. To find someone living in a center of secular intellectualism who not only believed in God but also displayed that belief in action astounded him. Chesterton also admired the confidence that Frances's Anglo-Catholicism gave her. Having been so susceptible to the influences of irreligious thought himself, with what he regarded as terrible results, he esteemed the independence of mind fostered by her faith, considering it "the unique quality that cut her off from the current culture and saved her from it."[85] In Frances, then, he saw incarnated his own growing senses of dogma's freeing power and of how religious belief could undergird cultural rebellion.

As they courted, Chesterton wrote often to Frances about his spiritual state. He had mused earlier that "the right way is the Christian way;"[86] but his theism was not transformed into orthodox Christianity instantly, as vestiges of Unitarianism remained:

> I am not a Catholic. . . . I belong to the same sect as Plato, Lo-O-Tse, Epictetus, Sohnya Maini, Shakespeare, Goethe, St. Paul, Hiawatha,

---

ald and Tadie, *Riddle of Joy*, 18. Stratford Caldecott thus astutely calls Chesterton's spirituality "'eucharistic' . . . a joy in existence overflowing into thanks" ("Was Chesterton a Theologian?" *Chesterton Review* 24 [November 1998]: 479).

84. Walter Conn, *Christian Conversion* (New York: Paulist Press, 1986), 227. Emphasis in original.

85. Chesterton, *Autobiography*, 149–50.

86. Chesterton, c. 1893–94 notebook, quoted in Barker, *Chesterton*, 63.

Prof. Huxley, the Cid, Walt Whitman, Jesus Xt, and Mr. Rudyard Kipling. The same church included many more. The odd thing is that it hasn't been founded yet.[87]

His philosophical convictions were only deepening, though, for he asserted at roughly the same time that "I *am* right about the Cosmos, and Schopenhauer and Co. are wrong."[88] Frances began introducing Gilbert to her Anglo-Catholic friends and spiritual advisers, making her the agent of his first regular contact with orthodox Christians; he credited her explicitly with leading him from Unitarianism to Anglicanism.[89] She hence deserves Chesterton's poetic appellation of her as the one "who brought the cross to me." As Chesterton associated with this group, his embryonic orthodoxy became more defined.

He was particularly influenced by Conrad Noel, the curate who presided over his 1901 marriage to Frances. If he was growing increasingly frustrated with his day's high culture, Chesterton had also absorbed many of its prejudices about religion's putatively unintellectual nature. He was much surprised, then, when Noel seemed to be the sole participant in a debating society who showed "all the advantages of having been tolerably trained in some sort of system of thinking." This was a major epiphany for Chesterton, for it promised him a means of integrating his metaphysical and ethical insights with the theism arising from his principle of gratitude; indeed, one of his work's central themes would be this rationality of religion. He also deemed Noel an "uncompromising rebel" against post-Christian intellectual trends like Nietzscheanism, and thus began to see more clearly how doctrinal faith could inspire cultural dissent, despite disagreeing later with Noel's pro-Communist politics.[90]

Yet neither wife nor friend could convert Chesterton to orthodox Christianity by themselves. As always, he had to think the matter through for himself. His debates, though, were no longer solely internal. Having become a journalist shortly before his marriage, Chesterton could now discuss the matters most on his mind in public forums. He

---

87. Chesterton to Frances Blogg, 23 March 1899, Chesterton Archives, British Library.
88. Chesterton quoted in Ward, *Chesterton*, 138. Emphasis in original.
89. Ward, *Chesterton*, 282.
90. Chesterton, *Autobiography*, 154–55.

claimed that he began moving closer to orthodoxy during his early lectures. He became increasingly convinced that people embraced the various replacements for ancestral religion not as liberation from dead dogmas, but out of desperation to believe in anything at all: "I saw Israel scattered on the hills as sheep that have not a shepherd; and I saw a large number of sheep run about bleating eagerly in whatever neighborhood it was supposed that a shepherd might be found." Chesterton soon started asserting that loss of allegiance to the Good Shepherd had produced this scene, that traditional Christianity was the source of meaning from which his culture had wrongly deviated. Perhaps remembering his own pain and confusion, he saluted those who retained humane values in an era he deemed increasingly dominated by Darwinism and Nietzscheanism. But he feared that these outlines of both personal and social sanity were filled in insufficiently: "they held [these ideals] less firmly than they might have done, if there had been anything like a fundamental principle of morals and metaphysics to support them."[91]

Chesterton's own statement of what he felt that fundamental principle is was not immediately forthcoming, though. He continued to define himself negatively, as against modern theology and philosophy, leaving his affirmation of orthodox Christianity largely implied. He used this reactive tactic in a lengthy 1903–4 public controversy with Robert Blatchford, but the best example of this phase of his thought is *Heretics* (1905). In this volume, Chesterton criticized thinkers he deemed modern monomaniacs, who take a part of the truth and substitute it for the whole (such as Kipling, Shaw, Wells, and Joseph McCabe). He also sought to persuade a culture seemingly obsessed with efficiency and material success that philosophy is worth disputing about at all. In attempting to prove the primacy of theory, he stressed its practicality:

> the most practical and important thing about a man is still his view of the universe. We think that for a landlady considering a lodger, it is important to know his income, but still more important to know his philosophy. . . . There is nothing which is so weak for working purposes as this enormous importance attached to immediate victory. There is nothing that fails like success.

91. Ibid., 170.

This defense of the primary importance of philosophy became a constant concern of Chesterton's work, as did other themes introduced in this book, including the idea that progress depends on a *telos*. He even identified himself as a Christian (as he had when debating Blatchford), asserted that man is a dogma-making animal, and posited a link between religious mysticism and sanity. Yet, even though he was moving toward the tenets of High Anglicanism at this time, he did not develop his understanding of those purportedly sane Christian dogmas.[92] He still had a clearer sense of what he was saying "no" to than of what commanded his assent. As one reviewer of *Heretics* put it, "Mr. Chesterton perceives a thousand truths: but he perceives no consistent body of truth."[93]

His positive assertion of his beliefs was also occasioned by debate, however. G. S. Street said in another review of *Heretics* that he would begin to worry about his philosophy when Chesterton stated his own. Chesterton took this opportunity to set down at last the beliefs he had been formulating since recovering from the Slade breakdown. The result was *Orthodoxy* (1908), which one reviewer dubbed unwittingly the product of a "heart whose strength, sweetness and sanity have survived self-consciousness."[94] As such remarks suggest, this intensely personal statement of how Chesterton came to believe in orthodox Christianity is not a work of apologetics as such. It was intended as a reply to Street's challenge, whatever its accidental evangelical effects.

The beginning of *Orthodoxy* further illuminates Chesterton's interest in the prophet role. His notebooks reveal that this issue was much on his mind, especially after his breakdown and recovery. As he came closer to orthodoxy, he began to see prophecy as a dangerous temptation. His era's prophets, as he described them in *Heretics*, all had what he judged an

---

92. Chesterton, *Heretics*, 41–45, 206, 196, 207; and Wills, *Man and Mask*, 88.

93. R. W. L., *Black and White*, 8 July 1905 (Conlon, *The Critical Judgments*, 104). David Dooley has made a thoughtful and spirited case that Chesterton was a more committed dogmatic Christian at this stage of his career than is commonly realized ("Foreword" to *Collected Works*, vol. 1, 7–34). Yet Dooley concedes that Chesterton's positive beliefs still remained more implied and incidental in these early controversies, awaiting their "fuller exposition" (26) in later works like *Orthodoxy*. David Fagerberg is thus more correct to claim that Chesterton at this time was "learning Christianity by a sort of *via negativa*" (*The Size of Chesterton's Catholicism* [Notre Dame, Ind.: University of Notre Dame Press, 1998], 8).

94. B. S., *Manchester Guardian*, 29 September 1908 (Conlon, *The Critical Judgments*, 168).

unbalanced understanding of truth. Remembering his own temporary adoption of such a scheme, he distrusted similar secular, anthropocentric explanations of meaning. Yet he also recognized these thinkers' cultural power, and thus felt compelled to advocate his counter-vision of gratitude. But "that notion of seeing a vision was dangerously near to my old original natural nightmare,"[95] as, on its own, "somebody would have seen its promising possibilities in the direction of perversion or insanity."[96]

Only orthodoxy resolved this dilemma for Chesterton, for in it he discovered that his truth was not his alone. He confessed that he had shared "all the idiotic ambitions of the end of the nineteenth century . . . I tried to be some ten minutes in advance of the truth"; but he found that "I was eighteen hundred years behind it . . . I did try to found a heresy of my own; and when I had put the last touches to it, I discovered that it was orthodoxy."[97] Orthodoxy supplied an intellectual structure and a tradition that sanctioned his insights, thereby removing the temptation to pride in his own thoughts, and hence inducing the humility he felt he needed to propound his views without fear of lapsing into monomania. In orthodox Christianity, Chesterton found a place where his truths would be balanced by other truths, and thus assure that "in that sane spiritual society . . . optimism will never be turned into an orgy of anarchy or a stagnation of slavery, and that there will not fall on any one of us the ironical disaster of having discovered a truth only to disseminate a lie."[98] Orthodoxy, then, became his source of sanity because it prevented the devolution into chaos, servility, and lies that he had depicted in *Thursday* as sanity's greatest foes.

The humility that arose from accepting the equilibrium of orthodoxy helped Chesterton settle the problem of prophecy. If post-Christian prophets were distinguished by their pride in a single idea, Chesterton would become their mirror image: a jester. According to Wills, a prophet takes himself completely seriously, but the jester is marked by "a deliberate exaggeration and self-mocking animation."[99] From this

---

95. Chesterton, *Autobiography*, 328.   96. Chesterton, *Where All Roads Lead*, 48.
97. G. K. Chesterton, *Orthodoxy* (1908; reprint, Garden City, NY: Image Books, 1959), 12.
98. Chesterton, *Where All Roads Lead*, 50.   99. Wills, *Man and Mask*, 49.

standpoint, the critic is free to focus on his subject rather than himself, thus explaining Chesterton's remark that he always took his ideas, but never himself, seriously.[100] Moreover, this understanding of his role explains Chesterton's frequent use of self-deprecatory humor: "the great prophet or martyr has to be laughed at, and what is much worse, to be laughable . . . humanity must, if it [is] to have faith, learn how to play the fool."[101] Finally, this self-perception clarifies Chesterton's frequent insistence that he was not a prophet, despite being dubbed one often.[102] Yet his peers also labeled him a jester and, given his sense of what a prophet is, his denials of the latter role were accurate.[103] But Knox's judgment in his eulogy is not incompatible with Chesterton's assertion: what they both suggested is that when heresy is orthodox, only a humble jester can be a true prophet.

In addition to shaping his later writing's form, orthodoxy also enriched its content. The metaphysical and ethical insights that Chesterton had formed over the last decade now gained a specifically theological grounding. For example, sanity became a distinctly religious issue. In *Or-*

---

100. For an interesting gloss on this notion, see Chesterton, *ILN*, 18 November 1911.

101. Undated manuscript fragment, Chesterton Archives, The British Library.

102. Chesterton was dealing with this issue almost literally until his dying day, as he insisted in the last article he wrote that "I have never set up to be a prophet. . . ." ("In Reply to Critics," *G. K.'s Weekly*, 11 June 1936). See also *ILN*, 15 September 1928.

The British Library's Chesterton Archive contains numerous depictions of Chesterton as a prophet by his contemporaries, as does Conlon, *The Critical Judgments*. This perception persisted posthumously. Christopher Hollis, for example, combined the sense of Chesterton as both prophet and rebel in a 1948 BBC talk, "Prophet of the Counterattack" (reprinted in *The Listener*, 25 November 1948); and Maurice Rickett wrote a pamphlet entitled *G. K. Chesterton: A Christian Prophet for England Today* in 1950. See even more recent such designations in, e.g., Malcolm Muggeridge, "GKC," *New Statesman*, 23 August 1963; Adrian Hastings, *A History of English Christianity, 1920–1985* (London: Collins, 1986), 175; William Oddie, "A New Kind of Saint?" *Catholic World Report* (June 1995): 59, 61; Pearce, *Wisdom and Innocence*, viii, 185, 203, 302, 316, 350, 386, 391, 441; Stephen Medcalf, "The Innocence of G. K.," *TLS* (20 December 1996): 9.

103. For contemporaneous evaluations of Chesterton as a jester, see, e.g., Conlon, *The Critical Judgments*, 85, 90, 144, 174, 240–42, 349; and Pearce, *Wisdom and Innocence*, 255. For posthumous uses of this classification, see Peter Milward, "G. K. Chesterton's Faith and Journalism," *Chesterton Review* 7 (November 1981): 355; J. M. Cameron, "Innocent at Home," *New York Review of Books* 30 (28 April 1983): 23. Michael Asquith apparently saw Chesterton fulfilling both roles, as he entitled an article "G. K. Chesterton: Prophet and Jester." *The Listener*, 6 March 1952.

thodoxy, Chesterton argues that modern insanity arises from overconfidence in human powers, especially reason. Echoing his own crisis, he asserts that "the men who really believe in themselves are all in lunatic asylums," and that "the madman is not the man who has lost his reason. The madman is the man who has lost everything except his reason." Immurement in reason can promote either rationalism and materialism or his own temptation, the solipsism that begins with belief in self and ends with the person believing in nothing and no one, "alone in his own nightmare." Either of these extremes denies the Incarnational idea that Being is a mixture of matter and spirit. In contrarily accepting this intricacy, Chesterton claimed, the orthodox Christian acquires a balanced view of both the self and the cosmos: "The Christian admits that the universe is manifold and even miscellaneous, just as a sane man knows that he is complex." Hence, when the mental scales tip too far in favor of reason, mysticism restores perspective by stressing that everything is not rationally comprehensible. Similarly, when the spiritual grows too strong, orthodoxy emphasizes the power and goodness of reason and matter. In either case, Christianity is the "philosophy of sanity" because it preserves "this balance of apparent contradictions that has been the whole buoyancy of the healthy man."[104] Chesterton's persistent need for balance was now met by orthodox Christianity.

Chesterton stresses in *Orthodoxy*, though, that this balance is dynamic. In contrast to the Aristotelian ideal of extremes blending into a golden mean through dilution of their passions, he contends, Christian balance consists of the simultaneous existence of seeming antitheses, each in its purest form. Thus the orthodox Christian is concurrently a passionate lover of good and a ferocious hater of evil: "St. Francis, in praising all good, could be a more shouting optimist than Walt Whitman. St. Jerome, in denouncing all evil, could paint the world blacker than Schopenhauer." This idea is an advance on Syme's distinction between esteem for the goodness of Being generally and hatred of specific evils; and Chesterton linked it explicitly to his acceptance of orthodoxy:

---

104. Chesterton, *Orthodoxy*, 14, 18, 19, 26, 24, 27, 16, 28. For a foreshadowing of some of these points, see Chesterton, "A Wild Reconstruction" (1901), in *Lunacy and Letters*, 34–36. This essay is in many ways a germinal version of *Orthodoxy*.

the idea of this combination is indeed central in orthodox theology. For orthodox theology has specially insisted that Christ was not a being apart from God and man, like an elf, nor yet a being half human and half not, like a centaur, but both things at once and both things thoroughly, very man and very God.[105]

Being both fully divine and fully human, Chesterton thought, Christ could give the greatest affirmation possible to all that He had made by becoming one with it and dying for it, a fact that should make any willful perversions of this good creation especially abhorrent to the orthodox Christian. Once again, then, the Incarnation was decisive in shaping Chesterton's views of balance: believing in it helped him to extract what he considered the valid insights contained in optimism and pessimism while avoiding their purported extremism, and retaining, if refocusing, their rightly passionate intensity.

Chesterton's own experience had convinced him of how precarious this balance of sanity is, and he found this view also confirmed by orthodoxy. Because the Christian balance is one of undiluted extremes, he held, it is always teetering on the brink of heresy and insanity. Strict limits are thus necessary to prevent catastrophic deviations: "an inch is everything when you are balancing. The Church could not afford to swerve a hair's breadth on some things if she was to continue her great and daring experiment of the irregular equilibrium."[106] Thus his embryonic idea of dogma's freeing power became clearer under orthodoxy's influence. The Church was responsible for setting the lines of excellence; once done, a believer could exercise his vital powers along them without the constant fear of falling into madness. Chesterton's overall accent on what he considered Christian orthodoxy's essential sanity was so compelling to one reviewer that he called *Orthodoxy* itself "an antidote to insanity."[107]

Yet the allegedly complex balance of orthodoxy attracted Chesterton not just because of its apparent sanity, but also due to what seemed its

---

105. Chesterton, *Orthodoxy*, 96, 92. David Jones marked a passage exemplifying this logic in his copy (72).

106. Chesterton, *Orthodoxy*, 100.

107. R. A. Scott-James, *Daily News*, 25 September 1908 (Conlon, *The Critical Judgments*, 161).

realism. In what became a central theme of his career, he asserted that Christianity's complexity matched life's: "It not only goes right about things, but it goes wrong (if one may say so) exactly where the things go wrong. Its plan suits the secret irregularities, and expects the unexpected." This holistic harmony with life as lived separated Christianity from more simplistic schemes to him, for "a stick might fit a hole or a stone a hollow by accident. But a key and a lock are both complex. And if a key fits a lock, you know it is the right key."[108]

The key metaphor helps connect orthodoxy and Chesterton's childhood. His first memory was of a man carrying a key across a bridge in his father's toy theater; he used this image more than once when describing the Church.[109] Though his breakdown destroyed his boyhood's ideals, Chesterton remembered the time itself happily, and he advocated viewing the world with childlike wonder continually. Orthodoxy grounded these memories and sentiments in a theology that he felt was resilient against the forces that had shattered his youthful cosmology. It provided the dynamic balance between the virtue of personal innocence and the knowledge of good and evil, permitting one to be as a little child while putting away childish things. In enabling Chesterton to reintegrate his childhood into his beliefs, then, orthodox Christianity provided him with the fullest measure of personal and intellectual coherence that he had known since his collapse: it is "like my father in the garden . . . for it is my father's house. I end where I began—at the right end. I have entered at last the gate of all good philosophy. I have come into my second childhood."[110] This is not Sunday's wicked garden, but the refuge of one who has awakened from that nightmare, "the only paradise still left virgin and unspoilt enough, in the imagination of a man who has turned the seven heavens upside down."[111]

The simile of Church as father is also telling in explaining the psychol-

---

108. Chesterton, *Orthodoxy*, 82–83.

109. Chesterton, *Autobiography*, 331; and *The Collected Works of G. K. Chesterton*, vol. 2, *The Everlasting Man* (San Francisco: Ignatius Press, 1986), 347.

110. Chesterton, *Orthodoxy*, 157–58. Chesterton used the idea of a second childhood often when referring to his conversion(s). See, e.g., *Autobiography*, 88, 234; and "The Second Childhood," in *Collected Poems*, 81.

111. Chesterton, *Poet and Lunatics*, 233. See also *Stevenson*, 81–82.

ogy of Chesterton's conversion. Even before his personal orthodoxy was very developed, he claimed that "Christianity seeks after God with a most elementary passion it can find, the craving for a father."[112] Conversion theorists posit that this search for an authoritative, yet personal and loving, picture of the divine motivates many religious journeys, and that trusting acceptance of its presence in a particular religion is a critical moment in the conversion process.[113] And Chesterton's discovery of it in orthodox Christianity was significant not only at this time, as this need for authority would also be crucial in his later movement to Roman Catholicism. In 1908, though, such confessional differences mattered less to him. He desired an authoritative account of Being, and orthodoxy convinced him due to what seemed its continuous correspondence with reality. Whereas he had concluded that the force behind Spiritualism tells lies, he came to profess orthodox Christianity not because it "told this truth or that truth, but [it] has revealed itself as a truth-telling thing."[114] In accepting its dogmas, he had recaptured the innocent assurance of always knowing the differences between right and wrong and truth and falsity that his father had given him in the garden, much like another Father in another Garden.

Chesterton considered this rebirth an occasion for gratitude, and his philosophy of gratitude was deepened by orthodoxy. Referring, as he frequently did, to the morality he learned in childhood fairy tales, Chesterton rehearses in *Orthodoxy* his discovery that the fact of existence itself demands gratitude, which in turn demands a giver to be thankful to. He then introduces a corollary to this principle, the Doctrine of Conditional Joy. To him, the gift of existence comes with restrictions and prohibitions, but he did not regard these limits as unfair: as he is not the

---

112. Chesterton, *The Speaker*, 17 November 1900; quoted in David Dooley, "Chesterton in Debate with Blatchford: The Development of a Controversialist," in Macdonald and Tadie, *Riddle of Joy*, 209. Chesterton also contended contemporaneously that "the element of authority in human life cannot be too highly valued" ("A Wild Reconstruction," 37).

113. See Emilie Griffin, *Turning: Reflections on the Experience of Conversion* (New York: Doubleday, 1980), 46; and John Dunne, *A Search for God in Time and Memory* (New York: Macmillan, 1969), 222. Jonathan Rose argues that attempts to recover one's childhood were especially strong among Edwardians. Rose, *The Edwardian Temperament, 1895–1919* (Athens: Ohio University Press, 1986), 178–98.

114. Chesterton, *Orthodoxy*, 157.

Creator and thus received existence as a pure gift, it did not seem onerous to accept whatever ontological preconditions the giver established as the capacity for enjoying all the benefits of Being. This attitude strengthened Chesterton's sentiment of humility, for given the great grace of existence itself, "one may well be modest and submit to the queerest limitations of so queer a kindness." In his mind, this insight into natural law taught by myths gained its fulfillment and a specifically theological sanction from orthodoxy's doctrine of the Fall: "A box is opened, and all evils fly out. A word is forgotten, and cities perish. A lamp is lit, and love flies away. A flower is plucked, and human lives are forfeited. An apple is eaten and the hope of God is gone."[115] Chesterton's ethical notion that humble, grateful acceptance of the gift of Being and its concomitant limits is the way to happiness was thus verified for him by the Christian dogma that it was precisely proud ingratitude and the arrogant ambition of creatures to be like God that precipitated the human race's aboriginal calamity.

The doctrine of original sin also clarified Chesterton's position on optimism and pessimism. His intuitive conclusion that Being is fundamentally good despite commonly witnessed evils was confirmed by the Christian teaching that all created things, being from God, are good, but that people, by abusing the gift of freedom, bring much sorrow on themselves. The pessimist is too proud to see good in anything, and the optimist is so proud as to feel that he can find good in everything. To Chesterton, though, the orthodox Christian admits his sins humbly while simultaneously celebrating his special place in creation. Echoing Newman's notion of the "greatness and littleness of man," Chesterton asserts, "In so far as I am Man I am the chief of creatures. In so far as I am *a* man I am the chief of sinners. . . . One can hardly think too little of one's self. One can hardly think too much of one's soul."[116]

For Chesterton, then, the doctrine of original sin offered the basis for true optimism that he had been seeking. While his remark that original sin is "the only encouraging view of life" may sound odd initially, it

---

115. Ibid., 55, 58, 56. See also *A Gleaming Cohort* (London: Methuen, 1926), 171–74.
116. Chesterton, *Orthodoxy*, 94–95. Emphasis in original. See also *The Collected Works of G. K. Chesterton, Sidelights*, (San Francisco: Ignatius Press, 1990), 611; and "Consulting the Encyclopedia," in *The Common Man* (New York: Sheed & Ward, 1950), 243–44.

flows logically from the premises adduced in *Orthodoxy*. If one denies original sin, he thought, one must accept the persistently flawed state of human nature as normative. Such resignation can only foster despair, for there is no way to redeem the time. In believing in original sin, however, Chesterton held, one contends that people are fallen from a higher dignity that they can be restored to by cooperating with God's grace. Hope is thus the virtue marking this idea's adherents, for they anticipate ultimate deliverance from evil. That salvation and justice come only in the next life, but they do come. Those who disclaim original sin, though, not only lack an effective remedy for evil in this life, but also have no logical reason for positing the existence of an afterlife. Even if they do foresee an eternity, it must be a frightening extension, rather than a transformation, of temporality, for they cannot rationally claim to recover something they have denied losing. Chesterton thus concluded that only by accepting implication in the aboriginal calamity can the primordial joys of paradise be regained: only if people have fallen, can they rise.[117] Greene would also be attracted by this logic, feeling that the doctrine of original sin provided the best explanation of, and hope for salvation from, evil.

Finally, belief in original sin gave impetus to Chesterton's ideas about rebellion. He had long feared that both optimism and pessimism produce quietism, either by asserting that no change is needed, or that any change is pointless. Orthodox Christianity resolved this problem for him, though, in a way that encapsulates many foregoing themes. To Chesterton, the gift of existence establishes a primary, unconditional loyalty to Being. Recognition of its essential goodness stimulates love of it and that love, in turn, fosters hatred of its flaws and a wish to correct them. Moreover, the fact of freedom, another gift, enables one to conduct these reforms. Change, then, is both desirable and possible.[118] Yet

---

117. G. K. Chesterton, "The Outline of the Fall," *G. K.'s Weekly*, 25 September 1926: 25. See also *Autobiography*, 171.

118. Chesterton had discerned this aspect of Christianity even when his own attitude was more detached: "this universal paradox of the union between a seraphic contentment and a desire for drastic change was no more exemplified than in Christianity . . . improvement comes only from hope, and hope only comes from satisfaction." *Daily News*, 16 September 1901.

that change must take a specific shape. As Chesterton would insist consistently, reform implies form. But he felt most post-Christian revolutionaries were nihilists. Lacking any clear idea about what to construct after destroying the status quo, they ultimately fail to act at all, for "as long as the vision of heaven is always changing, the vision of earth will be exactly the same. No ideal will remain long enough to be realized, or even partly realized."[119] Modern radicals, then, are really conservatives.

The true rebel, as in *Thursday*, is the person with a fixed goal. In *Orthodoxy*, however, the novel's metaphysical defense of common things is enriched by Christianity. For Chesterton, orthodoxy's "chief merit" is that "it is the natural fountain of revolution and reform." He maintains that "my vision of perfection assuredly cannot be altered; for it is called Eden. . . . For the orthodox there can always be a revolution; for a revolution is a restoration." This formula is the theological foundation of his radical conservatism, his desire to uproot his current culture so as to re-root it in Christian tradition, the stable measure by which he judged the status quo flawed. In orthodox Christianity Chesterton found the principles for which he had already taken up the standard validated:

> in so far as we value democracy and the self-renewing energies of the west, we are much more likely to find them in the old theology than the new. If we want reform we must adhere to orthodoxy. . . . By insisting specially on the transcendence of God, we get wonder, curiosity, moral and political adventure, righteous indignation—Christendom.[120]

Orthodoxy's ability to answer his need for authority enhanced this aspect of traditional Christianity's appeal to him, for he claimed contemporaneously that a source of surety was essential for successful rebellion: "Tell me how we shall do it without authority? Tell me how you will have an army of revolt without discipline?"[121]

Orthodoxy, then, had become the basis of Chesterton's outlook. The insights he had groped toward individually were now confirmed and elaborated by a broad heritage of belief and behavior. This Christian

---

119. Chesterton, *Orthodoxy*, 107. For the continuity of this view, see, e.g., *The Thing*, 139.
120. Chesterton, *Orthodoxy*, 138, 109–10, 134. For a remarkably similar restatement of this conviction decades later, see "Notes," *G. K.'s Weekly*, 26 April 1934, 115.
121. Chesterton, "The Anarchist," 127.

legacy gave his private ideas a public framework, thereby freeing him from the perceived temptation of founding a personal heresy, and empowering him to become a humble jester for what he deemed two-thousand-year-old truths. Chesterton also acquired an expansive, active, and adventurous understanding of sanity. Orthodoxy further supplied what seemed an authoritative, realistic standard for judging experience, plus a way of recapturing his childhood happiness, hence restoring, yet strengthening, the innocence lost so traumatically at the Slade. Moreover, belief in original sin liberated him from what he saw as the fatalism of optimism and pessimism by stressing the importance of free will, even as it enriched his principles of gratitude and conditional joy. Orthodoxy thus gave Chesterton both motive and means for his rebellion against modernity: even as others looked ahead to seemingly sterile secular utopias, he would look back to Christendom for his ideal order, for he felt that if humans had abused the gifts of freedom and creation through sin, they could also reform themselves and the world through right uses of their wills. If *Heretics* had lacked a consistent body of truth, then, *Orthodoxy* was marked, as one reviewer noted, by "strict coherence . . . he has pinned himself down to his subject, and unfolds his thesis with system."[122]

Faith Without a Pope: Chesterton's Early Catholicism

But Chesterton's spiritual flux did not cease with his full acceptance of orthodoxy. Indeed, even at the time that he wrote *Orthodoxy*, he was wondering which church was most orthodox. Charting his spiritual journey's last stage, from Anglo to Roman Catholicism, is a vexing task, for his published writing is largely silent on this transition's timing. However, his work and reports of those who knew him well suggest a rough chronology. What might be called his "notional assent" to Roman Catholicism began around the time he penned *Orthodoxy*. His "real assent" can be dated at least to a near-fatal illness he suffered during the Great War. He made his final decision to be received some time in the early 1920s, as he perceived the Anglican Church becoming more Modernist. He still delayed,

---

122. R. A. Scott-James, *Daily News*, 25 September 1908 (Conlon, *The Critical Judgments*, 159–60). Other readers, though, found the case too inseparable from its advocate. See, e.g., Conlon, *The Critical Judgments*, 165, 170–71.

though, hoping that Frances would also convert, but in 1922 he finally could wait no longer and became a Roman Catholic.

Despite his youthful prejudices, Chesterton was attracted from early on to a proportionately greater amount of Roman Catholic culture and belief than most of his peers were. An 1894 Italian holiday fostered a lifelong affinity for Rome and medievalism, even if his initial fascination lacked a religious basis or a corresponding interest in the Italianate model of the Church and its doctrines. However, he was contemporaneously praising Roman Catholicism as more "ecstatic," if more "morbid," than liberal Christianity.[123] Moreover, his early notebooks reveal an intense interest in the Virgin Mary, a devotion hardly encouraged by the Protestant cum secular culture of his rearing. If these drawings and poems generally portray her as a female archetype or a sister instead of as the Mother of God, he nonetheless confessed later that it was the "very idea of Our Lady" that began to draw him out of Protestantism, as she had almost always emblemized Roman Catholicism to him: "The instant I remembered the Catholic Church, I remembered her; when I tried to forget the Catholic Church, I tried to forget her."[124]

There were also several early personal Roman Catholic influences on Chesterton. He had met Hilaire Belloc by late 1900, and even attended Midnight Mass with him that Christmas.[125] He met Father John O'Connor (the loose inspiration for the Father Brown stories) in 1904, who, like Conrad Noel, showed Chesterton that a cleric could derive intellectual vitality from his faith. Additionally, Chesterton's close friend Maurice Baring became a Roman Catholic in 1909, and his beloved brother, Cecil Chesterton, followed four years later. Gilbert also befriended Roman Catholic apologist Wilfrid Ward and his family around this time. It was through Ward that Chesterton met Lord Hugh Cecil, with whom he had a pivotal conversation. Chesterton thought that he was a Catholic, but their talk produced crucial discoveries about both Lord Hugh and himself: "The strongest impression I received, was that he was a Protestant.

---

123. Chesterton, *Basil Howe*, 96.
124. Chesterton, *Where All Roads Lead*, 39; and *The Collected Works of G. K. Chesterton*, vol. 3, *The Well and the Shallows* (San Francisco: Ignatius Press, 1990), 463. For earlier evidence of this belief, see the drafts of "Ave Maria" (1891–93) in *Collected Poetry: Part I*, 111–16; and Maisie Ward, *Return to Chesterton* (London: Sheed & Ward, 1952), 237–38.
125. Pearce, *Wisdom and Innocence*, 52.

I was myself still a thousand miles from being a [Roman] Catholic; but I think it was the perfect and solid Protestantism of Lord Hugh that fully revealed to me that I was no longer a Protestant."[126] This revelation was vital for Chesterton, for he now became convinced that he would find orthodoxy in Catholicism. While at this time an Anglo-Catholic, that title's latter term mattered most to him, for (as he put it in 1910) he was now certain that "every human being would end up either in utter pessimistic scepticism or in the Catholic creed."[127] These various contacts made him consider more deeply the possibility that Roman Catholicism might be that orthodox creed's true home, thus illustrating Waugh's theorem that personal examples are often as, or more, persuasive in effecting a conversion than doctrines alone.[128]

Chesterton, though, could not neglect intellectual issues, and he began pouring over Roman Catholic claims. Some of his journalism from the period around *Orthodoxy*'s composition indicates deepening doubts about the Anglican Church's ability to combat theological Modernism, thus confirming Dorothy Collins's judgment that he was struggling with the question of moving to Rome as early as 1907.[129] Chesterton at this time seemed to be trying to uphold the Tractarian *via media*, asserting

---

126. Chesterton, *Autobiography*, 249.

127. G. K. Chesterton, *William Blake* (1910; reprint, London: House of Stratus, 2000), 57.

"I did not start out with the idea of saving the English Church, but of finding the Catholic Church. If the two were one, so much the better; but I had never conceived of Catholicism as a sort of showy attribute or attraction to be tacked on to my own national body, but as the inmost soul of the true body, wherever it might be." *The Collected Works of G. K. Chesterton*, vol. 3, *The Catholic Church and Conversion* (San Francisco: Ignatius Press, 1990), 72–73. See also Pearce, *Wisdom and Innocence*, 278–79.

128. "[E]ntering into the system even socially brought an ever-increasing certitude upon the original question." Chesterton, *Autobiography*, 179. For Waugh's view, see "Come Inside," in *The Essays, Articles and Reviews of Evelyn Waugh*, ed. Donat Gallagher (Boston: Little, Brown & Co., 1984), 366–68.

129. Dorothy Collins to A. L. Maycock, 26 January 1959, Chesterton Archives, The British Library. Except for Frances, Collins may have been the person who knew Chesterton best. Far from having been just his secretary, she was treated as a member of the Chesterton family, and lived with them from 1926–36.

Her speculations are substantiated by Chesterton's portrayal of Roman Catholic monks as counter-modern rebels in a 1907 story ("A Nightmare," in *Collected Works*, vol. 14, 87–90). See also his 7 December 1907 letter to the *Nation*, in which he referred to the "collective authority in religion" represented by Roman Catholicism; and his 18 January 1908 *Daily News* column, in which he defended sacramental confession.

that Anglicanism can be both English and Catholic. Asked by an opponent in 1907 if he was a Roman Catholic, Chesterton replied:

> I am not. I shall not be until you have convinced me that the Church of England is really the muddle-headed provincial heresy that you make it out . . . the whole point of that [Oxford] Movement was to maintain that a man in the Church of England was not a man 'deprived of the right to appeal' to the authority that can alone maintain dogma.

The issue of authority also loomed large in a 1909 debate between Chesterton and Robert Dell in the *Church Socialist Quarterly*. Dell, a rare Roman Catholic convert Modernist, had called traditional Catholicism the most reactionary force in Europe. Chesterton thus found himself defending Roman Catholicism against one of its own. He judged Dell's advocacy of Modernism the best case against it, claiming his foe upheld "a nightmare vision of the universe . . . [a] modern relapse into chaos" ruled by the pride of scientists and artists, *Thursday*'s crusaders against ancient institutions. Seeing the ghosts of his own breakdown continuing to haunt the modern mind, Chesterton argued that only orthodox Catholicism supplies the dogmas that can repel these anarchic forces of pessimistic, skeptical disillusion and insanity; and he would consistently criticize the Modernist "dislike of dogmas." Yet he also revealed his continued uncertainty about the location of the authority that maintains them: "About the seat of this Catholic authority I do not disguise from anyone that I am still in some doubt; and I agree much more with the high Anglicans than the Roman Modernists. Nevertheless, I never felt so near to Mr. Dell's communion as after I had read his attack on it."[130] Thus Chesterton was not being disingenuous when he asked G. S. Street to challenge him on this question in *Orthodoxy*.[131] He was genuinely unsure, and probably desired the opportunity to ponder this issue systematically, as he had done with his creed after Street's review of *Heretics*.

Yet such a challenge was not forthcoming, and his thinking about the choice of Canterbury or Rome at this time was episodic and implied.

---

130. Chesterton quoted in Ian Boyd, "Chesterton's Anglican Reaction to Modernism," in *Chesterton & the Modernist Crisis*, ed. Aidan Nichols (Saskatoon, Canada: Chesterton Review Press, 1990), 15, 27, 31; and G. K. Chesterton, preface to *Modernism and the Christian Church*, by Francis Woodlock (London: Longmans, Green & Co., 1925), v.

131. Chesterton, *Orthodoxy*, 13.

Nonetheless, enough hints exist to show the direction in which his mind was moving. In *Heretics,* for instance, he chides modern Anglicans for lacking clearly defined dogmas. In *Orthodoxy,* Roman Catholics are associated with democracy and peasants, and specifically Roman doctrines and disciplines like papal infallibility and clerical celibacy are mentioned favorably.[132] In fact, one reviewer of *Orthodoxy* asserted (though not complimentarily) that "it is really difficult to see how he can avoid Roman Catholicism."[133] His fiction from this period is equally revealing. Even *Thursday* contains favorable references to Catholicism, as in Syme's assertion that "we are all Catholics now."[134] Chesterton's attraction to Roman Catholicism at this juncture is even clearer in *The Ball and the Cross* (1909).

This novel resembles Greene's *Monsignor Quixote,* depicting a journey that occasions an intellectual debate which helps convert a materialist to Roman Catholicism. Yet while Greene's protagonists are friends, Chesterton's two characters begin as mortal enemies. Evan MacIan, a Scottish Catholic, attacks James Turnbull's atheist newspaper office following what MacIan regards as a blasphemous article about the Virgin Mary. Already in choice of plot material, Chesterton is revealing the press of Roman Catholic issues on his mind. MacIan and Turnbull seek to settle their disagreement through a duel, but they are inhibited by a secular society that deems such conflicts, especially over matters of purported personal preference like religion, barbaric. They are finally incarcerated in a lunatic asylum by Prof. Lucifer, who symbolizes the evils of scientism and secularism's judgment that a religious sensibility is a form of insanity, an assessment MacIan and Turnbull take as confirmation of their own sanity due to its crazy origin. Finally, aided by a previously imprisoned monk named Michael, they incinerate the asylum and Turnbull converts. Michael defeats Lucifer again.[135]

---

132. Chesterton, *Heretics,* 45; and *Orthodoxy,* 10, 40, 48, 148, 90, 156.

133. Anon., *The Observer,* 4 October 1908 (Conlon, *The Critical Judgments,* 172).

134. Chesterton, *Thursday,* 7, 10, 12, 42, 64, 68, 83–84. He also asserted contemporaneously that "the meaning of the last thirty years is that everybody—Churchmen, Nonconformists, Baptists and Unitarians—have been sucked closer to Rome. Peg out on your mental map the contour of thought say ten years ago, and you will find that in the interval it has swept towards Catholicism" (*Daily News,* 13 December 1907).

135. Martin Gardner suggests intriguingly that this novel was Chesterton's fictionalization of his contemporaneous journalistic disputes with Robert Blatchford (Gardner, introduction to *The Ball and the Cross,* by G. K. Chesterton [New York: Dover, 1995], iv–v).

While rich in many Chestertonian themes, the novel does highlight its author's spiritual state at the time he composed it. MacIan is specifically identified as a Roman Catholic, not an Anglican, as is one of the heroines. France is contrasted positively to England, in part because of its Roman Catholic heritage. Chesterton also includes some eloquent passages about the doctrine of transubstantiation, a bitterly divisive issue in the Anglican Church then, belief in which was considered a sign of papist predilections. Finally, and perhaps most tellingly, Prof. Lucifer remarks to Turnbull that "this Catholicism is a curious thing . . . it soaks and weakens men without their knowing it, just as I fear it has soaked and weakened you," an assessment cognate with Chesterton's later account of his initial attraction to Rome.[136] It is thus understandable that one of the novel's reviewers thought that Chesterton had already become a Roman Catholic—and even warned that "he is in danger of its becoming an *idee fixe* with him."[137]

Personal and public evidence from this time buttresses Chesterton's fictional hints of his religious leanings. John O'Connor claimed that Chesterton told him in the late spring of 1911 that he had decided to join the Roman church, as even the best kind of Anglicanism was "only a pale imitation."[138] Some of Chesterton's contemporaneous public remarks substantiate O'Connor's story. In March of that year, for instance, he had referred to "Rome" as the exemplary form of the Christian Church.[139] In addition, on 18 November 1911 he told a Cambridge audience that he was more inclined than ever to see both Greek Orthodoxy and Anglicanism as further from truth than Roman Catholicism.[140] The

---

Similarly, Pearce sees the tale as a parable of the Chesterton-Shaw relationship (*Literary Converts* [London: HarperCollins, 1999], 57). Many of its themes are also prefigured in Chesterton, "A Nightmare," 87–90.

136. G. K. Chesterton, *The Ball and the Cross* (London: Watts, Gardner, Darnton & Co., 1909), 315; and *The Catholic Church and Conversion*, 89–90. See also *Ball and Cross*, 87, 205–6, 24, 228, 48, 226, 230–31.

137. F. G. Bettany, *The Sunday Times*, 27 February 1910 (Conlon, *The Critical Judgments*, 224).

138. Michael Ffinch, *G. K. Chesterton* (San Francisco: Harper & Row, 1986), 201.

139. Chesterton to *The Nation*, 18 March 1911; reprinted in *Chesterton Review* 13 (May 1987): 146–47.

140. See *Chesterton Review* 12 (August 1986): 297.

longstanding issue of authority was at the forefront of Chesterton's mind throughout this period, and Rome's position on this question was beginning to claim his conscience.

But other issues of conscience were holding him back. Initially, and most importantly, was Frances. Chesterton felt unpayably indebted to her for bringing him to orthodoxy in the first place. She was untroubled by his doubts about Anglicanism, and she had also been grieved permanently by her Roman Catholic convert brother's 1906 suicide. Gilbert was thus loathe to trouble her on such an affecting subject, particularly given his deep dependence on her for the practical aspects of his religion. Moreover, his family was reacting coolly to Cecil's flirtations with the Scarlet Woman, and G. K. did not want to introduce further tensions. Finally, he was not yet so convinced by Roman Catholicism that he felt morally required to convert. He could pause to test his belief, while also waiting for the opportune moment to discuss the matter with his family. These intellectual and personal reasons are what kept Chesterton from immediately embracing Rome, not, as Dale asserts, a "lack of social 'acceptability'" in Roman Catholicism.[141]

"My Husband and the Catholic Church": Illness and Transformation

Intellectual acceptance and practical action converged more closely a few years later. In late November 1914, Chesterton succumbed to the pressures of overwork and various familial and religious anxieties. He became comatose around Christmas and was near death. Uncertainty about his religious intentions added to Frances's ensuing strain. According to O'Connor, G. K. had intimated his Rome-ward leanings to Frances before he fell ill, but had not made his wishes clear; and her letters to O'Connor at this time show that fears about upsetting Gilbert's family, who had only accepted Cecil's conversion grudgingly, were foremost in her mind.[142] During a period of lucidity, however, Gilbert apparently in-

---

141. Dale, *Outline*, 203. Being a self-declared rebel against his culture, such social scruples would hardly have hindered Chesterton from going over to Rome. In fact, orthodox Roman Catholicism's dissent from post-Christian mores only heightened its attraction for him.

142. John O'Connor, *Father Brown on Chesterton* (London: Frederick Muller, 1937), 95; and Ward, *Chesterton*, 385–86.

dicated that he desired to be received so that he could die a Roman Catholic. Frances confided this matter to Josephine (Mrs. Wilfrid) Ward:

> I think I would rather you did not tell anyone just yet of what I told you regarding my husband and the Catholic Church.... I don't want the world at large to be able to say that he came to this decision when he was weak and unlike himself ... in God's good time he will make his confession of faith—and if death comes near him again I shall know how to act.[143]

Chesterton would repeat this wish to die a Roman Catholic years later, but its presence here indicates that his commitment to Roman Catholicism had undergone a significant development. Rather than just accepting its teaching intellectually, he now embraced Roman Catholicism with his whole being, desiring its blessing as he faced his judgment. In Gabriel Marcel's terms, in the course of this illness, Chesterton moved from a "belief that" orthodox Roman Catholic doctrine was intellectually accurate to a "belief in" its ability to redeem his soul. Additionally, according to Vincent McNabb, Chesterton claimed to have had a "mystic swoon" shortly before emerging from his coma in which he was addressed by Belloc's late wife (who had persuaded Cecil to become a Roman Catholic), an experience that gave further emotional texture to Gilbert's growing resolve to follow his brother's course.[144] The fact that G. K. Chesterton did not act on this conviction for almost a decade, though, has led many scholars to underemphasize this incident and the crucial transformation it effected in his attitude toward Rome.[145]

---

143. Frances Chesterton to Josephine Ward, 21 March 1915 (Ward, *Chesterton*, 387).

144. McNabb's report of this incident is reprinted in *Chesterton Review* 22 (February & May 1996): 258–59.

145. For example, Ffinch (233–36) and Coren (215–16) briefly rehearse this episode's events, but do not assess its spiritual significance. Pearce (*Wisdom and Innocence*, 214–20) is more sensitive to this incident's religious dimensions, but does not recognize its central importance for Chesterton's spiritual development. Dale's interpretation is full of missteps. Her assertion that Chesterton cared chiefly about "matters of daily discipline and habits," and not doctrinal differences between Anglo and Roman Catholicism, mistakes ephemerals for essentials. It was precisely doctrinal issues, like the locus of dogmatic authority and the forgiveness of sins that drew Chesterton away from Anglicanism, even leading him to accept disciplines, like early morning Mass, that he disliked greatly (see Ward, *Chesterton*, 547). Had such habits been his primary concern, he never would have become a Roman Catholic.

Why he did not act immediately after his recovery in the spring of 1915 is hard to ascertain. Chesterton once mentioned "mental fatigue" as an obstacle to Roman Catholic conversions, and the ensuing months and years brought many exhausting burdens on his own head and heart.[146] His prompt adoption of Cecil's newspaper during his brother's military service was demanding, and Cecil's 1918 death from an illness contracted during his stint in uniform devastated Gilbert. Moreover, after this tragedy, he presumably did not wish to add to his parents' grief by taking an action he thought would upset them. His scruples about Frances were also stronger than ever after the scare he had given her. Finally, while he may have become deeply committed to Roman Catholicism by this time, "action was always the weakest side of Chesterton. His talent and duty were to use his brain."[147] Especially as Frances showed no sign of moving to Rome, he lacked the practical motivation to take that step; and he may well have been intimidated by the prospect of having to make his way in a new spiritual home without her assistance.

Nevertheless, he took the duty to use his brain seriously, and continued to ponder Catholic issues. For example, he reviewed "with enthusiasm" Knox's *Reunion All Around*, which satirized the bent of some Anglicans to downplay doctrinal differences with Nonconformists in the name of Christian fellowship, and he concurrently chided such tendencies poetically in "The Higher Unity." The incident that provoked Knox's novel "proved decisive to some hesitating members of the Anglo-Catholic party who, in the language of the set, 'poped.'"[148] Chesterton's own decision to "pope" finally came in the early 1920s, and Knox and some of the issues raised in his book were crucial to it. The final stages of Chesterton's march to Rome were marked by a couple of dramatic events, growing disaffection with Anglicanism, and sustained self-examination.

This is also where Dale makes her "social acceptability" argument. These misunderstandings make it unsurprising that she considers Frances's consultation of O'Connor and Mrs. Ward "odd," despite longtime friendships with both of them, and the vital issues at stake (*Outline*, 202–3).

146. "Mr. Chesterton on Obstacles to Conversion," *The Tablet*, 9 June 1923, 774.
147. Wills, *Man and Mask*, 151. See also Ward, *Chesterton*, 445–46.
148. Evelyn Waugh, *Monsignor Ronald Knox* (Boston: Little, Brown & Co., 1959), 117; Chesterton, *Collected Poems*, 168–69.

"The Thing That I Would Do if I Returned to My Own Land": Travel and Commitment

In mid-1919, the *Daily Telegraph* commissioned Chesterton to write a series of articles about Jerusalem (which later became *The New Jerusalem*), and he sensed that this trip might assist his spiritual journey. He told Baring that his sojourn was "not wholly unconnected with the serious things" that they had been discussing since at least 1913, and his intuitions did not fail him.[149] During this trip (from December 1919 to April 1920), he had two experiences that were pivotal in his religious development. First, seeing where Christ lived and died heightened his sensitivity to Christianity's historicity and the consequent importance of tradition.[150] His sense that *Orthodoxy*'s "democracy of the dead" was found most fully in the communion of saints preached by Rome, an idea he had tentatively broached as early as 1911, achieved startling clarity when he heard Benediction in the Church of the Ecce Homo on Palm Sunday: "my train of thought, which really was one of thought and not fugitive emotion, came to an explosion."[151]

While Chesterton stresses here, as he usually did, his conversion's intellectual nature (an emphasis shared by Greene, Dawson, and Jones), it also had an undeniable emotional component, as the second crucial incident illustrates.[152] Following this highly charged trip to Palestine, the Chestertons returned to Britain by way of Italy. Arriving in Brindisi on Easter Sunday, they attended a Catholic Mass, as no Anglican service was available. The church they visited contained a statue of the Virgin Mary,

---

149. Chesterton to Baring, quoted in Ward, *Chesterton*, 442. For the dating of this discussion to at least 1913, see Chesterton's note on a 22 August 1913 letter from Baring, Chesterton Archives, The British Library.

150. See Chesterton quoted in Coren, *Gilbert*, 222; and Chesterton, "Bethlehem and the Great Cities," in *The Spice of Life and Other Essays*, ed. Dorothy Collins (London: Darwen Finlayson, 1964), 138–39.

151. Chesterton to Baring, undated 1919 letter, quoted in Ward, *Chesterton*, 447.

152. Chesterton's clearest and most vigorous assertion of his conversion's rational character is in *Christendom in Dublin* (London: Sheed & Ward, 1932), 56–58. The Ecce Homo experience itself may have had a more emotional dimension than he admitted. His use of "explosion" as a metaphor is one that William James associated with the more emotional elements of conversion. See *The Varieties of Religious Experience* (1902; reprint, New York: Modern Library, 1929), 195.

before which Gilbert prayed and made "the freest and the hardest of all my acts of freedom," promising her "the thing that I would do, if I returned to my own land."[153] He was committing himself to trust God, through Mary's mediation, to see him safely to his spiritual home.

Upon arrival in Britain in April, he plunged back into work, but thoughts arising from his trip were ever-present. Despite the greater certainty he had gained recently and his promise to Mary, Chesterton continued to worry about how Frances would react to his choice. He was also facing the fear of full commitment many converts feel as they make their final decision, claiming later that he had had "fears of something that had the finality and simplicity of suicide." Having pondered these issues for so long and so intensely, the enormity of what he was contemplating was especially clear: "the more I thrust the thing into the back of my mind, the more certain I grew of what Thing it was."[154]

"Like a Farewell": Thoughts After Lambeth

He was also becoming more sure that the Anglican Church was not that Thing. As Newman had, Chesterton was coming to believe that there was no third way possible between Protestantism and Roman Catholicism, at least given the direction he thought the contemporary Anglican Church was taking. He complained to Baring in mid-1920 that the decisions of that year's Lambeth Conference, which had been held in July and August, were a sign that the English Church had "done something decisively Protestant or Pagan."[155] He never specified more clearly what in that conference's conclusions troubled him so, but some inferences are possible.

While theological Modernism was not discussed explicitly at this conclave, it was part of the meeting's intellectual atmosphere, being this period's "most characteristic theology."[156] Anglo-Catholics detected its influence in the conference's most important declaration, the "Appeal to All Christian People." This letter sought to encourage Christian unity in

---

153. Chesterton, *The Well and the Shallows*, 463.
154. Chesterton, *The Catholic Church and Conversion*, 93. See Griffin, *Turning*, 122–23, for this hesitation as a frequent attitude of converts at this stage of the process.
155. Chesterton to Maurice Baring, 1920, n.d. (Ward, *Chesterton*, 456).
156. Hastings, *English Christianity*, 232.

the wake of the Great War, but many Anglo-Catholics thought it made too many doctrinal concessions to Protestants, particularly Presbyterians. A Catholic faction strongly opposed these facets of it, but was outvoted.[157] Given this background, it is easy to understand Chesterton's distress. The very unionist tendencies he and Knox had satirized a few years before were now apparently becoming the predominant force in his church. The Catholicism that had always been his chief priority was seemingly sacrificed to the goal of unity; and the indifferentist impatience with doctrinal divisions that he had condemned in *The Ball and the Cross* appeared to be growing increasingly influential in what he had considered his spiritual refuge from ascendant secularity.

The 1920 Lambeth Conference issued further statements that contradicted Chesterton's outlook. For instance, it addressed the personally salient issue of Spiritualism. Although ultimately reproving it, the Lambeth report expressed sympathy for the impulses behind it and what it deemed its partial truths.[158] These conclusions would thus have seemed an insufficient repudiation of what Chesterton had long regarded as a pagan and potentially maddening system, a case of praising by faint damns. He even cited "my spiritual biography" as a reason for his disquiet with Lambeth.[159] Beyond these specific issues, though, the intellectual tone of the Lambeth deliberations seems to have upset Chesterton. Its treatment of Spiritualism is indicative of the conference's generally moderate approach, whose eventual edicts were based on an "irreducible minimum" of dogma that was "more qualified than it had ever been."[160] This highly nuanced approach was antithetical to Chesterton's desire for clear, uncompromising authority in religious matters, and he told Baring that "the insecurity I felt in Anglicanism was typified in the Lambeth Conference."[161] As he elaborated a few years later,

---

157. Alan M. G. Stephenson, *Anglicanism and the Lambeth Conferences* (London: SPCK, 1978), 128–54.

158. See *The Lambeth Conferences (1867–1948)* (London: SPCK, 1948), 28–29, 48–49, 106–13.

159. Chesterton to Baring, 1920, n.d. (Ward, *Chesterton*, 456–57).

160. Roger Lloyd, *The Church of England, 1900–1965* (London: SCM Press, 1966), 409. See also *The Lambeth Conferences*, 140.

161. Chesterton to Baring, 1920, n.d. (Ward, *Chesterton*, 456). See Stephenson, *Anglicanism*, 145, for other reaction echoing this concern.

any church claiming to be authoritative, must be able to answer quite definitely when great questions of public morals are put.... But Protestant churches are in utter bewilderment on these moral questions—for example on birth control, on divorce, and on Spiritualism ... the Church of England does not speak strongly. It has no united action. I have no use for a Church which is not a Church militant, which cannot order battle and fall in line and march in the same direction.[162]

All these concerns highlight Chesterton's opposition to what he considered Anglicanism's growing accommodation of modernity. Its perceived doctrinal timidity and consequent willingness to compromise dogmas, and to sympathize with fashionable movements like Spiritualism, all seemed microcosmic of the longtime struggle in the Anglican Church between those who tried to reconcile it with post-Christian culture and those who deemed such concessions tantamount to surrender of its uniqueness. Having been drawn to orthodoxy by what he saw as its counter-modern, rebellious outlook, Chesterton was clearly among those who wished to keep the church unlike the current world. As that group's sway appeared to wane, and the majority seemingly eschewed explicitly Catholic convictions, he felt that his search for Catholicism in Anglicanism had ended. He concluded that the principles he hoped to preserve against Modernist pressures were being jettisoned by accommodationist Anglicans; only in Rome, where rebellion against modern irreligion was the rule, did unequivocal orthodoxy appear to prevail.

Yet Chesterton's perception that Catholics were no longer welcome in the Anglican Church at this time may seem mistaken. Adrian Hastings has argued convincingly that the 1920s inaugurated "the golden age of Anglo-Catholicism," and that it was Protestant forces in the church who were on the defensive for much of this decade. But even that Catholicism owed much to the liberal and Modernist Catholic theology that Chesterton had long opposed, as, from the century's early years, twentieth-century Anglo-Catholics had been steadily replacing Tractarian orthodoxy with a religion influenced by Roman excommunicate George Tyrrell, in which "ritual remained ... but dogma had been largely

---

162. Chesterton to the *Toronto Daily Star*, quoted in O'Connor, *Father Brown*, 140–41.

washed away,"[163] along with "the burden of the original apostolic deposit."[164] Moreover, it is also plausible that Lambeth's proclamations only added impetus to a decision that Chesterton had already largely made. His experiences in the Holy Land and Italy had strengthened his resolution to become a Roman Catholic; and sensing that Anglicans—even Anglo-Catholics—were dallying indecisively with, if not capitulating to, modern movements that he thought Christianity must combat confidently made it easier for him to fulfill his vow to Mary. In fact, he stressed to Baring that only personal problems now prevented him from sharing his friend's church. Discussing an Anglo-Catholic Congress he had addressed in the summer of 1920, Chesterton maintained,

> I felt it like a farewell . . . many of them besides myself would be Roman Catholics rather than accept things that they are quite likely to be asked to accept—for instance, by the Lambeth Conference. . . . I am concerned most, however, about somebody I value more than the Archbishop of Canterbury; Frances, to whom I owe much of my own faith. . . . [I must] talk the whole thing over with her, and then act as I believe.[165]

The Thing(s): Why Chesterton Became a Roman Catholic

That long conversation would last for two more years. If he remained a nominal Anglican during this time, though, Rome had claimed Chesterton's soul. Crucial traits of orthodoxy that he had long praised were fulfilled in Roman Catholicism. For example, his desire for authority now became focused in the papacy: his craving for a father was finally satisfied by the Holy Father. Chesterton had been moved as early as 1914 by the clarity Roman Catholicism derived from having a single center of definitive doctrine. But as the Anglican trumpets seemed more uncertain, he became increasingly impressed by Roman Catholicism's constancy, regarding its ability to keep its core beliefs intact and fresh over the ages as "the strongest of all the purely intellectual forces" that

---

163. Hastings, *English Christianity*, 195–96. See also Hugh McLeod, *Religion and Society in England, 1850–1914* (New York: St. Martin's Press, 1996), 190.
164. Aidan Nichols, "Chesterton and Modernism," in *Chesterton & the Modernist Crisis*, 162.
165. Chesterton to Baring, 1920, n.d. (Ward, *Chesterton*, 456–57).

spurred his conversion.[166] He judged ultimately that this faith's capacity for consistent truth-telling rested on its fidelity to the rock on which the Way, Truth, and Life had founded His Church. Recalling his first memory and *Orthodoxy*'s imagery, Chesterton concluded that

> he who is called Pontifex, the Builder of the Bridge, is called also Claviger, the Bearer of the Key; and that such keys were given him to bind and loose when he was a poor fisher in a far province, beside a small and almost secret sea.[167]

Chesterton also considered such a clearly defined center of authority a further deterrent to founding a personal heresy. In accepting papal teaching as his binding guide in faith and morals, he could remain sure of being a jester, a humble servant of traditional truths and their teller. As his reaction to Lambeth suggests, Chesterton thought that his day's Anglicanism was in peril of becoming a home of proud prophets, due to its lack of an agreed authoritative teaching office. Italianate Catholicism's emphasis on the papacy thus assuaged Chesterton's crucial theological and personal need for an external source of dogmatic surety.[168] This importance that he attached to papal authority led him to intimate finally that accession to it is Roman Catholicism's defining trait: "the Church is not a movement or a mood or a direction, but the balance of many movements and moods; and membership of it consists of accepting the ultimate arbitrament which strikes the balance between them."[169] In becoming a Roman Catholic, then, Chesterton "both affirmed himself by reverting to his truest self, and he denied himself by submitting to the authority of the Church, thereby escaping that ideological solipsism to which he often refers, and with which was associated his sense of sin."[170]

---

166. Chesterton, *Where All Roads Lead*, 29. See also *ILN*, 29 August 1914, which, tellingly, eulogized Pius X.

167. Chesterton, *Autobiography*, 331.

168. "The lack of discipline which allowed the Anglican Church to harbor those who were spokesmen for ideas which he felt were definitely destructive to Christianity was another factor which convinced him that it was not the True Church, which could be found nowhere but under the authority of the Pope." Dorothy Collins to A. L. Maycock, 26 January 1959, loc. cit. See also Woodlock, *Modernism*, 28.

169. Chesterton, *Chaucer*, 341.

170. Kevin L. Morris, "Chesterton's Conversion: Hesitation and the Recovery of Infancy," *Chesterton Review* 18 (August 1992): 380. See also Hunter, *Explorations in Allegory*, 134.

Chesterton's great respect for the papacy, however, did not foster the fideism exemplified in his fiction by Evan MacIan; indeed he contended that "it would be better to reject the Faith than to accept it as an unreasonable thing."[171] Rather, Chesterton believed that accepting authoritative direction in the absolutes of doctrine and ethics provided the framework and freedom necessary to make debate on probables possible and profitable. He had long held that "men should agree on a principle, that they may differ on everything else;"[172] and he found this conviction fulfilled in Roman Catholicism: "[Roman] Catholics know the two or three transcendental truths on which they do agree; and take rather a pleasure in disagreeing on everything else." To Chesterton, then, this integrated variety made dogmatic Catholicism the foundation of "an active, fruitful, progressive and even adventurous life of the intellect."[173] He even asserted that the papacy's global perspective enables it to avoid parochial preconceptions, and thus use its authority to buttress progressive forces within the Church.[174] Chesterton hence concluded that the See of Peter's occupant was able to utter the clearest, most consistent, and most liberating definitions of the lines of excellence that he had found set down by orthodoxy initially; to him, these declarations complemented reason's fruits: a Roman Catholic "believes in following his reason as far as it will go; and because, so far as it does go, it points in a direction which the authority of the Church continues."[175]

Another power bestowed on the original Pontifex, that to bind and loose, was also vital to Chesterton's acceptance of Roman Catholicism. He argued that the sacrament of penance was his main motive for becoming a Roman Catholic, as he thought only this religion claimed to "get rid of" his sins. This desire accords well with some of orthodoxy's other attractions for him. First, Chesterton held that if he had been able to confess his dark adolescent fantasies liturgically, rather than brooding over them, his descent into madness would have been arrested, for con-

---

171. Chesterton, *Christendom in Dublin*, 57. See also *As I Was Saying* (New York: Dodd, Mead & Co., 1936), 32.
172. G. K. Chesterton, *A Miscellany of Men* (New York: Dodd, Mead & Co., 1912), 144.
173. Chesterton, *The Thing*, 265, 299. See also *ILN*, 15 September 1923; and *Chaucer*, 285.
174. Chesterton, *Chaucer*, 186–87.
175. Chesterton, *The Weekly Dispatch*, 22 November 1925, op. cit. See also *ILN*, 29 August 1914.

fession is "the end of mere solitude and secrecy." This belief not only displays the Slade crisis's persistent influence, but it also helps accent another aspect of his opinion of the penitential sacrament. To Chesterton, every confession is like a conversion. He felt that confession restores the innocence lost by sin, just as his acceptance of orthodoxy had helped return his child's-eye view of the world. One thus enters a second childhood both when he adopts orthodox Christianity, as well as each time he reaffirms commitment to it by ceremonial repentance and atonement: the Roman Catholic believes that "in that dim corner, and in that brief ritual, God has really remade him in His own image . . . he is only five minutes old."[176]

Confession also strengthened Chesterton's philosophy of gratitude. To him, it provided the outlet for contrition and forgiveness when Being is treated ungratefully; and, in doing so, it affirmed his belief in the Janus face of freedom in a fallen world: whereas other faiths may offer ways to say "thank you," he thought only Roman Catholicism supplies a mandatory, sacramental way to declare "I'm sorry" too. Confession further enriched the corollary principle of conditional joy, as genuine repentance becomes the cost of forgiveness and the consequent resumption of full enjoyment of Being: "The gift is given at a price, and is conditioned by a confession."[177] Finally, Chesterton felt that the penance following confession was integral to preserving sanity, for it reinstated the balance disrupted by sin. Writing of medieval Catholics five years before his reception, he described views that became his own: "Extravagant humiliation after extravagant pride for them restored the balance of sanity."[178] This singularly Roman Catholic sacrament thus fulfilled many of the insights that had originally drawn Chesterton to orthodoxy.

Besides confession, Chesterton held that he ultimately became a Roman Catholic due to its "Truth, which may also be called Reality."[179] Orthodox Christianity's realism, its accordance with Being's complexity de-

---

176. Chesterton, *Autobiography*, 96, 329, 319–20.

177. Ibid., 320.

178. G. K. Chesterton, *A Short History of England* (London: Chatto & Windus, 1917), 80. Confession's importance to him became even clearer in his post-reception writings. For example, the unifying theme of *The Secret of Father Brown* (London: Cassell, 1927) is the potential for sin in all people and the consequent need for sacramental atonement.

179. Chesterton, *Autobiography*, 320. See also *Where All Roads Lead*, 27.

scribed in *Orthodoxy*, was finally fully present for him in Roman Catholicism, "which is realistic above all things."[180] He felt not only that "medieval religion was more realistic than modern idealism and optimism," but that it also surpassed other forms of Christianity on this count.[181] Believing that Protestants had substituted single truths for the whole Truth, he concluded that full Christian realism existed in either Anglo or Roman Catholicism. Chesterton became convinced that only Roman Catholicism has always held, and does always hold, a full complement of Truth, due to what he considered its unswerving fidelity to its origins and tradition. The Anglo-Catholic, by contrast, has only partial access to Catholicism because of his limited assent to its truth-claims: "Whilst you may be more or less of an Anglo-Catholic, you *cannot* be more or less of a Catholic."[182] In particular, Chesterton argued that Anglo-Catholicism's lack of a certain center of authority led its adherents to define their doctrines ephemerally by reacting to current concerns instead of striving for full continuity with Christianity's heritage: the Anglo-Catholic fights heresies of "the moment . . . the fallacies are merely fashions, and the next fashion will be quite different. And then *his* orthodoxy will be old-fashioned, but not ours."[183] As Chesterton believed that "an inch is everything when you are balancing," these seemingly small imbalances shaped his ultimate choice decisively.

As, in *Orthodoxy*, Chesterton had designated orthodox Christianity's ability to preserve this complex balance the "philosophy of sanity," it is unsurprising that his distinction between Roman Catholicism and other worldviews—and its corollary that "all [Roman] Catholicism is a balance"[184]—led him to conclude that the "central sanity is the philosophy of the Catholic Church."[185] Unlike Protestants or Anglo-Catholics,

---

180. Chesterton, *The Weekly Dispatch*, 22 November 1925, op. cit.
181. Chesterton, *ILN*, 1 September 1928.
182. "Mr. Chesterton on Obstacles to Conversion," 774. Emphasis in original.
183. Chesterton, *Where All Roads Lead*, 40. Emphasis in original. He made the same point in a 14 February 1923 letter to Baring: "The Church, as the Church and not merely as ordinary opinion, has something to say to philosophies which the merely High Church has never had occasion to think about. If the next movement is the very reverse of Protestantism, the Church will have something to say about it; or rather has already something to say about it" (Ward, *Chesterton*, 458).
184. G. K. Chesterton, *The Superstitions of the Skeptic* (London: W. Heffer & Sons, 1925), 36.
185. Chesterton, *The Catholic Church and Conversion*, 104.

Chesterton felt, an orthodox Roman Catholic holds "the complete philosophy which keeps a man sane; and not some single fragment of it . . . which may easily drive him mad."[186] Specifically, he thought Roman Catholic realism alone affirms completely the traditional, even tragic, truths that are necessary to keep away the maddening, constantly haunting, specter of Spiritualism; it is the "key" to sanity:

> Now a Catholic starts with all this realistic experience of humanity and history. A Spiritualist generally starts with the recent nineteenth-century optimism, in which his creed was born, which vaguely assumes that if there is anything spiritual, it is happier, higher, lovelier and loftier than anything we yet know . . . [it is] another optimistic fashion that there are no devil-worshipers—or no devils. But there are. That is the fact of experience that is the key to many mysteries, including the mysterious policy of the Roman Catholic Church.[187]

Chesterton further connected sanity, tradition, and realism, as well as justified counter-modern rebellion, in an essay penned six years after his reception:

> In nine cases out of ten the Church simply stood for sanity and social balance against heretics who were sometimes very like lunatics. . . . A study of the true historical cases commonly shows us the spirit of the age going wrong, and the Catholics at least relatively going right. It is a mind surviving a hundred moods . . . those who know the Catholic practice find it not only right, but always right when everything else is wrong.[188]

It is because Roman Catholicism has an autonomous source and standard of truth that it can stand outside its times and criticize them. Possessing an unbroken tradition and the authoritative truth-telling power embodied in the papacy, Chesterton believed, orthodox Roman Catholic

---

186. Chesterton, *The Thing*, 307.
187. Chesterton, "The Dangers of Necromancy," in *The Common Man*, 95.
188. G. K. Chesterton, "Why I Am a Catholic," *The Outline*, 28 January 1928. He anticipated this idea and rhetoric in *The Ball and the Cross* (148), giving further credence to the view that he was moving to Rome from the century's first years: "Catholic virtue is often invisible . . . because it is always sane; and all fashions are mild insanities. . . . The Church always seems to be behind the times, when it is really beyond the times; it is waiting till the last fad shall have seen its last summer. It keeps the key of a permanent virtue." See also *Lunacy and Letters*, 122.

dogmas free their adherents to rebel against secularist heresies: "it is still common to regard conversion as a form of revolt. And as regards the established convention of much of the modern world, it is a revolt." The "fixed goal" demanded for effective action in *Orthodoxy* was now supplied for Chesterton by Rome. Only it seemed to have the breadth of experience and accuracy of judgment necessary to prevent a person from mistaking the ephemeral for the eternal, plus the organs of discipline that Chesterton had long deemed essential to any army of revolt. He had long considered orthodoxy the source of this alternate affirmation needed to negate modern movements constructively. But he now concluded that this power was the "peculiar and solitary triumph of the Catholic faith" because it was the lone contemporary Christian church unwilling to cut down its creed to suit the irreligious mood of modern times: "The Catholic Church is the only thing which saves a man from the degrading slavery of being a child of his age."[189] In accepting the claims of a body for which, as Alan Gilbert puts it, "resistance, not accommodation, was the norm . . . [in which] marginality and conservatism were defenses against secularization," Chesterton thus gave his radical conservatism a spiritual home.[190] Once post-Christian norms were uprooted from British culture, it could be rerooted in the traditions of Christendom that, he felt, this church solely preserved in their purest forms.

Roman Catholicism, therefore, was the culmination of Chesterton's spiritual odyssey. Its singular sacraments and tradition met his need for complete, realistic, and authoritative truth, a longing that conversion theorists consider an essential element of many Roman Catholic receptions.[191] Its doctrines confirmed his principle of gratitude while its rituals provided a unique means of atonement for ingratitude, thus highlighting simultaneously the joys and responsibilities of freedom to him. Chesterton sensed that this church's unwillingness to give up its distinct traits in order to modernize enabled it to preserve what he considered the precarious balance of sanity. He hence thought it could ground his

---

189. Chesterton, *The Catholic Church and Conversion*, 65, 112, 110.

190. Alan Gilbert, *The Making of Post-Christian Britain* (London: Longman, 1980), 155.

191. See Conn, *Christian Conversion*, 183; and Karl Morrison, *Understanding Conversion* (Charlottesville: University Press of Virginia, 1992), 124.

condemnations of modern lunacy and be the standard for a healthier order. These yearnings had attracted him to Anglicanism, but its even tentative embrace of ideas he was convinced would produce personal and cultural catastrophe pushed him to an agonizing decision. Ironically, his impressions of confidence and freedom from regnant ideas are what had initially drawn Chesterton to Frances and her faith. With the failure of that religion to provide similar surety to him, though, he was now prepared to leave behind even the one who had brought the cross to him.

"My Name is Lazarus and I Live": Chesterton's Final Conversion

While the spirit seems to have been fully willing by late 1920, the flesh remained weak until 1922.[192] This hesitancy was not simply a case of Chesterton's usual slowness to action, for his feelings about Frances almost alone held him back. Some friends' impatience at what they deemed his glacial pace of deciding was becoming irritating, but he found more understanding assistance from Baring and Knox.[193] As an adult convert himself and a close friend to both Gilbert and Frances, Baring alone among Chesterton's intimates could appreciate G. K.'s difficulties. Knox was Baring's complement. He had become a Roman Catholic at a relatively young age (29) and was not close to Chesterton hitherto. But Chesterton had been his "idol" since boyhood, and he credited Chesterton with helping preserve his faith during a period of struggle with doubt.[194] He would now have the chance to similarly encourage his

---

192. Before departing in December 1920 to lecture in America, Chesterton wrote telling letters to Baring and O'Connor. He told Baring that "I have pretty well made up my mind about the thing we talked about. Fortunately, the thing we talked about can be found all over the world." To O'Connor, he echoed his post-Lambeth remarks to Baring, claiming that, upon his return, he would want to discuss "the most important things there are. . . . I feel it is also only right to consult with my Anglo-Catholic friends; but I have at present a feeling that it will be something like a farewell." (Both quoted in Pearce, *Wisdom and Innocence*, 253–54.)

193. Chesterton, *The Catholic Church and Conversion*, 188. Although he names no names, it became well known that Belloc, for one, eventually ceased hoping that Chesterton would convert to Roman Catholicism, thinking him attracted to it for aesthetic and romantic (i.e., wrong) reasons. Waugh also noted a growing frustration among Chesterton's friends with his caution, which he dated to 1915 (*Ronald Knox*, 198).

194. Ronald Knox to Frances Chesterton, 15 June 1936, Marion E. Wade Collection, Box 1, Folder 28, Wheaton College, Wheaton, Ill.

hero. Baring had known Knox since the late 1910s, and it was at his suggestion that Chesterton first contacted the priest in early 1922.

His letters to Knox from this period are as revealing a look at Chesterton's soul as exist. He believed that the meaning of his life depended on making this choice between churches correctly. He wished passionately to recover fully the lost innocence of childhood, and remained deeply affected by his struggle with solipsism:

> I am concerned about what has become of a little boy whose father showed him a toy theater, and a schoolboy whom nobody ever heard of, with his brooding on doubts and dirt and daydreams of crude conscientiousness so inconsistent as to be near to hypocrisy; and all the morbid life of the lonely mind of a living person with whom I have lived. It is that story, that so often came near to ending badly, that I want to end well.

The desire to die a Roman Catholic that had emerged during his Great War illness and is implied here had also appeared in an earlier letter to Knox;[195] and his father's death in the spring of 1922 increased Chesterton's desire to have the consolations of what he now considered the true faith when his own end came.[196] Yet even with his resolve stiffened, attending to his father's estate, and not wanting to upset his grieving mother any further, continued to delay his actual reception.

But he finally had to face his feelings about Frances forthrightly. Ever since he began to realize that he was a Roman Catholic, he had hoped to convince her to convert as well. Yet, perhaps smarting from his own encounters with overzealous yet well-meaning believers, he feared alienating her. He felt that the slightest touch could give her either great faith in or great hatred for Rome; an inch was everything in her balance.[197] To help insure that it tipped rightly, he called in John O'Connor, at Frances's

---

195. See Marion E. Wade Collection, Box 2, Folder 66. As Chesterton rarely dated his letters, it is impossible to know exactly when he wrote them, but their contexts suggest the above chronology. The earlier one is from early 1922. The other is probably from the spring of 1922. Knox's side of the correspondence has not survived.

196. See Chesterton to Knox, n.d., 1922, Chesterton Archives, The British Library.

197. See Chesterton to Baring, n.d., Chesterton Archives, The British Library; Chesterton to Knox, n.d., 1922, Chesterton Archives, The British Library; and Pearce, *Wisdom and Innocence*, 260.

request and with Knox's blessing. On 26 July 1922, O'Connor discussed the situation with both of them. The next morning he told Frances that only anxiety about her reaction was keeping G. K. from being received. O'Connor claimed that Frances said she would be greatly relieved if Gilbert so acted, for it would finally give them both the peace that his preoccupation had been preventing. But she also stressed that she could not move with him. Satisfied at last that Frances had consented, Chesterton arranged for his reception. On 30 July, he made his First Confession, to O'Connor, and was rebaptized by O'Connor and Dom Ignatius Rice, a friend of both Chestertons. He was now a Roman Catholic.

His first acts as one were, fittingly, to write notes of gratitude to Knox and Baring. He also comforted Frances, and wrote a presumably difficult letter to his mother. He stressed that he saw Roman Catholicism as the best way of sustaining humane ethical ideals (like honor, freedom, and charity) that his parents had taught him. Orthodoxy as found in Anglicanism had once provided that integration and continuity, but Chesterton concluded that only Rome now upheld such ancestral ideals unambiguously: the Anglican Church had lost its militancy for him, making its Roman counterpart the "one fighting form of Christianity." He assured her, with terrible understatement, that his decision was not precipitous, and ended by offering what was ultimately the chief reason for his action: "I believe it is the truth."[198] Finally, he wrote a poem reflecting this belief. Having at last taken this step, he felt rewarded with a certainty of conviction and an enhanced ability to differentiate between passing and permanent things; he now felt fully reborn:

> After one moment when I bowed my head
> And the whole world turned over and came upright
>
> . . .
>
> The sages have a hundred maps to give
> That trace their crawling cosmos like a tree,
> They rattle reason out through many a sieve
> That stores the sand and lets the gold go free:

---

198. Chesterton to Marie Chesterton, quoted in Ward, *Chesterton*, 466. Interestingly, he had referred to "that insatiably fighting thing, the Catholic Church" as early as 1904. See "The Style of Newman," in *A Handful of Authors*, ed. Dorothy Collins (New York: Sheed & Ward, 1953), 133.

And all these things are less than dust to me
Because my name is Lazarus and I live.[199]

"That Is What Is Meant By Having a Religion": Chesterton as a "Catholic Writer"

Now a member of what he saw as a militant church, Chesterton offered his pen as his chief weapon for defending his new faith against what he considered the insanities of secularist culture. He had published few, if any, directly apologetic works previously; but in the last fourteen years of his life, he wrote countless articles and at least four books of Roman Catholic apologetics, plus the bulk of his chief theological volumes, including studies of Francis of Assisi and Thomas Aquinas. Moreover, Roman Catholicism also infused his nonconfessional writings, especially his view of history. In fact, only his later fiction was less firmly imprinted by his new faith than his work in other genres.[200]

Is it hence correct to dub Chesterton a "Catholic writer"? This designation, which infuriated Greene and which Dawson and Jones also confronted, needs to be clarified. If it means that everything Chesterton wrote was meant to win converts or could only be understood by his co-religionists, then it is obviously false. Yet if it means that Roman Catholicism colored everything he wrote in some way, this is true and Chesterton did not deny it. Given his Victorian conception of the moral purpose of art, he felt that every author's writing is shaped and permeated by a set of convictions, and he asserted Catholicism's ability to serve this function as early as 1913.[201] It is not surprising, then, that in the years following his reception he considered his own governing principles to be Roman Catholic ones: "A Catholic putting Catholicism into a novel, or a song, or a sonnet, or anything else, is not being a propagandist; he is simply being a Catholic . . . even when it is not in the least propagandist, it

---

199. G. K. Chesterton, "The Convert," in *Collected Poems*, 387 (Greene took special note of this poem in his copy).

200. Chesterton's social and political ideas also became more explicitly linked to Roman Catholic doctrines, as will be shown in the companion history of these converts' social criticism.

201. "Catholicism is not a topic. It is not something one can mention on Tuesday but not on Friday. It is a way of looking at everything there is in the world." Chesterton, *The New Witness*, 30 October 1913.

will probably be full of the implications of my own religion; because that is what is meant by having a religion."[202] Because he believed orthodox Catholicism to be holistic, he contended that its core beliefs could accommodate the demands of distinct genres, and thus respect the difference between advocating its truth claims directly and crafting imaginative art with its complexion. Orthodox Roman Catholicism had become his way of understanding Being and it molded his presentations in all media, a development conversion theorists regard as a typical effect of religious conversion. Ian Boyd argues that this attitude was also a form of prophecy to Chesterton, that he was attempting to recall an errant people to their Christian roots by articulating that traditional faith to them in a wide array of culturally credible forms.[203]

While this goal had been true for years, Chesterton's reception into the Catholic Church gave his work greater focus and depth. Now without any reservations about the philosophy he was advocating, he could communicate his certainty and sense of fulfillment with clear conviction, as in the poem penned on the day of his reception. This absence of hesitation or defensiveness broadened his perspective, as he admitted in 1926: "with fuller convictions, one comes to have larger views."[204] Conversion also enhanced his sense of freedom from the tyranny of his times' norms. Chesterton held that a Roman convert can draw on fundamental alternatives from the full panoply of thought from two Christian millennia when assessing experience instead of being bound to only part of that legacy or to culturally current mores: he is "under vast domes as open as the Renaissance and as universal as the Republic of the world.

---

202. Chesterton, *The Thing*, 225.

203. See Conn, *Christian Conversion*, 112, 192; and Ian Boyd, "The Legendary Chesterton," in Macdonald and Tadie, *Riddle of Joy*, 59–60.

204. Chesterton, *ILN*, 24 July 1926. Knox echoed Chesterton's self-assessment, claiming that after his conversion, "his ideas seemed to grow even larger and more luminous." Ronald Knox, "G. K. Chesterton: The Man and His Work," in Conlon, *Half Century of Views*, 49. George Orwell, however, had a much more negative view of the effect of his conversion, lamenting that "Chesterton was a writer of considerable talent who chose to suppress both his sensibilities and his intellectual honesty in the cause of Roman Catholic propaganda." "Notes on Nationalism," in *The Collected Essays, Journalism and Letters of George Orwell*, ed. Sonia Orwell and Ian Angus (New York: Harcourt, Brace & World, 1968), 3: 365.

He can say in a sense unknown to all modern men certain ancient and serene words: *Romanus civis sum;* I am not a slave."[205]

Roman Catholicism's enrichment of Chesterton's lifelong themes is evident in many genres. For instance, his first Roman Catholic poems, *The Queen of Seven Swords*, are hymns to his long-beloved spiritual Mother; but his Mariology acquires an added imaginative dimension here by its association with the Roman Catholic sacrament of penance.[206] His post-reception thought's greater depth is also manifest in specifically apologetic works. For example, in *Orthodoxy* Chesterton held that in trying to found his own creed he was actually discovering something backed by the whole of Christendom. Discussing that insight in *The Thing* (1929), he held that "I should not have seen it quite [as] sharply and clearly; as I see it now." What had changed was his view of which creed best represents orthodoxy: the "old treasury of Christendom" is now deemed rich because of its "Catholic capital." As modern movements have spent that capital, trying to have Christian values without a credal foundation, only Roman Catholicism has been able to preserve either in undiluted form, due to its resolute resistance of post-Christianity.[207] Hence, Chesterton's acceptance of this faith refined his sense of where orthodoxy's principles are safely banked, even as this perception enriched his understanding of his new church. It is thus no surprise that he also wrote most of his main theological works only after 1922.[208]

The Everlasting Man (1925), Chesterton's theology of history, generally acknowledged to be his finest work, also best displays the deepening that resulted from his assent to Roman Catholicism. His only previous book-length work of history, *A Short History of England* (1917), had a more telescoped vision than *The Everlasting Man*'s. He had long contended that "there is no intelligible history without a religion";[209] but, although the *Short History* is favorably inclined to Catholicism, its Catholic elements are more implied than stated. Even if Dale is correct in suggesting that

---

205. Chesterton, *The Catholic Church and Conversion*, 94.
206. See Wills, *Man and Mask*, 164–65.
207. Chesterton, *The Thing*, 147, 151.
208. Mark Knight, "G. K. Chesterton and the Cross," *Christianity & Literature* 49 (Summer 2000): 495, n. 8.
209. Chesterton, *ILN*, 19 November 1910.

he had embraced Roman Catholicism inwardly by the time he wrote the *Short History*, it is a more tentative acceptance.[210] Chesterton was not fully committed to Roman Catholicism in 1917 and chose to concentrate more on history's matter than its meaning. The *Short History* is about history, now and in England, whereas *The Everlasting Man* attempts to assert history's overall significance. Only Chesterton's unequivocal adoption of a cosmology could supply the assuredness necessary to attempt such a bold project; and his effort in *The Everlasting Man* to bring an explanation of all history into clear focus finds his analysis inseparable from his faith, reflecting the increased confidence provided by his reception.

Like so many of his important works, *The Everlasting Man* began as a rebuttal. Wells had completed his *Outline of History* in 1919, in which he asserted that the purpose of past events had been to create modern humanity and society, which in turn are the embryo for even better people and eras in the future. Not surprisingly, then, he paid scant attention to religion. Considering secularism a healthier outlook due to its chronological primacy, he rejected the notion that past cultures could have owed their successes to something he regarded as barbaric superstition. Chesterton was a persistent critic of his friend's theses. He reviewed the *Outline* for the *Times*, and also advanced some of *The Everlasting Man*'s later arguments against it in a 1922 essay, *Where All Roads Lead*.[211] Three years later, he published *The Everlasting Man*, a work designed not merely as a response to Wells, "but to all histories based on a belief in linear progress."[212]

The Everlasting Man opens with a telling observation, as Chesterton stresses that his view of history and his religious faith are inextricably connected: "It is impossible, I hope, for any Catholic to write any book on any subject, above all this subject, without showing that he is a Catholic."[213] Whereas he had claimed in the *Short History* that without religion "there would never have been any English history at all," a specific

---

210. Dale, *Outline*, 209.

211. Compare especially *Where All Roads Lead*, 51–58, with *Everlasting Man*, 214–32. This essay, written very soon after his reception, is in many respects a germinal version of *The Everlasting Man*.

212. Ian Crowther, *G. K. Chesterton* (London: Claridge Press, 1991), 12.

213. Chesterton, *Everlasting Man*, 141.

faith rather than religion generally is now the key to his interpretation of history, revealing the extent of his religious development in the years separating these two books.[214] In making religion central to his view of history, Chesterton begins his analysis in a consciously counter-modern vein, and his specific arguments also follow this path. Instead of portraying history as a linear progression to the present, he posits three irruptions of qualitative differentiation: those separating humans from animals, Christ from all other humans, and Christianity from all other religions. In the case of human beings, he begins by rebutting Wells's claim that primitive cave drawings are a form of bestial superstition. As Jones would later, Chesterton asserts that cave paintings demonstrate that, from the species's earliest days, people, and only people, have sought to represent nature under other forms. He argues that the impulses behind art and religious worship are essentially the same, and that only rational beings possess them: "these natural experiences, and even natural excitements, never do pass the line that separates them from creative expression like art and religion, in any creature except man. . . . It was unique and it could make creeds as it could make cave-drawings."[215] To him, these artistic and sacramental impulses merge further in the myths that he contends humans, and humans alone, invent. Because only humans have the powers of speech and fancy, he posits, only they can attempt to explain their world imaginatively. Like any art form, this one also has a religious function for Chesterton, for he holds that most myths have tried to explain the ways of the divine to men, and have often involved the salvific death of a god or heroic god-figure.

Yet even the "sane heathenism" of the Roman Empire—"the highest achievement of the human race" to that point—was an insufficient theophany. Chesterton held that the Incarnation occurred when it did because "Man could do no more." With the Incarnation a new cosmos emerged that is "larger than the old cosmos."[216] To him, Christ is the

---

214. Chesterton, *Short History*, 41.

215. Chesterton, *Everlasting Man*, 181–82. Greene highlighted other instances of this idea in his copy. Chesterton had held this view for much of his career. See, e.g., *The Collected Works of G. K. Chesterton*, vol. 4, *What's Wrong with the World* (San Francisco: Ignatius Press, 1987), 166.

216. Chesterton, *Everlasting Man*, 307, 293, 309.

unique intersection of the human and holy trinities, being both Son of Man and Son of God. He thus fuses the material and the spiritual, the ephemeral and the eternal, within His person and thereby raises history to a higher ontological level: He makes the matter and meaning of history one. In Chesterton's view, Christ hence fulfilled all that was good in paganism, completing what was incomplete in ancient myths. Yet He also purged all falsehood from them, and so inaugurated a uniquely True understanding of Being, one that is more vital because it is unencumbered by error. As he put it in a contemporaneous story, "it divided truth from error with a blade like ice; but all that was left had never felt so much alive."[217] Christ has thus fixed forever the goal by which rebels and jesters can always call their ages to account, for He "incarnates Truth in the historical processes."[218]

Chesterton contends further that the Church Christ left behind after His Ascension continues this process. Chesterton maintains that orthodox Christianity distinguishes itself from all other faiths by claiming to have been founded by Truth Himself. He argues (in a passage Greene noted) that Christ alone of all religious founders claimed to be God; and, for Chesterton, someone whom he considers so self-evidently sane would only have made such an assertion if it was true. The Church, then, is His vicar, serving as the voice of Truth in history's final stage. Chesterton uses the key metaphor to express this belief that Christianity is qualitatively different due to its exclusive possession of Truth: "It definitely asserted that there was a key and that it possessed that key and that no other key was like it . . . there was undoubtedly much about the key that seemed complex; indeed there was only one thing about it that was simple. It opened the door."[219] Chesterton's repeated claim that orthodoxy is the outlook most in accord with Being had culminated in Roman Catholicism by this time. To him, the Roman Pontiff holds the keys of Peter.

Because the Church "fits the lock; because it is like life," Chesterton

---

217. G. K. Chesterton, *The Incredulity of Father Brown* (1926; reprint, London: Penguin, 1982), 146. See also *The Collected Works of G. K. Chesterton*, vol. 21, *The Resurrection of Rome* (San Francisco: Ignatius Press, 1990), 357–61, 455–56.
218. Wills, *Man and Mask*, 196.
219. Chesterton, *Everlasting Man*, 346–47.

believed that it has had the unique ability to merge phenomena previously considered incompatible, particularly mythology and philosophy. Whereas antiquity deemed myth and religion one thing and philosophy quite another, he declares, Catholicism rhymes these two roads to truth due to its historicity. He argued that no pagan myths claimed to be histories, but that the Gospels ground their validity in being accounts of actual events, thereby merging the mythological desire to tell tales with the philosophical search for truth: "The Catholic faith is the reconciliation because it is the realization both of mythology and philosophy. It is a story and in that sense one of a hundred stories; only it is a true story. It is a philosophy and in that sense one of a hundred philosophies; only it is a philosophy that is like life."[220] Chesterton hence specifies *Orthodoxy*'s dynamic balance here in the marriage of the imaginative and the rational powers under the Catholic Church's auspices, demonstrating further the enlargement of his vision following his reception.

He contends in *The Everlasting Man* that this combination and the Church that fosters it furnish the weapons for a continuous "revolution against the prince of the world."[221] He felt that similar rebellions had failed in the pre-Christian world, and he thought that the post-Christian era would suffer a kindred fate if it did not reform. Even as he defended what he saw as the tenuous orthodox Christian balance between philosophy and mythology, he sensed a modern reversion to the pre-Christian split, in the forms of rationalism and romanticism.[222] Believing that only Roman Catholicism had preserved this precarious equilibrium previously, Chesterton considered a Catholic revival essential for the successful rebellion against present-day (Prof.) Lucifers that would redeem his time. Although he had stated similar views formerly, *The Everlasting Man* uses history more explicitly than before as the foundation for contemporary evangelical hopes.

Holding that mirror of history up to nature, Chesterton deduces that Catholicism's foes had judged it dead many times in the past, "just as they do today." These "deaths of the faith"—Arianism, Albigensianism,

---

220. *Ibid.*, 380–81, 365, 378.

221. *Ibid.*, 313.

222. "[T]here are two tides in the world today—reason running one way and imagination the other." Chesterton, *ILN*, 21 April 1923.

Humanist skepticism, the Enlightenment, and Darwinism—were times when Catholicism seemed to have been buried by more up-to-date or progressive systems. But, he contends, orthodoxy returned after each heresy had departed, and cannot ever be eliminated permanently, because Catholicism is founded on the One Who conquered death: "it had a God who knew the way out of the grave." He uses these precedents deliberately to substantiate his belief that a similar Roman Catholic renascence was occurring in his own day: "we know that also in this last ending, which really did look to us like the final ending, the incredible thing has happened again; the Faith has a better following among the young men than among the old. When Ibsen spoke of the new generation knocking at the door, he certainly never expected that it would be the church-door."[223] Chesterton later extended this principle and hope to Western culture, the social order he considered founded on orthodox Catholicism, deeming it a civilization that "does decline, and has done so any number of times . . . [but it] has a way of managing to reappear, when its enemies have in their turn decayed." His peers are hence unwise to proclaim the "final extinction" of "this everlastingly dying creed and culture," for "today it stands erect and resurrected."[224] While Chesterton was overly sanguine about these religious and cultural revivals' extent, that very optimism arose from the confidence engendered by his reception. Indeed, all of *The Everlasting Man*'s main arguments were present embryonically in *Orthodoxy*, but had remained undeveloped for nearly two decades. The notions of humans being qualitatively different from animals, Christ being qualitatively different from all humans, and His Church being a revolutionary, eternally reviving institution are all sketched briefly in the earlier book.[225] But their elaboration awaited the deeper understanding of their significance that Chesterton acquired only with unqualified belief in Roman Catholicism. Only by embracing fully Roman Catholic teachings and traditions did Chester-

---

223. Chesterton, *Everlasting Man*, 383, 382, 387. Greene highlighted this analysis in his copy. Many of these points are prefigured in Chesterton's earlier writings. See, especially, *G. F. Watts* (London: Duckworth, 1904), 101; *Orthodoxy*, 101, 147, 149; and *Where All Roads Lead*, 29–30, 34–36, 40.
224. Chesterton, *Chaucer*, 373–74. See also *ILN*, 24 December 1921.
225. See Chesterton, *Orthodoxy*, 143–47.

ton think he had sufficient vision to see the matter and meaning of history steadily and wholly.

One literary form, however, does not display the fact or molding effects of his reception. Unlike Greene's experience, Chesterton's Roman Catholicism did not become his fiction's shaping force. He wrote fewer novels after converting and, with the significant exception of *The Return of Don Quixote*, these tales do not treat expressly Catholic issues or bear the stamp of a distinctively Catholic imagination. David Lodge has suggested persuasively that this anomaly in Chesterton's post-reception writing arises from a tension between full adherence to his new faith and his preferred fictional form of fantasy: "Chesterton's acceptance of the most precise and systematic of all Christian creeds imposed upon his thought a certain rigidity which did not combine easily with the form of fantastic novel he had developed."[226] While these commitments are not inherently exclusive, as Tolkien's work illustrates, it does appear that Chesterton found it harder to connect complete acceptance of Rome with romance than with any other genre.

Settling the Manichees: Chesterton and Thomism

On the whole, however, Roman Catholicism deepened Chesterton's thought. And it also broadened it. In particular, Thomistic philosophy and theology both fulfilled and transformed many of its central concerns. Chesterton had read the *Summa* by the time he wrote *Orthodoxy*, and his early writings contain the basic Thomist premise that faith and reason are allies, not antagonists, in the search for truth.[227] Moreover, he contrasted Scholasticism favorably with modern thought in *Heretics*.[228] Yet it was not until the impediments of doubt disappeared with his reception into the Church that the marriage of his mind with Thomas's could be fully fruitful: only when Chesterton possessed the "stupendous certitude" he attributed to Aquinas could he explain and apply Thomas's

---

226. David Lodge, "Dual Vision: Chesterton as a Novelist," in Conlon, *Half Century of Views*, 327.

227. See, e.g., Chesterton, *Thursday*, 11; and *The Innocence of Father Brown* (1911; reprint, London: Penguin, 1950), 24, 29. Hugh Kenner maintains that this theme is recurrent in the Father Brown tales. See *Paradox in Chesterton* (New York: Sheed & Ward, 1948), 129.

228. Chesterton, *Heretics*, 46.

teachings confidently.[229] The result of his growing surety was *St. Thomas Aquinas* (1933). In many respects, this book is the culmination of his thought, as lifelong themes find their resting place in Aquinas's system. *St. Thomas* is also a nonfictional allegory of Chesterton's own era, as he felt that Thomas's medieval foes had reemerged in modernity.

Initially, Chesterton's core principle of gratitude was ratified by Thomism. He saw Thomism's "primary and fundamental part" as "entirely the praise of Life, the praise of Being, the praise of God as the Creator of the World," for "Aquinas accepted things as God created them." Chesterton attributed this belief to Thomas's idea of *ens*. Aquinas held that even prior to essence or existence there is a principle of being within Being, that "something is something. . . . There *is* an Is."[230] This notion is the basis of philosophical realism, and it accords with Chesterton's view that the very fact of Being is a miracle meriting celebration and a sign that there is a Giver of this gift.[231] To both men, something is something, not nothing. And something is some thing, not a mental illusion. Thomism was also Chesterton's ultimate solution to his persistent fear of solipsism.

> In the Thomist, the energy of the mind forces the imagination outwards, but because the images it seeks are real things . . . things *not* to be found by staring inwards at the mind . . . the object *is* an object; it can and does exist outside the mind. . . . God made Man so that he was capable of coming in contact with reality.

Thomism further vanquished pessimism for Chesterton. If something is not only something, but the gift of a benevolent Creator, then Being's essential goodness becomes cause for the praise of Life. Modern pessimists who ask Hamlet's question are thus permanently rebuked by Thomas's philosophy: "To be—that is the answer." To Chesterton, then,

---

229. From page proofs of *St. Thomas Aquinas* in Chesterton Archives, The British Library.

230. *The Collected Works of G. K. Chesterton*, vol. 2, *St. Thomas Aquinas* (San Francisco: Ignatius Press, 1986), 483, 468, 529. Emphasis in original.

231. Chesterton recognized this link between his thought and Aquinas's retrospectively: "The truth presented itself to me, rather, in the form that where there is anything there is God. . . . I should have been amazed to know how near in some ways was my Anything to the *Ens* of St. Thomas Aquinas" (*Autobiography*, 148).

Thomism alone consistently and continually affirmed the primary loyalty to Being advocated in *Orthodoxy*, making it "the only optimist theology."[232]

Besides affirming Chesterton's basic principles, Thomism also substantiated his chief metaphors. He held that, in its time, Thomism "saved the sanity of the world"[233] by balancing faith and reason and that, for similar reasons, in his own day "the return of the Scholastic will simply be the return of the sane man." Thomism hence became the full "philosophy of sanity" depicted in *Orthodoxy*, for Chesterton thought its fidelity to Being's complexity refutes the extremes of spiritualism and materialism. It thus provides the dynamic, yet precarious, balance that prevents Christianity from deteriorating into either pure mythology or philosophy; what the Church had uniquely joined, Thomism keeps from being sundered.[234] Furthermore, Chesterton argued that Thomism preserves this balance because it is supported by the authority of the papacy. He felt that Thomism is especially vulnerable to heresy because, in so carefully balancing mysticism and reason, it lives on two dangerous edges simultaneously. It hence needs the Church's authoritative teaching power to keep it level: "Religion is a very terrible thing. . . . Authority is often quite as much needed to restrain it as to impose it . . . it is indulged in much saner proportion under Catholic Authority than in Pagan or Puritan anarchy."[235] No doubt Chesterton took the marriage of Thomism and papal authority in the encyclical *Aeterni Patris* as a comforting sign that the Church recognized this need to measure the lines of excellence carefully, aware that an inch is everything when you are balancing.[236]

Given the Church's rebuttal of modernity, though, allegiance to its authority meant rebellion against the dominant culture. Chesterton believed that the growing pessimism and irrationalism he discerned in his day made Thomism the best system to affirm when negating such

---

232. Chesterton, *St. Thomas*, 541–42, 489, 490. Emphasis in original.
233. Ibid., 487.
234. Chesterton, *The Well and the Shallows*, 475. See also Wills, *Man and Mask*, 170–71.
235. Chesterton, *St. Thomas*, 483.
236. Chesterton never commented directly on this 1879 encyclical. Yet Leo XIII's call for a Thomistic revival to help cure modern evils arising from adherence to "false" philosophies mirrors Chesterton's own understanding of the need for and importance of Thomism.

notions because Thomism "is the flat contrary of Modernism." If late-Victorian despair and the Great War had produced cultural chaos, Thomism would restore a cosmos. Chesterton contended that the secret of this system's past success was that it "was *not* a compromise with the world," and this is why he thought it could also be a regenerative force in contemporary British culture: "each generation is converted by the saint who contradicts it most."[237] His more general sense of Roman Catholicism as a source of rebellion and renewal was thus enriched by his contemplation of Thomism.

Moreover, Thomism crowned his career as a jester. If Chesterton had defended philosophy *per se* in *Heretics* and had tried to express his own theory in *Orthodoxy*, in *St. Thomas* he has refined his view to *a* theory: it is this particular articulation of orthodoxy that is now the "*only* working philosophy," as it is "the Thomist" who "begins by being theoretical, but his theory turns out to be entirely practical."[238] Hence the jester no longer upholds the idea of philosophy but the ideas of a philosophy. Wills thus calls *St. Thomas* the "completion" of *Heretics*, for in Thomism Chesterton found his "fixed goal" needed for effective practical action defined clearly in the "central philosophy of the West."[239] With his head and heart fixed on this objective tradition, he felt that his hands were free to implement its teachings in his own time.

That contemporary undercurrent is crucial to understanding *St. Thomas*. With the growing disillusionment of the rising generation induced in part by the Great War, and voiced by some literary Modernists, Chesterton dubbed spiritualism "the negative religion of our time" in 1927,[240] and decried the modern "sorts of scepticism which masquerade as mysticism" in 1931.[241] Witnessing this intensifying pessimism in his later years alarmed Chesterton, for he thought people were withdrawing from material realities into the imprisonment, and despair, of their own minds: "those who call themselves 'Modern' seem to have abandoned

---

237. Chesterton, *St. Thomas*, 434, 426, 424, 528. Emphasis in original.
238. Ibid., 542, 522. Emphasis added.
239. Wills, *Man and Mask*, 171.
240. Chesterton, "Defending the West," in *Chesterton Review* 15–16 (November 1989 & February 1990): 433.
241. Chesterton, *The Common Man*, 105.

the use of reason; they have sunk back into their own subconsciousness."[242] That way had lain madness for him, and he feared that interwar British culture as a whole might suffer a similar fate were some alternative not proposed to the "looming spectre of Spiritualism,"[243] as he posited (in 1926) that "we are under a wave of pessimism just now" that took a different shape from that of the 1890s, but required the same antidote of belief in the goodness of all facets of Being.[244] For him, that alternative and antidote was Thomism. He felt that the Middle Ages' great danger, which Thomas had rebutted, was renewed Manicheanism and Gnosticism. These dualist heresies held that matter is intrinsically evil, that life is thus a trial to be endured, and that the ultimate goal of believers is to escape from the prison of the body into a life of pure spirit. Chesterton contended that these doctrines had returned in secular form in his era: "there are a good many Manicheans among the Moderns." He also saw some theological Modernists as neo-Manicheans, including Anglicans E. W. Barnes and Dean Inge, whose beliefs he credited expressly with helping convince him to leave Canterbury for Rome. As Thomas had revived Aristotle to settle the Manichees of his day, then, Chesterton regarded a Thomistic renascence as the remedy for post-Christian pessimism and spiritualism: Thomas would again save the West from the "dreadful doom" of "abstract spirituality."[245]

Chesterton felt that Thomistic understandings of the Creation, Incarnation, and Atonement refuted those who deemed matter inherently depraved. Much as Jones would do, Chesterton stressed the Thomist belief that God affirmed the temporal and material not only by creating it, but also by becoming one with it and dying for it at a distinct moment in his-

---

242. Chesterton, *Sidelights*, 515. See also ibid., 605–11; *What I Saw in America*, 238; *Superstitions of the Skeptic*, 4–5.

243. Chesterton, *Chaucer*, 315.

244. *Observer*, 10 January 1926; and *Illustrated Sunday Herald*, 24 January 1926. See also *Avowals and Denials* (London: Methuen, 1934), 152–57. For a brilliant treatment of the common themes cutting across these two periods, see John Coates, "Chesterton and the Modernist Cultural Context," in *Chesterton & the Modernist Crisis*, 51–76. Chesterton had held since 1906 that one who is "conscious of his sub-consciousness" is "a madman in the most frightful and vivid meaning of the term" (*Lunacy and Letters*, 92).

245. Chesterton, *St. Thomas*, 485, 428; and preface to Woodlock, *Modernism*, iv. See also *Poet and Lunatics*, 124. His view of the Anglican thinkers is in *The Thing*, 295–96; O'Connor, *Father Brown*, 139–40.

tory: it was the "world" that God so loved. If matter itself is fundamentally good, Thomas continued, the means of perceiving it, reason and the senses, are also good, if flawed by original sin. Renunciation of this life and its powers is thus the ultimate act of ingratitude. To Thomas (and Chesterton) the Incarnation meant that "it was no longer possible for the soul to despise the senses, which had been the organs of something that was more than man. Plato might despise the flesh; but God had not despised it." Chesterton hence held that any Christian revival must begin with these premises, for "a Christian *means* a man who believes that deity or sanctity has attached to matter or entered the world of the senses."[246]

Yet he also argued that such a restoration must be a Catholic, Thomistic one, for not all Christians accept this central belief. Chesterton felt that modern Manicheanism was not limited to modernist pessimism, but was also a key facet of Protestant theology. Like Dawson, he had long asserted that modernity began with the Reformation.[247] He claimed that Catholicism's neo-Platonic, Augustinian strain, which Thomas had barely kept in equilibrium with Aristotelianism, regained prominence under Luther due to revulsion at logic-chopping late Scholastics. In developing an "elemental and emotional religion" that overemphasized the power of sin, Chesterton argued, Luther created a cosmology indistinguishable from the ancient Manichees or twentieth-century doomsayers: "all natural things were useless. Reason was useless. Will was useless ... That Protestantism was pessimism...."[248] Chesterton held further that "there never was a Modernism yet, but a Calvinist was at the bottom of it," an opinion only bolstering his belief that the lone hope for cultural rejuvenation was the philosophy that he thought Luther, Calvin, and the rest of the modern world had all rejected.[249] He concluded in the wake of his reception that the Catholic Church was the "one and only real champion" of natural goods like rea-

---

246. Chesterton, *St. Thomas*, 493, 437. Emphasis in original. He had expressed this theology's essence, but without the Thomistic categories, in "The Ballad of the White Horse": "For our God hath blessed creation / Calling it good ... Yet by God's death the stars shall stand / And the small apples grow" (*Collected Poems*, 257).
247. Chesterton, *Orthodoxy*, 30; and *ILN*, 12 June 1920.
248. Chesterton, *St. Thomas*, 548–49.
249. G. K. Chesterton, *Irish Impressions* (London: W. Collins Sons & Co., 1919), 188.

son in modern times,²⁵⁰ for Thomism's balanced validation of both the temporal and the transcendent was the "only creed in which the saints can be sane."²⁵¹

Subsequent attempts at a Thomistic revival largely proved ephemeral. But those later developments do not devalue Thomism's importance to Chesterton's worldview.²⁵² Thomism supplied a comprehensive, integrative system that confirmed the metaphysical and religious insights he had been developing since his Slade breakdown. His capacious intellectual appetite was sated by Thomas's equally abundant feast in a way no other theology probably could have done. Augustine's latent Platonism was too close to the idealism that had sent him into the abyss; he needed Thomas's realism as a secure starting point. Chesterton found his basic belief, that "it is good to be here," substantiated by Thomas's *ens*. Corollary principles of gratitude, cosmic optimism, the goodness of matter, and trust in reason and the senses then followed as logically for him as for Aquinas. Thomism hence filled in Chesterton's outline of sanity by rebutting "Manichean madness," and it provided a specific set of principles to jest for and rebel on behalf of.²⁵³ By refuting modern heresies, Chesterton thought, Thomism would fertilize the flowering of the Catholic Third Spring, in which traditional Christianity would again find its way out of the grave. He hoped to tend that garden in which the stone had been rolled away.

Ending in Beginning: Conclusion

Chesterton was both steward and sower in the field of orthodox Catholicism, for he drew on and shaped its British yield. For instance, he sensed similarities in his and Newman's outlooks throughout his career. He claimed in 1904 that Newman expressed the principle of wonder

---

250. G. K. Chesterton, "God and Intelligence in Modern Philosophy" (1925), in *Chesterton Review* 26 (August 2000): 291.

251. G. K. Chesterton, "St. Thomas Aquinas," *Spectator*, 27 February 1932.

252. Although Jay Corrin claims that Chesterton helped spark the neo-Thomist revival in England, its seed fell on largely rocky ground. While more successful temporarily in France and the United States, its chief figures are more venerated (or ignored) than studied in most contemporary Roman Catholic circles. Corrin, *G. K. Chesterton and Hilaire Belloc: The Battle Against Modernity* (Athens: Ohio University Press, 1981), xii.

253. Chesterton, *Sidelights*, 470.

even better than Whitman, and he compared *Orthodoxy* with Newman's *Apologia*.[254] Even more crucially, he noted Newman's role in establishing a tradition of Catholic counter-modern rebellion, even as he was struggling with his own decision about joining it. In 1907, for example, he cited Newman in reproving "the frightful danger of Liberalism" as the "chief blunder of our time;"[255] and in 1913, he called Newman's moral commentary "a revolt," a "protest of the rationality of religion as against the increasing irrationality of mere Victorian comfort and compromise . . . he has no followers in his own age: but very many in ours."[256] Even allowing for the underestimation of Newman's Victorian legacy, Chesterton's belief that Newman had helped start a movement of cultural protest rooted in his religion that remained vital in his own day is manifest. Once he joined the Catholic Church, Chesterton continued to invoke Newman's cultural critique, particularly his definition of liberalism, as ongoing defiance of the "anti-dogmatic principle" was integral to Chesterton's own dissent from modern unbelief.[257] These significant affinities thus validate Hastings's conclusion that Chesterton stands within the "tradition of Newman."[258]

Yet Chesterton also felt from the early 1900s that "we live in an age without shape or parallel."[259] He thus developed this legacy to focus its resources on what he deemed the new challenge of a uniquely potent

---

254. Chesterton, "Style of Newman," 131; and Wills, *Man and Mask*, 227, n. 15.

255. Chesterton, quoted in Boyd, "Anglican Reaction to Modernism," 16.

256. Chesterton, *Victorian Age*, 29, 31–32. One reviewer of this book held that Chesterton's "praise is all for Newman." Anon., *The Observer*, 23 February 1913 (Conlon, *Critical Judgments*, 308).

257. Chesterton, *St. Thomas*, 433, n. 2. Chesterton deemed this reference to Newman important enough to add it at the page-proofs stage. This continuity substantiates Sheridan Gilley's view: Chesterton's "whole life, like Newman's, was directed against liberalism in religion" ("A Tradition and Culture Lost, To Be Regained?" in *Catholics in England, 1950–2000*, ed. Michael Hornsby-Smith [London: Cassell, 1999], 42).

258. Adrian Hastings, "Some Reflections on the English Catholicism of the Late 1930s," in *Bishops and Writers: Aspects of the Evolution of Modern English Catholicism*, ed. Adrian Hastings (Wheathampsted-Hertfordshire: Anthony Clarke, 1977), 111. Chesterton's contemporaries made similar comparisons, in some cases even before he became a Roman Catholic officially. See, e.g., Alfred Brickel, "Cardinal Newman and Gilbert K. Chesterton," *Catholic World* 109 (September 1919): 744–52; and Theodore Maynard, "The Newman of a New Age," *Commonweal* 3 (2 December 1925): 96–97.

259. Chesterton quoted in Boyd, "Anglican Reaction to Modernism," 30.

hostility to traditional Christianity and its affirmation of objective, external, temporal reality in the early twentieth century. Moreover, he helped transmit the essential elements of this heritage of Roman Catholic rebellion against modern secularism to a growing number of converts who were taking places in it. Even if their specific applications of these shared norms differed from Chesterton's, Greene, Dawson, and Jones all avowed a conscious debt to him and, even more significantly, demonstrated an unconscious one. As Knox asserted, this generation was often "thinking Chesterton" without realizing it.[260] Before discussing some of these thinkers' spiritual odysseys, though, it is useful to recapitulate Chesterton's own journey.

There would have been little basis for predicting that the young G. K. Chesterton would become an orthodox Christian, much less an ardent Roman Catholic. His early religiosity was ethical and aesthetic, and his childhood happiness betokened a lifetime adherence to common upper-middle-class norms—a mixture of agnostic humanitarianism and vague "Progressive" leanings. What transformed Chesterton was his sensed encounter with evil at the Slade School. His introspective temperament had left him vulnerable to self-immurement, and his inherited values were unable to check that tendency's destructive consequences. With the inadequacy of those ancestral principles revealed, he began pursuing a more satisfying framework for his ever-active intellect.

Yet it was his heart that initially led him. Having found God through gratitude, he discovered orthodoxy through Frances. Contact with her and her circle convinced Chesterton that Catholic Christianity would supply the resources to retain sanity, resist secularity, and humbly jest against his age's false prophets. His Anglo-Catholicism was as sincere as Newman's had been; but changes he discerned in Anglicanism finally made continued allegiance impossible. Its apparent accommodation of modern trends that he expected religion to resist persuaded Chesterton that only Rome had the authority needed to maintain all ancient, orthodox dogmas against the pressures of a post-Christian culture. His passage was tempest-tossed, for he was forced to leave Frances on the shore behind him. Yet once inside the Church, he did not regret his voyage

---

260. Knox quoted in Ward, *Chesterton*, 524.

(and Frances did join him in 1926). Rather, free of any fundamental doubts for the first time since boyhood, his thought bloomed fully. Thomism gave his worldview coherence and completion.

In hindsight, it may seem almost inevitable that Chesterton would end up an orthodox Roman Catholic. To think so, however, is to underrate his struggle's seriousness and his spiritual development's distinct phases. Each choice was conditioned by specific events and resulted from careful, often anguished, deliberation. Those who have found his ponderous pace perplexing fail to understand one of Chesterton's chief convictions, that life is a story. To see that is to see a sensitive man considering religious questions as though his life depended on them, for he thought it did. He would write the conclusion to his own tale, hoping it would end well, but knowing that it might not. Finally, though, he did think he had attained a happy ending. In Thomistic Roman Catholicism Chesterton recovered fully the integrity and happiness of his childhood. Yet this second childhood was richer than his first, due to the wisdom he felt he had acquired in reaching it. In that sense he had gone around the world to come home. But what a journey it was.

CHAPTER 2

THE HEART OF THE MATTER
Mapping Graham Greene's Religious Journey

ONE CONVERT who was "thinking Chesterton" was Graham Greene. Greene was impressed by Chesterton even before Greene became a Roman Catholic, as the only autograph he sought as a youngster was "when I ran, in my school cap, after G. K. Chesterton, as he labored like a Lepanto galleon down Shaftesbury Avenue."¹ Though not an uncritical admirer, Greene retained this esteem for Chesterton throughout his long career. In 1944, for example, he rebutted the portrait of his predecessor as an ephemeral verbal prankster, asserting that Chesterton's religious writing saw what "was most lacking in our age";² and he re-

---

1. Graham Greene, *A Sort of Life* (New York: Simon & Schuster, 1971), 61 *(SOL)*.
2. Graham Greene, "G. K. Chesterton," in *Collected Essays* (New York: Penguin, 1969), 108 *(CE)*.

mained faithful to Chesterton into old age, implying in 1978 that "The Ballad of the White Horse" was a better poem than one by another mentor, "The Waste Land."[3] Moreover, Greene was eulogized upon his 1991 death as "Chesterton's successor" in British literary life.[4] While he shunned such labels when alive, they nonetheless point to essential similarities in these men's lives and ideas, affinities ignored by most scholars.[5]

In particular, both their worldviews were shaped decisively by youthful traumas occasioned by the contrast between happy boyhoods and an event that came to symbolize Evil. Their inability to comprehend these episodes from within their inherited outlooks helped make them susceptible to Catholicism's claims, which gave both men theological explanations for their adolescent crises and their metaphysical lessons. Moreover, this early encounter with evil became the focal point of each writer's dissent from what he regarded as modern religious and cultural norms. While Greene's conversion to Roman Catholicism was not as laborious a process as Chesterton's, his struggle with its teachings was dynamic until death. Furthermore, if his greater interest in sinners and seediness made him "no happy warrior,"[6] he still considered himself a recruit to Chesterton's "one fighting form of Christianity," albeit sometimes a member of its "Foreign Legion."[7] In short, despite his different path to and understanding of Catholicism, Greene was drawn to it, as Chesterton was, as balm for psychic wounds sustained in youth; also like his predecessor, he came to root his role as a counter-modern rebel in its precepts and ethos.

Although Greene and others have recounted elements of his religious biography, a comprehensive assessment of it has been possible only since 1991, and the attempts made since then have lacked nuance and accuracy.[8] This deficiency demands correction, for Greene's "theology is a

---

3. Greene, *The Observer*, 12 March 1978. Greene had twenty-one Chesterton titles in his library at his death, including most of Chesterton's major works. This library is held by John J. Burns Library, Boston College.

4. Anthony Grist, "News and Comments," *Chesterton Review* 18 (August 1992): 456.

5. See Adam Schwartz, "'It is Good to be Here': G. K. Chesterton's *The Thing* and the Thought of Graham Greene," *Faith & Reason* 21 (Spring–Summer 1995): 101–19.

6. Grist, "News and Comments," 456.

7. Greene, *SOL*, 169.

8. For example, his official biographer, Norman Sherry, has produced two exhaustive

radical part of his thinking and feeling, the evident principle of integration in his art."⁹ Only by understanding fully his spiritual voyage's course, then, will the chief factors in his intellectual vision and cultural commentary become clear. Yet this is not a journey without maps, as numerous mileposts stand out. The first is his youthful liberal Christianity, followed by the crisis at the Berkhamsted school that undermined his boyhood faith and dominated his consciousness permanently. The search for meaning this calamity sparked eventually led to his acceptance of Roman Catholicism in 1926. His subsequent explorations of that household of faith culminated in emphasis on metarational experience, doubt, and opposition to key changes associated with the Second Vatican Council. Throughout all these stages, though, Greene considered himself a rebel against modern culture. He thus further developed and applied the legacy of British Catholic protest that he inherited from the likes of Chesterton and Newman.

Sorts of Life: Art and the Man

Before trying to follow Greene's spiritual footsteps, however, it is important to recognize that he was a crafty cartographer. He guarded his privacy jealousy and claimed to disdain introspection, thus becoming notorious for misleading interviewers, while also admitting that his autobiographies were "only 'a sort of life.'"¹⁰ Yet one of his work's paradoxes is that despite these deceptions and disavowals, his fiction and criticism are saturated with references to his life: he is one of the most

---

tomes thus far (*The Life of Graham Greene*, vol. 1, 1904–1939 [New York: Viking, 1989], and *The Life of Graham Greene*, vol. 2, 1939–1955 [London: Jonathan Cape, 1994]) that provide a wealth of information, but are more concerned with narrative than analysis, especially when treating the religious aspects of Greene's life. Michael Shelden's *Graham Greene: The Man Within* (London: Heinemann, 1994) is more intellectually rigorous, but is marred fatally by unremitting hostility to Greene, which usually fosters the most cynical reading of the material possible. He does not think that Greene underwent any spiritual development (128), and judges his acceptance of Catholicism wholly tactical (127). Given his denial of the authenticity of Greene's conversion, Greene's religious journey does not engage Shelden's attention, and what commentary he does offer about it is so jaded and counterintuitive that it obscures some good insights about Greene's writing.

9. Francis Connolly, "Inside Modern Man: The Spiritual Adventures of Graham Greene," *Renascence* 1 (Spring 1949): 17.

10. Greene, *SOL*, 11.

indirectly autobiographical authors in modern British letters. As Michael Shelden claims, "The 'real' stories he told about himself may be less reliable than the encoded messages of his fiction."[11] Greene's dislike for direct self-examination, then, frequently provoked sublimation of such reflections into his creative writing. As helpful as his fiction is in deciphering the often ambiguous nonfictional charts he drafts, though, a direct relationship to his life should not be assumed in all instances, nor should the inventive power of imagination be denigrated. Greene told Evelyn Waugh, "I would certainly not attempt to hide behind the time-old gag that an author can never be identified with his characters. . . . At the same time I think one can say that a parallel must not be drawn all down the line and not necessarily to the conclusion of the line."[12] Thus while Greene is in his fiction, he is not wholly of it. He reserves, and often executes, the right of any imaginative artist to use personal experiences as the springboard for broader moral, religious, and political statements.

One principal way Greene simultaneously identified with and distanced himself from his characters was by using them to try to purge temptations from which he suffered. He was fascinated by numerous beliefs and actions that he judged would produce disastrous consequences if indulged, but whose attraction was too powerful to ignore. He considered these lines from Browning the epigraph for all his novels:

> Our interest's on the dangerous edge of things.
> The honest thief, the tender murderer,
> The superstitious atheist, demi-rep
> That loves and saves her soul in new French books—
> We watch while these in equilibrium keep
> The giddy line midway.[13]

Fiction indeed became his chief means of keeping his personal equilibrium, as Greene's characters frequently succumb to his own temptations, and suffer the fate he had foreseen for himself. Implicit in this process is the hope that by going to such extremes in his art, he can avoid doing so

---

11. Shelden, *Within*, 50.
12. Graham Greene, *Ways of Escape* (New York: Simon & Schuster, 1980), 263 *(WOE)*.
13. Greene, *SOL*, 117. See also Shelden, *Within*, 407–8.

in his life; allowing his characters to cross that giddy line midway enables him to remain on its safe side: "Writing is a sort of therapy—the way one writes, but also the experiences, the events in one's life which provide, however remotely, the basis for one's writing. . . . [I] try to cure anguish by giving it a symbolic representation. . . . I tamed certain nightmares in making use of them as a background."[14] Greene's self-assessment is confirmed by Anne Salvatore, who maintains that he often offers readers "the opportunity to experience an attitude that leads to disaster in its exaggerated form. . . . Greene allows the character's perspective to disclose its own disastrous effects." Through rhetorical devices like free indirect discourse, he was able to sympathize with his characters' dilemmas while also disapproving of their resolutions, thereby affirming his resistance to the temptations they could not withstand.[15]

Greene was not alone in sensing literature's purgative potential, as Chesterton, C. S. Lewis, and more recent critics have all noted the ability of authors to confront their dark sides in their writing.[16] But this pattern's prominence in his work has particular causes and nuances. Initially, Greene was a diagnosed manic-depressive. Creative writers are considered to be ten to twenty times more prone to this affliction than people in other professions, and some of those sufferers have asserted that their writing helped cast out demons that haunted them during depressive phases.[17] While Greene's writing was not motivated exclusively by such a desire, recognizing this connection to a specific medical condition helps illuminate his work's therapeutic aspect. Moreover, his psychological state and use of literature in coping with it helps explain his

14. Marie-Francoise Allain, *The Other Man: Conversations with Graham Greene* (New York: Simon & Schuster, 1983), 26, 135.

15. Anne Salvatore, *Greene and Kierkegaard: The Discourse of Belief* (Tuscaloosa: University of Alabama Press, 1988), 33, 41. See also Richard Freis, "Scobie's World," *Religion & Literature* 24 (Autumn 1992): n. 2.

16. G. K. Chesterton, *The Secret of Father Brown* (1927; reprint, London: Penguin, 1974), 12; C. S. Lewis, *A Preface to Paradise Lost* (London: Oxford University Press, 1960), 100 (highlighted by Greene in his copy); Dorothy L. Sayers, *The Mind of the Maker* (1941; reprint, San Francisco: HarperCollins, 1987), 49–59; Barbara Johnson, *A World of Difference* (Baltimore: Johns Hopkins University Press, 1987), 144–54.

17. William Grimes, "Exploring Writers' Links to Depression and Suicide," *New York Times*, 14 November 1994, B1. Greene was especially susceptible to this malady, as it also afflicted his paternal grandfather.

creation of "Hilary Trench," an alter ego he adopted during depressive periods when he "felt the need to express unpleasant aspects of his character." Greene's invention of such a figure reveals not only a desire to avoid responsibility for vicious thoughts by attributing them to Trench, but also implies the hope that if "Hilary" uttered such notions, Graham would not act on them. While Greene asserted at various points that he had killed Trench, "this gloomy and morbid double personality never left him," a point he acknowledged tacitly in a late novel.[18] *The Honorary Consul*'s Charley Fortnum has his own Hilary Trench, one he humorously names Mason: "It was always to Mason he attributed his worst errors and his worst failings."[19] Greene, then, found books and an invented doppelganger a way of disposing of his dubious desires temporarily, even if these devils never ceased to torment him fully. He always danced on the dangerous edge.

Prologue to Pilgrimage: Early Childhood and Its Discontents

With this key to Greene's personal map elucidated more fully, it is possible to retrace his specific spiritual steps. His family was like Chesterton's, being respectably middle class and conventionally liberal Christian. His maternal grandfather was a Bedfordshire clergyman until he defrocked himself after a crisis of conscience. Whether in reaction to this incident or not, Greene's parents showed no signs of being distinctively devout: "before my conversion I had no Church. My family was quite indifferent to these problems."[20] His father, Charles, was a liberal in both religion and politics, with a typically Victorian trust in human nature and belief in Progress.[21] He replaced doctrinal or devotional rigor in religious matters with heightened concern for ethics and aesthetics. His bywords were duty and purity, and he chose favorite scripture passages

---

18. Sherry, *Life*, 2: 67–8.

19. Greene, *The Honorary Consul* (1973; reprint, New York: Pocket Books, 1974), 117 *(HC)*. This device is prefigured in Greene, *The Third Man* (1949; reprint, New York: Pocket Books, 1974), in which "there was always a conflict" in the protagonist, Rollo Martins, for "Rollo wanted to hit out, but Martins was steady" (18, 27). Martins also occasionally uses his real name interchangeably with his pseudonym, Buck Dexter.

20. Allain, *Other Man*, 146.

21. See Humphrey Carpenter, *The Brideshead Generation* (Boston: Houghton Mifflin, 1990), 107.

based on "personal feeling for its beauty." In short, Charles was an "old-style believer in clean living and the good Christian life."[22] There is less evidence of Marion Greene's views, but some hints can be adduced. In Graham's autobiographical story "Under the Garden," for example, the protagonist's mother—who shares many of Marion's other traits—is described as a Fabian empiricist: "She had very decided views, you know, about any mysteries. . . . She wanted everything to be very clear."[23] If Graham was drawn to the dangerous edge, his sister recalled their mother as "very stable and practical. She was rational and had good sense."[24] Marion had little interest in religious topics, and often admitted her ignorance of various practices, an understandable attitude given her father's fate. She also seems to have shared her husband's benign view of human nature and his intense perception of propriety. In *The Ministry of Fear*, Arthur Rowe dreams of trying to convince his mother that he is a murderer, only to be rebuffed: "My little boy couldn't kill anyone. . . . My little boy wouldn't hurt a beetle," a translation of Graham's belief about Marion that "if one of us had committed murder she would, I am sure, have blamed the victim." She also once destroyed *Old Moore's Almanack* due to what she considered indecent advertisements.[25] The religious ambiance fostered by Greene's parents, then, was like that of many of their class: a no-nonsense, personal Christianity of the heart distrustful of spiritual enthusiasm, and dogmatic in matters of conduct, if not conviction.

Young Graham seems to have inherited his parents' conventional traits, including their indifference to religious issues. The religion he learned as a boy "went no deeper than the sentimental hymns" and the "prayers of a rather lay variety" said at school.[26] He found the Anglican liturgy "interminable," and was confirmed "only because it was expected of me." Nor was he troubled in his early years by this lack of deep religious roots. Until he was six, the Greenes lived in St. John's house of

---

22. Sherry, *Life*, 1: 45.
23. Greene, "Under the Garden," in *Collected Short Stories* (New York: Penguin, 1986), 177.
24. Elizabeth Greene conversation with Norman Sherry, 6 July 1984 (Sherry, *Life*, 1: 48).
25. Greene, *The Ministry of Fear* (1943; New York: Viking, 1982), 67; *SOL*, 19; Sherry, *Life*, 2: 28.
26. Greene, *SOL*, 164, 68.

Berkhamsted School, where Charles was housemaster. This was Graham's arcadian period, one he recalled with an impression of "tranquillity and happiness."[27] But this idyllic interval ended when Charles Greene succeeded Dr. Thomas Fry as Berkhamsted's headmaster in 1910.

While the full consequences of his father's decision for Graham were still years away, even the move from St. John's to the headmaster's house precipitated new anxieties in the youngster. Graham claimed that it was at age seven, "menaced by the approach of school and a new sort of life,"[28] that a recurrent nightmare about a witch in his linen cupboard began, an experience he judged in old age to have been more terrible than any waking danger he had faced.[29] He also tried unsuccessfully to conceal his ability to read, fearful that reading represented the "grim portal" to preparatory school, which he entered soon after turning eight. While the books he favored seem fairly normal for a boy of his time, the lessons he claimed to have learned from them are far less standard. For instance, he judged Kipling's *Baa Baa, Black Sheep* "a warning not to take happiness in childhood for granted."[30] Greene had always been very sensitive and had had some graphic early experiences of death; but he appears to have become more generally skeptical about happiness during his preparatory school years. His official biographer feels that this outlook intensified when he moved into Berkhamsted Junior School at age ten, and "began to be aware of cowardice, shame, deception and disappointment."[31]

Why Greene's disenchantment with human nature deepened at the Junior School is difficult to ascertain directly. It seems likely that a confluence of events, rather than a specific incident, conspired to blacken his mood. For one, the Great War coincided directly with his Junior School

---

27. Unpublished passage from *A Sort of Life* (quoted in Sherry, *Life*, 1: 254–55); and Greene, *SOL*, 31.
28. Greene, *SOL*, 32.
29. Graham Greene, *A World of My Own: A Dream Diary* (New York: Viking, 1992), xxii. His association of these years with bad dreams was enduring and finally given fictional form in his seventies when a character says of her son, "He's at the age for nightmares. I read somewhere that they come when school begins to threaten. I wish he hadn't got to go to prep school." (*The Human Factor* [1978; reprint, New York: Avon Books, 1979], 20.)
30. Greene, *SOL*, 25, 52. See also *CE*, 16.
31. Sherry, *Life*, 1: 8–9, 19.

years. He was little affected by the war personally, but it dominated the school's mood, especially its headmaster's. Like many liberals, Charles Greene was deeply disillusioned by the conflict, claiming to see "nothing but disaster" when contemplating it and its outcome.[32] Graham joined the O.T.C., but his clumsiness brought chidings that cut him more sharply than they would have a less sensitive soul. Charles and Marion had always been remote parents, but as Graham had to spend more time away from his siblings and nurses and endure the slings and arrows of outrageous classmates, this boy who had always craved solitude grew lonelier. He began a habit of truancy at age ten that became more ambitious the next year, when he was regularly absent from school altogether. Although these escapes were a clear sign that he was troubled, his parents appear to have responded with only conventional disciplinary measures. And Greene's misery at this time was not unrelieved. He still came home every night after school, and was able to anticipate happy holidays at his uncle's home.

Yet he claimed that even such intervals were shadowed by his apprehension of the contrasting environments on the two sides of the green baize door in his father's study that joined school and home: "There would be a slight smell of iodine from the matron's room, of damp towels from the changing rooms, of ink everywhere. Shut the door behind you again, and the world smelt differently: books and fruit and eau-de-Cologne."[33] As his thirteenth birthday approached, so did terror at the rite of passage it signified—becoming a boarder at his father's school: "I felt anything, even a romantic death, might happen to save me before my thirteenth year struck."[34] But this was only the first of Greene's many death wishes to be denied him. In September 1918, he went through the green baize door at the start of term, aware that he would not live at home again until the holidays. This door became a totem in his writing of what occurred after it closed. Indeed, he later visualized it shutting on a jail, a madhouse, even being the gates of Hell.

---

32. Sherry, *Life*, 1: 63.
33. Graham Greene, *The Lawless Roads* (1939; reprint, New York: Penguin, 1976), 13 *(LR)*.
34. Greene, *SOL*, 72.

"Where the Misery of Life Started": Graham Greene's Schooldays

Greene's reactions to his boarding school days are uncompromisingly acidic. His public school was "where the misery of life started,"[35] the place where "one met for the first time characters, adult and adolescent, who bore about them the genuine quality of evil."[36] His most feared death, drowning, was preferable to school. Moreover, *The Heart of the Matter*'s protagonist implies that his daughter's infant death was a blessing in disguise for "if my child had lived, she too would have been conscriptable, flung into some grim dormitory to find her own way."[37] To Greene, the public school system seemed designed "only for the convenience of the authorities and often works for the boy's unhappiness."[38]

Greene was particularly susceptible to this way of life's affects, as the "rhythm of boarding-school life was somewhat manic-depressive," but certain aspects of that system made this boy especially unhappy.[39] In particular, he was dismayed by what seemed his school's utter lack of privacy: in "the total absence of solitude, there was the horror" of the system.[40] He insisted in 1934 that "this intense inescapable communal life cannot be good for anyone. The least sensitive, the most sociable boy surely needs the opportunity to be alone," leaving unsaid how desperately this highly sensitive and solitary youngster had required such a chance. The chief motive for this deprivation of solitude was fears about masturbation and homosexuality, which Charles Greene felt especially acutely. While not singling out his father, Graham dismissed the reasoning behind his anxieties in indicting "the system['s] . . . cult of suspicion and its abnormal fear of sexuality": "It is a curious system, but one common to all public schools, which prevents a normal sexual relationship

---

35. Ibid., 14.
36. Greene, *LR*, 14. He further claimed that it was only after his boarding school years "that Evil came into my dreams." *Journey Without Maps* (1936; reprint, New York: Penguin, 1980), 181.
37. Greene, *SOL*, 86; and *The Heart of the Matter* (1948, 1971; reprint, New York: Penguin, 1978), 158 *(HOM)*.
38. Graham Greene, *The Old School* (London: Jonathan Cape, 1934), 250.
39. Bernard Crick, *George Orwell: A Life* (New York: Penguin, 1980), 70.
40. Allain, *Other Man*, 30.

and punishes harshly any temporary substitute."[41] Greene thus believed that the denial of privacy inherent in his father's regimen had been far more damaging than any sexual sins he might have been saved from committing. As this increased supervision and fear of illicit sex were standard practice at most schools, reflecting the societal consensus about such issues, Greene's harsh dissent is also evidence of the cultural rebel he was becoming.[42]

Given this claustrophobic reaction, it is not surprising that Greene used his school as a referent for stultifying confinements frequently in his adult writing. Characters often depict their schools as prisons, an analogy also invoked by one historian of the subject.[43] Furthermore, one of Greene's sharpest censures of his school experiences comes when he compares *The Ministry of Fear*'s infamous "sick bay," where people are unjustly incarcerated as insane, to his dormitory. In doing so, he joins Chesterton in a British literary tradition dating to the 1700s of portraying unfair madhouse confinements, while also providing an indirect personal assessment of his school years' impact on him: "Ahead of him was the green baize door he had never seen opened, and beyond that door lay the sick bay. He was back in his own childhood . . . looking in through the open door, he grew up—learned that adventure didn't follow the literary pattern, that there weren't always happy endings."[44] Finally, inverting Wordsworth, Greene said of this time in his life, "Hell lay about them in their infancy,"[45] a metaphor that "is the image that Greene most readily associates with his schooldays," and one Noel Annan also em-

---

41. Greene, *Old School*, 250–54. He had initiated this collection with the express purpose of presenting "studies of the horror of the public school." Greene diary entry of 22 July 1933 (Sherry, *Life*, 1: 492).

42. Noel Annan, *Our Age* (London: Weidenfeld & Nicolson, 1990), 42–43.

43. Ibid., 42. See, e.g., Greene, *It's a Battlefield* (1934; reprint, New York: Penguin, 1977), 17–19; *This Gun for Hire* (1936; New York: Viking, 1982), 147; "A Visit to Morin," in *Collected Short Stories*, 217; *HC*, 135; *Human Factor*, 13; *The Captain and the Enemy* (New York: Viking, 1988), 13.

44. Greene, *Ministry of Fear*, 155, 210. See also Andrew Scull, *The Most Solitary of Afflictions: Madness and Society in Britain, 1700–1900* (New Haven, Conn.: Yale University Press, 1993), 24, 348, n. 45; and Vieda Skultans, *English Madness: Ideas on Insanity, 1580–1890* (London: Routledge & Keegan Paul, 1979), 99–103.

45. Greene, *LR*, 14. See also Greene, *SOL*, 74; and *Brighton Rock* (1938; reprint, New York: Bantam, 1968), 65 *(BR)*.

ployed when discussing the climate that people like Greene confronted at public school.[46]

As such similarities suggest, Greene was hardly original in condemning his public school years. Annan has pointed out that Britain is unique in having an entire literary genre known as the "public school novel." While once a hagiographic medium, Greene came of age as this form of literature entered "the age of Almamatricide," in which titles like *Unwillingly to School* predominated.[47] But the duration and intensity of Greene's negative fixation on these years is nonetheless exceptional. Many Old Boys, after all, develop sentimental attachments to their schools, and either recant earlier criticisms or put them in perspective. Few have made critiques of these academies central elements of work done in their seventies and eighties. What specific circumstances drove Greene to greater truancy and even suicide attempts while at school, and shaped him enduringly?[48]

Two significant factors stand out, one a condition of his tenure at Berkhamsted, the other a particular incident and its consequences. First, Greene was in the unique position of being the headmaster's son, which immediately and permanently divided his loyalties. To make matters worse, his older brother was their house's head boy, which Graham thought isolated him further from his fellows: how could they trust someone so intimately connected to the intrusive and hated authorities? He felt like "the son of a quisling in a country under occupation.... I was surrounded by the forces of the resistance, and yet I couldn't join them without betraying my father and my brother."[49] Belonging to neither side in this constant conflict completely, "I was ostracized, I found myself in the situation of a leper."[50] Yet all Charles's sons had faced this fate and the rest had survived, even thrived. Graham, though, was also gangly, shy, and bookish, nor did he try to hide these traits. His official bi-

---

46. Philip Stratford, *Faith and Fiction: Creative Process in Greene and Mauriac* (Notre Dame, Ind.: University of Notre Dame Press, 1964), 52; and Annan, *Our Age*, 43.

47. Annan, *Our Age*, 44–47. See also Andrea Freud Loewenstein, *Loathsome Jews and Engulfing Women: Metaphors of Projection in the Works of Wyndham Lewis, Charles Williams, and Graham Greene* (New York: New York University Press, 1993), 103–18.

48. See Greene, *SOL*, 75–77, 88; and Sherry, *Life*, 1: 86–87.

49. Greene, *SOL*, 74.

50. Allain, *Other Man*, 27.

ographer concludes that such qualities only exacerbated the perception of abnormality occasioned by being his father's son, making survival in the conformist adolescent culture doubly difficult: he was "different and therefore a target for torment simply because he was different—the pack drives out the 'sport.'"[51]

Greene's keen sensitivity and deep loneliness made him highly vulnerable to the dynamics of relationships. This volatile potential was actualized by his interactions with two other boys, Lionel Carter and A. H. Wheeler; what he considered their conspiracy to betray his friendship was his final push into the abyss. Greene and his biographers are vague about exactly what happened, but some reconstruction of the essential events (which occurred in 1919–20) is possible. Carter is *The Lawless Roads*'s "Collifax," one of those who bore about him the genuine quality of evil and about whom Hell lay in his infancy. He tortured the young Greene physically and mentally. For the former, he used dividers, which became an emblem of cruelty in Greene's writing.[52] The latter was based on exploitation of Greene's distinctive status, something Carter would have understood particularly well: Carter's maternal uncle, Jacky Hill, was a master at Berkhamsted, so he also faced the problem of divided loyalties, albeit not as acutely as Greene did. This point has been either ignored or only glanced at by Greene's biographers, but it provides a plausible explanation for Carter's motives and success. By humiliating Greene, he could distract attention from his own situation; and, given their similar positions, he would have been able to estimate the most effective tactics for belittling Greene, either by imaginatively sympathizing with him, or remembering whatever taunting he may have suffered himself. In any case, he made this mental torment "the most [sic] terrible"[53] of the two kinds, and even earned his victim's grudging esteem for his "genius for evil."[54]

If Carter was the devil Greene knew, Wheeler was a demon in dis-

---

51. Sherry, *Life*, 1: 70.

52. See, e.g., Greene, *England Made Me* (1935; reprint, New York: Penguin, 1970), 83; *BR*, 48–49, 99, 104, 166; "The Basement Room," in *Collected Short Stories*, 102; *HOM*, 179; Sherry, *Life*, 1: 77.

53. Greene, "Prologue to Pilgrimage," quoted in Sherry, *Life*, 1: 77.

54. Greene, "The Lost Childhood," in *CE*, 17. See also *SOL*, 82. Greene named a villain in "The Bear Fell Free" "Carter," as he did a character in *Our Man in Havana* (1958) who is killed

guise. Wheeler (called "Watson" in *A Sort of Life*) was described by a fellow student as "one of those no-character people. I mean he was just there." As he and Carter left no known accounts of what happened at Berkhamsted, only speculation is possible about precisely what transpired between these three boys. Norman Sherry argues that Greene may have confided his interest in unpopular topics to Wheeler, only to have Carter discover this information and embarrass Greene by disclosing it.[55] While not fully persuasive, it is a far more plausible explanation than Shelden's unsubstantiated assertion of homosexual feelings between Wheeler and Greene ending in jealousy and humiliation when Wheeler joined forces with Carter.[56] Given Wheeler's apparently nondescript temperament, he could well have been pressured by the more charismatic Carter into forsaking Quisling's son and taking his rightful place in the resistance without realizing how much he had hurt Greene in the process. Indeed, Greene reports that when he and Wheeler met thirty years later, Wheeler reminisced about the good old days at school when the three of them were bosom pals; Greene added dryly, "His memory held a quite different impression from mine."[57]

Greene's immediate impression was a feeling of utter abandonment, and, whatever the exact facts, the pain of losing one of his few friends scarred his soul permanently. In 1940, he wrote that betrayal of friends is a worse sin than murder or robbery; and in 1957 he gave this definition of a nightmare: "when your best friend might suddenly without any reason turn into your worst enemy."[58] Despite efforts to purge this incident from his mind, Greene recognized his inability to ever write it out of his system fully, a judgment his work validates: "every few years a scent, a stretch of wall, a book on a shelf, a name in a newspaper, would remind me to lift the stone and watch the creature move its head toward the light."[59] If his years as a boarder were when the misery of life started,

---

by the protagonist. In addition, *The Ministry of Fear*'s Hilfe seems based in large part on Carter.

55. Sherry, *Life*, 1: 82–83.   56. Shelden, *Within*, 68–71.
57. Greene, *SOL*, 84.
58. Greene, *The Power and the Glory* (1940; reprint, New York: Penguin, 1983), 178 *(P&G)*; and Greene quoted in Sherry, *Life*, 1: 82.
59. Greene, *SOL*, 83. For the theme of the betrayal of friends in Greene's writing, see, e.g., *Battlefield*, 54; *The Confidential Agent* (1939; reprint, New York: Penguin, 1971), passim;

Greene felt Wheeler's betrayal initiated the "real misery of that time," one he never escaped.[60]

What made these matters so unmanageable for Greene was their cumulative effect. While any of these conditions and incidents might have been bearable in isolation, together they fostered the breakdown that he had been verging on since Junior School. He later generalized his suffering and blamed the public school system for encouraging betrayals, but his immediate reaction to his crisis was, like Chesterton, to turn further inward. When suicide attempts failed, he managed to function for a time after being forsaken, possibly aided by fantasies of committing cruelties on a neighbor girl, thereby transferring temporarily his feelings of pain and powerlessness.[61] On the last day of the 1920 summer holidays, though, Greene concluded that he could not return to school. He retreated to Berkhamsted Common, leaving his parents a note asserting that he would not come home until they assured him that he would not have to go back to school. His bad luck followed him in this scheme too, however, for his sister, Molly, apprehended him less than two hours after he departed. While a rather ignominious bit of absconding, these events remained important to Graham, as they appear in his fiction frequently.[62]

His parents were alarmed by his actions, having been ignorant of Carter's cruelties, which precipitated them. Although Carter was not expelled immediately, he did leave Berkhamsted in 1921 without completing his education, which, given his uncle's position at the school, may have been a compromise suitable to both families.[63] Even before Carter was dealt with, though, the Greenes had to determine what to do with Graham. Greene maintained that there was an almost immediate decision to send him to London for psychoanalysis, but Sherry has docu-

---

HOM, 164; *A Burnt-Out Case* (1960; reprint, New York: Penguin, 1977), 168; HC, 24, 31, 97, 115, 207, 228, 230, 241, 301; *Human Factor*, 56, 192, 222–23, 266; *Captain and Enemy*, 9–11, 140, 144, 167, 173. This theme is also central to the plots of *The Man Within*, *The Human Factor*, *The Third Man*, and *The Quiet American*.

60. Greene to Catherine Walston, 25 December 1950 (Sherry, *Life*, 2: 350).

61. Greene, *Old School*, 253; and *Journey*, 36–37.

62. See, e.g., *England Made Me*, 12–13, 20, 24; *P&G*, 47; *Ministry of Fear*, 70, 155, 173–74; HOM, 147; "The Basement Room," 111; *Human Factor*, 12–13; *Captain and Enemy*, 27.

63. Greene hints at such an explanation in his fiction. See, e.g., *England Made Me*, 83; *P&G*, 196; HOM, 164.

mented that he did not leave Berkhamsted until at least mid-1921.[64] It appears likely, then, that he became a day student until his treatment was arranged. Given that psychoanalysis was a young practice at this time, and his father's generally conservative approach to such matters, it seems sensible to conclude that Greene's departure was delayed for months by myriad inquiries and details.

The Burden of a Lost Childhood: The Influence of Greene's School Years

Before chronicling that period and its importance for his outlook, some reflection on this aboriginal calamity's significance is required, as it was the pivot for Greene's later thought. His intellectual and spiritual development is intimately tied to his reaction to his boarding school years, for they fostered the yearnings and themes that would dominate his work: "It was as if I had been supplied once and for all with a subject."[65] In particular, Greene held that these years provided both material and motive for becoming a writer. They also shaped the sort of writer and thinker he became by giving him a tragic view of life and a distrust of innocence, positions that helped lead him to Roman Catholicism. Finally, they furnished some of his foremost roles by teaching him the virtue of disloyalty and how to take the victim's side.

Simon Leys has argued that "the brutalities of boarding school can routinely maim sensitive children for life; occasionally they may also breed a genius."[66] In Greene's case, both results seem to have occurred. He admitted that his fixation on his schooldays was a kind of disease, but he considered it his writing's dynamic impetus: "the disease is also one's material. Cure the disease & I doubt whether a writer would remain."[67] He insisted that he had been infected at Berkhamsted:

> In all my books perhaps I return to the duality which has marked my life from the time that I was a pupil in the school at Berkhamsted whose head was my father. . . . Thanks to these books I've recaptured my ex-

---

64. Greene, *SOL*, 92–93; and Sherry, *Life*, 1: 92.
65. Greene, "The Lost Childhood," 16.
66. S. Leys, "Balzac's Genius and Other Paradoxes," *New York Review of Books* 42 (12 January 1995): 23.
67. Greene to Vivien Greene, 3 June 1948 (Sherry, *Life*, 2: 285).

perience of childhood, or rather of that part of it when I was a boarder, at twelve or thirteen. I've had no wish to do away with this cleavage; I've accepted it as one of the constants of my work and of my life. Perhaps it was the only way to exorcise the evil, for there's no doubt, it was a most unpleasant situation."[68]

In that sense, all Greene's novels are public school novels.

Yet these demons continued to haunt him. Even when he tried to generalize his experience, his own story remained transparent: "There are certain writers, as different as Dickens from Kipling, who never shake off the burden of their childhood.... All later experience seems to have been related to those months or years of unhappiness ... the best stories of Munro are all of childhood, its humor and its anarchy as well as its cruelty and unhappiness."[69] His contemporaries and critics also recognized the centrality of his school years and his consequent unhappiness to his creative vision. Douglas Jerrold held that Greene wrote "with feverish nostalgia of his schooldays, which he hated, and therefore loves to recall."[70] Moreover, many of his fictional creations share some form of this trait of their master, as "nearly all Greene's main characters reject their past, yet it is nevertheless the shaping influence of their character. The roots of their problems lie in harrowing childhood experiences."[71] These years' profound, painful effect on Greene's imagination, then, shaped his artistic doctrine: "the creative writer perceives his world once and for all in childhood and adolescence, and his whole career is an effort to illustrate his private world in terms of the great public world we all share."[72]

---

68. Allain, *Other Man*, 26–27.

69. Greene, "The Burden of Childhood," in *CE*, 99–101.

70. Jerrold quoted in Shelden, *Within*, 343. See also Peter Quennell, "The School at Berkhamsted: Two Views at Variance," in *Graham Greene: Man of Paradox*, ed. A. F. Cassis (Chicago: Loyola University Press, 1994), 11–15. This memoir is of particular interest because Quennell was at Berkhamsted with Greene.

Loewenstein (*Loathsome Jews*, 244–59) has also recognized the pivotal nature of Greene's youthful trauma to his worldview, but her analysis underplays the significance of the Carter-Wheeler episode in favor of a less substantiated emphasis on his relationship with his parents, one that is also overdetermined by contemporary psychological paradigms.

71. Robert Barnes, "Two Modes of Fiction," *Renascence* 14 (Summer 1962): 197.

72. Greene, "The Young Dickens," in *CE*, 83. Greene even asserted that living in a leper colony was preferable to returning to Berkhamsted when seeking material for a novel in the late 1950s (*SOL*, 74).

His school years also provided another, more specific motive for becoming a writer. To Greene, taking up his pen was a form of revenge against Carter and Wheeler. He wondered in 1971 whether "I would ever have written a book had it not been for Watson [Wheeler] and the dead Carter, if those years of humiliation had not given me an excessive desire to prove that I was good at something."[73] His need to overcome the degradation suffered at their hands was a potent bacillus of his disease. Yet he was never cured on this count either, as even in his last novel the protagonist recalls a desire to hurt only one person, "a boy called Twining who had made my life miserable" at school.[74] Greene recognized even in his first published novel that this wish "to show those men that I was someone to be considered" could easily become "a child's foolish and dangerous game with fire."[75] But his fury overwhelmed his sense of folly, and his efforts to prove himself persisted permanently, along with a correspondingly heightened fear of failure.[76]

Just as Greene's schooldays gave him sources and reasons for his writing, they also shaped the outlook he voiced in it. He took with him behind that green baize door the same liberal presuppositions that Chesterton had brought to the Slade. Having not been taught to believe in original sin and to believe in human nature's general goodness, neither man had intellectual and spiritual resources sufficient to comprehend his discovery of ideas and practices that contravened trusted assumptions about life's benignity. If their crises' proximate causes, such as impressionism and sadistic schoolboys, are hardly the best objective avatars of evil, subjectively they assumed disproportionate significance because of the cognitive dissonance they caused. Each man faced his challenge without adequate defenses; his worldview was thus rapidly and violently upended without any apparent means of reintegration. In Greene's case, Carter's cruelties "destroyed his illusions of man's heroic nature and so wrenched Graham's nature out of true . . . [by] sapping Graham's belief in his boyhood dreams and chivalric standards . . . faith

---

73. Greene, *SOL*, 84. See also Sherry, *Life*, 2: 350. Tellingly, he entitled an autobiographical fragment *The Revenge* (Greene Library, Burns Library).
74. Greene, *Captain and Enemy*, 44.
75. Graham Greene, *The Man Within* (1929; reprint, New York: Bantam, 1948), 113, 179.
76. Greene, *SOL*, 217, 219.

was not able to rescue him from his unbearable situation."[77] While not intrinsically wicked, then, the Slade and Berkhamsted symbolized evil to these authors because of the shock their systems suffered at these schools. Hence, just as Chesterton was troubled by the tensions tied to his Slade breakdown for much of his life, so Greene became preoccupied with "the discrepancy between the old liberal myths that had ruled his childhood and what his keen eye had showed" to be their flaws in his school setting.[78]

One of the central and enduring sources of Greene's new, more tragic attitude was the epiphany he had when reading Marjorie Bowen's *The Viper of Milan*. He read it when he was fourteen, as he was undergoing Carter's abuse, and found in an apparently commonplace adventure story a way to "explain the terrible living world of the stone stairs and the never quiet dormitory." He saw Carter as the villainous Visconti's objective correlative, and he deduced from this tale a leading tenet of his later thought:

> Goodness has only once found a perfect incarnation in a human body and never will again, but evil can always find a home there. Human nature is not black and white but black and grey. I read all that in *The Viper of Milan* and I looked round and I saw that it was so . . . religion might later explain it to me in other terms, but the pattern was already there—perfect evil walking the world where perfect good can never walk again.[79]

---

77. Sherry, *Life*, 1: 80–81, 85. *The Man Within* (138) offers fictional confirmation of this analysis: "The qualities he had built round himself were dreams only, which Andrews by one act had destroyed."

78. Judith Adamson, *Graham Greene: The Dangerous Edge* (New York: Macmillan, 1990), 5–6.

79. Greene, "The Lost Childhood," 16–17. His reprisal of the name Visconti for a key character in his 1969 novel *Travels With My Aunt* testifies to this tale's lasting impact on him. Brian Diemert is hence badly mistaken in asserting that "his selection of her novel for special comment is as good as any other choice he might have made from among the books he read in his childhood." Diemert, *Graham Greene's Thrillers and the 1930s* (Montreal & Kingston: McGill-Queen's University Press, 1996), 186, n. 16. Gwenn Boardman is even more wrongheaded in seeing Greene's professed debt to this story as a "long-standing literary joke." Boardman, *Graham Greene: The Aesthetics of Exploration* (Gainesville: University of Florida Press, 1971), 174.

Greene's mature assertion of his early discovery of this principle was not a retrospective judgment. A poem published when he was twenty-one also voices his beliefs in the greater vividness of life's dark side, and in the black hues haunting its brighter portion:

> Comfort and Fear—these two alone made Life.
> But while the Fear too often stood alone . . .
> The Comfort always had been mixed with fear.

The connection between this outlook and his school years is also substantiated by his early adult writings.[80] Like Chesterton's, then, Greene's basic view of human nature antedated his encounter with Roman Catholicism—or even any sustained religious reflection—and was rooted in his adolescent crisis. His conversion would ratify, rather than modify, his youthful convictions' essence.

This acceptance of a secular version of the Fall also promoted an early skepticism of innocence. While there is less boyhood evidence of this opinion, Greene's fiction and essays demonstrate that his school sufferings convinced him that moral corruption is almost instantaneous. To him, "innocence was a slobbering mouth, a toothless gum pulling at the teats, perhaps not even that; innocence was the ugly cry of birth,"[81] because even the "preposterously young" can have "complete theoretical knowledge of vice."[82] He admitted this attitude's personal roots in 1936, when he commented that a cinematic portrayal of childhood as a period of brutality, and "the more than human evil of the lying sadistic child," had "an authenticity guaranteed by one's own memories."[83] That he was remembering one specific sadistic child when formulating his broader

---

80. Greene, "Sad Cure," *The Cherwell*, 20 February 1926; quoted in Sherry, *Life*, 1: 11. Ellipsis in original. See also, e.g., *The Old School*, 7; *England Made Me*, 51; *Confidential*, 51; Shelden, *Within*, 93.

81. Greene, BR, 140–41. See also *The Man Within*, 24; *Confidential*, 20, 39–40, 49–51, 64; *Our Man in Havana* (1958; reprint, New York: Penguin, 1969), 31, 44. The difficulty in presenting Greene's contemporaneous thoughts on these and other issues connected with his breakdown is that his diary from that period is no longer extant, and he seems to have written few, if any, letters at that time.

82. Greene, *Confidential*, 50.

83. Greene review of *These Three*, *The Spectator*, 1 May 1936; reprinted in *Graham Greene on Film: Collected Film Criticism, 1935–40*, ed. John Russell Taylor (New York: Simon & Schuster, 1972), 72.

principle of the ruthlessness of youth is evident from later passages' rhetoric: "She was like a child with a pair of dividers who knows her power to injure. You could never trust a child not to use her advantage."[84] This suspicion of innocence thus reveals another way Greene's school years shaped his moral imagination. As with the tragic view of life, Roman Catholicism would provide theological categories for this insight, but would not change its substance.

Besides deriving thematic direction from his boarding school ordeal, Greene also acquired his most important rhetorical roles. In particular, his sense of being an unjustly persecuted outsider helped fertilize an already subversive temperament. He maintained that he had always had rebellious instincts, but that his unhappiness at school intensified them. For instance, he deemed his truancy and suicide attempts specific acts of rebellion.[85] In adulthood, he transmuted the necessity of divided loyalties suffered at school into "the virtue of disloyalty." Greene argued that to be a writer is to be a rebel:

> The writer is driven by his own vocation to be a Protestant in a Catholic society, a Catholic in a Protestant one, to see the virtues of the Capitalist in a Communist society, of the Communist in a Capitalist state.... Loyalty confines you to accepted opinions: loyalty forbids you to comprehend sympathetically your dissident fellows; but disloyalty encourages you to roam through any human mind: it gives the novelist an extra dimension of understanding.[86]

While this conviction is not unique to Greene's thought, it became integral to his persona, as even his most hostile biographer recognizes.[87]

His work demonstrates this principle's roots in his school experiences. Annan has argued that loyalty was one of the two ideals that public schools in Greene's time strove most to inculcate.[88] In asserting dis-

---

84. Greene, *HOM*, 179.
85. Greene, *SOL*, 94, 206, 80–81; and *LR*, 14.
86. Greene, "The Virtue of Disloyalty," in *Reflections*, ed. Judith Adamson (New York: Penguin, 1990), 268–69. See also Allain, *Other Man*, 111–12, 168.
87. See Shelden, *Within*, 5; and Val Ross, "A Portrait of the Biographer as a Chameleon," *The Globe and Mail*, 15 October 1994. Chesterton expressed a similar idea (*Illustrated London News*, 25 June 1932).
88. Annan, *Our Age*, 43.

loyalty as a virtue, then, Greene engaged in a specific act of subterfuge against the public school ethos. As the autobiographical protagonist of "Under the Garden" is told, "You'll have to forget all your schoolmasters try to teach you. . . . Be disloyal. . . . If you have to earn a living, boy, and the price they make you pay is loyalty, be a double agent."[89] Greene illustrated his sense of how high a price loyalty is through *England Made Me*'s Anthony Farrant. He escapes from his school but is sent back by his sister, Kate, only to be rewarded for his later adherence to the public school code by becoming a failed drifter. Such a depiction suggests that Greene used Anthony as a projection of his fears about what would have befallen him had his rebellion at Berkhamsted been similarly squashed. His transgressive temperament thus took its full form from his years behind the green baize door. The permanent state of disloyalty to both his fellows and his family that he experienced anxiously then became a source of creativity to Greene later by widening his sympathies. Although his acceptance of Roman Catholicism would become an essential element of this role by giving him something to affirm when he rejected modern culture, religion would again shape, rather than create, a fundamental part of his intellectual vision.

If Greene's school experiences taught him to broaden his sympathies through disloyalty, they also insured that his greatest sympathy would be with victims. Indeed Camus's dictum, in many ways, seems Greene's also: "Always take the victim's side." Greene thought this advocacy, like disloyalty, part of an author's function: "The writer, just as much as the Christian Church, is the defender of the individual."[90] He likewise stressed this attitude consistently, and claimed that even in Junior School, "I knew already in my heart that I belonged on the side of the victims, not of the torturers."[91] While this view was ratified at boarding school, it was also transformed significantly. If he gained even greater sympathy

---

89. Greene, "Under the Garden," 210, 202. He repeated this metaphor with specific reference to his own vocation in an *Evening Standard* interview of 9 January 1978: "a writer is always an agent: a double agent."

90. Greene, *Why Do I Write?* (London: Percival Marshall, 1948), 49.

91. Greene, *SOL*, 65. For its continuity in his thought, see, e.g., Sherry, *Life*, 2: 281; and Christopher Burstall, "Graham Greene Takes the Orient Express," in *Conversations with Graham Greene*, ed. Henry Donaghy (Jackson: University Press of Mississippi, 1992), 58.

for sufferers as his own pain intensified, his encounter with Carter and Wheeler also seems to have given his notions of victimization more nuance. Greene remarked that after his father interviewed him upon his return from the Common, other investigations began among the school's "innocent inhabitants."[92] This inquisition, coupled with Carter's early departure, persuaded Greene that a victim can quickly become a victimizer, and he expressed such a belief throughout his fiction. For instance, police officer Scobie—who always seeks to defend victims—supports what he thinks are innocent tenants against rapacious landlords: "But he soon discovered that the guilt and innocence were as relative as the wealth. The wronged tenant turned out to be also the wealthy capitalist, making a profit of five shillings a week on a single room, living rent free herself."[93] Greene's awareness of these kinds of moral subtleties originated in his reaction to his boarding school sufferings, and ultimately gave him a more precise doctrine than Camus's: "the writer should always be ready to change sides at the drop of a hat. He stands for the victims and the victims change."[94] Converting to Roman Catholicism would help him decide how to choose and when to change sides, but it was his years at Berkhamsted that gave him the sense of a duty to do so at all.

A World of His Own: London and Psychotherapy

If these motives, means, themes, and roles represent the long-term yield of Greene's struggle with his public school years, he also sought more immediate ways of coping with them. By July 1921, he had taken up residence in London with Kenneth and Zoe Richmond, who were his parents' antitheses in many ways. Kenneth was a self-trained psychiatrist who had also been deeply unhappy at his boarding school; and both were dedicated Spiritualists, who practiced lax child discipline and candor about sex. They offered Greene greater openness, intimacy, and warmth than he had experienced at Berkhamsted, and his six months with them was "the happiest period of my life." He held that it was largely the contrast with school that was so therapeutic, especially the cleanliness, solitude, and independence he enjoyed. But he also suggested that this period had its wrenching aspects, as his adolescent analysis

92. Greene, *SOL*, 92.
93. Greene, *HOM*, 20.
94. Greene, "The Virtue of Disloyalty," 269.

fostered a desire "to turn up every stone to discover what lay beneath, to question motives, to doubt."[95] Although some of these fruits, particularly doubt, became hallmarks of his mature thought, he believed consistently that self-discovery had high costs. He even emphasized in his later years that "I have no wish to know myself." Despite a lifetime of psychoanalysis, Greene never thought himself cured. While he considered his disease a necessary condition of his writing, his attempts to at least contain it were, from the first, often bitter medicine.[96]

Greene stressed consistently the limited efficacy of the Richmonds' treatments.[97] One thing they failed to supply was a persuasive religious explanation of his suffering. In fact, his time with them appears to have been the coup de grâce to any vestiges of his already-friable liberal Christianity. Whether it was their Spiritualist accent on "the god within you," Greene's reflections on his agonies, the geographic and mental distance from his parents, or some mixture of these factors, the product was a growing religious apathy: "I had emerged from my psychoanalysis without any religious belief at all, certainly no belief in the Jesus of the school chapel." Nor had he discovered a nonreligious means of personal reintegration. His claim that he returned to Berkhamsted "repaired" is thus overstated.[98] But this fragility was not immediately apparent. Outwardly, his roughly nine months at home were pacific, and he finished his education without undue emotional strain. Beneath the surface, though, he was still ruminating over the blow to his psyche struck by Wheeler and the now-absent Carter. One of his closest friends from this period recalls that he was "exuberantly skeptical and blithely pessimistic.... At each fresh insight he obtained into human absurdity or wickedness, his pallid, faintly woebegone face would assume an air of solemn glee."[99] It was as though such revelations vindicated the worldview his reactions to his boarding school suffering had stimulated.

---

95. Greene, SOL, 189, 102–3.
96. Allain, Other Man, 17. See also HC, 52; Human Factor, 21; Captain and Enemy, 99. Greene maintained that his school memories only became more painful with time, despite continued therapy (WOE, 47–48).
97. See, e.g., SOL, 128; WOE, 19; and Sherry, Life, 2: 285.
98. Greene, SOL, 117, 105.
99. Peter Quennell, quoted in Sherry, Life, 1: 111.

The Dangerous Edge of Things:
Oxford Atheism and Continued Disquiet

Greene took this psychological baggage with him from Berkhamsted to Balliol in autumn 1922. In many ways, his college years were a continuation of his response to his schooldays. For instance, he sustained his rebellious streak, especially regarding religion. In 1923, he published a tale of a pagan who takes over Heaven, to its inhabitants' delight. The next year, he depicted a demonic, Manichean Incarnation without a Resurrection. Satan assumes human form and is shot by an archbishop, who then fears God's justice for committing murder. As he lies dying, Satan tells the bishop not to fear God, for

> "I am God," said the man [Satan], and choked up fresh blood.
> "But if you are God . . . how can you die?"
> "I made myself man . . . a miracle . . . Very rash . . ."
> And in a bubble of bloodstained laughter God died.[100]

Greene's fascination with evil and its role in shattering his youthful religious beliefs is evident, as is the way such preoccupations were shaping his literary vision. Additionally, an Oxford friend recalled that "I've never heard atheism put forward better than by Graham" during these years.[101] Both imaginatively and logically, then, Greene seemed to be trying to put away what he considered his childish Christianity as he became a man.

Doing so, though, did not forestall deep psychological troughs. His most serious response to depression was renewed suicide attempts, as he played Russian roulette six times in the autumn and winter of 1923. His adolescent pain thus remained deep enough in his college years to provoke him to attempted self-destruction.[102] Greene eventually abandoned

---

100. Greene, "The Trial of Pan," *The Oxford Outlook* (February 1923): 47–50; and "The Improbable Tale of the Archbishop of Canterbridge," *The Cherwell*, 15 November 1924. See also Allain, *Other Man*, 41.

101. Robin Turton, April 1977 interview with Norman Sherry (Sherry, *Life*, 1: 127).

102. As an adult, Greene denied that he had meant to die in these incidents (Greene, *SOL*, 130; and Allain, *Other Man*, 49–50). But Oxford friends who knew of this habit felt that he was trying to end his life; his prior attempts to kill himself when depressed, his admission that he had not been cured by the Richmonds, and the fact that his later fiction and dreams

this practice, and took a second in history in spring 1925. Yet his discontent persisted, as evinced by his choice to sign up for a three-year tour in China with the British American Tobacco Company despite being deeply in love with his future wife. He admitted later that he had desired "to cut away from the past" by literally putting distance between himself and his background; his plan was also a direct defiance of his family's wish that he become a writer.[103] Greene saw the folly of his stubbornness soon, however, and the inability to escape one's past became a central theme of his work. He gave British American Tobacco notice in August 1925. A brief, unhappy spell as a tutor ended his opposition to writing for a living, as he decided in October of that year to try his hand at journalism. *The Times* was his ultimate goal, but he needed to gain experience at provincial papers first. He thus became a trainee subeditor at *The Nottingham Journal*.

The Human Factor: Greene and "Romantic Theology"

His November 1925 arrival in Nottingham inaugurated a crucial section of Greene's life, for it was here that he became a Roman Catholic on 28 February 1926. How did this convinced and convincing atheist come to embrace "the Scarlet Woman" so quickly? As with Chesterton, another woman helped bring the cross to him. Greene met Vivien Dayrell-Browning in early 1925 under curious, but fateful, circumstances. Like many atheists, he was deeply interested in what he opposed, as his Oxford stories indicate. And his disapproval of religious ideas did not imply misconstrual of them, as Edith Sitwell recognized in thanking him for a 1923 article about her poems: "I am not used to people understanding anything whatever about my poetry . . . as they do not understand the spiritual impulse behind the image. You have understood it all."[104] Yet at least one person thought his grasp of religious matters was not always so total. In a March 1925 essay Greene referred to those who "worship" the Virgin Mary.[105] He soon received a letter from "some ardent Catho-

---

associate Russian roulette with people actively seeking death all substantiate that apprehension. See Sherry, *Life*, 1: 159; Allain, *Other Man*, 172; Greene, *Dr. Fischer of Geneva or the Bomb Party* (New York: Avon Books, 1980), 110–11, 137–39; and Greene, *World of My Own*, 76.

103. Greene, *SOL*, 149; and Allain, *Other Man*, 42–43.
104. Edith Sitwell to Greene, 19 June 1923 (Sherry, *Life*, 1: 141).
105. *Oxford Outlook*, March 1925 (Sherry, *Life*, 1: 179).

lic," telling him that people do not "worship" Mary, they "venerate" her, even supplying the technical term, "hyperdulia."[106] That ardent Catholic was Vivien Dayrell-Browning. While Greene claimed in 1971 that he sought a meeting with her because he was fascinated intellectually by anyone who took these "subtle distinctions of an unbelievable theology" seriously, contemporaneous documents suggest that it was his strong sensitivity that was stirred, as he hoped to apologize for the offense he had given.[107] Whatever the motive, their early March encounter left him enamored.

Yet how could an earnest atheist and a committed Catholic hope for a future together? Vivien had converted to Roman Catholicism only two years before meeting Greene. She practiced her faith devoutly, and even published religious poetry. Nor was Greene her only suitor. Seemingly more compatible men (including David Jones's friend Harman Grisewood) also courted her. Greene discussed these difficulties with his cousin Claud Cockburn. Cockburn advised him to convert outwardly to Catholicism if it was necessary to marry Vivien, but to not let it affect his real convictions, counsel Cockburn came to regret when "the whole thing suddenly took off and became serious."[108]

As Cockburn suggests, Greene's motives for converting were more complex than just a desire to wed Vivien. The link between human love and divine love did nonetheless become central to Greene's religious thought. Charles Williams defined this principle as "romantic theology," and while there is no evidence that either writer influenced the other, their views are quite similar. Williams (inspired by Dante and Coventry Patmore) asserted that for a Christian, "the principles of Romantic Theology can be reduced to a single formula: which is, the identification of love with Jesus Christ, and of marriage with His life . . . this love is but the herald of religious love for God." Greene voiced a more naturalistic version of this idea in a story published during his stay with the Richmonds, but gave it full religious expression after his conversion.[109] In *The*

---

106. Greene to Marion Greene, 6 March 1925 (Sherry, *Life*, 1: 179).
107. Greene, *SOL*, 164; Sherry, *Life*, 1: 179–80.
108. Cockburn interview with Norman Sherry, 18 June 1977 (Sherry, *Life*, 1: 193).
109. Charles Williams, *Outlines of Romantic Theology*, ed. Alice Mary Hadfield (Grand Rapids, Mich.: William B. Eerdmans Publishing Co., 1990), 14, 64. See also Greene, "The

End of the Affair, for instance, Sarah Miles describes how her love for Maurice Bendrix brought her to God:

> Did I ever love Maurice as much before I loved You? Or was it really You I loved all the time? Did I touch You when I touched him? Could I have touched You if I hadn't touched him first . . . he gave me so much love and I gave him so much love that soon there wasn't anything left, when we'd finished, but You.

As she later tells Maurice, "I've fallen into belief like I fell in love." Even the more skeptical Bendrix comes to think that "the words of human love have been used by the saints to describe their vision of God, and so, I suppose, we might use the terms of prayer, meditation, contemplation to explain the intensity of the love we feel for a woman."[110] Another skeptic, *A Burnt-Out Case*'s Querry, articulates Greene's belief even more succinctly: "Perhaps it's true that you can't believe in a god without loving a human being or love a human being without believing in a god."[111]

Furthermore, the fact that Sarah, Bendrix, and Querry are all undergoing conversion or renewal experiences illustrates the role Greene felt human love played in his own conversion to a particular confession. This assessment was not retrospective, as a mid-1925 letter to Vivien attests: "I could worship *with* you, if you had your arms round me . . . when I see that Catholicism can produce something so fine all through, I know there must be something in it."[112] This more specific assertion of romantic love as the gateway to accepting a new religious faith (or to renewing a discarded one) is substantiated by Williams and conversion theorists, such as Walter Conn:

> But genuine love refuses to worship a limited good, no matter how lovable. It remains responsive to the demand of the call for "something more," the demand to "leave all things," to "go out," to "give oneself."

Creation of Beauty" (Sherry, *Life*, 1: 101). In his library, Greene had two copies of Patmore's *Angel in the House*, which Williams drew on in elucidating his notion of romantic theology. For a more general comparative analysis of Williams's and Greene's views of women and sex, see Loewenstein, *Loathsome Jews*, chaps. 5 and 6.

110. Graham Greene, *The End of the Affair* (1951; reprint, New York: Penguin, 1975), 123, 147, 47.

111. Greene, *Burnt-Out Case*, 114.

112. Greene to Vivien Dayrell-Browning (Sherry, *Life*, 1: 220). Emphasis in original.

If love goes beyond its immediate object, it is also experienced as originating beyond one's very self and existing beyond one's control; one experiences oneself as almost literally seized by the power of love's demand.[113]

Even though his own marriage failed, Greene continued to posit this connection between marriage and a creed, and he wrote wistfully of domestic life in his later fiction.[114]

Neither Williams nor Greene, though, confined the experiences associated with romantic theology to sacramental marriage.[115] Williams claimed to have known divine revelation through erotic passion not only with his wife, but also with Phyllis Jones, whom he met after he was married. While Williams only loved Phyllis in his heart, Greene gave more complete expression to his ardor for the woman who inspired similar feelings in him. Catherine Walston was also a Roman Catholic convert and Greene was her godfather. When they met in 1946, his marriage was only nominal, as he was living with Dorothy Glover. Catherine herself had conducted several affairs, with her husband's tacit consent. Greene eventually left Dorothy, for he felt that Catherine, unlike any previous mistress, was a source of spiritual renewal through physical love. In fact, their relationship in many ways mirrored his early years with Vivien. Whereas he had once wanted to worship with Vivien's arms around him, he now told Catherine that "it's odd how little I get out of Mass except when you're around." Moreover, just as Vivien had helped lead him into the Church, he credited Catherine with his "new Catholicism," and held that "the only way I can learn to love God more than you is with you." Greene understood the irony of such spiritual stimulation coming from a sinful union, but insisted consistently upon his religious renascence's authenticity. Catherine's importance to him from the standpoint of romantic theology is clear from a 1949 poem he wrote for her:

---

113. Walter Conn, *Christian Conversion* (New York: Paulist Press, 1986), 147. See also Williams, *Romantic Theology*, 30–33; and Emilie Griffin, *Turning: Reflections on the Experience of Conversion* (New York: Doubleday, 1980), 139.

114. See, e.g., *End of Affair*, 78, 105, 121; "Under the Garden," 214; *HC*, 99, 221; *Human Factor*, 49, 159; *Captain and Enemy*, 79, 100.

115. Indeed, Querry's case shows that Greene felt one could reach *agape* via *caritas* as well as *eros*.

> Did I ever love God before I knew the place
> I rest in now, with my hand
> Set in stone, never to move?
> For this is love, and this I love.
> And even my God is here.[116]

In Search of a Conversion: Myths and Motives

However much Greene's interpretations of romantic theology evolved and expanded, though, its origins were clearly in his passion for Vivien. But the intensity of his feelings at the time he sought instruction in November 1925 is not evident from his direct accounts of that period. He said that it was out of fairness, even from a desire to alleviate boredom, that he asked a priest to contact him: "it occurred to me, during the long empty mornings, that if I were to marry a Catholic I ought at least to learn the nature and limits of the beliefs she held."[117] In truth, Greene was hardly assured of winning Vivien's hand. While they had become engaged, she warned that the chances of their actually marrying were 80:1. Yet he was devoted to her, and knew that his prospects would improve if he took instruction, as her response of being "madly excited" at his decision confirmed.[118]

But Greene's choice was not based solely on marital calculations. Vivien was the proximate cause of his investigation of Roman Catholicism, but once his explorations began, he quickly found aspects of it independently appealing, as Chesterton had with Frances's Anglo-Catholicism. As he told Vivien shortly after starting his instruction, "I admit the idea came to me, because of you. I do all the same feel I want to be a Catholic now, even a little apart from you. One does want fearfully hard, something fine & hard & certain, however uncomfortable, to catch hold of in the general flux."[119] His fiction further confirms this facet of his conversion. Often in his work, an unbelieving man is drawn to a believing woman, not just for her own merits, but also for her faith's abili-

---

116. Sherry, *Life*, 2: 257, 232, 329, 279.
117. Greene, *SOL*, 164–65. See also Allain, *Other Man*, 144.
118. Vivien Dayrell-Browning to Greene, undated but some time in November 1925 (Sherry, *Life*, 1: 256).
119. Greene to Vivien Dayrell-Browning, 2 November 1925 (Sherry, *Life*, 1: 256).

ty to supply something absent from his psyche: "He had seen the effect of belief on many people. He knew it was regarded as a recipe for peace, an ingredient of courage. He waited for her to speak, to offer something of her faith."[120] The peace Greene sought from Vivien's faith was a way of keeping at bay the furies that had pursued him since boarding school. As he learned more about Catholicism, he concluded that it provided a uniquely compelling explanation of the evil he felt he had faced at Berkhamsted, as well as some hope for deliverance from it in ways no other faith or secular outlook offered.

Once again, though, Greene's direct accounts of his conversion are not fully reliable, and must be qualified to present a more accurate description of his decision. He claimed constantly that he became a Roman Catholic for completely intellectual reasons, stressing as late as 1979 that "my conversion was not in the least an emotional affair. It was purely intellectual."[121] Intellectual issues were genuine and significant motives in his choice and they need to be probed further. But his insistence on their exclusivity protests too much and veils emotional or metarational factors of at least equal importance. These components need to be highlighted, then, to balance Greene's disguising of them, and thus paint a more holistic portrait of his conversion.

Indeed, Greene's intellectualist mask slipped at times. He wrote to Vivien one night during his instruction, "I've suddenly realized that I *do* believe the Catholic faith. Rationally I've believed for some time, but only this evening imaginatively."[122] This admission reveals that even when he was learning about Roman Catholicism, he judged more than just intellectual acceptance of it necessary for true belief. Additionally, he claimed in 1936 that one of conversion's advantages is "a spiritual one."[123] Such rhetoric and contemporaneous testimony indicate that more than rational arguments prompted his own conversion. What

---

120. Greene, *Rumour at Nightfall* (New York: Doubleday, Doran & Co., 1932), 129–30. This motif is also used in, e.g., *The Man Within*, *This Gun for Hire*, *The End of the Affair*, and *The Living Room*.

121. Allain, *Other Man*, 144. See also *Journey*, 213, 17; *SOL*, 167–68; Sherry, *Life*, 1: 257; and Cassis, *Paradox*, 197, 342–43, 459.

122. Greene to Vivien Dayrell-Browning, undated. Emphasis in original; quoted in Sherry, *Life*, 1: 259, who dates it at sometime in December 1925.

123. Greene, *Journey*, 85. See also *Battlefield*, 140, 190–91.

were these nonrational factors? Beyond his love for Vivien, another person's character was crucial to Greene's choice. He disliked his instructor, Fr. George Trollope, at first, and this reaction could have had detrimental consequences, for even at this early stage Greene believed in the importance of personal example to conversion: "Personality seems to me to count an awful lot in belief. If the person, who upholds the doctrine, seems much too small for them, one doubts the doctrine. It's illogical of course."[124] Yet he admitted it was still a key principle to him, showing again that his budding faith did not feed on logic alone. His opinion of Trollope gradually improved, however, as he became impressed by the priest's "inexplicable goodness," something his school sufferings had led him to think was unavailable in a black and grey world.[125] Finding such a quality present in one who had dedicated his life to Catholicism stimulated Greene's interest in it further, as he sought to discern if there was more in heaven and earth than he had dreamt of in his youthful philosophy. Trollope's ethical presence, then, at the very least supplemented significantly his discursive teaching.

Yet, as with Chesterton, religion sometimes repulsed Greene emotionally as much as it attracted him. Greene admitted that as his reception drew closer, "the fun of the intellectual exercise was over. I had reached the limit of the land and there the sea waited, if I didn't turn back. I was laughing to keep my courage up."[126] As seen in Chesterton's case, this "last-ditch reluctance" is common in the conversion process;[127] Greene portrayed it artistically in *The End of the Affair* when Sarah declares to God that "I want to abandon everything, everybody but you: only fear and habit prevent me."[128] He later conceded that even after his reception there remained "a slight feeling of fear" because of uncertainty about his future course as a Catholic.[129] Besides sharing many converts' emotionally packed conceptions of love and fear, though, Greene also was confronting the peculiarly significant challenge of his school

---

124. Greene to Vivien Dayrell-Browning, 14 November 1925 (Sherry, *Life*, 1: 257).
125. Greene, *SOL*, 166. He recreated this state of mind in a later novel (*Human Factor*, 115).
126. Greene, *SOL*, 169.
127. Griffin, *Turning*, 122–23.
128. Greene, *End of Affair*, 53. See also *Reflections*, 209.
129. Greene to Ronald Matthews, quoted in Stratford, *Faith and Fiction*, 178.

years. It is crucial to understand that Greene's acceptance of Roman Catholicism was intimately connected to his life's central trauma rather than being solely the process of cool reasoning he depicts. His Berkhamsted breakdown was a central nonrational element of his conversion.

Emilie Griffin posits that conversion provides "a hope which the convert previously lacked: first, that the universe makes sense, and second, that it is possible to rely on God for help."[130] Greene made a cognate judgment, asserting that one of conversion's spiritual advantages is "being offered an insubstantial hope,"[131] and that "hope is the flame of the Christian religion."[132] His previous inability to find any such source of enlightenment and assistance concerning his school sufferings had promoted his suicide attempts and his glorying in pessimism: these had seemed the only honest reactions to a milieu that appeared insensitive to evil's existence and persistence. He admitted that when he applied for instruction, "I was ready to believe in the existence of evil . . . the evil which surrounded me prepared me for the paradoxes of Christianity;"[133] and he later told a friend that "I had to find a religion . . . to measure my evil against."[134] For Greene, that religion was Roman Catholicism, due to what he regarded as its unique emphasis on evil: "To be a Catholic is to believe in the Devil."[135]

Just as Chesterton argued that the doctrine of original sin was optimism's only valid basis, so Greene held that the Catholic acceptance of a malevolent, but created, force in Being is the best foundation for hope. He thought this paradox of Christianity made sense of the universe by enabling one to resist manifestations of evil rather than misunderstand or deny them, as he believed his liberal Christian parents and modern culture generally had done. If post-Christians and creeds like Anglicanism had "almost relinquished Hell" in his era, he noted, "no day passed

---

130. Griffin, *Turning*, 140.

131. Greene, *Journey*, 85.

132. Greene quoted in Penelope Gilliatt, "The Dangerous Edge," in Donaghy, *Conversations*, 147.

133. Allain, *Other Man*, 148.

134. Greene to Guy Elmes, quoted in Shelden, *Within*, 125.

135. Greene review of *After Strange Gods*, by T. S. Eliot, *Life and Letters* 10 (April 1934): 112. (The review is unsigned, but Stratford [*Faith and Fiction*, 132] and Shelden [*Within*, 126] have both identified Greene as its author.) See also *BR*, 247.

in a Catholic Church without prayers for deliverance from evil spirits 'wandering through the world for the ruin of souls.'"[136] Only an acknowledged enemy can be combated successfully, and Greene thought Roman Catholics alone had a fully accurate battle plan, due to their willingness to admit the enemy's presence and the strength of his positions. But, contrary to his Oxford Manichean tendencies, what Greene considered the Catholic emphasis on the Devil also assured him that no matter how powerful evil was in time, it could not conquer goodness in eternity, as symbolized by the Devil's created, and hence subordinate, status. God's help could thus be relied on, and would vindicate those who suffered and struggled against His foes: "deliver us from evil" became a promise rather than a pious platitude. In short, Roman Catholicism was "a strong antidote to mere apathetic pessimism in the presence of evil" for Greene, offering a hopeful alternative to what seemed the "tepidity, indifference or boredom" of secularist and liberal Christian responses to it.[137] By fighting the good fight, he believed, we shall overcome some day.

Greene's theological grapplings with his school experiences also influenced his depictions of evil's most obvious symbol, the devil's lair. This already-noted analogy between school and Hell now requires greater specification. Greene's interest in Hell during his instruction is evident from his remark to Vivien that this doctrine supplies "something hard, non-sentimental and exciting," some of the qualities he found attractive in Roman Catholicism generally and absent from his ancestral modernist Anglicanism, which had largely abjured this dogma.[138] While the eternal isolation traditionally associated with Hell is a frequent image in his writing, he also painted a picture more related to his school

---

136. Greene, *CE*, 40–41. See also, e.g., *Confidential*, 59, 84, 125, 128, 150, 171, 201.

Noel Annan (*Our Age*, 299) substantiates Greene's perception that mainline Christianity in their age minimized evil: "The liver and lungs were torn out of the old theology leaving the heart still beating. Compassion came from the heart, judgment disappeared. Personal evil and wickedness were no longer so sinful." Additionally, historian Tony Judt has reached a conclusion about modern culture quite similar to Greene's: "In our post-Christian world, discussion of Evil has a curious, anachronistic feel, rather like invoking the Devil." "At Home in This Century," *New York Review of Books* 42 (6 April 1995): 10.

137. Stratford, *Faith and Fiction*, 55.

138. Greene to Vivien Dayrell-Browning (Sherry, *Life*, 1: 260, who is imprecise about the exact date).

years. In relatively early novels, some characters are horrified by an eternity of pain, and a priest counsels a reluctant penitent, "Don't depend too much on God's mercy. He has given you this chance. He may not give you another.... Nothing left except pain."[139] Whereas Chesterton had seen pain as an antidote to solipsism, Greene viewed its infinite prolongation as the worst thing one could suffer. His attitude appears rooted in memories of what seemed at the time to be never-ending "mental torments of hellish intensity" perpetrated by Carter, an interpretation substantiated by Greene's comparison of his dormitory with Hell in *The Lawless Roads*.[140] His portrayal of Hell, then, shows the symbiosis between his school years and his conversion: Roman Catholicism met his psychic and emotional need for comprehending his crisis, even as his understanding and expression of religious doctrines were shaped by the pain of those years and his reaction to them.

Greene's discovery of a theology that could explain and provide hope for ultimate deliverance from the evil experienced in and symbolized by his school years gave him an emotional and spiritual succor that the mental stimulation of pondering arguments about God's existence could not. Yet the intellectual aspects of his choice that Greene stressed should not be ignored. Understanding the specific arguments he believed, and the degree to which he adopted them, will help clarify his basic conception of Catholicism, and will also prevent common mistakes when tracing its development. While he admired the all-embracing nature of Sarah's conversion in *The End of the Affair*, Greene admitted that his own, at least intellectually, was less total. The young atheist's "primary difficulty was to believe in a God at all,"[141] one his instruction resolved but not conclusively: "It was the arguments of Fr. Trollope at Nottingham which persuaded me that God's existence was a probability.... I eventually came to accept the existence of God not as an absolute truth but as a provisional one."[142] His choice of Roman Catholi-

---

139. Greene, *P&G*, 188. See also *BR*, 107; *P&G*, 76, 133; *Ministry of Fear*, 71.

140. Grahame Smith, *The Achievement of Graham Greene* (New York: Barnes & Noble, 1986), 12; and Greene, *LR*, 14.

141. Greene, *SOL*, 167. "I believe the whole bag of tricks, there's nothing I don't believe, they could subdivide the Trinity into a dozen parts and I'd believe" (*End of Affair*, 146).

142. Allain, *Other Man*, 144–45.

cism was similarly contingent: "[I] became convinced that at any rate this might be nearer the truth than the other religions . . . the arguments for Catholicism were more convincing than those of other religions."[143]

Greene's probabilism may have been molded by Newman, whose general influence he often admitted, but whatever its provenance, his acceptance of God and Roman Catholicism as probable rather than absolute truths demonstrates that a tension between belief and doubt existed in his thought from his earliest Catholic days.[144] Indeed, he claimed in some accounts of his conversion that his confirmation name, Thomas, was in honor of the doubting disciple, not the angelic doctor.[145] Like the disease of his school years, Greene considered this conflict in his religious thought a creative spur, as a passage from his final novel reveals. Speaking of the Captain with whom he has spent much of his life, the protagonist calls him "an eternal question-mark never to be answered, like the existence of God, and so, as all theologians do, I continue to write in order to turn the question over and over without any hope of an answer."[146] This stress on the struggle between belief and doubt couples with Greene's comment about his confirmation name to indicate that (unlike Chesterton, Dawson, or Jones) he found at least one answer, Thomism, unpersuasive. While he would accent his criticism of Scholasticism more in later years, along with his emphasis on doubt, both seeds were sown in his Catholicism's springtime.

As weighty as such intellectual issues were to Greene, though, why did he make them his conversion myth's focal point at the expense of his decision's equally substantial emotional and spiritual components? Two

---

143. Greene quoted in John Cornwell, "Why I Am Still a Catholic," in Cassis, *Paradox*, 459. His faith's probabilist nature was lifelong, as he claimed in 1986 that "I think there's a sporting chance that God exists . . . if there is a God, the Catholics probably come nearest to getting Him right" (quoted in John Mortimer, "'I'm an Angry Old Man, You See,'" in Cassis, *Paradox*, 436–37).

144. Greene highlighted numerous statements of the probabilist position by Newman in his copies of the Cardinal's works. See, e.g., Newman, *Apologia Pro Vita Sua*, ed. Charles Harrold (New York: Longmans, Green & Co., 1947), 18–19, 180–81; *The Letters and Diaries of John Henry Newman*, vol. 11, ed. Charles Dessain (London: Thomas Nelson & Sons, 1961), 60–61, 69; *The Letters and Diaries of John Henry Newman*, vol. 12, ed. Charles Dessain (London: Thomas Nelson & Sons, 1962), 289.

145. See *SOL*, 169; *Reflections*, 305; Sherry, *Life*, 1: 335. Cf. *Journey*, 101.

146. Greene, *Captain and Enemy*, 109.

reasons seem most plausible. First, Greene's psychological volatility made him suspicious of emotion. Stressing his conversion's intellectual aspects made it more difficult for himself or others to dismiss it as the manifestation of a manic period. As Richard Johnstone explains,

> Emotional belief carries with it the strong possibility of later disillusionment, if and when the tenets of the faith seem increasingly to diverge from reality. But if it is first established that the faith covers convincingly all aspects of reality, the possibility of disillusionment is eliminated. Greene's description of his faith as intellectually compelled is in effect a claim for the irrefutability of religion.[147]

Such a claim is also a cultural commentary. As post-Christian society prefers rational instead of spiritual explanations of reality, Greene felt that his conversion and the views arising from it had to be presented in the culturally accepted idiom of intellectual conviction to be credible. By depicting faith as compatible with (and indeed rooted in) reason, he was challenging radically secularism's dismissal of the sacred by asserting that religion is not inherently irrational.[148] He held that having so engaged an audience on its terms, "you can put over what you will of horror, suffering, truth."[149] He thus had both personal and tactical grounds for painting his reception as the product of reasoning alone.

Although these motives are understandable, they do not obviate the need to revise Greene's conversion myth. The simultaneous interplay of rational and nonrational factors vitiates the more schematic impression Greene leaves of acquiring notional assent in 1926, but real assent only with witnessing persecuted Mexican Catholics in 1938. While that trip led him to emphasize his faith's emotional dimension more, the nonrational element of his Catholicism was present in and from his conversion. Mexico's lawless roads intensified and publicized, rather than created, this aspect of his religion.

---

147. Richard Johnstone, *The Will to Believe* (Oxford: Oxford University Press, 1982), 63–64.

148. Conversion theorist James Fowler substantiates the underlying premise of Greene's approach: "so pervasive is the impact of the secularizing consciousness that even religionists and persons of faith have tended to accept the culture's truncation of belief into assent to a set of propositions or commitment to a 'belief system.'" *Stages of Faith* (San Francisco: Harper & Row, 1981), 13.

149. Greene review of *Rhythm on the Range*, *The Spectator*, 14 August 1936 (*Greene on Film*, 94).

Mapping Graham Greene's Religious Journey 147

Besides these broader thoughts and feelings, Greene, like Chesterton, was drawn to certain particularly Roman Catholic doctrines and practices. As was Chesterton, he was fascinated by sacramental confession; but, unlike his predecessor, Greene celebrated this sacrament often, at least during his early Catholic years. Confession allusions and motifs also pervade his fiction. The idea that sins could be wiped out by the sincere practice of a codified, required rite of contrition and sacredotally directed penance had special appeal to one so conscious of evil; it combined with his interest in doctrines about the Devil and Hell to reinforce his belief that Roman Catholicism was uniquely equipped to deal with evil in his day. He made this point indirectly in *The Ministry of Fear* when Arthur Rowe is unable to find anyone who will hold him morally responsible for murder, due to what Greene saw as post-Christians' desire to explain evil away by psychologizing it. Rowe's crime is treated as an instance of illness in need of cure rather than as a sin for which he is accountable; his inability to find a source of blame, and hence forgiveness, makes him unable to forgive himself, leaving him permanently crippled. Contrarily, Greene believed that a Catholic could "lose the burden of his fear and responsibility" even "after a lifetime of the most hideous crime" through sacramental participation in Christ's Atonement.[150] Yet, although he felt that psychoanalysis could not substitute for confession, his years with the Richmonds may have helped predispose his interest in this sacrament. Not only is a debate between a psychologist and a priest a central element of *The Living Room*, but Greene also analogized the two practices.[151]

In addition to this specific sacrament, Greene, again like Chesterton, was attracted to the general authority claimed by the Catholic Church. During his instruction, he denounced Anglicanism for substituting "sticky sentiment" for defined dogmas, and he continued to complain in later years that it lacked clear doctrinal standards:

> I've too often seen the absurdity, exemplified in the Anglican church, of a bishop remaining a bishop even though he doesn't believe in the Resurrection, nor even in the historical existence of Christ. There are cer-

---

150. Greene, *Burnt-Out Case*, 52; and Greene, *P&G*, 189.
151. See, e.g., *Human Factor*, 206; and Greene, *Orient Express* (1933; reprint, New York: Pocket Books, 1961), 138–41.

tain points of reference which cannot be abandoned, otherwise one might as well go and become a Buddhist or a Hindu. . . . So long as differences between the churches exist, those differences ought to be upheld, otherwise one becomes as foggy as the Anglicans.[152]

In Roman Catholicism, though, Greene thought that he had found not only lucidly expressed truths, but, as Chesterton also believed, a truth-telling institution. After a session with Fr. Trollope, he told Vivien that "it's quite possible after all to believe it at this early stage, because the acceptance and belief in the Church as a guide includes faith in everything I've still got to be taught."[153] He considered such a source of certainty the antidote to the apparent moral and intellectual flux of post-Christian culture (and faiths, like Anglicanism, that he felt had accommodated it), a point personified by Jules Briton in *It's a Battlefield* (1934). Jules, the only identifiable Roman Catholic in this novel, desires an authoritative, active alternative to what he sees as weightless worldliness, but which he fails to find in fashionable political ideologies: "He wanted something he could follow with passion, but Communism was talk and never action, and patriotism puzzled him. . . . He wanted someone to say to him: 'Do this. Do that. Go here. Go there.' He wanted to be saved from the counter and the tea urn, the 'Weights,' and the heartless flippancy of the cafe." For Jules, such salvation comes only from his Catholicism, which rebels assuredly against secularist ennui and asserts the presence of evil: "Always in the badly lit church, surrounded by the hideous statues of an uncompromising faith, listening to the certainty of that pronouncement—*péché, péché, péché*—he was given confidence, an immense pride, a purpose. However lost in the cafe . . . here he was at home."[154]

Yet, much as Greene may have sympathized with a faith like Jules's, his own was more tenuous. Just as his belief in God's existence was conditional, so was his obedience to His vicar. Greene came to disagree strongly with many of the Church's teachings, but he never broke with

---

152. Greene to Vivien Dayrell-Browning, 24 December 1925 (Sherry, *Life*, 1: 260); and Allain, *Other Man*, 158–59. He highlighted Newman's similar contention in *Letters and Diaries*, 12: 168. Greene often focused on arguments stressing the importance of dogma in his annotations of Newman and other authors.

153. Greene to Vivien Dayrell-Browning (Sherry, *Life*, 1: 259, who estimates its date as early December 1925).

154. Greene, *Battlefield*, 40–41, 140. See also Greene's review of *After Strange Gods*, 111.

it fully, often saying he was "a protestant inside the Church." What makes his case especially complex is that, unlike some dissenters, he continued to insist on the importance of dogma. As he put it in 1979, "I'm not in opposition to Rome. . . . I believe in the necessity of a minimum of dogmas, and I certainly believe in heresy. . . . If one considers oneself a Catholic, there are a certain number of facts which have to be accepted."[155] He felt that Catholics were taught the Truth and would be held accountable for that knowledge, but he was still willing to give only limited allegiance to the teacher. Once again, Greene was trying to balance on a dangerous edge. This tension is evident in his qualified support for controversial practices and doctrines like the Index and papal infallibility.[156] His studied ambiguity on these issues, being unwilling to support or condemn Church teaching wholeheartedly, is indicative of his general posture toward the Rock of Peter: "though it repulsed me, I couldn't help admiring its unyielding facade."[157] The Church's stolidity had enticed him, and he did not want it to repeat what he considered the Anglicans' mistake of sacrificing its standards to suit individual members' objections, including his own: the household of faith would not be worth residing in if it were remodeled to oblige every crazy uncle in the attic, even one named Graham Greene.

An "Added Dimension": Roman Catholicism and Greene's Worldview

Despite the intellectual contortions required to sustain such an outlook, Greene had compelling reasons to remain a Roman Catholic for the rest of his life. His new faith intersected with his post-Berkhamsted worldview to both validate and transform his vocation as a writer, his view of human nature, and his rhetorical and cultural roles. Initially, his

---

155. Allain, *Other Man*, 158–59. Greene's sense of the need for clear standards in Roman Catholicism also led him to be less ecumenically inclined than Dawson or Jones. He claimed in 1965 to be in "full agreement" with Vatican II's ecumenical spirit (Greene to Edward Quinn, 18 February 1965, Greene Papers, Folder B1 "P/Q", Burns Library), but qualified this position later: "I have reservations. I don't think we can expect to be ecumenical with Muslims and Buddhists . . . or even the Jewish faith. But I'm ecumenical in the Christian communities." Cornwell, "Still a Catholic," 471.

156. See *Yours Etc.: Letters to the Press, 1945–1989*, ed. Christopher Hawtree (New York: Penguin, 1989), 39, 206, 248 (*YE*).

157. Greene, *SOL*, 193.

conversion shaped his opposition to literary Modernism. Greene maintained that "I was in revolt against the Bloomsbury School,"[158] whom he accused of creating characters who "wandered like cardboard symbols through a world that was paper-thin." He attributed Forster's and Woolf's ultimately insubstantial fiction to their loss of "the religious sense," and "with the religious sense went the sense of the importance of the human act. It was as if the world of fiction had lost a dimension."[159] He hence concluded that the religious imagination could best restore that missing humanistic dimension because "human beings are more important to believers than they are to atheists. If one tells oneself that man is no more than a superior animal, that each individual has before him a maximum of eighty years of life, then man is indeed of little importance."[160] To Greene, though, such "unimportance in the world of the senses is only matched by his enormous importance in another world," making characters with "the solidity and importance of men with souls to save or lose" the stuff of lasting literature.[161] He admitted that "my conversion gave my books an added dimension,"[162] and it was this stress on the religious sense that distinguished his work from the Modernists': "Greene's assumption diverges from modernism, too, because his definition of self includes a soul and an active relationship with God."[163] His adolescent crisis had impelled him to write, but his conversion gave sharper definition to his poetics.

Does this mean that Greene was a "Catholic writer"? While often dubbed one, he detested this label, preferring to call himself "a writer who happens to be a Catholic."[164] His reasons for shunning the Catholic writer designation seem twofold. One appears to be pique at critics who (in Waugh's terms) believe a Catholic artist should craft "only advertising brochures setting out in attractive terms the advantages of Church mem-

---

158. Cornwell, "Still a Catholic," 466. See also James MacArthur, "To the Heart of the Master," *Globe and Mail*, 19 January 1991, D5.
159. Greene, "Francois Mauriac," in *CE*, 91.
160. Allain, *Other Man*, 152.
161. Greene, "Francois Mauriac," 91–92.
162. Greene quoted in Dinesh D'Souza, "Beyond Marx and Jesus," *Crisis* 2 (May 1988): 20.
163. Salvatore, *Greene and Kierkegaard*, 81.
164. Greene, *WOE*, 77. See also Allain, *Other Man*, 149–50.

bership."[165] Donald Costello has shown that Greene's work was frequently reviewed in such terms, judging that "the Catholic press has not examined Greene's work primarily as literature . . . their major interest is in the relative achievements of various Catholic authors . . . viewed not generally as 'literary men' but specifically as 'Catholic authors.'"[166] Beyond being offended by such criticism's often patronizing tone, Greene felt that adhering consciously to the norms connoted by "Catholic writer" would be artistically stifling: "Literature has nothing to do with edification . . . doubt and even denial must be given their chance of self-expression."[167]

Yet such a demand is not incompatible with being a "Catholic writer," when that term is defined properly. What the critics who exasperated Greene misunderstood was the distinction between apologetics and fiction. Whereas the advocate lays out a brief for his church, the imaginative artist paints a world in Catholic colors. All points on the spectrum are present, though, given the holistic nature of both Catholicism and literature: since each addresses all aspects of human nature and life, describing temptation, sin, doubt, and denial, as well as repentance, redemption, and faith, excluding any of these hues produces both bad Catholicism and bad literature. In a more temperate moment, Greene (like Chesterton) recognized these differences and reconsidered the notion, if not the nomenclature, of a Catholic writer: "The apologist writes for a certain type of reader; the novelist addresses all . . . if one is Catholic, he doesn't have to try to be 'Catholic.' Everything that he says or writes inevitably breathes Catholicism."[168] Moreover, Greene once proposed an anthology of writings presenting "human life criticized from a Catholic standpoint."[169] Such statements encapsulate his writing's

---

165. Evelyn Waugh, "Felix Culpa?" *The Tablet* CXCI (5 June 1948): 352–54.
166. Donald Costello, "Graham Greene and the Catholic Press," *Renascence* 12 (Autumn 1959): 20–21.
167. Greene, *Why Do I Write?* 32.
168. Greene quoted in Père Jouve and Marcel More, "Table Talk With Graham Greene," in Donaghy, *Conversations*, 26. R. W. B. Lewis comments insightfully that Greene's fiction is "not applied Catholicism; it is absorbed Catholicism . . . he writes from a peculiar vision of life which [is] given intellectual content by the vocabulary of Catholicism." *The Picaresque Saint* (Philadelphia: J. B. Lippincott, 1956, 1958), 225.
169. Greene notes, Alan Redway Papers, Box 3, Folder 3, Georgetown University.

shaping vision. His rejection of a misconstrued label should not obscure Roman Catholicism's centrality to his worldview. Similarly, while Greene is regularly dubbed a prophet because of his political prescience, he did not assign himself this role nor discuss it much, even as he nonetheless used prophetic tropes often, especially in travelogues and topical essays.[170]

In addition to molding his general artistic perspective, Greene's conversion also helped define further his tragic view of life and his suspicion of innocence. Initially, he translated his ethical perception that human nature is black and grey into more specifically theological terms. Writing from a Roman Catholic perspective of the same Berkhamsted experiences that had inspired his initial insight, Greene declared:

> And so faith came to one—shapelessly, without dogma, a presence above a croquet lawn, something associated with violence, cruelty, evil across the way. One began to believe in heaven because one believed in hell, but for a long while it was only hell one could picture with a certain intimacy.

Evil was vividly present in his dorm's congestion and tauntings, but Goodness was much fainter, even where he might have expected to find it in full color: "The Anglican Church could not supply the same intimate symbols for heaven; only a big brass eagle, an organ voluntary." Only with instruction in Roman Catholicism, Greene maintained, did he begin to see some lighter shades of grey: "The Mother of God took the place of the brass eagle: one began to have a dim conception of the ap-

---

Greene's sense of this identity persisted. In 1985, for instance, he told Shusaku Endo that he hoped Endo would "continue writing 'Catholic' literature as if on his behalf" if Greene predeceased him (George Bull, "A Literary Love Affair," *Chesterton Review* 27 [February & May 2001]: 177).

170. See, e.g., Mariella Gable, *This is Catholic Fiction* (New York: Sheed & Ward, 1948), 35; Roger Sharrock, *Saints, Sinners and Comedians: The Novels of Graham Greene* (London: Burns & Oates, 1984), 14, 22, 241; Maria Cuoto, *Graham Greene: On the Frontier* (New York: St. Martin's, 1988), 92–93; John Desmond, "Book Reviews," *Religion & Literature* 23 (Summer 1991): 115–16; Grist, "News and Comments"; Leopoldo Duran, *Graham Greene: Friend and Brother* (London: HarperCollins, 1994), 56. Moreover, Walter Brueggemann suggests that taking the victim's side is part of the prophetic imagination (*The Prophetic Imagination* [Philadelphia: Fortress Press, 1978], especially chap. 5). For Greene's rare, undeveloped, treatment of prophets, see, e.g., WOE, 194; *Monsignor Quixote* (New York: Washington Square Press, 1983), 108–9; *The Quiet American* (1955, 1973; reprint, New York: Penguin, 1977), 157.

palling mysteries of love moving through a ravaged world."[171] The emotional and psychological effects of this aspect of his conversion have been discussed, but its theological roots also deserve definition.

The specific Roman Catholic doctrine that provided the theological vocabulary for Greene's insight, and that distinguished his new faith from his parents' version of Anglicanism, was original sin. Newman's assertion that humanity is implicated in an aboriginal calamity became Greene's mantra in his early Catholic years, summarizing for him the Roman Catholic attitude toward life.[172] Its appeal is unsurprising, for Newman's principle resonated with Greene's reflections on his school years, while raising them to a higher ontological level: "Roman doctrine, and particularly the doctrine of Original Sin, took into account that 'awful prison' that he perceived about him in his childhood . . . here is the boyhood pattern repeated in mature religious experience."[173] Beyond confirming his earlier impressions of human nature, belief in original sin also enabled Greene (as it did Chesterton) to escape his early pessimism by providing an eternal perspective on human evil. Regarding wickedness as an "intrinsic part of human life in every place" supplied a feeling of solidarity with a wide net of fellow sufferers, while thinking that God's goodness would eucatastrophically redeem such anguish offered a sense of "peace and patience and goodness, which includes, like the Roman virtue, courage and endurance . . . what right had an English Catholic to bitterness or horror at human nature."[174] He felt that his faith "guaranteed a happy ending," and speculated that "that's what the saints were at with their incomprehensible happiness—they had seen the end of the story when they came in and couldn't take the agonies seriously."[175]

Believing in original sin also affected Greene's views about innocence. In part, it deepened his skepticism, as he once suggested that, under this doctrine's rubrics, even a fetus might not be considered innocent.[176] Yet

171. Greene, *LR*, 14–15. See also *Rumour*, 179; *BR*, 50; *Captain and Enemy*, 12.

172. See *LR*, passim and Alan Redway Papers, Box 3, Folder 3, Georgetown University. Greene also took special note of this passage in his extant copy of the *Apologia*—which he could not have obtained before 1947—revealing this idea's persistent importance to him.

173. Stratford, *Faith and Fiction*, 55.

174. Greene, *LR*, 34, 96.

175. Greene, *Confidential*, 65–66. See also "At Home," *CE*, 333–36.

176. Greene to *The Times*, 13 November 1981 (*YE*, 205).

he also seems to have thought that baptism can cleanse a soul from original sin's stain, as after his own rebaptism he felt that he "had taken up the thread of life from very far back, from as far back as innocence."[177] Ultimately, though, he concluded that no soul can remain white for long in a black and grey world. Although it is better to baptize people than not, he held, the sacrament's efficacy diminished the longer one waited, as a "tardy baptism is not the same, after the world has taken its tarnishing account."[178] In Greene's mind, then, the sacraments are merely meliorative; they can contain essentially fallen human nature's worst aspects temporarily, but cannot fundamentally alter it. This interpretation of original sin helped him comprehend Carter's instinctive cruelty: in a world of such rapid corruption, it would not be unusual to find a schoolboy who bore about him the genuine quality of evil.

The intersection of Greene's memories of his school years, his ensuing tragic view of life and distrust of innocence, and the translation of these beliefs into the Roman Catholic category of original sin became central to his outlook. He claimed in 1949 to be "preoccupied with the mystery of sin. It is always the foundation of my books."[179] In particular, his preoccupation with the specific sin of Carter and Wheeler's treachery led him to focus artistically on the most egregious example of the Fall in the Christian story:

> it was Greene's obsession with the act of betrayal that led him to the archetypal story that he has been rewriting, with endless variations, since *The Man Within:* the story of Holy Week, the story of betrayal and sacrifice. . . . That story, too, like the terms of Christian religion, came later and served to explain—by virtue of being the supreme instance of its kind—the pattern of human conduct already discovered.[180]

---

177. Greene, *Journey,* 102.
178. Greene, *LR,* 160.
179. Greene quoted in Jouve and More, "Table Talk," 17. George Steiner calls Greene's concentration on the economy of the Fall his "obsessive focus" ("Burnt-Out Case," *The New Yorker* 50 [28 October 1974]: 185); and Eugene Goodheart maintains that this "obsession with evil and suffering" also drove Greene's literary criticism ("Greene's Literary Criticism: The Religious Aspect," in *Graham Greene: A Revaluation,* ed. Jeffrey Meyers [New York: Macmillan, 1990], 42–43).
180. Lewis, *Picaresque Saint,* 227. In one of his Bibles, Greene highlighted John 13:21–30 and 18:2–3, which foretell and describe Judas's betrayal of Jesus.

Whether as overtly as in The Power and the Glory, or rendered into geopolitical terms as in The Quiet American, Greene sought to link his personal myth to its Christian exemplar in the hope of giving his own suffering wider significance. That he considered both stories connected to the aboriginal calamity he thought all humans become implicated in at an early age is clear from his frequent quotations of A. E.'s "Germinal": "In the lost boyhood of Judas/Christ was betrayed." Greene's conversion, then, gave him both a theology that ratified and enhanced the metaphysical intuitions he had gleaned from his breakdown, and a mythology that aided his imaginative expression of those lessons.

In addition to helping Greene form his general views of a writer's function and his assessment of human nature, acceptance of Roman Catholicism also helped define his specific roles as a rebel and a defender of victims. His already subversive temperament merged with his new faith to produce a posture of personal and cultural rebellion. Initially, Greene's conversion was a rebuke to his religious upbringing. Roman Catholicism's emphasis on evil and original sin gave him conceptual categories he had been seeking since his crisis, but ones that Charles and Marion Greene's cosmology could not supply. While he is rare among British Roman Catholic converts in not facing strong familial resistance to his decision, his choice was nevertheless a strong indictment of their beliefs. As Rose Macaulay remarked, Greene had "no affection for the C. of E. of his childhood; it was much too temperate and mild and benign for him. The R.C. church broke in his ears with a darker, more catastrophic thunder, and caught him up in it."[181] In replacing the brass eagle with the Mother of God, he was also replacing the liberal Christianity of his own mother and father with the more hard-edged theology of what became Holy Mother Church for him.

Yet, as Greene's continued closeness to his family indicates, his disloyalty's personal elements were less important than its conceptual components. He renounced his parents' outlook, not so much because it was

---

181. Rose Macaulay, "Hypnotized by the Church," in Cassis, Paradox, 105. Greene's experience thus exemplifies Hugh McLeod's judgment that "Anglicanism remained important in a negative way even for those who rebelled against their public school upbringing: the rebellion tended to include a bitter rejection of the religion that had held it together." McLeod, Religion and Society in England, 1850–1914 (New York: St. Martin's Press, 1996), 112.

theirs, but because he judged it an incorrect interpretation of life. Robert Evans has argued:

> The situation from which men like Greene rebel in the 20th century is that liberal optimistic view of the world nurtured by the Enlightenment and brought to fruition in the 19th century.... There is no original sin; man is by nature a good creature. For a long time now this has been the rationalist point of view. But Greene ... has rejected it ... after investigating the seediness of our world.[182]

In *The Ministry of Fear*, for example, Arthur Rowe attends a book sale during the Blitz and discovers "a Roman missal," which "was the only thing that spoke of war in the old quiet room.... 'Let not man prevail,' he read—and the truth of the appeal chimed like music. For in all the world outside that room man had indeed prevailed."[183] Greene had earlier judged the Blitz and World War II itself "the just and reasonable expression of human nature left without belief," and claimed that, unlike his secularist peers, he was prepared for those horrors, and given a hopeful perspective on them, by belief in original sin.[184] Additionally, at a crucial moment in Sarah's conversion in *The End of the Affair*, she has an epiphany while touring a "Roman church" with her husband: "I walked out of the church in a flaming rage, and in defiance of Henry and all the reasonable and the detached ... I dipped my finger in the so-called holy water and made a kind of cross on my forehead." This passage's importance for Greene's counter-modern rebellion becomes even clearer when it is recalled that "detached" is precisely how logical positivists like Ayer and Russell were referred to earlier in the book.[185] In short, Greene's writing affirms Roman Catholicism for what he considered its rejection of coldly rationalistic, anthropocentric optimism, due to its greater awareness of mystery and malevolence.

Besides opposing Catholicism's premises to some modern philosophies', Greene also portrayed his faith as contrary to modern social norms. Sarah asserts that religious goods stores "ought to have opaque

---

182. Robert Evans, introduction to *Graham Greene: Some Critical Considerations*, ed. Robert Evans (Lexington: University of Kentucky Press, 1963), xiv–xv.
183. Greene, *Ministry of Fear*, 79. See the prefiguring of this point in *P&G*, 150.
184. Greene, "At Home," 334–36. See also "Escape," in *Reflections*, 84–86.
185. Greene, *End of Affair*, 112, 84.

glass in their doors like rubber-goods shops"; a later novel's monastery similarly tempts girls in a school tour group: "the celibacy and the silence in the old building were like a provocative perfume . . . as though beyond it there might be secrets more interesting and perverse than anything the young men could offer."[186] Such daring analogies are Greene's way of asserting that, in a post-Christian culture, Catholicism is something socially illicit. That it is also described as consequently seductive reveals further how attractive he found Catholicism's transgressive aspect. Having already disavowed modern secularity, Greene had now discovered a worldview that shared his negation while also providing an enticing counter-*telos*. If, as he felt, his age would call this union a tawdry affair, for him it was like finding love in the ruins.

Furthermore, Greene saw Christ as a rebel, and argued that His example teaches that nothing "can kill the impetus of Christianity." Thus, no matter how pervasive post-Christianity becomes, "there will always exist pockets of Christian resistance," most likely found in Roman Catholicism, due to its consistent dissent from secularist trends.[187] To him, such fidelity to its heritage against these pressures makes rebellious Rome radically distinct from its modernizing counterparts: "It was not after all the question, can this Thing survive? it was, how can this Thing ever be defeated?"[188] An early novel presents Catholics as "conspirators against the larger world," and in later years Greene dubbed them "the spies of God."[189] Whether confronting modern thought's premises directly or using sexual and political analogies to the same end, then, his virtue of disloyalty is clearly within a tradition of counter-modern Roman Catholic rebellion. He summarized this fusion of his crisis-defined outlook with his new faith when he held that English Roman Catholicism "should produce revolutionaries," and his peers and critics have recognized this link between religion and rebellion as a hallmark of his

---

186. Ibid., 119–20; and *Monsignor Quixote*, 217. Chesterton held a similar view: "In our time theology is a secret pleasure; it is enjoyed in dark corners, like a vice" (*Illustrated London News*, 12 January 1907).

187. Greene, "The Last Pope," in *Reflections*, 118, 120. See also "The Last Word," in *The Last Word and Other Stories* (New York: Penguin, 1990), 16; and Greene to *The Times*, 10 September 1971 (*YE*, 154).

188. Greene, *CE*, 298.

189. Greene, *Rumour*, 224; and "Last Pope," 120.

thought.[190] While it originated in his reaction to his adolescent breakdown, then, Greene's faith-based disloyalty to modernity came to encompass his general attitude toward his time and, as will be shown, grounded some of his strongest criticisms of the Church itself.

Lastly, Greene's conversion both drew from and shaped his sympathy for victims. Conversion theorist James Fowler maintains that "in the direct experience of the negation of one's personhood or in one's identification with the negations experienced by others, visions are born of what life is *meant* to be.... The visions that form and inform Universalizing faith arise out of and speak to such situations as these."[191] Greene's boyhood torture and betrayal had already given him this experience and the imaginative sympathy with other sufferers it can engender. His conversion was both informed by this background and affected the form his sense of solidarity took. Initially, the historical persecutions of British Roman Catholics seem to have enhanced Greene's sympathy for this faith. He referred to this tradition of subjugation frequently, and saw Jesuit martyr Robert Southwell as an exemplar of the virtue of disloyalty, thus revealing his temperamental affinities with this often oppressed, rebellious minority. As V. S. Pritchett opined, "It was enjoyable for the Protestant to feel now that the English Catholics had been 'disloyal.'... Characteristically, Greene had chosen a minority."[192]

Whatever the extent of this motive in Greene's actual conversion, once he was a Roman Catholic, he found his faith congenial to his concern for the downtrodden. As with the other aspects of his worldview, his Catholicism and his stand for victims were symbiotic, Catholicism giving theological sanction to his prior position, while that earlier outlook shaped his religion in crucial ways. In an early novel, Greene illustrated the general relationship between sympathy and faith by a Roman Catholic woman's "readiness to defend": "he could recognize its charity, mercy, above all its limitless suffering." He reiterated this connection in

---

190. Greene, *CE*, 262. See also, e.g., Costello, "Catholic Press," 13, 19; Stratford, *Faith and Fiction*, 192–93.

191. Fowler, *Stages of Faith*, 204. Emphasis in original.

192. V. S. Pritchett, "The Human Factor in Graham Greene," in Donaghy, *Conversations*, 116. See also, e.g., *LR*, passim; "The Spy," in *CE*, 311; "The Virtue of Disloyalty," 268–70; Shelden, *Within*, 396.

later works, as when a recovering skeptic recalls a friend's dictum that "when one suffers, one begins to feel part of the human condition, on the side of the Christian myth."[193] Moreover, as in the case of betrayal, he also portrayed the crucified Christ as the ultimate victim.[194] Greene thus again conjoined his personal story to a communal myth, in this case by joining a group that had also endured unjust persecution, and was founded in memory of One who had suffered the greatest possible injustice. He thus gained endorsement and expansion of his earlier sympathy with the oppressed, eventually coming to the "pervasive belief" that it is in "solidarity with suffering, guilt, and weakness ... that God is most concretely present."[195]

Just as Greene's conversion affected his defense of victims, so did that role help mold his presentation of his religion. In particular, he used it to justify a more emotional expression of his faith. He declared consistently that witnessing persecuted Mexican Catholics' faith in 1938 had generated a hitherto absent emotional dimension of his own Catholicism. His response to what he observed seems genuine, but previous analysis has shown that Greene's religion had a strong emotional component long before this trip: his journey may have intensified that affective aspect, but it was not as transformative as he suggested.[196] What is especially interesting for the present purpose, though, is that he used his sympathy for victims to explain this alleged alteration in his religious views. Asked in 1979 when he had begun to "feel" his faith, Greene replied: "I recognized the first inroads during my visit to Mexico in 1938. *It's all bound up with my loyalty to the underdog—and so it has been ever since.* In Mexico the underdogs were the Catholics ... the fidelity of the believers assumed such proportions that I couldn't help being profoundly moved."[197] Greene thus used one element of his personal myth, sympathy for victims, to temper the intellectualist dimension of it described earlier. In doing so, he justifies his adjusted attitude as rooted in principle rather than just

---

193. Greene, *Rumour*, 298; and *Burnt-Out Case*, 186.
194. See his 1 April 1948 poem quoted in Sherry, *Life*, 2: 294.
195. Terry Eagleton, *Exiles and Emigres* (New York: Schocken, 1970), 130.
196. See, e.g., Donaghy, *Conversations*, 58, 86; Cuoto, *Frontier*, 220. Greene even conceded cautiously that "probably emotion had been astir before" this trip (WOE, 80).
197. Allain, *Other Man*, 145–46. Emphasis added.

personal passion. By linking his Mexican experiences and the claimed ensuing evolution of his religious views to his long-standing concern for the dispossessed, he sought to inoculate them from efforts at delegitimization as mere emotional enthusiasm. Greene's trip to Mexico, then, remains a crucial part of his story (although not entirely for the reasons he implied), for his portrayal of it displays continued sensitivity to what he deemed post-Christian cultural norms, as well as how facets of his worldview interacted.

Greene's conversion, then, sanctioned and enlarged his adolescent outlook and became the basis of his rebuttal of modern secularism. Believing that Roman Catholicism restored the absent religious and humanistic dimension to literature, offered a more accurate reading of the human condition, and provided a set of countercultural principles and practices to affirm when refuting contemporary culture, especially a particular sympathy for victims, gave Greene continuity with his life's central event while providing a foundation for adult reflections. Even when specific views changed, these core convictions remained the heart of the matter. Greene often insisted that, however many discordant notes he struck, he never stopped singing out of a Catholic hymnal.

Bringing Faith to the Forefront: *Brighton Rock*

Following his conversion, Greene became a subeditor at his long-dreamed-of *Times*, and Vivien at last married him in October 1927. He was also writing novels, but only in 1929 was one published. *The Man Within* sold well, and Greene began to devote himself full time to writing. By the mid to late 1930s, after two dismal failures, he was making a respectable living by his pen. Although his early novels did not deal with explicitly Roman Catholic themes, they were "Catholic by omission," for they displayed "not only a vestigial sign of Christian conscience but, in opposition to the apathy and hostility of the irreligious world, a positive footing for a religious attitude."[198] That specifically religious attitude began to emerge in 1937, as Greene composed *Brighton Rock*. He claimed that only then was he ready to foreground Catholic themes in his fiction, and he admitted while writing this novel that it gave him more trouble

---

198. Stratford, *Faith and Fiction*, 188, 192.

than any previous tome.[199] The result, though, was a work that both voiced what will seem familiar themes and also broke important new ground in his rebellion against modernity.

Rhetorically, *Brighton Rock* exemplifies Greene's revolt against literary Modernism. He began it as a conventional thriller, like its immediate predecessor, *This Gun for Hire*. Whereas the earlier book's religious themes had remained latent, however, in *Brighton Rock* Roman Catholicism is "the frame of reference that informs its structure."[200] Besides making his main characters identifiably Catholic and having much of the plot develop from that fact's implications, Greene also used them to assert the critical importance of the human act he felt Modernism denied. He declared that a key theme of the novel is "the incommensurable consequences of any single act," and stressed that those repercussions are not limited to time.[201] The villainous Pinkie claims that a murder scene had "eternal importance," and his wife, Rose, deems their wedding night intercourse "an eternal act."[202] The centrality of damnation to the book further reveals Greene's literary linking of Catholicism with the transcendent dimension of fiction he found absent from Modernist art. *Brighton Rock,* then, embodies the counter-modernist, Catholic-based aesthetic that Greene was crafting concurrently in his literary criticism.

With respect to content, the themes of evil and innocence are vital to this novel. Pinkie Brown is only seventeen, but he heads a race-course gang, and is crueler than any of the other toughs or their bosses. There is much of Carter in him, from his youth (which Greene accents by calling him "the Boy") to his sadism to his readiness to betray more innocent people. He also embodies Greene's youthful unhappiness and his response to his crisis, as when Rose asks him if he believes Roman Catholicism is true:

"Of course it's true," the Boy said. ". . . Of course there's Hell. Flames and damnation . . . torments."

---

199. See *WOE*, 78; and Greene to David Higham, 7 November 1938, Alan Redway Papers, Box 3, Folder 3, Georgetown University.
200. A. A. DeVitis, "The Entertaining Mr. Greene," *Renascence* 16 (Autumn 1961): 14.
201. Greene to Ronald Matthews, quoted in Stratford, *Faith and Fiction*, 192.
202. Greene, *BR*, 177, 200.

"And Heaven too," Rose said with anxiety. . . .
"Oh, maybe," the Boy said, "maybe."

Pinkie's Catholicism, though, is more a Gnostic nihilism. He abhors pleasure, especially sex, and feels a "dim desire for annihilation." Instead of surrendering to God, then, he makes evil his good, making his profession of faith "Credo in unum Satanum."[203]

Pinkie's extreme attitudes and behavior arising from experiences and insights similar to Greene's illustrate Greene's use of fiction to purge dangerous temptations. With his pessimism distorting, rather than being transformed by, his Catholicism, Pinkie is what Greene visualizes he could have become in reaction to his school experiences: "As children we have all suffered punishments for faults we have not committed, but the wound has soon healed. With . . . Pinkie the wound never heals."[204] In recognizing this potential for unrelenting evil spurred by resentment of unjust persecution, and the need to exorcise it to begin healing, Greene tacitly reasserts his belief in original sin and, more overtly, in the possibility of damnation if one remains, like Pinkie, unrepentant to the last:

> An enormous emotion beat on him; it was like something trying to get in, the pressure of gigantic wings against the glass. *Dona nobis pacem*. He withstood it . . . it was as if the flames had literally got him . . . as if he'd been withdrawn suddenly by a hand out of any existence—

By creating such a character, Greene hoped to avoid such a fate.[205]

One signal of Pinkie's depravity and damnation is his treatment of his wife. He marries Rose not out of love, but to preclude her testifying against him at a possible murder investigation and trial. In an inversion of romantic theology, his rebuff of Rose's genuine, if sentimental, love is a sign of his rejection of God's mercy. His unwillingness to give himself at the human level mirrors, and contributes to, his withstanding God's

---

203. Greene, BR, 50, 164, 143, 165. Arthur Calder-Marshall maintains that *Brighton Rock* "was a working out of a conflict in Graham's nature . . . based upon Graham's own pre-conversion experience of evil. If Satan exists, God must" (quoted in Sherry, *Life*, 1: 637).

204. Greene, WOE, 75.

205. Greene, BR, 240, 243–44. Even after he claimed to stop believing in Hell, Greene observed in a discussion about the often congruent fates of writers and their characters, "I hope that I, at any rate, shall get the better of Pinkie" (Allain, *Other Man*, 176).

entreaties at the end of his life: "Pinkie's sexual revulsion keeps him from understanding that sexual love, if only imperfectly, mirrors God's love and gives a glimpse of divine union."[206] The clinching proof of Pinkie's damnation arises from this misunderstanding of marriage. On their wedding day, Rose asks him to record his voice. He tells her he has said something "loving" on the disk, but what Pinkie really records is "God damn you, you little bitch, why can't you go back home forever and let me be?" After his subsequent suicide, Rose believes that he is damned, but a priest reassures her that "if he loved you," he might be saved. She intends to validate this hope by playing the "loving" record, and the book closes with her approaching "the worst horror of all."[207] If human love can be a path to divine love, Greene felt, so can human hate pave the road to Hell.

Although Pinkie's is the clearest case of corrupted innocence in this novel, Rose's situation is more subtle than it may seem. Her tender years, rhetorical comparisons of her in the tale to the Virgin Mary, and her name's connotation of the medieval symbol of innocence have led some to suggest that she is a virtuous victim of Pinkie's wickedness. Yet Rose is not immune to Greene's belief in almost instantaneous corruption. She admits to having stolen even before meeting Pinkie, and reveals on their wedding night that she knows the real reason he married her, leading him to laugh with "infinite contempt and superiority at a world which used words like innocence."[208] Her corruption increases after her marriage, and it is only by the slimmest margin of hope that she fails to fulfill a suicide pact with Pinkie. While not the enthusiast for evil that he is, then, Rose is still not exempt from implication in the aboriginal calamity: she is grey to Pinkie's black.

"She Couldn't Burn if She Tried": Good and Evil versus Right and Wrong

In addition to raising such characteristically Greenean issues, *Brighton Rock* also accented a new distinction that is central to his counter-

---

206. Carola Kaplan, "Graham Greene's Pinkie Brown and Flannery O'Connor's Misfit: The Psychopathic Killer and the Mystery of God's Grace," *Renascence* 32 (Winter 1980): 122.
207. Greene, BR, 176, 247–48.
208. Ibid., 185.

modern rebellion. Greene divided humanity into two types, believers in Good and Evil, and believers in Right and Wrong. The former are teleologically oriented, stressing ends, theology and metaphysics, and the transcendent; while the latter are deontologically inclined, emphasizing means, ethics, and the solely natural and human. Yet Greene thought that only believers in the absolutes of Good and Evil are fully human, for their moral imaginations alone are attuned to the eternal dimension of existence; believers in the mediated reality of Right and Wrong have had their sensibilities attenuated by exclusive focus on ephemerals, making them a kind of subhumanity.[209] Such a classification recalls Augustine's discrimination between the City of God and the City of Man;[210] and it further echoes Kierkegaard's differentiation of the religious and ethical senses, language Greene also used.[211] While there is scant evidence of any influence the bishop of Hippo or the nineteenth-century Dane had on this aspect of his thought, a more concrete link exists to T. S. Eliot. Greene referred often to Eliot's 1930 essay on Baudelaire, which reveals affinities in the ideas and rhetoric that Greene used later to categorize approaches to life. Eliot asserts the difference between "*moral* Good and Evil which are not natural Good and Bad or Puritan Right and Wrong," and claims that "so far as we are human, what we do must be either evil or good. . . . It is true to say that the glory of man is his capacity for salvation; it is also true to say that his glory is his capacity for damnation."[212] These resonances led one scholar to contend that when Greene

---

209. Richard Hoggart used Greene's terminology coincidentally to describe their generation's working-class attitudes: "they do not think much about sin and grace, good and evil, but they are sure there is a difference between right and wrong" (quoted in Sharrock, *Saints, Sinners and Comedians*, 286, n. 6). Some "fundamental option" theologians also employ the rhetoric of Greene's polarity, but their definition of its substance is quite different.

210. Greene is often dubbed an Augustinian Christian, with varying degrees of accuracy. See, e.g., A. J. Neame, "Black and Blue: A Study in the Catholic Novel," *The European* 2 (April 1953): 29; Kathleen Nott, *The Emperor's Clothes* (Bloomington: Indiana University Press, 1954); D'Souza, "Beyond Marx and Jesus," 24; Ralph McInerny, "Graham Greene," *Crisis* 5 (May 1991): 55. Greene had Augustine's *The City of God* and *Confessions* in his library at his death.

211. Greene described *Brighton Rock*'s main theme as the contrast "between the ethical mind and the religious" (Greene to Nancy Pearn, 9 April 1937; in Sherry, *Life*, 1: 639). He claimed "a great admiration for Kierkegaard" (Cuoto, *Frontier*, 220), but never elaborated on the extent of this influence. For affinities in these two writers' views, see Salvatore, *Greene and Kierkegaard*.

212. T. S. Eliot, "Baudelaire," in *Selected Prose*, ed. John Hayward (London: Penguin, 1953),

began treating Catholic themes openly in his fiction, "it was as though to illustrate some of Eliot's critical pronouncements."[213]

Yet these ideas, and even some of their terminology, are latent in his pre-*Brighton Rock* work. Pritchett considered this issue a subliminal factor in his conversion, and Greene hints at this distinction in his earliest novels.[214] It becomes clearer in a 1934–35 set of essays about the "spoilt priest" Frederick Rolfe. Greene cites Eliot's views on Good and Evil in these articles, and begins implying more specifically that Right and Wrong is the ideology of secularists whereas Good and Evil is the belief of Catholics. He argues that, as Modernist art is missing an essential dimension, so moderns have a "much thinner reality, they are not concerned with eternal damnation." They thus react with "startled incredulity" to the likes of Rolfe, the perverse Catholic who asserted the importance of "eternal issues, of the struggle between good and evil, between vice that really demands to be called satanic and virtue of a kind which can only be called heavenly."[215] Greene pressed his idea of a perceptual chasm between Catholics and post-Christians further in 1937, chiding Shaw as "ignorant of the nature of evil," something that "ethical man" could not understand because "the ethical is much further from the good than evil is."[216]

It is in *Brighton Rock*, though, that Greene stitches these various strands together and weaves a deeply textured statement of his principle through the clash of the Roman Catholics, Pinkie and Rose, and modern secularist Ida Arnold (a name evoking archetypal liberal Matthew Arnold). While Pinkie resents Rose and her claims on him, he comes to think that "what was most evil in him needed her: it couldn't get along without goodness. . . . Good and evil lived in the same country, spoke

---

188, 194. Emphasis in original. Greene highlighted Lyndall Gordon's citation of the "so far as we are human what we do must be either evil or good" passage in *Eliot's Early Years* (Oxford: Oxford University Press, 1977), 12.

213. Stratford, *Faith and Fiction*, 132. See also Sharrock, *Saints, Sinners and Comedians*, 236; and Fred Crawford, *Mixing Memory and Desire: "The Waste Land" and British Novels* (University Park: Pennsylvania State University Press, 1982), 103–23. Greene's extant library contains most of Eliot's works.

214. Pritchett, "Human Factor," 116. See also, e.g., *The Man Within*, 51; *Rumour*, 4, 163, 194, 224, 239–40, 242, 268, 276; *Battlefield*, 44, 89, 168, 201–2; *Gun for Hire*, 12.

215. Greene, "Frederick Rolfe: Edwardian Inferno," in *CE*, 130–32.

216. Greene, *London Mercury*, September 1937 (*YE*, 66).

the same language, came together like old friends, feeling the same completion, touching hands beside the iron bedstead." Greene's belief in this inherent complementarity is conveyed further by the protagonists' names. Pink and rose are different hues of the same color rather than being poles of the spectrum. If crucially different, their contrast is muted by a fundamentally shared essence. Ida Arnold, however, uses an entirely different prism. Her mantra is "I know the difference between Right and Wrong;" but she cannot persuade Rose to forsake Pinkie on these grounds, due to a radical conceptual incompatibility between the women:

> Rose didn't answer; the woman was quite right; the two words meant nothing to her. Their taste was extinguished by stronger foods—Good and Evil . . . she knew by tests as clear as mathematics that Pinkie was evil—what did it matter in that case whether he was right or wrong?

Or, as Rose puts it more graphically, "Right and wrong. That's what she talks about. . . . As if she knew. . . . Oh, she won't burn. She couldn't burn if she tried."[217]

This last passage highlights the religious dimension of Greene's distinction, one that has a more explicitly Roman Catholic cast here than in its earlier incarnations. Greene emphasizes that it is Catholics who believe in Good and Evil because they comprehend those terms' theological analogs: "They were two Romans together in the grey street. They understood each other. She used terms common to Heaven and Hell." He contrasts this sensibility shared by Pinkie and Rose with Ida's mixture of superstition, spiritualism, and naturalism. Ida depends on a Ouija board for direction, and likewise relies on her understanding of what is "natural," frequently justifying her interpretations of actions as "It's human nature." Pinkie, conversely, mocks "those crazy geezers who touch wood, throw salt, won't go under ladders," and a confrontation between Rose and Ida reveals a radical difference in their conceptions of human nature. Whereas Ida considers people immutable slaves to their natural instincts—"'It's like those sticks of rock: bite it all the way down, you'll still

---

217. Greene, *BR*, 125, 199–200, 112. See also Smith, *Achievement*, 64–65; and Cates Baldridge, *Graham Greene's Fictions: The Virtues of Extremity* (Columbia: University of Missouri Press, 2000), 26–28.

read Brighton. That's human nature'"—Rose contends that humans can change their conduct, and are thus responsible for it to their freedom's supernatural source: "'Confession . . . repentance,' Rose whispered."[218]

Greene posits a similar distinction between Catholicism and liberal Christianity. He depicts a funeral that Ida attends as occurring in "a bare cold secular chapel which could be adapted quietly and conveniently to any creed." The service itself is a satire of religions that reject Hell, belief in a personal God, and dogma. The minister reassures mourners that disbelief in "the old medieval hell" does not mean a lack of assurance that the deceased "is already at one with the One," even if "we do not know what that One is with whom (or with which) he is now at one." Greene scorns such a minister as being "like a conjurer." To him, such compromises with agnostic sentiments mock authentic religious beliefs, and invalidate their practitioners' Christian credentials. Whereas priests and Pinkie and Rose "know what's what," in Ida's case, "she's ignorant," invincibly so.[219]

This general polarity between traditional Roman Catholic Good and Evil and modern, liberal Right and Wrong generates further dichotomies throughout the novel. For instance, as his use of a funeral to illustrate their broader differences suggests, Greene thought a cardinal contrast between these outlooks on life was radically opposed approaches to its end. He describes Ida's view of death as connected intimately to her belief in modern substitute religions that are fundamentally opposed to Catholicism:

> Death shocked her, life was so important. She wasn't religious. She didn't believe in heaven or hell, only in ghosts, ouija boards, tables that rapped and little inept voices speaking plaintively of flowers. Let Papists treat death with flippancy: life wasn't so important perhaps to them as what came after; but to her death was the end of everything.

Yet, to one Papist, Pinkie, "Death wasn't an end; the censur swung and the priest raised the Host."[220] This overtly Catholic imagery highlights

218. Greene, BR, 166, 103, 199. See also *Battlefield*, 170; *Confidential*, 155.
219. Greene, BR, 31–32, 164, 112. Rose Macaulay recalls Greene's assertions that "only R.C.s were capable of real sin because the rest of us were invincibly ignorant" (quoted in Sherry, *Life*, 1: 639).
220. Greene, BR, 32, 102. See also "Under the Garden," 172; and HC, 136.

Greene's contention that Good and Evil's belief in life everlasting is essentially Catholic, whereas Right and Wrong's veneration of temporal existence is typically post-Christian. The circumstances of Pinkie's own death are also a declaration of counter-modern rebellion, for "the Boy's suicide, performed before Ida, denies in its agony and despair her optimism and essential belief in the goodness of the natural life.... [It] asserts the reality and importance of death before a society which does its best to soften or ignore it."[221]

The eternal fate Pinkie feels he has consigned himself to is a further statement of cultural subversion. Eliot wrote in his Baudelaire essay that "the possibility of damnation is so immense a relief in a world of electoral reform, plebiscites, sex reform, and dress reform, that damnation itself is an immediate form of salvation—of salvation from the ennui of modern life, because it at last gives some significance to living." Pinkie personifies this proposition. His acceptance of damnation arising from his belief in Catholic Good and Evil gives his life meaning by asserting the eternal dimension of reality that Greene found missing from modern, Right and Wrong thinking, what Eliot called "modernist Protestantism."[222] Pinkie's sense of himself as a mortal sinner fills him with "a kind of gloomy hilarity and pride. He saw himself now as a full-grown man for whom the angels wept."[223] In short, in damning himself, he "is fully aware of his own metaphysical significance, and it is a criticism of the world that it cannot see this significance."[224] In affirming damnation as a viable negation of modern secularity, Greene dramatized his perception of his age's spiritual poverty. Pinkie's fate, then, symbolizes Greene's core contention that Roman Catholics alone had retained a vital religious sense in his day by resisting secularizing trends—such as the absolutizing of probables like mass production, plebiscites, and myriad reforms—that modern British culture and liberal Protestantism accommodated.

This premise and its implications did not go unchallenged by Greene's peers. Noting its presence in another novel, Orwell charged

---

221. David Kubal, "*Brighton Rock:* The Political Theme," *Renascence* 23 (Autumn 1970): 52.
222. Eliot, "Baudelaire," 193.   223. Greene, *BR*, 168.
224. Eagleton, *Exiles and Emigres*, 133.

Greene with holding that "it is better, spiritually higher, to be an erring Catholic than a virtuous pagan. . . . Catholics retain their superiority since they alone know the meaning of good and evil." Orwell's comments are a thoughtful check on some of the more extreme ramifications of Greene's division.[225] Even in Greene's mind, the belief in Good and Evil rigidly reserved to Roman Catholics in *Brighton Rock* included subscribers to other teleologies elsewhere. This more general contrast between thinking in absolutes and in probables became the core of his distinction; and it convinced him that he had more in common with atheists and Communists than with theological or political liberals, for "a writer who is a Catholic cannot help having a certain sympathy for any faith which is sincerely held."[226] Greene remained counter-liberal and counter-modern, but not on an exclusively confessional basis. His first explicitly Roman Catholic novel, then, exemplifies how he applied many of his worldview's constants, plus how some of these underlying beliefs found expanded expression. As these elements recurred often in subsequent works, it is more fruitful to focus henceforth on developments in his thought than on reiterating familiar formulas.

A Cosmic War: *The Power and the Glory*

Greene's next novel treating a particularly Catholic theme, *The Power and the Glory* (1940), seeks to show how a sinner can escape Pinkie's fate and become a saint. By making the last priest in repressive Mexico a

---

225. "The Sanctified Sinner," in *The Collected Essays, Journalism and Letters of George Orwell*, ed. Sonia Orwell and Ian Angus (New York: Harcourt, Brace & World, 1968), 4: 440–41. Some religious (but non–Roman Catholic) authors, like C. S. Lewis, expressed tacit agreement with Greene's separation, but without his strict denominational boundaries. See, e.g., Lewis, *The Screwtape Letters* (New York: Collier, 1982), 158, 165–66, 172; and *The Allegory of Love* (London: Oxford University Press, 1946), 42 (highlighted by Greene in his copy). Furthermore, Iris Murdoch dealt with the kinds of questions that Greene isolates for believers in Good and Evil, but from a clearly post-Christian standpoint. Murdoch seemed also to believe in this specific distinction, in her contrast between the "nice" and the "good" (*The Nice and the Good* [New York: Penguin, 1968]). See also Thomas Woodman, *Faithful Fictions: The Catholic Novel in British Literature* (Philadelphia: Open University Press, 1991), 142.

226. Greene, *WOE*, 94–95. See also *Rumour*, 163; *LR*, 37; *P&G*, 23; *Human Factor*, 106, 112, 115–16, 249–51. Martin Stannard has asserted that this idea was "surely the heart of the matter" of Greene's writing and life. Stannard, "Getting to the Heart of the Matter," *National Review* (6 February 1995): 68.

whiskey priest who fears pain but always does his duty, Greene is rebuking self-righteous piety. The priest's saga also develops some crucial extensions of Greene's counter-modern rebellion, as Mexico's persecution of Catholics becomes a microcosm of the clash between Catholicism and the "whole world" of modern secularism symbolized by that nation's socialist policies: "Mexico is a state of mind."[227] Neither the priest nor the lieutenant who pursues him are named, which adds to this morality-play aspect of the book, making it "a cosmic war in human terms" as well as an object lesson of what the rest of the modern world might face if present post-Christian trends continued, thereby revealing Greene's assumption of the prophet role.[228]

Their conflict illustrates, first, Greene's more expansive sense that belief in Good and Evil also underlies some non-Roman Catholic teleologies, as the lieutenant has a sincerely held faith in a secularist utopia. There is "something of a priest" in his walk; "he was a mystic, too." But what he has seen is a pessimistic, dark Darwinian vacancy, "a complete certainty in the existence of a dying, cooling world, of human beings who had evolved from animals for no purpose at all. . . . He wanted to destroy everything." Yet, unlike Pinkie (whose Gnostic asceticism he also shares), this man hopes to "begin the world again" by eliminating all that is "poor, superstitious, and corrupt." He further disdains "a different way of life," the Right and Wrong path of "ease, safety, toleration, and complacency." The priest senses such sympathetic similarities, saying that the lieutenant is "a good man," and is "so right" to condemn corruption in the Church.[229]

Yet, to the priest (and to Greene), he is "wrong too, of course." For all their likenesses, Good and Evil are finally opposites, and the lieutenant and priest represent the two loves that build two incompatible cities.

---

227. Greene, *LR*, 50, 224. "The violence Greene met everywhere in Mexico becomes a paradigm for a brutality widespread in the years immediately before the second world war, a phenomenon which has its roots in spiritual blankness for Greene, as well as in social deprivation" (Smith, *Achievement*, 4).

228. Sherry, *Life*, 1: 698.

229. Greene, *P&G*, 22, 24–25, 58, 194, 36, 140, 193. Although Greene extends the parameters of Good and Evil to cover secularist ideologies in this novel, he still consigns mainline Protestantism to Right and Wrong (161–75). This tendency recurs even in such a comparatively late novel as *The Comedians* (1965, 1966; reprint, New York: Penguin, 1968), 225.

Greene asserts (as Chesterton did) that secular ideologues love Humanity but Roman Catholics love humans. When talking to his illegitimate daughter the priest reflects, "That was the difference, he had always known, between his faith and theirs, the political leaders of the people who cared only for things like the state, the republic: this child was more important than a whole continent." Undergirding this distrust of abstract philanthropy is belief in original sin. The priest warns the lieutenant that "the heart's an untrustworthy beast" in a fallen world, and that those who seek to build republics of virtue are more subject to the implications of the aboriginal calamity than those who cling to what was built on the Rock of Peter:

> It's no good your working for your end unless you're a good man yourself. And there won't always be good men in your party. Then you'll have all the old starvation, beating, get-rich-anyhow. But it doesn't matter so much my being a coward—and all the rest. I can put God into a man's mouth just the same—and I can give him God's pardon. It wouldn't make any difference to that if every priest in the Church was like me.[230]

Because the Church does not ask more of fallen humans than they are capable of, Greene believed, it avoids the brutality and despair entailed in attempts to change human nature, or in efforts that assume a greater degree of righteousness than people can exercise consistently. Faced with the faithless human heart that says "love, love, love," but really means "self, self, self,"[231] Greene's priest prefers to trust the perfect love of God, which passeth understanding: "God *is* love.... We wouldn't recognize *that* love. It might even look like hate. It would be enough to scare us—God's love."[232]

Once again, then, Roman Catholicism's understanding of evil distinguishes it for Greene, and makes it superior to an alternative that he sees some merit in. In holding that no abiding city can be built on the flimsy foundation of fallen human love, but only on the unchanging love of

---

230. Greene, *P&G*, 193, 82, 199, 195. See also *Ministry of Fear*, 214; and *The Collected Works of G. K. Chesterton*, vol. 2, *St. Francis of Assisi* (San Francisco: Ignatius Press, 1986), 29–30.
231. Greene, HOM, 267. See also *End of Affair*, 23; *Burnt-Out Case*, 82, 118; HC, 262.
232. Greene, *P&G*, 199–200. Emphasis in original.

God, Catholicism explained the flaws of the irreligious ideological zealotry he witnessed in Mexico by furnishing a broader conception of human nature and relations than he felt such partisans possessed. In short, this novel is his "most clear-cut assertion of the validity of religious over political belief,"[233] as the latter offers "only man's imagination, but for the Catholic there is a tradition separate from man's interpretation of it" that provides objective, realistic, authoritative guidance and an eternal perspective on temporal affairs, whatever the character of its individual adherents.[234]

"The Worst Passion of All": Pity and Compassion in Greene

The question of how to express sympathy for humans without slipping into abstract inhumanity present in *The Power and the Glory* became the focus of Greene's next overtly Catholic novel, and marked an important departure in his thought. In establishing how to take the victim's side, he asserted another polarity, between pity and compassion. Even some sapient critics interchange these terms, but Greene distinguished sharply between them: "When you pity, you treat that person pitied as an inferior, whilst with compassion you're treating the person as an equal."[235] To him, compassion arises from egalitarian empathy, a sense of shared suffering that can exist only between equals. Pity, though, is this virtue's corruption, the belief that one knows what is best for another and hence can make even ultimate decisions about his destiny: compassion stands with victims, but pity stands over them. This notion was germinal in Greene's early work, but he first voiced it clearly in *The Ministry of Fear* (1943). He initially called this novel "The Worst Passion of All," to highlight his conviction that "pity is a terrible thing. People talk about the passion of love. Pity is the worst passion of all." In the book, Arthur Rowe murders his terminally ill wife out of the sense of superiority that Greene associated with pity. Unwilling or unable to share her suffering

---

233. Johnstone, *Will to Believe*, 95. See also Baldridge, *Virtues of Extremity*, 179–83.
234. Adamson, *Dangerous Edge*, 65.
235. Greene quoted in Burstall, "Orient Express," 55. Cf. Nathan Scott, Jr., *Craters of the Spirit* (Washington: Corpus Books, 1968), 213–17; Anthony Burgess, *The Novel Now* (London: Faber & Faber, 1971), 63.

compassionately, he instead moves selfishly to relieve his own anguish, yet convinced that he is motivated by regard for her welfare. Later on, though, he realizes that "he was trying to escape his own pain, not hers," and he draws the consequent conclusion that "pity is cruel. Pity destroys. Love isn't safe when pity's prowling round."[236]

Greene translated this jeremiad against pity into a Roman Catholic context in *The Heart of the Matter* (1948), with Catholic convert Henry Scobie replacing Rowe. While not innocent, Scobie is more grey than black at the novel's outset, having a rare reputation in the colonial police force for incorruptibility; Greene intended the book to show "how muddled a man full of goodwill could become once 'off the rails.'"[237] As with Rowe, his derailing's proximate cause is pity for his wife, which leads him to borrow money from a nefarious merchant to give her a holiday. Pity further precipitates corruption when Scobie breaks contraband regulations because he pities a ship's captain. It even leads him to begin an affair during his wife's absence, and then to kill himself upon her return so as to spare both women this triangle's pain. In short, his maxim becomes "Any victim demands allegiance."[238]

Although this motto may appear identical to Greene's sympathy for victims, this novel demonstrates what he considered the dangers of such an unlimited credo, and it does so using a Catholic motif. Greene thought pity's sense of superiority manifested the deadly sin of pride.[239] Scobie thinks sometimes that he is "the only one" who recognizes his responsibility to others, and this arrogance leads him to pity even those who do not wish him to do so. He admits that "I even plan for other people." Even when he realizes his folly, Scobie feels unable to change: "It is my job to look after the others. . . . I have left even the hope of peace for ever. I am the responsible man."[240] What makes Scobie think himself

---

236. Greene, *Ministry of Fear*, 200, 210, 98, 255. See also Sherry, *Life*, 2: 146; *Battlefield*, 126; *BR*, 197; *Third Man*, 123; *Quiet American*, 98.
237. Greene quoted in Carpenter, *The Brideshead Generation*, 401.
238. Greene, *HOM*, 206.
239. See Burstall, "Orient Express," 55; *WOE*, 125.
240. Greene, *HOM*, 122, 73, 224. In a hitherto ignored parallel, *It's A Battlefield*'s Conrad Drover is a remarkable secular counterpart to, and foreshadowing of, Scobie. He shares Scobie's corruption by pity, including an adulterous affair occasioned by feelings of pity (126–27), his belief that his actions have inescapable consequences (155), his great pride (160),

hopeless is his Catholicism. Just as his pride and pity infect his relationships with people, so they damage his tie to God. Scobie believes that he knows better than God what people need, for his pity lacks "the recognition of one's own utter neediness and dependency and, therefore, the humility and openness to faith possessed by compassion."[241] His usurpation of divine authority over human destinies results in a reversal of Christ's two love commandments: "God can wait, he thought: how can one love God at the expense of one of his creatures?" This distortion of romantic theology leads Scobie to take communion to please his wife while unrepentant for his adultery, which he believes will damn him. He tries to repent and put his soul before the happiness of his wife and mistress, but fails due to his pride's deadliest effect, his inability to trust God: "I've never trusted you. . . . I can't shift my responsibility to you. . . . I can't make one of them suffer so as to save myself. . . . You see it's an *impasse*, God, an *impasse*." The only resolution Scobie can envision is suicide, "the worst crime a Catholic could commit."[242]

Yet Scobie's crime is not Pinkie's. At one point, Scobie asserts that "love—any kind of love—does deserve a bit of mercy. One will pay, of course, pay terribly, but I don't believe one will pay forever." He is later said to love "in his way," that way being pity for victims. As his corruption accelerates, he begins to visualize God as a victim, picturing "the punch-drunk head of God reeling sideways" from absorbing his sins. As he lies dying from an intentional drug overdose, Scobie, like Pinkie, hears something "seeking to get in." But whereas Pinkie had closed his ears to the appeal, Scobie hears

> someone appealing for help, someone in need of him. And automatically at the call of need, at the cry of a victim, Scobie strung himself to act. He dredged his consciousness up from an infinite distance in order to make some reply. He said aloud, "Dear God, I love . . ."

While he dies before he can do more, Scobie's willingness to act shows that he regrets his suicide. In loving God by pitying Him as a victim and

---

and his exaggerated sense of exclusive responsibility (172). Even elements of his death scene resonate with Scobie's (197).

241. Freis, "Scobie's World," 61.

242. Greene, *HOM*, 187, 259, 257. Emphasis in original.

thinking He needs him, Scobie overcomes despair and thus avoids damnation, although the pride behind his repentance makes Purgatory a necessary stop on his path to sanctity.[243] In so revealing pity's insidiously destructive effects, one critic has held, Scobie is Greene's personal purgation of the temptation to pity.[244] This view is substantiated by Greene's strong sympathetic streak, several (although denied by the novelist) similarities between him and Scobie, and his admission that pride was his "own besetting sin."[245]

Between the Stirrup and the Ground: Greene and the "Appalling Strangeness of the Mercy of God"

In addition to connecting pride, pity, and Purgatory, Scobie's story also elucidates most clearly another central tenet of Greene's theology. At the end of *Brighton Rock*, the priest Rose consults tells her, "You can't conceive, my child, nor can I or anyone—the . . . appalling . . . strangeness of the mercy of God."[246] Greene developed this idea subsequently into the principle that even the smallest amount of openness to grace is sufficient to effect salvation. Scobie's case exemplifies this notion. Another conversation between a wife and a priest at a novel's conclusion raises this issue, and reinforces that Scobie's love for God, however wrongly expressed, was the needle's eye He needed to pull this obstinate camel through to eventual salvation. When Louise Scobie says that it is futile to pray for her husband because his suicide has surely damned him, Fr. Rank responds:

"For goodness' sake, Mrs. Scobie, don't imagine you—or I—know a thing about God's mercy."

"The Church says . . ."

"I know the Church says. The Church knows all the rules. But it doesn't know what goes on in a single human heart. . . . It may seem an odd thing to

---

243. Ibid., 210, 217, 237, 265. See also *Rumour*, 211; and *HC*, 253.

Scobie's eternal fate is intensely controversial. For analysis supporting the argument that he is bound for Purgatory, see Adam Schwartz, "Christianity's Dangerous Edge: 'Belief,' 'Faith,' and Doubt in Graham Greene's Writing," *Thematica: Historical Research and Review* 3 (May 1996): 15.

244. Stratford, *Faith and Fiction*, 236.

245. Burstall, "Orient Express," 55. See also Sherry, *Life*, 2: passim; *WOE*, 126; and *YE*, 179.

246. Greene, *BR*, 247. Ellipsis in original.

say—when a man's as wrong as he was—but I think, from what I saw of him, that he really loved God."

Against rigid readings of Church rules, Greene posited that God would use any sincere expression of faith or love as His material for redemption. During prayer, Scobie hears God's voice "lowering the terms every time it spoke like a dealer in a market," telling him that just staying alive is enough, despite his other sins: "So long as you live, the voice said, I have hope. There's no human hopelessness like the hopelessness of God."[247] Scobie resists at this point, but he finally does love God.

Similarly, Sarah's proposed deal with God in *The End of the Affair*—to begin believing in Him and to give up Bendrix if he survives an air raid—becomes the catalyst God needs to activate the latent grace of an infant baptism that she never knew had been performed. Greene ultimately extended this principle even to explicit atheists like Marx, postulating in *Monsignor Quixote* that the love of this "good man" for the poor "will certainly have saved him at the last."[248] Even as Greene defined his role as a defender of victims more precisely and continued his explorations of sin and its eternal consequences in *The Heart of the Matter*, then, he also laid the foundations of his later skepticism about Hell by imagining a wider net of divine sympathy than Church officialdom seemed to. This outlook thus belies the frequent misconstrual (especially by Anthony Burgess) of his theology as Jansenist.[249] In taking such a stance, Greene also reasserted his willingness to be a protestant inside the Church, when he thought strictness was suffocating its spirit.

A "Semi-Lapsed" Credo: "Belief," "Faith," and Doubt in Greene

Even as Greene's next major novel treating Catholic themes, *The End of the Affair* (1951), addressed the appalling strangeness of God's mercy

---

247. Greene, *HOM*, 272, 259. See also "Under the Garden," 202; and "Colette's Funeral Rites" (1954), reprinted in *The Portable Graham Greene*, ed. Philip Stratford (New York: Viking, 1972, 1973), 511–12.

248. Greene, *Monsignor Quixote*, 47.

249. See, e.g., Burgess, *The Novel Now*, 61; Burgess, "Politics in the Novels of Graham Greene," *Journal of Contemporary History* 2 (April 1967): 93–99; *YE*, 173–74; Bernard Violet, "A Rare Occasion: Graham Greene on TV," in Cassis, *Paradox*, 348–49; Cuoto, *Frontier*, 212.

and the issues concerning conversion discussed previously, it also was the pivot for a significant change in his religious views. He began to establish another polarity, between "belief" and "faith." He considered "belief" to be rational assent to points of propositional knowledge, be they those of the penny catechism or the Scholastic proofs of God's existence, based in the adherent's mind. "Faith," however, he regarded as metarational, founded largely on the believer's intuition and personal religious experiences. Greene defined his distinction most lucidly in 1979: "There's a difference between belief and faith. If I don't believe in X or Y, faith intervenes, telling me that I'm wrong not to believe. Faith is above belief. One can say that it's a gift of God, while belief is not. Belief is founded on reason."[250] Conversion theorist James Fowler substantiates this differentiation: "Belief" is the effort to "translate experiences of and relations to transcendence into concepts or propositions," whereas "faith" is "the relation of trust in or loyalty to the transcendent about which concepts or propositions—beliefs—are fashioned." In short, "logic of rational certainty is 'belief' and logic of conviction is 'faith.'"[251]

Greene's earlier work had contained this dichotomy, as in his 1936 contention that he had not been "converted to a religious faith" but "convinced by specific arguments" of a creed.[252] But he began to delineate it more clearly in *The End of the Affair*, as well as to stress a preference for faith over belief. The aforementioned scene when Sarah leaves a church and crosses herself in defiance of reasonable and detached people takes on added significance in light of this distinction. Immediately prefatory to their departure, her "very reasonable" husband had been invoking Pascal and Newman to persuade her that Roman Catholicism's mystical side fits within some rational system of "belief." Sarah, though, finds such efforts hollow compared to her immediate, confused feelings of love, hate, and gratitude toward the crucified Christ, a kind of "faith" that fosters her symbolic rebellion against arid intellectualism.[253] This

---

250. Allain, *Other Man*, 162–63. See also Violet, "Greene on TV," 347; Cuoto, *Frontier*, 212; Duran, *Friend and Brother*, 289; *Monsignor Quixote*, 178.

251. Fowler, *Stages of Faith*, 11, 102–3. Charles Williams expressed this same polarity in identical terms. See, e.g., *The Descent of the Dove* (London: Longmans, 1939), 123.

252. Greene, *Journey*, 213. See also Baldridge, *Virtues of Extremity*, 58–59.

253. Greene, *End of Affair*, 111–12.

scene illustrates the tension in Greene's mind between these two approaches to Catholicism and an altered resolution of it. Whereas his primary accent had previously been on his reception's intellectual nature, Sarah's rejection of such an outlook as a crucial step in her conversion demonstrates subtly his own assertion of its insufficiency and his approval of a more nonrational view.

This favoring of "faith" became more obvious in immediately subsequent works. For instance, when the eponymous protagonist of "A Visit to Morin" is accused of losing his faith, he responds angrily, "I never told you that. . . . I told you I had lost my belief. That's quite a different thing."[254] A similar conversation occurs in *A Burnt-Out Case* when Morin's successor, Querry, refuses to discuss the arguments for God's existence:

"Any sixteen-year-old student could demolish them. . . . I don't wish to believe."
"Then why do I get more sense of faith from you than from anyone here?"[255]

This dictional differentiation's implications are clarified further in *Monsignor Quixote* when the title cleric claims, "We can't always believe. Just having faith."[256] To Greene, then, it is "faith" that finally matters, for it endures after disbelief in formulas emerges.

Beyond clarifying this general distinction and preference, Greene's greater accent on "faith" quickened his criticism of Scholasticism. Morin and Monsignor Quixote's companion both criticize Thomistic arguments, and the lapsed Christian doctor in *A Burnt-Out Case*'s leper colony declares, "It's a strange Christianity we have here, but I wonder whether the Apostles would find it as difficult to understand as the collected works of Thomas Aquinas."[257] Greene had never been drawn to this theology, but his heightened stress on metarational experience made such

---

254. Greene, "Morin," 227. See also *The Living Room*, in *Three Plays* (London: Mercury, 1961), 68; *Loser Takes All* (1954, 1955; reprint, New York: Penguin, 1977), 51–52; *Quiet American*, 16; *Our Man in Havana*, 186.
255. Greene, *Burnt-Out Case*, 92. See WOE, 265, for Querry as Morin's successor.
256. Greene, *Monsignor Quixote*, 73.
257. Greene, "Morin," 224–25; *Monsignor Quixote*, 139; *Burnt-Out Case*, 58.

an "academic and systematic" approach even less compelling, especially when he compared it with those of mystics like John of the Cross and Theresa of Avila (to each of whom he was devoted), and that of the "genius" Augustine, whom Greene considered more original and poetic than Aquinas.[258]

Greene invoked Augustine, as well as the Spanish theologian Unamuno, in support of his intensified emphasis on "faith."[259] The distinction between "belief" and "faith" itself further recalls Gabriel Marcel's discrimination between "belief in" and "belief that," and Newman's between "notional" and "real" assent, already noted in connection with Chesterton. In addition, the Catholic Church has affirmed the general privileging of spiritual experiences over the formulas that express them, making Greene's position orthodox.[260] The way he articulated his view, though, led some to doubt its orthodoxy. After reading "Morin" and *A Burnt-Out Case*, Waugh, for example, thought that Greene had ceased to be a Catholic. He failed to understand Greene's differentiation between "belief" and "faith," and feared that characters' losses of belief represented "a recantation of faith" by their creator. Greene tried to clarify matters, but only partially succeeded.[261] Waugh's use of the two terms interchangeably has been repeated often, an insensitivity to dictional subtleties that has promoted similar misreadings of Greene's spiritual state in his later years.[262]

---

258. Duran, *Friend and Brother*, 112. John of the Cross substantiates Greene's distinction between "belief" and "faith" implicitly, as he claimed that "faith" is "like night to the intellect" (quoted in Scott, *Craters*, 221). Greene had John of the Cross's *Complete Works* (3 vols.) in his library at the time of his death.

259. See *Monsignor Quixote*, 90, 97–99; and WOE, 265–67.

260. See *Catechism of the Catholic Church*, Articles 156 and 170. Although this document was issued after Greene's death, it consolidates the Church's traditional teaching rather than presents any new doctrines. For evidence more contemporaneous with Greene, see J. C. Whitehouse, "Grammars of Assent and Dissent in Graham Greene and Brian Moore," *Renascence* 43 (Spring 1990): 158.

261. Waugh to Greene, 5 January 1961, in *The Letters of Evelyn Waugh*, ed. Mark Amory (New Haven, Conn.: Ticknor & Fields, 1980), 559. See also ibid., 556–60; and *The Diaries of Evelyn Waugh*, ed. Michael Davie (Boston: Little, Brown & Co., 1976), 774–75.

262. See, e.g., Sharrock, *Saints, Sinners, and Comedians*, 172, 176; Theodore Fraser, *The Modern Catholic Novel in Europe* (New York: Twayne, 1994), 95; John Updike, "The Man Within," *The New Yorker* 71 (26 June and 3 July 1995): 185; James Hitchcock, "Apologists—With

Inattention to nuance has also obscured how Greene's increased emphasis on "faith" led him to reinterpret his conversion indirectly. In *The End of the Affair*, for example, he wanted Bendrix to represent someone who cannot accept "the possibility of a God," the same problem that had bedeviled the young Greene. In Bendrix's case, though, it is not the probable truth of certain propositions that compels a "reluctant doubt of his own atheism," but a series of miracles worked by Sarah.[263] She has been empowered to do these by her secret baptism, which Bendrix the rationalist scorns, yet knows the stakes of: "it wasn't You that took, for that would have been magic and I believe in magic even less than I believe in You: magic is your cross, your resurrection of the body, your holy Catholic church, your communion of saints."[264] Yet it is precisely this magic that begins to pull Bendrix toward God, as it had Sarah. Greene's use of it as the motive force for the conversion of someone facing the same problem he had demonstrates how his growing fictional accent on "faith" highlighted nonrational elements of his conversion that he was simultaneously denying strenuously elsewhere. The tactical rationale for stressing a purely intellectual conversion elucidated earlier still may have governed his public remarks; but Greene's fiction displayed increasingly the side of his mind dissatisfied with a solely rational religion.[265] His previously noted suppression of other nonrational elements of his conversion and spiritual development indicates that the fictional tales should be trusted as guides to his spiritual state when they conflict with the teller's personal myth. The religion of his art qualifies the myth of his religion.

Greene's stress on "faith" is also crucial to his counter-modern rebellion, for it gives primacy to the mystical, intuitive, experiential, and in-

---

Angst and Without," *Crisis* 10 (March 1996): 38; Patrick Allitt, *Catholic Converts: British and American Intellectuals Turn to Rome* (Ithaca, N.Y.: Cornell University Press, 1997), 305–8. Thomas Woodman's designation of Greene's novels containing this notion as "post-Catholic" suggests a cognate misconception (*Faithful Fictions*, 93, 125).

263. Greene, *WOE*, 143.

264. Greene, *End of Affair*, 164–65.

265. For further evidence of this shift, from *A Burnt-Out Case*, see Schwartz, "Christianity's Dangerous Edge," 11–12. Moreover, Greene's only concession in direct writings that his religion may have had an emotional aspect before his Mexican trip came after he began accenting "faith" over "belief" (*WOE*, 80).

tangible over the claims of reason. His public protestations notwithstanding, his writings and devotional practice reveal that, within the Church, Greene was ultimately suspicious of theologies that seemed too reliant on reason and was more receptive to Catholicism's apophatic strain. Allowing for hyperbole, Morin's attitude essentially bespeaks his creator's: "I used to believe in revelation, but I never believed in the capacity of the human mind."[266] The religious experiences associated with "faith" not only were more genuine and enduring expressions of Catholicism to Greene, but they also contrasted it more sharply with what he considered an empiricist, rationalistic secular culture, and "the abstractions of the Methodists and Anglicans" and other Protestants whom he thought had accommodated modernity, as typified by his mother's religious outlook.[267] It was by cleaving to the "magical heart of the faith" and rejecting rationalism, Greene believed, that Catholicism would gain lasting adherents and remain a distinct, abiding agent in modern culture.[268]

Although Greene's discrimination between "belief" and "faith" was latent in his earlier work, his definition of it and his greater accent on "faith" were distinct events in his spiritual development. What precipitated this change? He claimed in 1984 that he retained faith in God's existence but had less belief over time, and that "my lack of belief stems from my own faults and failure in love."[269] His initial loss of belief seems linked to his fault in loving not wisely but too well. Explaining his lack of belief, Morin tells his visitor, "For twenty years, I excommunicated myself voluntarily. I never went to Confession. I loved a woman too much to pretend to myself that I would ever leave her. . . . I had cut myself off for twenty years from grace and my belief withered as the priests said it would."[270] Morin's experience was a translation of Greene's. The woman he excommunicated himself for, at first, was Catherine Walston. Their affair began in 1947, and he seems to have stopped going to confession and communion regularly by 1950 because of his refusal to leave

266. Greene, "Morin," 224.
267. Allain, *Other Man*, 146.
268. Greene, *P&G*, 154.
269. Greene to Leopoldo Duran, 30 April 1984; quoted in Duran, *Friend and Brother*, 289.
270. Greene, "Morin," 227.

her.[271] His next novel was 1951's *The End of the Affair*, with its heightened attention to the distinction between "belief" and "faith," and to the latter's primacy. These facts thus substantiate the hint of an explanation offered a decade later in "Morin," and imply that Greene was already feeling excommunication's effects.

Even after parting with Catherine in the late 1950s, Greene continued to have mistresses and to excommunicate himself. The longer he eschewed the sacraments, the more his "belief" declined, as he acknowledged in 1979: "It's my own fault.... I've broken the rules. They are rules I respect, so I haven't been to communion now for nearly thirty years.... In my private life, my situation is not regular. If I went to communion, I would have to confess and make promises. I prefer to excommunicate myself."[272] Yet he simultaneously stressed that his "faith" grew stronger. He had suggested previously, again through Morin, that that enhancement resulted from his loss of "belief": "my lack of belief is a final proof that the Church is right and the faith is true.... I know the reason why I don't believe and the reason is—the Church is true and what she taught me is true."[273] The fact that Morin no longer rationally assents to propositional knowledge confirms his metarational sense that what the Church teaches is true, for everything is unfolding as it foretold. If he excommunicated himself, he was instructed, his belief would wither and that is exactly what has occurred, just as it had for Greene after his voluntary separation from the sacraments. In fact, the novelist echoed his character when describing his own spiritual state in 1975: "I have very few beliefs now. But I continue to have a certain faith. I have the faith that I am wrong. And that my lack of belief is my fault. And that I shall be proved wrong one day."[274] His fundamental faith that the

---

271. See Sherry, *Life*, 2: 278, 324–25; and C. C. Martindale to Greene, 18 August 1951, Greene Papers, Folder F14 "Father Martindale." In sharp contrast to his earlier interest in, and frequent practice of, the sacrament of penance, Greene claimed by 1959 that "I neither like confessions nor confession boxes" (Madeline Chapsal, "The Business of the Writer," in Cassis, *Paradox*, 146).

272. Allain, *Other Man*, 161–62. Greene's self-excommunication, then, is a further example of his respect for the Church's authority even when he disagreed with or could not live up to specific teachings.

273. Greene, "Morin," 227. See also *Burnt-Out Case*, 158.

274. Greene quoted in John Heilpern, "On the Dangerous Edge," in Cassis, *Paradox*, 252.

Church is a truth-telling institution, then, was paradoxically validated and deepened by his loss of belief.

Even if Greene thought his faith in certain root principles was increasing during his "semi-lapsed" years, though, many strongly held specific beliefs were being jettisoned.[275] The two most significant ones for this analysis are original sin and Hell. It is hard to pinpoint exactly when Greene ceased believing in original sin, but his literary interest in it declined substantially after the mid-1950s. One chief symbol of it, cruel youths, disappeared from his fiction almost completely after 1954's "The Destructors." Additionally, beginning with 1955's *The Quiet American* his concern with innocence became more practical and political than ontological or theological. Furthermore, whereas he had claimed in 1949 that he was preoccupied with sin, eight years later he asserted, "I find it very difficult to believe in sin. . . . I have very little sense of it," a contention he reiterated subsequently.[276] By 1988, he was maintaining, "I believe in 'between the stirrup and the ground.' . . . Original sin does not mean anything much to me." Yet if that belief was no longer compelling, the experience that had made it attractive in his youth remained vital—"I certainly believe there is good and evil in the world"[277]—and his tragic view of life also remained intact, as Greene wrote in the mid-1960s that a situation like Papa Doc's Haiti "isn't abnormal. It belongs to human life. Cruelty's like a searchlight. It sweeps from one spot to another. We only escape it for a time."[278]

His disbelief in Hell as part of the theological explanation of evil is easier to chart. In a Bible given him in 1948, Greene highlighted numerous passages concerning Hell, indicating that this issue was at his mind's forefront as he was depicting Scobie's destiny, and was on the verge of beginning his voluntary separation from the sacraments. Scobie's fate itself established the basis for a skepticism about Hell through its assertion of how little openness to grace Greene felt is needed to effect God's appallingly strange mercy. He amplified this point subsequently, stress-

275. Allain, *Other Man*, 162.
276. Greene quoted in Philip Toynbee, "Literature and Life—2. Graham Greene on 'The Job of the Writer,'" *The Observer*, 15 September 1957, 3. See also Cassis, *Paradox*, 192.
277. Greene quoted in Cuoto, *Frontier*, 212.
278. Greene, *Comedians*, 162.

ing his growing conviction that few people will possess Pinkie's determination to resist completely God's varied and constant entreaties to offer the slight submission He requires.[279] The priest in *The Living Room* (1953) voiced this principle clearly: "Mercy is what I believe in. Hell is for the great, the very great. I don't know anyone who's great enough for Hell except Satan."[280] By the time of *Monsignor Quixote*, another priest was teaching that "it will need only the prayers of one just man to save any of us" from perdition, suggesting that even if a satanically wicked person did exist, he could still be saved if a righteous person pleaded with God on his behalf.[281] Greene concluded ultimately that "I can't bring myself to imagine that a creature conceived by Him can be so evil as to merit eternal punishment. His grace must intervene at some point."[282] The writer who had once asserted the "fallacy of the death-bed repentance," and warned that God's mercy is limited, eventually reversed himself entirely.[283] When one of his characters utters Greene's previous belief that it is a "sin to trust too much to His mercy," another has the last word: "Oh, they have a name for that too. . . . It's called presumption. Well, I'm damned well going to presume."[284]

As significant as these alterations in his religious outlook were, they should not obscure underlying continuities. Just as Greene retained his ethical sense of evil's perdurance after rejecting the doctrine of original sin as a compelling explanation of that fact, so he maintained that "even

---

279. Greene even tried, unpersuasively, to cast doubt on Pinkie's damnation in his later years. See Schwartz, "Christianity's Dangerous Edge," 17–18.

280. Greene, *Living Room*, 44. See also *Burnt-Out Case*, 81. Bendrix might have been a candidate for Hell in an earlier Greene novel, given his professed hatred for God; but *The End of the Affair* asserts that hatred is only the inverse of love, and Sarah's similar experiences, plus the rhetorical and structural biases of the book, all suggest that Bendrix will at last give in to the good temptation.

281. Greene, *Monsignor Quixote*, 64.

282. Allain, *Other Man*, 151. See also Duran, *Friend and Brother*, 289. Greene also noted Newman's squeamishness about (but continued belief in) Hell. See *Apologia*, 6; and *Letters and Diaries*, 12: 318–19.

283. Greene, *P&G*, 118. For similar cautions, see *BR*, 107–8, 178–79, 228; *HOM*, 210. Significantly, all such discussions are in works prior to *The End of the Affair*.

284. Greene, *Living Room*, 49. Greene quoted this passage endorsing presumption as expressing his personal views in a 2 December 1968 letter to Auberon Waugh. Greene Papers, Folder D7, "Waugh Family Ib."

if one persists in rejecting the idea of eternal damnation, how can one deny the existence of total evil?"[285] The tragic view of life that his school experiences had engendered and that had helped draw him to Roman Catholicism outlived his rational acceptance of certain Catholic beliefs, making him (in Karl Miller's phrase) "the novelist from Hell who ceased to believe in it."[286] Greene continued to find evil palpable in a world that he thought denied its persistence even after previously persuasive theological rationales were no longer convincing; and it was this intuitive and experiential knowledge that finally mattered more to him than doctrinal justifications.[287] If his "belief" in original sin and Hell faded, then, his "faith" that human nature is black and grey remained vivid until the end. Moreover, he also continued to affirm his desire for authority in his later years, even connecting his increased emphasis on "faith" to it. As he put it in 1982, "I believe less, and accept more, through obedience. For instance, I could easily do without the virgin birth. But my faith tells me I am wrong."[288]

Greene's acceptance of Roman Catholic authority had always been tenuous, though, and this tension intensified in his later thought. Coupled with disbelief in specific doctrines was an unsurprisingly greater accent on the general virtues of doubt. Greene remarked in 1979 that "I have, if you like, more doubts, but my faith has grown too."[289] "Faith" and doubt are both less tied to the sorts of formulas and propositions that he found less convincing and more constricting with time, making them "complementary and inseparable" elements of his later religious thought.[290] Of course, the author whose conversion was on only probable grounds and who took his confirmation name in honor of the doubting apostle had always been concerned with doubt, even during his days with the Richmonds, and there are traces of this theme in his early nov-

---

285. Allain, *Other Man*, 148.
286. Karl Miller, "Dirty Business," *TLS* (30 September 1994): 3.
287. For Greene's continued belief in modern culture's denial of evil, see, e.g., Gloria Emerson, "Our Man in Antibes," in Donaghy, *Conversations*, 130.
288. Greene quoted in Auberon Waugh, "Travels with 'The Complete Hero,'" in Cassis, *Paradox*, 359.
289. Allain, *Other Man*, 162.
290. Whitehouse, "Grammars," 161. Greene marked Eliot's comment that "doubt and uncertainty are merely a variety of belief," in Gordon, *Eliot's Early Years*, 118.

els.²⁹¹ However, like "faith," this topic became more prominent in his work from the 1950s. *The Quiet American*'s skeptic, Fowler, is conspicuously named Thomas; and in *A Burnt-Out Case* it is Father Thomas whose Catholicism is unsettled, while Querry's name suggests the act of questioning. Additionally, Greene held that "the key line" of *The Potting Shed* (1958) was "When you are not sure you are alive."²⁹² Moreover, he referred to his friend Kim Philby's "chilling certainty" and "logical fanaticism" in 1968, and in a novel partly based on the Philby affair published in 1978, he wrote unsympathetically of "a face which was ready to receive orders and obey them promptly without question, a conformist face."²⁹³ By the early 1980s he was claiming that his "only message" was "fallibility. Doubts."²⁹⁴

Doubt is one of *Monsignor Quixote*'s principal themes and Greene details what he considers its virtues in this 1982 novel. The eponymous monsignor and the lapsed Catholic, now Communist, ex-mayor of their town (named, of course, Sancho) debate their respective creeds constantly; but they also confess their respective doubts and argue without rancor. Greene thereby depicts doubt as a crucial check on the chilling certainty he detected in Philby and other creeds' untroubled true believers. He regarded some 1964 marginalia as *Monsignor Quixote*'s inspiration: "A good future [is] based on the failure always to believe. Comprehension and charity also follow. Violence comes when we are afraid to admit that we do not always believe. By violence we try to kill the doubt in ourselves."²⁹⁵ An accepted lack of surety, then, spurs that extra dimension of sympathy with another's views that Greene deemed crucial, and thus fosters tolerance by generating distrust of all systems that claim exclusive rectitude. As Quixote reflects, "a sense of doubt can bring men together perhaps even more than sharing a faith. The believer will fight

291. See, e.g., *Rumour*, 144; *Orient Express*, 177; *Battlefield*, 170; *Confidential*, 10; *HOM*, 210.
292. Greene to C. C. Martindale, 4 March 1958, Greene Papers, Folder F14, "Father Martindale."
293. Greene, "The Spy," 311; and *Human Factor*, 103.
294. Karel Kyncl, "A Conversation with Graham Greene," in Donaghy, *Conversations*, 171.
295. Greene annotation of Albert Camus, *Carnets, 1942–1951* (London: Hamish Hamilton, 1964), 81, Greene Library (also quoted in Cuoto, *Frontier*, 214). In further marginalia on this page, Greene wrote "20 years later I read this marginal note and see the birth of Monsignor Quixote."

another believer over a shade of difference; the doubter fights only with himself."²⁹⁶

Greene further saw doubt as intimately connected to free will and to the magical heart of Catholicism. A pivotal point in *Monsignor Quixote* is a dream the monsignor has in which Christ is rescued from the Cross by a legion of angels. This miracle proves "with certainty" that He is God's son, leaving "no ambiguity, no room for doubt and no room for faith at all."²⁹⁷ To Quixote, this is a nightmare, for two reasons. First, there is no choice about whether to accept Christianity. Having seen its truth demonstrated, one must confess it. Neither doubt nor faith are viable options, then, but only an unambiguous belief based on empirical data. In seeing little merit in such an irrefragable religion, Greene is asserting that the only genuine faith is a freely chosen one that could just as easily have been rejected. As C. S. Lewis put it, "There must perhaps always be just enough lack of demonstrative certainty to make free choice possible, for what could we do but accept if the faith were like the multiplication table?"²⁹⁸ To both Lewis and Greene, then, only a faith that can be doubted is worth believing in.

Beyond eliminating any role for free will, Greene felt, the Christianity of the monsignor's dream would also finally stagnate. Being based solely on sense knowledge, it would not engage the mystical and imaginative sensibility, which he considered the key to enduring faith. A believer in this sort of religion would be like someone in Marx's classless, stateless society in that he "would have no faith. The future would be there before his eyes. Can a man live without faith?"²⁹⁹ For Greene, this kind of creed is just another logical fanaticism, for "the absence of mystery, especially the mystery of a divine sacrifice and bodily resurrection, for Quixote robs reality and history of their ultimate significance by reduc-

---

296. Greene, *Monsignor Quixote*, 53.
297. Ibid., 68.
298. Lewis to Sheldon Vanauken, 17 April 1951; quoted in Humphrey Carpenter, *The Inklings* (Boston: Houghton Mifflin, 1979), 46. Greene highlighted Newman's statement of this conviction in rhetoric akin to Lewis's: "were we forced to believe, as we are forced to admit that two sides of a triangle are greater than the third, there would be no trial of our affections, nothing morally right in believing, or wrong in not believing" (*Letters and Diaries*, 12: 290).
299. Greene, *Monsignor Quixote*, 72.

ing all to the 'certitude' of human knowledge," with the concomitant ennui of complete clarity. To Greene, then, only a metarational, supernatural, ambiguous faith can remain vital; "doubt guarantees mystery" by asserting the limits of human abilities, thus keeping the unsure receptive to experiences that passeth understanding.[300] Greene's doubt is hence not the purely secular skepticism of liberalism, for it assumes that, however veiled to reason the mystical, transcendent realities are, they do exist objectively and can be glimpsed in moments of heightened spiritual sensitivity.

Similarly, Greene asserted concurrently that, as piquant a catalyst of faith as doubt is, some concrete signs of his religion's truth were also necessary. His chief touchstones were historical ones. Monsignor Quixote maintains that, despite absurdities in his devotional books, "I still have faith ... in a historic fact. That Christ died on the Cross and rose again."[301] Quixote's faith in these events and their historicity ultimately was also at the core of his creator's Christianity. Greene was fascinated by John 20:1–10, in which Peter and John race to Christ's tomb, find it empty, and thus believe in His Resurrection. Greene held in 1984 that this passage was "like *reportage*," and that this quality in it had helped him refute theologians who deny the Resurrection's historicity: "I can be interested in the *reportage* of a mystery: I am completely uninterested—even bored—by a spiritual symbol equally 'unhistoric' in Küng's sense as the *reportage*. The attempt to get rid of the fairy tale makes me for the first time in years begin to believe in it again."[302] More generally, when defining Catholicism's bedrock principles for him in 1979, Greene stated, "A man lived: Christ. He lived in history." For all his sympathy with magical, mystical religion, he also thought Catholicism needed a corporeal component to prevent it from becoming "fit only for a handful of visionaries."[303] Thus, as for Chesterton, conviction that the eternal had interpen-

---

300. John Desmond, "The Heart of (The) Matter: The Mystery of the Real in *Monsignor Quixote*," *Religion & Literature* 22 (Spring 1990): 72.

301. Greene, *Monsignor Quixote*, 76.

302. Greene to Duran, 30 April 1984 (Duran, *Friend and Brother*, 289–90). See also ibid., 186; Mortimer, "Old Man," 436; Cornwell, "Still a Catholic," 462. He noted these verses in a Bible given to him in 1948.

303. Allain, *Other Man*, 159. He noted Newman's stress on Catholicism's historicity in his

etrated the temporal at a particular, verifiable juncture as part of the economy of salvation was crucial to Greene's continued faith in Christianity.

Whatever historical surety Greene possessed, his coexistent stress on doubt has disturbed both foes and friends. His most hostile biographer deems it a coy mask, while one who borders on hagiography refers nervously to Greene's "false doubts."[304] Yet his stress on doubt was genuine and does not reflect diminished religious interest or ardor. Rather, as Karl Morrison notes, such a tendency has historically been considered a healthy part of the conversion process: "Continual doubt was the wellspring of continual conversion."[305] While some of his "beliefs" changed and dissipated, Greene's "faith" continued to deepen even as his doubts intensified, as he admitted. Novels like *The Honorary Consul* and *Monsignor Quixote* further testify to his spiritual sophistication and vitality in his later years, as does his concurrent "special curiosity" about, and preference for, Catholic fiction and authors.[306] Emphasis on doubt is also consistent with his counter-modern rebellion, for accenting it became another protest against inordinate belief in the human mind's capacity, and religious accommodations of that conviction. By asserting the inability of human beings to acquire certain knowledge and the undesirability of total surety, Greene again subverted both rationalistic culture and "unconvincing philosophical arguments" that he associated with certain theologies.[307] His stress on doubt, then, reveals continuity with other aspects of his worldview, as well as his continued active, authentic, fruitful engagement with Catholic principles. Some of his favorite lines from Browning sum up Greene's later religious views uncannily:

> All we have gained then by our unbelief
> Is a life of doubt diversified by faith.

---

copy of *An Essay on the Development of Christian Doctrine*, ed. Charles Harrold (New York: Longmans, Green & Co., 1949), 7.

304. Shelden, *Within*, 6; Duran, *Friend and Brother*, 78.

305. Karl Morrison, *Understanding Conversion* (Charlottesville: University Press of Virginia, 1992), 33.

306. Shirley Hazzard, *Greene on Capri* (New York: Farrar, Straus, Giroux, 2000), 45.

307. Greene, *SOL*, 168.

A Siren Song of Progress: Greene and Chardinean Theology

As unsatisfying as he found some schools of theology, Greene remained intrigued by the discipline in his later years. In particular, he was interested for a time in Teilhard de Chardin's work. While Greene's direct references to some of Chardin's ideas were approving, his fictional portrayals of them were more critical.[308] In *A Burnt-Out Case*, for instance, the leper colony's doctor, Colin, advocates a Chardinean notion of evolution:

> We are riding a great ninth evolutionary wave. Even the Christian myth is part of the wave, and perhaps, who knows, it may be the most valuable part. Suppose love were to evolve as rapidly in our brains as technical skill has done.... I think of Christ as an amoeba who took the right turning.

To Querry, though, "It sounds like the old song of progress," which Colin then defends, arguing that progress's benefits have been worth its costs, and that since change is inevitable, it is best to be "on the side of the progress which survives." Love's inability to keep pace with technical skill, however, prevents Querry's survival, as he is shot to death by a needlessly jealous husband, an event Greene presents as an "absurd" farce rather than the regrettable, but ineluctable, price of advance.[309]

His opinion of Chardinean ideas is even clearer in *The Honorary Consul*. The lapsed priest turned political revolutionary, Rivas, holds that there are coequal day and night sides of God that battle for supremacy: "It is a long struggle and a long suffering, evolution, and I believe God is suffering the same evolution that we are." When his friend, Dr. Plarr, echoes Querry's objections, Rivas utters a rebuttal akin to Colin's:

---

308. See *SOL*, 168; and Greene to C. C. Martindale, 13 June 1962, Greene Papers, Folder F14, "Father Martindale." His extant library contains Chardin's *The Phenomenon of Man* and Robert Speaight's biography of Chardin.

309. Greene, *Burnt-Out Case*, 124, 196. Otherwise perceptive analysts of Greene's work misunderstand his view of Chardinean theology in this novel. See, e.g., David Lodge, *The Novelist at the Crossroads* (London: Routledge & Kegan Paul, 1971), 115–16; Allitt, *Catholic Converts*, 305; Desmond, "Matter," passim. Cates Baldridge similarly misreads *The Honorary Consul* (*Virtues of Extremity*, 84–87).

But I believe in Christ . . . the day side of God, in one moment of happy creation, produced perfect goodness. . . . God's intention for once was completely fulfilled so that the night side can never win more than a little victory here and there. With our help. Because the evolution of God depends on our evolution. Every evil act of ours strengthens His night side, and every good one helps His day side. We belong to Him and He belongs to us. But now at least we can be sure where evolution will end one day—it will end in a goodness like Christ's.[310]

If some have considered this outlook orthodox, such a reading is neither accurate nor Greene's intention.[311] Rivas's theory is a monist version of the Manicheanism of Greene's 1924 Oxford story translated into a Chardinean vocabulary; and Greene intended it to be heretical: "I invented this for him because he's got to have his theology, as it were, as he had left the church and married. Well, I thought it would probably not be acceptable to the Catholic Church."[312] While Greene was more favorable to these ideas elsewhere, the novel's rhetoric confirms this assessment.[313] Like Scobie, who also went "off the rails," Rivas claims, "I pity Him," while also denying free will, and asserting his own authority over the Church's, deeming his beliefs Catholic ones, "whatever the bishops may say. Or the Pope."[314] Given Greene's previous portrayals of pity as a manifestation of monstrous pride, his stress on free will, and his emphasis on dogma's importance even when he did not fully accept specific doctrines, it is clear that Rivas's theology is not to be imitated.

Such employment of Chardinean ideas suggests distrust of their premises. In depicting a theology that attempts to reconcile Roman

---

310. Greene, *HC*, 261–62.

311. See Duran, *Friend and Brother*, 111.

312. Greene quoted in Emerson, "Antibes," 129. Thomas Wendorf sees a similar anti-Manicheanism in Greene's final novel ("Allegory in Postmodernity: Graham Greene's *The Captain and the Enemy*," *Christianity & Literature* 50 [Summer 2001]: 669); and, even as Greene professed agnosticism about the devil in his later years, he still held that "I can't believe there's a Devil and not a God" (Mortimer, "Old Man," 437). This persistent rejection of Manichean ideas is thus a further example of a religious insight outlasting an initially persuasive theological explanation in Greene's mind.

313. Israel Shenkner, "Graham Greene at 66," *New York Times Book Review*, 17 September 1971, 26.

314. Greene, *HC*, 253, 260, 262. See Emerson, "Antibes," 129, for his appraisal of Rivas as "off the rails."

Catholicism with modern ideas of progress and evolution as naive, brutal, and heretical, Greene demonstrated his own counter-modern standpoint. His tragic view of life is evident in his implication that moral progress and the capacity for love will not evolve as rapidly as technical skill in a black and grey world. He stressed this concern further a few years after writing *The Honorary Consul* by confessing that the growing nuclear threat provoked "almost the same sense of impotence before human 'malevolence'" as Hitler's technologically sophisticated means of mass slaughter had.[315] In both cases, technology was the servant of the worst, who were full of passionate intensity, while the best lacked all conviction of how to understand and oppose such horrors. In addition, Greene's empathy with individuals and his distrust of abstractions made him suspicious of any worldview that justified current pain in the name of distant, ethereal gains, as Colin's and Rivas's outlooks are painted as doing. Indeed, Rivas undermines his own theory at the novel's climax by refusing to kill a hostage, and by reverting to a traditional view of his priestly duties by trying to minister to a dying man, though doing so costs him his own life. An innocent life and an unshriven soul are finally not inevitable casualties of evolution for him, but things worth dying for; their present (and eternal) value is greater than any future temporal utopia's.[316] The sense in Greene's novels, then, is that Chardinean theology discounts evil, and is hence willing to downplay immediate suffering due to an ill-grounded ontological optimism. Beneath the hymns of praise to love and Christ, Greene heard the same old song of progress that had always struck a false note with him. This interpretation of Chardinean ideas is thus microcosmic of his strong suspicion of efforts to harmonize Catholicism with modernity.

"I Thought the Church and I Wanted the Same Thing": Vatican II

A similar wariness permeates much of his later opposition to Church practices, especially those connected with Vatican II. Greene's willing-

---

315. Allain, *The Other Man*, 148.

316. Indeed Rivas's fate and eventual renunciation of Chardinean ideas may represent Greene's efforts to purge his attraction to these notions imaginatively.

ness to be a protestant inside the Church did anything but abate in his later years, as his disbelief in original sin and Hell illustrates. Yet his discontent with Church teaching remained as nuanced as in his younger days. For example, he supported the Church's condemnation of abortion, but for that very reason rejected its prohibition of artificial contraception. Additionally, although Greene badly underestimated *Humanae Vitae*'s importance, he stressed that it was not an infallible statement, and tried to root his objections to it in defense of one's family rights and church tradition, indicating a desire to give his dissent an orthodox framework.[317]

His criticisms of the liturgical changes primarily associated with Vatican II were equally complex and even more deeply rooted in respect for tradition. Greene admired John XXIII and Paul VI, but he also opposed staunchly some of the major alterations in the Church identified with their papacies. The most significant issue for him was adoption of the vernacular Mass. He considered the Latin Mass symbolic of the Church's catholicity. In Mexico, attending Mass was "like going home—a language I could understand.... One knew what was going on."[318] It "was like any Sunday anywhere" in space or time.[319] He disliked vernacularization because it disrupted these continuities. Greene lamented that "since the change to the vernacular, when I travel, I can't follow the Catholic services; they're in a different tongue each time."[320] He joined Jones and other secular and religious intellectuals in signing a 1971 letter to Rome (as he did again in 1978) protesting plans to eliminate the Latin rite, which they deemed a "living tradition" that was an integral element of consistency in Western culture and the "history of the human spirit."[321] While suggesting that vernacularization itself might have some benefits, Greene was quite critical of the actual proposed English translations (as Dawson and Jones were); and he defended the Latin Mass on

---

317. See Allain, *Other Man*, 157, 166–67; *YE*, 247–48; and Greene's 1981 Jerusalem Prize acceptance speech.

318. Greene, *LR*, 48–49.   319. Greene, *P&G*, 175.

320. Allain, *Other Man*, 161.

321. "Appeal to Preserve Mass Sent to Vatican," *The Times*, 6 July 1971; reprinted in William Blissett, *The Long Conversation: A Memoir of David Jones* (Oxford: Oxford University Press, 1981), 154–55; and "Latin Mass Society Appeal," *Tablet*, 16 September 1978, 903.

similarly aesthetic grounds, agreeing with his co-signatories of the 1971 manifesto that this rite had inspired "a host of priceless achievements in the arts."[322] Beyond the changed language, Greene also objected to alterations in liturgical procedure, such as the abolition of the reading of the Last Gospel (from John) at Mass's conclusion, and "the freedom given to priests to introduce endless prayers—for the astronauts or what have you."[323]

Greene considered these changes a capitulation to misguided modern preferences and thus in need of opposition. Alan Gilbert argues that John XXIII "wanted a measure of accommodation ... so that the Church would cease to appear 'a museum of ancient artefacts.'"[324] Yet Greene considered some of those artefacts central to the Church's identity, energy, and appeal: he found them no less alive for being ancient, and he made them focal points of his resistance. His attitude is personified by the clash between Monsignor Quixote and a pro-council priest, Herrera, who urges Quixote to read a "more modern work of theology" and denigrates John's Gospel. Differences about the Church's *aggiornamento* finally foster a complete impasse, for Quixote "knew that he could never communicate with Father Herrera on anything which touched the religion they were supposed to share. Father Herrera was in favor of the new Mass." The old Mass becomes Quixote's (and Greene's) talisman against Herrera, the modernizing bishop who sent him, and all who would abandon tradition for the sake of accommodation. When Quixote tries to convince Sancho of the Church's constancy, Sancho retorts that Vatican II's changes belie the monsignor's case, for it has "put even Saint John out of date. . . . No longer at the end of Mass do you read" the Last Gospel. Quixote replies defiantly, "I still say those words," although not to the congregation. Instead of obeying the Church's new liturgical law, the monsignor subverts it, if only silently, to uphold what he considers Roman Catholicism's traditional spirit. His rebellion is even clearer when, having been banned by his bishop from saying Mass, Quixote dies

---

322. "Appeal to Preserve Mass," 154. See also Greene to Edward Quinn, 18 February 1965, Burns Library; and his 1967–68 letters to the International Committee on English in the Liturgy. Greene Papers, Folder B3, "Liturgy in English," Burns Library.

323. Allain, *Other Man*, 161.

324. Alan Gilbert, *The Making of Post-Christian Britain* (London: Longman, 1980), 156.

not only celebrating a liturgy, but a Latin one. His defiance, then, is not just of a particular bishop's abuse of authority but is also directed at a broader hierarchy that has imposed a troubling change, for "as long as he was speaking the Latin words he was at least happy," as was Greene when he attended (albeit authorized) Latin Masses said by Fr. Leopoldo Duran during the 1970s and '80s.[325]

Greene's distaste for these alterations may seem only a fondness for the familiar. Yet his opposition to the new liturgy was not obstructionist or based solely on personal preference for a particular rite. Rather, he judged it a logical extension of the challenge to irreligious and liberal mores that he felt Roman Catholicism had formerly uttered unequivocally. The 1971 letter to Rome deemed the new Mass a surrender to "the materialistic and technocratic civilization that is increasingly threatening the life of mind and spirit," and its authors dubbed themselves the "vanguard where recognition of the value of tradition is concerned."[326] To them, the Church's break with tradition in this area signaled a larger rift with its history generally, and with the faith of those who had admired its prior unwillingness to adapt to post-Christian norms. A defining principle of Roman Catholicism was being lost, they feared. Additionally, Greene (like Jones) thought the Church's sense of purpose in the modern era derived from this contrarian ethic, and that efforts to conciliate the dominant worldly culture would hence lessen Roman Catholicism's attractiveness. To him, "Catholicism becomes rather less interesting the more permissive it gets."[327] The Church is

> an organization which has to train for combat, one which demands self-sacrifice. . . . I'm convinced that the drop in vocations has to do with the fact that we don't put across clearly enough the attraction to be found in a difficult and dangerous calling. One enlists in a venture which is total. People are attracted to the Church where there's danger.[328]

---

325. Greene, *Monsignor Quixote*, 40, 65, 32–33, 215; Duran, *Friend and Brother*, 100. Greene's Requiem was in Latin.
326. "Appeal to Preserve Mass," 154.
327. Greene quoted in Roy Perrot, "Graham Greene: A Brief Encounter," in Cassis, *Paradox*, 201.
328. Allain, *Other Man*, 157–58.

In short, Greene was far from "taking the transformations of the church with equanimity."[329] Rather, he thought that the new Mass might presage a new Church as welcoming of secularizing ideas as mainline Protestantism was, thus leaving pernicious aspects of modern culture unchecked, tradition untransmitted, counter-modern Christians and their allies without a spiritual home, and, ultimately, Catholic churches as empty as those of other denominations that had joined together what he felt God had put asunder.

Greene's sense of what constitutes a proper Roman Catholic response to modern culture, and its implications for liturgy and practice, ultimately illustrates the trend Knox identified. Greene's conception of the Church was rooted in the particular model prevalent when he was received, and he regretted what he regarded as injudicious deviations from that paradigm: his approach to the Church's attitudes and actions was hence conditioned by these normative perceptions arising from his conversion. While never admitting this aspect of his thought outright, Greene did offer indirect evidence of it, as in Rivas's (perhaps unintentionally) revealing confession in *The Honorary Consul*:

> I thought the Church and I wanted the same thing. . . . Even if I cannot love, I see no reason to hate . . . if I feel any emotion for the Church, it is regret, not hate. I think she could have used me easily for a good purpose if she had understood a little better. . . . I am sorry not to have had more patience. Failures like ours are often just failures of hope.[330]

A Burnt-Out Case?: The Persistence of Greene's Roman Catholicism

Did Greene's hope in Roman Catholicism finally fail him? Statements like these and his frequent criticism of Church positions and practices have led some to wonder whether he remained a Roman Catholic until the end.[331] Careful consideration of his always complex Catholicism, though, discloses that Greene managed to keep at least a foot in the church door. *The Honorary Consul* again supplies a window on his soul.

---

329. Allitt, *Catholic Converts*, 308. See also James Hitchcock, "Post-Mortem on a Rebirth: The Catholic Intellectual Renaissance," *American Scholar* 49 (Spring 1980): 224.

330. Greene, *HC*, 250–51, 284. See also *WOE*, 267.

331. See, e.g., McInerny, "Greene," 55–56; Fraser, *Modern Catholic Novel*, 95.

Mapping Graham Greene's Religious Journey

Like Morin's insistence that he retained faith even after losing belief, Rivas emphasizes to Dr. Plarr, "I never left the Church. Mine is only a separation, Eduardo, a separation by mutual consent, not a divorce. I shall never belong wholly to anyone else."[332] That Greene saw his voluntary excommunication as a sign of only "semi-lapsed" status is also evident from his identical reply to two separate interviewers who asked if he still felt pursued by God in his later years: "I hope that He is still dogging my footsteps."[333] That hope was grounded in a conviction of his fundamental orthodoxy, as revealed by his reaction to Duran's 1975 Spanish book about his work: "I wish it could appear in English, for in England I am regarded as a bit of a heretic."[334] Greene's sense that he remained within at least a penumbra of grace, and his further desire to leave this life with its benefits, is demonstrated both by his wish to be anointed if he was near death, and by his 1968 comment that he did not fear a long death, for "it will enable me to make peace with God."[335] Acknowledging his faith's tortured nature, and his feeling that "many Catholics would prefer me to have left the religion altogether," Greene still considered himself open enough to grace for God's appallingly strange mercy to work on his soul.[336] In fact, he declared flatly in 1989 that his disagreement with certain Roman Catholic doctrines "doesn't mean that I have left the Church."[337]

How did Greene reconcile these beliefs with his frequent opposition to policies of the church that he thought he never left? Initially, he made yet another distinction, between the Church's "two constituent elements: the divine and the human." He believed that the Church's divine truths would endure despite their human adherents' flaws; and he felt its

---

332. Greene, *HC*, 250.
333. See Allain, *Other Man*, 154; and Sherry, *Life*, 1: xxii.
334. Duran, *Friend and Brother*, 306.
335. Greene quoted in V. S. Naipaul, "Graham Greene," in Donaghy, *Conversations*, 67. For somewhat differing accounts of Greene's death, see Shelden, *Within*, 486–87; and Duran, *Friend and Brother*, 342–44. Both reports agree, though, that he wanted and received extreme unction.
336. Greene quoted in Norman Lebrecht, "Commitment to Central America and a Passion for Religion," in Cassis, *Paradox*, 392.
337. Greene quoted in Alberto Huerta, "Graham Greene's Way," *The Tablet*, 10 August 1991, 967.

hierarchy in particular was all too human, due to the corrupting influences of power.[338] His unwillingness to spare his church's leaders from his general distrust of power shows the continuity of that aspect of his thought, his underlying tragic view of life, and the depth of his character's rebellious dimension. Yet it is crucial to realize that, for Greene, "the Church is not the hierarchy."[339] He dubbed Mexican peasants the "population of heaven" in 1938, and reiterated this conviction nearly fifty years later: "the Church does not belong to the Archbishop, it belongs to the Catholic people," such as the Nicaraguan poor who worshipped with "faith and fervor."[340] Such common parishioners had the "simplicity and clarity" that he thought the hierarchy lacked;[341] Monsignor Quixote considers them his instructors: "Oh, I don't teach them. They teach me." The curia could tamper with the liturgy and misread the signs of the time, but the Church was solid at its core, which contained more than a spark of its divine element. Like his monsignor, then, Greene was a religious populist, a "Catholic in spite of the Curia."[342]

But Greene also felt that the Curia could correct its mistakes, and he offered many of his criticisms to this end. For instance, he was grateful that the Church "recognized its errors" in initially ignoring the plight of Mindszenty in Hungary and Wyszynski in Poland by asking their forgiveness and making them cardinals.[343] While Paul Johnson judged Greene's efforts at fraternal correction a case of a convert trying to "teach his fellow-Catholics their business," Duran offers a less arrogant motive, saying that he made these statements because "he loved the Church."[344] Duran's assessment may seem naive, but such a rationale becomes more plausible when Chesterton's dictum that one only seeks to reform what one loves is recalled. Maybe Greene was "thinking Chester-

338. Duran, *Friend and Brother*, 101. See also, e.g., *YE*, 3, 25, 138; and Duran, *Friend and Brother*, 106.
339. Greene to the *Tablet*, 2 February 1983 (*YE*, 212).
340. Greene, *LR*, 44; and Greene to *The Times*, 20 March 1986 (*YE*, 232-33). See also *Quiet American*, 49; *Getting to Know the General* (Toronto: Lester & Orpen Dennys, 1984), 120; and Cornwell, "Still a Catholic," 471.
341. Greene quoted in Duran, *Friend and Brother*, 106.
342. Greene, *Monsignor Quixote*, 66, 177.
343. Duran, *Friend and Brother*, 102.
344. Johnson quoted in *New Statesman*, 7 November 1959 (*YE*, 95); Duran, *Friend and Brother*, 101.

ton" again: "The devotee is entirely free to criticise.... Love is bound; and the more it is bound the less it is blind.... Can he hate it enough to change it, and yet love it enough to think it worth changing?"[345] The fact that Greene continued to consider himself a Catholic even when criticizing Church leadership and practices pointedly was his affirmative answer.

The broader perspective offered by conversion theory also helps substantiate the permanence of Greene's Catholicism. E. D. Starbuck concluded that "persons who have passed through conversion, having once taken a stand for the religious life, tend to feel themselves identified with it, no matter how much their religious enthusiasm declines."[346] Following his reception, Greene made Catholicism an integral aspect of his identity, a component he struggled with constantly but never surrendered, even when he lost belief in what had been some signal Catholic doctrines to him. He called the faith engendered by his conversion a "virus from which one could never be cured." His use of a similar metaphor for his school experiences is highly revealing, as these had led him to Roman Catholicism and both remained deep down in the heart of him, so deep they became a part of him. As he put it in 1982 when his brother described an auto accident in which he had smashed into a church even though he could see the church coming toward him, "That is the fate of all the Greenes."[347] No matter how much he swerved and detoured along the way, Graham never went off the rails completely, and he finally reached the destination he had never fully turned back from. His journey was always with maps.

Greene's sojourn also drew from, echoed, and extended other modern British Catholic pilgrimages and protests. Besides admiring and being influenced by Newman and Chesterton, Greene also continued their rebellion against the liberal "anti-dogmatic principle," even unto the point of self-excommunication when his respect for what he saw as Catholic truth clashed with his rejection of specific doctrines and disciplines. But he also felt that one of this principle's chief developments—

---

345. G. K. Chesterton, *Orthodoxy* (1908; reprint, New York: Image Books, 1959), 71–72. Greene had a copy of *Orthodoxy* in his library at the time of his death.

346. Starbuck quoted in William James, *The Varieties of Religious Experience* (1902; reprint, New York: Modern Library, 1929), 252–53. James agreed with this judgment.

347. Duran, *Friend and Brother*, 97, 265.

the denial of aboriginal evil driven by a dream of human perfectibility—had grown more pervasive and perilous in his day. If he is rightly seen as carrying on the Tractarian (and Chestertonian) critique of liberalism, then, he did so because dogmatic Catholicism's rebuttal of it supplied what he held was most lacking in his own age, an acute recognition of the permanently flawed state of temporal life and human nature, a condition that Hannah Arendt considered the particular intellectual problem for Greene's generation of writers.[348] To Greene, only the ancient bark of Peter had the correct coordinates and seaworthy sailors to navigate safely these treacherous rapids of fallen human life, and thus avoid the shipwrecks he thought were suffered by modern secularism and liberal Christianity. Lifelong passage on this vessel, even if only in the lifeboat, was hence necessary for an eternally sound landing.

"Like A Birthmark": Conclusion

Before charting some of his eminent peers' journeys, a last reading of Greene's spiritual voyage is in order. Although intentionally unclear about much of his interior life, he provided many clues to its course, especially in his fictional characters' struggles. What emerges is the tale of a deeply sensitive child unprepared by his parents' worldview for the ostracism and abuse he underwent at boarding school due to his unique status. These years and the shock they gave his tender system incarnated evil for him, and hence shaped a tragic view of life, a suspicion of innocence, a sympathy for victims, even when they change, and a target for his rebellious temperament in the form of modern outlooks that seemed fundamentally naive. Psychotherapy salved these wounds only temporarily, for it could not account persuasively for the evil men do, nor could the liberal Anglicanism Greene grew up with. Cynical pessimism seemed his only honest choice.

Yet love called him out of his virtual despair and, despite his infidelity to Vivien, he never forgot how human passion had led him to divine grace. Despite tactical protestations to the contrary, he accepted Roman

---

348. Hannah Arendt, "Nightmare and Flight" (1945); reprinted in *Essays in Understanding*, ed. Jerome Kohn (New York: Harcourt Brace & Co., 1994), 133. See also Cuoto, *Frontier*, 28; and Maurice Cowling, *Religion and Public Doctrine in Modern England* (Cambridge: Cambridge University Press, 1985), 2: 334.

Catholicism as both rationally probable and emotionally satisfying. It became the guiding force in his life and writing from his career's outset, for its doctrines of original sin and Hell provided an explanation of evil that ratified theologically Greene's antecedent tragic sensibility, while also offering hope of overcoming the aboriginal calamity's effects. His adopted religion also molded other elements of his prior worldview, such as giving him a cause that transcended secular justifications for rebellion, and prompting him to feel compassion for victims rather than pity. It also spawned new notions, such as the distinction between belief in Good and Evil and in Right and Wrong, plus a framework for condemning literary Modernism.

Even when his respect for Church rules led him to excommunicate himself, with a consequent diminution of "belief," Greene's "faith" grew, as he stressed more strongly the metarational side of Catholicism. Even doubt became a spur to faith, for he felt it freed him from a rationalistic form of religion that had become more untenable with time. Yet these changed views did not lessen his sense of evil nor his desire to combat a culture that he thought discounted or ignored it. When Catholics seemed to be accepting the kind of thinking he had abandoned even before joining the Church, his opposition was resolutely clear. But he also held that the Church could and should be brought around. His novels had stressed that hate is the inverse of love, so what appeared to some as scorn for, or renunciation of, his faith was actually, in Greene's mind, his assertion of its value to him.

Labor of love or not, Greene's continuous conversation with his faith was an often enervating struggle. Yet in the midst of his agony, he managed to hold on to the beliefs that Christianity is historically true, and that Roman Catholicism was the variety of it most loyal to its essential heritage in his time, and thus the one best suited to rebel against an irreligious culture that devalued or denied the existence and persistence of evil. As with his whiskey priest, Greene's Catholicism was "like a birthmark." His interest was on the dangerous edge of things, but these core convictions kept his equilibrium and prevented him from crossing the midway mark on that giddy line. Perhaps it was another case of "thinking Chesterton," for an inch really was everything when Greene was balancing.

CHAPTER 3

CHRISTOPHER DAWSON'S PROGRESS IN RELIGION

Tradition, Inheritance, and the Dynamics of World History

WHILE LECTURING in America in the early 1930s, Greene's mentor, T. S. Eliot, was asked which of his contemporaries was the most powerful intellectual influence in Britain. He could have selected such still esteemed figures as his Bloomsbury friends, Chesterton, Auden, or Shaw; but Eliot chose a different name: Christopher Dawson.[1] Dawson's sway spanned the ideological and theological spectra, and also extended across the Atlantic. Barbara Ward, Russell Kirk, the Catholic Worker

---

1. Christina Scott, *A Historian and His World: A Life of Christopher Dawson* (New Brunswick, N.J.: Transaction Publishers, 1992), 210.

movement, Lewis Mumford, agnostic Arnold Toynbee, and even the deeply anti-Catholic Dean Inge all saluted his work. In recent decades, though, and especially since his 1970 death, Dawson's writing has been comparatively ignored.[2] Indeed, by 1997 Jeffrey Hart could conclude cor-

---

2. He is omitted, for example, from *Historians of Modern Europe*, ed. Hans Schmidt (Baton Rouge: Louisiana State University Press, 1971), which includes Toynbee and J. L. Hammond. John Kenyon's synoptic survey of modern British historians (*The History Men: The Historical Profession in England since the Renaissance* [Pittsburgh, Pa.: University of Pittsburgh Press, 1983]) also seems ignorant of Dawson's work, despite Kenyon's interest in the relationship between history and sociology, metahistories, and the role of historian as prophet, all topics central to Dawson's approach. Although more familiar with these themes and Dawson's work generally, Maurice Cowling offers only a breezy rehearsal of it, and puzzlingly dismisses him as a "glib" thinker, who "lacked a sense of difficulty and concentration" (*Religion and Public Doctrine in Modern England* [Cambridge: Cambridge University Press, 1985], 2: 336–39).

Christina Scott's biography is the only lengthy, comprehensive account of Dawson's life and career currently available. Her purpose is more to tell his story and present his thought than to treat particular elements of it in depth. The book thus does not provide detailed analysis of subjects like his religious development and its effect on his historical and cultural views, although it does supply much useful data. Daniel O'Connor's *The Relation Between Religion and Culture According to Christopher Dawson* (Montreal: Librairie Saint-Viateur, 1952) is similarly limited by its avowed attempt to be "a synthesis" of Dawson's work, and is further weakened by (necessarily) lacking the perspective that comes with studying the entire Dawson corpus. Patrick Allitt provides a rich comparison of Dawson's life and ideas to those of Carlton Hayes in *Catholic Converts: British and American Intellectuals Turn to Rome* (Ithaca, N.Y.: Cornell University Press, 1997), 237–75; but his analysis's broad scope and parallel structure preclude detailed, nuanced treatment of Dawson's biography and views. Some more targeted articles have appeared in *The Dawson Newsletter*, *The Chesterton Review*'s issue devoted to Dawson (May 1983), and essay collections like *The Dynamic Character of Christian Culture: Essays on Dawsonian Themes*, ed. Peter Cataldo (Lanham, Md.: University Press of America, 1984); *Christianity and Western Civilization*, ed. Wethersfield Institute (San Francisco: Ignatius Press, 1995); and *Eternity in Time: Christopher Dawson and the Catholic Idea of History*, ed. Stratford Caldecott and John Morrill (Edinburgh: T&T Clark, 1997). The best of these pieces, though, only reveal how fecund Dawson's work is and thus encourage further analysis of it, by suggesting other lines of inquiry.

Dawson's work was beginning to be marginalized near the end of his life (see, e.g., E. I. Watkin, "Tribute to Christopher Dawson," *The Tablet*, 4 October 1969, 974; David Knowles, "Obituary: Christopher Dawson," *The Tablet*, 6 June 1970, 558; and Daniel Callahan, "Christopher Dawson," *Commonweal*, 12 June 1970, 284). Fernando Cervantes and John Lukacs have each attributed this development to Dawson's being a Catholic, amateur historian of wide-ranging interests in an increasingly post-Christian, professional society that emphasized specialization, trends that have only intensified since his death and thus, they imply, further contributed to his being ignored by current scholars (Cervantes, "A Vision to

rectly that "today he is not much noticed intellectually."[3] But this condescension of posterity is no excuse for continuing to disregard a figure so many notable thinkers of diverse ideologies and interests united in praising. His peers' appraisals help demonstrate that Dawson was one of the leading lights of twentieth-century British Catholic thought. Detailing his religious development, its effect on his work in his fields of history and cultural studies, as well as its relationship to his concerns about his own culture, will illuminate the ideas that had this broad impact. And it will also situate them within the heritage of British Roman Catholic rebellion against modern secularism.

More precisely, Dawson's religious path was similar to Chesterton's and Greene's, although with some key differences. Like the other two converts, Dawson's youth was especially decisive in shaping his adult outlook; but unlike them, his early years were saturated with religion and even exposure to traditional Catholicism. Yet this background did not prevent him from sharing his fellows' fate of an adolescent crisis and loss of faith that affected him enduringly, one that set him too on the road to Rome, in this case both literally and figuratively. His 1914 conversion resulted from an intricate investigation of Roman Catholicism's facets, and this deliberate habit of mind persisted as his new faith became his intellectual gyroscope. Whether he was analyzing history or

---

Regain?: Reconsidering Christopher Dawson," *New Blackfriars* 70 [October 1989]: 448; Lukacs, "Order and History," *Intercollegiate Review* 28 [Spring 1993]: 50–52). Moreover, Allitt has pointed out that the kind of sweeping syntheses Dawson wrote became unfashionable among his historian successors, who focused on microhistory and thus excluded metahistorians like Dawson from the historiographical mainstream (*Catholic Converts*, 271–72). While Russell Hittinger has claimed that Dawson's "greatness was made possible in large measure precisely because he avoided the narrow and often petty constraints of professional, academic institutions" (Hittinger, "The Great Historian of Culture," *University Bookman* 33, no. 4 [1993]: 14), Cervantes's, Lukacs's, and Allitt's interpretations of Dawson's standing in the scholarly world remain plausible, certainly more so than Russell Kirk's unsubstantiated assessment that "Dawson's studies are winning the day" (Kirk, "The High Achievement of Christopher Dawson," *Chesterton Review* 10 [November 1984]: 436). David Jones sensed such a tendency already in the 1950s. See Jones to René Hague, 11–12 January 1955; reprinted in *Chesterton Review* 23 (February & May 1997): 108.

3. Jeffrey Hart, "Christopher Dawson and the History We Are Not Told," *Modern Age* 39 (Summer 1997): 212. See also Gerald Russello, "The Relevance of Christopher Dawson," *First Things* (April 2002): 46.

the development of cultures, or pondering the destiny of his own civilization, Catholicism was Dawson's constant conceptual framework. His broad knowledge of other eras and beliefs, however, fostered a more ecumenical attitude than was common amongst his contemporaries, and thus generated tension with some co-religionists. Nevertheless he was always an orthodox Catholic, a commitment that helped shape his distress at the mid-century liturgical changes. Moreover, however crucial he deemed it to understand the principles driving modern culture, he also always rebelled against them resolutely. In fact, part of his rationale for studying history and other cultures was to discover parallels and criteria from the past and other orders by which he could warn his times of the perils attendant upon a post-Christian age. Dawson, then, adopted the roles of both rebel and prophet against modern secularism, forms he found best substantiated by Roman Catholicism.

"A Detached Fragment From the Past": The Childhood of a Rebel

Dawson grew up in secluded areas like Hay-on-Wye and Craven. He thus learned early to live a solitary life, and to rely on his family heavily for intellectual and spiritual nourishment. He hence felt as strongly as Chesterton and Greene did that his first years had shaped his life definitively: "no one could owe more to childhood impressions than I did. In fact it was then I acquired my love of history, my interest in the differences of cultures and my sense of the importance of religion in human life, as a massive, objective, unquestioned power that entered into everything and impressed its mark on the external as well as the internal world."[4] The religion that made this impression was a mixture of various Christian traditions. His maternal grandfather, William Bevan, was an old High Church clergyman, who served the Church of Wales for fifty-six years at Hay, and was staunchly anti-Catholic. His grandson called his living "a sort of Anglican theocracy . . . there was a complete unification of political, religious, economic and social authority and influence."[5] Bevan's daughter, Mary, inherited his Anglicanism and anti-

---

4. Dawson quoted in Scott, *Historian*, 15.
5. Christopher Dawson, *Tradition and Inheritance* (1949; reprint, St. Paul, Minn.: The Wanderer Press, 1970), 11.

Catholicism. But this prejudice did not dissuade her from marrying Anglo-Catholic Henry Dawson, perhaps in part because his mother was firmly Protestant. Indeed she had raised him as a strict Protestant and he had only become an Anglo-Catholic later under the Oxford Movement's influence. Yet Henry's Catholic sympathies set the new family's religious tone, as he used Catholic devotional books, and replaced traditional Victorian family prayers with Terce and Compline. Another Catholic bent was his interest in mysticism, and one of Christopher's friends thought his library on the subject befitted a monastery.[6] Henry indicated the intensity of his Catholic beliefs further by moving the family from Hay to his ancestral area of Craven in 1896, a decision his son later ascribed to cultural and religious motives: it manifested "a conscious desire to recover contact with lost family traditions . . . [in] reaction against the rootlessness of nineteenth century culture . . . his return to Craven was in part a deliberate reaction against the Protestant tradition and an attempt to recover lost spiritual roots in a past which he felt to be Catholic."[7]

Henry's Catholic-based act of counter-modern rebellion had direct and long-term effects on Christopher. For one thing, living in Craven enhanced his youth's Catholic ethos by expanding its presence from the home to the larger community. In retrospect, he saw that climate of opinion as a macrocosm of his father's protests against Protestant hegemony:

> Nowhere was the destruction of the monasteries more bitterly resented than in Craven. . . . The fall of the abbeys left a gap in northern culture which was never filled either by the Church of England or the Nonconformists and the attempt of the new yeoman class to fill it by the foundation of the village grammar schools that are a characteristic feature of Craven was but a superficial solution.

Hence, Dawson's first impression of Craven was of an objective correlative to Catholic disquiet with modernity. He deemed it a cell of Catholic culture defined by resistance to Protestantism and industrialism: its *"genius loci"* is one that "has survived the religious revolution of the six-

---

6. See Scott, *Historian*, 18, 22, 54; and Dawson, *Tradition and Inheritance*, 28.
7. Dawson, *Tradition and Inheritance*, 18, 28.

teenth century and the industrial revolution of the nineteenth century," a perception that "remains with me" as an adult.[8] Even though these remarks came long after his conversion, and thus may have been colored by that choice, they still disclose telling evidence about the Catholic element of Dawson's boyhood and his overall worldview. However much his memories were shaped by subsequent events, the theme of Catholicism as a source of rebellion on behalf of traditional, religious culture attributed to childhood experience here was still central to his mature outlook. Dawson's desire to locate its commencement in his own origins is hence a key sign of its importance to him.

Beyond these more specifically religious issues, Dawson also believed that his childhood generated other intellectual and psychological attitudes, ones that would be crucial to his later conversion. As the foregoing analysis suggests, he valued both personal and cultural continuity highly, and he regarded this veneration of tradition as a product of his youth. Even before his father's return to his Craven roots, for instance, what Christopher felt most at Hay was "the continuity of the present with the remote past." Additionally, he asserted that "the principle of authority played a large place in our lives . . . and yet the sense of discipline and order was stimulating and not repressive." Lastly, Dawson sensed being a cultural outsider as a child: "the world that I had accepted as the solid foundation of my own life and the life of my family and the life of England was not the world of my contemporaries, but a detached fragment of the past which had somehow managed to survive on the margin between the present and the past."[9]

"Strange and Distasteful": Schooldays and a Crisis of Faith

Like Chesterton and Greene, Dawson regarded these early years as "a solitary and secluded boyhood in which I was extremely happy."[10] Yet, also like them, he found the end of this age of innocence particularly wrenching. As did Greene, Dawson "loved the freedom and the absence of social constraint" of his boyhood, and it is thus not surprising that he also loathed the regimentation and conformism of English boarding

---

8. Ibid., 25–26, 27.
9. Ibid., 12, 16, 30–31, 17–18.
10. Dawson quoted in Scott, *Historian*, 27.

schools.¹¹ He hated Bilton Grange school from his arrival at age ten in 1899 and never warmed to it over the next four years. The dissonance with his home life that created this misery was both cultural and cognitive. He shared Greene's gawkiness, had a weak constitution, was a loner, and contemned organized games. Moreover, Dawson thought his classmates lived by norms very different from those he had inherited, and he hence felt isolated from "a horde of savages with no common interests or ideas or beliefs or traditions."¹²

The most significant difference in ideas, beliefs, and traditions between home and school for Dawson was religious. To him, the school chapel's liberal Christianity was "more ethics than religion, and a haze of vagueness and uncertainty hung around the more fundamental articles of Christian dogma,"¹³ a theology he found "strange and distasteful" compared to his boyhood Anglo-Catholicism.¹⁴ This contrast did not instantly shake his received religion, though, as "home influences" helped blunt the clash's immediate impact on him.¹⁵ Yet this religious tension festered during his education's subsequent stages. Dawson entered Winchester public school in 1903. Unlike Greene, he began to recover psychologically during his brief tenure there, as it was the "most religious and traditional" leading English school, and catered to traditionalists and intellectuals.¹⁶ Pupils had more autonomy than was customary, for example, and games were (relatively) de-emphasized. He was still confronting Establishment Anglicanism, which in schools like Winchester at this time had an "emphatically Protestant and rather vaguely Evangelical note"; but he continued to find countervailing forces more in accord with his Catholic upbringing.¹⁷

One such compensatory home influence was his great-uncle, William

---

11. Dawson, *Tradition and Inheritance*, 29.

12. Dawson quoted in Scott, *Historian*, 31.

13. Christopher Dawson, "Why I Am a Catholic," *Catholic Times*, 21 May 1926; reprinted in *Chesterton Review* 9 (May 1983): 110–13.

14. Dawson quoted in Scott, *Historian*, 32.

15. Dawson, "Why I Am a Catholic," 110.

16. E. I. Watkin, "Christopher Dawson," *The Commonweal* (27 October 1933): 608. See also Scott, *Historian*, 33.

17. Adrian Hastings, *A History of English Christianity, 1920–1985* (London: Collins, 1986), 74–75.

Dawson, a High Church Christian Socialist who (like his nephew) had been influenced by the Tractarians in his youth. Additionally, perhaps as a spiritual manifestation of his claustrophobic reaction to school life, Christopher began to cultivate his father's interest in mysticism, with its stress on a solitary, personal, unmediated encounter with God. Lastly, he felt that visits to Winchester Cathedral taught him "much more" than did his religious instruction in school by supplying a "greater sense of the magnitude of the religious element in our culture and the depths of its roots in our national life than anything one could learn from books. Nor was it merely a question of widening one's historical sense; it also deepened one's spiritual sense of religion as an objective reality far transcending one's private experience," exactly the impression of religion he recalled from his childhood.[18]

Dawson bid farewell to the Cathedral and Winchester itself in mid-1904, after a severe bout of bronchitis. Upon recovery in summer 1905, he was sent to a Bedfordshire tutor named Moss. This retired cleric provided Dawson with an atmosphere similar to that Greene breathed while with the Richmonds, and there are close parallels in what each gained and lost during his respite from formal education. Physically and psychologically, the next three years were highly beneficial for Dawson. He was with Moss until 1906 and then went to other private tutors in Oxford and Germany. In each case, the relaxed pace of life and rural environment mirrored his boyhood's setting, and his health greatly improved. Private instruction also restored his youth's great personal freedom, and he used it to read widely in various fields. And other pupils he lived with seem to have been more serious and tolerant than previous classmates had been. Dawson thus echoed Greene's appraisal of his interval, calling it "one of the happiest periods of his life."[19]

A further source of happiness was his friendship with another Moss student, E. I. Watkin. But the circumstances of their meeting in 1905 hardly hinted at the lifelong closeness that would develop. According to Watkin, their first encounter occasioned a furious argument that ended

---

18. Christopher Dawson, *Education and the Crisis of Christian Culture* (New York: Henry Regnery, 1949), 12.
19. Scott, *Historian*, 36.

with his forcing the back of a chair down upon Dawson's head.[20] The topic that incited this violence was religion, and the altercation reveals a crucial change that had occurred in Dawson's views. Watkin at this time was a devout Anglo-Catholic, but some time between late 1904 and this incident Dawson had lost his ancestral faith. The tension between his home life's Anglo-Catholicism and his school days' liberal Christianity that had been building for over five years now burst, so that, like Greene, "I lost faith in religion altogether for the time being."[21]

In particular, Dawson perceived a clash between two principal components of his childhood, as he began to detect an absence of authority in Anglo-Catholicism. While at school, he started to sense that "the Anglo-Catholic position was weak in the very point where it claimed to be strongest. It was lacking in authority. It was not the teaching of the official Church, but of an enterprising minority which provided its own standard of orthodoxy." This skepticism about his boyhood creed was enhanced when his "official pastors and masters—bishops, headmasters, clergymen and tutors—looked askance at it."[22] Not only did Dawson discern an inconsistency in his childhood cosmology, then, but, like Chesterton, he was also unable to defend his youthful ideas against challenges from his new environment. If home influences kept these conflicts' consequences at bay temporarily, they could not compensate entirely for such contradictions, and they seem to have lost their ability to soothe Dawson's soul fully by mid-1905. By 1906, the resulting spiritual turmoil led him to share Chesterton's near-solipsism at a comparable period, as Dawson posited that "there appears to me to be no certainty except my own existence." A year later he was allowing that Christianity might be "a possibility among other possibilities," but added that he had "not the slightest conviction" of its truth.[23] He appears to have been a vigorous advocate for this agnosticism, as Greene was at Oxford, for Watkin recalled finding his points "too difficult to answer for my comfort."[24]

---

20. Watkin quoted in M. D. Knowles, "Christopher Dawson, 1889–1970," *Proceedings of the British Academy,* 1971 (Oxford: Oxford University Press, 1973), 441.
21. Dawson, "Why I Am a Catholic," 111.
22. Ibid., 110–11.
23. Dawson quoted in Scott, *Historian,* 37–38.
24. Watkin quoted in Knowles, "Dawson," 441. All this evidence refutes James Hitch-

Dawson's internal debate continued over the next year, and by the time he went up to Oxford in 1908 he had regained some basic belief in Christianity. Childhood influences were again vital to his spiritual development. Dawson held that his boyhood impressions of religion's objectivity and authenticity were so strong that he could not surrender them, even when he lacked a sustaining rational basis for believing: "I could not acquiesce altogether in a view of life which left no place for religion. If religion, of whatever kind, has taken an important place in one's early life, the complete absence of it leaves a sensible gap in one's experience." In Greene's terms, then, even when bereft of "belief," Dawson retained "faith." Dawson acknowledged this distinction implicitly, arguing that "however much I lacked intellectual grounds for faith, I could not doubt that the spiritual side of life represented something real which could not be explained away as mere illusion." His recovery of Christianity initiated a life-long preference for metarational and intuitive experience rather than rational proofs in religious matters.[25] One crucial example of "faith" for his spiritual renewal was mysticism, which "made so strong an impression on my mind that I felt that there must be something lacking in any theory of life which left no room for these higher types of character and experience."[26] These factors helped produce a religious renascence by mid-1908. While studying in Germany that summer, for instance, he lamented life in what seemed a post-Christian society: "This country is most dreadful. People get on so very well without religion . . . they examine Christianity as if it was a kind of beetle. . . . This is a most soul-destroying place."[27] Dawson's emergence from agnosticism, then, highlights the continued importance of childhood episodes and sensibil-

---

cock's claim that Dawson "seems not to have passed through the crucible of doubt" during his religious journey ("Post-Mortem on a Rebirth: The Catholic Intellectual Renaissance," *American Scholar* [Spring 1980]: 220).

25. Dawson, "Why I Am a Catholic," 111. See also, e.g., c. 1909 essay on mysticism, quoted in Scott, *Historian*, 56; *Enquiries: into Religion and Culture* (New York: Sheed & Ward, 1934), 193, 195; *Medieval Essays* (New York: Sheed & Ward, 1954), 109; Dawson to *The Catholic Herald*, 23 March 1956.

26. Dawson, "Why I Am a Catholic," 111. Indeed, roughly a year after he re-accepted faith, Dawson claimed that Christianity is essentially mystical. Dawson manuscript on mysticism. Dawson Manuscripts, University of St. Thomas, St. Paul, Minn.

27. Dawson quoted in Scott, *Historian*, 40.

ities to him, along with the growing significance of suprarational experiences to his religion. It also suggests the biographical roots of his later claim that religion is the central factor in both personal and cultural life.

If Dawson's school years and his accompanying crisis did not become a subtext of his adult writing (as they did for Chesterton and Greene), their severity should not be discounted. The disorienting contrast with his happy home and the spiritual discontent it fostered not only affected him deeply at the time, but scarred him lastingly. He claimed that Bilton Grange forever prejudiced him against "England of the Diamond Jubilee, schoolboys, schools and even against the Midlands," where it was located. Winchester had been comparatively congenial objectively, but his subjective feelings toward it were still far from fond. When a friend called it a "kill or cure" school, for example, Dawson replied, "It maims." Nor were these sentiments literary hyperbole. When it was time to choose a school for his son, for instance, Dawson, his wife, and a friend set out to visit a possibility. Nearing its gates, though, Dawson exclaimed, "I can't face it," and read in a nearby woods while the others toured the grounds. Hence, his reticence to discuss these years and their absence, even by implication, from his work should not indict his daughter's belief that they had "a disastrous and permanent influence on his whole life."[28]

A "Half-Hearted" Anglican: Dawson at Oxford

While Dawson considered himself a Christian upon arrival at Trinity College in Michelmas term, 1908, and even resumed the practice of Anglo-Catholicism, he sensed that this recovery of faith was not his spiritual journey's end. He stressed that the state of his soul as he went up was one of "half-hearted" Anglo-Catholicism, as he remained "without intellectual conviction" in it: despite the importance he accorded "faith," Dawson's powerful mind also required the intellectual infrastructure of "belief" for him to have a holistic religious identity.[29] This spiritual restlessness helped dictate his course of studies. Dawson began reading for a history degree, and he focused on the philosophy of history and religion, as his personal and scholarly concerns were coalescing.

---

28. Scott, *Historian*, 31, 34, 81, 31.
29. Dawson, "Why I Am a Catholic," 112.

For example, although he had read Augustine's *City of God* previously, it was the "greatest influence of all on his thought at this time."[30] His interest in mysticism led him to von Hügel during this period as well. Moreover, his initial encounter with "The Ballad of the White Horse" came as an undergraduate, and he later told Chesterton that it "first brought the breath of life to this period for me when I was fed up with Stubbs and Oman and the rest of them."[31] Finally, a 1911 essay was cool to Henry VIII's and Cromwell's monastic confiscations, implying that on one of the English Reformation's foundational acts, young Dawson saw the Roman Catholics as the more aggrieved party.[32] He was thus gravitating toward Catholic authors and themes as he sought intellectual and spiritual sustenance, even as the existing Anglo model of Catholicism remained rationally unsatisfactory to him. Watkin, who seems to have been in a similar position, had "poped" in the summer of 1908, but his best friend was hesitant even to consider such a step: "at the time I knew nothing of [Roman] Catholicism as a living religion." Watkin himself recalled debates between them that had demonstrated how far Dawson was from joining his new church.[33] In the following year, however, three crucial events occurred to hasten his coming inside.

A Series of Links: Rome, Tractarians, and Love

First, at Easter 1909, Dawson made his maiden trip to Rome. He was invited by Watkin's family, and his initial impressions of the eternal city are a reminder that his qualms about modern society antedated his conversion, for he deemed Rome "much less spoilt by modernization" than he had anticipated.[34] The party attended Holy Week services and an audience with Pius X, but Dawson was most affected by his exploration of religious and historical sites. Like Chesterton during his sojourn in Italy at an equivalent age, Dawson discovered "a new world of religion and culture," although he asserted a relationship between these factors more

---

30. Scott, *Historian*, 45.
31. Dawson to Chesterton, 1 June 1932; reprinted in *Chesterton Review* 9 (May 1983): 136.
32. Christopher Dawson, "History of St. Alban's Abbey from 1300 to the Dissolution of the Monasteries," Dawson Manuscripts.
33. Dawson, "Why I Am a Catholic," 111; and Watkin quoted in Knowles, "Dawson," 442.
34. Scott, *Historian*, 48.

promptly than his predecessor had, perhaps because of his childhood memories of such a synergy. To Dawson, Rome provided the knowledge of Roman Catholicism as a living religion that he had previously lacked: "I realized for the first time that Catholic civilization did not stop with the Middle Ages, and that contemporary with our own national Protestant development there was the wonderful flowering of the Baroque culture."[35] The baroque would be an enduring enthusiasm of his, for Dawson's understanding of it suited crucial elements of his spiritual makeup.

Dawson thought the baroque emphasized mysticism and metarational religious experience. He held that its art led him to the work of Greene's favorite mystics, Sts. Theresa and John of the Cross, "compared to whom even the greatest of non-Catholic religious writers seem pale and unreal."[36] Indeed, he later called the baroque a "mystical spirituality," making it a clear exemplar, then, of "faith."[37] Yet he also judged it a source of "belief," claiming that one reason he valued the baroque era highly was that it created positive theology.[38] The baroque also represented what Anglo-Catholicism no longer did, "the reassertion of the power of religion and the authority of the Church."[39] Lastly, R. V. Young implies that the baroque resonated with Dawson's sense of being a protester against modern culture: "The culture of the Baroque, then, is the concrete manifestation of the attempt to curb the forces of nationalism, secularism, and social disunity that emerged with the Reformation and the more extreme elements of Renaissance humanism. There is a very real sense in which the Baroque is Catholicity embattled."[40]

The fusion of religion and culture that Dawson saw in the baroque stimulated his historical imagination as well as his religious outlook. On Easter Sunday, he visited the church of the Ara Coeli, built on the Capitol's summit. Sitting where Gibbon had when moved to write his *Decline*

---

35. Dawson, "Why I Am a Catholic," 111.

36. Ibid., 112. Dawson had known of St. John of the Cross, at least, before this trip, having written a hymn to him at age 15 (Scott, *Historian*, 56).

37. Christopher Dawson, "The European Revolution," *Catholic World* 179 (May 1954): 90.

38. Dawson to John J. Mulloy, 22 April 1954, Dawson Correspondence, University of St. Thomas, St. Paul, Minn. Dawson defined positive theology as, essentially, patristic studies.

39. Dawson, "The European Revolution," 89.

40. R. V. Young, "Christopher Dawson and Baroque Culture," in Cataldo, *Dynamic Character*, 131.

and Fall, Dawson was similarly inspired. He wrote later that year in his journal of "a vow" made at Easter in the Ara Coeli to write a history of culture, and asserted that "however unfit I may be I believe it is God's will I should attempt it."[41] His remark recalls Newman's cognate sense of vocation generated by an Italian journey, and Dawson's treatment of that incident is an enlightening gloss on his own epiphany.

In 1833, Newman was touring Italy and when in Rome, Dawson claimed, he was moved by "a Christianity so unlike that which he had known,"[42] an almost direct translation of Dawson's own remembered reaction to Italian Catholicism as something "different to anything I had known" in Britain.[43] Additionally, Newman "began to think that I had a mission" while on this journey. Dawson read Newman's *Apologia* shortly after returning from Italy, and this passage is marked in his copy.[44] Even more revealing, though, is his later portrayal of Newman's mind-set at this time, for Dawson's rhetoric expands the *Apologia*'s spare text in a way deeply resonant with his 1909 journal entry: "he was overwhelmed by a growing sense of his personal mission—of a divine power setting him apart for some high purpose and leading him he knew not where."[45] Such close linguistic likenesses indicate that, on this topic as well as many others, Dawson disclosed as much, or more, about himself as he did Newman when discussing his Oxford forerunner, as Newman's work and age were the subjects in which Dawson "felt most at home."[46] Though Newman was less enthusiastic about Italianate Catholicism than other converts were, then, the fact that Dawson's similar epiphanies about Roman Catholicism occurred during exposure to this form of that faith remains significant: in being impressed by its vitality, emphasis on authority, and difference from British faiths, Dawson was exemplify-

---

41. Dawson quoted in Scott, *Historian*, 49.
42. Christopher Dawson, *The Spirit of the Oxford Movement* (London: Sheed & Ward, 1933), 59.
43. Dawson, "Why I Am a Catholic," 111.
44. John Henry Newman, *Apologia Pro Vita Sua*, ed. A. Dwight Culler (Boston: Houghton Mifflin, 1956), 53. Dawson's library is held by the University of St. Thomas, St. Paul, Minn.
45. Dawson, *Spirit of Oxford Movement*, 59.
46. Scott, *Historian*, 116. Even a hostile critic of Dawson's work shares this judgment, calling his thought "essentially Tractarian" (Cowling, *Religion and Public Doctrine*, 2: 336).

ing the appeal this model of the Church had for many British converts.

The courtship leading to the marriage of Newman's and Dawson's true minds was initiated shortly after Dawson's return from Rome when he heard a lecture by the Cardinal's biographer, Wilfrid Ward; his newfound interest in the Oxford Movement was the second event of 1909 that sharpened his spiritual development. His father and great-uncle had been drawn to Anglo-Catholicism by reading the Tractarians, but Christopher's exposure to them repelled him from his ancestral theology, due to the substantial difference between his day's Anglo-Catholicism and that embraced by Henry and William Dawson. As seen in Chesterton's case, Anglo-Catholicism's early-twentieth-century drift from Tractarianism toward a liberal and Modernist theology that preserved ritual but eschewed dogma and the apostolic deposit was increasingly disturbing tradition-minded Anglo-Catholics. Their ranks included not only Chesterton, but also members of Dawson's generation, most notably fellow Oxfordian Ronald Knox. The solitary Dawson, however, had little contact with such contemporaries. To him, it was by studying the Oxford Movement that he gained insight into numerous questions concerning Anglo-Catholicism that had long been troubling him, plus substantiation of some of the fresh impressions he had acquired in Italy.

In general, he seems to have begun considering Newman's judgment of the *via media* a forecast of Anglo-Catholicism's fate in his own era. In his copy of the *Apologia*, Dawson highlighted both Newman's hope that Anglo-Catholicism could be a "substantive religion," rather than just a negation of Roman Catholicism and Protestantism, and his later conclusion that this solution was not viable, for the Anglican Church "may be a great creation, though it be not divine."[47] Dawson's later book on the Oxford Movement revealed how these seeds of doubt had finally reached fruition in his own mind, as he accented this theme of Anglo-Catholicism's insufficiency, and translated it into his own times' terms. He held that "the modern Anglo-Catholic" lacks substance, in part, because he attempts "to explain away the Reformation" by denying its revolutionary basis and effects. Moreover, Dawson considered Anglo-Catholic successes in ritual and worship vitiated by the "remarkable advance of Liberal-

---

47. Newman, *Apologia*, 83, 315.

ism and Modernism in matters of faith," precisely the trends he felt the Oxford Movement had been founded to oppose, and whose presence in current Anglican theology also troubled Chesterton and Knox. As Dawson detected these ideas "in the very bosom of the Anglo-Catholic party itself," he concluded (like Chesterton and Knox) that it could no longer uphold traditional Christianity against modern challenges, for "Liberal Protestantism seems to posses no inherent principle capable of withstanding the growing pressure of secularized culture."[48] Dawson's germinal sense during his Oxford years that Newman's fears about Anglo-Catholicism's untenability had been realized in his epoch, along with its consequent capitulation to tendencies that Dawson had always found distasteful, then, helped move him closer to Newman's ultimate religious decision.

More specifically, investigating the Oxford Movement helped Dawson confront the persistent issues of authority and an intellectual basis for religious belief. Not only did he note Newman's description of John Keble as someone who guided himself "by authority," but he also highlighted the Cardinal's depiction of Roman Catholicism as "a great objective fact," the very language Dawson used to denote religion's impression on him in boyhood and at Winchester Cathedral.[49] Moreover, he later argued that one of the Oxford Movement's hallmarks was that it "stood for Authority and Tradition against Liberalism," a position that Dawson had believed since his schooldays was being abjured by its Anglo-Catholic successors in his age.[50] Finally, he found the positive theology that he had discovered in the baroque present in British culture in the Tractarians, although he thought it had been displaced by liberalism and Modernism in contemporary Anglo-Catholicism.[51] The Oxford Movement thus manifested to Dawson both his long-standing and newfound religious concerns in a specifically British theological setting, even as the perceived di-

---

48. Dawson, *Spirit of Oxford Movement*, 105, 138, 134.

49. Newman, *Apologia*, 272, 314.

50. Dawson, *Spirit of Oxford Movement*, 134. For the continuity of this assessment of the Oxford Movement in his thought, see Dawson, "Christianity and Modern Civilization," 1958, Dawson Manuscripts.

51. See Christopher Dawson, "The Catholic Revival in England," 1960, Dawson Manuscripts.

vergence between the Tractarians and their ostensible descendants started to suggest to him that these needs could no longer be satisfied in his national church.

Besides appealing to Dawson on particularly theological grounds, the Oxford Movement accorded with his broader cultural outlook and burgeoning rhetorical roles. Dawson's dismay with modern culture was growing during his undergraduate years. Watkin recorded his friend's 1911 complaint that "our age was one of earnest skepticism and great change;"[52] these sentiments evolved into a principle by the time of Dawson's book on the Oxford Movement, wherein he defined a "Modernist" as one who feels that "there are no eternal truths and no divine law other than the law of change." Newman was clearly a soulmate on this score, and Dawson marked passages in the *Apologia* concerning the importance of dogma, liberalism's alleged threat to it, and Roman Catholicism's being the sole safe harbor from modern secularism. He also judged Newman and his associates deliberate dams against this storm, revealing in his adult work how his longtime cultural concerns shaped his scholarly interpretation of this movement. To Dawson, the Oxford Movement's significance was "above all" its "acceptance of the Liberal challenge. It stood *pro causa Dei* against the apostasy of the modern world," and its "fundamental note" was "its *anti-modernism*."[53] His embryonic sense as a student that the Tractarians shared his cultural disquiet, but that current Anglo-Catholicism had abandoned Newman's conception of Christianity as a "counter-kingdom" by accommodating liberalism and Modernism, was thus additional encouragement to explore his predecessor's final source of that kingdom which is not of this world.

In addition to being a cadre of counter-modern rebels to Dawson, he also deemed the Tractarians a band of prophets. He argued later in his career that Newman especially was a prophet, and that this role was his most important one during his Oxford years.[54] Furthermore, he asserted

---

52. Watkin diary entry of 1 May 1911; quoted in Scott, *Historian*, 53.
53. Dawson, *Spirit of Oxford Movement*, 136, 134. All emphases in originals.
54. Christopher Dawson, "Newman and the Sword of the Spirit," *The Sword of the Spirit*, August 1945; reprinted in *The Dawson Newsletter* 9 (Spring/Summer 1991): 12.

that Newman "was profoundly conscious of the heavy price that the prophetic vocation entails."[55] While there is no apparent evidence that Dawson was thinking in such specific terms about himself during his own Oxford days, Watkin did note in 1912 that his friend was "eager for apologetic work."[56] If the particular rhetorical strategy he would employ was unclear, Dawson had at least decided, then, to engage his culture actively from a religious standpoint, a commitment he likely expected to be costly given his 1911 contention that his era was dominated by skepticism and radical change.

If the Oxford Movement's impact on Dawson was not instantly transformative, that initial encounter did stimulate the mature opinions adduced here. Dawson claimed consistently to be more interested in and familiar with Newman's Tractarian years. Moreover, his biographer testifies that the *Apologia* had "a considerable influence on his own conversion."[57] At a time when Dawson's search for spiritual order was intensifying, and when he had just been impressed favorably by Roman Catholic culture, studying the Oxford Movement exposed him to the progenitors of the theological position he claimed to hold, plus the course of their religious developments. Seeing Newman's doubts about Anglo-Catholicism verified by its contemporary avatar's apparent infidelity to the Tractarian heritage of counter-modern witness helped deepen his long-standing discontent with his inherited faith; watching some predecessors with a kindred worldview ultimately traverse the road to Rome further beckoned Dawson down that path.

Yet culture, theology, and history were not his only maps. Like Chesterton and Greene, a central way to Dawson's soul was through his heart. The third crucial event of 1909 was his meeting Valery Mills. He was drawn to her instantly, but Valery had no sudden special feelings for him, and marriage did not seem feasible on other counts. Neither was financially secure, but there was an even more serious obstacle: Valery was a Roman Catholic. The Millses cared little about the religious issue, as Valery's Catholic mother had wed a (now dead) Protestant, and was

---

55. Dawson, *Spirit of Oxford Movement*, 60.
56. Watkin undated 1912 diary entry; quoted in Scott, *Historian*, 57.
57. Scott, *Historian*, 50.

resolved not to inflict on another the prejudice she had faced from her family. Dawson's father was also unlikely to oppose the match, given his strong Catholic (if not Roman Catholic) sympathies. His mother's anti-Catholicism, though, led her to regard marrying outside the Anglican Church as "an act of desertion."[58] Sensing the wrench that he would throw into family relations, and seeing that Valery did not reciprocate his intense feelings, Dawson told only Watkin of his love.

Such reticence ceased to be viable in late 1912. A trip to Rome was again vital for Dawson's life and faith. This time, however, it was Valery who visited Italy and was inspired with a sense of vocation. After an audience with Pius X, Valery "knew that there was something she must do to change her life"—she must marry Christopher.[59] Upon returning to Oxford in mid-1913, she decided to accept his proposal and the expected Dawson family row ensued. His mother and sister were angered, and his paternal grandmother was not even told, lest she alter her will. Even William Dawson, who liked Valery, castigated Rome's requirements that the children of mixed marriages be raised Roman Catholics. Such reactions offended the Mills family, with one cousin claiming that the Dawsons were acting as though Christopher wanted to marry a chorus girl.

For Christopher's part, he sought to assure Valery that their religious views were compatible. Shortly before their engagement, he told her that he was not, and never had been, a Protestant. He recalled his boyhood's Catholic ethos, noted that his closest friends had been Catholics, and that he had chosen Catholic writers for spiritual guidance. Like Newman, Chesterton, and Knox, he had been drawn consistently to orthodox Catholic Christianity and, like them, his membership in the Anglican church was contingent on its having room for those beliefs: the more Anglo-Catholicism appeared to become a species of liberal Protestantism, the less loyalty Dawson felt to it. He implied that these growing doubts about his ancestral faith might soon lead him to share Valery's church as well as her creed: "if you believe the Catholic Church to be the one true church you cannot think that God's grace would bring us so far and no further."[60] Such remarks, plus Valery's memory of her happy

58. Ibid., 60.
59. Ibid.
60. Dawson to Valery Mills, undated July 1913 letter; quoted in Scott, *Historian*, 61.

"mixed" family, perhaps indicate why (unlike Vivien Dayrell-Browning) she did not make conversion a condition for marrying a non-Roman Catholic.

Valery was not the only Roman Catholic to whom Dawson was close in these crucial years. One of his best friends at Oxford, for instance, was a then-Jesuit scholastic, Francis Burdett, who was both highly intelligent and a mystic. Yet Dawson thought that the chief personal influence on him at this time was Watkin. Watkin introduced his shy friend to other Roman Catholics, and they lived together in the 1910–11 academic year. Their frequent discussions' impact was clear to Watkin by early 1912, when he found the bent of Dawson's thought "more pronounceably orthodox than ever. I hope he may yet be a [Roman] Catholic."[61] Dawson himself singled out his "closest friend" for special credit in his most extensive account of his conversion and, after seeing Watkin for the last time, Dawson told his death-bed nurse, "he made me a Catholic."[62] Even if Watkin was first among equals, though, he was still part of a wider Roman Catholic network that included Valery, Burdett, and other associates. According to conversion theorist Emilie Griffin, such personal examples are a frequent factor in the conversion process, particularly in its final stages, as the convert senses "being surrounded. . . . God, through his believing friends and acquaintances, and even through the opinions of non-believers, [begins] to 'close in' on him."[63] While not a proponent of romantic theology, Dawson did consider personal relations crucial to conversion and religious development. In his own case, he felt that "I was learning more from my Catholic friends than anything I could learn from books,"[64] and he later generalized this principle: "no people has ever been converted to Christianity by a learned apologetic or by mysticism, important as these things are. . . . Where there is direct spiritual communication through a saint or an evangelist, you always find results, but where it is a matter of routine organization and activities, you do not."[65]

---

61. Watkin undated spring 1912 diary entry; quoted in Scott, *Historian*, 57.

62. Dawson, "Why I Am a Catholic," 112; and Scott, *Historian*, 207.

63. Emilie Griffin, *Turning: Reflections on the Experience of Conversion* (New York: Doubleday, 1980), 100.

64. Dawson, "Why I Am a Catholic," 112.

65. Dawson to John J. Mulloy, 30–31 December 1956; reprinted in *The Dawson Newsletter* 11 (Spring 1993): 15.

Coming Inside: Why He Was a Roman Catholic

As necessary as the witness of loved ones was to his conversion, though, Dawson thought it insufficient without accompanying rational confidence: if he favored "faith" to "belief," he was still unwilling to profess Roman Catholicism until he was persuaded intellectually of its truth. Dawson remembered his undergraduate position as "trying to live on Catholicism from outside ... in this kind of spiritual eclecticism, which subsists on Catholic ideals but lacks the foundation of intellectual conviction."[66] He considered this position unsustainable and thus sought those rational underpinnings, confident that God would lead him along what he apprehended was an arduous path: "the way of the intellect is always difficult even for men within the Church but it is always safe to trust that God will do his part."[67] He graduated from Oxford in 1911 and spent the next two years on this difficult road, taking the "careful and conscientious approach to Catholicism" he later ascribed to Newman, as he read scripture, commentaries, patristics, and the Tractarians.[68]

In particular, Dawson claimed that he could not yet see Roman Catholicism as a unity. The writings of Sts. Paul and John resolved this problem, for after investigating them, "I realized that the Incarnation, the Sacraments, the external order of the Church and the internal working of Sanctifying Grace were all parts of one organic unity, a living tree, whose roots are in the Divine Nature and whose fruit is the perfection of the Saints." Comprehending the doctrine of sanctifying grace seems to have been decisive for his acceptance of Roman Catholicism's truth-claims. He held that he had long been ignorant of this dogma, but that its scriptural presentation, and elucidations of it by Augustine and Aquinas, "removed all my difficulties and uncertainties and carried complete conviction to my mind. It was no longer possible to hesitate," and so he decided to be received.[69]

---

66. Dawson, "Why I Am a Catholic," 112.
67. Dawson to Valery Mills, undated July 1913 letter; quoted in Scott, *Historian*, 61.
68. Dawson quoted in Scott, *Historian*, 62. He noted Newman's similar description of a like period in his life (*Apologia*, 81).
69. Dawson, "Why I Am a Catholic," 112–13. The Roman Catholic Church defines the doctrine of sanctifying grace as follows: "The grace of Christ is the gratuitous gift that God

If these issues served as the more proximate causes of Dawson's conversion by convincing him that Roman Catholicism could be his long-sought intellectual foundation of faith, this church also met other persistent needs. For one thing, his desire for authority, which had been frustrated for years in Anglicanism, was now fulfilled: "Dawson saw in the authority of Rome an attractive alternative to the seeming discontinuity of his own Anglican congregation."[70] He believed that "if we wish to be religious we must submit to religious authority."[71] His impression that current Anglo-Catholicism and liberal Christianity rejected this premise led him to renounce them in favor of a church that he thought had possessed from its earliest days "a system of ecclesiastical organization and a principle of social authority that distinguished it from all the other religious bodies." Whereas he had considered Anglo-Catholicism's standards of orthodoxy the products of its members' preferences since his schooldays, Dawson now came to regard Roman Catholicism's leaders as the spiritual descendants of Jesus's apostles, and thus representatives "not of the community but of the Christ, who had chosen them and transmitted to them His divine authority." In describing the views of St. Irenaeus (whom he read during his conversion's final stage), Dawson

---

makes to us of his own life, infused by the Holy Spirit into our soul to heal it of sin and to sanctify it. It is the *sanctifying* or *deifying grace* received in Baptism. It is in us the source of the work of sanctification. . . . Sanctifying grace is an habitual gift, a stable and supernatural disposition that perfects the soul itself to enable it to live with God, to act by his love." *Catechism of the Catholic Church*, Articles 1999 and 2000. Emphasis in original.

Neither Dawson's account nor his biographer's explain any further why this particular doctrine was so crucial to him, nor do his extant papers clarify this matter. From the standpoint of conversion theory, Dawson's understanding of sanctifying grace seems to have been the point at which his religious reflections reached a kind of critical mass that impelled him to the further, and final, stage of wholehearted acceptance. Griffin (*Turning*, 63) describes this aspect of the conversion process: "a number of ideas and arguments are collected from various sources; the mind works away at them; then, sometimes in a sudden burst of energy, a sorting and ordering occurs not sequentially, but all at once . . . a hint is given, a clue or lead which suggests a solution, and the mind works furiously to piece together a framework or a conclusion." Sanctifying grace appears to have been that catalytic clue for Dawson.

70. Arnold Sparr, *To Promote, Defend and Redeem: The Catholic Literary Revival and the Cultural Transformation of American Catholicism, 1920–1960* (New York: Greenwood Press, 1990), 105.

71. Christopher Dawson, *The Modern Dilemma* (London: Sheed & Ward, 1932), 106.

summarized his own outlook: "it is the Roman Church that is the center of unity and the guarantee of orthodox belief."[72]

For Dawson, as for Chesterton, that unity and guarantee were especially centered in the papacy. He held that "as Peter had possessed a unique position among the Twelve, so the Roman Church, which traced its origins to St. Peter, possessed an exceptional position among the churches."[73] Also like Chesterton, Dawson's earliest memory, of a Pontifex, was the psychological seed brought to fruition by this aspect of his conversion, for his most distant recollection was a line from a poem about Bran the Blessed: "He who will be chief, let him be a bridge."[74] The Roman Catholic chief personified to Dawson not only the bridge between Christ and humanity, but also certain cherished cultural roles. He invoked St. Bernard's ideal of "the prophetic and apostolic mission of a true Pope set over the nations to destroy, and root up, to build and to plant."[75] To retain the autonomy Dawson deemed essential to these functions of prophet and rebel, as well as to protecting traditional, orthodox teachings against ephemeral enthusiasms, he judged that the pope needed the disciplinary tool of infallibility. Demonstrating his affinities with Italianate Catholicism, Dawson saw Vatican I's promulgation of this doctrine as necessary in an increasingly secular world to help preserve the Church's independence from hostile cultural and political forces, and to maintain it as a certain center of spiritual unity, one of the very qualities that had drawn Dawson Romeward in the first place.[76]

Roman Catholicism's emphasis on authority, epitomized by that of the papacy, allowed Dawson to reintegrate two esteemed boyhood principles that had been sundered for years. Since his schooldays, authority and religion had seemed antitheses, but his conversion harmonized them again. Dawson's reception, therefore, restored youthful psychological unity, albeit under a different theological rubric. This dimension of

---

72. Christopher Dawson, *The Making of Europe* (London: Sheed & Ward, 1932), 31–33 (MOE).

73. Dawson, MOE, 31.

74. Dawson, *Tradition and Inheritance*, 13.

75. Dawson, *Religion and the Rise of Western Culture* (London: Sheed & Ward, 1950), 246–47.

76. See Christopher Dawson, "Liberalism and Ultramontanism: Pius IX and the Vatican Council," c. 1958–62, Dawson Manuscripts.

his conversion thus typifies not only the importance of authority that conversion theorists find common among Roman Catholic receptions, but also the recovery of childhood sensibilities that they consider a frequent product of the conversion process.[77]

Beyond supplying Dawson with authority, Roman Catholicism also validated his closely related veneration of tradition. He asserted "the incomparable importance for Catholicism of tradition," arguing that this stress on a vital, institutionalized continuum between past and present was what makes it a "fuller, more concrete, and more organic" form of Christianity than any other Christian sect or denomination:

> It is the bearer of a living tradition which unites the present and the past, the living and the dead, in one great spiritual community which transcends all the limited communities of race and nation and state. Hence, it is not enough for the Catholic to believe in the Word as contained in the sacred Scriptures, it is not even enough to accept the historic faith as embodied in the creeds and interpreted by Catholic theology, it is necessary for him to be incorporated as a cell in the living organism of the divine society and to enter into communion with the historic reality of the sacred tradition.[78]

Central to his contention that the Catholic Church was the legitimate, living legate of historical Christianity was belief in the apostolic succession. As with Newman, pursuing the historical question of which current Christian church had an unbroken tie to Christ's twelve, and hence to Christ Himself, was a principal element of Dawson's conversion.

Although he reached Newman's conclusion, Newman did not guide Dawson along this particular path. Rather, he credited liberal Protestant theologian Adolf von Harnack, who "never knew how much he contributed to the process of my conversion."[79] Harnack posited in his *History of Dogma* that the Reformation and its Protestant successors had

---

77. See Walter Conn, *Christian Conversion* (New York: Paulist Press, 1986), 183, 200; James Fowler, *Stages of Faith* (San Francisco: Harper & Row, 1981), 16; Griffin, *Turning*, 168; John Dunne, *A Search for God in Time and Memory* (New York: Macmillan, 1969), 129–30.

78. Christopher Dawson, "The Kingdom of God and History," in *Christianity and European Culture*, ed. Gerald Russello (Washington, D.C.: The Catholic University of America Press, 1998), 210.

79. Dawson interviewed in *The Sign*, December 1958; quoted in Scott, *Historian*, 63.

broken fully with their Catholic past (rather than just its abuses), and thus cut themselves off willfully and wholly from what Dawson considered their authenticating connection to the apostles. Thus, "what to Harnack was a return to the primitive gospel was to Dawson an irreparable breach with the Christian past."[80] It was this radicalism that Dawson felt current Anglo-Catholics sought to explain away in their view of the Reformation, one their abjural of the apostolic deposit shared.[81] But Dawson's sense of the Reformation as a religious revolution helped persuade him that his ancestral faith was, at best, schismatic, and that Roman Catholicism was the sole historically uninterrupted link to Christianity's founders and Founder: "this work of divine restoration has been carried on continuously and indefectibly for nineteen centuries by the Church" and the Church alone.[82]

Besides providing historically grounded theological content to his yearnings for authority and tradition, orthodox Roman Catholicism also resonated with Dawson's rhetorical roles. He believed that the Western Church had a long-standing heritage of cultural rebellion, arguing that its primitive incarnation appealed "above all" to those

> who revolted against the spiritual emptiness and corruption of the dominant material culture, and who felt the need of a new spiritual order and a religious view of life. And so it became the focus of the forces of disaffection and opposition to the dominant culture in a far more fundamental sense than any movement of political or economic discontent. It was a protest not against material injustice but against the spiritual ideals of the ancient world and its whole social ethos.[83]

He felt that only Roman Catholicism upheld this tradition of Christian countercultural witness in the modern era. To him, the Catholic cosmology was "a challenge to the whole secular view of history which is tending to become the faith of the modern world" because, unlike liberalism

---

80. Aidan Nichols, "Christopher Dawson's Catholic Setting," in Caldecott and Morrill, *Eternity*, 32. This argument's enduring impact on Dawson is evident from his rehearsal of it nearly forty years later (see Dawson to the *Catholic Herald*, 6 January 1956).

81. Conversely, he saw the Oxford Movement's appeal to the apostolic succession as its "essential principle" (Dawson, *Spirit of Oxford Movement*, 92).

82. Christopher Dawson, "Christian Culture," *The Commonweal* 61 (1 April 1955): 678.

83. Dawson, MOE, 26–27.

or Communism, it directs life towards a supernatural end.[84] Moreover, he held that "Protestantism succeeded in accommodating itself to the modern environment by the abandonment of metaphysics and dogma and a concentration on ethical ideals," as he had discerned in his school chapel and his day's Anglo-Catholicism, but that "Catholicism could not live in an atmosphere of subjective idealism and moral pragmatism. It was forced to go into the desert." It was therefore "not compromised by the bankruptcy" of dominant notions, and could hence keep the case for orthodoxy alive in a post-Christian age.[85] For Dawson, then, Roman Catholicism was Chesterton's one fighting form of Christianity, the sole avatar of that faith that had retained its subversive legacy and thus that alone opposed regnant cultural forces he had long seen as pernicious.

Beyond resisting secular blandishments themselves, Dawson also felt, Christians must alert others to these perceived threats. Once again, he approached this aspect of Christianity historically, arguing that the "prophetic element is an essential part of the Christian tradition."[86] Like rebellion, he found this traditional facet of Christianity best upheld in his day by Roman Catholicism: "the Catholic interpretation of history preserves the prophetic and apocalyptic sense of mystery and divine judgment."[87] Indeed, he held that Catholicism fuses the roles of rebel and prophet, making the papacy a microcosm of the Church's mission. He saw the Catholic idea of the prophetic role as the witness of the Church against the world, a notion he rooted in scripture and patristics.[88] He vested this specific fidelity to origins in Roman Catholicism due to his sense that this church alone was faithful as a body to its roots generally: if Protestants and Anglo-Catholics no longer resist the secular world in modern times, neither will they utter radical warnings to it.[89]

---

84. Dawson, "The Kingdom of God and History," 211.

85. Christopher Dawson, "General Introduction," in *Essays in Order* (New York: Macmillan, 1931), xvi.

86. Christopher Dawson, *The Judgment of the Nations* (New York: Sheed & Ward, 1942), 153.

87. Christopher Dawson, *Religion and the Modern State* (London: Sheed & Ward, 1935), 81 (RMS).

88. See Dawson to Douglas Horton, 23 November 1958, Dawson Correspondence.

89. Indeed, Dawson suggested that Protestantism is not a prophetic religion. See *The Formation of Christendom* (New York: Sheed & Ward, 1967), 291.

Roman Catholicism attracted Dawson, then, because it ratified and fulfilled many preexistent religious and cultural longings. His trip to Rome and discovery of the baroque made Roman Catholicism seem a still-thriving religious culture, one containing enriching examples of faith forms that had long moved him, like mysticism, while also suggesting the possibility of an authoritative, intellectually persuasive theology. Pulled by these experiences, he was further pushed by the Tractarians, for studying the Oxford Movement deepened Dawson's doubts about Anglo-Catholicism. He not only noted Newman's conclusion that it was impossible to have orthodox Catholicism without Rome, but he also perceived contemporary confirmation of that conviction in current Anglo-Catholicism's apparent capitulation to liberalism and Modernism. Affective relationships with Roman Catholics complemented his more distinctly spiritual and rational reflections.

Yet intellectual issues were decisive. Reading scripture and theology persuaded Dawson that Roman Catholicism was an integrated explanation of Being, and that it offered the grace needed for salvation. Moreover, investigating history convinced him that this church alone had an authentic authority and tradition. His study of the past also proved to him that Roman Catholics were the lone present-day Christians who preserved corporately the historical Church's rebellious and prophetic response to the profane's powers and principalities. In short, Roman Catholicism gave Dawson what he felt would be a lasting basis for the kind of religion he had known as a boy and had mourned the loss of since his schooldays: a coherent, certain, vital contrast to modernity that was validated by reason, history, spiritual and cultural experience, and the examples of those he loved.

"Wreckage" and Writing: Conflict and Commencement of a Career

Yet friction with some of his beloved made this decision difficult for Dawson. He had decided definitively by the fall of 1913 to convert, but was not received until 5 January 1914.[90] There were no delays on the Roman Catholic side, as his priest instructor required only two meetings,

---

90. Scott, *Historian*, 62.

due to Dawson's erudition. The obstacles lay in the convert's relations with his family. His mother, still bruised by his engagement to Valery, was further wounded by what she considered an additional affront: if marrying a Roman Catholic was an act of desertion in her mind, actually becoming one was tantamount to treason. His sister reacted similarly, and a permanent rift developed between them. His father's response was milder, but still disapproving. Although a Catholic in religion, his son recalled, Henry thought "no man has the right to leave the church to which his fathers belonged," an ironic position given that investigating another, more explicitly religious, kind of tradition had helped spur Christopher's decision to depart the Anglican Church.[91]

Although Dawson's family reacted more harshly to his choice than Chesterton's or Greene's did, conversions often spur such grave feelings. To the convert, this response is what Emilie Griffin calls "wreckage": "the inadvertent damage done to the fabric of one's personal relationships by a conversion: an action which seems like a betrayal to those left behind." In fact, Dawson's familial difficulties seem more typical of the fate of modern British Catholic converts, as Newman, Hopkins, Jones, and Waugh faced similar hostility and estrangement.[92] Common or not, Dawson was affected deeply by his family's response, even if it was expected and did not shake his conviction in his choice. The tension it created combined with stress that had built up during years of religious struggle and anxiety about marrying Valery to bring him to the "brink of a nervous breakdown."[93]

Shortly after his reception, Dawson joined Valery and her mother in Florence for three months. The physical and psychological distance from Britain, sense of relief at having made his religious decision, and being with his betrothed all brightened his mood. But soon after returning to Oxford, this inner peace was threatened by the Great War's outbreak. Events were kind to him, though, as his best friend was not in the trenches (Watkin was a pacifist), and his war work consisted chiefly of teaching in a Franciscan school, with a brief stint in Admiralty Intelligence. His frailty had exempted him from military service and, after a medical judg-

---

91. Dawson, *Tradition and Inheritance*, 28.   92. Griffin, *Turning*, 153.
93. Scott, *Historian*, 65.

ment that Dawson could never hold a steady job, his father granted Christopher an annual allowance that enabled him to wed Valery in 1916. Settled domestically and religiously, he could now direct his energies undistractedly toward fulfilling the vow he had made at the Ara Coeli.

Not by Reason Alone: Roman Catholicism and Dawson's Worldview

Dawson had begun preparing his promised history of culture intensively since his conversion, but his reading prefatory to his reception was certainly complementary; this relationship would be a hallmark of his future writing. His grouping of his love for history, his interest in different cultures, and the importance of religion as his childhood's dominant impressions should be recalled, for the fusion of these factors defined his adult scholarship. Not only did he approach Catholicism through history and culture, but once converted, his religious beliefs also became his hermeneutic. He shared Chesterton's and Greene's sense that a Catholic writer is one whose faith infuses his work without violating its genre's standards.[94] Dawson summarized his own synergistic approach on his seventieth birthday: "All my life for fifty years I have been writing on one subject and for one cause—the cause of Christendom and the study of Christian culture."[95] Before examining the specific relationship between his religious beliefs and his interpretations of history and cultures, though, it is necessary to see how orthodox Roman Catholicism shaped his more general outlook, as these assumptions underlay all facets of his work.

For example, although the doctrine of original sin was not as crucial an issue in Dawson's conversion as in Chesterton's and Greene's, he did argue that professing a tragic view of life distinguishes traditional Catholics sharply from modern anti-dogmatists: "in comparison with the optimism of liberalism the Christian view of life and the Christian interpretation of history are profoundly tragic. The true progress of history is a mystery which is fulfilled in failure and suffering and which will only be revealed at the end of time."[96] Dawson argued further that modern

---

94. See 1959 Dawson memo, Dawson Correspondence.
95. Dawson quoted in Scott, *Historian*, 197.
96. Dawson, "The Kingdom of God and History," 212. His annotations of the *Apologia*

optimistically innocent denials of the basic flaw in human nature taught by Christianity had eroded religious safeguards against its effects, risking chaotic brutality: "we have discovered that evil too is a progressive force and that the modern world provides unlimited prospects for its development," due to its rejection of original sin.[97] Moreover, he thought only Roman Catholicism upheld this doctrine corporately in his era: in accommodating liberalism and its facile optimism, Anglo-Catholics and Protestants had ceased admitting the "limitations of human nature" and thus promoted a dangerously untenable ethics of aboriginal innocence.[98]

Dawson also held that Catholic and modern worldviews had divergent ideas of human identity. He contended consistently that people are naturally religious.[99] He saw this hypothesis as the one most in accord with the experience of Catholic mystics;[100] further biographical origins of this premise are revealed by recalling his assertion that boyhood impressions of religion's objectivity and authenticity convinced him that any theory of life excluding such phenomena is inherently deficient. Dawson judged such a belief common to most of history, but felt that Western thought since the Renaissance had tended in a contrary positivistic direction, in which rationalistic empiricism is exalted and "religion is reduced to subjective feeling and moral activity." Yet, he argued, so discounting religion's place in the human personality is not only false, but also dangerous. Believing that "man cannot live by reason alone,"[101] Dawson declared that a post-Christian society only perverts, rather than eliminates, the religious impulse: "the fact that religion no longer finds a place in social life does not necessarily involve the disappearance of the religious instinct. If the latter is denied its normal expression, and driven

---

reveal that, as with Greene, Newman's assertion of an aboriginal calamity impressed Dawson greatly; he also praised Newman's sensitivity to evil and suffering against liberal and Progressive optimism (Dawson, *Spirit of Oxford Movement*, 38–39).

97. Dawson, *Judgment of Nations*, 5.
98. Dawson, *Essays in Order*, xvi.
99. See, e.g., Christopher Dawson, *The Age of the Gods* (Boston: Houghton Mifflin, 1928), 23; Dawson to Dom Bede Griffiths, 27 April 1957, Dawson Correspondence; and *Formation*, 24–25.
100. Dawson, *Enquiries*, 194. David Jones highlighted this passage in his copy.
101. Christopher Dawson, "Christianity and the New Age," in *Essays in Order*, 190.

back upon itself, it may easily become an anti-social force of explosive violence."[102] Denied its natural satisfaction, such a "spiritually undernourished" culture will seek sustenance in "substitute religions" of class, race, or the will-to-power, any of which becomes "a kingdom of darkness."[103] His catastrophic tone illustrates his assumption of the prophet's role, and may have been partly due to a belief that only Roman Catholics upheld the traditional Christian anthropology in his day. To him, Protestants had "jettisoned the theological traditions of Protestant orthodoxy" in their efforts to "come to terms with the modern world,"[104] which had made them "exclusively this-worldly," a fate Anglo-Catholics would likely share as they espoused secularizing forces like liberalism and Modernism.[105]

Dawson's assertions of the differences between Roman Catholicism and modern mores (and religions that had accommodated them) on these root questions of human nature and identity are miniatures of his general claim that the two cosmologies are incompatible. He depicted "the modern European" as someone essentially concerned with temporal life and material needs, and with religion as a moral influence,[106] and who thus accepts "no hierarchy of values, no intellectual authority, and no social or religious tradition," the very things Dawson praised Roman Catholicism for preserving.[107] Although he felt that ideologies predicated on these norms "dominated the whole spirit of modern civilization," Dawson insisted that orthodox Catholicism could not coexist peacefully with them.[108] He argued that Catholicism was "more traditionalist and more realist" than Protestantism and that it rejected the idea of "an inevitable law of progress" that he felt grounded both liberal and Protestant idealism, thus creating "an irreconcilable opposition of princi-

---

102. Christopher Dawson, *Progress and Religion* (1929; reprint, Peru, Ill.: Sherwood Sugden & Co., 1992), 228 *(P&R)*. Jones highlighted this passage in his copy.

103. Christopher Dawson, "Foundations of European Order," *Catholic Mind* 42 (May 1944): 314.

104. Dawson, *Essays in Order*, ix.

105. Dawson, RMS, 108.

106. Dawson, MOE, 108.

107. Dawson, *P&R*, 228 (highlighted by Jones in his copy).

108. Christopher Dawson, "Catholicism and the Bourgeois Mind," in *Dynamics of World History*, ed. John J. Mulloy (New York: Sheed & Ward, 1958), 200.

ples."¹⁰⁹ Dawson further posited a "fundamental disharmony" between bourgeois and Christian civilization, and asserted that the religious view of life is equally at odds with liberal rationalism and socialist materialism.¹¹⁰ Given such forces' current cultural ascendancy, he cautioned, Catholic protesters against them would be a small minority of dissenters. But Dawson concluded that this status would help Roman Catholics avoid imitating what he saw as liberal Protestantism's and Anglo-Catholicism's failure to retain their integrity: "I do not think that Christianity can ever compete with these forms of mass culture on their own ground. If it does so, it runs the danger of becoming commercialized and politicized and thus of sacrificing its own distinctive values. . . . Christians stand to gain more in the long run by accepting their minority position and looking for quality rather than quantity."¹¹¹

"Religion is the Key of History": Dawson's Metahistorical Methodology

Dawson's specific approach to history and his interpretations of particular periods contain many of these assumptions and also reveal further ways in which Roman Catholicism guided his scholarship. As has been noted, his tragic view of life led him to deem belief in Progress an untenable "belief in human perfectibility."¹¹² Rather, following Augustine, he argued that the "true history of the human race is to be found in the process of enlightenment and salvation."¹¹³ So regarding progress as an essentially spiritual rather than a temporal evolution, Dawson rejected readings of history that he considered predicated on immanent linearity, especially the Whig interpretation. He held that "modern historians" often saw history as an "inevitable movement of progress that culminates in the present state of things." But he judged this approach "fundamentally unhistorical," for it denies the past any autonomy or in-

---

109. Dawson, "The Kingdom of God and History," 209.
110. Dawson, "Catholicism and the Bourgeois Mind," 200; and "The New Leviathan," in *Enquiries*, 18.
111. Christopher Dawson, "The Challenge of Secularism," *Catholic World* 182 (February 1956): 326–27. For an earlier incarnation of this view, see "Prevision in Religion," in *Dynamics*, 102.
112. Dawson, *P&R*, 4–5.
113. Christopher Dawson, "St. Augustine and His Age," in *Enquiries*, 252.

tegrity, ending in the "Pharisaic self-righteousness of the Whig historians or, still worse, the self-satisfaction of the modern Philistine."[114] This rebuttal of one of his discipline's prevailing models, inspired in part by his religious convictions, thus localizes further Dawson's dissent from modern intellectual presuppositions.

He also translated his belief that people are naturally religious into a tool of historical analysis. Shortly before Dawson's conversion, Watkin recorded that his friend found "revelation the necessary key to the interpretation of history,"[115] a conviction that Dawson uttered in almost identical terms over three decades later: "Religion is the key of history."[116] Such a charting of the stream of time flows logically from a belief that its sailors are essentially beings with souls to save or lose; but Dawson considered it unfashionable among modern historians: "I have tried to write a history that does not leave out everything that matters, in the academic fashion, and that gives a proper place to spiritual factors."[117] Once again, his belief that spiritual factors are what matter, and that they are ignored by academic historians, helped enhance his sense of being a rebel both culturally and professionally. He attributed his view that spiritual elements are primary in understanding history, in part, to childhood exposure to myths and legends: "In this way I discovered very early that history was not a flat expanse of time, measured off in dates, but a series of different worlds and that each of them had its own spirit and form and its own riches of poetic imagination."[118] In his maturity, Dawson refined this Romantic notion into a more specific, religiously orient-

---

114. Dawson, *MOE*, xvi. Dwight Culler has argued that the Whig view of history is essentially modern, that it could only have arisen in a culture that felt that "anyone who looked forward to or anticipated the modern world was peculiarly interesting." *The Victorian Mirror of History* (New Haven, Conn.: Yale University Press, 1985), 74.

115. Undated Watkin diary entry from spring 1912; quoted in Scott, *Historian*, 58.

116. Christopher Dawson, *Religion and Culture* (London: Sheed & Ward, 1948), 50. He later attributed these words to Lord Acton (*Religion and Rise of Western Culture*, 7). Chesterton made almost identical statements. See *Illustrated London News*, 27 September 1930; and *The Common Man* (New York: Sheed & Ward, 1950), 211.

117. Dawson to G. K. Chesterton, 1 June 1932, *Chesterton Review* 9 (May 1983): 136. For an explicit rejection of a religious reading of history by one of Dawson's chief peers, see E. H. Carr, *What is History?* (New York: Vintage, 1961), 96.

118. Dawson, *Tradition and Inheritance*, 30.

ed principle: "in my view and dominating my whole life work, the key problem is that of Theology and History."[119]

Such an anti-materialist perspective, not surprisingly, helped Dawson reject positivism: "the essence of history is not to be found in facts but in traditions," which include mythical and religious elements.[120] His emphasis on tradition, another legacy of childhood, also promoted a less expected, and precocious, methodology. As early as the late 1920s and early 1930s, he was anticipating the Annales school's tenets, as he wrote of treating history as an "organic process," and of attending less to politics and diplomacy and more to "permanent social and economic forces that determine the life of peoples." He also welcomed interdisciplinary approaches, claiming, for instance, that history and sociology are indispensable complements in the study of social life.[121] Yet whereas the Annales writers and some who merged history and sociology verged in determinist and positivist directions, Dawson's stress on theology sent his efforts down a different road.

Admitting that rigorous study of underlying structures and statistics was a prerequisite for acceptable scholarship, Dawson stressed that mastery of these techniques "will not produce great history." Rather, he claimed that significant historians possess "a universal vision transcending the relative limitations of the particular field of historical study . . . a universal metahistorical vision of this kind, partaking more of the nature of religious contemplation than of scientific generalization, lies very close to the sources of their creative power."[122] But, he warned, even the best metahistorians risk becoming too abstract, a flaw he saw in Toynbee: "my fundamental criticism of Toynbee's great work is that it is too telescopic and that a true science of human cultures must be based on a more microscopic technique of anthropological and historical research."[123] He sympathized with Toynbee's efforts, though, and his own

---

119. Dawson to John Mulloy, 22 August 1953; quoted in Russell Hittinger, "The Metahistorical Vision of Christopher Dawson," in Cataldo, *Dynamic Character*, 50, n. 9.

120. Dawson, "The Kingdom of God and History," 198.

121. Christopher Dawson, "Sociology as a Science" (1934), in *Dynamics*, 19–21. See also *Age of Gods*, passim.

122. Christopher Dawson, "The Problem of Metahistory," in *Dynamics*, 293.

123. Christopher Dawson, "Arnold Toynbee and the Study of History," in *Dynamics*, 403–4.

practice of metahistory is another example of Dawson's challenge to modernity, as his peers recognized. In 1958, for example, Hayden White deemed Dawson one of the "rebel historicists" who reject "the main stream of English historical thought," the "historiographical empiricism" dominant since Hume.[124]

"The Very Heart of Christianity": A Catholic Theology of History

For Dawson, the foundation of his own rebellious, metahistorical vision was his religion. He asserted that such a basis was an intrinsic component of Christian belief:

> the Christian view of history is not a secondary element derived by philosophical reflection from the study of history. It lies at the very heart of Christianity and forms an integral part of the Christian faith. Hence there is no Christian "philosophy of history" in the strict sense of the word. There is, instead, a Christian history and a Christian theology of history, and it is not too much to say that without them there would be no such thing as Christianity.[125]

Sensing such an intimate connection between Christianity and history led him to maintain further that accepting orthodox Christian truth-claims supplies a key to understanding all historical periods and cultural achievements.[126] To Dawson, that key was the doctrine of Divine Providence. Believing that God is governing the universe in accord with His laws and is directing history to the fulfillment of His revealed promises and prophecies means that a Christian "knows, however obscurely, the goal towards which the world is moving."[127]

Yet he held that even some orthodox, yet non-Roman Catholic, Chris-

---

124. Hayden White, "Religion, Culture, and Western Civilization in Christopher Dawson's Idea of History," *English Miscellany* 9 (1958): 247–49. Subsequent scholars have echoed White's judgment. See, e.g., Hittinger, "Metahistorical Vision," 11–12; James A. Raftis, "The Development of Christopher Dawson's Thought," *Chesterton Review* 9 (May 1983): 116, 131; and Dermot Quinn, "Christopher Dawson and the Catholic Idea of History," in Caldecott and Morrill, *Eternity*, 70.

125. Christopher Dawson, "The Christian View of History," in *Dynamics*, 234.

126. Dawson to John J. Mulloy, 22 August 1953, Dawson Correspondence.

127. Christopher Dawson, *Christianity in East & West*, ed. John Mulloy (1959; reprint, Peru, Ill.: Sherwood Sugden & Co., 1981), 119.

tians still lacked the accompanying understanding of history. In 1951, for instance, he lamented that even C. S. Lewis was questioning the possibility of a Christian interpretation of history.[128] Dawson regarded his own church as the firmest and fullest repository of this relationship, declaring more than once that "there is a natural affinity and concordance between the spirit of Catholicism and the spirit of history, and it is no accident that the modern historical tradition should have been born and nourished in the Catholic Church."[129] Revealingly, he called the baroque the father of this heritage, one he felt current Protestants and Anglo-Catholics had rejected either by accommodating what he saw as immanentized eschatologies, like liberalism or socialism; or by positing a radical divorce between the sacred and profane, a view he detected in Karl Barth's followers.[130] While this assessment of non-Roman Catholic views of history seems too sweeping (it does not, for example, account for his criticism of Lewis, who opposed immanentist and Barthian outlooks as fervently as Dawson did), it is another instance of Dawson's belief that Roman Catholicism was the most faithful modern exponent of the Christian tradition.

Just as Dawson saw orthodox Catholicism and modernity as generally antithetical, so he asserted that the Christian view of history, as best articulated by Roman Catholicism, was distinctly counter-modern. He felt that the Christian outlook's emphasis on transcendent providence set it at odds with materialistic and rationalistic explanations of history. Given what he deemed modern thought's empiricist biases, however, he regarded these secular philosophies as ascendant, and concluded that present-day students of culture neither knew of the Christian theology of history nor believed in it.[131] Convinced of its truth, though, he nonetheless specified this view's components and employed it consistently in his writing, indicating again the connection between his religious beliefs and his cultural rebellion.

---

128. Dawson, "The Christian View of History," 234.

129. Dawson, *RMS*, 83. See also *Edward Gibbon* (London: Proceedings of the British Academy, 1934), 9.

130. See Dawson to John J. Mulloy, 22 April 1954, Dawson Correspondence; and Dawson, *Dynamics*, 233, 283.

131. Dawson to John J. Mulloy, 22 August 1953, Dawson Correspondence.

As Chesterton did, Dawson identified stress on the Incarnation and Christianity's consequent historicity, plus the purported uniqueness of this faith and the Church that perpetuates it, as the hallmarks of a Christian approach to history. Dawson argued that bridging the worlds of spirit and matter was the "historic function of religion,"[132] one orthodox Christianity fulfilled, as Jesus "is not merely a moral teacher or even an inspired hierophant of divine truth, but God made man, the Savior and restorer of the human race, from whom and in whom humanity acquires a new life and a new principle of unity."[133] From his earliest writing, Dawson insisted that this "central doctrine of the Christian faith is also the center of history," and, like Chesterton, he deemed this merger of the eternal and the temporal the key event in history because it effected a qualitative change in Being.[134] He asserted that God's becoming human raised humanity to a higher level by creating the possibility of "uniting organically the whole of man, body and soul, sense and spirit, with a higher spiritual principle, thus making of him a new creature." In taking all things unto Himself, Christ offered humanity the sanctifying grace that was so vital an issue in Dawson's conversion; he considered this potential for universal redemption and glorious transformation the "essential doctrine of Christianity."[135] Following Augustine's schema, Dawson argued that this revolutionary ontological change caused by Christ ended purely human history and inaugurated the Kingdom of God, making "the progressive extension of the Incarnation by the gradual incorporation of mankind into this higher unity" the proper focus of Christian thought and action. The Christian view of history is hence a contemplation of the divine irruption in time and its consequences.[136]

The claim that this Incarnation and redemption had happened at a particular point in time as part of a historical process, that Christianity is an essentially historical religion, was also crucial to Dawson's outlook

---

132. Dawson, *Religion and Culture*, 22.
133. Dawson, "The Kingdom of God and History," 201.
134. Dawson, "The Christian View of History," 235.
135. Christopher Dawson, "The Nature and Destiny of Man," in *God and the Supernatural*, ed. Father Cuthbert (London: Longmans, Green & Co., 1920), 69.
136. Dawson, *P&R*, 155. See also Dawson to John J. Mulloy, 22 August 1953, Dawson Correspondence.

(as it was to Chesterton's and Greene's). He held that Christianity redeemed the messianic promise of Judaism, itself a historical faith,[137] and that Christians found that culmination in the life of a specified man in a certain place at a distinct moment, "a Galilean peasant executed under Tiberius."[138] He insisted further that God's temporal intervention had historical consequents as well as antecedents, especially in the apostolic ministry and the Church's tradition.[139] Belief in Christianity's historical character was central to Dawson for two closely related reasons. First, he argued that since human nature is a blend of spirit and matter, a satisfactory religion must appeal to both facets. While many worldviews suit only the spiritual side, he thought, Christianity's historical nature makes it sensitive also to tangible needs, ones he deemed it in some ways more vital to meet: "the religious instinct finds its fullest and most concrete satisfaction in the historical field—through faith in an historical person, an historical community, and an historical tradition," exactly what he felt Christianity, and especially Catholicism, offered.[140] For all his stress on metarational experience and metahistory, then, he (like Greene) thought the concrete was crucial, particularly in religious matters.

He thus considered this Christian commitment to history a check on the excessive abstraction he found exemplified by Toynbee's work. Dawson held from early on that Christianity is not "an abstract theory of salvation,"[141] but is rather "a concrete reality. It is the spiritual order incarnated in a historical person and in a historical society."[142] Just as the Christian religion meets both spiritual and material needs, then, so its interpretation of history is equally sensitive to the transcendent significance and the temporal data of events: "the Absolute and the Finite, the Eternal and the Temporal, God and the World were no longer conceived as two exclusive and opposed orders of being.... The two orders interpenetrated one another." To Dawson, this merger of the meaning and matter of history into an inextricable bond that avoids the centrifugal pressures of gnosticism and positivism was orthodox Christianity's ge-

---

137. See, e.g., "Nature and Destiny," 70; P&R, 149, 154; Essays in Order, 216; RMS, xvii.
138. Dawson, "The Christian View of History," 235.
139. Dawson, undated, untitled manuscript, c. 1958–62, Dawson Manuscripts.
140. Dawson, P&R, 244.   141. Dawson, Essays in Order, 216.
142. Dawson, Modern Dilemma, 107.

nius; R. V. Young judges that belief in this equilibrium is what distinguished Dawson's thought from that of equally ambitious materialists and fellow metahistorians.[143] Yet this theology's balance is tenuous, for its assertion of precise synergy between history's purpose and substance leaves it "vulnerable to having the meaning altered by neglect or distortion of the matter," or vice versa.[144] Like Chesterton and Greene, Dawson felt that an inch is everything when you are balancing.

It was orthodox Christianity's, and especially Roman Catholicism's, ability to hew successfully to that straight, but narrow, line that Dawson thought made it unique. He argued as early as 1931 that the Catholic Church "alone possesses a tradition that is capable of satisfying the whole of human nature and that brings the transcendent reality of spiritual Being into relation with human experience and the realities of social life." He developed this thesis and its implications throughout his life.[145] He felt that Protestants and Anglo-Catholics had forsaken such comprehensiveness in his era and succumbed to narrow fanaticisms,[146] leaving his church the sole keeper of that all-embracing equilibrium midway between idealism and historicism that sets apart the Christian approach to history: "the Catholic interpretation of history differs from any other in its combination of universalism with a sense of the uniqueness and irreversibility of the historic process."[147] It was this fusion that he found absent from other faiths. Admitting that Judaism and Islam are historical religions, Dawson thought their denial of the Incarnation fostered theologies of history similar to the Barthians', ones positing a personal, providential deity, but One distant and radically distinct from the profane. He believed that the Jewish sense of salvation was ultimately transferred from "the historical to the cosmic plane," and that in Islam "the bridge between God and Man was broken, and the Divine Omnipotence

---

143. Dawson, *P&R*, 155–56, 245; and Young, "Dawson and Baroque Culture," 127. Dermot Quinn contends similarly that "this balance of eschatology and incarnation is the central element of Dawson's historical imagination" ("Dawson and Historical Imagination," *Chesterton Review* 26 [November 2000]: 483).

144. Hittinger, "Metahistorical Vision," 6. See also Dawson, *P&R*, 245.

145. Dawson, *Essays in Order*, 226. See *East and West*, 28, for an almost identical reiteration nearly thirty years later.

146. See Dawson to Charles Marital-de Witte, 24 March 1947, Dawson Correspondence.

147. Dawson, *RMS*, 80. See also *Formation*, 12.

once more reigned in lonely splendor."[148] He deemed Eastern religions even less compatible with Christianity, considering them spiritualist faiths that denied the essential goodness of the material universe. So at odds with Christianity's affirmation of the material and the temporal did Dawson find this outlook that he thought "the only basis" for an understanding between Christianity and Eastern religions is at "the philosophic level. . . . There is no room for a strictly *theological* understanding."[149] To Dawson, then, the divine intimacy with Being manifested in Christ gives His followers alone a view of history that is equally faithful to both His natures, and is thus sufficiently sensitive to history's theological complexity; and he singled out Roman Catholicism for upholding this principle from his earliest work.

Dawson judged Christianity unique not only in its beliefs, but also in its historical impact. Like Chesterton, he felt that it had arisen at a time when humanity had exhausted its possibilities, thereby introducing a qualitatively new dimension to history. He held that without Christian monotheism's intervention, Western religion would have aped Eastern faiths' blend of polytheism and spiritualism.[150] Christianity, though, brought something that the Greek and Roman world "could not produce from itself or by its own power." Rather than being a new form of ancient religions, it was of a "different order to the philosophies and ideologies of men," for its message of sanctifying grace "recreated the world from within . . . it was the divine seed of a new world miraculously springing up in a world that seemed worn out and under sentence of death."[151] In Dawson's mind, part of this uniqueness resulted from Christianity's rebelliousness, as it was an "irreconcilable alternative to the whole dominant religio-political system." Conceding that Christian cultural dissent was a bequest of Judaism, he still insisted that the new

---

148. Dawson, *P&R*, 155, 162. Jones annotated the passage on Islam heavily in his copy. See also *MOE*, chaps. 8–9; and "The Christian View of History," 236–39. Dawson confessed near the end of his career that he had not yet found a satisfactory way of treating the rise of Islam and its relation to Christian culture (Dawson to Leslie Bullock, 6 June 1961, Dawson Correspondence).

149. Dawson, *East and West*, 10–11. Emphasis in original. See also *P&R*, 126–41; *Dynamics*, 187; *Enquiries*, 295–96.

150. See Dawson to Arnold Toynbee, 5 November 1954, Dawson Correspondence.

151. Christopher Dawson, *Beyond Politics* (New York: Sheed & Ward, 1939), 89–90.

religion exhibited "absolute novelty" in basing its protest on "the life of a historical personality."[152] If the Christian standard of cultural criticism remained ultimately eternal, he also felt it was incarnated in the words and deeds of that Galilean peasant executed under Tiberius for His challenge to Judeo-Roman mores. To Dawson, then, Christianity was unparalleled in both its devotion to history's matter and meaning, and its transformative effects on human nature and culture, ones he considered subversive of prevailing norms from its inception.

Dawson thought that Christ also affirmed history by instituting a Church to carry on His work. He argued that Catholics consider the Church and Christian culture to be a continuous extension of the Incarnation, and that this organic connection to Christ empowers the Church to continue His integrating and sanctifying role in history: "it is her mission to transform the world by bringing every side of human existence and every human activity into contact with the sources of supernatural life."[153] Just as Catholic theology does not scorn the concrete, then, neither does its institutional expression, for the Church is "not an abstraction like Humanity or an ideal like that of so many religious and political sects. It is a true society with its own visible institutions and objective laws and an intense consciousness of its social identity."[154] But he also considered the Church "the only true society" because it alone "has its source in a spiritual will."[155]

As these claims suggest, Dawson ascribed part of the Church's truth to its asserted ability to preserve in actuality the theoretical balance between universality and historicity. To him, the Church is simultaneously a historical institution and a representative (and earthly foretaste) of a universal spiritual society that exists eternally. It thus uniquely affirms time without being confined to it: "The Church exists in history, but it

---

152. Christopher Dawson, "The Roman Empire and the Birth of the Christian Church," in *Religion and World History: A Selection from the Works of Christopher Dawson*, ed. James Oliver and Christina Scott (New York: Image, 1975), 153. For the link between Jewish and Christian rebels, see Dawson, *Formation*, 68–69.

153. Dawson, *Beyond Politics*, 114–15. See also *The Crisis of Western Education* (1961; reprint, New York: Image, 1965), 122; and Dawson to John J. Mulloy, 26 September and 1 October 1962, Dawson Correspondence.

154. Dawson, *Formation*, 296.

155. Dawson, *Enquiries*, 257.

transcends history so that each of its temporal manifestations has a supernatural value and significance."[156] He thought Roman Catholicism best upheld this ideal, being both "a real society, not an imaginary or invisible one," and a "universal society, not a national or local one."[157] Dawson saw the Church's militancy as another link with its Founder, for he felt that this organ was the temporal continuation of Christ's challenge to established orders. He believed that the Church's role as a counter-kingdom had not changed since the days of Christ or the early Church. In his time, Dawson thought that the Church's ability to be in the world but not of it made it an especially compelling alternative to irreligious materialism, because it neither neglects nor idolizes the tangible. It is a "universal spiritual society whose feet are firmly planted in history and whose Head is divine: a Society which possesses no less objective reality and juridical form than a State, while at the same time its action extends to the very depths of the individual human soul." Allowing that the perceived dominance of secular ideas made it difficult for modern man to comprehend and accept this incarnational concept, Dawson nonetheless stressed that those who so confront modern unbelief are imitating Christ and His first followers.[158]

Dawson detected these characteristics of the Christian Church in all orthodox followers of Jesus, but he contended that Roman Catholicism was the fullest and surest source of them in his era. Besides holding that Roman Catholicism was the straightest historical line back to Christ through the apostolic succession, that Anglo-Catholicism and Protestantism had lost the balance between time and eternity by becoming either wholly of or divorced from the world, and that Roman Catholics alone remained rebels against secular trends, Dawson also argued that his church had best preserved the ideal of unity that came from its being founded by a single, concrete person: "As the Christian faith in Christ is faith in a real historical person, not an abstract ideal, so the Catholic faith in the church is faith in a real historical society, not an invisible communion of saints or a spiritual union of Christians who are divided into a

---

156. Christopher Dawson, *The Historic Reality of Christian Culture* (New York: Harper Torchbooks, 1960), 58. See also ibid., 117–20; and *Crisis Western Education*, 113, 133.

157. Dawson, *Modern Dilemma*, 110. See also *RMS*, 149–50.

158. Dawson, *East and West*, 215–17.

number of religious groups and sects."[159] Dawson thus suggested that Catholicism is more inherently committed to the idea of a single Christian church than other denominations are. Additionally, he deemed Roman Catholicism best suited to catalyze this necessary unity, due to its emphasis on authority and its willingness to resist beliefs contrary to Christian traditions. Judging his church the "one great social and spiritual institution which is the visible embodiment of divine authority and supernatural truth,"[160] Dawson claimed that "the Catholic Church is no less necessary to Christianity, for without it the latter would become no more than a mass of divergent opinions dissolving under the pressure of rationalist criticism and secularist culture."[161] This church alone preserves the balance between historicity and universality, thus reaffirming the traditional Christian respect for the temporal while also transcending ephemeral cultural trends corrosive of unity and necessary protest. Such an analysis begs many questions, especially since conflict over authority and attitudes toward the profane had sparked much of the Christian disunity Dawson hoped to heal. But it is an evident example of his overall belief that Roman Catholicism was the leading guardian of the Christian heritage, and the best hope of its perpetuation, in modern times.

Enquiries into Dawson's Intellectual Inheritance: Augustine and Aquinas

Before demonstrating how Dawson applied his Christian interpretation of history to particular periods, it is necessary to situate it theologically. As his conversion reading indicates, Dawson drew on Augustinianism and Thomism in forming his outlook. Some Augustinian aspects have already been adduced, but it is vital to see how closely Dawson identified with the bishop of Hippo. He acknowledged Augustine's influence (although he once declined to write a book on the saint),[162] and the

---

159. Dawson, "The Kingdom of God and History," 210.
160. Christopher Dawson, "Future of Christian Culture," *The Commonweal* 59 (19 March 1954): 597.
161. Dawson, *Modern Dilemma*, 111.
162. See O'Connor, *Relation*, x; and Dawson to Miles Waldman, 16 February 1948, Dawson Correspondence.

affinities in their thought have led Dawson critics to posit correctly that his worldview was "essentially Augustinian."[163] Dawson deemed Augustine's work seminal in shaping the approach to history he had inherited: "it is impossible to exaggerate the influence of St. Augustine's thought on the development of the Christian view of history and on the whole tradition of Western historiography."[164] He credited Augustine with founding the idea of history as a linear, dynamic process that ends in the realization of God's providential purpose, with defining human dignity as central to this process, and with advocating the Church's role as cultural leaven. More personally, Dawson saw Augustine's religion as a "philosophy of spiritual experience" that was "the source of Western mysticism."[165] Finally, he judged Augustine a rebel against his time's secular attitudes, arguing that he divested the state of its divine aura, and thus freed citizens to shape a new order based on true transcendent norms.[166]

Dawson's assumptions and analysis reveal his adoption of Augustinian attitudes. For example, he often evoked Augustine's distinction between the cities of man and of God. Moreover, his writing about Augustine and his age frequently contained a contemporary subtext. Indeed, he appears to have seen himself in a position akin to Augustine's, being present at the eclipse of a powerful empire and its culture, one he sought to rebuild on an orthodox Christian basis even if it meant enduring the execration of a majority wedded to pagan practices, which hence dishonors prophets: "the spiritual reformer cannot expect to have the majority on his side. He must be prepared to stand alone like Ezekiel and Jeremy. He must take as his example St. Augustine besieged by the Vandals at Hippo."[167]

---

163. John Mulloy, "Christopher Dawson and G. K. Chesterton," *Chesterton Review* 9 (August 1983): 227. See also Scott, *Historian*, 73, 99; Hittinger, "Metahistorical Vision," 19–20; Quinn, "Historical Imagination," 482. White ("Dawson's Idea of History," 249–50) also sees this aspect to Dawson's thought, but his reading of Augustine is too dualistic.

164. Dawson, "The Christian View of History," 241.

165. Dawson, *MOE*, 63.

166. Dawson, *Enquiries*, 258.

167. Dawson, *Religion and Rise of Western Culture*, 147. See also, e.g., *RMS*, xv–xvi; *Enquiries*, 213, 216; and "Notes on Secularism," c. 1950s, Dawson Correspondence.

Dawson's taking of Augustine as an example for his own religiously based reform is often sensed, at least in broad terms, by Dawson scholars;[168] the extent to which Thomism influenced his work is more disputed.[169] Dawson himself judged his thought within the tradition of medieval English Scholasticism,[170] and he praised Aquinas often, especially for introducing the Greek Fathers' ideas of grace into Western Christianity.[171] Beyond that resonance with personally salient spiritual issues, Dawson found many of his ideas about the Christian view of history present in Thomism. Like Chesterton, he felt that Thomas had settled the Manichees and all who disdain the material. To Dawson, this reaffirmation of the Incarnation's validation and sanctification of the concrete was Aquinas's "fundamental principle."[172] He hence also held that Thomism exemplified the orthodox balance between historicity and universality: "the whole Thomist synthesis" is governed by "the concordance in difference of the two orders—of Nature and Grace, of Reason and Faith, of the temporal and the spiritual powers." He saw this equilibrium's reiteration as the "essential significance" of Scholasticism.[173] If Augustine kept Dawson from becoming of the world, then, Thomas insured that he remained in it. Dawson also saw in Thomism the potential

---

168. Numerous scholars have noted the parallels between Dawson's and Augustine's historical situations and roles, but most seem to find it coincidental, and none have addressed directly whether or to what extent Dawson assumed this role consciously. See, e.g., Scott, *Historian*, 166; Knowles, "Obituary," 558; E. J. Oliver, "The Religion of Christopher Dawson," *Chesterton Review* 9 (May 1983): 165; and Nichols, "Dawson's Catholic Setting," 34.

169. Horton Davies, for instance, dubs Dawson England's "leading neo-Thomist" (*Worship and Theology in England*, vol. 5 [Princeton, N.J.: Princeton University Press, 1965], 184); and White ("Dawson's Idea of History," 264) asserts that his work demonstrates "how a Scholastic view of religion may be turned into a criterion of historical interpretation," a reading Norman Cantor substantially echoes (*Inventing the Middle Ages* [New York: Quill, 1991], 329–30). Defining neo-Thomism more narrowly, though, Hitchcock judges that Dawson was seen as "an interesting anomaly" due to his use of scholarly rather than neo-Scholastic norms in his work, a point that has some validity but seems to understate Dawson's use of Thomistic categories ("Post-Mortem," 220). Mulloy contrasts Dawson's Thomism with Chesterton's, finding the latter the more "ardent disciple," a view that also underemphasizes the Thomistic cast of Dawson's thought ("Dawson and Chesterton," 227).

170. See Dawson to John J. Mulloy, 19 January 1957, Dawson Correspondence.

171. Mulloy, "Chesterton and Dawson," 231.

172. Dawson, *P&R*, 173–75. Jones highlighted these passages in his copy.

173. Dawson, *Formation*, 242. Jones highlighted this passage in his copy.

for a "really catholic philosophy of history,"[174] one that has "held fast to the old tradition"[175] of Christendom and whose "dominant spirit" is a thirst for unity.[176]

The stress on unity—the idea that all truth is God's truth—is the facet of Thomism most evident in Dawson's writing. From early on, he contended that "Catholicism stands essentially for a universal order in which every good and every truth of the natural or the social order can find a place"; he applied this ideal more specifically, arguing, for instance, that there is no inherent incompatibility between science and religion.[177] Dawson also posited the corresponding Thomistic notion that people naturally seek the good, meaning that misdirected inclinations can be redirected toward ultimate goodness. He thus thought that even a post-Christian culture should not be despaired of: "every way of life" is "a potential way to God," for even ill-chosen goods can be the media by which "the universal good is apprehended and through which these cultures are oriented towards the good that transcends their own power and knowledge."[178] As indebted as he was to Augustine and Aquinas, though, Dawson was not uncritical of them or their followers. For example, he deemed his day's Thomists too focused on metaphysics and not enough on social theory.[179] Moreover, despite seeing parallels between his times and earlier eras, Dawson was sensitive to each age's vicissitudes, and thus emphasized the limits to such analogies. He enjoined his era's scholars to draw on principles found in Augustine and Aquinas, but to express them in fresh ways befitting changed cultural conditions.[180]

Catholicism and the Historian's Mind: A Religious Reading of World History

Dawson's idea of a Christian approach to history had more than theoretical and theological implications. It also governed how he interpret-

---

174. Dawson, "The Kingdom of God and History," 206.
175. Dawson, *Formation*, 22.
176. Dawson, *Religion and Rise of Western Culture*, 237.
177. Dawson, *Essays in Order*, vi. See also *Modern Dilemma*, 89–90.
178. Dawson, *Religion and Culture*, 62. Jones highlighted this passage and noted it on the flyleaf of his copy.
179. See Dawson to John J. Mulloy, 30 July 1954, Dawson Correspondence.
180. Dawson to Dom Bede Griffiths, 24 August 1957, Dawson Correspondence.

ed specific eras and events. He was not a specialist in a single period, as his interests ranged from prehistory to modernity, so sampling his scholarship in each area is the best means of revealing his faith's common shaping influence. Dawson's contention that religion is the key of history is evident in his earliest book, on prehistoric Europe and the ancient East. He argued that the ancient world underwent an enormous cultural change in the fourth millennium B.C. and that its trigger was "the temple and the religious conceptions which it stood for . . . the Sacred City appears at the dawn of history as the essential organ of the higher civilization." He further claimed that in Sumer the temple was the core and mainspring of community life, that Egyptian exceptionalism arose from "a religious idea," and that ancient Chinese civilization owed its stability to a "theocratic tradition."[181] Even in the pre-Christian world, then, Dawson saw religion as the central social and historical factor, and it served as his intellectual gyroscope when navigating a wide sea of diverse material.

The same integrating principle persisted when he focused more on Europe. His interpretation of the Roman Empire, for example, rebukes Gibbon's implicitly. Rather than deeming the Empire and Christianity antitheses, Dawson, again following Augustine (and Newman), discerned continuity. He held that the process of unification that ended in the Empire's foundation was a providential preparation for the Church, and that the new Christian Rome was "destined to inherit the Roman tradition and to preserve the old ideal of Roman unity in a changed world."[182] Furthermore, his lifelong analogies between Roman days and his own centered on religious issues, as in his belief that "the Church is being brought back to the same situation in which she began . . . a persecuted minority in an anti-Christian world state," with the hopeful assertion that "it was under those conditions that the Church achieved her greatest triumph and exercised her most far-reaching influence on civilization."[183] Hence, Dawson's religion not only led him to see Christian-

---

181. Dawson, *Age of Gods*, 113, 123, 159, 162.

182. Dawson, *MOE*, 23–24. See also Dawson, *Medieval Essays*, 39; and *Dynamics*, 333–36, 340–41.

183. Dawson, "Newman and the Sword of the Spirit," 13. See also Christopher Dawson, "The Outlook for Christian Culture Today," *Cross-Currents* 5 (Spring 1955): 132; and *Modern Dilemma*, 25.

Tradition, Inheritance, and World 249

imperial connections as that era's most vital data, but also to assess the Church's role positively and to regard its behavior as a model for the mid-twentieth century.

Dawson's view of the Middle Ages bore his faith's imprint even more deeply, and thus challenged conventional historiographical and cultural views more radically. He rejected the term "Dark Ages" on religious grounds: "to the Catholic they are not dark ages so much as ages of dawn," for this era saw the West converted, Christian civilization founded, and Catholic art and liturgy created. He held that "it is very difficult for anyone who is not a Catholic to understand the full meaning of this great tradition," for the monastic formation and preservation of a distinctly Christian culture in the midst of material ruin is "difficult for the modern who views all history *sub specie humanitatis* to appreciate, since to him 'the Day of Man' is the only possible object of a reasonable man's devotion." Dawson nonetheless judged these years "the most creative age of all," for they generated the "very culture itself—the root and ground of all the subsequent culture achievements."[184] As he did with Roman times, Dawson also compared its successor epoch to his own. He contrasted favorably a society "weak and immature like European civilization during the Dark Ages," which "recognizes its own limitations, and bows before the kingdom of the spirit," with the arrogant "victorious material civilization of our own age,"[185] one not even dark "with the honest night of barbarism."[186] He thus contested both what he saw as secularist scholarly misreadings of this era, and popular clichés positing modernity's self-evident superiority to this ostensibly benighted interlude.

This close link between Dawson's Catholicism and his historical judgments might foster expectations of a strict identification of Christianity with the Middle Ages. Hayden White and others have criticized him on these grounds, accusing him of "withdrawing into the Middle Ages," and of being part of the Catholic medievalism they associate with

---

184. Dawson, *MOE*, xvii, xviii–xix, xv. One reviewer of this volume judged it rebellious: "his book marks a complete break with many historical conventions and traditions." Patrick Healy, "Constructive Dark Ages," *The Commonweal* 17 (4 January 1933): 275.
185. Dawson, "Nature and Destiny," 81.
186. Christopher Dawson, "The End of an Age," *The Criterion* 9 (April 1930): 387.

Chesterton and Belloc.[187] Such inferences may seem logical, but a careful reading of Dawson's work reveals their inaccuracy. He refused to equate this single epoch with the universal faith that he thought undergirded it, stating explicitly that "Christian culture is not the same thing as medieval culture. It existed before the Middle Ages began and it continued to exist after they had ended."[188] Rather than trying to arrest historical development by retreating into a bygone era, Dawson insisted that "there have been many Christian cultures and there may be many more" because "the concept of Christian culture is far wider than that of the Middle Ages."[189] Moreover, he censured the Oxford Movement and Catholic revivalists for idealizing this period, complaining that Catholics were "too obsessed with the Middle Ages," and that this fixation undercut such writers' credibility.[190] He denied flatly ever having been a Bellocite; he belonged (along with Jones) to the Order Group, a collection of Catholics who opposed what they deemed the Chesterbellocian idea that Catholics are necessarily medievalists.[191] While an inaccurate reading of Chesterton's position, if not Belloc's, Dawson's adherence to it does reveal how far he was from holding the romantic view of the Middle Ages often ascribed to him.

His refusal to posit a rigid identity between Catholicism and medievalism does not mean, however, that he found the period lacking in virtues. Recognizing that what is Catholic is not necessarily medieval, and what is medieval is not necessarily Catholic, Dawson still felt that "there has never been an age in which European culture was more penetrated by the Catholic tradition, or in which Catholic ideals found a

---

187. White, "Dawson's Idea of History," 279, 277. Cowling also tends toward this misreading (*Religion and Public Doctrine*, 2: 339), as does Joseph Pearce, *Wisdom and Innocence: A Life of G. K. Chesterton* (San Francisco: Ignatius Press, 1997), 414. A good contemporaneous example is Justus George Lawler, *The Catholic Dimension in Higher Education* (Westminster: The Newman Press, 1959), 10, 205, 211–16.

188. Christopher Dawson, "Education and Christian Culture," *The Commonweal* 59 (4 December 1953): 217.

189. Dawson, *Medieval Essays*, 1.

190. Dawson quoted in Paul Foster, "The Making of Europe," *Chesterton Review* 9 (May 1983): 141. See also "The Outlook for Christian Culture Today," 131; and *MOE*, xvii.

191. See Dawson to John Mulloy, 23 April 1955; and *Order* memo, 19 October 1928, Dawson Correspondence.

fuller expression in almost every field of human activity."[192] In particular, he thought the Middle Ages saw the development of an organic, communitarian social order grounded in religious principles, one he deemed revolutionary, the source of Western science and culture, and an exemplar of European unity.[193] He also saw monks as rebels against secular practices, and held that the "prophetic spirit" is what gave medieval culture its distinctive spiritual energy and moral prestige.[194] To him, these practices and attitudes were not confined to their original culture, because they were rooted in a transcendent faith. If of medieval genesis, they had become a dynamic part of the Church's spiritual patrimony, making them as applicable to the modern age that had thus far rejected them as to the medieval era that had embraced them fully. If he did not join some Catholics in idealizing the Middle Ages, then, he did deem medieval culture "Christian culture *par excellence*," and considered its underlying principles of both perennial and particular value and validity.[195]

This respect for medieval times and culture made Dawson wary of what he deemed the twin destroyers of its synthesis. He argued that the Renaissance and the Reformation combined to upset the orthodox Catholic, medieval balance between the temporal and the transcendent, as each movement exaggerated one facet and denigrated the other: "the sixteenth century saw the first great European revolution, a revolt carried out by the Italian Renaissance in the name of the purity of culture and by the German Reformation in the name of the purity of the Gospel. The Middle Ages were rejected by the humanists as barbarous and by the reformers as superstitious and corrupt."[196] In Chesterton's terms, the Renaissance stressed philosophy, the Reformation, mythology.

To Dawson, "the apotheosis of Humanity" was Renaissance culture's "central idea." He held that the humanists rejected dependence on the supernatural, and hence cleaved religion from reason, and focused their

---

192. Dawson, *Formation*, 280.
193. See, e.g., *P&R*, 166; *Religion and Rise of Western Culture*, 11, 206–7, 229–30, 270–71; "The European Revolution," 87, 92–93. He described medieval culture as a revolution in a 1940s draft of an undated letter (Dawson Correspondence).
194. Dawson, *Medieval Essays*, 68; and *Religion and Rise of Western Culture*, 164.
195. Dawson, *Formation*, 280, 160.
196. Dawson, "The European Revolution," 88.

efforts on this newly independent rational sphere. He felt that such anthropocentrism changed its advocates' ideas of nature, history, and ethics, thus ultimately, if unintentionally, fueling secularization: the Renaissance

> introduced a new set of ideal values (or set an ideal value on human activities) which were not necessarily secular but were essentially natural ... in Thomism these values were strictly subordinated to religious and supernatural ends, whereas the humanists regarded them as ends in themselves and gave them an autonomous significance.[197]

Yet Dawson's religious beliefs persuaded him that even a finally anti-Christian movement depended on Catholic Christianity for its inspiration and impetus. He insisted that the qualitative change in Being effected by Christ and perpetuated by the Church had made a return to purely pagan classicism impossible. However much humanism was the rediscovery of man and the natural world, the discoverers were not natural men, but Christians: "It was from the accumulated resources of their Christian past that they acquired the spiritual energy to conquer the material world and to create the new secular culture."[198] In Dawson's mind, Christian men create even heathen things.

He regarded the Reformation as the Renaissance's mirror. If the Renaissance had virtually divinized human nature and powers like reason, Dawson (like Chesterton) saw in the Lutheran emphasis on human depravity "the supreme example of the anti-humanist spirit, the enemy of moderation and human reason,"[199] one "entirely alien in spirit from the culture of the Italian Renaissance."[200] Thus, although approached from the opposite direction, Dawson thought the Reformation ultimately reached the Renaissance's secular destination. He held that the Protestant stress on individualized, spiritualized religion privatized faith and

---

197. Christopher Dawson, *The Dividing of Christendom* (New York: Sheed & Ward, 1965), 67, 46. See also "End of an Age," 389; and *Enquiries*, 108–9.
198. Dawson, "End of an Age," 397.
199. Dawson, *Crisis Western Education*, 32.
200. Dawson, *P&R*, 180. For all his stress on Luther, Dawson thought Calvin more important for English history (See Dawson to Michael Mason, 9 July 1957, Dawson Correspondence). He called the English Reformation itself a divergence from "the Catholic way ... into the waste lands of sectarianism" (*Medieval Essays*, 270).

left the public sphere unprotected from secular pressures. Lacking a unifying religious basis for social life, civilization became "private and domestic ... [it] was entirely destitute of the communal spirit and of the civic traditions which had marked the ancient and the medieval city." The "production of wealth" replaced the praise of God as the social ethic, and "left every other side of life," including religion, "to private initiative."[201] Nor was materialism the only beneficiary of religion's divorce from culture and its consequent compartmentalization. Dawson believed that the reformers' accent on national churches fostered emphasis on national differences instead of religious similarities. He argued that as the universal Church became more an abstract spiritual ideal than a social reality, the ensuing growth of separate Christian societies undermined people's sense of belonging to a tangible, global church and culture. They thus became susceptible to nationalistic sentiments, promoting the secularization of Christian culture, as the community of place replaced the communion of saints as one's chief allegiance.[202]

But, as with the Renaissance, Dawson felt that the reformers could not escape their Catholic roots fully. Even more so than the Renaissance, he held, the Reformation was intimately tied to Catholicism. The humanists, after all, had classical Mediterranean Hellenism to reprise, although this recovery was shaped by Christianity; but the northern European Protestants had "no older tradition of higher culture," and thus could only declare cultural independence by "a remolding and transforming of the Christian tradition itself in accordance with [their] national genius." Hence, "the Renaissance of Northern Europe is the Reformation."[203] As finally antithetical as he found these two movements, then, Dawson deemed each an effort to purify Catholic Christianity gone awry. If the Renaissance made men gods and the Reformation saw them as beasts, neither upheld the medieval ideal of a Christian citizen. With religion separated from cultural life as either too irrational or too personal, Dawson found the ensuing vacuum filled by lesser facets of life now disproportionately magnified in social significance. If these out-

---

201. Christopher Dawson, *Christianity and Sex* (London: Faber & Faber, 1930), 25.

202. See Dawson, "The Christian Church and the Democratic State," 1958, Dawson Manuscripts.

203. Dawson, *P&R*, 178.

comes seem far removed from medieval Catholicism, he still saw that faith as the driving, if unconscious, force behind them, illustrating the extent of his belief that religion is the key of history.

Yet he did not exempt Catholics from responsibility for Christendom's breakup. He attributed the loss of Christian unity in the age of the Renaissance and Reformation in part to a failure of spiritual leadership by the Church, a lesson he suggested contemporary Catholics had yet to learn.[204] His view of the Counter-Reformation was also ambivalent. On the one hand, and not unexpectedly, Dawson praised the baroque as an antidote to the perceived excesses of the humanists and reformers, calling it "the desecularization of the Renaissance," and contrasting its passionate intensity favorably to the "sober pietism" of the Protestant north. He also claimed in 1954 that the Counter-Reformation restored the universality and the unity of Christianity and culture that had characterized the medieval synthesis.[205] But Dawson qualified this contention a decade later, stressing the Counter-Reformation's Latin nature and the ensuing hostility it encountered in northern Europe, a development he thought partially responsible for the secularization of Western culture.[206] On the whole, then, he seemed to feel that Catholics had not confronted the Renaissance and the Reformation as effectively as they should have, either historically or in his day.

Dawson saw the Enlightenment as the intellectual culmination of trends loosed by earlier secularizing forces. He posited that the Enlightenment spawned a new breech between philosophy and mythology, this time among humanists, as "the one-sided rationalism of the Encyclopedists provoked the one-sided subjective emotionalism of Rousseau and the Romantics." But he found this split's products even more radically removed from their dynamic religious source than their sixteenth-century predecessor had been: "Rationalism had lost its spiritual inspiration and romanticism lacked its intellectual order and its sense of form. Thus the disappearance of the Christian element in humanism has involved the

---

204. Dawson, W[?]immer Lecture, 1960, Dawson Manuscripts; and "Education and Christian Culture," 219.
205. Dawson, "The European Revolution," 89–90.
206. Dawson, *Dividing*, 161.

loss of its vital quality." In place of Christianity, Dawson thought, the Enlightenment combined the Renaissance's belief in human goodness and progress with a hostility to tradition and mystery that also precipitated a qualitative break with the earlier classicists, making neither rationalism nor romanticism "the true representative of the earlier humanism."[207] He held this new outlook responsible for the "complete secularization of Western culture";[208] his view of it somewhat anticipated Peter Gay's thesis that the Enlightenment marked the rise of a distinctly *"modern paganism, emancipated from classical thought as much as from Christian dogma."*[209] While Gay would find this standpoint liberating, though, Dawson deemed it superficial and constricting due to its sensed inability to treat transcendent and tragic topics. To Dawson, Enlightenment thought "shut its eyes to everything but the natural virtues of the human heart, and salved the wounds of humanity with a few moral platitudes."[210]

As hostile to religion as Dawson judged the Enlightenment, he still analyzed it in religious terms, calling it "religious in origin, although it was anti-religious in its results."[211] He thought that the *philosophes* sought consciously to replace Catholic dogma with a kindred universal philosophical orthodoxy of science and reason.[212] As with its cultural antecedents, he felt that Catholics had not responded effectively to the threat of this "new religion."[213] He regarded the Church's attempts to coerce *philosophes* and their followers as "the supreme example" of how religious persecution defeats its own aims and serves its foes'.[214] Moreover, he saw the 1773 dissolution of the Jesuits as the turning point in the

---

207. Dawson, "End of an Age," 398. See also *Dynamics*, 35; and Dawson, "Religion and the Romantic Movement," *The Tablet*, 1937; reprinted in *The Dawson Newsletter* 13 (Spring 1995): 1–6, 4.

208. Dawson, *East and West*, 83.

209. Peter Gay, *The Enlightenment: An Interpretation: The Rise of Modern Paganism* (New York: Norton, 1966), xi. Emphasis in original.

210. Dawson, *Enquiries*, 303.

211. Christopher Dawson, *The Gods of Revolution* (London: Sidwick & Jackson, 1972), 15. Although published posthumously, much of this book had been composed in the 1930s.

212. Dawson, *P&R*, 203.

213. Dawson, *Enquiries*, 303.

214. Dawson, *Gods of Revolution*, 15.

Enlightenment's victory, for it destroyed "the only force" within the Church capable of contesting the Encyclopedists' anti-Christian propaganda successfully.[215]

Dawson did detect capable critics of the Enlightenment, though, and he described them also in religious terms. If the institutional Church was insufficient to this task, he lauded individual Catholics, like Joseph de Maistre, with whom he identified and whom he said had the "spirit of a Hebrew prophet."[216] Moreover, he argued that Rousseau had a "genuinely religious temperament," and that his idealism was a "reaction against the secularization of the modern state and an attempt to recover that sense of spiritual community which Christian society possessed in the past."[217] Although holding that Romanticism played a vital role in secularization, Dawson also thought it more patient of baptism than rationalism. He asserted a clear link between Romanticism and mysticism,[218] and claimed that Romanticism's inspiration was the culture of medieval Christendom. He posited further that this renewed interest in medieval culture at first focused on its poetry and art, but ineluctably penetrated to its theological roots; and he claimed that only a lack of time prevented the writers Novalis and Wackenroder from becoming Roman Catholics, while he cited other Romantics, like Friedrich von Schlegel and Adam Müller, who did convert.[219] As debatable as any of these claims is individually, they reveal collectively how much Dawson's Catholicism shaped his view of the Enlightenment's nature and causes, as well as the responses to it.

He adopted a similar approach to the French Revolution, the last major epoch or event he studied systematically. From early on, Dawson considered the revolution the practical expression of Enlightenment

---

215. Dawson, *Dividing*, 274.

216. Dawson, "Religion and the Romantic Movement," 3. For his identification with Maistre, see Dawson to John J. Mulloy, 19 January 1957, Dawson Correspondence.

217. Dawson, *Dividing*, 268, 278.

218. Dawson, "Religion and the Romantic Movement," 6.

219. Dawson, "Introduction to the 19th Century: The Two Trends of Catholic Revival and the Growth of Revolutionary Liberalism," 1958, Dawson Manuscripts; "The Catholic Revival in the 19th Century and the Oxford Movement," 1961, Dawson Manuscripts; and "Religion and the Romantic Movement," 5. See also Dawson to Daniel O'Connor, 16 December 1939, in O'Connor, *Relation*, xi.

Tradition, Inheritance, and World 257

philosophies, and he thought this ideological radicalism was what gave the revolution its historical significance.[220] He regarded the uprising as the tangible triumph of the secularization that had been growing steadily in modern Western culture at a theoretical level.[221] In Burkean fashion, he criticized the use of "abstract concepts of Reason and Truth and Civilization as weapons to attack every truth and to undermine the foundations on which the actual historic structure of European culture rested."[222] Dawson also judged the French Revolution one of the "modern influences" that had contributed to contemporary problems, but that Catholics were inclined to underestimate, due to their purported fixation on the Middle Ages.[223]

As he did with other such movements, like the Renaissance, Reformation, and Enlightenment, Dawson assessed the French Revolution by religious, Catholic standards. He claimed that the revolutionaries adopted the *philosophes'* conscious anti-Catholicism by undertaking a radical reconstruction of the Church according to Enlightenment principles, plus measures of positive de-Christianization.[224] These policies signaled to him how fundamentally hostile to Catholicism the revolution was: "it was a religion of human salvation, the salvation of the world by the power of man set free by Reason. The Cross has been replaced by the Tree of Liberty, the Grace of God by the Reason of Man, and Redemption by Revolution."[225] If the Enlightenment was a qualitative break with the Renaissance, Dawson thought, the revolution was an equally substantial split from the Reformation: "In sheer material destruction of monasteries and churches, in confiscation of property and abrogation of privileges, the Age of the Revolution far surpassed that of the Reformation; it was in fact a second Reformation, but a frankly anti-religious one."[226]

---

220. See, e.g., an entry in a pre-1920s notebook, Dawson Manuscripts; *Beyond Politics*, 72; *Crisis Western Education*, 153–54; *Gods of Revolution*, 60. This link between the Enlightenment and the revolution is debated contentiously by historians of the period. Cf. P. N. Furbank, "Nothing Sacred," *New York Review of Books* 42 (8 June 1995): 53.
221. Dawson, "The Catholic Revival in the 19th Century and the Oxford Movement."
222. Christopher Dawson, *Understanding Europe* (1952; reprint, New York: Image 1960), 192.
223. Dawson quoted in Foster, "Making of Europe," 141.
224. Christopher Dawson, "Rationalism and Revolution," 1957, Dawson Manuscripts.
225. Dawson, *Gods of Revolution*, 75.
226. Dawson, "Religion and the Romantic Movement," 1. See also *Dividing*, 276.

As with the Enlightenment's foes, Dawson also appraised counterrevolutionaries in religious terms. Besides inspiring specific figures like Maistre, Dawson held, there was a general revival of Catholicism in the postrevolutionary era that was inseparable from a concurrent reaction against rationalism and revolutionary abstractions.[227] Nor were these predecessor rebels all intellectuals. To Dawson, the revolution ultimately failed because the common people abhorred assaults on their ancestral faith, and thus conducted popular campaigns in its defense that dashed the revolutionaries' hopes.[228] Dawson's overall treatment of this episode reveals again how his similar devotion to that faith shaped his historical judgments. He felt that historians had neglected such detailed attention to religious issues and the use of a religious hermeneutic when reflecting on the revolution in France; but Toynbee judged in 1972 that this focus and approach is exactly what made his contribution to French Revolution historiography original and valuable.[229]

This survey of Dawson's assumptions about history and his specific readings of particular periods, events, and movements reveals a highly developed, consistently applied analytical framework rooted in orthodox Roman Catholicism. Toynbee was not alone in seeing this perspective as the distinguishing trait of Dawson's historiography, as peers and reviewers generally noted his Catholicism's centrality to his analysis. Their appraisals of this vision's validity, though, were more mixed. Roman Catholics usually praised Dawson, but so did some not noticeably religious historians. Harry Elmer Barnes, for instance, held that he "almost measures up to the pattern of the ideal historian" suggested by James Harvey Robinson; Barnes downplayed Dawson's tendency to select views that "clash the least with Catholic dogma," arguing that "not even the most militant Protestant or skeptical historian" could disqualify his contributions on such grounds.[230] But the importance of Dawson's Catholicism

227. Christopher Dawson lecture notes for "The Catholic Revival in France," 1960, Dawson Manuscripts.
228. Dawson, "Rationalism and Revolution"; and *Gods of Revolution*, 89–90.
229. See Dawson, "Rationalism and Revolution"; and Arnold Toynbee, introduction to *Gods of Revolution*, x.
230. Harry Elmer Barnes, review of *Dynamics*, American Historical Review 63 (October 1957): 77–79. For similar judgments, see H. A. L. Fisher, review of *The Making of Europe*, English Review 55 (July 1932): 98; Crane Brinton, review of *Dynamics*, Speculum (April 1958): 273;

to his work also drew sharp criticism. Christopher Hill, for example, dubbed him "a diligent Roman Catholic publicist with a considerable and genuine interest in history," but "not a great historian."[231] While such a judgment is unsurprising coming from a committed Marxist, even a devout counter-modernist, but dedicated Protestant, like Reinhold Niebuhr echoed it. Arguing that "a tight dogmatism does not make for good historiography," Niebuhr felt that Dawson's interpretations were often "strictly controlled by dogmatic Catholic presuppositions."[232] Such a breakdown of responses is not unexpected. Dawson consciously made his religion central to his scholarship, thus inviting assessment of its role as the key factor in evaluating his writing. Paradoxically, but understandably, readers without such a firm commitment of their own saw his standpoint as just a different interpretative perspective that provoked no strong emotional reaction. Those with an equally defined, but differing, theoretical or religious outlook, though, had more at stake personally, and thus engaged his first principles, generating more severe, if insoluble, criticisms. Like any historian of clearly expressed beliefs, Dawson risked alienating those who disagreed with his premises; yet it was those very core ideas that both friend and foe saw as his work's significant and distinctive facet.

Religion and Culture: Dawson's Approach to Cultural Studies

Dawson faced a similar situation when he turned from history to cultural studies, as when he gave the prestigious Gifford Lectures at the University of Edinburgh in 1947 and 1948. His claim that his interest in other cultures began in boyhood should be recalled, as he seems to have followed his father in this avocation. As an adult, Dawson *fils* considered this field the only one to which he had made an original contribution.[233]

---

and Alexander Murray, introduction to *The Making of Europe*, by Christopher Dawson (Washington, D.C.: The Catholic University of America Press, 2003), xxxiv.

231. Hill quoted in Scott, *Historian*, 171. His remarks appeared originally in the *Spectator* in September 1956.

232. Reinhold Niebuhr, "What's a Mote to One is a Beam to Another," *New York Times Book Review*, 13 March 1960, 18. See also White, "Dawson's Idea of History," 279, 285–86.

233. See Scott, *Historian*, 20–21; and Dawson to John J. Mulloy, 5 July 1955, Dawson Correspondence.

Toynbee and others would find originalities in his historiography as well, but his work in cultural studies is marked by the same intricacy of thought and underlying assumptions.

In a definition that greatly influenced T. S. Eliot, Dawson called a culture "the way of life of a particular people adapted to a special environment."[234] Also like Eliot, he saw his model of culture as sociological. Inspired by P. G. F. Le Play and his British successors at *The Sociological Review* (such as Patrick Geddes), Dawson held from early on that culture is the "fundamental social reality" on which all other social phenomena depend; he insisted often that he used the term in its sociological sense.[235] John Mulloy has argued that the close-knit circumstances of Dawson's youth predisposed him to such a model because of its focus on small units in which "the basic elements which constitute a society are more easily perceived," as they were by Dawson in Hay-on-Wye and Craven.[236] Whatever the cause, Dawson considered this approach to culture a bridge between anthropology, sociology, and history, thus offering a basis for an integrated, interdisciplinary attitude to cultural studies like the one he recommended to historians.[237]

Dawson also rejected many contemporary conceptions of culture. For instance, he opposed any system predicating cultural development solely on economic and political advance, a position he deemed "diametrically opposed to the dominant social philosophy of the modern world, whether individualist or socialist."[238] To Dawson, wealth and power are corrupting influences, and when they become the chief focus of a fallen people's way of life, the vision without which cultures perish dims: "a

---

234. Dawson, *P&R*, 55. Reviewing Eliot's *Notes Toward the Definition of Culture*, Dawson called Eliot's definition of culture as the whole way of life of a people "my own." "Mr. T. S. Eliot on the Meaning of Culture," *The Month* n.s., 1 (March 1949): 152. Eliot acknowledged a general debt to Dawson's work in this volume. See Eliot, *Christianity and Culture* (New York: Harcourt Brace Jovanovich, 1988), 83.

235. Dawson, "Sociology as a Science," 19–20. For Le Play and his successors' importance to Dawson, see Scott, *Historian*, 72–73; and Dawson to Daniel O'Connor, 16 December 1939, in O'Connor, *Relation*, x.

236. John J. Mulloy, "Dawson on the Individual and Society," *The Dawson Newsletter* 10 (Fall 1992): 12.

237. Dawson to John J. Mulloy, 1 July 1954, Dawson Correspondence.

238. Dawson, *Enquiries*, vi.

civilization may prosper externally and grow daily larger and louder and richer and more self-confident, while at the same time it is decreasing in social vitality and losing its hold on its higher cultural traditions."[239] If he denounced what he considered liberal and Marxist models of culture for their materialism, though, he also condemned the idealism he associated with R. G. Collingwood for eliminating culture's physical aspects completely. He was more taken with Spengler's and Toynbee's paradigms, but finally found each seriously flawed. While praising Spengler's emphases on cultures' organic development, their nonrational factors, and the sensitive study of their particulars, Dawson disputed his chief conclusions. For one thing, he held that Spengler's stress on the peculiar evolution of individual cultures ignored cross-fertilization between cultures. Dawson found this hermetic idea of culture irreconcilable with the whole course of history, "which is nothing but a vast system of intercultural relations." Moreover, he did not deem civilization an ossified form of culture, as he felt Spengler did, but rather the time of greatest openness to those external influences that he thought Spengler dismissed.[240] Dawson saluted Toynbee for seeing the "absurdity" of Spengler's approach, and for treating transcultural and nonmaterial issues in his synoptic study of history. Yet he finally judged Toynbee's analysis too relativistic, culturally in early work and theologically in later volumes. He felt this interpretative framework was oversimplified and thus both inaccurate and inadequate.[241]

While Dawson stressed his differences with the likes of Spengler and Toynbee, it is important to note that the aspects of their work he lauded were those challenging modern conventions. Indeed, as this approval and his other theoretical comments suggest, he saw his writings on culture as integral to his own rebellion against modern norms. Part of the reason he welcomed Eliot's work was that it highlighted "those great primary elements of culture—family, region and religion" that Dawson

---

239. Dawson, P&R, 9. See also Christopher Dawson, "Hope and Culture: Christian Culture as a Culture of Hope," *Lumen Vitae* 9 (July–September 1954): 426–27. Chesterton voiced a similar view (*Illustrated London News*, 2 August 1924).

240. Dawson, *Dynamics*, 387, 381, 385. One contemporary called Dawson "a Catholic Spengler." Mason Wade, "A Catholic Spengler," *The Commonweal* (18 October 1935): 605.

241. Dawson, "Arnold Toynbee and the Study of History," 392, 397.

thought modern investigators neglected, but that he deemed essential.²⁴² In addition, he felt that his epoch's idea of culture had become "a sublimated abstraction," rather than the organic reality he thought Spengler rightly stressed.²⁴³ Finally, he charged that academic overspecialization and capitulations to scientism had hindered both the interdisciplinary approach he favored, and the use of analytical paradigms that accented nonempirical evidence like literature and religion. In short, Dawson thought he was "ploughing a lone furrow" due to his dissent from what he considered modern attitudes toward culture.²⁴⁴

As with his historical scholarship, Dawson rooted this portion of his rebellion in religion. Just as he asserted that people are naturally religious and that religion is the key of history, so he believed that religion is the basis of culture. He held this opinion before his conversion, as revealed by his childhood sense of living in an Anglican theocracy, his lament for the cultural gap he thought Craven had suffered due to the monasteries' dissolution, and his impressions of Winchester Cathedral, Rome, and the baroque. Additionally, he claimed that reading Ernst Troeltsch's work in 1912 generated a desire to study the relationship between religion and culture systematically.²⁴⁵ His conversion deepened this conviction, and it became central to his view of cultural development.

Dawson stressed this dynamic from his earliest writing, and summarized it in his first set of Gifford Lectures: "We cannot understand the inner form of a society unless we understand its religion. We cannot understand its cultural achievements unless we understand the religious beliefs that lie behind them."²⁴⁶ Avoiding what he considered the flaw of idealism, Dawson upheld the importance of tangible factors, like economics, customs, and laws; but he also insisted that these material activities and relations could be practiced properly only under the aegis of a spiritual

---

242. Dawson, "Mr. T. S. Eliot on the Meaning of Culture," 152.

243. Christopher Dawson, "The Study of Christian Culture as a Means of Education," *Lumen Vitae* 5 (March 1950): 175.

244. See Dawson to Douglas Horton, 25 February 1958; Dawson to John J. Mulloy, 1 July 1954 (both in Dawson Correspondence); and Christopher Dawson, "Ploughing a Lone Furrow," in *Christianity and Culture*, ed. J. Stanley Murphy (Baltimore: Helicon Press, 1960), 17.

245. Dawson referred to reading Troeltsch in a 1934 autobiographical sketch (Dawson Correspondence).

246. Dawson, *Religion and Culture*, 50. See also *Age of Gods*, 22–23; and *P&R*, viii.

and moral order.[247] He argued that religion fuses these various facets of life into the common way of life all people share by integrating "the inner world of spiritual aspiration with the outer world of social activity." It was this harmony that he found absent from modern, post-Christian society, declaring that in societies founded on faith, ones "so opposed to our own," life is "internally unified" and the "same spirit" pervades its members' multifarious manual, intellectual, and spiritual labors.[248] He saw the lack of a unifying spiritual ethic as "a relatively modern and anomalous phenomenon,"[249] but one that had already led to "the impoverishment of our whole culture" by 1929. He thus became increasingly anxious when pondering continued post-Christianity, for he held that "a society which has lost its religion becomes sooner or later a society which has lost its culture."[250] Indeed, he deemed this axiom "the central conviction which has dominated my mind ever since I began to write."[251]

Religion and the Rise (and Fall) of Western Culture

Dawson applied this dynamic and concern particularly to Western civilization. He contended that Catholic Christianity is the basis of Western culture. While rejecting Belloc's crude identification of Europe with the Faith, Dawson did assert that "the true foundation of the European community is nevertheless a spiritual one and it finds its center in Catholicism, for the Catholic Church is the living heart of the Christian tradition as Christianity is the spiritual basis of the European tradition."[252] He also insisted that traditional Christianity had imparted its

---

247. See Christopher Dawson, notes for "The Study of Catholicism in relation to the study of Christian culture," c. 1958–62, Dawson Manuscripts; and *Formation*, 44.

248. Dawson, *Enquiries*, 70–71.

249. Dawson, *Religion and Culture*, 49.

250. Dawson, *P&R*, 249, 233 (Jones highlighted these passages). Dawson further suggested that, absent a religious basis, a civilization also becomes inhuman because it denies humanity's essentially religious nature. See "Foundations of European Order," 314; and *Understanding Europe*, 229–30.

251. Dawson, *Enquiries*, vi.

252. Dawson, introduction to *The Necessity of Politics*, by Carl Schmitt (London: Sheed & Ward, 1931), 12. He explicitly rejected Belloc's equation in a 23 April 1955 letter to John J. Mulloy (Dawson Correspondence). In a 5 January 1945 letter to Harman Grisewood (Dawson Correspondence), Dawson listed humanism, the rule of law, and the principle of nationality, along with Christianity, as the essential sources of European culture.

uniqueness to the civilization it created. For example, Dawson held that Christianity gave Western culture an unmatched dynamism. Believing that history is the arena of salvation and that it is moving toward an eternal climax, he claimed, "Christian culture involves a ceaseless effort to widen the frontiers of the Kingdom of God."[253] He felt this expansiveness further differentiated the civilization founded on this faith: "what distinguishes Western culture from the other world civilizations is its *missionary character*—its transmission from one people to another in a continuous series of spiritual movements."[254] He saw this evangelical spirit and its attendant moral earnestness as the "essential characteristics" of Western civilization, even in the degraded form of post-Christian imperialism.[255]

As the reference to imperialism suggests, Dawson (like Chesterton) believed that Christianity had penetrated the West's cultural ethos so deeply that post-Christian societies were living off their Christian and Catholic capital. His study of Troeltsch may have stimulated this idea, for the German held a similar view.[256] For Dawson's part, he maintained that "the new social ideals and secular forms of cultures themselves represent partial and one-sided survivals of the Christian social tradition," as modern ideologies and institutions like democracy, nationalism, liberalism, socialism, humanitarianism, and Progress were all secular surrogates for Christianity that had been fostered by it and were rooted in it. But he felt that these imbalanced substitutes could not survive for long on their own. He declared that since secularism "did not create these moral ideals, so, too, it cannot preserve them. It lives on the spiritual capital that it has inherited from Christian civilization, and as this is exhausted something else must come to take its place."[257]

While sure that the religious impulse itself could never be driven out of a culture fully and that Christianity was likewise everlasting, Dawson

---

253. Dawson, "The Outlook for Christian Culture Today," 131.
254. Dawson, *Religion and Rise of Western Culture*, 18. Emphasis in original.
255. Dawson, "The Study of Christian Culture as a Means of Education," 180. See also Dawson to Charles Marital-de Witte, 24 March 1947, Dawson Correspondence.
256. See Scott, *Historian*, 72.
257. Dawson, RMS, xxi, 64. For his explications of these ersatz religions, see, e.g., *P&R*, 242–43; *Modern Dilemma*, 47–49; RMS, xxi; *Judgment of Nations*, 21–22; *Understanding Europe*, 20.

did contend that a specific culture could lose its Christian foundation through generations of neglect and deliberate apostasy. He feared that this was happening to modern Europe. He argued that modern criticism of traditional Christianity had furthered the secularization of European culture, thereby eroding that civilization's basis: "Instead of uniting Europe in a new spiritual unity, it had helped to destroy the spiritual tradition to which European culture owed its unity and its very existence."[258] As Christianity waned, he warned, so would the virtues lauded in its secular substitutes. Rather than having more liberty, equality, fraternity, democracy, and social advance without Christianity, Europe would decay into some type of "'totalitarian' secularism," like Communism or Fascism.[259] As Dawson held that Protestantism had abetted secularization and that current Anglo-Catholicism had capitulated to it, he judged that effective European resistance to what he saw as modern paganism and its potentially destructive impact could be found only in Roman Catholicism. He felt his church alone still upheld a corpus of traditional Christian principles that had been the basis of Western civilization historically and remained so, if only unconsciously.[260] Once again, then, his rebellion against modern irreligion rested on his belief that Roman Catholicism was the sole current institutional defender of the historical Christian faith and the culture rooted in it.

Dawson's Notes Toward the Definition of a Christian Culture

Since he believed the West is essentially Christian, and that these unconscious assumptions could and should be reawakened, Dawson's idea of a Christian culture deserves consideration. As with his study of culture generally, he focused on its Christian variety's sociological character. If a culture is the whole way of life of a particular people, then Christian culture is "the Christian way of life in its historical development," not just its theology and liturgy.[261] And, he stressed, religion, qua

---

258. Dawson, P&R, 217. See also East and West, 203–4.
259. Dawson, RMS, 65. See also Crisis Western Education, 90.
260. See draft of Dawson to the editor of the Glasgow Observer, 8 August 1947, Dawson Correspondence.
261. Dawson, "Christian Culture," 678. See also "The Challenge of Secularism," 329.

religion, is as much the basis of this culture as of any other: "The only true criterion of a Christian culture is the degree in which the social way of life is based on the Christian faith. However barbarous a society may be, however backward in the modern humanitarian sense, if its members possess a genuine Christian faith they will possess a Christian culture. . . ."[262] Dawson thought such a society's integrating principle was rooted, like the Christian approach to history, in the Incarnation, as it asserts a synergy between the sacred and profane.[263] This order is thus "essentially a sacramental culture which embodie[s] religious truth in visible and palpable forms," making it also "essentially humanist" in that "there is nothing human which does not come within its sphere and which does not in some way belong to it."[264] Yet, as with the Christian theology of history, Dawson insisted that a Christian culture's respect for the things of this world does not mean conformity to it. He held that Christian culture had traditionally been in revolt against secular culture, but that Rome alone upheld this legacy as a body in his day.[265]

Dawson felt Roman Catholicism represented these aspects of Christian culture better than other denominations. If his day's Anglo-Catholicism risked becoming wholly immanentized by its embrace of liberalism and Modernism, he thought, Protestantism had the opposite tendency. To him, Christianity's Incarnational basis makes it an inherently "culturally creative force," as it reaffirms Christ's sanctification of the temporal by being salt, light, and leaven.[266] But the Protestantism of Luther and Calvin failed his tests of a Christian culture. He deemed it anti-sacramental, being "as ferociously iconoclastic as the early Moslems," and hence also "the very antithesis of Humanism."[267] Moreover, he thought current Protestants like Barth went "further than Calvin himself in their denial of human values."[268] For Dawson, this purported

---

262. Dawson, *Historic Reality*, 14.
263. Dawson to John J. Mulloy, 26 September and 1 October 1962, Dawson Correspondence.
264. Dawson, "The Challenge of Secularism," 328.
265. See Dawson to John J. Mulloy, 11 November 1957, Dawson Correspondence.
266. Dawson, "Hope and Culture," 428.
267. Dawson, "The European Revolution," 90.
268. Dawson, "Christianity and the Humanist Tradition," *Dublin Review* 226 (Winter 1952): 2.

hostility to culture was another Protestant contribution to the sacred's disappearance from modern life, as it helped erect "a barrier between religion and life which contributed so largely to the progressive secularization of Western culture"[269] by destroying the "medieval unity of religion and social life."[270] As that referent suggests, he found such views radically incompatible with Catholicism. To him, "it has always been the tendency of Catholicism to incarnate itself in culture,"[271] as "the Catholic ideal" is to order the whole of life towards unity "not by the denial and destruction of natural human values, but by bringing them into living relation with spiritual truth and spiritual reality."[272] Given this basic, and in his mind insuperable, difference between the two theologies, he held that it is Catholics who "have to keep alive the concept of Christian culture in a secular world."[273] Dawson's outlook may seem tendentious, but as faithful a Protestant and severe a critic as Niebuhr felt it had some validity: "It is also plausible to accuse Protestantism of being either too individualistic or as allowing for the secularization of culture. Undoubtedly it is the genius of Catholicism to do justice to the social character of both religion and of human existence."[274]

Because he considered Roman Catholics best suited to carry out this traditional task, Dawson was alarmed by many of his co-religionists' apparent ignorance of their heritage. He lamented that even in 1950 "there is still no common Catholic culture"; he worried that Roman Catholics were more and more under the sway of "the increasing secularization of English culture," as agents of secular culture (like the cinema and press) had greater influence on Catholics than the organs of Catholic culture had on the non-Catholic majority.[275] Indeed, he concluded in 1956 that the average English Catholic "shares the general atmosphere of modern

---

269. Dawson, "Hope and Culture," 430.
270. Dawson, "Christianity and the Humanist Tradition," 5.
271. Dawson, *Formation*, 14.
272. Dawson, *Essays in Order*, vii.
273. Dawson, *Crisis Western Education*, 149. "There are many, especially among the Protestants and the sectarians, who look on Christianity and culture as alien from one another.... In their extreme forms such views are irreconcilable with Catholicism." Dawson, "The Challenge of Secularism," 329.
274. Niebuhr, "Mote to One," 18.
275. Dawson, "The English Catholics 1850–1950," *Dublin Review* 217 (Winter 1950): 10–11.

secularized Western culture."[276] As Dawson rested his hopes for Christian re-enculturation on Catholics, yet not only found them ill-prepared for this vocation but also capitulating further to modern irreligion along with the rest of society, it is not surprising that his interest in education grew over the years.

Dawson's work in cultural studies did not cover as many periods nor fill as many volumes as his historical scholarship, but it still drew substantial commentary from his peers. Fellow Roman Catholics were among his most favorable critics. E. I. Watkin, for example, called his friend "first and last" a scholar of "human culture in general but most particularly of Christian culture."[277] Moreover, the eminent Thomist Etienne Gilson held that Dawson's Gifford Lectures provided him with what he had lacked for forty years.[278] Yet noted non-Roman Catholics also praised his writing on culture. Besides Niebuhr's concession, Eliot told Dawson that he valued his opinion in this field more highly than anyone else's.[279] And C. S. Lewis called his first set of Giffords "exactly what I wanted . . . a great treat."[280] A less laudatory non-Catholic, however, was Ananda Coomarssway, who in 1956 charged him with what later thinkers would call Eurocentrism: "there are still men like Christopher Dawson for whom 'the future of Western culture' and 'the fate of humanity' are one and the same thing."[281] There were fewer such critiques, though, than future ages more attuned to issues of cultural pluralism would be inclined to offer.

As with his historiography, the centrality of Dawson's religion to his cultural works was noted often. Edwin Halsey judged that his stress on religion's role in culture formation was his "unique contribution" to this field. John Mulloy also found his "specific contribution" to cultural studies to be his insistence that a culture is an organic unity of spiritual and

---

276. Christopher Dawson, "Civilization in Crisis," *Catholic World* 182 (January 1956): 251.
277. Watkin, "Tribute to Christopher Dawson," 974.
278. Gilson to Frank Sheed, 22 August 1950, Dawson Correspondence.
279. T. S. Eliot to Dawson, 8 February 1949, Dawson Correspondence.
280. C. S. Lewis to Dawson, 27 September 1948; quoted in Scott, *Historian*, 158–59.
281. Ananda Coomarssway, "Responsibility of the English-Speaking People," *Cross-Currents* 6 (Winter 1956): 37. Dawson dealt with the kinds of issues raised by Coomarssway two years later in "Is the Church Too Western?" (1958); reprinted in *The Dawson Newsletter* 11 (Summer 1993): 14–16.

natural elements, while Richard Janet has concluded more recently that Dawson's stress on this synergy has "deeply influenced" some Catholic intellectuals.[282] But, as was also the case with his historical work, readers debated the value of a particularly Catholic focus and framework. A recent critic (himself a Catholic prelate) commends the nuclearity of Dawson's Catholicism for giving his cultural analysis "warmth and sympathetic penetration."[283] Yet Hayden White felt this commitment led Dawson to demonize other faiths, accusing him of attributing "all the evils of the modern Western world" to Protestantism.[284] If an exaggeration, this charge does show the extent to which Dawson's religion also shaped this facet of his work, and how it helped drive reception of these writings. Indeed, most recent scholars of his cultural studies, chiefly Roman Catholics, continue to focus on how his faith served as his critical vision's foundation.[285]

Uniting the "Scattered Forces of Christendom": Dawson and Ecumenism

The pivotal importance of Dawson's religion to his scholarship and his sharp distinctions between Catholicism and other faiths does not mean that he shunned other creeds or their adherents. His desire for unity and integration, and a belief that cultural cohesion finally rested on religious reunification, made him a proponent of ecumenism from early on.[286] Tellingly, he judged the Oxford Movement's "great and perhaps

---

282. Edwin Halsey, "Christopher Dawson," *Integrity* 4 (June 1950): 47; John J. Mulloy, "Continuity and Development in Christopher Dawson's Thought," in *Dynamics*, 430; and Richard Janet, "'Cold, Bare Ruined Choirs'?: Reflections on the Nature of Catholic History," in *Catholicism at the Millennium*, ed. Gerald Miller and Wilburn Stancil (Kansas City, Mo.: Rockhurst University Press, 2001), 8.

283. Rembert Weakland, foreword to *Religion and the Rise of Western Culture*, by Christopher Dawson (New York: Image Books, 1991), n.p.

284. White, "Dawson's Idea of History," 279. Another respected peer, Hugh Trevor-Roper, likewise found it "inconceivable" that "so learned a scholar should appear, in this one respect, so parochial." Trevor-Roper, "Books in General," *New Statesman and Nation*, 11 March 1950, 276.

285. See, e.g., *Christianity and Western Civilization*, especially the essays by Joseph Koterski, James Hitchcock, and Glenn Olson.

286. For Christian unity as the precondition for European cultural unity, see, e.g., *RMS*, 138–39; *Religion and Culture*, 217 (Jones highlighted this passage in his copy); *Formation*, 298.

unique importance" to be "the intimacy of social contact" that it created between Catholics and Protestants for the first time since the Reformation.[287] Moreover, the Order Group thought it struck its notes in a "more ecumenical key" than the Chesterbellocians.[288] At a more personal level, Dawson often attended Evensong after his conversion—asserting, when queried about the Catholic Church's view of this practice, "I never ask."[289] Finally, correspondents regularly saw him as an ecumenist, an impression his replies reinforced.

Dawson's reading of the signs of his time led him to regard Christian reunification as especially propitious and pressing in his era. He held that the split in Christendom occasioned by the Renaissance and Reformation had begun to heal in the nineteenth century with the rise of interdenominational missionary societies.[290] He thought that this movement toward unity had intensified in his day, aided by a similar secular push, concluding in the early 1940s that "the present age is more favorable to the cause of unity than any time since the Middle Ages."[291] His sense of ecumenism's promise was given urgency by his conviction that it was also a crucial component of confronting post-Christianity. Like C. S. Lewis, Dawson deemed the core beliefs uniting all orthodox Christians more important than whatever separated them, especially in an era he found hostile to religious belief of any kind: "our position today is no longer that of a Catholic minority in a Protestant society, but that of a religious minority in a secular or neo-pagan civilization . . . we have to deal not with the validity of Anglican orders but with the existence of the human soul and the ultimate foundations of the moral order."[292]

---

287. Dawson, *Formation*, 8–9.

288. Knowles, "Obituary," 558. See also *Order* memo, 19 October 1928, Dawson Correspondence.

289. Dawson quoted in Scott, *Historian*, 149.

290. See Christopher Dawson, "The Movement Towards Christian Unity in the Nineteenth and Twentieth Centuries," 1960, Dawson Manuscripts. In particular, he noted the Evangelical Alliance of 1846 and the 1860 World Missionary Conference at Edinburgh.

291. Dawson, *Judgment of Nations*, 181. See Christopher Dawson, "European Literature and the Latin Middle Ages," *Dublin Review* 224 (Spring 1950): 32–33, for the secular movement toward European unity.

292. Christopher Dawson, "English Catholicism and Victorian Liberalism," *The Tablet*, 1950; reprinted in *The Dawson Newsletter* 11 (Fall 1993): 9.

Dawson even felt that the majority's disdain for religion could be beneficial, if it led Christians to a more unified understanding of, and deeper devotion to, their shared faith:

> if Christianity becomes a minority religion, if it is threatened by hostility and persecution, then the common cause of Christianity becomes a reality and not merely a phrase, and there is a center round which the scattered forces of Christendom can rally and reorganize.... It may even be that the very strength of the forces that are gathering against the Church and against religion will make for unity by forcing Christians together, as it were, in spite of themselves.[293]

Whatever the cause of this unity, Dawson thought it essential if Christianity was to resist secular ideologies successfully. To that end, he opposed Catholic provincialism. While he had been moved by Craven's splendid Catholic isolation, Dawson cautioned that such an approach also contains dangers. He held that since Christendom's breakup began, Catholics had tended to adopt a "purely defensive attitude, to live, as has been said, in a state of siege." He sympathized with this perceived need to simply preserve the faith, especially given the inauspicious historical and demographic position of British Catholics and the present post-Christian setting. But he also warned that this truculent strategy can ultimately imperil the cause it seeks to defend by fostering that ignorance of the Catholic heritage that so disturbed him, and thus creating "a culture-less Catholicism, a society of Christian barbarians."[294] Dawson's ardent belief in Catholicism as the root and leaven of Western culture, though, provoked admonitions against this tendency to retreat into a Christian ghetto out of dismay at secularism's seeming strengthening in his era. He felt that if Catholics forsook Britain as irredeemably pagan, their withdrawal would only help make it more pagan.[295] To him, then, Roman Catholics cannot accommodate modern unbelief; but their required rebellion must confront post-Christianity actively and directly,

---

293. Dawson, *Judgment of Nations*, 181–82.

294. Dawson, "Education and Christian Culture," 219. Interestingly, Halsey ("Dawson") credited Dawson with helping to move the Church out of "that state of siege in which it had been living for four centuries."

295. See Dawson to Douglas Woodruff, 20 August 1947; and Dawson to Bernard Wall, 9 September 1946, Dawson Correspondence.

and should seek out all people of good will to "work for a real restoration of Christian culture rather than merely to fight a defensive action in a purely conservative spirit."[296]

Dawson advocated these ecumenical ideals not only in writing, but also through extensive participation in two organizations during the early 1940s. The first was the Sword of the Spirit. The Sword took its vision from Arthur Cardinal Hinsley, who (goaded by Dawson and Barbara Ward) founded it following the fall of France in 1940. Hinsley wanted both to inoculate British Catholics against charges of dual loyalty, and to institutionally unite people of good will in Britain and abroad against the totalitarian threat to traditional Western ideals. The Sword was thus "the first Catholic attempt to found an Ecumenical movement in England."[297] Hinsley named Dawson its vice president, indicating that he should be its leading spirit and guiding light.[298] Its early days were filled with promising successes. Not only was there wide international interest, but other British churches were receptive to Hinsley's pleas for a common defense of Western culture. The Sword's zenith was a two-day interdenominational meeting on social and international issues held in May 1941 under the joint patronage of Hinsley and the Archbishop of Canterbury. A week after this convocation, the previously suspicious Anglican *Church Times* called the gatherings "a remarkable demonstration of a united Christian front." In June, *The Friend*, a Quaker newspaper, dubbed the Sword an "immense advance," because it revealed a Catholic willingness to cooperate with other churches, and promoted ideas that were "radical and far-reaching."[299]

These practices and notions were too radical and far-reaching for many conservatives in all denominations, though. Numerous Anglican and Free Church clergy were chary of close cooperation with Roman Catholics, doubts that were only confirmed by some Catholics' attitudes and behavior.[300] Clerics like Victor White and Archbishop Peter Amigo

---

296. Dawson, *Crisis Western Education*, 131.

297. Scott, *Historian*, 139. Dawson had also been involved previously with the Committee for War Aims, which had concerns related to those of the Sword.

298. Hinsley to Dawson, 16 January 1941, Dawson Correspondence.

299. *Church Times*, 16 May 1941; and *The Friend*, 27 June 1941.

300. See Michael Walsh, "Ecumenism in War-Time Britain: The Sword of the Spirit and Religion and Life," part 1, *Heythrop Journal* 23 (July 1982): 243–58, and part 2, *Heythrop Journal*

objected to interdenominational meetings and held that joint prayer services could be seen as an abdication by Roman Catholics of their claim to exclusive truth. Hinsley found such ideas parochial, asserting that "I am wholeheartedly with the idea of *leaven*," an opinion Dawson echoed consistently.[301] Dawson's and Hinsley's views, though, were finally defeated. In August 1941, hardliners in the hierarchy persuaded the Sword to restrict full membership to Roman Catholics. A month later, Hinsley's two chief theologians affirmed this position, and advised further that public religious events be excluded from the Sword's activities. Dawson considered such strictures a death blow, arguing that such a regimen would reduce the Sword to a "sort of Better Britain movement which could be done better under purely secular auspices."[302] However, most of the British hierarchy supported the exclusivist position, and it was ultimately endorsed by Rome. Hinsley bowed to this formidable opposition, but resigned the Sword's presidency in 1942 and died in 1943. Dawson remained active in the Sword, but grew increasingly disenchanted, especially after Hinsley's successor, Bernard Cardinal Griffin, redefined its principles in a way Dawson felt would further complicate relations with non-Roman Catholic associate members.[303] By 1947, he was wishing that the Sword would disband rather than betray its ecumenical foundations any further, comparing it to a broken-down coach without a driver.[304] He thought it was no longer worth traveling on a vehicle that had reversed direction from its original destination of ecumenical outreach.

He had a similar experience at the *Dublin Review*. Hinsley named him editor of the venerable *"Dublin"* in 1940, one of many parallels to Daw-

---

23 (October 1982): 377–94; Stewart Mews, "The Sword of the Spirit: A Catholic Crusade of 1940," in *The Church and War*, ed. W. J. Sheils (Oxford: Blackwell, 1983) 425–26; Thomas Moloney, *Westminster, Whitehall and the Vatican: The Role of Cardinal Hinsley, 1939–43* (London: Burns & Oates, 1985), 198–99.

301. Hinsley to Dawson, 30 August 1941; quoted in Scott, *Historian*, 145. Emphasis in original. See also, e.g., Dawson to Hinsley, 1 September 1941; and Dawson, undated essay on the Sword (Dawson Correspondence).

302. Dawson to Hinsley, 4 November 1941; quoted in Moloney, *Westminster*, 200.

303. See Dawson to A. C. F. Beales, 6 May 1947, Dawson Correspondence.

304. Dawson to John Murray, 5 August 1947, Dawson Correspondence. For the Sword's later years, and its growing Roman Catholic exclusiveness, see M. Vivian Brand, *The Social Catholic Movement in England, 1920–1955* (London: Pageant Press, 1963), 197–200.

son's work with the Sword. Dawson saw the journal as an instrument for upholding Western culture in a time of totalitarianism, both in its editorials and its welcome of pieces from refugee writers. He also made it a deliberately ecumenical review, encouraging contributions from any defender of the West regardless of religious affiliation, a contrast to the *Dublin*'s traditional focus on more exclusively Catholic concerns.[305] Lastly, Barbara Ward was his assistant editor, thus mirroring part of the Sword's division of labor. The *Dublin* also imitated the Sword's early success. Dawson drew continental and international interest, while also cultivating thoughtful, but non-Catholic, Britons like A. D. Lindsay. Just as the Sword's expansiveness inspired conservative opposition, though, so did the *Dublin*'s.

Douglas Jerrold (whose firm published the *Dublin*) was especially disturbed by its editorial direction. For a time, he saw Dawson as a good czar being misled by leftist Ward. But Dawson made clear in 1942 that he opposed Jerrold's die-hard conservatism, and wanted the journal to be a front for neither Catholic rightists nor leftists.[306] Jerrold then tried to remove him from the editorship, but was blocked by Hinsley. Jerrold finally ousted Dawson in 1944 on the pretext that the *Dublin*'s editor should live in London. Dawson, though, was sure that he had been deposed because of his editorial policy, and later observers have agreed that his identification with Hinsley's ecumenism cost him this post. Once again, his ecumenical sympathies were too strong for powerful conservatives and left Dawson estranged from an organization he had entered with high hopes.[307]

Dawson's ecumenical efforts and rocky relationship with Catholic conservatives does not mean, however, that he was at all a religious rela-

---

305. "[T]he appeal is limited neither to Catholics only nor to the citizens of France and Britain alone. The Christian cause at the present moment is also the common cause of all who are defending our civilization against the blind assault of mass despotism and the idolatry of power which has resulted in a new paganism that is destructive of all moral and intellectual values." Christopher Dawson, "Editorial Note," *Dublin Review* 207 (July 1940): 3.

306. See Dawson to Robert Speaight, 27 August 1942; Speaight to Dawson, 30 August 1942; and Dawson to Speaight, 5 September 1942, Dawson Correspondence.

307. See Dawson to A. Farquharson, 6 February 1946, Dawson Correspondence; and Nichols, "Dawson's Catholic Setting," 43–44. Dawson continued to write for the *Dublin* after his dismissal, though.

tivist. Indeed he consistently rebuked the Toynbean idea that all world religions are equally valid parallel traditions of revelation.[308] Among Christians, he thought genuine reunion could only occur if Roman Catholicism were recognized as Christianity's normative form;[309] such a view follows logically from his belief that Roman Catholicism is the authentic successor of the apostles and the most faithful preserver of historical Christianity. He argued further that because this religion is uniquely True, it is thus the sole satisfactory solution to post-Christian dilemmas. To him, the Catholic Church was the "only power" capable of "overcoming the spiritual disorder of the modern world,"[310] for it is the "only power" that stands for the "deeper spiritual realities and traditions which secular civilization has lost and for lack of which is dying."[311] When a rabbi called such remarks harmful to interfaith efforts, Dawson revealed his view of ecumenism's limits. He replied that Catholics feel that their faith has a unique, providential mission, and that to downplay that conviction for the sake of congenial interfaith ties would be to sacrifice religious truth to social convention.[312]

Dawson's approach to ecumenism may hence seem quite conservative overall. Indeed, nothing in his ideas contradicts current Roman Catholic teaching on this topic.[313] If his quarrels with his day's conservatives appear antiquated, then, it must be emphasized that his notions were precocious. His era's Catholic Church gave interfaith outreach a much lower priority; and if measures like joint prayer and interdenominational meetings have become accepted and encouraged, they were not always so welcome. In fact, Dawson's work itself was often more influential among non-Catholics, like Eliot and Toynbee.[314] If his views on ec-

---

308. See, e.g., Dawson to Toynbee, 5 November 1954, Dawson Correspondence; Dawson to Bede Griffiths, 30 July 1957, Dawson Correspondence; Dawson, "Education and the Study of Christian Culture," *Studies* 42 (Autumn 1953): 295.
309. See Dawson to Andrew Beck, 10 April 1944, Dawson Correspondence.
310. Dawson, *East and West*, 216.
311. Dawson quoted in "1,247 Graduated from St. John's," *New York Times*, 15 June 1959, 22.
312. Dawson to Jacob Sodden, undated. Sodden had written to Dawson on 16 June 1959 to criticize the St. John's speech reported in the *New York Times*. Dawson Correspondence.
313. See *Catechism of the Catholic Church*, Articles 820–22.
314. See Scott, *Historian*, 148, 213; Edward Norman, *Church and Society in England, 1770–1970* (Oxford: Clarendon Press, 1976), 364–65; Hastings, *English Christianity*, 238; and

umenism no longer seem advanced, it is because of how much the Church has adjusted its position on this issue rather than being a sign of any grievous misunderstanding or extraordinary rigidity by his conservative contemporaries.

"I Hate the Changes in the Liturgy": Dawson and the Changing Church

Dawson's ideas of ecumenism, its limits, and the extent of change within the Church that he considered wise all shaped his attitude toward its liturgical reforms and Vatican II. His ecumenical bent led him to welcome the council initially, believing that it could promote mutual understanding between Catholics and Protestants. He even delayed publishing a series of lectures on the return to Christian unity in anticipation of any ecumenical action it might take.[315] But his ultimate reaction to Vatican II and related developments, like Greene's and Jones's, focused more on internal church matters, particularly alterations in the liturgy. While touted as necessary reforms by their advocates, Dawson deemed these changes disquieting exacerbations of disturbing trends.

Even in the 1950s, he was distressed by tendencies within the Catholic Church that seemed antagonistic to his reasons for joining it. For instance, he chided certain Catholic theologians for their "philistine and patronising" view of the baroque. Dawson charged in 1958 that these interpretations, which criticized the baroque for an overly materialistic concern with cultural forms, ignored its "great achievement" in "mysticism and the interior life," factors that were central to his conversion. He feared that these misreadings indicated the growth of a "Puritan movement within the Church" that would bring inside its doors the Protestant divorce between religion and culture. This anxiety did not abate with time, as he reproved "pro-Lutheran utterances" by the Catholic press more than a decade later.[316] Despite his precocious ecumenical

---

Gerald Russello, "Christopher Dawson: Is There a Christian Culture?" *Commonweal*, 5 April 1996, 21.

315. Dawson to John J. Mulloy, 5 February 1959, Dawson Correspondence. These lectures are available in manuscript at the University of St. Thomas.

316. Scott, *Historian*, 176, 175, 206.

sympathies, then, Dawson thought the Church would be ill-advised to adopt what he saw as sectarian theological errors.

Dawson also worried that Catholic officialdom was increasingly concerned with "belief" rather than "faith," and that it risked accommodating worldliness in the process. Already in 1942, Jones was reporting that Dawson found "a belief in effecting things by organization and formulas etc. etc. (among Catholics) growing rather than lessening." By adopting a utilitarian mind-set and focusing on the external formulas and formalities of religion, Dawson felt, Catholics risked losing a love of truth for its own sake, and for the metarational experiences that he saw as Christianity's dynamic core and that had helped attract him to Rome. In such a scenario, he warned, Roman Catholicism finally becomes essentially indistinguishable from irreligious ideologies, as "'propaganda' is universally dominant in the Church as outside it, and once you yield interiorly to the propagandist attitude you're sunk."[317] Like Greene, therefore, Dawson saw many traits of Catholicism that had initially drawn him to it being undercut within the Church during his later years.

Dawson's apprehensions about contemporary Roman Catholicism's commitment to upholding its heritage against modern cultural pressures crystallized, as did Greene's and Jones's, around the issue of liturgical reform. His Anglo-Catholic upbringing implanted a love of ritual in Dawson, and he was especially devoted to the Latin Mass, regarding it as the linguistic articulation of Roman Catholicism's universal validity:

> The existence of a common liturgical language of some kind is a sign of the Church's mission to reverse the curse of Babel and to create a bond of unity between the peoples. The nations that are still divided from one another by the barriers of race and language leave their divisions and antipathies at the door of the Church and worship together in a tongue which belongs to none and yet which is common to all.[318]

---

317. David Jones to Harman Grisewood, 1 June 1942; quoted in Scott, *Historian*, 141. See also Dawson to J. H. Oldham, 18 April 1942, Dawson Correspondence. He echoed these concerns nearly fifteen years later in a letter to Watkin (Scott, *Historian*, 175).

318. Dawson to Col. Ross-Duggan, 18 June 1953; quoted in Scott, *Historian*, 206.

Against charges that this rite reflected a Western bias, Dawson countered in 1958 that using Latin gives worship a "universal and supertemporal character which is accentuated by its music, which is so remote from the modern West. For what has the Mass to do with Western culture? It is the eternal offering of an eternal priesthood."[319] He believed that, although this ritual had originated in the West, its eternal dimension allowed it to transcend that genesis, thus making it equally appropriate for all societies.

Yet Dawson was not a liturgical reactionary. He regarded the sacraments around which the liturgy is built as absolutes, but their specific ritual expressions as relative, and hence subject to change for good cause.[320] It was the particular adjustments made in the 1950s and 1960s that he criticized, then, rather than the idea of change itself, for he judged the new rites ill-considered and insufficient replacements. For example, he saw the loss of rituals like Gregorian chant as unfortunate and unnecessary; he even opined that Anglicanism conserved Catholic ceremonials better than the current Roman church.[321] Finally, although (like Greene) he did not consider the vernacular liturgy an inherently flawed idea, Dawson deemed its manifestation in his day a poorly translated "stunt," one that provoked a rare flash of anger: "I hate the changes in the liturgy."[322] He did not live to sign the 1971 appeal to retain the Latin Mass that Greene did. But the statement's stress on this rite's importance to Christian and Western culture, and on the need for the Church to resist modern technocracy's encroachments, is in the spirit of Dawson's objections to the Church's mid-century course, as substantiated by the presence of like-minded friends (such as Jones, Watkin, and Dawson's son-in-law, Rivers Scott) among its signatories.

These cultural complaints were the core of Dawson's opposition to the Church's modifications, and they arose from his historical sensibility and long-standing veneration of tradition. He thought that any benefits

---

319. Dawson, "Is the Church Too Western?" 15.

320. See Dawson to John J. Mulloy, 26 September and 1 October 1962, Dawson Correspondence.

321. See Knowles, "Obituary," 558; and M. D. Knowles, "Christopher Dawson, 1889–1970," 442.

322. Dawson quoted in Scott, *Historian*, 175, 205.

Tradition, Inheritance, and World   279

the alterations brought did not compensate for their break with centuries of practice. Conceding that the Church should be flexible when crafting specific articulations of its universal beliefs, he still cautioned that "it has its own internal tradition which it maintains with the most scrupulous fidelity and which it can never surrender." He felt further that upholding this heritage is especially vital in a post-Christian age: "though the Church no longer inspires and dominates the external culture of the modern world, it still remains the guardian of all the riches of its own inner life and is the bearer of a sacred tradition," one belonging not just to Catholicism but also to the culture founded on that faith.[323] Even if the Catholic liturgy is not limited to the West, it has played a crucial role in shaping that civilization, and such a legacy demands respect.

To part with it or any of its facets, Dawson hence asserted, is to draw the Church closer to the world by depriving it of elements that distinguish it from the regnant agnostic milieu, as well as to relinquish pieces of the Western patrimony. Doing so can be licit, but, in his mind, the motive and replacement needed to be more compelling than those offered by his day's liturgical reformers. To treat tradition lightly was another symptom of what Dawson considered a dangerous flirtation with the modern temper by some Catholics, and was one of the cultural tendencies he had sought to combat through his conversion. He thought that resisting its perceived presence within the Church would preserve Roman Catholicism's proper role as defender of historical Christianity and the culture created by it for his generation, while also preventing the disenfranchisement of his ancestors in the democracy of the dead. As David Knowles summarizes, Dawson felt that if Roman Catholics abandoned so many components of the liturgical structure created by centuries of Christian Europe, particularly when Christianity was already a weakened cultural force, they would betray "a precious legacy held on trust."[324]

Dawson's views on the changes in the Church during the latter part of his life, like Greene's, exemplify the pattern described by Knox. Having

---

323. Dawson, "The Outlook for Christian Culture Today," 135–36. See also Dawson to *The Catholic Herald*, 28 September 1951.
324. Knowles, "Obituary," 558.

joined the Church largely because it represented the most complete form of traditional Christianity to him, Dawson used that perception persistently as the standard for measuring its behavior. Hence, when the facets of Catholicism that he had found most congenial during his conversion seemed threatened by apparent accommodations of modernity, he began to consider the Church at risk of renouncing its fiduciary responsibilities. His objections thus indicate the firm hold Dawson's conversion experiences had on his religious vision: the Church of his early impressions remained a wiser model of stewardship to him than did its later reality.

Critic and Questioner: Dawson's Rhetorical Roles

Although these changes disturbed Dawson greatly, they did not damage his fundamental faith fatally, as he remained a devout Roman Catholic until death. If his convictions' content has been specified, further attention to their forms is required before his religious development can be assessed fully. Douglas Woodruff's tribute, that "the essential things which Christopher Dawson had to say were unpopular," reveals that even the kind of conservative Catholic with whom Dawson often disagreed discerned the role of a rebel that pervaded his career.[325] If this was his chief rhetorical identity, Dawson, like Chesterton, was also concerned with, and was seen as exhibiting, a prophetic one.

Beyond his praise of the likes of Newman and Maistre for being prophets, and his attraction to Roman Catholicism, the papacy, and medieval times because of their perceived embodiment of Christianity's prophetic dimension, Dawson himself was often deemed a prophet. For example, contemporaries compared him to Jeremiah, Amos, and Hosea.[326] Some reviewers considered this designation a compliment. Edwin Halsey, for instance, concluded in 1950 that he "retains the role of the true prophet."[327] Other critics acknowledged this role but disap-

---

325. Douglas Woodruff, "Obituary: Christopher Dawson," *The Tablet*, 6 June 1970, 558. For a more recent cognate classification of his thought, see Lukacs, "Order and History," 50–51.

326. V. A. Demant, *Theology of Society* (London: Faber & Faber, 1947), 187; and White, "Dawson's Idea of History," 265, n. 34.

327. Halsey, "Dawson," 48. See also Charles Donovan, "The Tradition Behind Our Learning," *America*, 8 April 1961, 85; and Knowles, "Obituary," 558.

proved of it or sought to downplay it. Andrew Beck, in 1943, found Dawson too influenced by the Old Testament prophets, while Crane Brinton stressed in 1958 that he "is in no sense a wild man, a prophet of doom."[328] Some of his work's most recent analysts have also used this appellation, usually favorably.[329]

Unlike Greene, who also was so dubbed, but like Chesterton, Dawson showed a conscious interest in this role. He suggested that prophets exercise an essential social function, especially in a secular age, by keeping a culture's natural religious yearnings on a positive course.[330] He reflected on the subject of prophecy from at least the 1920s and often appeared to assume this posture rhetorically. Even as late as 1960, he declared that "the important thing is to make people realize the predicament in which our modern civilization stands and the danger of allowing it to drift," clearly the prophet's function.[331] Yet Dawson never called himself one. In addition to his personal humility, he also at times seemed to assert a conflict between being a prophet and a rebel. Even as he praised Roman Catholicism and the papacy for rhyming these roles, he also contrasted writers who "consciously accept the prophetic role" with those who are the "critics and questioners . . . disturbed by the prevailing trends . . . who tried to maintain or restore a certain standard of moral or civilized values."[332] Although Dawson appeared to regard American culture as particularly prone to this split, his sense of incompatibility between these roles, at least in some instances, remains instructive about his own preferences. If he did not always see a need to select between them, his reluctance to claim the prophetic mantle implies that, when choice was required, he judged it more vital to be a rebel than a prophet. His own work and its reception, however, reveal that a prophet can also

---

328. Beck quoted in Scott, *Historian*, 148; and Brinton, review of *Dynamics*, 273.

329. See, e.g., *The Catholic Writer*, ed. Ralph McInerny (San Francisco: Ignatius Press, 1991), 34; *Christianity and Western Civilization*, 12, 52; and Caldecott and Morrill, *Eternity*, 1, 17, 34, 54, 94.

330. See Dawson, *Religion and Culture*, 83.

331. Christopher Dawson, *America and the Secularization of Modern Culture* (Houston, Tex.: University of St. Thomas Press, 1960), 31. See also, e.g., his 1920s notes on the Hebrew prophets in Dawson Manuscripts.

332. Christopher Dawson, "The Tradition and Destiny of American Literature," *The Critic*, November 1957; reprinted in *The Dawson Newsletter* 12 (Fall 1994): 2.

be, and be seen as, a critic and questioner of prevailing trends, who tries to restore moral values.

Refusing All Compromise: Conclusion

The nature of Dawson's warnings and protests against dominant ideals helps situate his thought among other British Catholic questioners and critics of post-Christianity. His biographer judges that, of Dawson's many affinities with Newman, he "above all" shared the Cardinal's distaste for secularist anti-dogmatism and its developments.[333] But Dawson also held that "the gulf which separates the world of Newman's *Loss and Gain* . . . from the world of George Orwell's *1984* or Koestler's *Darkness at Noon* is not one that can be measured in terms of years or generations."[334] Dawson thought that his era was facing a uniquely menacing manifestation of liberalism's ramifications, especially its disregard for precedent, due to the unprecedented ascendancy of confident agnosticism. He felt that by the early twentieth century, "the goal of the Liberal Enlightenment and Revolution had been reached and Europe at last possessed a completely secularized culture,"[335] a milieu that was utterly unlike that met by Newman or any other ancestor and one in which "civilization has cut adrift from its old moorings and is floating on a tide of change. Custom and tradition and law and authority have lost their old sacredness and moral prestige."[336] As Anglo-Catholics concurrently forsook the Tractarian reverence for tradition, Dawson decided that Roman Catholicism was the lone corporate twentieth-century defender of the heritage of orthodox Christianity and its culture against regnant irreligion and its repercussions. His cautions about the Church's course at the end of his life were thus fueled, in part, by anxiety that his age might behold the further erosion, and perhaps eclipse, of this integral element of Catholic identity and of religion's historical role as "the guardian of tra-

---

333. Christina Scott, Biographical Note to *The Spirit of the Oxford Movement and "Newman's Place in History,"* by Christopher Dawson (London: Saint Austin Press, 2001), xiv.

334. Dawson, "English Catholicism and Victorian Liberalism," 9.

335. Dawson, "End of an Age," 387.

336. Dawson, "Civilization in Crisis," 246. See also *P&R*, 228; "End of an Age," 391; *Christianity and Sex*, 5; *Tradition and Inheritance*, 32; *Religion and Culture*, 49; "Education and Christian Culture," 220.

dition."[337] Without vigilance against growing disrespect for precedent within Roman ranks, he feared, his generation might see the rising tide of Western secularism loosen even the Rock of Peter from its moorings and finally engulf it and the remnants of the civilization built upon it, a concern that Greene and Jones echoed.

While Dawson's religious views did not go through the manifold stages of Chesterton's or the substantive shifts of Greene's, then, they did not lack dynamism. If he defined his core convictions comparatively early, his application of them to diverse fields and his responses to cultural and internal church developments gave his vision constant vitality, even as it was driven by different forces than his fellow converts'. Whereas Chesterton's spiritual journey was spurred by a search for sanity and a childlike celebration of Being, and Greene's by a desire for a persuasive explanation of evil, Dawson's was impelled by a reverence for history and religion's cultural fruits.

His religiously drenched childhood, especially the faith of his father, fostered and temporarily satisfied these yearnings. But schoolboy exposure to liberal Christianity generated tension with Dawson's inherited Anglo-Catholicism, and he eventually could not sustain the incongruity between his memories and desires and their sensed inadequate expression in current Anglicanism. While his ensuing agnosticism was short-lived, due to his boyhood religious experiences' emotional force, Dawson remained dissatisfied intellectually with his recovered Anglo-Catholicism, yet could not conceive of a more viable option. The confluence of events of 1909, though, revealed a previously unimagined possibility. Seeing Roman Catholicism as a living religion by witnessing its cultural manifestations, starting to study the counter-modern Tractarians who approached Christianity through history and often ended up in Rome as a result, and falling in love with a Roman Catholic, while deepening other such friendships, all began to suggest a solution to his quest. He nevertheless moved slowly, as he faced intellectual difficulties and emotional anxieties connected with a conversion to Roman Catholicism. But these strains did not deter him from finally accepting a faith he concluded was the most coherent, historically valid form of Christianity,

---

337. Dawson, *Religion and Culture*, 50.

one that also reintegrated childhood virtues, like authority and tradition, that seemed absent from contemporary Anglicanism, offered the grace he felt required for beatitude, and alone confirmed his rebellion and prophetic witness against modernity.

Orthodox Roman Catholicism became his work's basis. Drawing on venerable Catholic theologies, Dawson held that a religious, Catholic Christian perspective could supply a wider and more accurate reading of history and cultural development than secularist views, without sacrificing scholarly standards. His stresses on metahistory, the centrality of religion to human nature, history, and culture, and the singularity of Christianity and the culture it created all stood in conscious contrast to modern empiricist, historicist, and Progressive approaches. This standpoint helped produce what Dawson and others deemed his most useful and original insights; and his peers also saw it as being rebellious and as integral to his outlook, even if they did not always praise its effect on his interpretations.

The wide range of material to which Dawson applied this perspective combined with his sympathetic study of his subjects to help shape an ecumenical sensibility that rejected retreat into a Catholic bunker, and that provoked considerable conservative opposition. However much Dawson valued dialogue between faiths, though, he always saw Roman Catholicism as the only source of ultimate unity. To him, it alone provided the proper balance between spirit and matter, universality and historicity, religion and culture, that allowed men and cultures to respect the world without being conformed to it. He feared the Church was deviating from these norms near the end of his life under the assaults of a puritan separation of religion and culture from one side and a bureaucratic, utilitarian proclivity that disrespected tradition from the other, and he was thus anxious about alterations of the ancient liturgy. If he was in the vanguard on ecumenism, but the rearguard on liturgical change, Dawson's motive was the same in both cases: he favored engaging other religions and post-Christian culture, but only in ways faithful to the heritage of historical Christianity as conserved by the Roman Catholic Church.

To Dawson, such conservatism was fundamentally radical, for it required a comprehensive rebuttal of modern mores. From his first years in Craven to his last days in Budleigh Salterton, he challenged modern culture and thought Christians were obliged to combat its secularist trends. He judged early on that Roman Catholicism was the sole church so corporately committed in his age, and that it thus had a special duty not just to resist post-Christianity, but also to voice the ideals of the "counter-kingdom" that he saw as the source of Christian cultural renewal. Were the current Church to abjure this role, it would betray its ancestors and crush the only hope for a recreated Christendom. His sense that being a Catholic entails being a counter-modern rebel, then, helped govern Dawson's conversion, animate his scholarship, and mold his view of the Church's internal conduct. Even his use of prophetic tropes served this belief and was secondary to it.

This elaborate tapestry of essentially unified thought gained him eminent admirers, but its central thread of orthodox Roman Catholic rebellion against modern irreligion also brought him prominent critics and perhaps less lasting influence than some of his peers. Dawson recognized these risks early on, but set his eyes on what he deemed a greater prize, one he thought attained by those he felt were most worth imitating:

> All through the spiritual decline of the modern world there have been men and women who refused all compromise, and maintained the ideal of the Christian life in all its fullness . . . [this was] typical of the situation of the Christian ideal in the modern world. It was forced to separate itself from the main stream of modern life, and so, in spite of its abiding vitality, it could not dominate or modify the circumstances that governed the lives of the majority of men. The life of the saints was a witness against the modern world, rather than an example to it.[338]

338. Dawson, *Enquiries*, 305–6.

CHAPTER 4

FINDING HARBOR WITH A REMNANT

David Jones's Religious Voyage

SHORTLY AFTER Dawson's 1970 death, David Jones, a friend of four decades, wrote that "I not only am greatly indebted to him, but had a great affection for him. . . . I was astonished at the lack of appreciation he received."[1] Jones's eulogy was the climax of a long-standing admiration for Dawson. In the preface to his 1952 poem, *The Anathemata*, for instance, Jones gave Dawson primary acknowledgment, claiming to feel "especially indebted" to the historian.[2] He reiterated this conviction of-

---

1. Jones to Roland Mathias, undated draft, David Jones 1985 Purchase. Group A, Box II/25, The National Library of Wales, Aberystwyth (hereafter, NLW).

2. David Jones, *The Anathemata: Fragments of an Attempted Writing* (London: Faber & Faber, 1952), 36.

ten, as when he exclaimed a year later that "Christopher D. has taught me so much of what very little I know."³

But Jones was not just a Dawsonian disciple. Acclaimed as an innovative visual artist even before he began publishing verse in the 1930s, his poetry rapidly won praise from esteemed peers, including some who also lauded Dawson.⁴ T. S. Eliot, for one, judged Jones's first poem, *In Parenthesis*, "a work of genius," and also hailed his "equally remarkable" *The Anathemata*.⁵ W. H. Auden had even higher regard for *The Anathemata*, calling it "the greatest long poem written in English in this century," while deeming *In Parenthesis* "the greatest book" about the Great War that he had read. He further dubbed Jones one of the modern poet-critics "from whom I have learned most."⁶ Among Jones's co-religionists, Waugh reviewed his debut poem in 1937 as "in many places, above Mr. Eliot,"⁷ while one-time neighbor Greene called *The Anathemata* "a really new thing" in 1953, and in 1980 judged *In Parenthesis* "among the great poems of this century."⁸ Sigfried Sassoon also deemed *In Parenthesis*

---

3. Jones letter draft, 29 January 1953 (addressee illegible), David Jones 1985 Purchase. Group C, Box 1, NLW. See also, e.g., Jones to René Hague, 11–12 January 1955; reprinted in *Chesterton Review* 23 (February & May 1997): 108. Jones owned most of Dawson's books. His extant library is in the David Jones Collection, Department of Printed Books, NLW.

4. Although Jones's paintings, engravings, and the like reveal many facets of his outlook, the current analysis will be confined to his literary work, as a proper iconography of the visual material would require sustained separate treatment and would be less immediately indicative of how his religious and cultural convictions developed. For the common concerns in Jones's visual and written art, see Thomas Dilworth, *The Shape of Meaning in the Poetry of David Jones* (Toronto: University of Toronto Press, 1988), 3–36; and Dilworth, "David Jones's *The Deluge*: Engraving the Structure of the Modern Long Poem," *Journal of Modern Literature* 19 (Summer 1994): 5–30. But also note Derek A. G. Shiel's caution against occluding the distinct nature of each genre in which Jones worked ("David Jones the Maker," *Chesterton Review* 23 [February & May 1997]: 162).

5. T. S. Eliot, introduction to *In Parenthesis*, by David Jones (London: Faber & Faber, 1937, 1963, 1978), vii *(IP)*. Jones returned these plaudits consistently, in 1937 calling Eliot "the greatest English poet of our own time" *(IP,* 212, n. 42), and declaring in 1962 that "the greatest influence on me was Tom Eliot" (Richard Wald, "'I Don't Think I'm Modern,'" *New York Herald Tribune*, 8 July 1962, 11). He owned most of Eliot's books.

6. W. H. Auden, *A Certain World* (New York: Viking, 1970), 372–73; and Auden quoted in Dilworth, *Shape*, 3.

7. Evelyn Waugh, "A Mystic in the Trenches"; reprinted in *The Essays, Articles and Reviews of Evelyn Waugh*, ed. Donat Gallagher (Boston: Little, Brown & Co., 1984), 196.

8. Greene to Jones, 23 February 1953, David Jones 1985 Purchase. Group C, Box 5, NLW; and Graham Greene, *Ways of Escape* (New York: Simon & Schuster, 1980), 42.

"important," but confessed that *The Anathemata* was "quite beyond me."[9]

Such tributes were not confined to Christians or contemporaries. At a 1938 party, Yeats sought Jones out for a salute. To William Carlos Williams, *The Anathemata* was "tough but rewarding," yet "too much for me."[10] And, even as he chided Jones's thought severely in 1959, Frank Kermode still deemed its premises "essential to the production of the kind of art most people are prepared to call important."[11] More recently, Seamus Heaney has acknowledged Jones's influence on his work, as have Geoffrey Hill and Basil Bunting, the latter stressing that he is utterly unsympathetic to Catholicism.[12] By the late 1980s, scholars were calling Jones "the major Roman Catholic poet in English in this century,"[13] and even "the most important native British poet of the twentieth century."[14]

As impressive as this catalogue of applause is, James Campbell was still correct to contend in 1995 that "Jones remains a relatively obscure figure among twentieth-century British poets."[15] His writing's recondite nature accounts partly for this persistent relative neglect, as does his fealty to "an abiding religious faith and a sense of Western rootedness that is shared by few poets in this age."[16] But his chronic anonymity also has more specific scholarly causes. Given his work's allusive nature and depth, almost all criticism of it has hitherto been exegetical. If necessary, valuable, and still incomplete, Campbell claims rightly that this intensely focused literary archeology has made Jones scholarship "rather insular."[17] In particular, there has been no satisfactory systematic analysis of

---

9. Sassoon quoted in Joseph Pearce, *Literary Converts* (London: HarperCollins, 1999), 346.
10. Dilworth, *Shape*, 3.
11. Frank Kermode, *Puzzles and Epiphanies* (London: Routledge & Kegan Paul, 1962), 29.
12. Dilworth, *Shape*, 6, 360–61.
13. Joseph Schwartz, "Editor's Page," *Renascence* 38 (Winter 1986): 66.
14. Dilworth, *Shape*, 368.
15. James Campbell, review of Kathleen Henderson Staudt, *At the Turn of a Civilization*, *Religion & Literature* 27 (Summer 1995): 105. Jones's conspicuous absence from Patrick Allitt's survey of Anglophone Roman Catholic convert thinkers highlights graphically this ongoing neglect of his work, even by careful scholars studying fields in which Jones was a signal figure. Allitt, *Catholic Converts* (Ithaca, N.Y.: Cornell University Press, 1997).
16. Kathleen Henderson Staudt, *At the Turn of a Civilization: David Jones and Modern Poetics* (Ann Arbor: University of Michigan Press, 1994), 194.
17. James Campbell, 105.

how Jones's *thought* evolved, and how these reflections on religion and culture belong to the legacy of British Roman Catholic reactions to modern civilization.[18] Tracing his religious beliefs' development and their interplay with his cultural criticism will thus not only provide further conceptual frameworks for assessing Jones's work, but will also reveal his stance as an orthodox Roman Catholic rebel against modern secularism.

Unlike Chesterton, Greene, and Dawson, Jones did not appear to undergo a single galvanizing crisis of faith. Rather, he believed from an early age in the importance of sacramental action and grew progressively disenchanted with what seemed staunch hostility to such practices in his received Protestantism. Although his service in the Great War affected Jones permanently, it played only an ancillary role in his 1921 conversion. He was far more swayed by the link he saw between art and sacrament, his belief that his age was increasingly opposed to these activities (ones he deemed human nature's defining traits), and his eventual conclusion that only Roman Catholicism had the doctrines and authority necessary for effective rebellion against dehumanizing modern technocracy.

After his conversion, Jones found these views validated and elaborated by Thomism, and he used them and other insights to develop a theol-

---

18. For example, the first full-scale biography of Jones has only just appeared and has been little noticed (Keith Alldritt, *David Jones: Writer and Artist* [London: Constable & Robinson, 2003]). The next most extensive biographical work is William Blissett's *The Long Conversation: A Memoir of David Jones* (Oxford: Oxford University Press, 1981). But, being a memoir, it is necessarily anecdotal rather than analytical. Thomas Dilworth's *The Shape of Meaning* incorporates some discussion of the development of Jones's religious and cultural views, but as its primary focus is on elucidating each poem sequentially, it is unable to present a sustained exposition of the chief tenets of Jones's thought. Elizabeth Ward's *David Jones: Mythmaker* (Manchester: Manchester University Press, 1983) is admirable for its effort to see Jones as a cultural thinker, establish context for his writing, and raise pointed questions about his views; but it is finally marred by insufficient attention to the elements of Jones's religious outlook and by ideological hostility to his opinions, which produces tendentious and mistaken analysis of some crucial aspects of his work. Kathleen Henderson Staudt's *At the Turn of a Civilization*—the only other work to focus intently on Jones as a cultural critic—is outstanding for its treatment of gender issues in his writing and thoughtful in assessing his place in literary thought, as well as in documenting some key influences on his views, but is weakened considerably by underestimation of the centrality of Jones's religious beliefs to his outlook. Moreover, even some of his best critics have not drawn fully on the verse published posthumously as *The Roman Quarry and Other Sequences*, ed. Harman Grisewood and René Hague (London: Agenda Editions, 1981) *(RQ)*.

ogy of history centered on Christ's Passion. He thought this pivotal event was re-presented sacramentally in both war and the Mass, thereby fusing his most important personal experience with his chief intellectual and religious concerns. Jones expanded this belief in the Eucharist's ability to recall one specific past event by asserting the dynamic nature of all tradition, alleging that the past remains really present in the present. He finally held that Christ and His ritual re-calling fulfilled their mythic and factual forerunners and successors, but without compromising their uniqueness; Jones thereby gained theological sanction for his personal passion for unity. Because he considered modern culture hostile to this sacramental sensibility and concern for continuity, Jones opposed the Church's liturgical changes as capitulations to the very forces he had become a Roman Catholic to combat. His theology similarly helped inspire qualms about what he deemed some of literary Modernism's aesthetic premises, even as he adopted its forms in his verse. In warning about the decay of vital aspects of human nature and culture, and in resisting the trends he blamed for this degeneration, while affirming what he saw as a proper Roman Catholic alternative, then, Jones assumed the roles of both prophet and rebel against modernity.

"The Years of Becoming": Childhood and Its Seeds

Like Chesterton, Greene, and Dawson, Jones believed that childhood experiences shape adult outlooks decisively: "there are root things imbibed in childhood which, I think, condition one at a deep level throughout one's life."[19] He judged the inhabitants of these "years of becoming"[20] of "the most primary importance," for it is through these people and events that "'all the rest' is already half sensed long before it is known."[21] The religious people and practices that Jones knew during these crucial years were similar to Dawson's early influences. His parents' marriage was also religiously mixed, although the reverse of Dawson's. Alice Bradshaw, her son asserted, learned "the purest Catholic doc-

---

19. Jones to Sir Gilbert Inglefield, 8 June 1968 (draft), David Jones 1985 Purchase. Group C, Box 17, NLW.

20. David Jones, "The Tutelar of Place," in *The Sleeping Lord and Other Fragments* (London: Faber & Faber, 1974), 59 *(SL)*.

21. Jones, *The Anathemata*, 41.

trine" in her Rotherhithe High Church parish, but conformed to James Jones's Low Church Evangelicalism as a condition of marriage.[22] James was a lay reader in his congregation, and, like many of his generation, distrusted Catholic theology and practices deeply. Yet his son did not escape early exposure to Catholicism. In 1900, for instance, one of Alice's friends mentioned guardian angels in David's presence, leading him to ask his mother embarrassing questions about these beings "which Daddy says can't be proved from the Bible, but that someone called Dr. Pusey got it from what he calls Papists."[23]

This was not the only awkward moment caused by Jones's youthful explorations of Catholicism. He was certain from about age six that he would be an artist, for trying to represent objects and events under new forms was "as natural a desire as, say, stroking the cat."[24] As well as being the germ of his mature notion that men are essentially artists, his boyhood symbolic sensibility had immediate implications for his religious behavior. For example, six-year-old David decided on Good Friday that it would be "a 'good thing' to make a recalling" of Christ's death by constructing a cross from two beams and processing around the yard with it.[25] Upon beholding this sight, James Jones admonished his son that "there were people called Roman Catholics who did that sort of thing ... but that true Christians carried their cross in their hearts."[26] Yet David still felt impelled to ritual and symbolic action. As a teen, "something almost in the nature of a compulsion" made him begin kneeling at the *Incarnatus* portion of the creed during Sunday services. This was a common Roman Catholic custom, but his fellow Low Churchmen scorned such behavior as "papistical."[27] When rebuked by his mother,

---

22. Jones quoted in Blissett, *Conversation*, 17.

23. David Jones, "Fragments of an Attempted Autobiographical Writing," *Agenda* 12–13 (Winter–Spring 1975): 99. Jones deemed his mother the more influential of his parents (Jones to Vernon Watkins, 17 April 1962, David Jones Collection, Box 1/Folder 58, John J. Burns Library, Boston College).

24. Jones, "Fragments of an Attempted Autobiographical Writing," 102.

25. Jones to René Hague, 9–15 July 1973, in *Dai Greatcoat: A Self-Portrait of David Jones in His Letters*, ed. René Hague (London: Faber & Faber, 1980), 247 *(DGC)*.

26. Blissett, *Conversation*, 126. See also Peter Orr, "Mr. Jones, Your Legs Are Crossed," *Agenda* 15 (1977): 112.

27. Jones to René Hague, 9–15 July 1973 *(DGC, 247)*.

David responded plaintively, "I just *have* to kneel at those words,"[28] for he thought that they "demanded this bodily action."[29] From early on, then, Jones was willing to rebel against received norms, and to do so on behalf of distinctively Roman Catholic principles and practices.

This early tension between what Jones learned at home and his instincts' instructions persisted for years, but remained largely latent. He lacked Greene's and Dawson's catalyst for their adolescent crises, as he persuaded his parents to send him to art school rather than public school, but he was spared the trauma that Chesterton underwent at the Slade. He matriculated at Camberwell Art School in 1909, at age fourteen. His instructor there was A. S. Hatrick, whom Jones later called "a kind of oblique Catholic influence" for introducing him to the postimpressionism that would play a fateful role in his later religious development. Although there was no immediate impact on his beliefs, Jones did recall that his attempts at figure composition were usually of "some medieval subject introducing a vested priest," indicating that the link between art and sacrament was becoming a growing preoccupation, as were two other subjects that he would muse over much in his maturity: medievalism and the Mass.[30] For the most part, though, Jones (like Dawson during his Oxford years) concentrated on mastering his chosen crafts' techniques and remained an active, if unenthusiastic, Anglican.

As his Camberwell curriculum lacked commercial or academic applications, Jones had become anxious about his future by 1914. With neither career nor church supplying direction for or passion in his life, Jones, like many similarly situated members of his generation, saw the Great War's outbreak as "an excitement . . . and something of a solution,"[31] by offering the opportunity of "getting into history."[32] He enrolled in the Royal Welch Fusiliers. Unlike Graves and Sassoon, he was not an officer in that famous regiment, but his service as a private left him no less deeply

---

28. Jones quoted in Orr, "Mr. Jones," 112. Emphasis in original.
29. Jones to René Hague, 9–15 July 1973 (*DGC*, 248).
30. Jones to René Hague, 9–15 July 1973 (*DGC*, 246).
31. Blissett, *Conversation*, 116.
32. Jones quoted in Nesta Roberts, "Sign of the Bear," *Guardian*, 17 February 1964, 7. See also Jonathan Miles, *Backgrounds to David Jones* (Cardiff: University of Wales Press, 1990), 89–93.

touched by the war than his poet peers were: "the forward area of the West Front had a permanent effect upon me and has affected my work in all sorts of ways."[33] Besides inspiring frequent direct references to his war experience, these years also conditioned his choice of subject matter, and even his rhetoric when discussing seemingly unrelated issues, in poetry, essays, and letters. If all Greene's novels are public school novels, then, all Jones's writings are Great War writings. He enlisted in January 1915, left for France in December, and was stationed in trenches until being wounded at the Somme in July 1916. He rejoined his unit three months later near Ypres, and moved with them to the Bois Grenier sector in September 1917, remaining there until early 1918. A case of trench fever, though, spared him from combat during the German offensives of March and April 1918. Jones was demobilized in 1919.

"An Uninitiated Bloke": Jones and Wartime Roman Catholicism

The war's role in shaping many of Jones's chief beliefs effected his religious views in three crucial ways. First, unlike many of his peers who entered the war with a tepid religion, the ubiquity and threat of death did not undermine his faith. Rather, he told William Blissett, he had "a deep irrational conviction that he would survive it, recalling the psalm, 'A thousand shall fall at thy right hand. . . .'" Jones ascribed this confidence to a sense similar to that felt by Newman and Dawson at comparable chronological points in their lives, one of "vocation and a sense of having hardly begun to learn his art, let alone exercise it."[34] The connection between religion and art was again central to his thoughts; this belief that he was being spared to make something beautiful for God began combining with two specific wartime occurrences to bring Jones closer to the conviction that Roman Catholicism was the best venue for exercising his perceived vocation.

Like Graves, Jones was impressed by the courage Roman Catholic chaplains exhibited in staying at the front to give extreme unction to dy-

---

33. David Jones, *Epoch and Artist*, ed. Harman Grisewood (London: Faber & Faber, 1959), 28 (*E&A*). See also Ward, *Mythmaker*, 215.

34. Blissett, *Conversation*, 122. See Jones's use of this psalm in *IP*, 158.

ing soldiers; he was especially taken with Father Daniel Hughes (the model for *In Parenthesis*'s Father Larkin), whom he met in October 1916, discussed Roman Catholicism with, and even borrowed a devotional book from.[35] Yet beyond these moving personal examples of Catholicism, Jones was affected profoundly and lastingly by witnessing the celebration of another Roman sacrament some time in 1916 or early 1917. If uncertain about exactly when or where this incident occurred, he recalled vividly searching for firewood and encountering an abandoned farm building that seemed a promising source of tinder. Peering through a chink in its wall, where he expected vacancy he instead saw inside "a sacerdos in a gilt-hued *planeta,* two points of flickering candlelight . . . and kneeling in the hay beneath the improvised *mensa* were a few huddled figures in khaki." Never having seen a Mass firsthand before, Jones was unsure what part of it he was observing and he departed promptly, feeling "like an uninitiated bloke prying on the Mysteries of a Cult." Yet, he claimed, this momentary glimpse of the central Roman Catholic rite "made a big impression on me." His verse substantiates this perception, for, as Vincent Sherry notes, many of Jones's Mass poems are written from the standpoint of an outsider seeing the ceremony for the first time.[36]

In particular, Jones asserted that he was drawn to the unific power he discerned in the celebration of the Eucharist. One of his chief preoccupations was a passion for unity. His youthful artistic apprehension that things can be reproduced in different forms seems to have bred a belief in the essential interconnectedness of all Being, and in the artist's duty to testify to this harmony. Jones appears to have found this conviction as natural as the desire to draw, for he asserted later in life that "a 'desire and pursuit of the whole' is native to us."[37] He elaborated this notion as

---

35. See Blissett, *Conversation,* 126–27. Graves's views are in *Goodbye to All That* (New York: Anchor Books, 1985), 189–90, a volume that was one of Jones's favorite Great War books.

36. Jones to René Hague, 9–15 July 1973 (*DGC,* 248–49). See also Vincent Sherry, "David Jones and Literary Modernism: The Use of the Dramatic Monologue," in *Craft and Tradition: Essays in Honor of William Blissett,* ed. H. B. De Groot and Alexander Leggatt (Calgary: University of Calgary Press, 1990), 246–47. John Breslin maintains further that "this first Mass, observed also through a slat, is the *fons* for all the liturgies that appear in Jones's poetry" ("David Jones: The Shaping of a Poet's Mind," *Renascence* 38 [Winter 1986]: 88).

37. David Jones, "A Christmas Message, 1960," in *The Dying Gaul and Other Writings,* ed. Harman Grisewood (London: Faber & Faber, 1972, 1978), 168 (*DG*).

an adult, arguing that "the ultimate problem" is "to make a whole, a unity, out of varying parts,"[38] and that "the arts abhor any loppings off of meanings or emptyings out, any lessening of the totality of connotation, any loss of recession and thickness through."[39] In distinctly religious matters, he favored scripture verses like "I have not lost of them a single one" and the psalm "about Jerusalem being builded as a city 'where parts are united in me,'" which he thought should be "the artists' text or motto."[40] He held further that "the thing which I sensed more than all else at Mass long before I became a Catholic and afterwards was precisely that oneness," and that he had this impression from his first peek through that front-line peep hole.[41]

This experience was vital to his spiritual development because it was the first time that any sort of formal worship had suited his catholic sensibility. His youth's putatively more egalitarian theology had failed to convey a sense of connected commonality: "I felt immediately that oneness between the Offerant and those toughs that clustered round him in the dim-lit byre—a thing I had never felt remotely as a Protestant at the Office of Holy Communion in spite of the insistence of Protestant theology on the 'priesthood of the laity.'"[42] Even allowing for these remarks' retrospective nature, it does seem clear that as Jones's sense of his vocation as an artist intensified during the war, contact with Catholics and their rites suggested to him that this faith affirmed long-held beliefs that he had not found validated by his ancestral church. If Jones entered the war an apathetic Anglican, then, he left the trenches well on the way to Rome. He held that he was "'inside' a Catholic"[43] by mid-1917, as "I became aware or half-aware, by a kind of 'unity of indirect reference' that the claims of the Patriarch of the West could not for long be resisted."[44]

38. Jones quoted in Dilworth, *Shape*, 155.
39. Jones, *The Anathemata*, 24.
40. Jones undated letter fragment, David Jones 1985 Purchase. Group A, Box V/I, NLW.
41. Jones undated manuscript, David Jones 1985 Purchase. Group A, Box 1/16, NLW.
42. Jones to René Hague, 9–15 July 1973 (*DGC*, 249).
43. Jones to René Hague, 23 February 1972; quoted in Dilworth, *Shape*, 120. See also Jones to Bernard Bergonzi, undated, c. 1960s, (draft), David Jones 1985 Purchase. Group B, Box 1/9, NLW.
44. Jones undated manuscript, David Jones 1985 Purchase. Group C, Box 2, NLW.

Yet Jones managed to resist them for four more years. He remained an Anglican communicant for the rest of the war, even as he was rethinking his spiritual allegiance in light of his wartime experiences. Like Chesterton, who behaved similarly at a comparable point in his journey from Canterbury to Rome, Jones found it hard to take decisive action of any kind. Moreover, as drawn to Roman Catholicism as he was temperamentally and emotionally, he was still ignorant or skeptical of many aspects of its theology. Finally, like Dawson, he knew that a decision to "pope" might strain family ties, especially with his father. Thus, by the time of demobilization, Jones was moving from the stage in the conversion process identified by Emilie Griffin as "Desire" to that of "Dialectic," all the while being sensitive to the "wreckage" that might result from making this choice.[45] He was hardly idle as he continued his musings as a civilian, for he entered the Westminster School of Art in 1919. His interests defied popular tastes, as he focused more on visionaries like Blake and El Greco than on the then-fashionable postimpressionists. Yet it was postimpressionism that ultimately helped Jones become a Roman Catholic.

"The Whole Gamut of Making": Art and Sacrament

Understanding this apparently incongruous connection requires elucidating some key aspects of Jones's worldview. While these statements come from his later writings, their essential logic underlay his thought as he was pondering whether or not to convert. First, Jones argued that people are fundamentally artists. As with his desire for unity, he generalized what he considered "natural" to himself as a child: "man's natural activity [is] the activity we call 'art.'"[46] Jones held that this trait distinguished humans from all other beings, as "man is the only artist and only artists are men."[47] But, demonstrating his passion for unity, he extended this definition's reach deep into the past and far into the future: "we were *homo faber, homo sapiens* before Lascaux and we shall be *homo faber, homo sapiens* after the last atomic bomb has fallen."[48] To Jones, then, to

---

45. Emilie Griffin, *Turning: Reflections on the Experience of Conversion* (New York: Doubleday, 1980), 29, 152–53.
46. David Jones, "Art and Sacrament," in *E&A*, 149.
47. David Jones, "Art and Democracy," in *E&A*, 94.
48. Jones quoted in René Hague, *A Commentary on The Anathemata of David Jones*

be an artist is what it means to be made in the image and likeness of God: God-the-Creator makes a gift of this quality to His human creatures, and only His human creatures (albeit on a reduced scale), and thereby establishes an essential identity between Himself and them. As Dorothy L. Sayers put it (in a book Jones owned), when the Genesis author looks at man,

> he sees in him something essentially divine, but when we turn back to see what he says about the original upon which the "image" of God was modeled, we find only the single assertion, "God created." The characteristic common to God and man is apparently that: the desire and the ability to make things.[49]

Others (including Chesterton and Tolkien) held similar views, but Jones also saw an intimate connection between art and sacrament.[50] He argued that art and sacrament both re-present phenomena under new forms: if God is substantially present under the material accidents of bread, wine, water, oil, and the like, so too is an artist's model essentially existent within the paint, stone, metal, or even words out of which an artefacture is made. Taking Hogarth's *Shrimp Girl* as an example, Jones held that this painting and the Eucharist each attempt to "show forth, recall and re-present, strictly within the conditions of a given art and under another mode, such and such a reality. It is a *signum* of that reality and it makes a kind of anamnesis of that reality . . . we have whatever is denoted under 'Shrimp Girl' really present under the form of paint." He allowed that Hogarth's inspiration from life is not "'really present' in the

---

(Toronto: University of Toronto Press, 1977), 29. Brenda Fowler has echoed Jones recently, arguing that "most paleoanthropologists now agree" that it is with the emergence of "symbolic expression," like cave art, that "we first recognize human beings as they are today" ("Where Did He Go?" *New York Times Book Review*, 17 December 1995, 21).

49. Dorothy L. Sayers, *The Mind of the Maker* (1941; reprint, San Francisco: HarperCollins, 1979), 22.

50. See Chesterton, *A Handful of Authors*, ed. Dorothy Collins (London: Sheed & Ward, 1953), 80, and *The Collected Works of G. K. Chesterton*, vol. 18, *Robert Louis Stevenson* (San Francisco: Ignatius Press, 1991), 53; and Tolkien, "On Fairy Stories," in *Poems and Stories* (Boston: Houghton Mifflin, 1994), 162–63. In 1952, Jones listed Tolkien among the fifty "living or recently living authors" to whom he was indebted (*The Anathemata*, 36), but it is not clear if he read this particular essay or not. See also Thomas Woodman, *Faithful Fictions: The Catholic Novel in British Literature* (Philadelphia: Open University Press, 1991), 124–27.

particular sense used by the theologians" of Christ's asserted actual indwelling within consecrated bread and wine, but is so "in a certain analogous sense." Jones nonetheless regarded this analogy as direct enough to conclude that "the art of man is essentially a sign-making or 'sacramental' activity."[51]

Jones thus deduced further (as Chesterton did) that if people are artists at root, they are also intrinsic sacramentalists. He argued that "man is not only man-the-maker but man the maker, user and apprehender of signs . . . a sign-making element however minimal, obscure and hard to define does adhere to all human artefactures."[52] The scope of *homo faber*'s ranks thus extend to *homo significator*'s: "we have at least 60,000 years and *maybe a hell of a lot* longer, of evidence of this 'ere *signa*-making in man . . . man is *essentially* a creature of sign and *signa*-making, a 'sacramentalist' to the core," and will be as long as human beings remain the kind of creatures they are.[53] Part of being made in God's image, then, is using signs to make visible His invisible reality and presence.

Jones held that this link between art and sacrament was an inchoate intuition until early 1919, when he began pondering their relationship in connection with his reflections about whether to join the Church of Rome. He was assessing competing Christian views of the Eucharist intently at this time, as these doctrines resonated with his sacramental sensibility and were a key point of dispute between Catholics and Protestants during this era. He and his classmates were concurrently debating the nature of art, and Jones found these two concerns synthesized in his mind by discussions of postimpressionist theory: "Then, with relative suddenness, the analogy between what we called 'the Arts' and the things that Christians called the eucharistic signs became (if still but vaguely) apparent. It became increasingly evident that this analogy applied to the whole gamut of 'making.'"[54]

The common ground that he saw beneath this avant-garde aesthetic

---

51. Jones, "Art and Sacrament," 158, 160, 174–75, 161. See also *DG*, 220, n. 19.
52. Jones, "A Christmas Message, 1960," 169.
53. Jones to René Hague, 8–16 June 1966 (*DGC*, 221–22). Emphasis in original.
54. Jones, "Art and Sacrament," 171. See also Jones undated manuscript, David Jones 1985 Purchase. Group B, Box V/4, NLW; and Horton Davies, *Worship and Theology in England* (Princeton, N.J.: Princeton University Press, 1962, 1965), 4: 122, and 5: 301.

David Jones's Religious Voyage 299

and traditional Roman Catholic sacramentalism was a shared stress on re-presentation. To Roger Fry (Britain's chief postimpressionist theorist), a proper art work is "an equivalence, not a likeness."[55] Jones found this idea akin to the Catholic dogma of transubstantiation:

> "post-impressionist" is a useful term *spelt without caps*—for in *basic idea* it means that a work is not an "impression" of "nature" but a made "thing[,]" a *signum* of a reality of some sort . . . it had quite a lot to do with my seeing the Sacraments of the Church as fitting in perfectly with all human *poiesis*—nothing could be more "post-impressionist" in *that sense* than what the Church predicated of the Mass, where "sign" & "thing signified" are said to be one.[56]

Jones recalled trying to explain this perceived connection to some fellow students, using the same kind of comparison he later employed in discussing Hogarth: he argued that an artefact may be made of pencil or paint, but is actually a particular "human body or a hill slope under the form of those materials . . . a Miss Price under the appearance of chalk or paint." His Catholic colleagues deemed this idea dangerous because it seemed to equate human creation with the Creator's becoming one with His creatures in the sacraments. Jones thus initiated his later caveat, that this relationship was *"by analogy,"* yet with the same later insistence that postimpressionism and Roman Catholicism have "a very similar intention." If his Catholic compatriots were skeptical of this schema, though, he also conceded that dedicated postimpressionists would also have denied his link.[57]

Eccentric as his interpretation may have been, Jones upheld it persistently, for it provided intellectual and theological justification for his lifelong sense of the essential similarity between what he considered the defining and uniquely human activities of art and sacrament. In particular, Jones started to see the Mass as the exemplary work of art. He asserted that during his Westminster days he began believing that "the Mass,

---

55. Fry quoted in Dilworth, *Shape*, 10.
56. Jones to William Blissett, 11–12 June 1967 (Blissett, *Conversation*, 45–46). Emphasis in original.
57. Jones to René Hague, 19 January 1973; quoted in Dilworth, *Shape*, 10. Emphasis in original. See also Jones to William Blissett, 11–12 June 1967 (*Conversation*, 45–46).

involving as it did, bodily manual acts, said words, and a whole complex of interrelated forms was, as it were, the prototype or supreme model, analogically speaking, of all the arts of man."[58] The unifying urge implied in that statement was more explicit elsewhere, as when he described the Lascaux cave paintings in the language of eucharistic theology:

> And see how they run, the juxtaposed forms,
> brighting the vaults of Lascaux; how the linear is wedded
> to volume, how they do, within, in an unbloody manner,
> under the forms of brown haematite and black manganese on
> the graved lime-face, what is done, without,
>   far on the windy tundra
> at the kill
> that the kindred may have life.[59]

To Jones, then, the Mass's archetypal nature allowed it to subsume all works of art, even those made prior to its institution.

Jones focused on the circumstances of that inauguration in asserting the Mass's artistic essence. He argued that when God took on human nature, the Creator of necessity became an artist and a sacramentalist: "He placed Himself in the order of signs," as Jones often quoted from theologian Maurice de la Taille. Hence, He could only provide for His temporal re-presentation by means of art and sacrament, making the Mass inherently a re-calling, for it is done by men in memory of a man, all of whom are re-presenters at root:

> unless man is of his essential nature a *poeta*, one who makes things that are signs of something, then the central act of the Christian religion is totally without meaning. How can there be a manual act that makes *anamnesis* unless man is man-the-maker, and thus *poiesis* his native and authentic mode of apperception and in the end his only mode?[60]

---

58. Jones to Saunders Lewis, undated 1971 fragment, David Jones 1985 Purchase. Group B, Box V/6, NLW.

59. Jones, *The Anathemata*, 60 (highlighted by Greene in his copy). Jones accented this point further in a 4 September 1971 letter to Grisewood: "As for the Lascaux caves . . . the superb forms of the great horned creatures with a dart or two depicted in flank or neck, is about the nearest thing to the acts and words of the inutile Oblation of the Coena Domini" (*DGC*, 232–33). See also *DG*, 168.

60. Jones, preface to *E&A*, 13.

Jones asserted further that this Christian commitment to artefacture extends even to the materials that Christ blessed and that a priest consecrates. Bread and wine, rather than wheat and grapes, are used because they are works of human hands as well as fruits of the earth and vine: "Something has to be made by us before it can become for us his sign who made us. This point he settled in the upper room."[61] Yet, Jones concluded, since this re-calling is of He who made us, the Creator Himself, it is qualitatively different from all other art works: it is directly re-presentational whereas they are only so analogically. To Jones, because the Mass is "a sign which *is* the reality it signifies," it "extends and fulfills" these other arts' intent.[62] If he agreed that

> from dear and grave Demeter come
> > germ of all:
> of the dear arts as well as bread.
> To institute, to make stable
> to offer oblations

he still insisted that when a priest breaks a consecrated host over a chalice

> he parts that, which—
> > under the sign of that creature—
> can do more than any grain.[63]

If it took years for Jones to elaborate this complex interpretation of the Mass's artistic nature, the epiphanies behind it and the general relationship between art and sacrament gleaned in his Westminster days were immediately crucial to his conversion. The more he connected what he had long felt about art and religion with Roman Catholic theology, the more Jones began to consider the animus to sacramental action he had faced as a boy an integral part of Protestantism. He was coming to the conclusion that "the *essence* of Protestantism is that the Xtian reli-

---

61. Jones, *The Anathemata*, 31. For this view in his verse, see ibid., 82, 157–58, 187, 205; *SL*, 76; *RQ*, 106.

62. Angela Dorenkamp, "Time and Sacrament in *The Anathemata*," *Renascence* 23 (Summer 1971): 188. Emphasis in original.

63. Jones, *The Anathemata*, 230, 227.

gion is a matter of inclination of the heart and soul, an interior disposition," whereas Catholicism holds that "certain manual cult actions and verbal formulae are of the *essence* of the Xtian religion," and that Catholics so stress sacramental action not due to scriptural or traditional injunctions "but because such is the nature of man."[64] Specifically, he became convinced that the queries about the Eucharist that beset his mind at this time were best answered by Roman Catholicism:

> [I] was formally received into the Catholic Church on precisely that understanding that the Mass was not a commemorative service of thanksgiving or a common meal such as I had known from childhood, but an actual and effectual sacrifice as concrete and as real . . . as that other penetration of the timeless into time . . . the Incarnation.[65]

Jones was thus finding in Catholicism a faith whose central rite seemed both to satisfy his need for unity and to ratify his definition of human nature intellectually and aesthetically.

"There is No Almost": Gratuity, Utility, Rebellion, Authority, and Eric Gill

But Jones was still groping toward these conclusions in 1919. It was at this point that a chain of friendships was forged that ultimately helped secure his entry into the Church of Rome. Jones held that it was chiefly his friendships with some Catholic fellow students at Westminster that persuaded him to receive "formal instructions in what I inwardly felt."[66] Though somewhat skeptical of the path he was taking, at least one Catholic schoolmate thought Jones's sense of direction sound enough to help him pilot his course. This was Frank Wall, whom Jones met in 1919 and in whom he confided his attraction to Roman Catholicism. Wall in turn introduced him to Chesterton's friend John O'Connor, who began playing the part in Jones's spiritual story that Ronald Knox performed contemporaneously in Chesterton's. Jones and O'Connor were soon having long talks, for the priest shared Jones's intense interest in the relationship between art and religion. In fact, he translated Maritain's *Art and Scholas-*

---

64. Jones to René Hague, 8–16 June 1966 (*DGC*, 222). Emphasis in original.
65. Jones undated letter draft, David Jones 1985 Purchase. Group C, Box 2, NLW.
66. Jones to Saunders Lewis, undated 1971 letter fragment, op. cit.

ticism, which elaborated Jones's core ideas in Thomistic terms and influenced him greatly when he read it after his reception. Also in 1919, Jones received Chesterton's *Orthodoxy* as a sketch club prize in January. It is unclear when he read it, but Blissett comments more generally that "Chesterton was a germinating presence for David Jones in the seedtime of his soul,"[67] and Jones did praise *Orthodoxy* particularly when discussing Chesterton in 1972.[68]

Another Chestertonian, though, had perhaps the most important impact on Jones's conversion. On 29 January 1921, at O'Connor's behest, Jones and Wall visited Eric Gill, himself a recent Roman Catholic convert (1913), at Gill's "cell of good living" in Ditchling. Jones recalled leaving this meeting feeling that, at least temporarily, "the labyrinth [was] illuminated, the muddle shake[n] out into a discernible figure."[69] This relationship was catalytic in shaking out many of Jones's muddles, for it was only eight months after they met that he formally became a Roman Catholic. Indeed, he credited Gill with convincing him of "the truths of the Church."[70] Gill's conversion had been impelled by many of the forces that were driving Jones's. He too, for instance, believed that people were artists at root, and he had been attracted to the Roman Catholic liturgy and Eucharistic teachings.[71] Jones also found Gill's aesthetic views in accord with his interpretation of postimpressionism and Catholicism, an outlook Jones deemed out of the artistic mainstream: "he was concerned with the making of 'things' rather than with expressing a mood, and there is no other important artist living at all like that."[72]

---

67. William Blissett, "David Jones and the Chesterbelloc." Blissett omitted this line from the published version of this article, which is in *Chesterton Review* 23 (February & May 1997): 27–55. Thanks to Ian Boyd, the *Review*'s editor, for allowing me to read the manuscript version quoted here.

68. Blissett, *Conversation*, 109.

69. David Jones, "Eric Gill," in *E&A*, 296.

70. Jones quoted in Dilworth, *Shape*, 6.

71. See Eric Gill, *Autobiography* (London: Jonathan Cape, 1940), 39. Gill's statement of being drawn to Catholicism because of the Mass and related issues is in an undated essay on the liturgy by him that Jones kept in his papers (David Jones 1985 Purchase, Group A, Box III/36, NLW).

72. Jones, "Eric Gill as Sculptor," in *E&A*, 293. For Gill's views on postimpressionism, see Adrian Cunningham, "Primary Things: Land, Work, and Sign," *Chesterton Review* 22 (February & May 1996): 81.

Finally, he thought Gill shared his love of unity, another trait Jones saw as rebellious: "His great passion was to make a unity of all his activities. . . . This same determination to effect order in life, as well as in art, separates him somewhat from most of his contemporaries."[73]

Gill also helped shape more specific aspects of Jones's worldview, ones that helped give the latter's theological deliberations a sense of urgency. Gill partly inspired what one critic calls the "foundation of all Jones's analysis of culture and history and the key to understanding his poetry," his distinction between gratuity and utility.[74] Jones contended that whenever something is made, one of two motives predominates. If the maker has a gratuitous attitude, he is spurred by delight in the act of creation, works for the personal satisfaction derived from exercising one's artistic essence, and thus has an integrated relationship to the finished product. In short, the gratuitous maker lives to work. To Jones, this approach was genuine art's sine qua non, for he believed that "where there is no delight there is no art;"[75] that man's "greatest achievements . . . have been at least largely of an extra-utile nature"[76] because such intransitive making is his "one birthright;"[77] and that such efforts hence harmonize "the whole of his nature, with sensitivities ranging from flesh to fur to foliage and every kind of creatureliness to activities of the intellect, to perceptions of the spirit."[78] If, contrarily, utility governs one's making, Jones felt that efficiency is the endeavor's hallmark, for it is being done for pragmatic ends and usually at the behest of another, thus fostering alienation between the maker and what he produces. This person, then, works to live. Jones deemed this outlook the enemy of authentic art, for in it the "inutile has no place—only what serves and actually effects a so-called practical end is to be permitted."[79]

---

73. Jones, "Eric Gill," 298. See also Gill, *Autobiography*, 100.

74. Dilworth, *Shape*, 65. Late in life, Jones called this distinction the "pivot round which all one has ever stated depends" (Jones to Harman Grisewood, 4 September 1971 [*DGC*, 231]).

75. David Jones, "Art in Relation to War," in *DG*, 129.

76. Jones to Harman Grisewood, 4 September 1971 (*DGC*, 232).

77. Jones, "Art in Relation to War," 150.

78. Jones undated manuscript for *The Listener*, David Jones 1985 Purchase. Group C, Box 1, NLW.

79. Jones to Alun Jones, 26 February 1972 (draft), David Jones 1985 Purchase. Group A, Box II/28, NLW.

Consequently, utility plays Jacob to a worker's Esau, depriving him of his one birthright by eliminating delight and the pursuit of personal satisfaction from work: "We do not expect men to know the 'artists' joy' (as they call it) when engaged in these servile tasks." Far from unifying human nature, then, the "strictly utile" deals with "only a fraction of man's nature," a spiritual restriction that Jones judged analogous to a physical sterilization or castration.[80]

Jones felt that a balance between gratuitous and utilitarian motives is present in all art works, but feared that in his epoch the utile was achieving an unparalleled primacy.[81] He held that "the characteristic works of our present technocracy . . . seek the 'utile,'"[82] which promotes preoccupation with devices that "serve a definable purpose and are in no sense made as *signa* of something other than themselves."[83] In this kind of culture, "the symbolic life (the life of the true cultures, of 'institutional' religion, and of *all artists* . . . is progressively eliminated—the technician is master." To Jones, such a milieu, in which "the utile is the sole factor determining the forms, and the symbolic loses altogether its central and presiding position,"[84] was "truly new" in man's experience as an artist.[85]

The roots of this distinction appear to be in Jones's childhood. His father was a printer, and David recalled watching him trying laboriously to satisfy clients' demands by following procedures that seemed "an unnatural art process with no scope for invention."[86] As will be shown, Jones's war service gave additional existential basis to this discrimination. But he only encountered an intellectual formulation of it in the same setting

---

80. Jones, "Art in Relation to War," 150–51; and Jones undated manuscript for *The Listener,* op. cit.

81. See, e.g., "Wales and Visual Form," in *DG,* 89–90; and "A Christmas Message, 1960," 169.

82. Jones, "The Utile," in *E&A,* 181.

83. David Jones, "Notes on the 1930s," in *DG,* 44–45.

84. David Jones, "Religion and the Muses," in *E&A,* 103, 104, n. 2. Emphasis in original.

85. Jones to Dr. Crichton Miller, c. 1946–47, Harman Grisewood Papers, Box 5, Folder 28, Georgetown University, Washington, D.C. Sayers had cognate convictions and expressed them extensively, making comparative exploration of hers and Jones's analyses a potentially fruitful line of inquiry. See, e.g., *Mind of Maker,* 217–25; and Dorothy L. Sayers, *The Whimsical Christian* (New York: Collier Books, 1987), 49–51. Besides *The Mind of the Maker,* Jones also owned Sayers's *Unpopular Opinions* and *Why Work?*

86. Blissett, *Conversation,* 72.

that began to connect art and sacrament for him, as postimpressionist theorists like Fry and Clive Bell also distinguished between objects made principally for "use" and those fashioned primarily to be "enjoyed," with true art falling into the latter category. And Chesterton also hinted at this dichotomy in a passage of *Orthodoxy* that Jones marked.[87] Although Jones's mature definition of this opposition would draw further from thinkers like Maritain, it was Gill who immediately nurtured it.

Jones maintained that Gill considered a sensed modern tendency "of seeking first utility" a central cause of cultural degradation.[88] Gill resisted this perceived trend both in his writing and in his attempts, as at Ditchling, to set up communities of craftsworkers as independent of industrial technology as possible. In particular, Jones claimed that Gill championed an approach predicated on the centrality of delight and personal satisfaction in all spheres of making, that "all men should first of all, and most of all, be concerned to do their jobs well. That the good of the work should come first and be their natural concern, as also their natural delight." He held further that Gill's dedication to this ideal motivated his membership in "that movement against the exploitation of man as workman which has been and is the characteristic defect of our society." Despite later differences they had on these matters, then, their conversations and Jones's visits to Ditchling in 1921 gave intellectual affirmation and an objective correlative to Jones's nascent sense of the importance of preserving a gratuitous aesthetic and ethic in an age ruled increasingly by the utile.[89] Even more significantly, Gill influenced, and possibly impelled, its eventual religious expression: Jones's impression of their fundamental affinity on certain crucial points contributed to his conversion by offering an example of a like-minded associate who had ultimately found Roman Catholicism the faith most in accord with these views.

---

87. Dilworth, *Shape*, 65; and Chesterton, *Orthodoxy* (1908; reprint, New York: Image Books, 1959), 54.

88. Jones, "Wales and Visual Form," 81.

89. Jones, "Eric Gill," 302, 300. For their later differences, see Tony Stoneburner, "Notes on Prophecy and Apocalypse in a Time of Anarchy and Revolution: A Trying Out," in *Literature in Revolution*, ed. G. A. White and C. Newman (New York: Holt, Reinhart & Winston, 1972), 268–70.

More specifically, the burgeoning distinction between gratuity and utility abetted Jones's conversion in several ways. First, this differentiation flowed from and helped shape his basic belief about human nature. Jones argued that the gratuitous facet of art is what makes it a uniquely human activity. He conceded that both animals and humans are makers. But, he held, because only people have free will, and are thus liberated from the determining power of instinct, they alone can express gratuitous intention in their work: they alone can choose to make something beautiful, for the sole purpose of delight, rather than just fashioning what the standards of efficiency require. Thus "it is the intransitivity and gratuitousness in man's art that is the sign of man's uniqueness."[90] In such a schema, where a human is defined as a creative creature who is "inescapably committed to the extra-utile,"[91] then, "an act of art is essentially a gratuitous act."[92] As, for Jones, what goes for art also holds for sacrament, he judged that "things that are the signs of something other, together with those signs that not only have the nature of a sign, but are themselves, under some mode, what they signify" both "partake of the extra-utile and of the gratuitous," and that this trait is what makes creating them distinctly human actions.[93] Finally, he extended this reasoning to the sacrament that he saw as the archetypal artefact:

> So he crouches kindly and with attention, careful of the
> saving formulas, precise in the work of his hands. The
> gold tissue crumples, the transfigured man contracts over
> his work.
> It's a lover's work here.[94]

This mature portrayal of the Mass as a delight-filled making is an elaboration of the link between gratuity and Roman Catholicism that Jones was beginning to formulate in the late 1910s and early 1920s. In line with his growing sense of the radical difference between Protestant and Catholic theology, he began to think that all Christians used signs and

90. Jones, "Art and Sacrament," 148–49.
91. Jones to Harman Grisewood, undated draft, David Jones 1985 Purchase. Group B, Box V/6, NLW.
92. Jones, "Art in Relation to War," 164.
93. Jones, *The Anathemata*, 29. See also "Use and Sign," in *DG*, 183.
94. Jones, "The Old Quarry, Part One," in *RQ*, 115.

acted gratuitously, but that only Catholicism was based on this behavior. Given his beliefs in an essentially artistic human nature, a fundamental similarity between art and sacrament, and Christ's placement of Himself in this order of signs, Jones claimed, even long after he converted, that all His followers were committed to the importance of making: "no artefacture no Christian religion." He held that at both a Mass-house and a Meeting-house, Christians perform certain manual operations with material elements and proclaim that these things are done as a deliberate signification.[95] Yet, as has been shown, the doctrinal disputes about this Eucharistic rite that he discerned in the late 1910s and early 1920s convinced Jones that Catholicism alone had sacramentalism as its theological core.

In his mind, the Catholic emphasis on re-presentation in the Eucharist thus dedicates Roman Catholics particularly to sacrament's counterpart, art, and to gratuity, the foundation of both: "In contrast with some beliefs the belief of the Catholic Church commits its adherents . . . to the belief that things of all sorts can, are, and should be given special significances, set aside, made other, raised above the utile to the status of *signa* and revered with corporeal, manual acts."[96] As Catholicism was unique in being not only an incarnational religion, but one dedicated to "an *art-form* (the Mass) as the principal vehicle of grace and the core of the whole matter,"[97] he thought it alone among Christian creeds was rooted in his fundamental assumption about human nature: "the Catholic religion inescapably and centrally rests on the presupposition that extra-utile acts, signs or sacraments are not only valid and effectual but are connatural to man *qua* man."[98]

Jones's conviction that Catholicism distinctly and radically affirms art, sacrament, and gratuity theologically became the heart of his faith. But he considered these principles and practices challenged by modern cul-

---

95. Jones, *The Anathemata*, 31; and "Art and Sacrament," 163–64.

96. Jones, "A Christmas Message, 1960," 167.

97. Jones to Desmond Chute, 29 December 1952, in *Inner Necessities: The Letters of David Jones to Desmond Chute*, ed. Thomas Dilworth (Toronto: Anson-Cartwright, 1984), 26. Emphasis in original.

98. Jones to the *Tablet*, n.d., David Jones 1985 Purchase. Group C, Box 2, NLW. See also *DG*, 169–70.

ture even before he converted. From early on, he was apprehensive that modern civilization's apparent prioritization of the utile would erode the basis of art, sacrament, human nature, and, later, Roman Catholicism. He seems to have first discerned this perceived peril during his war service, as the tension between utility and gratuity, and concern about the former's ascendancy, is a crucial subtext of *In Parenthesis*. Jones claimed in its preface that "a rubicon has been passed between striking with a hand weapon as men used to do and loosing poison from the sky as we do ourselves," feeling that these more efficient means of waging war were somehow alien to the nature of *homo faber* and *homo significator*: "We who are of the same world of sense with hairy ass and furry wolf and who presume to other and more radiant affinities, are finding it difficult, as yet, to recognize these creatures of chemicals as true extensions of ourselves, that we may feel for them a native affection." In the poem itself, a memorial hymn of mechanism, "Casey Jones," drowns out a Christian song of praise, "O, How a Rose 'Ere Blooming," on Christmas; and the "regular discharges" of an artillery gun similarly muffle "the careful artistry of the prayers" at a Sunday service.[99] Even allowing for its retrospective nature, Jones's testimony and his extensive focus on this issue in his recalling of the war decades later indicate that his anxieties about the utile's sensed growing cultural predominance were troubling him in the trenches, and were thus part of the mental makeup with which he pondered whether or not to become a Roman Catholic.

In threatening to displace gratuity from its previously privileged place as making's primary motive, Jones believed, the ascendant emphasis on utility imperiled the basis of art. He argued consistently that "our age, the age of technical perfections, of function, of material efficiently directed towards a material end, is of its nature . . . anti-symbolic,"[100] and it thus finally excludes those dedicated to the extra-utile: "as the artist is concerned precisely with making things that are *signa* of some otherness (no matter what) his works would appear to have no essential and crucial place in such a situation were the matter carried to its logical conclusion." While Jones did not think his culture had yet reached this point, he

---

99. Jones, *IP*, xiv, 68, 107.
100. Jones, "Art in Relation to War," 136.

grew progressively less hopeful about its prospects.[101] Of course, what menaced art in his view also jeopardized sacrament. Believing that "Technological Man" is alienated from gratuity and the other "thought-modes of Man-the Artist, with which a sacramental religion is necessarily bound up," Jones concluded that the sacramentalist is as irrelevant as the artist in such a cosmology.[102] He thought this marginalization was also unfolding steadily in his day: "In a manner of speaking the priest and the artist are already in the catacombs."[103] He feared particularly the potential implications of this cultural transformation for what he considered the supreme Christian art and sacrament, anxieties he voiced by portraying a technocratic soldier's mess as a perverted utile Mass:

> See! I break this barrack bread, I drink with you, this issue cup,
> I salute, with you, these mutilated signa, I with you have cried
> with all of us the ratifying formula: *Idem in me.*[104]

So preoccupied was Jones with the threat he discerned from the utile that he even asserted the impossibility of finding "a single spoon" that does not offend the senses.[105]

He dismissed possible criticism of such a concern's apparent triviality by saying that it reflected regard for the "fundamental desires of all men, of Man."[106] Indeed, Jones's close attention to the purported modern preference for the utile does become more explicable in light of his idea of human nature. If people are artists and sacramentalists at root, a cultural trend that delegitimizes gratuitous making thus threatens to create a society of subhumans. Distress about this aspect of the utile's alleged dominance also seems to have originated in his war service, for technological war's dehumanizing effects is a frequent theme of *In Parenthesis*,

---

101. Jones, "Notes on the 1930s," 45. In a 1968 letter to Mr. Gommon, Jones claimed that "the obsession with the utile, etc. is much more ubiquitous in 1968 than it was in 1941, the dilemmas and problems . . . are more acute and more complicated." David Jones 1985 Purchase. Group C, Box 1, NLW.

102. Jones, "A Christmas Message, 1960," 174. See also Jones to Desmond Chute, 29 December 1952 (*Inner Necessities*, 25–27).

103. Jones, "Religion and the Muses," 103.

104. Jones, "The Tribune's Visitation," in *SL*, 58.

105. Jones, "The Utile," 181.

106. Ibid.

and these experiences became a metaphor for the state of Western culture in his later poetry.[107] At a more theoretical level, he claimed that

> the effect of obsession with "technocracy", the "utile" . . . [is] to alienate the mind of the creator we call "man" from all that has hitherto belonged to him as "man-the artist", man the "sign" or "sacrament-maker", & so be deprivative of the perceptions & acts that belong to man as "poeta."

The end result is "a kind of sub-man."[108] He found modern culture rife with this potential to a "unique degree" as, "more than any previous civilization," it compels its inhabitants to "sub-human (because entirely material utile and functional) activities."[109] Others echoed his cautions. Sayers, for one, wondered whether by confining men to "uncreative activities and an uncreative outlook, we are not doing violence to the very structure of our being"; to C. S. Lewis, a radical empiricism foreboded "the abolition of man."[110]

Unlike these two Anglicans, however, Jones also saw the utile as a singular threat to Roman Catholicism. Since he regarded this theology as predicated particularly on gratuity, he thought its basic claims were challenged more directly by technocracy than Protestantism's were. Jones argued that the utile's alleged rise to cultural power had affected "the Catholic thing in a special way," for its fundamental denial of gratuity struck at Catholicism's core stress on the primacy of extra-utile, sacramental behavior.[111] He thus deemed Catholicism "of necessity alien to the basic positivism of our present civilization"; but his view of Protestantism led him to conclude that these churches were not so threatened by, and hence not so necessarily hostile to, the utile.[112] Recalling his defi-

---

107. See *IP*, 37, 61, 66, 67, 89; and *RQ*, 187–211. Such passages illustrate Paul Fussell's argument that many writers whose outlooks were shaped by this war came to feel that "'modern society' is largely a continuation of the army by other means" (*The Great War and Modern Memory* [Oxford: Oxford University Press, 1975], 320).
108. Jones to René Hague, 19 January 1973; quoted in Hague, *Commentary*, 248.
109. Jones, "Wales and Visual Form," 90.
110. Sayers, *Mind of Maker*, 185; and Lewis, *The Abolition of Man* (New York: Macmillan, 1947), esp. 67–91.
111. Jones to René Hague, 8–16 June 1966 (*DGC*, 223).
112. Jones to the *Tablet*, undated draft, David Jones 1985 Purchase. Group A, Box I/1, NLW.

nition of Protestantism's essence as a proper interior disposition, Jones asserted that

> leaving aside the truth or otherwise of the Catholic belief in this matter, it is clearly at odds with the thought process which conditions all men of our essentially positivist, desacramentalized civilization, whereas a religion of the mind, of aspirations of interior "faith" issuing in "good works", is not, fundamentally, at odds with "modern man",

who Jones thought often aspired to these ideals in secular form.[113] He articulated these judgments most clearly in his later work, but they accord with his impressions developing during the late 1910s and early 1920s that Protestantism is indifferent or opposed to sacrament, that Catholicism in contrast is rooted in it, and that defending the gratuitous sensibility behind art and sacrament was increasingly important for preserving human nature's basis in an age he felt was growing steadily more antagonistic to that foundation.

As these aspects of Jones's analysis of the utile imply, his impression of its threat helped fashion his sense of being a rebel. Since his age's dominant cultural ideal denies the basis of artistic activity, he held, makers of all kinds must thus subvert the utile's hegemony. Artists are deliberate "witnesses to values elsewhere neglected," for their gratuitous making presents a "reaction against the functionalism, the *Materialismus*, the utility, the technics" in their delight-filled affirmations of the extra-utile.[114] Amongst this cloud of witnesses are also those devoted to sacrament. To Jones, "the occupation of all priests and of the whole sacramental system" all "runs counter to the main trend of our technocracy, for it presupposes the primacy of the extra-utile." He pointed especially to monks, whom he felt (as Chesterton and Dawson did) had historically protected art and sacrament.[115] But such succor from the past was in-

---

113. Jones to René Hague, 8–16 June 1966 (*DGC*, 222–24).
114. Jones, "Art in Relation to War," 138.
115. Jones to the *Tablet*, undated draft, David Jones 1985 Purchase. Group C, Box 1, NLW. For Jones on monks, see, e.g., "The Myth of Arthur," in *For Hilaire Belloc*, ed. Douglas Woodruff (1942; reprint, New York: Greenwood Press, 1969), 212–16. He heavily annotated Dawson's treatment of monasticism and its rebellious implications in *Medieval Essays* (London: Sheed & Ward, 1953), 68. For Chesterton's view, see "The New Dark Ages," *Sign* (July 1927): 12.

sufficient for his present purposes, for he continued to insist that "all artists are against the current of the age in a way perhaps they've never been before," as the modern utile seeks uniquely to exclude gratuity utterly as a valid facet or mode of making.[116] For Jones, this provocation was so fundamental that retaliatory acts of artistic and sacramental subversion were equally radical: "it is indeed 'human nature' that is rebelling—it is man-as-artist that is in rebellion."[117]

This former private's sense of being behind the lines against an overpowering foe made the Church Militant an especially appealing ally. His impression of the fundamental incompatibility between Roman Catholicism and the utile led Jones to regard this church as being as inherently rebellious against modern norms as he thought art, sacrament, and human nature are. He reiterated consistently that this basic disparity between technocracy's devaluation of sacrament and the Catholic affirmation of it means that the Church (unlike some kinds of Protestantism) cannot make peace with modern culture because it confronts the utile at the level of first principles.[118] Collaboration thus not being an option if Roman Catholics wish to preserve their integrity, they must necessarily join the underground: "There can be no *aggiornamento* there."[119] *The Anathemata* crystallizes this sense of traditional Catholicism as a besieged redoubt of gratuity:

> The utile infiltration nowhere held
> creeps vestibule
> is already at the closed lattices, is coming through each door.

---

116. Jones quoted in *The Poet Speaks*, ed. Peter Orr (London: Routledge & Kegan Paul, 1966), 98.

117. Jones, "Art in Relation to War," 159. Jones's contemporaneous critics generally recognized his own art's rebellious intent, although they accented different aspects. See, e.g., Herbert Read, "A Malory of the Trenches," *London Mercury* 36 (July 1937): 304; Harold Rosenberg, "Aesthetics of Crisis," *The New Yorker* 40 (22 August 1964): 114; and Bernard Bergonzi, *Heroes' Twilight* (London: Constable, 1965), 204.

118. See, e.g., Jones to Mr. Gommon, undated 1968, op. cit.; and "A Christmas Message, 1960," 172.

119. Jones to the *Tablet*, undated draft, David Jones 1985 Purchase. Group A, Box I/1, NLW.

> The cult-man stands alone in Pellam's land: more precariously than he knows he guards the *signa:* the pontifex among his house-treasures . . .[120]

Though Jones only made these connections fully years after his conversion, they were the fruit of reflection that was already underway earnestly in the late 1910s and early 1920s.

His attempt to begin systematizing these impressions at the time seems to have benefited from his contact with Gill. Beyond their other affinities, Jones also portrayed Gill as a rebel. He thought that being committed to gratuity made Gill "an oddity" by definition in a utile age, but he also maintained that his mentor's work possessed a "different *kind* of otherness" due, in part, to his religion.[121] Gill's defiant advocacy of developed views akin to Jones's embryonic intuitions hence helped persuade Jones that his growing identification with a faith seemingly based on sacrament was the warp of a seamless garment whose woof was his dissent from what appeared to be a progressively anti-symbolic era; this intellectual garb eventually became his battle armor. Newly enlisted himself, Gill was eager to sign up another recruit to this crusade.

Impressed as he was by those in the trenches of this cultural conflict's Catholic sector, Jones's choice of this unit finally rested on confidence in those giving the orders. Despite hating "staff-wallahs" in other contexts, he felt that the uprising against the utile needed a clear chain of command. From early on, Jones sensed a decline of traditional standards in art and life, and he came to think that Roman Catholicism alone offered an authoritative structure that affirmed the norms he considered consonant with human nature. Just as he judged the Mass the exemplary art work, he saw the "hierarchical organism of the Church" as "a supreme and confirmatory archetype of all that we had taken for granted in the creative works of man," and it was "owing to a half-conscious apperception of this that some of us became Catholics."[122] The Church's dogmatic dedication in its sacramental doctrines to the validity and centrality of

---

120. Jones, *The Anathemata*, 50.
121. Jones, "Eric Gill as Sculptor," 288–90. Emphasis in original.
122. Jones undated manuscript, David Jones 1985 Purchase. Group A, Box I/16, NLW. See also *DGC*, 44.

gratuity only ratified what Jones had long considered natural. But he deemed authoritative statements of this principle vital in his era to protect "what is natural to man" from the hegemonic "false theory" of sub-human utility, and he concluded that such prophylactic edicts would only be voiced by the Catholic Church.[123] If Protestantism in the main lacked substantive contrasts with the utile, its want of a single, conclusive source of obligatory beliefs also left it susceptible generally to what Jones saw as spurious secularist standards. Roman Catholicism, though, offered both a clash of absolutes with modern mores, and a definite means of establishing unequivocal norms, which its adherents acknowledged as binding.

For Jones, accepting this authority created greater confidence in combating the utile. He held that "certain ideas implicit or explicit in Catholic Dogma . . . have had a considerably liberating effect" on him, especially those about art.[124] Like Chesterton, then, Jones felt that when the heart is fixed on what both deemed a truth-telling (or truth-ratifying) institution, the hands are free to defy contrasting secularist notions. Faith in the Church's judgment and a commitment to accede to it provided, in his mind, the discipline essential to any successful insurgence. While many Protestants would form their strategy for dealing with modern unbelief ad hoc, and thus be overrun easily or prone to collaborate, the Catholic, not needing to reason out the whys of every plan, could focus fully on engaging his portion of the line. Jones saw himself as part of such a well-trained army under a competent general, declaring that "the Catholic Church whose supreme pontiff is the Bishop of Rome is waging celestial warfare of global extension" on behalf of gratuity.[125] Like Chesterton, Greene, and Dawson, then, Jones was finally convinced that Roman Catholicism was the only form of modern Christianity that was structured corporately to supply a certain and consistent articulation of particular core principles. It was thus, they thought, immune from contrary irreligious cultural trends and hence able to spearhead resistance to

---

123. Jones autobiographical manuscript, 5 September 1935, David Jones 1985 Purchase. Group B, Box V/5, NLW.

124. Jones to H. S. Ede, 5 September 1935, David Jones 1985 Purchase. Group C, Box 15, NLW.

125. Jones undated manuscript, David Jones 1985 Purchase. Group C, Box 2, NLW.

them. This issue's decisive nature is unsurprising, as conversion theorists note that a desire for authority is often crucial to Roman Catholic receptions.[126]

In Jones's case, Gill's influence was again instrumental. Perhaps with his mother's religious background in mind, Jones (like Newman, Chesterton, and Dawson) seems to have held out hope that he could find plenary Catholicism in the Anglican church. On his first visit to Ditchling, though, he recalled, Gill

> drew a triangle symbolizing the Catholic Church, and asked me what it was. I said, "A triangle." Then he drew what looked like a triangle except that its sides did not quite meet at the top, and he asked, "Now, what is this?" I said, "It is almost a triangle." He answered, "There *is* no almost-a-triangle; either it is a triangle or it is not."

Jones remembered further that the "non-triangle" represented the Anglican Church for, in this view, Anglicanism's rejection of papal teaching authority precludes its being fully Catholic.[127] It is hence one of those varieties of Protestantism more likely to connect its lines by embracing current cultural movements, due to the absence of constitutional brakes on such accommodation found within Roman Catholicism. Jones claimed that Gill used this triangle analogy to symbolize "absolute certainty." While not immediately persuasive, he admitted that the logic behind Gill's demonstration remained "peculiarly salutary" for him.[128] Indeed, the final stages of Jones's deliberations during the next few months of 1921 were dominated by the questions of whether one could be a Catholic Anglican, and of his relationship to his ancestral faith generally.

John O'Connor counseled Jones (as he would Chesterton a year later) that converting to Roman Catholicism would be the flowering, rather than sundering, of at least some religious roots, an issue especially weighty to one so concerned with unity. O'Connor insisted repeatedly that "there are lots of things in Anglicanism which are remains of Cath-

---

126. See, e.g., Walter Conn, *Christian Conversion* (New York: Paulist Press, 1986), 183.

127. Jones quoted in Thomas Dilworth, review of Blissett, *The Long Conversation*, *Chesterton Review* 9 (November 1983): 379. Emphasis in original.

128. Jones, "Eric Gill," 296–97. Jones consistently lamented the absence of a central doctrinal authority in Anglicanism and its perceived effects. See, e.g., Jones to Harman Grisewood, 6 July 1964 (*DGC*, 208).

olic Truth.... All they need is showing as they really are, renovating, and removing from corrosive action of error—of the tares growing with the wheat." He also stressed the idea of probabilism (which also would be crucial for Greene), telling Jones that it was a capital error to require "mathematical certitude" in this spiritual and moral question. Jones revisited Ditchling in early August, to O'Connor's delight. He was studying the Catholic catechism concurrently, and was impressed by its simplicity and lucidity. Perhaps feeling that reacquaintance with Gill had emboldened Jones, O'Connor tried to persuade him on 10 August that he was ready to be received. He reminded Jones of his lifelong knowledge of and interest in Catholicism, and urged him to transcend the hesitancy born of uncertainty that conversion theorists deem a frequent element of a convert's final steps: "Your trouble is largely nervousness at the untried. When you feel the ocean under you, you will feel that swimming is the only natural thing to do."[129]

Whether moved by this reasoning, by conversations with Gill, or a combination of these factors and the accumulated effects of his own reflections, Jones decided to take the plunge less than two weeks after receiving this letter.[130] He was conditionally rebaptized by O'Connor on 7 September 1921. His journey to Rome, begun on the Western front four years before, now ended in Chesterton's one fighting form of Christianity. Indeed, Jones took as his confirmation name the warrior archangel's, Michael, as he enlisted in the spiritual army he thought was waging celestial warfare. Although penned in a slightly different context, a passage from *In Parenthesis* crystallizes lucidly this sense that, in becoming a Roman Catholic, Jones was joining a small cell of countercultural insurgents, as well as the circumstances of his wartime attraction to this church and its central rite:

---

129. Thomas Dilworth, "The Letters of John O'Connor to David Jones," *Chesterton Review* 23 (February & May 1997): 59–62. For last-minute qualms as a common facet of conversions, see Griffin, *Turning*, 122–23.

130. Jones's final decision to be received occurred sometime before 24 August 1921, for his father wrote to him on that day reacting to a letter in which David had announced his intention to convert.

> Come on night's fall for ambuscade.
> Find harbour with a remnant.
> Share with the proscribed their unleavened cake.
> . . .
> Seek a way separate and more strait.[131]

While Jones acknowledged generously those (like Hughes, Wall, O'Connor, and Gill) who had helped him choose this new path, he stressed the role of personal example in faith less than Chesterton, Greene, or Dawson did. There are hints of romantic theology in his art, some inspired by his brief engagement to Gill's daughter, Petra, during the early 1920s. Yet he also asserted (unlike Charles Williams) that "'Romantic Love'" is "quite different from the Christian sacramental thing of marriage," making it a less likely conduit of grace.[132] Jones never addressed this issue in detail, but it seems plausible that the lack of a romantic element in his conversion and later spiritual life, his retiring nature, lingering pain from his breakup with Petra, and perhaps a reaction to the unconventional sexual practices of Eric Gill (who seemed to believe that establishing a connection between human and divine love suspended traditional Christian sexual mores) all helped make him charier of conflating love of neighbor and love of God than his peers were.[133]

Another form of love was implicated more directly in Jones's decision to become a Roman Catholic. Like Dawson, he was convinced of his choice's correctness, yet he also knew it would pain his family. In fact, it seems likely that entailed in Jones's fears about renouncing aspects of his Anglican heritage was concern that the sea of faith would become a Styx between himself and his father. David told James Jones of his decision in late August 1921. David warned that it was futile to argue, but James still registered objections. They were based on points of Protestant theology that had long troubled his son. He held that Roman Catholic sacramentalism was equivalent to idolatry; argued that in response to the purported want of authority, Roman Catholics displace scripture from its proper

---

131. Jones, *IP,* 66.
132. Jones to Harman Grisewood, 27 June 1959 (*DGC,* 177).
133. Fiona MacCarthy, *Eric Gill: A Lover's Quest for Art and God* (New York: E. P. Dutton, 1989).

primacy; and insisted that this church "is and always has been the enemy of progress and Enlightenment." Such a response from a devout Protestant thus ratified ironically David's belief that his affirmation of sacrament and negation of modernity were best voiced and upheld authoritatively by Rome. There was no lasting family breach, but some tension appeared to linger.[134] As in Dawson's case, the wreckage resulting from this decision was never pieced together fully. Yet in making this choice, David Jones also was finally able to unify his aesthetic perceptions with his religious principles, thereby achieving a psychic integration unknown even in childhood. As William James (and others) noted, this process by which "a self hitherto divided, and consciously wrong inferior and unhappy" becomes "unified and consciously right superior and happy" due to a "firmer hold upon religious realities" is a hallmark of conversion experiences.[135]

Some Jones readers have claimed that witnessing the Great War's carnage was a more crucial factor in effecting his conversion.[136] Although his war experience played a vital role in his ultimate decision, it has already been shown that, unlike Graves's or fellow Catholic convert Sassoon's, Jones's religious views were not traumatized by what he saw at the front. Rather, the war was more a backdrop for Jones's conception of the cultural concerns that were central to his conversion: as he was discerning the utile's hegemony through battlefield developments, he was also gaining immediate knowledge of a faith seemingly founded on gratuity and thus opposed intrinsically to what he regarded as modern technocracy's dehumanizing course. In that sense, Jeremy Hooker is correct to say that "the place in which David Jones experienced chaos was also

---

134. James Jones to David Jones, 24 August 1921, David Jones 1985 Purchase. Group C, Box 8, NLW; and Blissett, *Conversation*, 17, 67, 127.

135. William James, *The Varieties of Religious Experience* (1902; reprint, New York: Modern Library, 1929), 186. See also C. G. Jung, "Psychotherapists or the Clergy?" in *Modern Man in Search of a Soul*, trans. W. S. Dell and Cary F. Baynes (New York: Harcourt, Brace & World, 1933, 1966), 236–38, 243; and John Dunne, *A Search for God in Time and Memory* (New York: Macmillan, 1969), 223.

136. See, e.g., Stoneburner, "Prophecy and Apocalypse," 266–67; Neil Corcoran, *The Song of Deeds: A Study of The Anathemata of David Jones* (Cardiff: University of Wales Press, 1982), 96; and Kathleen Raine, "David Jones Remembered," in Merlin James, *David Jones 1895–1974: A Map of the Artist's Mind* (London: Lund Humphries, 1995), 62.

where he perceived the form of a great order."[137] If his march to Rome began in the Great War, then, Jones (as his confirmation name indicates) always had a greater war in mind, for he believed that "the first of all wars, which began in heaven . . . is not over yet."[138]

Ditchling Days: Maritain as Mentor

While Catholicism ratified rather than created most of the main tenets of his battle plan, Jones's worldview did gain enrichment and elaboration from his post-conversion study of Catholic theology. He took up residence at Ditchling in late 1921. If he did not become an unquestioning disciple of Gill's, some of the work Jones studied during his tenure in Sussex had a lasting impact on his religious ideas. One of the most seminal thinkers he read during this period was Jacques Maritain. He suggested that Maritain was as crucial an influence on his thought as Gill, especially his *Art and Scholasticism*, which Jones first read in 1923.[139] In particular, Maritain's writing helped Jones refine his ideas about the link between art and sacrament, and the distinction between gratuity and utility.

Art and Scholasticism reaffirmed Jones's belief that re-presentation is the purpose of art, for Maritain held that art manifests in a material a definite "radiation of Being," making any work of art a "sign."[140] As Jones's understanding of Catholic theology broadened, he began accenting this asserted transubstantiatory aspect of art and sacrament more, concluding ultimately that artists and priests have the same function in the post-Ascension world. Although he thought pre-Christian artists and ritualists had achieved analogically the fusion of spirit and matter that Christ accomplished directly, Jones also believed that makers who live following His physical presence are especially required to re-present this synergy, so as to show forth the ongoing salvific indwelling of the Logos

---

137. Jeremy Hooker, "In the Labyrinth: An Exploration of *The Anathemata*," in *David Jones: Man and Poet*, ed. John Matthias (Orono: University of Maine Press, 1989), 280. Even Jones's harshest critic acknowledges the primacy of cultural motives in his conversion (Ward, *Mythmaker*, 20–21).

138. Dilworth, *Shape*, 116.

139. See Dilworth, review of *The Long Conversation*, 376; and Jones, "Autobiographical Talk," in *E&A*, 30.

140. Maritain quoted in Dilworth, *Shape*, 10.

with the temporal. For Jones, art became "essentially a conjoining of two things, matter and spirit,"[141] making the central question for artists in the ages after Christ whether they "'fill up' in their arts 'what is lacking' to the continuing processes of conjoining heaven and earth, or do they not?"[142] The priest's role in continuing this process of conjunction comes, in Jones's mind, from his ability to make Christ as really present in each Mass as He was in Palestine in the days of Caesar Augustus: "the babe of real, substantial, mortal flesh ... was neither more or less a *signum* of the Eternal Logos, than the *signa* on the altar."[143] In seeing both art and sacrament as fundamentally incarnational, as well as gratuitous, then, Jones found further reason for declaring the Mass the model art work.

He posited the identity of these vocations, while implying another piquant aspect of them and his sense of modernity's hostility to these roles, most clearly in a later poem:

> It takes a bit of priest, Iscariot, to make the best
> prophet—and, as we see, the best poet. Turn that over,
> in that anti-clerical head of yours—you'll find it sober
> if unfamiliar truth—O I know well these offices are made
> to be antipathetic—that's typical, that's the cant of the age.[144]

There appears to be a greater tension between artist and priest elsewhere, but Thomas Dilworth has shown that even those passages illustrate the complementarity, rather than contradiction, of these functions in Jones's mind.[145] The speed with which Jones adopted this belief and began working out its implications is revealed by Gill's 1928 appraisal that his protégé's current aesthetic was consciously incarnational: "for him, paint is stuff with which to materialize mental visions—in which to fuse the material with the spiritual." And even a far less friendly critic concedes the centrality of this idea to Jones's lifelong outlook, judging

---

141. Jones, "Wales and Visual Form," 92.
142. Jones, "Art in Relation to War," 142–43.
143. Jones to Harman Grisewood, undated draft, David Jones 1985 Purchase. Group B, Box V/6, NLW.
144. Jones, "The Agent," in *RQ*, 144. See also "Religion and the Muses," 103.
145. See Jones, "The Sleeping Lord," in *SL*, 82; and Dilworth, *Shape*, 333.

it "the single most fruitful consequence" of his three years in Sussex.[146]

Jones also drew on Maritain in elaborating and expanding the crucial notion of gratuity. Jones maintained in 1935 that the "most important" liberating dogma he learned from the Church was that "God made and sustains the whole show *gratuitously.*"[147] It was from Maritain specifically that he took the terminology of gratuity, for in *Art and Scholasticism* the philosopher declared that "art is gratuitous" intrinsically, and he also stressed delight as such making's hallmark.[148] He held further that only God can create entirely gratuitously (a point Jones accepted in his claim that all human making is a blend of gratuitous and utilitarian motives), while emphasizing that, due to this limitation on human making, "artistic creation does not copy God's creation, it continues it."[149] Jones posited a more elastic version of this latter point, though, often suggesting a near-identity between a human's gratuitous acts of creation and God's gratuitous act of Creation, thereby harmonizing again his pre-conversion aesthetic with his newfound theology.

In 1939, Jones echoed Maritain, arguing that humans "extend" divine creativity when they fashion things gratuitously.[150] By 1950, though, he had become bolder:

> I understand the theologians to say that God's creation of the cosmos was a gratuitous act: it is interesting therefore that it is that very quality of gratuitousness which we recognize in the creative works of man. . . . There is little or no point, so it seems to me, in stressing the differences of degree. I believe the tendency to stress those differences of degree and to posit a difference of kind comes from theorists rather than from workmen, from "philosophers" rather than from "makers."[151]

---

146. Eric Gill manuscript, 7 September 1928, David Jones 1985 Purchase. Group A, Box III/27, NLW; and Ward, *Mythmaker*, 34.

147. Jones to H. S. Ede, 5 September 1935, op. cit. Emphasis in original.

148. Maritain quoted in Staudt, *Turn*, 41. See also Breslin, "Shaping," 97.

149. Maritain quoted in Breslin, "Shaping," 98. For Maritain on God alone creating gratuitously, see David Blamires, *David Jones: Artist and Writer* (Manchester: Manchester University Press, 1971), 20.

150. David Jones, "Christopher Smart," in *E&A*, 287.

151. David Jones, "A Note on Mr. Berenson's Views," in *E&A*, 275.

As Jones matured intellectually, then, he seems to have concluded that the fine Scholastic distinctions of trained philosophers like Maritain obscured the artistic and imaginative power of asserting a fundamental relationship between human and divine gratuitous creativity. If it is overstatement to call these views "somewhat heterodox," it is clear that Jones's interpretation of Catholicism was governed by concerns antedating his conversion and his desire to unify these notions with his adopted creed's tenets.[152]

Jones was not alone in stating even this more daring equation, as Greene (for one) voiced similar ideas.[153] What distinguishes Jones's view of gratuity, though, is his explicit opposition of it to the utile. Maritain's work contains no such overt polarity, so Jones's adaptation of this concept to his own analysis reveals again his willingness to associate new theological terms freely with his perennial concerns. Elizabeth Ward thus concludes correctly that Maritain bequeathed to Jones not so much his philosophy itself, but "an intellectual basis for the emotional distrust of modernity" that Jones had felt increasingly in the years prior to arrival at Ditchling.[154] Additionally, Jones's positing of a theoretical bifurcation where none had existed before reveals further his thought's binary nature.[155]

---

152. Ward, *Mythmaker*, 23.

153. Greene, *A Burnt-Out Case* (1960; reprint, New York: Penguin, 1977), 81; and John Cornwell, "Why I Am Still a Catholic," in *Graham Greene: Man of Paradox*, ed. A. F. Cassis (Chicago: Loyola University Press, 1994), 465–66. For other thinkers' cognate views, see, e.g., Glenn Olson, "Cultural Dynamics: Secularization and Sacrilization," in *Christianity and Western Civilization*, ed. Wethersfield Institute (San Francisco: Ignatius Press, 1995), 114; and A. N. Wilson, *C. S. Lewis: A Biography* (New York: Fawcett Columbine, 1990), 87.

154. Ward, *Mythmaker*, 39. Jones's interest in Maritain outlasted his tenure at Ditchling and received further encouragement from the Order Group, for, as Harman Grisewood recalled, "Maritain was our philosopher" (Grisewood, "Remembering David Jones," *Journal of Modern Literature* 14 [Spring 1988]: 570).

155. Fussell has argued that polarized outlooks were a common outcome for those who experienced trench warfare in the Great War (*Great War*, 76, 79). Jonathan Miles, though, has held that Jones's polarized thinking resulted from his 1920s residence in the border area of Capel-y-ffin (*Eric Gill and David Jones at Capel-Y-Ffin* [Bridgend: Seren, 1992], 15). However, given the war's deep effect on his consciousness in so many other ways, it is more plausible that his attraction to Capel was a manifestation of an oppositional habit of mind developed in the trenches rather than this bifurcated vision's genesis.

The "Substantial Advantage" of Thomism

This habit of dichotomizing made theological dualism a strong temptation for Jones. In fact, Ward describes his outlook often as "dualistic," even asserting that he had a "Manichaean style of imagination."[156] Her use of these terms is imprecise, though, and yields an inaccurate reading of his worldview, for the theology Jones learned at Ditchling, and to which he assented essentially thenceforth, was distinctly Thomist. Jones was well aware of his attraction to dualistic theologies. He once professed Marcionism, a second-century gnostic heresy. One of Dawson's favorite Church Fathers, Irenaeus, persuaded him to abandon this belief, but the tug of dualism continued to condition Jones's religious views.[157] He conceded in 1942, for instance, that "I liked very much" some elements of Buddhism.[158] Studying Thomism aided his rejection of dualistic ideas, for it offered him (as it did Chesterton) a firmly incarnational theology, one committed to the corporeal. He found Thomism conducive to key aspects of his cosmology, like (as his use of Maritain's work shows) the sense of an intimate relationship between divine and human creativity, the connection between art and sacrament, and gratuity. At root, though, it was Thomism's insistence on the goodness of matter that drew Jones (as it did Gill), for he felt that this principle made the distinctly human activities of art and sacrament possible.[159]

Jones claimed that Roman Catholic theology had convinced him of "the reality of matter and spirit, that both are real and both good."[160] From this premise, he concluded that "the Catholic Church commits its adherents, in a most inescapable manner, to the body and the embodied . . . to sense-perception, to the contactual, the known, the felt, the seen, the handled," and hence also to "a certain mistrust of the unembodied

---

156. Ward, *Mythmaker*, 40.

157. Dilworth, *Shape*, 355; and Blissett, *Conversation*, 76. See Jones to Harman Grisewood, 18 May 1956 (*DGC*, 167–68), for his continued attraction to Marcionism despite "loath[ing]" its "ascetical thing."

158. Jones to Tom Burns, 10 May 1942, David Jones 1985 Purchase. Group B, Box I/16, NLW.

159. See Malcolm Yorke, *Eric Gill: Man of Flesh and Spirit* (New York: Universe Press, 1981), 41–46.

160. Jones to H. S. Ede, 5 September 1935, op. cit.

concept" that Jones remained drawn to.¹⁶¹ In particular, he cited often Aquinas's claim that the body is a "substantial advantage." To Jones, the benefit humans derive from bodies is that having one allows them to interact gratuitously with other matter in a way that neither pure spirits nor creatures without souls are able to: "Without our corporeality, there could not be 'making' or 'makers', there could then not be that making which is done at the altar. The incorporeal intelligences (angels) are incapable of Ars and the animals are incapable of Ars. It is we alone of all creation that are capable of Ars, of sign, of sacrament."¹⁶² Thomism's emphasis on the goodness of the material thus enriched theologically Jones's aesthetic insight that people, and only people, are gratuitous makers while also helping him combat further the dualistic beliefs whose pull he never seems to have escaped fully.

Belief in the resurrection of the body was another crucial dogmatic validation of its importance for Jones, one Blissett judged close to his "deepest religious concern."¹⁶³ As early as 1927, Jones was accenting, in Thomistic terms, his impression of the Church's insistence that "man is *incomplete* without body—hence the 'Resurrection of the body' . . . she says that whatever *is* of the 'essence' of our bodies (and not merely accidental) we shall have for all eternity—as separate individuals."¹⁶⁴ He referred to this teaching often, and his interest in the body's role in the economy of salvation and its fate after death also fostered concern for proper burial rites. He considered "a religious care for the dead" a sacrament and thus a sign of humanity, one practiced "because of the sacredness of bodies." Whether a culture affirmed this principle or not became a test of its vitality for Jones, for he endorsed Dawson's dictum that only dying civilizations forget their dead.¹⁶⁵

---

161. Jones, "A Christmas Message, 1960," 167.
162. Jones, undated draft of "Poets and Mystics," David Jones 1985 Purchase. Group C, Box 1, NLW. For his invocations of Aquinas on the body, see, e.g., *E&A*, 165–67; *DG*, 176; *DGC*, 240. For a similar view in Chesterton's work, see *A Miscellany of Men* (New York: Dodd, Mead & Co., 1912), 145–46.
163. Blissett, *Conversation*, 67.
164. Jones to H. S. Ede, 4 November 1927 (*DGC*, 45). Emphasis in original.
165. Jones, *The Anathemata*, 61, n. 2; and "The Roman Quarry," in *RQ*, 19, n. 40. See also Christopher Dawson, *The Age of the Gods* (New York: Houghton, Mifflin, 1928), 23–24, 421 (highlighted by Jones).

Jones thought modern technocracy failed this test, for he deemed it uniquely hostile to the body, whether alive or dead: "more than any previous civilization it tends to disembody man."[166] His war years appear to have been crucial in shaping this belief. He saw mechanized warfare as particularly adverse to the body's sacredness and integrity, depicting industrial weapons and the wounds they impart as historically unprecedented:

> Properly organized chemists can let make more riving
> power than ever Twrch Trwyth;
> more blistered he is than painted Troy Towers
> and unwholer, limb from limb, than any of them fallen at
> Catraeth
> or on the seaboard-down, by Salisbury . . .

The large number of casualties caused due to this technological progress are met by a technological answer. Instead of burying all the dead individually,

> They bright-whiten all this sepulchre with powdered chloride of lime. It's a perfectly sanitary war.

But, to Jones, these "chemical-corrupted once-bodies" have lost the recognition, connoted by a discrete grave, of the separate individuality that he thought they will have eternally:

> They've
> served him barbarously—poor Johnny—you wouldn't desire him, you wouldn't know him for any other.

These Johnnies are at least buried in some sense, though. In the heat of battle, Jones contended, modern warriors disregard even remedial rituals for their slain comrades, behavior he found antithetical to an ancestral human impulse. There is "no maker to contrive his funerary song," for

> this aint a bloody Wake
> for these dead, who will soon have their dead
> for burial clods heaped over.

---

166. Jones, "Wales and Visual Form," 90.

> Nor time for halsing
> nor to clip green wounds
> nor weeping Maries bringing anointments
> neither any word spoken
> nor no decent nor appropriate sowing of this seed
> nor remembrance of the harvesting
> of the renascent cycle
> and return
> nor shaving of the head nor ritual incising for these *viriles* under each tree.[167]

Jones's invocation of so many traditional rites for the dead both illustrates his impression of utile civilization's uniqueness and rebukes its perceived break with millennia of human behavior. Beyond these cultural disputes with modern norms, he added a distinctly religious one. Arguing that "a moralist or man of ethic, [or] a man who holds a religion of pure spirit . . . need not, I suppose, see what all the fuss is about,"[168] Jones asserted that Roman Catholicism's dedication to the body made its adherents implacable foes of all alleged modern efforts to dis-grace the material: "It commits them to the 'creaturely.'"[169] Besides adding texture to his pre-conversion affirmations, then, Jones's interpretation of this aspect of Thomism also gave him additional reason to rebel against his culture, and to do so from a particularly Roman Catholic standpoint.

The repudiation of disembodied abstractions and commitment to the individual integrity of bodies and matter that Jones took from Thomism also led him to accent the importance of the particular and of limits. Echoing a view of Maritain's that he endorsed, Jones asserted that the artist, "of his nature, deals in the contactual and the particular."[170] He held that this insight arose initially from his being a visual artist, but he also stressed that Catholic theology had taught him the incarnational principle that "in each particular the general should shine out, and that

---

167. Jones, *IP*, 155, 43, 155, 174.
168. Jones to Desmond Chute, 29 December 1952 (*Inner Necessities*, 26).
169. Jones, "A Christmas Message, 1960," 167.
170. David Jones, "On the Difficulties of One Writer of Welsh Affinity Whose Language Is English," in *DG*, 31. For Maritain's view, and Jones's approval of it, see Miles, *Backgrounds*, 42–43.

without the particular there can be no general for us men."[171] He made this opinion part of his artistic credo, insisting often that "our business here below is to make the universal shine out from the particular," but under a crucial condition: "the concrete, the exact dimensions, the contactual, the visual, the bodily, what the senses register, the assembled data [come] first—*then* is the 'imagination' freed to get on with the job. The vague, the fanciful, the generalized have no place," especially when it comes to abstract ideas.[172] Gill held as early as 1930 that Jones was abiding by this standard in his visual art, a judgment Blissett seconded later for his poetry.[173] Similarly, Jones stressed the importance of limits. He argued that the artist "must work within the limits of his love. There must be no mugging-up, no 'ought to know' or 'try to feel'; for only what is actually loved and known can be seen *sub specie aeternitatis*."[174] Despite the begged questions in this theorem, Jones claimed to adhere to it firmly in his own work, even at the cost of making it opaque to some audiences. His critics generally confirm his fidelity to this norm, and Blissett has substantiated Jones's implication here that this dedication to limits in artistic work derived partially from his understanding of Catholicism.[175]

Jones held further that modern culture contradicted his concern for the particular and limits. He argued that "awareness of the importance of what is particular" is in "conflict with our present technological civilization, which flattens out and standardizes the diversity of all created things."[176] He ascribed this devaluation of the discrete in part to the apparent ascendancy of his fellow converts' bête noire, abstraction, in aesthetics: "Those actually engaged on what are now called 'the Arts' sometimes give the impression of being more interested in movements, aims, trends and ideologies than in the nature of Ars herself," which is to deal

---

171. Jones to H. S. Ede, 5 September 1935, op. cit. See also Dilworth, *Shape*, 117; and Blissett, *Conversation*, 39.

172. David Jones, "James Joyce's Dublin," in *E&A*, 304, 306. Emphasis in original. For the importance of adhering to this norm when dealing with abstract ideas, see, e.g., *DGC*, 89; *DG*, 82; and *E&A*, 210.

173. See Blissett, *Conversation*, 153.

174. Jones, *The Anathemata*, 24.

175. William Blissett, "The Syntax of Violence," in Matthias, *Man and Poet*, 206. See also Blamires, *Artist and Writer*, 59; *IP*, x; *The Anathemata*, 9–43.

176. Jones, undated manuscript, David Jones 1985 Purchase, Group B, Box V/5, NLW.

in the contactual and particular.¹⁷⁷ He also felt that "ancient limits are transgressed" often in modern times, which is "never, in itself, a good."¹⁷⁸ He again drew on his war experiences, for part of what troubled Jones about modern war was its total nature. His distress at technological conflict's boundless destruction and what it connoted is clear in his use of a common trope of Great War writing, the "first shell":

> Out of the vortex, rifling the air it came—bright, brass-shod, Pandoran; with all-filling screaming the howling crescendo's up-piling snapt. The universal world, breath held, one half second, a bludgeoned stillness. Then the pent violence released a consummation of all burstings out; all sudden up-rendings and rivings-through—all taking-out of vents—all barrier-breaking—all unmaking. Pernitric begetting—the dissolving and splitting of solid things.¹⁷⁹

To Jones, then, modern society had brought disaster on itself by forsaking ancestral boundaries due to its utilitarian, single-minded fascination with what could be done if everything was seen as possible. For him, traditional Catholicism's commitment to contrary principles thus offered a refuge from this physical and cultural suicide: if Pandora's box could never be closed again, the tabernacle built on the Rock of Peter still contained a Body that could never die.

Jones's sense that the convictions he had deduced from Thomism were besieged in his epoch made him especially wary of beliefs that he thought lacked a forthright dedication to the temporal. Even when acknowledging appealing aspects of Buddhism, for example, he still concluded that "it's a rum business."¹⁸⁰ Moreover, he disclaimed any attrac-

---

177. Jones, "The Utile," 183.
178. David Jones, "The Viae," in *E&A*, 192.
179. Jones, *IP*, 24. See also "Art in Relation to War," 133.
For the "first shell" as a common theme in Great War literature, see William Blissett, "*In Parenthesis* Among the War Books," *University of Toronto Quarterly* 42 (Spring 1973): 283. As Jones wrote so much later than most other Great War writers and was familiar with their work, it is possible that he knew the significance of this motif, and thus sought to invest his use of it with a potent dose of cultural criticism.
180. Jones to Tom Burns, 10 May 1942, op. cit.

tion to Islam, and singled out Muslim iconoclasm when depicting this faith.[181] This antipathy extended to other forms of Christianity. For instance, in line with his view of Protestantism's essence, Jones condemned "totally unsacramental and unintellectual" Calvinistic Methodism.[182] But he was also suspicious of a figure many Roman Catholics revere: Augustine of Hippo. He invoked Augustine throughout his poetry, yet he also deemed the saint "'wrong' about all kinds of things."[183] Specifically, Jones (perhaps betraying his own insecurity in this regard) felt that Augustine never renounced his early dualism sufficiently. For example, he noted Dawson's analysis of Augustine's "sympathy with the Platonic tradition," and added a telling annotation: "a blood still too much."[184] Whereas Greene tended to an Augustinian attitude and Dawson blended Augustinianism and Thomism in his work, Jones's experience with disembodied beliefs made him, like Chesterton, fully confident only in the Angelic Doctor's diagnoses and prescriptions.

Likewise, Jones lacked Greene's and Dawson's enthusiasm for mysticism. He claimed in 1927 to "loathe the word mystic," and he elaborated theologically on this disdain in 1935: "it is important to be anthropomorphic, to deal through and in the things we understand as men—to be incarnational. To know that a beef-steak is neither more nor less 'mystical' than a diaphanous cloud."[185] By 1971, he professed not to read or understand mystics.[186] Yet even in these later days, Jones was unable to persuade himself fully of a critique of pure spirit, for he told Dilworth (who only knew him during his final three years) that he was not a mystic, but "I wish to God I were."[187] But even if Jones was haunted persistently by disembodied theologies and practices, his adoption of Thomism's em-

---

181. Blissett, *Conversation*, 136; and Jones, *The Anathemata*, 147.

182. Blissett, *Conversation*, 105.

183. Jones to Jim (probably H. S. Ede), undated 1953, David Jones 1985 Purchase. Group C, Box 2, NLW. See also *The Anathemata*, 50, 167; "The Book of Balaam's Ass," in *RQ*, 201; "The Wall," in *SL*, 13.

184. Dawson, *Medieval Essays*, 47.

185. Jones to H. S. Ede, 4 November 1927 (*DGC*, 45); and Jones to H. S. Ede, 5 September 1935 (Matthias, *Man and Poet*, 110).

186. Blissett, *Conversation*, 72.

187. Dilworth, *Shape*, 24. It is thus somewhere between ironic and incisive that Waugh's review of *In Parenthesis* was entitled "A Mystic in the Trenches."

phasis on the body; his stress on its role in making; his consequent concern for its integrity, for its fate after death, for rites dealing with it, and for the particular and limits; and his intense wariness about other beliefs and behaviors, all indicate that this inclination was not his imagination's dominant force. Thomas Whittaker's conclusion is hence a just corrective to Ward's: "Jones was no obsessive dualist of doubtful Christianity but an empirical artist who approached the paradoxes of Christian non-dualism through the medium of the things that *homo faber, homo sapiens* is enabled to make."[188]

Jones's years of imbibing Thomism at Ditchling concluded in 1924. Due to intra-community disputes, the Gill family moved to Capel-y-ffin, where Jones spent much of 1924–26. But his period as Gill's apprentice was ending, although he would continue to visit the Gills and even made a community they formed at Pigotts in 1928 his chief abode from 1929–33. As Jones began spending more time in London, he met members of the future Order Group, whom he credited with helping refine his mature worldview.[189] By 1928, he had also made a portentous decision in his artistic career, as he began drafting the first passages of *In Parenthesis*: "I had no idea of what I was letting myself in for."[190]

Hanging on the Axile Tree: Jones's Theology of History

Indeed, it took Jones nearly a decade to write and publish this poem, for he was interrupted by a serious breakdown, from 1933 to 1936. He ascribed it to the effects of the war, early domestic troubles, and overreaching his capacities in his visual art. His writing may have added to the strain, for he was embarking on a new art form, revisiting his war experiences, and, in the process, starting to develop an intricate theology of history.[191] In answer to a question he would pose poetically years later—"Ah! what shall I write?"—Jones (who had long been interested in history) began to see the past as the poet's *materia;* and he sought to ex-

---

188. Thomas Whittaker, "Homo Faber, Homo Sapiens," in Matthias, *Man and Poet*, 484.
189. See *DGC*, 185, 190; and Grisewood, "Remembering David Jones," 568–71.
190. Jones, "Fragments of an Attempted Autobiographical Writing," 108.
191. See Jones to Dr. Crichton Miller, op. cit.; Jones to Harman Grisewood, 12 January 1935, Grisewood Papers, Box 2, Folder 3; Jones to John H. Johnston, 27 April 1962, David Jones 1985 Purchase. Group B, Box I/9, NLW; and *DGC*, 124.

plain its meaning by placing Christ, His redemptive death, and what Jones considered re-presentations of Himself and His sacrifice at its center.[192]

Before elucidating this historical hermeneutic's specific elements, some of its underlying premises need to be established. First, perhaps inspired by his devout upbringing and his youthful sense that art and sacrament are intrinsic to human nature, Jones posited that people are naturally religious. He maintained that this impulse appears even in those who renounce traditional creeds: "those who reject the postulates of supernatural religion are no less bound than are the men of religion by the allurements of *a* Prudentia . . . we *all* are committed to a Prudentia of sorts."[193] Thus, Jones concluded, all differences are theological differences, even those to which unbelievers are a party. As one of his technocratic characters puts it about Roman disputes with the occupied Jews,

> Religion? Why certainly, that's at the bone of it—
> same as everywhere, what I call the unhappy fallacy.[194]

While this speaker considers religion a failure of logical thinking, his Thomistic creator insisted frequently on the particularly rational nature of Roman Catholicism. Reflecting again the tension between his mind's discursive and mystical sides, Jones did occasionally discuss religion's metarational facets, Greene's "faith."[195] Yet, perhaps to compensate for what seemed too strong an attraction to these aspects, he accented

---

192. David Jones, "A, a, a, Domine Deus," in *SL*, 9. For his lifelong interest in history, see Jones to John H. Johnston, 27 April 1962, David Jones 1985 Purchase. Group B, Box V/6, NLW; and Jones quoted in Paul Hills, "Making and Dwelling Among Signs," in *David Jones, Artist and Poet*, ed. Paul Hills (Aldershot: Scolar Press, 1997), 84. For history as the poet's material for making, see *The Poet Speaks*, 104.

Jones's interest in a theology of history would also have been stoked by reading Maritain and knowing Order Group members Dawson and Martin D'Arcy, all of whom wrote extensively on this topic.

193. Jones, "Art and Sacrament," 146–47. Emphasis in original. He also noted Dawson's assertion of this contention in *Enquiries* (London: Sheed & Ward, 1934), 194.

194. Jones, "The Old Quarry, Part Two," in *RQ*, 158.

195. In an undated fragment, for example, he wrote of "the supreme folly of pretending that what is proposed for our belief is anything other than something totally beyond our understanding, and impatient of analysis, yet answering to some deeps in our make-up." David Jones 1985 Purchase. Group A, Box V/5, NLW.

Catholicism's "belief" components more often. For example, he stressed that the Mass's celebrants represent "rational man" and offer a "rational sacrifice," and he referred repeatedly to the Mass's offertory prayer, which asks God to, among other things, "make reasonable" the gifts of bread and wine.[196] As Jones shared Greene's sense of living in a rationalistic, positivistic age, he may also have felt his need to highlight Roman Catholicism's rational dimension to gain a hearing for its tenets, thereby adding a cultural motive to his personal ones for this emphasis.

Thinking that those who make everything, including history, are religious at root and that his own faith was based in reason, he thus felt that only a theo-logic can explain history's meaning fully. To Jones, history mattered because of its link to eternity: "Time is already big by sacred commerce with the Timeless courses."[197] This outlook resulted from his tragic view of life. Jones believed in original sin, sure that "something pretty fundamental has gone awry, and certainly that great misery and appalling wrongness abounds and that the lachrymose valley is the habitat of most (if not all)" people.[198] Such a cosmology finds no reason for hope within history itself. For Jones, hope and history can rhyme by using a transcendent grammar, but only by employing such a syntax:

> It is a kind of cowardice to look on history and not to despair if we confine ourselves to the natural order ... it can be objectively "all right" only if we pre-suppose an "other-world" order ... there is no decent escape from the *lacrimarum vale* ... if we open all the cupboards and bring out all the skeletons and consider the frustration which history past and present offers as a "pattern," [we] are compelled, if we presume to a shadow of optimism, to posit the necessity of other-world values.[199]

Thus, while that "day when Clio has no more to muse about" shadows Jones's work, this is not a sign of historical pessimism, as Ward thinks.[200]

---

196. Jones, *The Anathemata*, 202, n. 2, 30. See also ibid., 49, 64, 230; *IP*, 162; *SL*, 58; and *RQ*, 92.
197. Jones, *The Anathemata*, 213.
198. Jones to Harman Grisewood, 9 October 1971 (*DGC*, 234). See also *SL*, 20.
199. Jones, "Art in Relation to War," 154–55.
200. Jones, *The Anathemata*, 208. For the apocalypse backdrop, see, e.g., *IP*, 2, 8, 36, 114–16, 120–24, 135, 156, 160, 163, 167; *The Anathemata*, 49, 68, 121, 125, 130, 136, 151, 160, 236; *SL*, 24; *RQ*, 40, 71–72, 105.

Rather, belief in that other-world order and its values gave him a cosmic optimism like that which Chesterton also found in Christianity: history is objectively "all right" because apocalypse is followed by eschaton.

To avoid the absorption in entirely other-worldly orders that he sought to elude, however, Jones thought a theology of history, like any intellectual system, should be rooted in the particular. He thus stressed what he (like Chesterton, Greene, and Dawson) considered the historicity of Christianity, and its consequent commitment to letting the facts of actual events limit its claims, an outlook he felt orthodox Roman Catholicism upheld especially. Jones held that Christ affirmed history by entering it, not as an apparition, but as a tangible actor in a certain setting:

> not at any time, but
> at this acceptable time.[201]

Due to this divine validation of the discrete, "the Incarnation commits Xtians to an inescapable concern for time and place, site and event."[202] Among Christian churches, Jones felt, Catholicism's distinctive dogmatic dedication to the body and embodied also made it specially devoted "to history, to locality, to epoch and site."[203] He also accented Catholicism's commitment to historicity in his verse. A priest character, for example, finds the names of actual past persons "more credible" than those of figures from "a most wondrous tale."[204] But Jones regarded even the wondrous tale told in the Christian story itself as limited by factual parameters. His description of the Christmas liturgy's Gospel reading evinces this belief. At the word *voluntatis*, which ends this reading, the deacon,

> however much he would wish to continue proclaiming his wonder-tale, he must break off the recitation of this true *historia* and be silent.[205]

---

201. Jones, *The Anathemata*, 58.
202. Jones, undated manuscript, David Jones 1985 Purchase. Group A, Box IV/16, NLW.
203. Jones, "A Christmas Message, 1960," 167.
204. Jones, "The Sleeping Lord," 84.
205. Jones, *The Anathemata*, 220.

No embellishment of this wonderful tale is allowed, for that would violate its integrity as a true history, and thereby undermine a principle Jones judged central to the Christian, and especially Roman Catholic, cosmology.

In the Christian schema, God not only became one with the temporal, though. He also died to redeem it and its actors at a specific point and place in time ("under Pontius Pilate"); it is this event that Jones made central to his understanding of history.

> [I]t is incumbent upon all Christians to believe, and it is a central dogma of the Catholic Church, that the Redemption of the World was accomplished once for all at a certain date in time and at a specified site, that is, on Calvary.[206]

Jones claimed once that it was while composing *The Anathemata* that he had occasion to "consider the Tree of the Cross as the axial beam round which all things move."[207] But he also admitted that Christ's Passion became "almost an obsession" at a young age, as, when assigned scripture to study, he usually skipped the appointed passages and instead read accounts of the Passion.[208] His Good Friday cross-carrying in the family garden at age six tends to confirm this sense of a lifelong concern for the Crucifixion, and some of his early visual art also substantiates it. Jones's fascination with the subject persisted, as he even kept a nail in a chalice in his room as a constant reminder of Christ's death.[209] Whereas Chesterton and Dawson tended to find God's becoming human at all the apex of time's course, Jones was more specific, thinking that the even more astonishing assertion that this God-man had died to save His fallen crea-

---

206. Jones, "Art and Sacrament," 167.

207. David Jones, "Wales and the Crown," in *E&A*, 39. Eliot also used the term "axle-tree," although neither poet seems to have learned the term directly from the other (T. S. Eliot, *Four Quartets* [New York: Harcourt Brace Jovanovich, 1988], 15). Dilworth suggests that Jones learned this phrase from an art teacher, Walter Baynes ("From *The Deluge* to *The Anathemata*: Engraving Towards Poetry," in Hills, *Artist and Poet*, 46).

208. Jones, undated manuscript, David Jones 1985 Purchase. Group C, Box 15, NLW.

209. Kathleen Raine, "David Jones and the Actually Loved and Known," in Matthias, *Man and Poet*, 63. His "obsession" with scriptural accounts of the Passion also lasted. In a notebook, for example, he listed ten Bible verses, almost all of which concern this event. David Jones 1985 Purchase. Group C, Box 11, NLW.

tures was the supreme fact of history. The poet hence shared Greene's intense interest in Holy Week's events, although Jones focused more on Christ's death itself than on His betrayal.

In his verse, Jones recalled the Crucifixion constantly through diction, imagery, even by making it the setting and narrative locus of many passages and entire poems. These depictions range widely to posit the centrality of Christ's death. *The Anathemata*, for instance, utilizes the traditional metaphor of the Church as a ship and highlights material likenesses between a ship's keel and mast and Christ's Cross, while also alluding to "The Dream of the Rood" and analogizing the mythical tree that held the cosmos together—the Yggdrasil—to the actual axial beam round which Jones thought all things move.[210] He was not alone in asserting that everything hangs on this "Axile Tree," but his tendency to subsume such seemingly disparate referents under its aegis confirms the starkness of Guy Davenport's observation: for Jones, "the purpose of the evolution of the world was to raise the hill Golgotha, grow the wood for the cross, form the iron for the nails and develop the primate species Homo sapiens for God to be born a member of."[211]

Besides stressing the Passion's nuclearity, Jones also accented his belief in its historicity. Continuing his struggle with dualism, he held that the Crucifixion happened

> Not on the far fair-height, unbodied, where men of mind
> clamber the steep concepts . . .
> Not on any hill nor not on unseen
> unknown other-height the masters of concept postulate,
> but here in this demarcated place to touch and cross with
> iron, to see with this flesh-eye.[212]

Jones's concern for this authenticating particularity made him especially interested in dating the Passion's events. He again used various contexts, from conventional historical ones to nautical, mythological, and astro-

---

210. Jones, *The Anathemata*, 173, 200. See also *DG*, 216.

211. Guy Davenport, "In Love With All Things Made," *New York Times Book Review*, 17 October 1982, 9. For the importance of the Crucifixion to Christian thought generally, see Hague, *Commentary*, 7–8.

212. Jones, "The Roman Quarry," 43. See also *The Anathemata*, 53.

logical references, to help convey his sense of the Crucifixion's specific, temporally conditioned character. Hence the sailor's question,

> What bells is that
> when the overcast clears on a Mars' Venus-Day
> Selene waxed, the sun in the Ram?

can be answered by the chronicler:

> In the seven hundred and eighty-third year of the Urbs,
> . . .
> Under the fifth procurator
> of Judaea
> In the third or fourth
> severe
> April
> of the ten, sharp
> Aprils of his office.
> On Ariel mountain
> on Flail-floor Hill
> (here the articulated instrument of wood and here the
> bruised flesh for the wheat-offering.)
> . . .
> But eighteen days to the Maying.
> . . .
> they would be sounding six bells
> and the first dog-watch relief
> can bide a full hour yet.[213]

In again employing so many different media to emphasize the importance of establishing as precisely as possible when Christ's Passion transpired, Jones was also reiterating its pivotal importance in history to him. In his mind, not only had the world developed to make this sacrifice possible, but time itself was measured properly by reference to this episode: the Crucifixion was thus both the *center* of history and the center of *history*.

Jones, like Chesterton and Dawson, considered his idea of history in express contrast to modern presuppositions. He contended that "the

---

213. Jones, *The Anathemata*, 96, 185–88, 239. See also ibid., 157–58; *RQ*, 140–41; *SL*, 109.

fond but sustaining belief of most men" in his epoch was the Progressive notion of "things 'getting better' in every way borrowed from the evolutionary theory" that posits the "inevitable progress of the whole man."[214] He rejected this idea on three counts. First, Jones argued that there is no progress in the definitive human activity of art: "there is no improvement in the arts. Picasso is no improvement over Lascaux . . . the works are different but no better than each other in a temporal progression."[215] He relied mainly on archeological evidence to make this case, claiming it revealed that "in some respects we have not again equaled" prehistoric artistry, "let alone surpassed it." Chesterton and Eliot held a similar belief (one echoed by archeologists subsequently).[216] But Jones's adherence to it was especially significant for his rebellion against modern mores, because it established a radical disagreement with his impression of progressive principles: if the distinguishing human trait is static, he felt, human nature itself must likewise be fixed.

Jones's specific religious beliefs also shaped his rebuttal of Progressive ideologies. His tragic view of life, for example, led him (as it did Chesterton) to assert that unalloyed progress is impossible, as there is never any gain without some loss. Jones characterized believers in the "legend of general progress" as holding that the loss of present goods is justified because they will be replaced by different, yet better, future goods: "there is a sort of accumulating credit to which we are heirs." To him, though, this notion was bankrupt, for it read only one side of the ledger: "history is more of a rake's progress than the conservation of 'goods.' . . . If we inherit advantages from such deaths—that's all to the good, but the gain makes the loss no less real."[217] Jones's claim that the Crucifixion is the central moment in history further contradicted his perception of progressive ideas. If history climaxed in a.d. 30, it cannot still be improv-

---

214. Jones to Harman Grisewood, 18 November 1970 (*DGC*, 229–30).
215. Jones quoted in Dilworth, *Shape*, 381, n. 40.
216. Jones, *The Anathemata*, 76, n. 1 (marked by Greene). See also *DGC*, 228; Chesterton's *Illustrated London News* columns of 22 July 1922 and 10 December 1932; Eliot, *Selected Essays, 1917–1932* (New York: Harcourt, Brace & Co., 1932), 6; Corcoran, *Song of Deeds*, 21; and Marlise Simons, "French Scientists Date the Oldest Cave Paintings," *New York Times*, 8 June 1995, A4.
217. Jones, "Art in Relation to War," 153–54. See also Chesterton, *Illustrated London News*, 23 August 1930.

ing two millennia later. He allowed that material advances can occur over time, but insisted that only one moral change in human nature had transpired since the Fall, and that it occurred when Christ's death opened the possibility of salvation to all men. Hence, while Jones posited that history since Christ's Ascension has been moving linearly toward the apocalypse and eschaton that he often pondered, he did not think its actors' basic character could develop further following His Atonement.[218] Despite Jones's wariness of some of Augustine's ideas, then, his theology of history's structural subversion of whiggish schemas was perfectly Augustinian. Finally, his use of beliefs gleaned partially from Catholicism in this facet of his rebellion against modernity ironically affirms his father's view of the Church as a foe of progress.

Yet Jones felt that some in the Church shared the alleged modern obsession with progress, particularly Teilhard de Chardin. Like Greene, Jones sympathized with some of Chardin's ideas, especially his stress on unity. But he finally found their theologies of history irreconcilable. For instance, he held that "Teilhard knew nothing about the arts,"[219] and thus did not recognize their fixed nature nor their makers' "static condition."[220] Jones also thought Chardin upheld the legend of general progress. He deemed his own view that losses are entailed in any gain "incompatible with the idea of necessary progress, no matter how spiritualized," as in Chardin's Omega Point, and he thus "fears and with-

---

218. The structure of *In Parenthesis* illustrates Jones's belief, for his poem's construction mirrors that of his view of Christianity. Both appear to proceed to a seemingly sequentially premature high point, Christ's Passion and Dai Greatcoat's boast, which comes halfway through the poem. Dai is a Christ figure, as his boast reveals, for he is the soldier who has never died nor faded away but has been omnipresent in history, just as Christ said that "before Abraham was, I am." Both are everlasting men. Following their respective moments of greatest prominence on the historical and poetic stages, though, there is no decline, as one might expect, even though Christ's death has redeemed human nature and Dai's boast has covered all military history to his own time, leaving nothing more to talk about. Instead, both history and the poem remain linear. As history moves toward the eschaton, *In Parenthesis* moves toward its own apocalypse, the Battle of the Somme, and its Last Judgment, as the Queen of the Woods decides which fallen soldiers merit redemptive laurels. The poem, then, depicts imaginatively what Jones thought had occurred, and will happen actually, as history moves toward both its chronological and teleological end.

219. Jones quoted in Dilworth, *Shape*, 381, n. 40.
220. Jones, "Use and Sign," 178.

draws from Teilhard" on this issue.[221] Finally, and most fundamentally, Jones felt that Chardin failed to see the utile's catastrophic implications for art and sacrament: "He does not *seem* to note that with the astounding advances of both 'pure' and 'applied' science, the notion of *signa*, or 'sacrament,' becomes more and more alien to the men of our megalopolitan technocracy."[222] Thus, also like Greene, what regard Jones had for Chardin's views was outweighed by his apprehension that they were a facile accommodation of modern mores.

As Jones was forming these core beliefs in the need for a theology of history, the historical nature of Christianity and of what he saw as both its central dogma and history's central event, and his sense that these views were out of the modern mainstream, he was also seeking subjects for his verse. In line with his maxim that an artist must use what he knows and loves when making a work, Jones turned to his war memories. He certainly was intimately acquainted with these incidents, and he even had some affection for them, especially recollections of his fellow Tommies. In crucial ways, his means of evaluating these events was to fuse his memories of life on the line with his emerging theology of history. As he felt that participating in the war was getting into history, it is unsurprising that Jones related the troops' experiences to what he regarded as time's axile episode.

He suggested that war re-presents the Crucifixion because its sacrificed innocents are analogously akin to the Sacrificed Innocent. He theodicized the seemingly senseless slaughter of innocent soldiers that he had seen by linking their fate to that of Christ, in his mind the ultimate unjustly killed innocent. He posited that as Jesus' unwarranted death was not in vain, for He saved humanity from sin and was raised from the dead, so too will soldiers be redeemed if they fall in needless battles like the Somme. This pledge suffuses *In Parenthesis*, as when the troops reach France on "the third day, which was a Sunday." The poem's conclusion develops this eschatological promise most clearly, as the Queen of the Woods moves among the Somme's slain carrying laurels, which symbolize salvation:

221. Blissett, *Conversation*, 67.
222. Jones to William Noon, 5 December 1965; quoted in Noon, *Poetry and Prayer* (New Brunswick, N.J.: Rutgers University Press, 1967), 342–43, n. 52. Emphasis in original.

> Her awarding hands can
> pluck for each their fragile prize.
> She speaks to them according to precedence. She knows
> what's due to this elect society.

She is able to choose a biblically significant contingent of "twelve gentlemen" who will, in another connotatively charged description, "reign with her for a thousand years."[223] Through this fusion of original imagery and traditional Christian rhetoric, then, Jones made clear his sense of a typological link between those who shared the matter of history with him and the chief actor in the incident he thought gave temporality its meaning.

He denied at one point making this link in *In Parenthesis*, but the tale tells another story; and Jones admitted elsewhere that "I think that all our miseries and sufferings can be seen as in some way part of the whole anabasis and passion of" Jesus.[224] In *In Parenthesis* his joining of the misery and suffering of war to Christ's Passion is most explicit as the Battle of the Somme draws nigh. The night before the assault, while "some of them were already fallen to sleep," other soldiers stay awake in agony:

> you can't believe the Cup wont pass from
> or they wont make a better show
> in the Garden.

Yet this hope is vain, for sleepers and wakeful are

> . . . in a like condemnation
> to the place of a skull.

The bayonet (suggesting the lance that pierced Christ's side) is an infantryman's cross.

> you have not capacity for added fear only the limbs are leaden
> to negotiate the slope and rifles all out of balance, clumsied
> with long auxiliary steel
> seem five times the regulation weight—

---

223. Jones, *IP*, 9, 185.
224. Jones quoted in Dilworth, *Shape*, 131. His denial is in *DGC*, 246.

suggesting Christ's five wounds. Just as the battle begins, "the sun [is] gone out," and later on in the fighting "the earth had quaked." A wounded private wonders "do they divide the spoils at the Aid-Post" (which recalls soldiers "bunched to cast lots" earlier in the poem), while others pray to "Mother of Christ under the tree" or "suffering Jesus."[225]

Jones continued to posit this analogy after *In Parenthesis* and applied it to other battles. In "The Book of Balaam's Ass," for example, he uses it to treat the Passchendaele campaign, as dying troops again call "On Mary because of her secret piercing," and "On the Word seen by men because He was familiar with the wounding iron."[226] Moreover, Jones's sense of the homophonic resemblances between that battle's setting and Holy Week's events demonstrates starkly how extensively his imagination was dominated by Christ's death: "it is the site-name that made it as famed & held in the memory of soldiers & civies alike in post-war years." Other authors also found the place evocative, but for more tangible, onomatopoeic reasons, such as its slush and slop. While Jones was aware of the dismal physical conditions there and in war generally, they were not primary in his mind.[227] Instead, he had discovered a paradigm that explained his life's principal practical experience to him theologically, and he used it even more boldly over time, relating more distant historical, and even mythical, wars and warriors to Christ.[228]

As Jones's difference with other writers on Passchendaele's significance intimates, his development of the link between war and Christ's Passion was part of his rebellion against modern unbelief. Other Great War authors (especially Wilfrid Owen) linked their comrades in arms to Christ. Yet while some of them employed this analogy ironically or even homoerotically, Jones's use of it was typological and sincere. John Johnston has highlighted the core differences in Owen's and Jones's approaches. He argues that Owen tended to pity the soldiers' sacrifice, whereas Jones's attitude was closer to Greene's idea of compassion, and that the key to this contrast was Jones's un-ironic use of his religion:

---

225. Jones, *IP*, 146, 158, 154, 156, 164, 180, 187, 127, 177, 173.
226. Jones, "from The Book of Balaam's Ass," in *SL*, 107–8.
227. Jones to René Hague, 14 December 1973; quoted in Dilworth, *Shape*, 356. See also Jones to René Hague, {11 December?} 1973 (*DGC*, 252); and Fussell, *Great War*, 16.
228. See, e.g., *The Anathemata*, 84; *SL*, 65–69, 72–73, 75; *RQ*, 75, 80, 151–52.

Jones was as fully aware as Owen of the sacrificial aspects of the conflict. He sees the sacrifice, however, in terms of Christian ritual and symbolism.... The modern soldier, Jones suggests, dies as the scapegoat or as the lamb; the ancient rite of expiation is re-enacted on a vast scale ... but [his] death is not pitiful because it is significant in terms of ... Christian sacrifice and expiation.[229]

In asserting this model's validity in the face of unprecedented carnage, Jones thus set himself apart from Owen and many other Great War writers, who brought to it the same skepticism that their suffering had fostered toward Christianity and tradition generally. In short, there was an "altogether different point of departure of my stuff from ... blokes like Rupert Brooke right on through Sassoon and even Owen and Graves."[230]

To Jones, though, war was not the only re-creation of the Crucifixion in the post-Ascension era. He also held that the Mass re-called this event, and he owed this belief, in part, to his other formative settings, Ditchling and the Order Group. Specifically, Jones adopted the thesis of theologian Maurice de la Taille concerning the Eucharist. De la Taille saw the Last Supper and the Crucifixion as seamless parts of a single salvific act. To him, the Supper was a "representative ... unbloody" oblation that pledged Christ to its fulfillment in the "real, even bloody" immolation on the Cross: "There was a sacrifice at the Last Supper, but it was the sacrifice of redemption; and there was a sacrifice on the Cross, but it was the self-same sacrifice, continued and completed. The Supper and the Cross made up one complete sacrifice." Given this continuous relationship between the Supper and the Cross, he went on, if the Mass re-presents the Supper (as is held generally in Catholic theology), then it also necessarily re-enacts the immolation on the Cross:

---

229. John H. Johnston, *English Poetry of the First World War* (Princeton, N.J.: Princeton University Press, 1964), 333–34. See also Jon Silkin, *Out of Battle: The Poetry of the Great War* (Oxford: Oxford University Press, 1972), 329; Fussell, *Great War*, 116–20, 287–88, 298; John Wolffe, *God and Greater Britain* (London: Routledge, 1994), 239–43; Barton Friedman, "Tolkien and David Jones: The Great War and the War of the Ring," *Clio* 11 (Winter 1982): 126; and Vincent Sherry, "'Unmistakable Marks': Symbols and Voices in David Jones's *In Parenthesis,*" *Critical Quarterly* 25 (Winter 1983): 65. Ironically, Jones criticized Owen for making what he considered too close an identification between Jesus and the Tommies (*DGC*, 245–46).

230. Jones to Harman Grisewood, 22 May 1962 (*DGC*, 188).

What the Supper still lacked, the Mass presupposes. The work of the Cross completes both sacrifices. The Mass would not be at once a complete sacrifice if the Cross had not gone before; no more than the Supper could attain its sacrificial fulfillment without the Cross intervening. The Cross is the center . . . it divides from one another the two sides of the Eucharistic horizon: the side of Christ, looking forward to it, and the side of the Church, looking back upon it.[231]

The only difference between these offerings, he concluded, is that the Mass is an "unbloody" one. Although "real repetition of the slaying is excluded," the Mass remains a "true sacrifice" because "we do as a memorial what he did as a prefiguration of his own passion." In essence, the synergy of the two events it re-presents enables the Mass to use the forms of one to re-call both: "We offer it by the same rite that Christ used before us, by the rite of consecration, which in our hands as in His constitutes a mystical-sacramental-symbolic-representative immolation, wherein lies the real and actual, the visible, audible, tangible oblation of what is represented, namely of the immolation of Calvary."[232]

Jones gave both 1921 and 1923 as the date of his initial exposure to this theory. René Hague suggests that he may have started to posit this relationship between the Last Supper, the Crucifixion, and the Mass as early as 1920; Jones himself implied that he was crafting such an idea before his conversion, remarking that one reason he became a Catholic was his conclusion that "the Protestant tradition, especially with regard to the Supper, Calvary, and the Mass seen as one continuous whole, would not hold."[233] Even if he had begun to forge such a theorem on his own, though, his years at Ditchling offered sustained exposure to de la Taille's ideas and also to their foes, as Gill's associate Vincent McNabb was a chief critic of de la Taille. But Jones was unpersuaded by his warnings; and the Order Group piqued his interest in de la Taille further, for member Martin D'Arcy was a leading advocate of his fellow Jesuit's theory, and Jones cited often his primer on it *(The Mass and the Redemption)*.

---

231. Maurice de la Taille, *The Mystery of Faith and Human Opinion: Contrasted and Defined*, trans. J. B. Schimpf (London: Longmans, Green & Co., 1930), 231–32, 242–43.

232. Ibid., 231, 233–35.

233. Jones to Harman Grisewood, 14 January 1973, David Jones 1985 Purchase. Group C, Box 15, NLW. See also Hague, *Commentary*, 4.

Jones judged de la Taille's writing one of the formative works in shaping his outlook, and called him "my favorite theologian" as late as 1972.[234]

Why did this rather technical theology so impress Jones? For one thing, the two men shared certain core beliefs, such as the centrality of the Cross to both secular and sacred history. Moreover, de la Taille's theory allowed Jones, the lover of unity, to harmonize what he saw as the archetypal art work and central rite of Christian worship with what he deemed history's axile episode; indeed he felt that de la Taille's thesis had given "unity to various propositions of our religion touching the relationship between the Mass, Calvary and the Supper."[235] This theory also illuminated aesthetics for Jones. In positing that the symbolic act of the Supper was an intimate and constituent facet of Christ's actual death, de la Taille bolstered Jones's sense of the transubstantiatory nature of all sign-making. As Hague puts it, de la Taille's claim of a synergy between the symbolic and actual sacrifices enabled Jones "to relate that supreme sign to what is done by the artist, when a gesture, of hand, of the faculty that orders words ... brings into being a reality that goes beyond the mark on the paper or the sound vibrating in the air."[236] Jones voiced this idea most tellingly when he called the artist "an inveterate believer in 'transubstantiations' of some sort ... it will matter to the artist what kind of 'bread' is available to him when he presumes to 'show again under other forms' the eternal things, and art is nothing if it fails in this."[237]

To Jones, though, art was not only re-presentational, but also gratuitous; de la Taille's work enriched this view as well by substantiating Jones's differentiation between gratuity and utility. The poet argued that this distinction reaches "its highest conceivable level (for Catholics, anyway)" in noting the discriminations and connections between

> the *Oblatio* at the Supper, a ritual act and words wholly extra-utile, and the entirely utile acts whereby he who was already self-oblated was made fast by iron hooks to the wood of the *stauros*. We speak of the "Al-

---

234. Jones to William Blissett, 18 April 1972; quoted in Blissett, *Conversation*, 93. See also *DGC*, 188.
235. Jones, "The Fatigue," in *SL*, 36, n. 1.
236. Hague, *Commentary*, 7. See also de la Taille, *Mystery*, 103 (noted by Jones on the flyleaf of his copy).
237. Jones, "Art in Relation to War," 136.

tar of the Cross" only on the *presupposition* that the extra-utile ritual oblation at the Supper had already placed Our Lord in the state of a victim awaiting immolation . . . the *inutile and* the *utile* are both involved—otherwise the rite at the supper and the execution on the Tree have no substantial connection nor, necessarily, the Sacrifice of the Mass with both.[238]

Yet, as he found modern civilization becoming fixated on the utile exclusively, Jones believed his culture would be unable to grasp this balance, one he felt inhered in all art as well. Due to its denial of gratuity and symbol, then, "the modern world would have to substitute for each Mass an actual crucifixion if it would make the Mass integrated with itself," exactly what de la Taille had insisted the Eucharist's sacramental nature was designed to exclude.[239] As with Maritain's work, his fellow Frenchman's fed not only Jones's theology and aesthetic theories, but also the rebellion against modern technocracy they occasioned.

De la Taille's ideas appear often in Jones's writing. Jones parroted the theologian's notions in his prose, and he further expressed them poetically, as when he depicted Christ

> consummating in the unlit noon-dark
> on Moel-y-Penglog
> the Oblation made at the lighted feast board.[240]

De la Taille's thesis also informed Jones's verse structurally. In a Passion narrative in *The Anathemata*, for instance, the Last Supper and the Agony in the Garden are immediately succeeded by a description of a Mass, a substitution comprehensible only if the Mass is equivalent to the events that followed those of Holy Thursday chronologically.[241] Hence, if other Christian writers (like Greene and Charles Williams) displayed a de la Taillean understanding of the Eucharist at times, none made it as central to his intellectual and creative approach as Jones did. Paul Hills's judgment is thus sound: "The reenactment of Christ's sacrifice on Calvary in

---

238. Jones to Harman Grisewood, 4 September 1971 (*DGC*, 231). Emphasis in original.
239. Jones, "Art in Relation to War," 136.
240. Jones, "The Sleeping Lord," 83. ("Moel-y-Penglog" is Welsh for "Skull-Hill.") See also "The Fatigue," 36; "Art and Sacrament," 168; and "The Agent," 143, n. 23.
241. Jones, *The Anathemata*, 227. See also "The Kensington Mass," in *RQ*, 87–96.

the ritual of the Mass was the essential mystery of which, ultimately, all David Jones's art was a celebration and reconnaissance."[242]

Hills's use of a military term is unwittingly apt, for the poet who first saw a Mass during wartime brought his understanding of the liturgy's relationship to the Last Supper and the Crucifixion to his reflections on war. As both war and the Mass re-present the Crucifixion for Jones, he compares them frequently in *In Parenthesis*. Indeed, he portrays soldiering in distinctly de la Taillean terms. For example, Jones suggests that enlistment was a kind of unbloody oblation that will only achieve completion in the bloody immolation of actual combat. Hence "all they'd piled on since enlistment day" both culminates and is transformed on the evening the troops enter the theater of battle:

> a whole unlovely order this
> night would transubstantiate, lend some grace to.

Similarly, as the Mass is an essential re-presentation of the Crucifixion to Jones, so "the liturgy of their going-up" has "an apostolic actuality, a correspondence with the object" of warfare for him.[243]

Tradition and Inheritance: The Maker as Rememberer

If *In Parenthesis* centered on the bloody re-enactments of Christ's Passion in war, concern with its unbloody counterpart became more intense in Jones's subsequent work. Harman Grisewood and René Hague explain that the parallel between a present-day Mass and Christ's past Passion so preoccupied Jones that all the poems he penned after *In Paren-*

---

242. Paul Hills, "The Pierced Hermaphrodite: David Jones's Imagery of the Crucifixion," in Matthias, *Man and Poet*, 425. For Greene's use of these ideas, see, e.g., *Rumour at Nightfall* (New York: Doubleday, Doran & Co., 1932), 211; *The Power and the Glory* (1940; reprint, New York: Penguin, 1983), 95; *The Heart of the Matter* (1948, 1971; reprint, New York: Penguin, 1978), 224; *Monsignor Quixote* (New York: Washington Square Press, 1983), 76, 141. For Williams, see *Outlines of Romantic Theology*, ed. Alice Mary Hadfield (Grand Rapids, Mich.: William B. Eerdmans Publishing Co., 1990), 14–15; and *War in Heaven* (1930; reprint, Grand Rapids, Mich.: William B. Eerdmans Publishing Co., 1994), passim. There is no evidence that either author read de la Taille, though. Jones also noted this idea in Gregory Dix, *The Shape of the Liturgy*, 2d ed. (London: Dacre Press, 1945), 393.

243. Jones, *IP*, 27–28. This general topic is limned excellently in Thomas Dilworth, *The Liturgical Parenthesis of David Jones* (Ipswich: Golgonooza Press, 1979).

thesis were "parts of a single Mass poem."²⁴⁴ Its most significant fragment, and the next one published, was *The Anathemata*, which he claimed outright was about matters apt to stir in his mind "as often as not 'in the time of the Mass.'"²⁴⁵ Not only are the actions and theology of the Mass this poem's starting points and referents for its musings on history and culture, but its structure is informed by the liturgy's. As Dilworth notes, Jones's verse seeks to render various prior eras as concurrent facets of a vital present just as the Eucharist makes the historical events of Christ's Supper and Passion actual at each Mass.²⁴⁶ To Jones, then, the priest's power to re-present directly a particular past event in a current Eucharist is mirrored analogously by the artist's ability to show forth the general real presence of the past in the present: "A re-calling of the past, the handing on of what has been received, not by any means to live in the past but to understand that the past lives in us; all such notions are a kind of *anamnesis,* an effectual re-presenting."²⁴⁷

Jones had long stressed the importance and persistent force of tradition, what Eliot called a perception "not only of the pastness of the past, but of its presence."²⁴⁸ Jones's conviction that "tradition is part of ourselves" appeared first in his visual art;²⁴⁹ but it also became essential to his written work, for it met a criteria of gratuity: "These continuities are about the only thing that bring me a measure of delight."²⁵⁰ He thought that part of the artist's purpose is to attest to these continuities. He argued that "the thing called 'the past'" is what the artist draws on when he "'shows forth,' 'recalls,' 're-presents' and 'discovers,'" making the poet a "rememberer."²⁵¹ But this memory must not be selective:

---

244. Harman Grisewood and René Hague, introduction to *RQ*, xix–xx, xviii.
245. Jones, *The Anathemata*, 31.
246. Dilworth, *Shape*, 172–73, 255. See also Jeremy Hooker, *Poetry of Place* (Manchester: Carcanet Press, 1982), 39; and "Two Letters from David Jones," *Agenda* 11–12 (Autumn–Winter 1973–74): 20.
247. Jones undated letter draft, David Jones 1985 Purchase. Group A, Box V/14, NLW.
248. Eliot, *Selected Essays*, 4.
249. Jones, "The Agent," 147, n. 28. For this idea in his visual art, see Michael Ayrton, quoted in *DGC*, 157.
250. Jones quoted in Hague, *Commentary,* 30.
251. David Jones, "Past and Present," in *E&A,* 139, 141.

> We must be careful not to isolate one part of tradition, especially not to both isolate a part and then to develop and embroider it, so that at length it loses all affinity to, and all contact with, the complex of the ancient deposits . . . all the time we should feel, along with the contemporary twist, application, veneer, or what you will, the whole weight of what lies hidden—the many strata of the thing.[252]

Finally, Jones held that the struggle to preserve this unity must not sacrifice what celebrating continuity gave him: even when facing the profoundest contradictions, the artist "must resolve them all, not losing one, and still create delight."[253] He was not alone in regarding poets as "remembrancers & conservators of the things of the Island"; and he praised those, like Eliot, who shared this understanding of their role.[254]

Jones's sense of the poet as a rememberer established another distinct affinity with the priest in his mind. As an artist uses the past as his *materia* for recalling generally, so a priest uses the specific materials of bread and wine in his re-presentation due to their link to the past: "those signs were not regarded as mere symbols . . . [but] as a sacred tradition to be handed on because it was a *traditio* 'received of the Lord.'"[255] Moreover, Jones judged the Mass itself faithful to traditions of both the Church and sign-making generally:

> He does what is done in many places
> what he does other
>   he does after the mode
> of what has always been done.[256]

This fundamentally conservative function of art and sacrament makes even a priest character who questions the poet's claim to a corresponding role admit that poets,

---

252. Jones, "The Myth of Arthur," 190.
253. Jones, "Art in Relation to War," 141.
254. Jones, "The Sleeping Lord," 82. See also E&A, 140; The Anathemata, 163, n. 3; and RQ, 98.
255. Jones, "Art and Sacrament," 162.
256. Jones, The Anathemata, 243.

whatever else they were,
they were men who loved the things of the Island, and so did he.²⁵⁷

Jones thus argued that the cultural forces that he thought imperiled the poet and priest generally also endangered this facet of their role, along with their remembered and beloved things of the Island's heritage. In the same vein as his judgment of civilizations based on their treatment of their predecessors, Jones held that customary beliefs about human nature derived from secular and Christian legacies are "objective measuring rods" capable of assessing the extent to which various eras allow man "to behave in most accord with his nature as a creative creature."²⁵⁸ Unsurprisingly, he felt modernity failed this test of tradition. Not only did he think the utile threatened this norm's content in its perceived animus to art and sacrament, but he also deemed it disdainful of the principle of a living past generally, which Jones saw as a necessary component of gratuitous making.

To Jones, the "main trend of our time" is uniquely "one of a cutting-off from the past."²⁵⁹ He felt that the utile's pragmatic bent fostered focus on present achievement and future gains, plus scorn for seemingly inferior, and now dead, past attitudes and actions. A later poem's servant of such a "megalopolitan technocracy" crystallizes this conviction:

> Only the neurotic
> look to their beginnings.
>
> We are men of now and must strip as the facts of now would have it.²⁶⁰

Reiterating a crucial theme, Jones claimed contrarily that whatever benefits presentism and futurism held, adhering to them entails losses. He warned that the neglected past "will not be easily recoverable" once lost, and that a culture's designated rememberers would suffer most from this privation.²⁶¹ Asserting that artists "stand on the scaffold of a corporate

---

257. Jones, "The Sleeping Lord," 82.
258. Jones, "Art in Relation to War," 161.
259. Jones, "Use and Sign," 181.
260. Jones, "The Tribune's Visitation," 51–52. See also E&A, 82.
261. Jones, "A London Artist Looks at Contemporary Wales," in DG, 37.

tradition," he lamented in 1941 that "we have no such tradition, nor can have within seeable time, neither in the secular nor the religious realm, and our best artists are therefore not likely to be really satisfactory in that sense at all"; he symbolized this sentiment further in his poetry by portraying a priest who fears for his failing memory.[262] Jones thus worried that gratuitous making itself might become impossible if his culture persisted in ignoring its *materia,* for "one 'thinks' in those obsolete or becoming-obsolete terms."[263] In short, "either you have it all or (in the long run) you won't have it at all."[264] The utile's apparent renunciation of tradition thus became another reason for believing that it threatened the signature human trait and was hence a path to subhumanity.

In turn, then, tradition became a further resource for counter-modern rebellion. Jones contended that anyone who "inherits and reflects the traditional mood" of Britain is "a man of the diaspora," because its heritages "have been or are being destroyed by a new type of civilization."[265] As the artist depends particularly on these deposits for making, however, Jones held that he has a special obligation to defy utile dehumanization:

> in our present megalopolitan technocracy the artist must still remain a "rememberer" . . . of things which tend to be impoverished, or misconceived, or altogether lost or willfully set aside in the preoccupations of our present intense technological phase, but which, none the less, belong to man.[266]

He remained hopeful (as some of the "Last Romantics" did) that these acts of subversive preservation would be the prelude to a future epoch more favorable to tradition and the art he thought it generates. He used phoenix imagery to convey this belief in even some of his bleakest poetry, and he expressed it more directly in *The Anathemata*:

---

262. Jones to the *Tablet*, 5 September 1941, David Jones 1985 Purchase. Group A, Box I/1, NLW; and *SL*, 82.
263. Jones, "On the Difficulties of One Writer of Welsh Affinity Whose Language Is English," 31–34.
264. Jones, "Use and Sign," 181.
265. Jones, "Wales and Visual Form," 88–89.
266. Jones statement to the Bollingen Foundation, 1959, in *DG*, 17.

> You never know, captain:
> What's under works up.[267]

One reason Jones felt his rebellion might succeed ultimately was his link of his defense of tradition to his religion. Unlike most of the Last Romantics, he saw his sense of the past's vitality substantiated by Roman Catholic theology. He held that one thing that made him inwardly a Catholic during the war was a growing belief that "it was She who alone represented the tradition of the Xtian West."[268] Thus, "it was a longing, and a deep need, not to lose connection with these historic origins, that, in part, caused" him to convert.[269] Unsurprisingly, the Mass epitomized this Catholic commitment to continuity for Jones, as he felt its ceremonials re-presented the Western patrimony in a unique way:

> it (the Latin Liturgy) was in a positive way the direct oral and aural and sacral link with the whole past, with the rise of our religion in the Greco-Roman world of the late Roman world, just as the vestments of the sacred ministers afforded a visual and visible continuity with that world ... that continuity constituted something deeply felt—indefinable but inextricably bound up with what had made them.[270]

While not as crucial to his conversion as to Chesterton's or Dawson's, then, Catholicism's culturally conservative character enhanced its appeal to Jones: if both he and it believed that the past persisted in the present, he felt, then the Church could preserve the *materia* of making until the utile's assault had been withstood and reversed by subversive artists and sacramentalists, as well as be an armory for these guerrillas of gratuity and grace.

This reverence for tradition pervades Jones's thought and verse. In *In Parenthesis*, for instance, he began a lifelong claim that modern wars (like the two world wars) participated actually in a broader heritage of battle,

---

267. Jones, *The Anathemata*, 164. See also *SL*, 64; and Graham Hough, *The Last Romantics* (1947; reprint, London: University Paperbacks, 1961).

268. Jones to the *Tablet*, undated draft, David Jones 1985 Purchase. Group A, Box I/8, NLW.

269. Jones undated manuscript, David Jones 1985 Purchase. Group C, Box 10, NLW.

270. Jones to Tony Stoneburner, undated draft, David Jones 1985 Purchase. Group A, Box II/1, NLW. See also Jones to Richard Shirley Smith, 13 November 1961, in *Ten Letters*, ed. Derek Shiel (London: Agenda Editions, 1996), 40.

and hence were explicable in its terms, a standpoint at odds with most renderings of these conflicts.[271] Tradition's intrinsic importance was especially central to *The Anathemata*. Jones conceived this poem as a re-presentation of "those things which have made us all—of this island,"[272] as it "takes our Western-Xtian tradition for granted, just as it takes for granted our island deposits, Celto-Teutonic-Latinic."[273] He tried to communicate his conviction that these deposits remain vital through various devices, ranging from the use of Welsh to localize, and hence make immediate, the traditional Christian narratives of the Nativity and the Passion to his frequent references to fossil-containing limestone, which thus became an objective correlative of the past's continued presence in the present.[274] Jones deemed the difficulties many readers had in comprehending these techniques a sign of the cultural impoverishment he thought attendant upon a utile age: "on the whole people are somewhat dim about the content of a work that deals with objective traditions; that is perhaps to be expected."[275] Such an attitude may have been somewhat presumptuous, as even fellow traditionalists like Auden and Eliot found this poem difficult; but it also accords perfectly with Jones's sense of being a rebel against modernity.

Despite his frustration with misreadings of *The Anathemata*, Jones continued to uphold his idea of tradition. A reviewer noted that the final sequence of poems that he published in his lifetime "move the mind through a supra-historical 'present' in which there is no distinction between what happens *now* and what happened *then*," a view later critics echoed.[276] Moreover, one scholar called his published essays a reminder

---

271. See, e.g., *IP*, 79–84, 89; *DG*, 127–28; *The Anathemata*, 73, 90, 105, 160, 174, 177, 186–87, 231; *SL*, 110.

272. Jones to H. S. Ede, 17 December 1952 (*DGC*, 155). Emphasis in original.

273. Jones to William Hayward, 10 December 1957, in *Letters to William Hayward*, ed. Colin Wilcockson (London: Agenda Editions, 1979), 17.

274. See *The Anathemata*, 183–243; and Dilworth, *Shape*, 232.

275. Jones to Raymond Garlick, 21 December 1952, David Jones 1985 Purchase. Group C, Box 17, NLW.

276. Robert Nye, "Poetry," *The Times*, 28 March 1974, 14. Emphasis in original. See also Staudt, *Turn*, 177. Simon Lewty has made the intriguing suggestion that this aspect of Jones's work gives his corpus the character of a palimpsest ("The Palimpsest," in Hills, *Artist and Poet*, 54–64).

of "the profound significance of tradition."[277] Finally, fellow poet Guy Davenport appraised Jones's importance by referring to this theme in 1982: "What makes him so special? The answer will have to be 'tradition.'"[278] Like Faulkner, then, Jones felt that the past was not dead, it was not even past; but he also felt that this was no longer self-evident to his day's readers. Extraordinary measures, like the extensive notes he appended to his poems, thus seemed necessary if he was to preserve and, he hoped, revive this sensibility.[279]

Teste David: Rhyming All Things in the Transforming Power of Christ

Jones also found myth intimately tied to tradition. Not only were particular myths part of the living deposit that he thought artists drew on, but also he felt that, being works of art, myths generally shared the remembering purpose of all authentic making. To him, "the function of genuine myth" is "to conserve, to develop, to bring together, to make significant for the present what the past holds, without dilution or any deleting, but rather by understanding and transubstantiating."[280] Eliot also deemed positing "a continuous parallel between contemporaneity and antiquity" the "mythical method"; he held that artists of his era who used it did so in response to modern disenchantment and its effects: "It is simply a way of controlling, of ordering, of giving a shape and a significance to the immense panorama of futility and anarchy which is contemporary history."[281]

Jones's approach to myth was similarly counter-modern. He argued, for instance, that his era's demystifiers had ruined the term "myth" by

---

277. Joseph Schwartz, "Editor's Page," 66.

278. Davenport, "All Things Made," 9.

279. "Jones's notes are an educational technique. He is trying to make it possible for his contemporaries to get something of the vitality that he himself feels in the symbols, images, and references that the modern world has largely discarded . . . he is attempting to break down the isolation of the twentieth century and to reestablish the continuities of human experience." Blamires, *Artist and Writer*, 134–35.

280. Jones, "The Myth of Arthur," 200.

281. T. S. Eliot, "*Ulysses*, Order and Myth," *The Dial* (November 1923): 483. Dilworth (*Shape*, 27–28) speculates that Jones may have adopted this notion from Eliot, but his evidence is more suggestive than conclusive.

equating it with fiction, and he thus used "mythus" to approximate the Greek *mythos*, "a word uttered, something told." Moreover, he referred sardonically to

> speaking most factually
> and, as the fashion now requires, from observed data.[282]

He also insisted that the transcendent legacies found within myths, but allegedly excluded by utile moderns, must be preserved along with more tangible elements of the deposits that contemporary rememberers upheld: "the waste land before us is extensive; and it is certain that in our anabasis across it we shall have reason to keep in mind the tradition of our origins in both matter and spirit."[283] These beliefs have led more than one critic to share Andrew Campbell's view that Jones's thought is marked by opposition between "the deadly superficiality of the modern world and the vital depth of history and myth."[284]

While accurate in identifying Jones's counter-modern intent, the relationship between history and myth in his mind is more complicated than such analyses recognize. Although Jones claimed that history and mythology are the poet's materials, his sense of how they interact contains a contradiction, one only resolved fully by the application of his religious beliefs.[285] He suggested often that myth is in some way truer than fact, that (in Stephen Tonsor's terms) myth possesses a "higher kind of truthfulness . . . a living, experiential truth which escaped the neat categories of logic and rational analysis."[286] Jones held that "myth proposes for our acceptance a truth more real than the historic facts alone discover,"[287] and thus "historia" acquires full meaning only when it is

---

282. Jones, *The Anathemata*, 40 (n. 1), 216.
283. Jones, "The Myth of Arthur," 199.
284. Andrew Campbell, "Strata and Bedrock in David Jones's *The Anathemata*," *Renascence* 46 (Winter 1994): 117. See also Bergonzi, *Heroes' Twilight*, 199–200.
285. See *The Poet Speaks*, 104.
286. Stephen Tonsor, "The Use and the Abuse of Myth," *Intercollegiate Review* 15 (Spring 1980): 67.
287. Jones, *The Anathemata*, 124, n. 3. For a similar view in Chesterton's work, see, e.g., his *Illustrated London News* columns of 12 September 1908 and 29 September 1928.

> intermeddled with potent and light-
giving, life-giving, cult-making mythos.²⁸⁸

Were this Jones's outlook consistently, Elizabeth Ward's conclusion that he had "an essentially mythological understanding of history" would be inescapable.²⁸⁹

Yet this view undercuts Jones's intense concern for the particular and concrete, for the very facts of history. Demonstrating again the tension between his mind's mystical and rational sides and his attempts to mediate it, Jones also asserted at points that, rather than being rivals, myth and fact are partners in producing history. For example, he depicted the god Mars's rape of the mortal Ilia as generating Roman history:

> departed myth
> left ravished fact
> till Clio, the ageing mid-wife, found her
> nine calends gone
> huge in labor with the Roman people.²⁹⁰

This portrait of a complementary relationship of two distinct agents restores a balance between myth and fact in Jones's outlook; but use of the male-female trope also suggests a continued tension between these forces in his mind, albeit one he considered fruitful.

As with other temptations to weaken his attachment to the factual, Jones's strongest source of resistance to the tug of intangible myth was his Christianity. More than bringing the two discrete forces of myth and fact into a union that makes history, he claimed, Christ's hypostatic union established synergy between them by subsuming them within His single person, an act that gave meaning to history. In C. S. Lewis's phrase, in Christ, "Myth became Fact." Jones elaborated this notion by arguing that the Incarnation intertwined Hebraic myth and Hellenistic fact inextricably: "Yahweh and the Logos [are] the same God."²⁹¹ This idea had obvious appeal to one so passionate about unity.

288. Jones, "The Kensington Mass," 92.
289. Ward, *Mythmaker*, 126.
290. Jones, *The Anathemata*, 86. See also ibid., 129; and "The Agent," 147, n. 27.
291. Blissett, *Conversation*, 136. See also C. S. Lewis, "Is Theology Poetry?" in *The Weight of Glory and Other Addresses*, ed. Walter Hooper (New York: Collier, 1980), 84; and Tolkien, "On Fairy Stories," 179.

Further reflecting that love of wholeness, Jones contended additionally that, being both myth and fact, Christ is the fulfillment of each. Like Hopkins, he believed that all things rhyme in Christ: "There is only one tale to tell even though the telling is patient of endless development and ingenuity and can take on a million variant forms." For instance, Jones referred often to a line in the *Dies irae*, "teste David cum Sibylla," to stress his sense that the factual psalmist and the mythical priestess both attested anachronistically to the signs of the end-time revealed by Christ. He also deemed Christ the epitome of dying god and sacrificial hero legends as diverse as those of Cronos, Odysseus, Apollo, John Barleycorn, King Arthur, and Odin. He depicted another mythological form of this allegedly single story when he portrayed the Christmas Gospel as telling of how from "before all time Minerva is sprung from the head of Jove," an analogy he claimed one pope had proposed "to express the Eternal Generation of the Word . . . which alone makes sense of this particular birth in time." Jones's agreement with such comparisons thus led him to dub myth "an extra-revelational body of tradition."[292]

Yet David testified that fact could also fit this definition. He depicted numerous Christ antetypes and successors from history, including such conventional ones as Abel, Isaac, Joseph, and the prophecies of Virgil's Fourth Eclogue, plus some idiosyncratic selections, like Absalom, the Welsh king Llywelyn (d. 1282), and Elusian and Nemian priests. But in all of them, he argued, "the Mystery of the Incarnation was anticipated" or puppeted.[293] Jones also held that the Church imitates its founder's harmonizing power in its rites and ceremonials, as he often asserted the continuity of its customs with pre-Christian "palladic foreshadowings" of them.[294] Maritain too saw such myths, historical figures, and rites ful-

---

292. Jones, *The Anathemata*, 35, 221 (n. 3), 40 (n. 1). See also ibid., 62, 68–69, 96, 141, 192, 217, n. 2, 225, 227–28, 242; *DGC*, 168; *DG*, 214–16; *IP*, 62, 200–1, n. 42; *SL*, 27, 32, 55 (n. 1), 65–69, 92, 99; *RQ*, 18, n. 36, 107; and Ward, *Mythmaker*, 193–94. One scholar, though, argues that the Sybil's stories "were at odds with the dominant Christian culture" (Michael Gorra, "Taking the Freud Out of Mother Goose," *New York Times Book Review*, 19 November 1995, 7).

293. Jones, *IP*, 196, n. 22. See also *IP*, 39, 50, 62, 89, 153, 162, 167, 175, 181–82, 184, 186, 196 (n. 22), 211–12 (n. 42); *The Anathemata*, 213, 218 (n. 4); *SL*, 27, 66 (n. 1), 71 (n. 1), 89 (n. 1), 103; *RQ*, 95, 115ff., 140, 148–49, 195; Dilworth, *Shape*, 277–78.

294. Jones, *The Anathemata*, 50. See, e.g., ibid., 85, n. 4, 127 (n. 12, especially), 162, n. 7, 168, n. 1, 202, n. 2, 228–30; *SL*, 108–9; and *RQ*, 159–60, 202–3.

filled in Jesus and His Church; but Jones gave this belief far greater stress, for it enabled him to reconcile his faith with his unific impulses theologically.[295]

Jones's heavy accent on unity, though, has sometimes obscured his further belief that because Christ is a singular synthesis of myth and fact, He also transforms them:

> if there's continuity
> here, there's a new beginning

as well.[296] Jones argued that attempts "to level down Jesus Christ to just one of countless dying gods ... ignores some important facts," for "there are some elements in the Christian story which ... transform the pattern completely." Revealing again his concern for the particular, he held that it was precisely the factual nature of the Christian mythus that set it apart, as its purportedly unique historicity allowed it to revolutionize its genre: "The very incidents which may strike us as the most poetic and mythological ... are inextricably interwoven by the evangelists with down-to-earth existence at its most personal, its most prosaic and even squalid; and it is precisely in this that they see the saving mystery." This focus on temporality "reverses the normal process of folk-memory, which, we know, tends to mythologize history; now it is rather the mythological pattern that is embodied in historical fact."[297] In becoming fact, then, the Christ-myth ceases to be solely mythical, for its actuality makes it "the only *true* myth."[298] Hence even the myths analogously in accord with Christianity are corrected and completed by this factual creed: "Though 'Minerva springs eternally from the head of Jove,' the Eternally Begotten could not have become begotten on a creature except by a creature's pliant will."[299] This argument that God's interaction with particular actors at definite moments in time alters positively and

---

295. For Maritain's views, see Blamires, *Artist and Writer*, 19.

296. Jones, *The Anathemata*, 51. For underestimations of this aspect of Jones's thought, see, e.g., Blamires, *Artist and Writer*, 128–29; Corcoran, *Song of Deeds*, 87–89; Hills, *Artist and Poet*, 13–15, 132–40.

297. Jones undated manuscript, David Jones 1985 Purchase. Group A, Box V/15, NLW.

298. Dorenkamp, "Time and Sacrament," 187. Emphasis in original.

299. Jones, *The Anathemata*, 128, n. 5. See also Dilworth, *Shape*, 363; Campbell, "Strata and Bedrock," 129.

forever the ethereal quality of myths evinces again Jones's use of Christianity's discerned devotion to the concrete as theological inoculation against dualistic, ahistorical schemas.

He did not find fact unaffected by Christ, though. Jones held that the mythological aspects of Christ and Christianity gave history its meaning. As shown in the discussion of his theology of history, Jones believed that the Incarnation revealed that history's particular incidents all revolved around the nucleus of Christ. It is from the "hill-site" that "will germinate the nova vita," for Christ's life, and especially His death, have given the temporal flow of events the metaphysical purpose of gathering all things unto Him.[300] Revelation hence completes and consecrates this extra-revelational body of tradition as well without canceling it. As William Lynch puts it, Christ "is a new level, identical in structure with, but higher in energy than, every form or possibility of the old" order of facts that He entered.[301] For Jones, Christianity's chief rite also transforms its liturgical cousins. To him, these other rites were only symbolic or commemorative, but in the Mass, the sign actually becomes what is signified every time certain acts are done in memory of their originator. As the Mass re-presents the Myth made Fact, it adds "the delight and depth" missing from precursor ceremonies of either mythmakers or fact-men:

>   that salvific mummery
>   they used day by day
>   . . .
>   staged the
>   happy fault, could sing about the Golden Tree, more than
>   blind makers tell in cool translucent numbers.[302]

If, in the poet's mind, myth is transformed by Christ's factual nature, then, so is fact made qualitatively different by His mythical qualities. Other thinkers (like Chesterton, Lewis, and Tolkien) shared this sense of orthodox Christianity's transforming power over myth and fact; but it was more central to, and more overt in, Jones's work, for it allowed him

---

300. Jones, "The Old Quarry, Part Two," 167.
301. William Lynch, *Christ and Apollo* (New York: Sheed & Ward, 1960), 192.
302. Jones, "The Book of Balaam's Ass," 206.

to balance his impression of historicity's importance with his conviction that Christianity had still established a transcendent teleology.[303]

Jones's attempt to sustain such balanced positions was part of his rebellion against modern culture. He (like Chesterton) argued that the tenuous synthesis between myth and fact created by Christianity was at risk of splintering in his era: "our modern age is dividing it out in a way that has perhaps never been divided out before."[304] With the utile supposedly claiming exclusive legitimacy for fact, Jones worried that those who rejected positivism's perceived hegemony would assert its mirror of an uncompromising accent on disembodied myth. His friend, Desmond Chute, called *The Anathemata* a declaration of such fears in a review that Jones claimed "expressed so much of my intention."[305] Chute accepted Jones's claim that their epoch was uniquely hostile to gratuity and perforce to art and sacrament. Still following Jones, he held further that "an almost manichean disdain of the secular" had developed among some in reaction to this utile materialism, meaning that "no religious synthesis, no integration of forms" would be possible if these divisive trends persisted. He saluted Jones for issuing this warning.[306] Jones's opposition to the utile for sundering what he felt orthodoxy had singularly joined thus reveals how (again like Chesterton) he generalized personal fears about dualism to anxiety about the modern cultural condition. Moreover, his stress on Roman Catholicism's commitment to the body and embodied, its synergistic doctrine of transubstantiation, and the special peril he thought the utile posed to the Church suggests that he saw it as the form of Christianity most likely to uphold this balance between myth and fact corporately in his day.

---

303. See Adam Schwartz, "Theologies of History in G. K. Chesterton's *The Everlasting Man* and David Jones's *The Anathemata*," *Chesterton Review* 23 (February & May 1997): 65–83; *They Stand Together: The Letters of C. S. Lewis to Arthur Greeves*, ed. Walter Hooper (London: Collins, 1979), 427; and Tolkien, "On Fairy Stories," 180.

304. Jones quoted in *The Poet Speaks*, 102. See also *E&A*, 178; and *DG*, 136–37.

305. Jones to Desmond Chute, Corpus Christi, 1953 (*Inner Necessities*, 83). See also *DG*, 49.

306. Desmond Chute, review of *The Anathemata*, *Downside Review* 71 (Summer 1953); reprinted in *Inner Necessities*, 96.

"Buggering Up the Mass": Jones and Liturgical Change

Jones's emphasis on unity also gave him a strongly ecumenical temperament, although the mechanics and limits of religious outreach preoccupied him far less than they did Dawson. Yet like Dawson (and Greene) he welcomed the Second Vatican Council initially, hoping that it would improve relations between the Church and non-Catholics.[307] Also like the other converts', though, Jones's enthusiasm was short-lived. Indeed, he became an even harsher critic of the council than either Dawson or Greene, for he saw many of the changes it instituted as tampering with his faith's central aspect in what he concluded was a misguided and dangerous attempt to accommodate modern presentist and positivist predilections.

As the council began promulgating its decisions, Jones started to display qualms. While still pleased at the new ecumenical atmosphere it had created, he was also anxious about the conclave's ultimate impact: "I'm thinking now of the Roman Liturgy . . . chaps who talk about it don't see that it's a culture crisis more than a religious one. . . . I don't see saying the *glorio in excelsio* and the *Credo* in English is any help." Such concerns became the crux of his reservations, for (like Greene and Dawson) Jones focused his criticism of the council on the liturgical alterations it approved, and (again like them) he saw his opposition to these changes as part of a broader rebellion against modern culture. Unlike his peers, though, this issue became a virtual obsession with Jones: his personal papers, for example, contain hundreds of manuscript pages devoted to this topic alone.[308]

Such intensity is understandable in light of the Mass's centrality to his conversion and subsequent faith. Having been drawn to Catholicism by what he considered this rite's unific and re-presentational aspects, Jones was scrupulous about their conservation. Like Dawson, he had thus opposed liturgical changes long antedating Vatican II's and, in doing

---

307. See Jones undated letter fragment, David Jones 1985 Purchase. Group C, Box 1, NLW.

308. Jones undated letter fragment, David Jones 1985 Purchase. Group C, Box 9, NLW. The bulk of his papers concerning this subject are in David Jones 1985 Purchase. Group C, Boxes 9–10, NLW.

so, had set himself apart from friends like Gill, O'Connor, and Tom Burns.[309] As early as 1940, for instance, he complained that the Church had "lost all sense of shape, and the significance of their own stuff."[310] His specific objections (both pre- and postconciliar) were often to alterations with particularly personal resonance. For example, he pleaded poignantly against abolishing the practice of kneeling at the *Incarnatus*, lest his adopted church become as hostile to this "natural" behavior as his inherited one had been.[311] Jones was also especially attentive to the Good Friday liturgy, seeing it as the exemplary ritual re-calling of the central event in history. For instance, his belief in the actual re-presentation effected in the Eucharist led him to think that a mid-1950s edict authorizing general Communion distribution on Good Friday *"is all wrong . . . the rite of G.F. should show forth the total derelication of that part of the mythus . . . 'the real Absence.'"*[312] He also deemed this decision "a break" with traditional conceptions of Good Friday.[313]

But Jones also had less directly personal objections to changes in the liturgy. As he judged the Latin Mass the oral, aural, sacral, and visible link between Roman Catholic worshipers and the whole Western past, Jones was suspicious of the vernacular liturgy's implications. In 1962, he argued that it was getting harder to "keep any sort of liaison with the past. . . . Yet the Church would seem, by Her zealous retention of Latin, and by much besides, not to under-value the enriching, salutary, humanizing, and spiritualizing power of an inherited tradition."[314] Two years later,

---

309. See Stoneburner, "Prophecy and Apocalypse," 268–70; Gill undated essay on the liturgy, David Jones 1985 Purchase. Group A, Box III/36, NLW; Felicitas Corrigan, "The Prescience of Father Brown," *Chesterton Review* 21 (November 1995): 473–85; and Tom Burns, *The Use of Memory: Publishing and Further Pursuits* (London: Sheed & Ward, 1993), 150.

310. Jones to Tom Burns, 14 September 1940, David Jones 1985 Purchase. Group B, Box 1/16, NLW. He expressed cognate concerns embryonically in "Beauty in Catholic Churches," *Blackfriars* 7 (1926): 438–41.

311. Blissett, *Conversation*, 50; and Jones to the *Tablet*, undated, David Jones 1985 Purchase. Group C, Box 1, NLW.

312. Jones to Harman Grisewood, 7 February 1956 (*Inner Necessities*, 19, n. 10). Emphasis in original.

313. Jones to René Hague, 11–12 January 1955, 109. See also Jones, *DG*, 100; and *E&A*, 260–61.

314. Jones to the *Tablet*, 6 February 1962 (draft), David Jones 1985 Purchase. Group C, Box 1, NLW.

though, as the change to the vernacular was being mooted, he was more uneasy, warning that the Latin liturgy is an "integral part of our Western heritage.... It's a terrible thought that the language of the West, of the Western liturgy, and inevitably the Roman chant, might become virtually extinct."[315] By 1967, he thought that awful vision had materialized: "The Chant is pretty well gone and there seems no *pietas* for immemorial forms and the language of the Latin West is virtually out."[316] Jones deemed this linguistic declension exacerbated by the translations adopted for English speakers, and he thus shared Greene's and Dawson's distaste for them. He contemned new English renderings of ancient prayers and texts repeatedly, remarking most memorably that they were "rather like being given processed cheese when you have ordered Double Gloucester." This criticism arose from his passion for unity. Convinced that the arts abhor any loppings off of meaning, he saw the supreme art form as especially harmed by any lessening of recession and thickness through it; he considered this totality of connotation lost in the new translations.[317] Finally, the poet felt that vernacularization represented hasty capitulation to the worst aspects of modern thought generally: "the reasons are utile and so-called 'practical.'... At root, I don't believe it's a 'religious' matter at all. I believe it's only part of the Decline of the West."[318]

As this passage indicates, Jones's fundamental rationale for opposing the liturgical reforms came from the heart of his rebellion against modern technocracy. If he believed that these alterations reflected the utile's bias against tradition, and thus threatened Roman Catholicism's continuity with the past, he also thought they imperiled his creed's gratuitous, sacramental core. Jones argued that the reformers were trying to reconcile Roman Catholicism and modern culture, and that, "given the present 'streamlining' obsession of our megalopolitan civilization, a certain utile, mechanistic, and uniformative spirit will be detected in the deliberations of the Church, often, if not always, at the expense of *poiesis*,"

---

315. Jones to Harman Grisewood, 6 July 1964 (*DGC*, 209).

316. Jones to William Blissett, 16 May 1967; quoted in Blissett, *Conversation*, 38.

317. Jones to Harman Grisewood, 23 March 1961; quoted in Dilworth, *Shape*, 31. See also *The Anathemata*, 217, n. 4; *SL*, 109–10, n. 2; Jones to Richard and Juliet Shirley Smith, 17 August 1961 (*Ten Letters*, 36).

318. Jones to Harman Grisewood, 6 July 1964 (*DGC*, 209).

so long as this attempted rapprochement persists.[319] Beyond being an abjural of what Jones had long considered Catholicism's distinctive principle, he also feared that if the supreme art form yielded to the utile, the other arts would find it even more difficult to withstand positivism's purported hegemony. Indeed the 1971 appeal to save the Latin Mass that he and Greene signed contains a distinctively Jonesean passage: "In the materialistic and technocratic civilization that is increasingly threatening the life of mind and spirit in its original creative expression—the word—it seems particularly inhuman to deprive man of word-forms in one of their most grandiose manifestations."[320]

Jones countered that, instead of changing the liturgy to suit the times, the Church should use its traditional rites as focal points of rebellion on behalf of its foundational premise of gratuity.

> [A]bove all else, we need to be continuously reassured by the Church that no matter what the present Zeitgeist may be or how ubiquitous its sway, She is clearly contrary to it. We need a reinforcement rather than a diminution of precisely those things and modes of thought which are in fact being played down or eliminated.[321]

Were the Church to quit resisting the utile, he warned in 1967, it would endanger its survival by eliminating its raison d'être: "When one considers the essential positivism that determines our present civilization-phase, whereby the entire notion of sign or sacrament is necessarily alien, it is hard to see how a religion wholly dependent upon sacrament can suffer radical 'modernization' without contradicting its primary presupposition."[322] If the Church cedes the gratuitous character of its central rite to these pressures of positivism, Jones deduced, it soon ceases to be the Church: "if you deny that principle then you deny the basis upon which our religion of sacrament is founded."[323]

---

319. Jones to Father Crichton, undated draft, David Jones 1985 Purchase. Group C, Box 1, NLW.

320. "Appeal to Preserve Mass Sent to Vatican," *The Times*, 6 July 1971; reprinted in Blissett, *Conversation*, 154–55. His own avowal of this idea is in a notebook held in David Jones 1985 Purchase. Group C, Box 11, NLW.

321. Jones undated letter fragment, David Jones 1985 Purchase. Group A, Box I/16, NLW.

322. Jones to the *Times*, 17 November 1967 (draft), David Jones 1985 Purchase. Group A, Box II/18, NLW.

323. Jones to the *Tablet*, undated, David Jones 1985 Purchase. Group A, Box I/8, NLW.

As he examined the Church's brass, though, this private found few willing to stay in the trenches with him. Jones descried "an almost fatal blindness" concerning *"signum* and *sacramentum"* among the hierarchy, which made them unaware of how the changes they approved could precipitate a suicidal surrender to the utile.[324] Whatever their good intentions, these clerics "by no means appear aware of those 'enemy dispositions.'"[325] In short, Jones felt that the remnant he had found harbor with faced an ignorant mutiny among its officers that was changing the course and fundamental design of an ancient, yet still seaworthy, vessel, and thus was risking spiritual shipwreck for its passengers and remaining crew. Or, as he put it more graphically, the Church's continued viability was imperiled because "those buggers in the Curia"[326] had "buggered up the Mass."[327]

Yet, much as Jones detested the liturgical changes instituted during his later years, he (like Greene and Dawson) remained "loyal to the Vexillum."[328] Indeed, he was not an obscurantist, as he found "tedious" those who fought the Church's alterations because they "just want, out of mere custom, to have no change."[329] Like Greene's and Dawson's, then, Jones's opposition was aroused by the nature of the changes that were adopted, not the fact of them. Moreover, he did not think the modernizers were wholly triumphant, for he signed the 1971 appeal in the belief that the Vatican might yet adjust its decision, and he took "a little comfort" from the permission some churches received to retain the traditional rites.[330] Finally, he also seemed to share Greene's sense that the Church is not the hierarchy, as he found solace in the devotion to the ancient liturgy of friends like Dawson and Saunders Lewis. Despite the anguish caused by the actions of the Church's leaders, then, Jones believed

---

324. Jones to Tom Burns, 2 July 1971, David Jones 1985 Purchase. Group B, Box 1/16, NLW.
325. Jones to the *Tablet*, undated draft, David Jones 1985 Purchase. Group C, Box 2, NLW.
326. Jones quoted in Orr, "Mr. Jones," 124.
327. Jones quoted in Michael Alexander, "David Jones," in Matthias, *Man and Poet*, 67.
328. Blissett, *Conversation*, 132.
329. Jones to Harman Grisewood, 6 July 1964 (*DGC*, 207).
330. Blissett, *Conversation*, 71. According to Orr ("Mr. Jones," 124), Jones himself had to celebrate the *Novus Ordo* only rarely, as his nursing home's priest was "too far into the vale of years to learn new-fangledness."

in staying on board, doing what he could to replot the course (but not necessarily along exactly the same points as before), and standing by his mates. After a half-century's service in this armada, he would, if need be, go down with the ship.

Yet the fact that he considered himself in such a precarious position at all remains instructive, for it reveals how much the beliefs that prompted his conversion shaped his subsequent Catholicism. Jones had become a Roman Catholic because he thought this faith affirmed liturgically and theologically his concerns about unity and gratuity. So long as the Church upheld these convictions against the sensed spread of a mind-set contemptuous of the past and oriented toward the purely practical, he dwelt in the household of faith relatively comfortably. Yet when its managers seemed ready to dispense with what he regarded as its most valuable heirlooms to bring the place up to date, he became a less cooperative tenant. Like Greene and Dawson, then, Jones's pre-conversion principles had become so symbiotic with his conception of Catholicism that he saw his protest on their behalf as a defense of its distinctive traits against an institution that he thought had once championed them staunchly, but that now seemed less fervent.

Sacramentalist, Seer, Subversive: A Writer's Roles

Jones's misgivings about the Church's possible conflict with cherished convictions displayed in these liturgical qualms raise the question of how his faith interacted with other facets of his outlook. For example, was he a "Catholic writer"? This is a contentious matter among Jones scholars, and Jones is partly responsible for this discord, as his attitude toward this label was ambiguous.[331] Like Greene, he wished to avoid its propagandistic connotations; he even used rhetoric akin to Greene's, claiming that "my intention has not been to 'edify,'"[332] and calling himself an "artist who happens also to be a Catholic" more than once.[333] Yet Jones also declared that numerous notions about art were ideas that "I must owe my indebtedness to Her alone in,"[334] and he felt that these con-

---

331. See, e.g., Ward, *Mythmaker*, 3; Blamires, *Artist and Writer*, 174; Hills, *Artist and Poet*, 13–15, 63; Dilworth, "Letters," 62–63; and Corcoran, *Song of Deeds*, 7–8.
332. Jones, *The Anathemata*, 33.
333. See Jones, "The Arthurian Legend," in *E&A*, 211; and "Art and Sacrament," 144.
334. Jones to H. S. Ede, 5 September 1935, op. cit.

cepts "had a continuous effect on all my work."³³⁵ As with Greene, then, it appears that Jones shunned a particular label to keep the distinction between art and apologetics clear, but that, also like Greene (and Chesterton and Dawson), he felt that Roman Catholicism played a fundamental shaping role in his making. Indeed, as Jones held that art and Catholicism are both radically gratuitous, "Catholic artist" was more a redundancy than an oxymoron to him: "though there is no such thing as 'Catholic art' . . . the postulates of our religion presuppose that man is such and such a creature and the kind of creature presupposed will be found to involve the nature of art."³³⁶ Thus, if some critics have a point in saying that Jones's use of Catholicism was often highly personal, others are also right to deem it his work's informing vision, for this faith fused his aesthetic, cultural, and religious perceptions. Dilworth sums it up nicely: "Catholicism is integral to what Arnold would call Jones's 'criticism of life.' . . . It supplies an all-inclusive vision of life and a sense of integral relationship between matter and spirit that helps interpret the content of his poetry and even places poetry itself in a metaphysical context."³³⁷

But what of other contexts? Kathleen Staudt posits "the difficulty of classifying him or assimilating him to the mainstream of Anglo-American modernism."³³⁸ Jones had a carefully nuanced view of this literary movement, as he adopted its techniques but eschewed some of its chief philosophical tenets, and his objections to Modernist aesthetics were shaped in part by his religious beliefs. For one thing, as Dilworth notes, the stress on continuity that Jones derived partially from his faith is "exceptional among modernist writers, for whom the present primarily contrasts with the past."³³⁹ Moreover, Jones likewise rejected formalism. Redolent of Greene's criticism of the Bloomsbury novelists, Jones rebuked the idea that an artist is free to "concern himself solely with the 'form,'" claiming it yielded "an emptiness and aridity and dehumanized art-form."³⁴⁰ In his own art, he held, "the 'form' & the constantly changing 'forms' were de-

---

335. Jones 2 May 1966 manuscript, David Jones 1985 Purchase. Group C, Box 15, NLW.
336. Jones, "Art and Sacrament," 144.   337. Dilworth, Shape, 5–6.
338. Staudt, Turn, 192.
339. Dilworth, Shape, 63. See also Blamires, Artist and Writer, 12.
340. Jones undated letter, David Jones 1985 Purchase. Group B, Box V/6, NLW. See also DGC, 46.

termined by the 'content.' . . . I cannot conceive of myself proceeding in any other way."[341] He also mocked what he considered the Modernist over-emphasis on form:

> form indeed
> . . .
> —it matters—can't you see it matters—
> it's the only thing one can
>   speak of
>   with any conviction
>   with any certainty
>   I don't know about the
> *splendor veri.*[342]

Yet Jones did believe that he had been exposed to truth's splendor. His religious convictions, like Greene's, helped prompt him to rebut Modernism by prioritizing content over form in making: the Muses "must know how to behave to the Queen of the Moral Virtues and must curtsey to the Queen of the Sciences."[343]

For similar reasons, Jones also opposed the stress on subjectivity that he felt marked much Modernist art, some contrary judgments of his work notwithstanding.[344] Like Eliot and Sayers, Jones argued that art should transmit tradition (albeit in a distinctly personal way) rather than the author's individual experiences and emotions. He held that his own work is "pretty straightforward really, compared with most modern 'personal experience' and 'psychological' kinds of poetry . . . the things written of are not personal to me, but are the inheritance of us all."[345] Postimpressionism and Gill's thought helped inspire this dedication to objectivity, as both stressed that art is an objective re-presentation and not a subjective impression of a model.[346] Jones also worried that "the

---

341. Jones to Desmond Chute, 4 February 1953 (*Inner Necessities*, 48). See also *Ten Letters*, 23.

342. Jones, "The Old Quarry, Part Two," 164.

343. Jones, "Art and Democracy," 95.

344. See, e.g., "Religious Writing," *Times Literary Supplement*, 17 August 1956, xiv; John Holloway, "A Perpetual Showing," *Hudson Review* 16 (Spring 1963): 127.

345. Jones to H. S. Ede, 17 December 1952 (*DGC*, 155–56). See also Eliot, *Selected Essays*, 7–11; and Sayers, *Mind of Maker*, 121.

346. See Jones, *E&A*, 171–72, 293; and Dilworth, *Shape*, 11.

tide of subjectivism"[347] would drown the traditions he wished to keep vital, as "so quickly do works date in an age of individual experiment."[348] His dislike of "'self-expression'" in art was fed further by the fears of mental self-immurement that he shared with Chesterton.[349] In fact, Gill argued that the Thomism that taught Jones the goodness of matter as well as mind also supplied Aristotelian objectivity in both thought and art, which the poet called his "main conviction" in aesthetics in 1951. As Blissett puts it, Jones's "theology of the Logos put a limit to syntactical license" by providing an external standard of content against which to measure his formal creativity: his muse always remembered to curtsey.[350] These indictments of some of Modernism's chief traits thus reveal that his work cannot be assimilated to Anglo-American Modernism's mainstream, for it swims against that current as part of his wider rebellion against modern culture. In classifying Jones within a movement whose methods he borrowed without their attendant ideology, Davenport's designation of him as a "non-modernist modernist" is apt; although to dub Jones further a "counter-modern modernist" may be even more accurate.[351]

If Jones's views of Catholicism and Modernism were textured, so was his attitude toward some rhetorical roles. For instance, peers and critics have consistently dubbed him a prophet. But, like his fellow converts, Jones denied directly any assumption of this mantle.[352] He referred to "not being a prophet" himself, and claimed that "rather than being a seer or endowed with the gift of prophecy," the poet generally is a rememberer and transmitter of tradition, a rhetorical humility that makes him more of a jester.[353] Characters in his verse offer similar demurrals. Yet

---

347. Jones, "Art and Sacrament," 172. 348. Jones, "Eric Gill as Sculptor," 292.
349. Jones, *The Anathemata*, 12.
350. Jones quoted in Dilworth, *Shape*, 11; Blissett, "Syntax of Violence," 206; Gill ms., 7 September 1928, op. cit.
351. Guy Davenport, "Stanley Spencer and David Jones," in De Groot and Leggatt, *Craft and Tradition*, 261. See also Blamires, *Artist and Writer*, 12.
352. The most extended case for this classification is Kathleen Henderson Staudt, "What's Under Works Up: The Prophetic Modernism of David Jones," in Hills, *Artist and Poet*, 158–71. Some scholars, though, have dissented from this opinion. See, e.g., Noon, *Poetry and Prayer*, 229; Shiel, "Jones the Maker," 162.
353. Jones, 2 May 1966 manuscript, op. cit.; and *The Anathemata*, 35.

just as some of them are prophets despite their contrary claims, so their creator identified far more strongly with this role than he suggested overtly.³⁵⁴ One of Jones's chief dicta, "the virtue of art is to judge," also defines part of the prophet's function. Moreover, he adverted (both directly and allusively) to Hebrew prophets, and also identified with them indirectly. Hence, when he asks, "Ah! what shall I write?" he recalls Jeremiah's "Ah, Lord God! . . . I know not how to speak," and Isaiah's "What shall I cry out?" each of which is followed by God's vow to put wisdom in the man's mouth.³⁵⁵

Furthermore, a more direct allusion to Isaiah undermines Jones's separation of poetry and prophecy by conflating these functions lyrically:

> for Tyrannosaurus
> must somehow lie down with herbivores, or, the poet lied,
> which is not allowed.³⁵⁶

Recalling his direct equation of poet, priest, and prophet, this passage suggests that Jones believed that rememberers and prophets share the common purpose of being truth-tellers. As such people must often make unpopular judgments, it follows that (like Dawson) Jones also intimated that the prophetic office was best exercised in the modern age by members of what he considered both the foremost Christian truth-telling institution and the one least acceptable to the utile. He noted approvingly, for instance, the contention of Dawson and others that Protestantism is not a prophetic religion, and it is a distinctly Roman Catholic character who "wails like a minor prophet."³⁵⁷ Thus, as was the case for Chesterton, Greene, and Dawson, Jones's disavowals of this role cannot withstand the testimony his rhetoric adduces. Whatever his motives for claiming he knew not how to speak, he had both the structure

---

354. See, e.g., *IP,* 142; *The Anathemata,* 159; and Staudt, *Turn,* 148.

355. See Jeremiah 1:6; Isaiah 40:6. These references were suggested originally in, respectively, Ward, *Mythmaker,* 166; and Staudt, *Turn,* 35. Maritain cited the Jeremiah passage in *Art and Scholasticism.*

For other assumptions of the prophet's role, see, e.g., *IP,* 84; *SL,* 95–96. The general themes of prophecy and of distinguishing true from false prophets are also central to "The Book of Balaam's Ass."

356. Jones, *The Anathemata,* 74.

357. Jones, *IP,* 117. See also Dawson, *The Formation of Christendom* (New York: Sheed & Ward, 1967), 291; and Dix, *Shape of Liturgy,* 72.

and vocabulary to do more than wail, as many readers saw; and, to him, this ability to witness to truth was intertwined with his adopted faith.

Jones's identification with figures who were often vilified for challenging their day's established opinion, plus his general sense that the beliefs he upheld were besieged in his era, reinforces his role as a rebel. As with "Catholic art," Modernism, and prophecy, various readers described Jones as being out of the modern mainstream, one even claiming that his work *"required* a sense ... of marginalization, of embattlement, of pursuance-in-despite."[358] Unlike his view of those other categories, though, Jones's assumption of this persona contained no ambiguity nor denial. Asked if he felt that "you are very much against the current of the age," Jones replied, "Well, yes, appallingly so in one way," due to his defense of gratuity. Pressed further to state whether "you like the world in which we live now," he responded flatly, "No, I don't like it at all."[359] As was customary, he generalized this personal position, thereby agreeing with Greene implicitly that, in modernity, to be a writer is to be a rebel. In a utile age, "poetry is to be diagnosed as 'dangerous' because it evokes and recalls, is a kind of *anamnesis*."[360] And, as sacrament also has this gratuitous function, Jones concluded that art "shares the honors of sabotage with the tradition of religion" in modern culture.[361] Thus since (as Staudt puts it) Jones thought "the role of the poet [is] at once subversive and sacramental," and that Roman Catholicism best upholds the sacramentalism affirmed in the subversion of pure utility, William Noon is right to see that (as with prophecy) there is synergy between the roles of rebel and Catholic artist in Jones's mind: "he is as much aware as anyone that the Catholic artist is out of step with the cultural trend in today's corporate civilization. What long ago began as a religious crisis ends as an overall crisis for the culture of modern times."[362]

---

358. Merlin James, *Map of the Artist's Mind*, 49. Emphasis in original. See also, e.g., Kermode, *Puzzles*, 35; Stephen Spender, "Civilization vs. Culture," *New York Times Book Review*, 18 February 1979, 9; Corcoran, *Song of Deeds*, 5, 18; Ward, *Mythmaker*, 2, 65; Jeremy Hooker, *The Presence of the Past* (Bridgend: Poetry Wales, 1987), 17; Staudt, *Turn*, 2.

359. *The Poet Speaks*, 98, 102.

360. Jones, *The Anathemata*, 21. See also "Art in Relation to War," 123.

361. Jones, "Religion and the Muses," 100.

362. Staudt, *Turn*, 135; and Noon, *Poetry and Prayer*, 229. Cf. Ward, *Mythmaker*, 23.

A Fairly Honorable Defeat(?): Conclusion

Jones was not alone among orthodox British Catholics in sensing such an inextricably interconnected crisis, though his definition of it was distinctive. Heaney, for instance, saw Jones "picking up where the Oxford Movement left off."[363] Yet, although Jones felt that the unprecedented primacy of utility had commenced in the 1800s, he thought that this "Break" was not fully consolidated until the early twentieth century, and thus posed a uniquely acute challenge to his day's makers: by the 1920s, there was "an objective 'newness,' not brought about by, or from within, the activity we call 'the arts,' but from a civilizational change, causing, I should think, a greater metamorphosis than any historic or proto-historic change known to us." As the century went on, he descried the "onward and rapid acceleration" of this novel hegemony, until its sway reached even into that last dogmatic, institutional citadel of the traditional supremacy of gratuity, the Roman Catholic Church.[364] As he extended the protest against modern secularism and its developments enounced by the likes of Newman and Chesterton, then, Jones was as convinced as Greene and Dawson of the particularly perilous position of his own epoch.

It was this apprehension of his age's spiritual and cultural course that drove David Jones's religious development. Many of his key beliefs, such as people being essentially makers, the significance of symbolic action and its gratuitous basis, a desire for unity, and the Crucifixion's centrality, were all present in some form from childhood. Unlike Chesterton, Greene, or Dawson, though, no single episode transformed Jones's religious expression of this worldview. Rather, he was impelled toward Roman Catholicism by a gradual accumulation of evidence that persuaded him that this religion was best equipped to voice and defend these ideals in an era he considered increasingly hostile to them.

Jones found his inherited form of Protestantism insufficient on these counts early on. But despite some limited youthful exposure to Catholi-

---

363. Seamus Heaney, "Now and in England," *Spectator*, 4 May 1974, 547.
364. Jones, "Notes on the 1930s," 44. See also "Beauty in Catholic Churches," 438–41; *The Anathemata*, 15–16; Jones to Harman Grisewood, 11 January 1962 (*DGC*, 186); Jones to Mr. Gommon, op. cit.

cism, it was only at art school and in war that he acquired personal and liturgical knowledge of this kind of Christianity and was inspired to study its doctrines carefully. Spurred by a growing apprehension that modern culture was increasingly and uniquely devoted to solely utilitarian considerations, Jones began to find Roman Catholicism in accord with his contrary beliefs, especially when he linked its sacramentalism to postimpressionist aesthetics. Yet, despite deeming himself an inward Catholic by the late 1910s, he still thought he could remain an outward Anglican. In 1921, though, Eric Gill persuaded him that only Rome had the authority needed to uphold their shared beliefs about art and sacrament, and John O'Connor assured him that converting would actually enrich many aspects of his inheritance. If taking this difficult step had some of the personal repercussions that Jones had feared, it also integrated his aesthetic and religious perceptions with a theology fully for the first time.

Once received, Jones's approach to his new faith remained motivated by his prior concerns for gratuity and continuity, and his sense that Roman Catholicism was the form of Christianity best able to resist cultural trends that threatened what he saw as these core human characteristics. He rooted his theology of history in these long-standing concerns. In positing the Crucifixion and its liturgical re-enactment as being still points in a turning cosmos, Jones rebuked Progress in favor of continuity without sacrificing linearity; he also linked all myths, facts, and rituals to their Christian analogs fundamentally without surrendering his belief in the transforming power of the Incarnation and its sacramental re-calling. Similarly, the stress he derived from Thomism on what seemed Catholicism's especially incarnational outlook helped him resist tempting dualistic beliefs. Jones thus found in orthodox Roman Catholicism a balance between fact and myth, matter and spirit, that preserved what he had long deemed human nature's essential qualities against both the utile's perceived peril and the dangers he saw in overreacting to that challenge.

He was consequently alarmed by apparent deviations from this equilibrium within the Church. In cases like Chardinean theology or liturgical changes, Jones thought, attempts to accommodate modern culture would only erode the Church's foundation by diminishing its connections to the past and its sacramentalism. Having long considered Roman Catholicism his epoch's last corporate defender of these signature human traits, this Catholic artist thus brought his prophecy and rebellion against modernity into his spiritual home in his later years: if crucial questions were not asked, he feared, the Church would become as vast a waste land as he thought existed outside its doors. Even his poetic style was a focused tactic in his cultural protest, as use of Modernist methods coincided with consistent, Catholic criticism of key facets of Modernist aesthetics.

Jones saw that his campaign of subversion against the utile might be a losing battle, and that it could contribute to the ignorance of his work that persists, even among Catholics. But he believed in fighting on, certain that even such a defeat would be fairly honorable, for it would be in defense of the qualities that make people what they are:

> I do feel that what, for short, I'll call "our attitude" is now something of a "lost cause." That's O.K. "Lost causes" are almost always the right causes.[365]

This old soldier would not just fade away.

365. Jones to Harman Grisewood, 21 October 1953 (*DGC*, 159).

CONCLUSION

"I MAKE EACH DAY MY REVOLUTION"

JONES ONCE reiterated his belief that causes that seem lost in modernity are right from the standpoint of transcendent truth with a nod to a fellow cosmic optimist: "nothing succeeds like failure, as Chesterton might say."[1] This epigram is an apt epitaph for the entire Third Spring. As verdant a flowering in many fields of intellectual activity as this twentieth-century revival of British Roman Catholicism was, these converts' shared hope of routing out modern secularism from their culture's soil and planting anew a traditional Christian ethos failed to strike deep roots. Within both Britain and the Church itself, the beliefs and norms that Chesterton, Greene, Dawson, and Jones opposed became more pervasive during their lives and afterwards. Yet this broad pragmatic failure is in a sense the measure of their success as cultural dissenters. In offering consistent, stalwart rebuttals of modernity's first principles and their perceived religious and cultural consequences from a distinctly Roman Catholic perspective, these four authors helped carry forward a heritage of religious protest against liberal agnosticism and its allegedly secular, progressive, presentist, and utilitarian ramifications into the conditions of their era. In the process, they demonstrated that a never-large, often-persecuted faith could be so compelling to a widely disparate collection of the century's foremost minds that each man would choose to confess

---

1. Jones to Harman Grisewood, 20 July 1935, in *Dai Greatcoat: A Self-Portrait of David Jones in His Letters*, ed. René Hague (London: Faber & Faber, 1980), 75.

it, despite its unpopularity (and that of traditional religion generally at this time) and the sacrifices such a decision often entailed. If these rhetorical prophets were without honor among their own, their clear and steadfast articulation of their convictions still left a lasting legacy of radical, Roman Catholic challenge to the dominant climate of opinion in major spheres of modern British letters.

Writing of Eric Gill, Greene complained that "in this country Catholicism which should produce revolutionaries produces only eccentrics."[2] However true of Gill, it was not so for the author nor for Chesterton, Dawson, or Jones. All of them urged radical cultural transformation and remained devoted to this ideal even when the likes of Gill and Waugh retreated from the world into eccentricity. Each thinker's dismay with the modern milieu arose in youth, as received convictions failed to accord with his experiences, precipitating what John Barbour labels "deconversion" from his inherited belief system.[3] In religious matters, though to varying extents, the converts thought the faith they learned as boys did not account persuasively for human limitations and evil; was insensitive to the discerned wisdom, beauty, and persistent vitality of the past; and was unable to establish definitive standards of belief. As they sensed that their age was embracing more fully ideas they saw as maddening, naive, narrow, or destructive of human identity's core, each sought intellectual and spiritual affirmation of his alternate principles and his hopes for preserving and eventually reviving them. Faced with what seemed the unprecedented ascendancy of irreligious and anti-traditional beliefs in the century's dawning decades, each man came to deem resolute protest against dominant notions and norms essential to this desired conservation and revitalization. Under diverse conditions, and with differing degrees of rapidity and enthusiasm, all of them concluded that customary Catholic Christianity best upheld their convictions; and that only its Roman version—particularly the Italianate form this faith was taking in

---

2. Graham Greene, "Eric Gill," in *Collected Essays* (New York: Penguin, 1969), 262.

3. "A 'disjunction between theory and experience' often generates the elements constitutive of deconversion: intellectual doubt, moral criticism of an inadequate way of life, emotional upheaval and rejection of a community or a conception of society." John Barbour, *Versions of Deconversion: Autobiography and the Loss of Faith* (Charlottesville: University Press of Virginia, 1994), 206.

Britain—possessed the legitimate constitutional mechanisms to voice these countercultural contentions authoritatively and unswervingly.

Crucial to developing this certainty for all four was not only extensive reflection, but also the examples of others who found similar surety in this faith, even if the converts' choices often pained still others close to them. Once each man was received, orthodox Roman Catholicism—and especially its incarnational emphasis on the goodness of both spirit and matter, and an ensuing integrated equilibrium between them—became central to his personal and religious identity; Catholicism also supplied the intellectual framework and vocabulary that he used to articulate his rebellion against modern secularity. All of them deemed their thought enriched by veins of traditional Catholic theology like Augustinianism and Thomism (even as they differed about which lode had the most valuable ore), while they commonly eschewed what they saw as impoverished accommodationist systems advocated by the likes of theological (and literary) Modernists and Teilhard de Chardin. Similarly, although the converts clashed about the merits of mysticism, each regarded Christianity's claim to be a distinctly historical creed as essential to his faith and pondered the theological implications for history of the Incarnation and Redemption. Having so absorbed Roman Catholicism into their mind-sets, these thinkers all confronted what it meant to be a "Catholic writer," and each insisted that this perspective was not inimical to scholarly or creative freedom, but instead provided a distinct grammar and lexicon for discussing current and universal themes. All four, then, remained critically engaged with their times, avoiding the shoals of withdrawal from modern life or capitulation to its regnant beliefs. In so dissenting consistently from his age's prevailing norms while not despairing of its redemption, each author used prophetic tropes to warn his fellows against continued neglect of their traditional faith and heritage and to call for renewal of that patrimony. The writers hence desired both to uproot modern post-Christian mores thoroughly and to reroot Britain in customary Christian and ancestral ideals. They were thus all radical conservatives.

Yet the converts' staunch challenge to their culture also curbed their practical effectiveness. Over the course of these men's lives, both British society and the Catholic Church grew less sympathetic to their outlook.

In Britain, the eclipse of traditional Christianity that suffused the intelligentsia in the twentieth century's first years eventually became a culturewide phenomenon. Even those who dispute whether Britain became secularized by the end of the century agree that as the years progressed, and particularly since the 1960s, it was increasingly less animated by the orthodox, or "official," Christianity that Chesterton, Greene, Dawson, and Jones wanted to restore.[4] Church attendance and denominational identification declined consistently for traditional faiths, while disregard for, and even defiance of, their teachings—on matters from cohabitation to cloning—combined with continued acceptance of modern trends like specialization to erode their overall cultural authority. As Alan Gilbert puts it, "As religion has become a segmental activity in modern society, with denominational associations representing merely one involvement among many for people moving in a pluralistic, differentiated social environment, it has lost its traditional, normative role over social life generally."[5]

Even as British society as a whole became less favorable to traditional notions of religion and its role in civilization as the century went on, so too did Roman Catholics, both in Britain and institutionally, ease their hostility to modern culture. The growing adaptation by British Catholics to their nonorthodox Christian society that Dawson had apprehended in the 1950s accelerated, especially from the 1960s. The ebbing of official religion also brought greater tolerance and the collapse of some of the most virulent anti-Catholic prejudices. As Roman Catholics exploited ensuing new opportunities and began to enter the postwar middle class and to assume prestigious political and social positions, their previously

---

4. See, e.g., Grace Davie, *Religion in Britain Since 1945: Believing Without Belonging* (Oxford: Blackwell, 1994); John Wolffe, *God and Greater Britain: Religion and National Life in Britain and Ireland, 1843–1945* (London: Routledge, 1994), 254–64; Paul Badham, "Religious Pluralism in Modern Britain," in *A History of Religion in Britain*, ed. Sheridan Gilley and W. J. Sheils (Oxford: Blackwell, 1994), 488–502.

5. Alan Gilbert, *The Making of Post-Christian Britain* (London: Longman, 1980), 108. See Davie, *Religion in Britain*; and *Catholics in England, 1950–2000*, ed. Michael Hornsby-Smith (London: Cassell, 1999), for the most current chartings of the dips in church attendance and denominational affiliation over the century. See also, e.g., Warren Hoge, "Britain Lowers Gay Consent Age, Creating Single Standard," *New York Times*, 23 June 1998, A11; and "Britain Gives Green Light for Embryo Cloning," www.nytimes.com, 23 January 2001.

homogeneous subculture fragmented. With it crumbled the assumption that being a Roman Catholic automatically made one distinct from, and opposed to, dominant British principles and structures. Ideas and practices that once marked British Catholics as singular and separate members of society—like bans on religiously mixed marriages, divorce, and contraception—were no longer matters of consensus in the Roman Catholic community, as increasing numbers of its members adopted the larger society's approval of such modern beliefs and behaviors. This escalating social and cultural assimilation in the latter part of the century led Michael Hornsby-Smith to conclude in 1987 that "in the four decades since the Second World War English Catholics have very largely converged both structurally and culturally to the norms of the wider society."[6] His judgment that Roman Catholicism no longer seemed an alternative to prepotent mores is ratified further by the precipitous drop in the average annual number of conversions during this period: from 1959 to 1962, for instance, there were an average of 12,490 a year (with a peak of 13,735 in 1959), but a decade later only 4,436 (with a low of 3,897 in 1972).[7] And, Patrick Allitt noted in 1997, this pattern also prevailed among the group from which the Church had drawn British converts disproportionately in modern times: "conversion of intellectuals has continued up to the present but has been a less distinctive feature of postconciliar

---

6. Michael Hornsby-Smith, *Roman Catholics in England* (Cambridge: Cambridge University Press, 1987), 211. In addition to that work, see Hornsby-Smith, *Roman Catholic Beliefs in England* (Cambridge: Cambridge University Press, 1991); Hornsby-Smith, "Recent Transformations in English Catholicism: Evidence of Secularization?" in *Religion and Modernization: Sociologists and Historians Debate the Secularization Thesis*, ed. Steve Bruce (Oxford: Clarendon Press, 1992), 118–44; and Adrian Hastings, *A History of English Christianity, 1920–1985* (London: Collins, 1986), 562–63, for sociological and statistical substantiation of the conclusions summarized in this paragraph. For the persistence, and intensification, of these trends through the 1990s, see Hornsby-Smith, *Catholics in England, 1950–2000*, passim.

7. Hastings, *English Christianity*, 580. It might be argued that the Catholic Church still has countercultural appeal to some, particularly Anglicans disturbed by their church's 1992 decision to ordain women to the priesthood. But the number of conversions resulting from this development has not been large, nor have they, as yet, included any thinkers comparable to those received during the century's early years. Moreover, although the overall number of Catholic conversions rose to nearly six thousand per annum by the late 1990s, this figure is still less than half the average total that was prevalent at the zenith of Roman receptions in the late 1950s and early 1960s (Hornsby-Smith, *Catholics in England*, 13).

Catholicism than it was in the hundred and twenty years before the [Second Vatican] council."[8]

As Allitt's analysis implies, British Catholics also responded, in part, to the greater openness to modern mentalities that the Church commenced corporately with Vatican II. While its pronouncements were consistent with traditional Catholic doctrine, the council's symbolic changes, such as the alterations in the Mass, signaled to many Catholics that their church no longer saw uncompromising challenge of modernity as a hallmark of its identity. Bernard Bergonzi captured this mood even before the conclave had concluded:

> the climate of English Catholicism has changed extraordinarily in a very short time, reflecting of course, the impact of Pope John and the Second Vatican Council. . . . In the Universal Church the 400-year period of the defensive post-Tridentine reaction has come to an end; and in England there are signs of the decline of the "ghetto mentality" and Catholic exclusiveness. . . . It is perhaps a mark of psychological immaturity to be emotionally and aesthetically attached to particular liturgical forms; but it is quite a common reaction . . . the change-over could be rather traumatic for many admirable but uninformed Catholics.[9]

This sort of response to the council's changes was precisely what Greene, Dawson, and Jones had feared, both in its accommodationist content and its patronizing tone; and such sentiments were one reason they judged the liturgical modifications an unwise concession to post-Christian pressures. Both in Britain and globally, then, Roman Catholics were distancing themselves from the nineteenth-century Italianate model of the church that had enticed the converts and that had become their normative ecclesiological standard.[10]

---

8. Patrick Allitt, *Catholic Converts: British and American Intellectuals Turn to Rome* (Ithaca, N.Y.: Cornell University Press, 1997), x.

9. Bernard Bergonzi, "The English Catholics," *Encounter* 24 (January 1965): 29–30. Hornsby-Smith has judged that the "overwhelming majority" of British Roman Catholics favored these changes ("The Roman Catholic Church in Britain Since the Second World War," in *Religion, State, and Society in Modern Britain*, ed. Paul Badham [Lewiston, N.Y.: Edwin Mellen Press, 1989], 89). For a deft fictional depiction of this period, see David Lodge, *How Far Can You Go?* (London: Secker & Warburg, 1980).

10. Moreover, William McSweeney has argued that the principle of binding authority so integral to the Italianate model was itself undermined by Vatican II's theology and many

As both culture and church moved further away from their ideals, the converts' influence waned. Even though distinguished contemporaries praised their work, Dawson and Jones worried often that it was not read widely, anxieties that have proved well-founded;[11] and while Greene's books remained both commercially successful and seriously studied, critics frequently compartmentalized his "Catholic" works to a series of early volumes, downplayed his religion's presence in those written after the mid-1950s, and rarely explored his later output's counter-modern elements in detail.[12] Chesterton's writing also was increasingly ignored in the decades after Vatican II, a neglect David Lodge attributed in 1970 to changes in both British culture and the Catholic Church:

> Chesterton is read more and more selectively by fewer and fewer people.... The Modern Movement in literature, which Chesterton and Belloc either opposed or ignored, has become classical for our culture, and their own work looks thin and faded in comparison.... And the ideas for which they stood have largely lost their relevance.... The Chester-belloc's brand of Catholicism ... triumphalist, proselytizing, theologically conservative, Europe-oriented—is hardly congenial to the mood of the Church since Pope John XXIII and the Second Vatican Council.[13]

Roman Catholics' subsequent willingness to reject the hierarchy's edicts publicly, as epitomized by the widespread dissent from *Humanae Vitae*. McSweeney, *Roman Catholicism: The Search for Relevance* (New York: St. Martin's Press, 1980).

11. See, e.g., Dawson to G. K. Chesterton, 1 June 1932; reprinted in *Chesterton Review* 9 (May 1983): 136; Christina Scott, *A Historian and His World: A Life of Christopher Dawson* (New Brunswick, N.J.: Transaction Publishers, 1992), 128; David Jones, *The Dying Gaul and Other Writings*, ed. Harman Grisewood (London: Faber & Faber, 1972, 1978), 32–34; Jones to Vernon Watkins, 16 April 1962, in *Letters to Vernon Watkins*, ed. Ruth Pryor (Cardiff: University of Wales Press, 1976), 61.

12. See, e.g., Roger Sharrock, *Saints, Sinners and Comedians: The Novels of Graham Greene* (London: Burns & Oates, 1984), 17, 126, 196, 273–74; Bernard Bergonzi, "Contemporary British Fiction," *The Critic* (1989): 71; John Desmond, "Book Reviews," *Religion & Literature* 23 (Summer 1991): 121; John Updike, "The Man Within," *The New Yorker* 71 (26 June and 3 July 1995): 185; Allitt, *Catholic Converts*, 308; Robert Royal, "The (Mis)Guided Dream of Graham Greene," *First Things* (November 1999): 17.

13. David Lodge, *The Novelist at the Crossroads* (London: Routledge & Kegan Paul, 1971), 145. Although there has been a subsequent revival of interest in Chesterton's work, it remains limited, particularly in academic circles, and only a minority of Catholics educated since Vatican II are familiar with his writing.

Lodge himself typifies a growing trend among post-Vatican II British Catholic writers: an intellectual who writes from a standpoint shaped decisively by Roman Catholicism and about Catholic issues, but without a counter-modern edge, and even against the cultural criticisms voiced by his forebears.[14] While some authors, like Paul Johnson and Muriel Spark, follow more closely the model established by Chesterton and his fellow converts, protest against modernity ceased being a defining trait of twentieth-century British Roman Catholic thought in the immediate postconciliar era. As Bergonzi noted, starting in the 1960s "we have seen the emergence of intellectuals who, though intensely Catholic in their convictions, share the characteristic tone and modes of discourse of most other English intellectuals and are concerned with exploration rather than defense."[15] Thus, be it in Britain or the Church, the Third Spring's seed was largely swept away by the prevailing winds of change.

Yet it is their very willingness to sail against these winds that defines these four thinkers' achievement and legacy. In contesting their era's core principles, and in doing so from an identifiably Roman Catholic perspective, these authors used their considerable skills to obtain a hearing for ideals that were increasingly at odds with the tenor of their time. In fields ranging from journalism to fiction to poetry to history and cultural studies, they offered a fundamental alternative to their epoch's regnant precepts, and made their interpretations of a hitherto marginalized faith a constituent element of their age's climate of opinion. Even if their outlook was not widely persuasive immediately, it did attract the attention and admiration of many eminent peers, and its initial failure does not preclude future success. The Church itself has been rethinking its entente with modern culture under John Paul II, whose governing style accents papal authority and hierarchy, and whose thought echoes the Third Spring's critique of secularism.[16] Likewise, the growing appeal in Britain

---

14. See, especially, *The British Museum Is Falling Down* (London: MacGibbon & Kee, 1965); *How Far Can You Go?*; and "The Catholic Church and Cultural Life" (1980), in *Write On* (London: Secker & Warburg, 1986), 32–37. See also Bernard Bergonzi, "The Decline and Fall of the Catholic Novel," in *The Myth of Modernism and Twentieth Century Literature* (New York: St. Martin's Press, 1986), 179–87.

15. Bergonzi, "English Catholics," 28. Cf. Patrick Allitt, "A New Era of Converts," *Crisis* 8 (January 1994): 38.

16. Even the Latin Mass that the converts prized is somewhat renascent. See Peter

of sects that operate *"outside* the values and assumptions of the modern, secular world," like Pentecostalism, has led one respected scholar of its religions to posit that such movements may have "considerable" success in the future, and that "the Catholic Church may opt for a sectarian orientation to the wider secular culture," thus taking a position akin to the converts' stance of engaged protest.[17] Moreover, J. C. Whitehouse suggests that attempts to sustain a distinctively Catholic thought and art will succeed cognitively and aesthetically only if they are based in such a countercultural ethic.[18] But even if the post-Christian worldview remains dominant, Chesterton, Greene, Dawson, and Jones pose a challenge that its defenders disregard at the price of a truncated understanding of their own standpoint and of the genres in which they work.

Whatever the future holds, however, students of Britain's past will have the record of a movement that confronted modern unbelief at its roots, one that blossomed in an atmosphere more hostile to traditional religious growth of any kind than at any prior point in British history, and one that hence made Roman Catholicism part of twentieth-century British culture to an extent that could scarcely have been foreseen when this revival germinated. Eliot's eulogy of Chesterton thus suits the whole Third Spring: claiming that Chesterton had "revolutionary designs," Eliot argued that even if his ideas

> appear to be totally without effect, even if they should be demonstrated to be wrong—which would perhaps only mean that men have not the good will to carry them out—they were *the* ideas for his time that were fundamentally Christian and Catholic. He did more, I think, than any man of his time . . . to maintain the existence of the important minority in the modern world.[19]

Steinfels, "New York to Hear Mass in Latin, Language of Catholic Discontent," *New York Times*, 12 May 1996, 1, 9.

17. Alan Gilbert, "Secularization and the Future," in Gilley and Sheils, *History of Religion*, 519. Emphasis in original. For an account of current controversies within British Roman Catholicism concerning the appropriate extent of its engagement with contemporary culture, see William Oddie, "Bell-Curve Catholics," *Catholic World Report* (July 1996): 22–25. Cf. Thomas Woodman, *Faithful Fictions: The Catholic Novel in British Literature* (Philadelphia: Open University Press, 1991), 164.

18. J. C. Whitehouse, *Vertical Man* (London: Saint Austin Press, 1999), 12–13.

19. T. S. Eliot, *The Tablet*, 20 June 1936; reprinted in *G. K. Chesterton: The Critical Judgments*,

This, then, was the paradox of the Third Spring: the wedding of their cultural rebellion to their adopted religion that limited these intellectuals' influence both in the culture and the Church is also what denotes the nature of their contribution to each. The particular niche their work occupies in the history of British thought depends on their having been both Roman Catholic and counter-modern. Just as Newman's "resistance to the spirit of the age . . . assured that he would be judged a failure according to its liberal standards," so some have judged the early-twentieth-century converts unsuccessful because they could not effect cultural reconversion and would not endorse their church's modernization. Yet as Newman also held that a Roman Catholic is one who "fears no barbarian or heretical desolation, whose creed is destined to last unto the end," so his descendants in rebellion felt that keeping alive what they considered an authentic, counter-modern Catholic Christian approach to life and letters in an increasingly post-Christian era, even in occasional defiance of the Church's leadership, would ultimately be vindicated.[20] In that sense, the Third Spring was an even more remarkable occurrence than the Second, for it bloomed in a cultural climate dominated more extensively than its ancestor's had been by those who regarded all customary spiritual flowers as weeds.

To the likes of G. K. Chesterton, Graham Greene, Christopher Dawson, and David Jones, nothing succeeded like failure in such an epoch, for it proved that they had kept faith with what they deemed an enduring set of convictions. Agreeing with Chesterton that "we do not believe that there are any lost causes; we do not admit that there are any hopeless loyalties; and we should come back to our religion at last, if its temples were as deserted as Stonehenge," all four converts continued to combat the trends of their times, even amid apparent defeat, defection, and desolation. However concerned some of them grew about the current course of the Church or the culture, none of them lost his fundamental faith or hope in the religion and legacy that he had embraced as the best answer to modern agnosticism and secularism. Each was driven by "the hopeless hope; sometimes called the forlorn hope," sometimes called the cosmic

---

ed. D. J. Conlon (Antwerp: Universitaire Faculteiten Sint-Ignatius, 1976), 531–32. Emphasis in original.

20. Robert Pattison, *The Great Dissent: John Henry Newman and the Liberal Heresy* (Oxford: Oxford University Press, 1991), 6; and Newman quoted in ibid., 49.

optimism, that they were upholding an alternative of everlasting truth when rejecting contemporary conventions, and that persistent, reflective, and intensive expression of these beliefs could eventually persuade free people to refresh their heritage and so redeem the time.[21] An American counterpart, Samuel Hazo, has voiced their vision:

> The causes
> I believe in rarely win.
> The men and women I admire
> most are quietly ignored.
> . . .
> Regardless, I believe
> that something in me always was
> and will be what I am.
> I make each day my revolution.
> . . .
> I want to shout in every dialect
> of silence that the world we dream
> is what the world becomes,
> and what the world's become
> is there for anyone's re-dreaming.
> . . .
> The range
> of plus is no less infinite
> than minus . . .
> I learn that going
> on means coming back
> and looking hard at just one thing.
> That rosebush, for example.
> . . .
> And just like that the rose
> in all its whiteness blooms
> within me like a dream so true
> that I can taste it.
> And I do.[22]

---

21. *The Collected Works of G. K. Chesterton*, vol. 5, *The End of the Armistice*, ed. Frank Sheed (San Francisco: Ignatius Press, 1987), 661.
22. Samuel Hazo, "No Is the Father of Yes," in *Nightworks* (Riverdale-on-Hudson, N.Y.: Sheep Meadow Press, 1987), 83–84.

SELECT BIBLIOGRAPHY

The roster of published and unpublished primary sources is meant to be comprehensive. The list of secondary sources, though, is limited to standard studies in these fields, and to those that have particular bearing on twentieth-century British Catholicism and its setting, and on conversion, especially as manifested in the lives and works of Chesterton, Greene, Dawson, and Jones. Journals that were consulted regularly are listed separately, with only especially pertinent articles from their pages receiving a discrete entry.

Published Primary Sources

G. K. Chesterton

Alarms and Discursions. London: Methuen, 1910.
All Is Grist. London: Dodd, Mead & Co., 1932.
All I Survey. London: Methuen, 1933.
The Apostle and the Wild Ducks. Ed. Dorothy Collins. London: Paul Elek, 1975.
As I Was Saying. London: Methuen, 1936.
The Autobiography of G. K. Chesterton. Vol. 16 of *The Collected Works of G. K. Chesterton.* San Francisco: Ignatius Press, 1988.
Avowals and Denials. London: Methuen, 1934.
The Ball and the Cross. London: Watts, Gardner, Darnton & Co., 1909.
The Blatchford Controversies. Vol. 1 of *The Collected Works of G. K. Chesterton.* San Francisco: Ignatius Press, 1986.
The Catholic Church and Conversion. Vol. 3 of *The Collected Works of G. K. Chesterton.* San Francisco: Ignatius Press, 1990.
Charles Dickens, The Last of the Great Men. New York: The Readers Club, 1942.
Chaucer. Vol. 18 of *The Collected Works of G. K. Chesterton.* San Francisco: Ignatius Press, 1991.
Christendom in Dublin. London: Sheed & Ward, 1932.
The Collected Poems of G. K. Chesterton. London: Methuen, 1933.
Collected Poetry: Part I. Vol. 10 of *The Collected Works of G. K. Chesterton.* San Francisco: Ignatius Press, 1994.
The Colored Lands. New York: Sheed & Ward, 1938.
Come to Think of It. London: Methuen, 1930.

The Common Man. New York: Sheed & Ward, 1950.
The Crimes of England. Vol. 5 of *The Collected Works of G. K. Chesterton.* San Francisco: Ignatius Press, 1987.
"Culture and the Coming Peril." *Chesterton Review* 18 (August 1992): 333–43.
"The Day of the Lord." *American Review* 1 (April 1933): 76–79.
The Defendant. London: J. M. Dent & Sons, 1901.
"The Distributist." *The Commonweal* 12 (8 October 1930): 569–70.
The End of the Armistice. Vol. 5 of *The Collected Works of G. K. Chesterton.* San Francisco: Ignatius Press, 1987.
Eugenics and Other Evils. Vol. 4 of *The Collected Works of G. K. Chesterton.* San Francisco: Ignatius Press, 1987.
The Everlasting Man. Vol. 2 of *The Collected Works of G. K. Chesterton.* San Francisco: Ignatius Press, 1986.
Fancies versus Fads. New York: Dodd, Mead & Co., 1923.
The Flying Inn. London: Methuen, 1914.
G.K.C. as M.C. London: Methuen, 1929.
A Gleaming Cohort. London: Methuen, 1926.
A Handful of Authors. Ed. Dorothy Collins. New York: Sheed & Ward, 1953.
Heretics. Vol. 1 of *The Collected Works of G. K. Chesterton.* San Francisco: Ignatius Press, 1986.
"Human Nature and the Historians." *Catholic World* 104 (March 1917): 721–30.
The Incredulity of Father Brown. 1926. Reprint, London: Penguin, 1958.
The Innocence of Father Brown. 1911. Reprint, London: Penguin, 1950.
Irish Impressions. London: W. Collins Sons & Co., 1919.
Lunacy and Letters. Ed. Dorothy Collins. New York: Sheed & Ward, 1958.
Manalive. 1912. Reprint, London: Penguin, 1947.
The Man Who Was Thursday. 1908. Reprint, New York: Dover, 1986.
The Mask of Midas. Ed. Geir Hasnes. Trondheim, Norway: Classica forlag AS, 1991.
A Miscellany of Men. New York: Dodd, Mead & Co., 1912.
The Napoleon of Notting Hill. 1904. Reprint, New York: Dover, 1991.
The New Jerusalem. London: Hodder & Stoughton, 1920.
Orthodoxy. 1908. Reprint, New York: Image Books, 1959.
The Outline of Sanity. Vol. 5 of *The Collected Works of G. K. Chesterton.* San Francisco: Ignatius Press, 1987.
The Paradoxes of Mr. Pond. New York: Dodd, Mead & Co., 1937.
The Poet and the Lunatics. New York: Dodd, Mead & Co., 1929.
The Resurrection of Rome. Vol. 21 of *The Collected Works of G. K. Chesterton.* San Francisco: Ignatius Press, 1990.
The Return of Don Quixote. London: Chatto & Windus, 1927.
Robert Louis Stevenson. Vol. 18 of *The Collected Works of G. K. Chesterton.* San Francisco: Ignatius Press, 1991.
St. Francis of Assisi. Vol. 2 of *The Collected Works of G. K. Chesterton.* San Francisco: Ignatius Press, 1986.
St. Thomas Aquinas. Vol. 2 of *The Collected Works of G. K. Chesterton.* San Francisco: Ignatius Press, 1986.
The Scandal of Father Brown. 1929. Reprint, London: Penguin, 1978.

The Secret of Father Brown. 1927. Reprint, London: Penguin, 1974.
Selected Essays of G. K. Chesterton. London: Methuen, 1949.
A Shilling for My Thoughts. London: Methuen, 1916.
A Short History of England. London: Chatto & Windus, 1917.
Sidelights on New London and Newer York. Vol. 21 of *The Collected Works of G. K. Chesterton.* San Francisco: Ignatius Press, 1990.
The Spice of Life and Other Essays. Ed. Dorothy Collins. London: Darwen Finlayson, 1964.
The Superstitions of the Skeptic. London: W. Heffer & Sons, 1925.
The Thing: Why I Am a Catholic. Vol. 3 of *The Collected Works of G. K. Chesterton.* San Francisco: Ignatius Press, 1990.
Thomas Carlyle. Vol. 18 of *The Collected Works of G. K. Chesterton.* San Francisco: Ignatius Press, 1991.
Utopia of Usurers and Other Essays. Vol. 5 of *The Collected Works of G. K. Chesterton.* San Francisco: Ignatius Press, 1987.
Varied Types. New York: Dodd, Mead & Co., 1903.
The Victorian Age in Literature. 1913. Reprint, Oxford: Oxford University Press, 1946.
The Well and the Shallows. Vol. 3 of *The Collected Works of G. K. Chesterton.* San Francisco: Ignatius Press, 1990.
What I Saw in America. Vol. 21 of *The Collected Works of G. K. Chesterton.* San Francisco: Ignatius Press, 1990.
What's Wrong with the World. Vol. 4 of *The Collected Works of G. K. Chesterton.* San Francisco: Ignatius Press, 1987.
Where All Roads Lead. Vol. 3 of *The Collected Works of G. K. Chesterton.* San Francisco: Ignatius Press, 1990.
"Why I Am a Catholic." Vol. 3 of *The Collected Works of G. K. Chesterton.* San Francisco: Ignatius Press, 1990.
William Blake. London: Duckworth, 1910.
William Cobbett. London: Hodder & Stoughton, 1925.
The Wisdom of Father Brown. 1913. Reprint, London: Penguin, 1970.

Christopher Dawson

The Age of the Gods. New York: Houghton Mifflin, 1928.
America and the Secularization of Modern Culture. Houston, Tex.: University of St. Thomas Press, 1960.
Beyond Politics. New York: Sheed & Ward, 1939.
"Catholics in the Modern World." *The Tablet* (27 May 1950): 419–21.
"The Challenge of Secularism." *Catholic World* 182 (February 1956): 326–30.
"Christian Freedom." *Dublin Review* 211 (July 1942): 1–8.
"Christianity and Culture." *Dublin Review* 208 (April 1941): 137–49.
Christianity and European Culture: Selections from the Work of Christopher Dawson. Ed. Gerald Russello. Washington, D.C.: The Catholic University of America Press, 1998.
"Christianity and the Humanist Tradition." *Dublin Review* 226 (Winter 1952): 1–11.
"Christianity and Oriental Culture." *The Commonweal* 67 (29 November 1957): 222–26.

Christianity and Sex. London: Faber & Faber, 1930.
Christianity in East and West. Ed. John J. Mulloy. 1959. Reprint, LaSalle, Ill.: Sherwood Sugden & Co., 1981.
"Civilization in Crisis." *Catholic World* 182 (January 1956): 246–52.
The Crisis of Western Education. New York: Sheed & Ward, 1961. Reprint, New York: Image Books, 1965.
"Dealing with the Enlightenment and Liberal Ideology." *The Commonweal* 60 (14 May 1954): 138–39.
"Democracy and the British Tradition." *Dublin Review* 212 (April 1943): 97–103.
The Dividing of Christendom. New York: Sheed & Ward, 1965.
Dynamics of World History. Ed. John J. Mulloy. New York: Sheed & Ward, 1958. Reprint, LaSalle, Ill.: Sherwood Sugden & Co., 1978.
"Education and Christian Culture." *The Commonweal* 59 (4 December 1953): 216–20.
Education and the Crisis of Christian Culture. New York: Henry Regnery, 1949.
"Education and the State." *The Commonweal* 65 (25 January 1957): 423–27.
"Education and the Study of Christian Culture." *Studies* 42 (Autumn 1953): 293–302.
Edward Gibbon. London: Proceedings of the British Academy, 1934.
"The End of an Age." *The Criterion* 9 (April 1930): 386–401.
"English Catholicism and Victorian Liberalism." *The Tablet* (1950). Reprinted in *The Dawson Newsletter* 11 (Fall 1993): 8–10.
"The English Catholics, 1850–1950." *Dublin Review* 224 (Winter 1950): 1–12.
Enquiries: into Religion and Culture. New York: Sheed & Ward, 1934.
Essays in Order. New York: Macmillan, 1931.
"European Literature and the Latin Middle Ages." *Dublin Review* 214 (Spring 1950): 31–37.
"The European Revolution." *Catholic World* 179 (May 1954): 86–95.
The Formation of Christendom. New York: Sheed & Ward, 1967.
"Foundations of European Order." *Catholic Mind* 42 (May 1944): 313–16.
"The Foundations of Unity." *Dublin Review* 211 (October 1942): 97–104.
"Future of Christian Culture." *The Commonweal* 59 (19 March 1954): 595–98.
The Gods of Revolution. London: Sidwick & Jackson, 1972.
The Historic Reality of Christian Culture. New York: Harper Torchbooks, 1960.
"Hope and Culture: Christian Culture as a Culture of Hope." *Lumen Vitae* 9 (July–September 1954): 425–30.
Ideas and Beliefs of the Victorians. Ed. BBC. London: Sylvan Press, 1949.
The Judgment of the Nations. New York: Sheed & Ward, 1942.
"The Making of Britain." *The Tablet* 168 (5 December 1936): 781–82.
The Making of Europe. London: Sheed & Ward, 1932. Reprint, Washington, D.C.: The Catholic University of America Press, 2002.
Medieval Essays. New York: Sheed & Ward, 1954. Reprint, Washington, D.C.: The Catholic University of America Press, 2002.
The Modern Dilemma. London: Sheed & Ward, 1932.
"The Nature and Destiny of Man." In *God and the Supernatural*, ed. Father Cuthbert. London: Longmans, Green & Co., 1920, 57–84.
"The New Decline and Fall." *English Review* 53 (September 1931): 413–21.

"On Jewish History." *Orbis* 10 (Winter 1967): 1247–56.
"The Outlook for Christian Culture Today." *Cross-Currents* 5 (Spring 1955): 127–36.
Progress and Religion. London: Sheed & Ward, 1929. Reprint, Peru, Ill.: Sherwood Sugden & Co., 1992. Reprint, Washington, D.C.: The Catholic University of America Press, 2001.
Religion and Culture. London: Sheed & Ward, 1948.
Religion and the Modern State. London: Sheed & Ward, 1935.
Religion and the Rise of Western Culture. London: Sheed & Ward, 1950.
"Religion and the Romantic Movement." *The Tablet* (1937). Reprinted in *The Dawson Newsletter* 13 (Spring 1995): 1–6.
"Religion and the Totalitarian State." *The Criterion* 14 (October 1934): 1–16.
Religion and World History: A Selection from the Works of Christopher Dawson. Ed. James Oliver and Christina Scott. New York: Image Books, 1975.
"Religious Liberty and the New Political Forces." *The Month* 183 (January 1947): 40–7.
The Spirit of the Oxford Movement. London: Sheed & Ward, 1933.
"The Study of Christian Culture as a Means of Education." *Lumen Vitae* 5 (March 1950): 173–86.
"Toynbee's Odyssey of the West." *The Commonweal* 61 (22 October 1954): 62–67.
"The Tradition and Destiny of American Literature." *The Critic* (November 1957). Reprinted in *The Dawson Newsletter* 12 (Fall 1994): 1–4.
Tradition and Inheritance. St. Paul, Minn.: The Wanderer Press, 1970.
"T. S. Eliot on the Meaning of Culture." *The Month*, n.s., 1 (March 1949): 151–57.
Understanding Europe. London: Sheed & Ward, 1952. Reprint, New York: Image Books, 1960.
"Why I Am a Catholic." *Catholic Times* (21 May 1926). Reprinted in *Chesterton Review* 9 (May 1983): 110–13.

Graham Greene

Brighton Rock. 1938. Reprint, New York: Bantam, 1968.
A Burnt-Out Case. 1960. Reprint, New York: Penguin, 1977.
The Captain and the Enemy. New York: Viking, 1988.
Collected Essays. New York: Penguin, 1969.
Collected Short Stories. New York: Penguin, 1986.
The Comedians. 1965, 1966. Reprint, New York: Penguin, 1968.
The Confidential Agent. 1939. Reprint, New York: Penguin, 1971.
Dr. Fischer of Geneva or The Bomb Party. New York: Avon Books, 1980.
The End of the Affair. 1951. Reprint, New York: Penguin, 1975.
England Made Me. 1935. Reprint, New York: Penguin, 1970.
Getting to Know the General. Toronto: Lester & Orpen Dennys, 1984.
Graham Greene on Film: Collected Film Criticism, 1935–40. Ed. John Russell Taylor. New York: Simon & Schuster, 1972.
The Heart of the Matter. 1948, 1971. Reprint, New York: Penguin, 1978.
The Honorary Consul. 1973. Reprint, New York: Pocket Books, 1974.
The Human Factor. 1978. Reprint, New York: Avon Books, 1979.
In Search of a Character. New York: Viking, 1961.

It's a Battlefield. 1934. Reprint, New York: Penguin, 1977.
Journey Without Maps. 1936, 1946. Reprint, New York: Penguin, 1980.
The Last Word and Other Stories. New York: Penguin, 1990.
The Lawless Roads. 1939. Reprint, New York: Penguin, 1976.
The Man Within. 1929. Reprint, New York: Bantam, 1948.
The Ministry of Fear. 1943. Reprint, New York: Viking, 1982.
Monsignor Quixote. 1982. Reprint, New York: Washington Square Press, 1983.
Orient Express. 1933. Reprint, New York: Pocket Books, 1975.
Our Man in Havana. 1958. Reprint, New York: Penguin, 1969.
The Portable Graham Greene. Ed. Philip Stratford. New York: Viking, 1973.
The Power and the Glory. 1940. Reprint, New York: Penguin, 1971.
The Quiet American. 1955, 1973. New York: Penguin, 1977.
Reflections. New York: Penguin, 1990.
Rumour at Nightfall. New York: Doubleday, Doran & Co., 1932.
A Sort of Life. New York: Simon & Schuster, 1971.
This Gun for Hire. 1936. Reprint, New York: Viking, 1982.
Three Plays. London: Mercury Books, 1961.
"The Seed Cake and the Love Lady." *Life and Letters* 10 (August 1934): 517–24.
The Third Man. 1949. Reprint, New York: Pocket Books, 1974.
Ways of Escape. New York: Simon & Schuster, 1980.
"While Waiting for a War." *Granta* 17 (Autumn 1985): 13–29.
Why Do I Write? London: Percival Marshall, 1948.
A World of My Own: A Dream Diary. New York: Viking, 1992.
Yours Etc.: Letters to the Press, 1945–1989. Ed. Christopher Hawtree. New York: Penguin, 1989.
Greene, Graham, ed. *The Old School: Essays by Divers Hands*. London: Jonathan Cape, 1934.

David Jones

The Anathemata: Fragments of an Attempted Writing. London: Faber & Faber, 1952, 1972.
"Beauty in Catholic Churches." *Blackfriars* 7 (1926): 438–41.
Dai Greatcoat: A Self-Portrait of David Jones in His Letters. Ed. René Hague. London: Faber & Faber, 1980.
The Dying Gaul and Other Writings. Ed. Harman Grisewood. London: Faber & Faber, 1972, 1978.
Epoch and Artist. Ed. Harman Grisewood. London: Faber & Faber, 1959.
"Fragments of an Attempted Autobiographical Writing." *Agenda* 12–13 (Winter–Spring 1975): 96–108.
In Parenthesis. London: Faber & Faber, 1937, 1963, 1978.
Inner Necessities: The Letters of David Jones to Desmond Chute. Edited and introduced by Thomas Dilworth. Toronto: Anson-Cartwright, 1984.
Letters to Vernon Watkins. Ed. Ruth Pryor. Cardiff: University of Wales Press, 1976.
Letters to William Hayward. Ed. Colin Wilcockson. London: Agenda Editions, 1979.
"The Myth of Arthur." In *For Hilaire Belloc*, ed. Douglas Woodruff. 1942. Reprint, New York: Greenwood Press, 1969, 174–218.

The Roman Quarry and Other Sequences. Ed. Harman Grisewood and René Hague. London: Agenda Editions, 1981.
The Sleeping Lord and Other Fragments. London: Faber & Faber, 1974.
Ten Letters. Ed. Derek Shiel. London: Agenda Editions, 1996.

Secondary Sources

Adamson, Judith. *Graham Greene: The Dangerous Edge.* New York: Macmillan, 1990.
Aeschliman, M. D. "The Prudence of John Henry Newman." *First Things* no. 45 (August–September 1994): 36–39.
Ahlquist, Dale. "Unlearning Our History Lessons: Chesterton as a Historian." Paper delivered at the Midwest Chesterton Conference, Milwaukee, Wis., June 1996.
Alexander, Calvert. *The Catholic Literary Revival.* Milwaukee: Bruce Publishing Co., 1935.
Allain, Marie-Francoise. *The Other Man: Conversations with Graham Greene.* New York: Simon & Schuster, 1983.
Allitt, Patrick. *Catholic Converts: British and American Intellectuals Turn to Rome.* Ithaca, N.Y.: Cornell University Press, 1997.
———. "A New Era of Converts: From Newman and Dawson Until Today." *Crisis* 8 (January 1994): 33–38.
Allott, Kenneth, and Miriam Farris. *The Art of Graham Greene.* New York: Russell & Russell, 1951.
Annan, Noel. *Our Age.* London: Weidenfeld & Nicolson, 1990.
Arendt, Hannah. *Essays in Understanding.* Ed. Jerome Kohn. New York: Harcourt Brace & Co., 1994.
Auden, W. H. *A Certain World.* New York: Viking, 1970.
———. "Adam as a Welshman." *New York Review of Books* 10 (March 1963): 12.
———. "The Heresy of Our Time." *Renascence* 1 (Spring 1949): 23–24.
Badham, Paul, ed. *Religion, State, and Society in Modern Britain.* Lewiston, N.Y.: Edwin Mellen Press, 1989.
Baker, J. Robert. "'The Space of an Upturned Coffin': Tragedy in *The Heart of the Matter.*" *Literature and Belief* 12 (1992): 43–52.
Baldridge, Cates. *Graham Greene's Fictions: The Virtues of Extremity.* Columbia: University of Missouri Press, 2000.
Barbour, John. *Versions of Deconversion: Autobiography and the Loss of Faith.* Charlottesville: University Press of Virginia, 1994.
Barker, Dudley. *G. K. Chesterton: A Biography.* New York: Stein & Day, 1973.
Barnes, Robert. "Two Modes of Fiction: Hemingway and Greene." *Renascence* 14 (Summer 1962): 193–98.
Baron, Xavier. "Medieval Arthurian Motifs in the Modernist Art and Poetry of David Jones." *Studies in Medievalism* 4 (1992): 247–69.
Beales, Derek, and Geoffrey Best, eds. *History, Society, and the Churches.* Cambridge: Cambridge University Press, 1985.
Beck, G. A., ed. *English Catholics 1850–1950.* London: Burns & Oates, 1950.

Bell, Julian. "Moon Behind the Clouds: The Wounded Vision of David Jones." *TLS* (5 April 1996): 9–10.
Belloc, Hilaire. *The Place of Gilbert Chesterton in English Letters*. New York: Sheed & Ward, 1940.
Bergan, Brooke. "Sacred Site: The Poetics of Piety." *Religion & Literature* 22 (Spring 1990): 39–57.
Berger, Peter. *Facing Up to Modernity*. New York: Basic Books, 1977.
———. *The Sacred Canopy: Elements of a Sociological Theory of Religion*. Garden City, N.Y.: Anchor Press, 1969.
Bergonzi, Bernard. "Contemporary British Fiction." *The Critic* 43 (1989): 70–84.
———. "The English Catholics." *Encounter* 24 (January 1965): 19–30.
———. *Heroes' Twilight: A Study of the Literature of the Great War*. London: Constable, 1965.
———. *The Myth of Modernism and Twentieth Century Literature*. New York: St. Martin's Press, 1986.
Black, Frederick. "Chesterton and Madness." *Chesterton Review* 15 (August 1989): 327–39.
Blamires, David. *David Jones: Artist and Writer*. Manchester: Manchester University Press, 1971.
Blissett, William. "David Jones and the Chesterbelloc." *Chesterton Review* 23 (February & May 1997): 27–55.
———. "David Jones: Himself at the Cave-Mouth." *University of Toronto Quarterly* 36 (April 1967): 259–73.
———. "*In Parenthesis* Among the War Books." *University of Toronto Quarterly* 42 (Spring 1973): 258–88.
———. *The Long Conversation: A Memoir of David Jones*. Oxford: Oxford University Press, 1981.
———. "To Make a Shape in Words." *Renascence* 38 (Winter 1986): 67–81.
Block, Ed, Jr. "G. K. Chesterton's *Orthodoxy* as Intellectual Autobiography." *Renascence* 49 (Fall 1996): 41–55.
Boardman, Gwenn. "Greene's 'Under the Garden': Aesthetic Explorations." *Renascence* 17 (Summer 1965): 180–90.
Boyd, Ian. *The Novels of G. K. Chesterton*. London: Paul Elek, 1975.
———. "Sacramental Parodies: G. K. Chesterton and Muriel Spark Confront the Spiritualists." *Chronicles* 20 (December 1996): 12–15.
Brand, M. Vivian. *The Social Catholic Movement in England, 1920–1955*. London: Pageant Press, 1963.
Braybrooke, Patrick. *Some Catholic Novelists: Their Art and Outlook*. Milwaukee: Bruce Publishing Co., 1931.
Breslin, John. "David Jones: The Shaping of a Poet's Mind." *Renascence* 38 (Winter 1986): 83–102.
Brickel, Alfred. "Cardinal Newman and Gilbert K. Chesterton." *Catholic World* 109 (September 1919): 744–52.
Brown, W. Dale. "'To Be a Saint': Frederick Buechner's *The Final Beast* and Rewriting Graham Greene." *Religion & Literature* 24 (Summer 1992): 51–65.
Bruce, Steve. *Religion in Modern Britain*. Oxford: Oxford University Press, 1995.

―――, ed. *Religion and Modernization: Sociologists and Historians Debate the Secularization Thesis*. Oxford: Clarendon Press, 1992.
Brueggemann, Walter. *Finally Comes the Poet: Daring Speech for Proclamation*. Minneapolis: Fortress Press, 1989.
―――. *Hopeful Imagination: Prophetic Voices in Exile*. Philadelphia: Fortress Press, 1986.
―――. *The Prophetic Imagination*. Philadelphia: Fortress Press, 1978.
Budd, Susan. *Varieties of Unbelief: Atheists and Agnostics in English Society, 1850–1960*. London: Heinemann, 1977.
Burgess, Anthony. *The Novel Now*. London: Faber & Faber, 1971.
―――. "Politics in the Novels of Graham Greene." *Journal of Contemporary History* 2 (April 1967): 93–99.
Burns, Tom. *The Use of Memory: Publishing and Further Pursuits*. London: Sheed & Ward, 1993.
Caldecott, Stratford, and John Morrill, eds. *Eternity in Time: Christopher Dawson and the Catholic Idea of History*. Edinburgh: T&T Clark, 1997.
Callahan, Daniel. "Christopher Dawson." *Commonweal* 92 (12 June 1970): 284.
Cameron, J. M. "Innocent at Home." *New York Review of Books* 30 (28 April 1983): 23–26.
Campbell, Andrew. "Strata and Bedrock in David Jones's *Anathemata*." *Renascence* 46 (Winter 1994): 117–31.
Campbell, James. Review of *At the Turn of a Civilization*, by Kathleen Henderson Staudt. *Religion & Literature* 27 (Summer 1995): 105–6.
Canovan, Margaret. *G. K. Chesterton: Radical Populist*. New York: Harcourt Brace Jovanovich, 1977.
Cantor, Norman. *Inventing the Middle Ages*. New York: Quill, 1991.
Carey, John. *The Intellectuals and the Masses: Pride and Prejudice Among the Literary Intelligentsia, 1880–1939*. New York: St. Martin's Press, 1994.
Carpenter, Humphrey. *The Brideshead Generation*. Boston: Houghton Mifflin, 1990.
Carroll, Warren. "Chesterton's Christ Centered View of History." *Faith & Reason* 13 (1986): 299–312.
Cassis, A. F., ed. *Graham Greene: Man of Paradox*. Chicago: Loyola University Press, 1994.
Cataldo, Peter, ed. *The Dynamic Character of Christian Culture: Essays on Dawsonian Themes*. Lanham, Md.: University Press of America, 1984.
Cervantes, Fernando. "A Vision to Regain?: Reconsidering Christopher Dawson." *New Blackfriars* 70 (October 1989): 437–49.
―――. "Progress and Tradition: Christopher Dawson and Contemporary Thought." *Logos: A Journal of Catholic Thought and Culture* 2 (Spring 1999): 84–108.
Chadwick, Owen. *The Secularization of the European Mind in the Nineteenth Century*. Cambridge: Cambridge University Press, 1975.
―――. *The Victorian Church*. 2 vols. London: Adam and Charles Black, 1971–72.
"Christopher Dawson." *Jubilee* 8 (April 1961): 24–27.
Cleary, J. M. *Catholic Social Action in Britain, 1909–1959: A History of the Catholic Social Guild*. London: Catholic Social Guild, 1961.

Coates, John. *Chesterton and the Edwardian Cultural Crisis.* Hull: Hull University Press, 1984.
———. "Chesterton as a Literary Critic." *Renascence* 49 (Fall 1996): 5–21.
Collini, Stefan. *Public Moralists: Political Thought and Intellectual Life in Britain 1850–1930.* Oxford: Clarendon Press, 1991.
Conlon, D. J., ed. *G. K. Chesterton: A Half Century of Views.* Oxford: Oxford University Press, 1987.
———, ed. *G. K. Chesterton: The Critical Judgments.* Antwerp: Universitaire Faculteiten Sint-Ignatius, 1976.
Conn, Walter. *Christian Conversion.* New York: Paulist Press, 1986.
Connolly, Francis. "Inside Modern Man: The Spiritual Adventures of Graham Greene." *Renascence* 1 (Spring 1949): 16–23.
Consolo, Dominick. "Music as Motif: The Unity of *Brighton Rock.*" *Renascence* 15 (Fall 1962): 12–20.
Corcoran, Neil. *The Song of Deeds: A Study of The Anathemata of David Jones.* Cardiff: University of Wales Press, 1982.
Coren, Michael. *Gilbert: The Man Who Was G. K. Chesterton.* London: Jonathan Cape, 1989.
Corrigan, Felicitas. "The Prescience of Father Brown." *Chesterton Review* 21 (November 1995): 473–85.
Corrin, Jay P. *G. K. Chesterton and Hilaire Belloc: The Battle Against Modernity.* Athens: Ohio University Press, 1981.
Costello, Donald. "Graham Greene and the Catholic Press." *Renascence* 12 (Autumn 1959): 3–28.
Cowling, Maurice. *Religion and Public Doctrine in Modern England.* 2 vols. Cambridge: Cambridge University Press, 1980–85.
Cox, Gerald, III. "Graham Greene's Mystical Rose in Brighton." *Renascence* 23 (Autumn 1970): 21–30.
Crawford, Fred. *Mixing Memory and Desire: "The Waste Land" and British Novels.* University Park: Pennsylvania State University Press, 1982.
Crowther, Ian. *G. K. Chesterton.* London: Claridge Press, 1991.
Culler, A. Dwight. *The Victorian Mirror of History.* New Haven, Conn.: Yale University Press, 1985.
Cunningham, Adrian. "Primary Things: Land, Work, and Sign." *Chesterton Review* 22 (February & May 1996): 73–87.
Cuoto, Maria. *Graham Greene: On the Frontier: Politics and Religion in the Novels.* New York: St. Martin's Press, 1988.
D'Arcy, Martin. *The Meaning and Matter of History: A Christian View.* New York: Farrar, Straus & Cudahy, 1959.
D'Cruz, Doreen. "Comedy and Stasis in Greene's *The Comedians.*" *Renascence* 40 (Fall 1987): 53–63.
D'Souza, Dinesh. "Beyond Marx and Jesus." *Crisis* 2 (May 1988): 19–24.
Dale, Alzina Stone. *The Outline of Sanity: A Biography of G. K. Chesterton.* Grand Rapids, Mich.: William B. Eerdmans Publishing Co., 1982.
Daly, Carson. "The Amphibolic Title of *The Anathemata.*" *Renascence* 35 (Autumn 1982): 49–63.

———. "Hills as Sacramental Landscape in *The Anathemata*." *Renascence* 38 (Winter 1986): 131–39.
Davenport, Guy. "In Love With All Things Made." *New York Times Book Review* (17 October 1982): 9.
Davie, Grace. *Religion in Britain Since 1945: Believing Without Belonging*. Oxford: Blackwell, 1994.
Davies, Horton. *Worship and Theology in England*. Vols. 4–5. Princeton, N.J.: Princeton University Press, 1962–65.
Davis, Robert Murray. "The Rhetoric of Mexican Travel: Greene and Waugh." *Renascence* 38 (Spring 1986): 160–68.
de Groot, H. B., and Alexander Leggatt, eds. *Craft and Tradition: Essays in Honor of William Blissett*. Calgary: University of Calgary Press, 1990.
de la Taille, Maurice. *The Mystery of Faith and Human Opinion: Contrasted and Defined*. Trans. J. B. Schimpf. London: Longmans, Green & Co., 1930.
Deane, Patrick. "David Jones, T. S. Eliot, and The Modernist Unfinished." *Renascence* 47 (Winter 1995): 75–88.
Demant, V. A. *Theology of Society: More Essays in Christian Polity*. London: Faber & Faber, 1947.
Desmond, John. "The Heart of (The) Matter: The Mystery of the Real in *Monsignor Quixote*." *Religion & Literature* 22 (Spring 1990): 59–78.
DeVitis, A. A. "The Church and Major Scobie." *Renascence* 10 (Spring 1958): 115–20.
———. "The Entertaining Mr. Greene." *Renascence* 14 (Autumn 1961): 8–24.
———. "Greene's *The Comedians*: Hollower Men." *Renascence* 18 (Spring 1966): 129–36, 146.
Diemert, Brian. *Graham Greene's Thrillers and the 1930s*. Montreal & Kingston: McGill-Queen's University Press, 1996.
Dilworth, Thomas. "David Jones's *The Deluge*: Engraving the Structure of the Modern Long Poem." *Journal of Modern Literature* 19 (Summer 1994): 5–30.
———. "The Letters of John O'Connor to David Jones." *Chesterton Review* 23 (February & May 1997): 57–63.
———. *The Liturgical Parenthesis of David Jones*. Ipswich, U.K.: Golgonooza, 1979.
———. Review of *The Long Conversation: A Memoir of David Jones*, by William Blissett. *Chesterton Review* 9 (November 1983): 376–80.
———. *The Shape of Meaning in the Poetry of David Jones*. Toronto: University of Toronto Press, 1988.
Donaghy, Henry J., ed. *Conversations with Graham Greene*. Jackson: University Press of Mississippi, 1992.
Donoghue, Denis. *England, Their England: Commentaries on English Language and Literature*. Berkeley: University of California Press, 1989.
———. "A Novel of Thought, Action, and Pity." *New York Times Book Review* (26 February 1978): 1, 43.
Donovan, Charles. "The Tradition Behind Our Learning." *America* (8 April 1961): 85.
Dorenkamp, Angela. "Time and Sacrament in *The Anathemata*." *Renascence* 23 (Summer 1971): 183–91.
Dunne, John. *A Search for God in Time and Memory*. New York: Macmillan, 1969.

Duran, Leopoldo. *Graham Greene: Friend and Brother.* London: HarperCollins, 1994.
Eagleton, Terry. *Exiles and Émigrés.* New York: Schocken, 1970.
Eaker, J. Gordon. "G. K. Chesterton Among the Moderns." *Georgia Review* 13 (Summer 1959): 152–60.
Eco, Umberto. *Apocalypse Postponed.* Ed. Robert Lumley. Bloomington: Indiana University Press, 1994.
Eliot, T. S. *Christianity and Culture.* New York: Harcourt Brace Jovanovich, 1988.
———. *Essays: Ancient & Modern.* London: Faber & Faber, 1936.
———. *To Criticize the Critic.* New York: Farrar, Straus & Giroux, 1965.
———. "*Ulysses,* Order, and Myth." *Dial* 75 (November 1923): 480–83.
Evans, Robert O., ed. *Graham Greene: Some Critical Considerations.* Lexington: University of Kentucky Press, 1963.
Fagerberg, David. *The Size of Chesterton's Catholicism.* Notre Dame, Ind.: University of Notre Dame Press, 1998.
Fairchild, Hoxie Neale. *Religious Trends in English Poetry.* Vol. 6. New York: Columbia University Press, 1968.
Fay, Teresita, and Michael Yetman. "Scobie the Just: A Reassessment of *The Heart of the Matter.*" *Renascence* 19 (Spring 1977): 142–56.
Feske, Victor. *From Belloc to Churchill: Private Scholars, Public Culture, and the Crisis of British Liberalism, 1900–1939.* Chapel Hill: University of North Carolina Press, 1996.
Ffinch, Michael. *G. K. Chesterton.* San Francisco: Harper & Row, 1986.
Finn, James. "Graham Greene as Moralist." *First Things* no. 3 (May 1990): 20–29.
Foster, Joseph. *Contemporary Christian Writers.* New York: Hawthorn Books, 1963.
Foster, Paul. "The Making of Europe." *Chesterton Review* 9 (May 1983): 137–42.
Fowler, James. *Stages of Faith: The Psychology of Human Development and the Quest for Meaning.* San Francisco: Harper & Row, 1981.
Fraser, Theodore. *The Modern Catholic Novel in Europe.* New York: Twayne, 1994.
Freis, Richard. "Scobie's World." *Religion & Literature* 24 (Autumn 1992): 57–78.
Friedman, Barton. "Tolkien and David Jones: The Great War and the War of the Ring." *Clio* 11 (Winter 1982): 115–36.
Fussell, Paul. *Abroad: British Literary Traveling Between the Wars.* Oxford: Oxford University Press, 1980.
———. *The Great War and Modern Memory.* Oxford: Oxford University Press, 1975.
———. *Wartime.* Oxford: Oxford University Press, 1989.
Gable, Mariella. *This Is Catholic Fiction.* New York: Sheed & Ward, 1948.
Gardiner, Harold. "Graham Greene: Catholic Shocker." *Renascence* 1 (Spring 1949): 12–15.
Gaston, G. A. "The Structure of Salvation in *The Quiet American.*" *Renascence* 31 (Winter 1979): 93–106.
Gilbert, Alan. *The Making of Post-Christian Britain.* London: Longman, 1980.
Gill, Eric. *It All Goes Together.* London: The Devin-Adair Co., 1944.
Gilley, Sheridan. "Chesterton's Politics." *Chesterton Review* 21 (February & May 1995): 27–47.
Gilley, Sheridan, and W. J. Sheils, eds. *A History of Religion in Britain.* Oxford: Blackwell, 1994.

Gleason, Philip. "Christopher Dawson and the Study of Christian Culture." *Chesterton Review* 9 (May 1983): 167–71.
Glicksberg, Charles. "Graham Greene: Catholicism in Fiction." *Criticism* 1 (Fall 1959): 339–53.
Goldpaugh, Tom. "On the Traverse of the Wall: The Lost Long Poem of David Jones." *Journal of Modern Literature* 19 (Summer 1994): 31–53.
Gorra, Michael. "Taking the Freud Out of Mother Goose." *New York Times Book Review* (19 November 1995): 7.
Grafton, Anthony. "The Soul's Entrepreneurs." *New York Review of Books* 41 (3 March 1994): 33–37.
Grainger, J. H. *Patriotisms: Britain 1900–1939*. London: Routledge & Kegan Paul, 1986.
Grennen, Joseph. "The 'Making of Works': David Jones and the Medieval Drama." *Renascence* 45 (Summer 1993): 211–24.
Griffin, Emilie. *Turning: Reflections on the Experience of Conversion*. New York: Doubleday, 1980.
Grimes, William. "Exploring Writers' Links to Depression and Suicide." *New York Times* (14 November 1994): B1, B4.
Grisewood, Harman. "Remembering David Jones." Introduction and Notes by Thomas Dilworth. *Journal of Modern Literature* 14 (Spring 1988): 565–76.
Grist, Anthony. "News and Comments." *Chesterton Review* 18 (August 1992): 455–56.
Gross, John. *The Rise and Fall of the Man of Letters*. London: Weidenfeld & Nicholson, 1969.
Gwyn, Dennis. *A Hundred Years of Catholic Emancipation*. London: Longmans, Green & Co., 1929.
———. *The Second Spring, 1818–1852*. London: Catholic Book Club, 1944.
Hague, René. *A Commentary on The Anathemata of David Jones*. Toronto: University of Toronto Press, 1977.
Halsey, Edwin. "Christopher Dawson." *Integrity* 4 (June 1950): 47–49.
Harmer, Ruth Mulvey. "Greene World of Mexico: The Birth of a Novelist." *Renascence* 15 (Summer 1963): 171–82.
Hart, Jeffrey. "Christopher Dawson and the History We Are Not Told." *Modern Age* 39 (Summer 1997): 211–24.
Hastings, Adrian. *A History of English Christianity, 1920–1985*. London: Collins, 1986.
———, ed. *Bishops and Writers: Aspects of the Evolution of Modern English Catholicism*. Wheathampsted-Hertfordshire: Anthony Clarke, 1977.
Hazo, Samuel, ed. *The Christian Intellectual: Studies in the Relation of Catholicism to the Human Sciences*. Pittsburgh, Pa.: Duquesne University Press, 1963.
Hazzard, Shirley. *Greene on Capri*. New York: Farrar, Straus, Giroux, 2000.
Heaney, Seamus. "Now and in England." *Spectator* (4 May 1974): 547.
Hein, Rolland. "G. K. Chesterton: Myth, Paradox, and the Commonplace." *Seven: An Anglo-American Literary Review* 13 (1996): 13–24.
Helmstadter, Richard, and Bernard Lightman, eds. *Victorian Faith in Crisis*. London: Macmillan, 1990.

Hetzler, Leo. "Chesterton's Childhood: The Golden Key 1874–1886." *Chesterton Review* 21 (August 1995): 297–313.
Heyck, T. W. "The Decline of Christianity in Twentieth-Century Britain." *Albion* 28 (Fall 1996): 437–53.
———. *The Transformation of Intellectual Life in Victorian England*. New York: St. Martin's Press, 1982.
Hills, Paul, ed. *David Jones, Artist and Poet*. Aldershot: Scolar Press, 1997.
Hitchcock, James. "Apologists—With Angst and Without." *Crisis* 10 (March 1996): 34–38.
———. "Christopher Dawson." *American Scholar* 62 (Winter 1993): 111–18.
———. "Post-Mortem on a Rebirth: The Catholic Intellectual Renaissance." *American Scholar* 49 (Spring 1980): 211–25.
———. *The Recovery of the Sacred*. New York: Seabury Press, 1974.
Hittinger, Russell. "The Great Historian of Culture." *University Bookman* 33, no. 4 (1993): 14–17.
Hollis, Christopher. *G. K. Chesterton*. London: Longmans, Green & Co., 1950.
———. *The Mind of Chesterton*. London: Hollis & Carter, 1970.
Holloway, John. "A Perpetual Showing." *Hudson Review* 16 (Spring 1963): 122–30.
Holmes, J. Derek. *More Roman Than Rome: English Catholicism in the Nineteenth Century*. London: Burns & Oates, 1978.
Hooker, Jeremy. *Poetry of Place*. Manchester: Carcanet Press, 1982.
———. *The Presence of the Past: Essays on Modern British and American Poetry*. Bridgend, Mid Glamorgan, Wales: Poetry Wales Press, 1987.
Hornsby-Smith, Michael. *Roman Catholics in England*. Cambridge: Cambridge University Press, 1987.
———, ed. *Catholics in England, 1950–2000*. London: Cassell, 1999.
Houle, Shelia, B.V.M. "The Subjective Theological Vision of Graham Greene." *Renascence* 23 (Autumn 1970): 3–13.
Hughes, Catherine. "Innocence Revisited." *Renascence* 12 (Autumn 1959): 29–34.
Hughes, R. E. "*The Quiet American:* The Case Reopened." *Renascence* 12 (Autumn 1959): 41–42, 49.
Hughes, Trystan Owain. *Winds of Change: The Roman Catholic Church and Society in Wales, 1916–1962*. Cardiff: University of Wales Press, 1999.
Hunter, Lynette. *G. K. Chesterton: Explorations in Allegory*. New York: Macmillan, 1979.
Huxley, Aldous. *The Olive Tree and Other Essays*. London: Chatto & Windus, 1936.
Hylson-Smith, Kenneth. *The Churches in England from Elizabeth I to Elizabeth II*. Vol. 3, *1833–1998*. London: SCM Press, 1998.
Hynes, Joseph. "Two Affairs Revisited." *Twentieth Century Literature* (Summer 1987): 234–53.
Hynes, Samuel. *The Auden Generation*. London: The Bodley Head, 1976.
———. *Edwardian Occasions*. London: Routledge & Kegan Paul, 1972.
———. *The Edwardian Turn of Mind*. Princeton, N.J.: Princeton University Press, 1968.
———. *A War Imagined*. London: Athenaeum, 1991.
———, ed. *Graham Greene*. New Brunswick, N.J.: Prentice Hall, 1973.

Isley, William, Jr. "Knowledge and Mystery in Chesterton's *The Man Who Was Thursday.*" *Christianity & Literature* 42 (Winter 1993): 279–94.
Jaki, Stanley. *Chesterton: A Seer of Science*. Urbana: University of Illinois Press, 1986.
James, Merlin. *David Jones 1895–1974: A Map of the Artist's Mind*. London: Lund Humphries, 1995.
James, William. *The Varieties of Religious Experience*. 1902. Reprint, New York: Modern Library, 1929.
Jenkins, Philip. "Chesterton and the Anti-Catholic Tradition." *Chesterton Review* 18 (November 1992): 345–69.
Jennings, Elizabeth. *Seven Men of Vision: An Appreciation*. London: Vision, 1976.
Johnston, John. *English Poetry of the First World War*. Princeton, N.J.: Princeton University Press, 1964.
Johnstone, Richard. *The Will to Believe*. Oxford: Oxford University Press, 1982.
Jung, C. G. *Modern Man in Search of a Soul*. Trans. W. S. Dell and Cary F. Baynes. New York: Harcourt, Brace & World, 1933, 1966.
Kaplan, Carola. "Graham Greene's Pinkie Brown and Flannery O'Connor's Misfit: The Psychopathic Killer and the Mystery of God's Grace." *Renascence* 32 (Winter 1980): 116–28.
Kellogg, Gene. *The Vital Tradition: The Catholic Novel in a Period of Convergence*. Chicago: Loyola University Press, 1970.
Kenner, Hugh. *A Sinking Island: The Modern English Writers*. Baltimore: Johns Hopkins University Press, 1987.
———. *Paradox in Chesterton*. New York: Sheed & Ward, 1948.
———. "Seedless Fruit." *Poetry* 83 (February 1954): 295–301.
Kenyon, John. *The History Men: The Historical Profession in England since the Renaissance*. Pittsburgh, Pa.: University of Pittsburgh Press, 1983.
Kermode, Frank. *Puzzles and Epiphanies: Essays and Reviews, 1958–1961*. London: Routledge & Kegan Paul, 1962.
Kirk, Russell. *Eliot and His Age*. LaSalle, Ill.: Sherwood Sugden & Co., 1984.
———. "The High Achievement of Christopher Dawson." *Chesterton Review* 10 (November 1984): 435–38.
Knowles, David. "Christopher Dawson, 1889–1970." *Proceedings of the British Academy* 57 (1971). Oxford: Oxford University Press, 1973.
———. "Obituary: Christopher Dawson." *The Tablet* (6 June 1970): 558.
Knox, Ronald. *Captive Flames*. London: Burns & Oates, 1940.
———. *Literary Distractions*. New York: Sheed & Ward, 1958.
———. *A Spiritual Aeneid*. New York: Sheed & Ward, 1950.
Korda, Michael. "The Third Man." *The New Yorker* 72 (25 March 1996): 44–51.
Kubal, David. "Graham Greene's *Brighton Rock:* The Political Theme." *Renascence* 23 (Autumn 1970): 46–54.
Larson, Michael. "Laughing Till the Tears Come: Greene's Failed Comedian." *Renascence* 40 (Spring 1989): 177–87.
Leigh, David. "The Structures of Greene's *The Honorary Consul.*" *Renascence* 36 (Autumn 1985): 13–24.
Lester, John. *Journey Through Despair*. Princeton, N.J.: Princeton University Press, 1968.

Levi, Peter. "In Memory of David Jones." *Chesterton Review* 23 (February & May 1997): 217–21.
Lewis, C. S. *The Abolition of Man*. New York: Macmillan, 1947.
———. *The Problem of Pain*. New York: Collier Books, 1962.
Lewis, R. W. B. *The Picaresque Saint: Representative Figures in Contemporary Fiction*. Philadelphia: J. B. Lippincott Co., 1956, 1958.
Lloyd, Roger. *The Church of England, 1900–1965*. London: SCM Press, 1966.
Lodge, David. "Behind the Smoke Screen." *New York Review of Books* 42 (8 June 1995): 61–67.
———. "The Lives of Graham Greene." *New York Review of Books* 42 (22 June 1995): 25–28.
———. *The Novelist at the Crossroads*. London: Routledge & Kegan Paul, 1971.
———. *Write On: Occasional Essays '65–'85*. London: Secker & Warburg, 1986.
Loewenstein, Andrea Freud. *Loathsome Jews and Engulfing Women: Metaphors of Projection in the Works of Wyndham Lewis, Charles Williams, and Graham Greene*. New York: New York University Press, 1993.
Lukacs, John. "Order and History." *Intercollegiate Review* 28 (Spring 1993): 50–52.
Lynch, William. *Christ and Apollo: The Dimensions of the Literary Imagination*. New York: Sheed & Ward, 1960.
MacCarthy, Fiona. *Eric Gill: A Lover's Quest for Art and God*. New York: E. P. Dutton, 1989.
Macdonald, Michael H., and Andrew A. Tadie, eds. *G. K. Chesterton and C. S. Lewis: The Riddle of Joy*. Grand Rapids, Mich.: William B. Eerdmans Publishing Co., 1989.
———. *Permanent Things: Toward the Recovery of a More Human Scale at the End of the Twentieth Century*. Grand Rapids, Mich.: William B. Eerdmans Publishing Co., 1995.
Mackey, Aidan. "The Wisdom of G. K. Chesterton." *Canadian C. S. Lewis Journal* no. 90 (Fall 1996): 38–52.
Sister Marian, I.H.M. "Graham Greene's People: Being and Becoming." *Renascence* 16 (Autumn 1965): 16–22.
Maritain, Jacques. *On the Philosophy of History*. Ed. Joseph Evans. London: Geoffrey Bles, 1959.
Mathew, David. *Catholicism in England: The Portrait of a Minority: Its Culture and Tradition*. London: Eyre & Spottiswoode, 1936, 1948.
Mathias, Roland, ed. *David Jones: Eight Essays on His Work as a Writer and Artist*. Llandysul, Wales: Gomer Press, 1976.
Matthias, John, ed. *David Jones: Man and Poet*. Orono: University of Maine Press, 1989.
Maurois, Andre. *Points of View: from Kipling to Graham Greene*. New York: Frederick Ungar, 1968.
Maynard, Theodore. "The Chesterbelloc." Parts 1–4. *Catholic World* 110 (November 1919): 145–60; (December 1919): 319–30; (January 1920): 483–95; (February 1920): 617–29.
———. "The Newman of a New Age." *The Commonweal* 3 (2 December 1925): 96–97.

McCarthy, Mary. "Graham Greene and the Intelligentsia." *Partisan Review* 11 (Spring 1944): 228–30.
———. "Sheep in Wolves' Clothing." *Partisan Review* 24 (Spring 1957): 270–74.
McCauley, T. J. "Chestertonian Imprint: 20th Century." *Chesterton Review* 9 (May 1983): 182–86.
McClelland, V. Alan, and Michael Hodgetts, eds. *From Without the Flaminian Gate: 150 Years of Roman Catholicism in England and Wales, 1850–2000*. London: Darnton, Longman & Todd, 1999.
McCrum, Robert. "A Life in the Margins." *The New Yorker* 70 (11 April 1994): 46–55.
McGowan, F. A. "Innocent but Harmful." *Renascence* 7 (Autumn 1956): 44–47.
———. "Symbolism in *Brighton Rock*." *Renascence* 6 (Autumn 1955): 25–35.
McInerny, Ralph. "Graham Greene." *Crisis* 5 (May 1991): 55–56.
———, ed. *The Catholic Writer*. San Francisco: Ignatius Press, 1991.
McLeod, Hugh. *Religion and Society in England, 1850–1914*. New York: St. Martin's Press, 1996.
McSweeney, William. *Roman Catholicism: The Search for Relevance*. New York: St. Martin's Press, 1980.
Meath, Gerard. "Catholic Writing." *Blackfriars* 32 (December 1951): 602–9.
Medcalf, Stephen. "The Innocence of G. K." *TLS* (20 December 1996): 9.
———. "The Light from the Invisible Lamp." *Chesterton Review* 8 (August 1982): 244–51.
Meyers, Jeffrey, ed. *Graham Greene: A Revaluation*. New York: Macmillan, 1990.
Miles, Jonathan. *Backgrounds to David Jones*. Cardiff: University of Wales Press, 1990.
———. *Eric Gill and David Jones at Capel-Y-Ffin*. Bridgend, Mid Glamorgan, Wales: Seren, 1992.
Miller, J. Hillis. *The Disappearance of God*. Cambridge, Mass.: Harvard University Press, 1963.
Miller, Karl. "Dirty Business." *TLS* (30 September 1994): 3–4.
Milward, Peter. "G. K. Chesterton's Faith and Journalism." *Chesterton Review* 7 (November 1981): 347–55.
Moloney, Thomas. *Westminster, Whitehall and the Vatican: The Role of Cardinal Hinsley 1935–43*. London: Burns & Oates, 1985.
Montgomery, John Warwick, ed. *Myth, Allegory and Gospel*. Minneapolis, Minn.: Bethany Fellowship, 1974.
Morris, Kevin. "Chesterton's Conversion: Hesitation and the Recovery of Infancy." *Chesterton Review* 18 (November 1992): 371–83.
———. "The Mirror of Perfection: G. K. Chesterton's Interpretation of St. Francis of Assisi." *Chesterton Review* 22 (November 1996): 445–73.
Morrison, Karl. *Conversion and Text*. Charlottesville: University Press of Virginia, 1992.
———. *Understanding Conversion*. Charlottesville: University Press of Virginia, 1992.
Muggeridge, Malcolm. *Chronicles of Wasted Time: 2: The Infernal Grove*. New York: William Morrow & Co., 1974.

———. *Like It Was: The Diaries of Malcolm Muggeridge.* Ed. John Bright-Holmes. London: Collins, 1981.

———. *The Thirties: 1930–1940 in Great Britain.* 1940. Reprint, London: Weidenfeld & Nicolson, 1989.

Mulloy, John J. "Christopher Dawson and G. K. Chesterton." *Chesterton Review* 9 (August 1983): 226–32.

———. "Christopher Dawson on the Individual and Society." *The Dawson Newsletter* 10 (Fall 1992): 11–13.

Neame, A. J. "Black and Blue: A Study in the Catholic Novel." *The European* 2 (April 1953): 26–36.

Newman, John Henry. *Apologia Pro Vita Sua.* Ed. A. Dwight Culler. Boston: Houghton Mifflin, 1956.

———. *The Second Spring.* Ed. Francis Donnelly. London: Longmans, Green & Co., 1911.

Nichols, Aidan. *A Grammar of Consent.* Notre Dame, Ind.: University of Notre Dame Press, 1991.

———, ed. *Chesterton & the Modernist Crisis.* Saskatoon, Canada: Chesterton Review Press, 1990.

Niebuhr, Reinhold. "What's a Mote to One Is a Beam to Another." *New York Times Book Review* (13 March 1960): 18.

Nock, A. D. *Conversion.* Oxford: Oxford University Press, 1933.

Noon, William. *Poetry and Prayer.* New Brunswick, N.J.: Rutgers University Press, 1967.

Norman, Edward. *Church and Society in England, 1770–1970.* Oxford: Clarendon Press, 1976.

———. *The English Catholic Church in the Nineteenth Century.* Oxford: Oxford University Press, 1984.

———. *Roman Catholicism in England.* Oxford: Oxford University Press, 1985.

Nott, Kathleen. *The Emperor's Clothes.* Bloomington: Indiana University Press, 1954.

Nye, Robert. "Poetry." *The Times* (London) (28 March 1974): 14.

O'Brien, Conor Cruise. *Maria Cross: Imaginative Patterns in a Group of Catholic Writers.* London: Burns & Oates, 1963.

O'Connell, Marvin. "Dawson and the Oxford Movement." *Chesterton Review* 9 (May 1983): 149–60.

O'Connor, Daniel. *The Relation Between Religion and Culture According to Christopher Dawson.* Montreal: Librairie Saint-Viateur, 1952.

O'Connor, John. *The Catholic Revival in England.* New York: Macmillan, 1942.

O'Donoghue, Noel. "Chesterton and the Philosophical Imagination." *Chesterton Review* 24 (February & May 1998): 63–81.

———. "Chesterton's Marvelous Boyhood." *Chesterton Review* 10 (Fall–Winter, 1979–80): 101–15.

Oddie, William. "Bell-Curve Catholics." *Catholic World Report* 6 (July 1996): 22–25.

———. "Chesterton and History." 1993 Chesterton Lecture of The Chesterton Society, England, London, 27 September 1993.

———. "A New Kind of Saint?" *Catholic World Report* 5 (June 1995): 58–61.

Oliver, E. J. "The Religion of Christopher Dawson." *Chesterton Review* 9 (May 1983): 161–65.
Ombres, Robert. "The Cult Man Stands Precariously: David Jones and the Liturgy." *Chesterton Review* 23 (February & May 1997): 113–25.
Orr, Peter. "Mr. Jones, Your Legs Are Crossed: A Memoir." *Agenda* 15, nos. 2–3 (1977): 110–25.
———, ed. *The Poet Speaks*. London: Routledge & Kegan Paul, 1966.
Orwell, George. *The Collected Essays, Journalism, and Letters of George Orwell*. 4 vols. Ed. Sonia Orwell and Ian Angus. New York: Harcourt, Brace & World, 1968.
———. *The Road to Wigan Pier*. 1937. Reprint, New York: Berkeley Medallion, 1961.
Owen, Alex. *The Darkened Room: Women, Power and Spiritualism in Late Victorian England*. Philadelphia: University of Pennsylvania Press, 1990.
Pacey, Philip. *David Jones and Other Wonder Voyagers*. Bridgend, Mid Glamorgan, Wales: Poetry Wales Press, 1982.
Paine, Randall. *The Universe and Mr. Chesterton*. Peru, Ill.: Sherwood Sugden & Co., 1999.
Parkes, H. B. "Christopher Dawson." *Scrutiny* 5 (March 1937): 365–75.
Pattison, Robert. *The Great Dissent: John Henry Newman and the Liberal Heresy*. Oxford: Oxford University Press, 1991.
Pearce, Joseph. *Literary Converts: Spiritual Inspiration in an Age of Unbelief*. London: HarperCollins, 1999.
———. *Wisdom and Innocence: A Life of G. K. Chesterton*. San Francisco: Ignatius Press, 1997.
Perkin, Harold. *Origins of Modern English Society*. 1969. Reprint, London: Ark, 1985.
———. *The Rise of Professional Society: England Since 1880*. London: Routledge, 1989.
———. *The Structured Crowd: Essays in English Social History*. New Jersey: Barnes & Noble Books, 1981.
Perl, Jeffrey. *The Tradition of Return: The Implicit History of Modern Literature*. Princeton, N.J.: Princeton University Press, 1984.
Peterson, John. "What Chesterton Said." Paper delivered at the Midwest Chesterton Conference, Milwaukee, Wis., June 1993.
Pryce-Jones, David, ed. *Graham Greene*. New Jersey: Barnes & Noble, 1967.
Quinn, Bernetta. "David Jones." *Contemporary Literature* 14 (Spring 1973): 267–70.
Quinn, Dermot. "Christopher Dawson and Historical Imagination." *Chesterton Review* 26 (November 2000): 471–89.
Raftis, James A. "The Development of Christopher Dawson's Thought." *Chesterton Review* 9 (May 1983): 115–35.
Rahv, Philip. "Wicked American Innocence." *Commentary* 21 (May 1956): 488–90.
Rapp, Dean. "G. K. Chesterton's Criticism of Psychoanalysis." *Chesterton Review* 15 (August 1989): 341–53.
Read, Herbert. "A Malory of the Trenches." *London Mercury* 36 (July 1937): 304–5.
"Religious Writing." *Times Literary Supplement* (17 August 1956): xiv–xv.
Rodden, John. *The Politics of Literary Reputation: The Making and Claiming of "St. George" Orwell*. Oxford: Oxford University Press, 1989.

Rose, Jonathan. *The Edwardian Temperament, 1895–1919*. Athens: Ohio University Press, 1986.
Rosenberg, Harold. "Aesthetics of Crisis." *The New Yorker* 40 (22 August 1964): 114–22.
Ross, Val. "A Portrait of the Biographer as a Chameleon." *Globe and Mail*, 15 October 1994.
Russello, Gerald. "Christopher Dawson—Christ in History." *Crisis* 10 (April 1996): 28–30.
———. "Christopher Dawson: Is There a Christian Culture?" *Commonweal* 123 (5 April 1996): 19–21.
Salvatore, Anne. *Greene and Kierkegaard: The Discourse of Belief.* Tuscaloosa: University of Alabama Press, 1988.
Sarjeant, William A. S. "G. K. Chesterton at St. Paul's School." *Chesterton Review* 21 (August 1995): 315–41.
Sayers, Dorothy L. *The Mind of the Maker.* 1941. Reprint, San Francisco: HarperCollins, 1979.
Scanlan, Margaret. *Traces of Another Time: History and Politics in Postwar British Fiction.* Princeton, N.J.: Princeton University Press, 1990.
Schlesinger, Bruno. *Christopher Dawson and the Modern Political Crisis.* Notre Dame, Ind.: University of Notre Dame Press, 1949.
Schwartz, Adam. "Christianity's Dangerous Edge: 'Belief,' 'Faith,' and Doubt in Graham Greene's Writing." *Thematica: Historical Research and Review* 3 (May 1996): 2–29.
———. "'It is Good to be Here': G. K. Chesterton's *The Thing* and the Thought of Graham Greene." *Faith & Reason* 21 (Spring–Summer 1995): 101–19.
———. "Theologies of History in G. K. Chesterton's *The Everlasting Man* and in David Jones's *The Anathemata.*" *Chesterton Review* 23 (February & May 1997): 65–83.
Schwartz, Joseph. "Like a Birthmark." *Serran* (December 1963–January 1964): 18–19.
———. "The Theology of History in *The Everlasting Man.*" *Renascence* 49 (Fall 1996): 57–66.
———. "Traveling with My Aunt in Greeneland." Lecture delivered to the Milwaukee Chamber Theater, Milwaukee, Wis., 15 April 1996.
Scott, Christina. *A Historian and His World: A Life of Christopher Dawson, 1889–1970.* New Brunswick, N.J.: Transaction Publishers, 1992.
———. "The Meaning of the Millennium: The Ideas of Christopher Dawson." *Logos: A Journal of Catholic Thought and Culture* 2 (Spring 1999): 65–83.
Scott, George. *The R.C.s.* London: Hutchison & Co., 1973.
Scott, Nathan, Jr. *Craters of the Spirit: Studies in the Modern Novel.* Washington, D.C.: Corpus Books, 1968.
Scott, Winfrid Townley. "Delayed Shock of Recognition." *New York Herald Tribune* (8 July 1962): 3, 11.
Scull, Andrew. *The Most Solitary of Afflictions: Madness and Society in Britain, 1700–1900.* New Haven, Conn.: Yale University Press, 1993.
Sewell, Elizabeth. "G. K. Chesterton: The Giant Upside-Down." *Thought* 30 (Winter 1955–56): 555–76.

Sharrock, Roger. *Saints, Sinners and Comedians: The Novels of Graham Greene.* London: Burns & Oates, 1984.
Sheed, Frank. *The Church and I.* Garden City, N.Y.: Doubleday, 1974.
Sheils, W. J., ed. *The Church and War.* Oxford: Blackwell, 1983.
Shelden, Michael. *Graham Greene: The Man Within.* London: Heinemann, 1994.
Shenkner, Israel. "Graham Greene at 66." *New York Times Book Review* (17 September 1971): 2, 26.
Sherry, Norman. *The Life of Graham Greene.* Vol. 1, *1904–1939.* New York: Viking, 1989.
———. *The Life of Graham Greene.* Vol. 2, *1939–1955.* London: Jonathan Cape, 1994.
Sherry, Vincent. "David Jones's *In Parenthesis:* New Measure." *Twentieth Century Literature* 28 (Winter 1982): 375–80.
———. "'Unmistakable Marks': Symbols and Voices in David Jones's *In Parenthesis.*" *Critical Quarterly* 25 (Winter 1983): 63–73.
Shiel, Derek A. G. "David Jones the Maker." *Chesterton Review* 23 (February & May 1997): 157–63.
Silkin, Jon. *Out of Battle: The Poetry of the Great War.* Oxford: Oxford University Press, 1972.
Simon, John. "From Waste to Wonderland." *New Republic* 146 (28 May 1962): 21–23.
Sisson, C. H. "The Tradition of Defeat." *Times Literary Supplement* (7 July 1978): 755.
Skultans, Vieda. *English Madness: Ideas on Insanity, 1580–1890.* London: Routledge & Kegan Paul, 1979.
Smith, Grahame. *The Achievement of Graham Greene.* New York: Barnes & Noble, 1986.
Sonnenfeld, Albert. *Crossroads: Essays on the Catholic Novelists.* York, S.C.: French Literature Publications Company, 1982.
Sparr, Arnold. *To Promote, Defend, and Redeem: The Catholic Literary Revival and the Cultural Transformation of American Catholicism, 1920–1960.* New York: Greenwood Press, 1990.
Spears, Monroe K. "Shapes and Surfaces: David Jones with a Glance at Charles Tomlinson." *Contemporary Literature* 12 (Autumn 1971): 402–19.
Spender, Stephen. "Civilization vs. Culture." *New York Times Book Review* (18 February 1979): 9, 26.
———. *The Creative Element.* London: Hamish & Hamilton, 1953.
Stannard, Martin. *Evelyn Waugh: The Early Years, 1903–1939.* New York: Norton, 1986.
———. *Evelyn Waugh: The Later Years, 1939–1966.* New York: Norton, 1992.
———. "Getting to the Heart of the Matter." *National Review* 40 (6 February 1995): 67–68.
Staudt, Kathleen Henderson. *At the Turn of a Civilization: David Jones and Modern Poetics.* Ann Arbor: University of Michigan Press, 1994.
———. "The Language of T. S. Eliot's *Four Quartets* and David Jones's *The Anathemata.*" *Renascence* 38 (Winter 1986): 118–30.
Steiner, George. "Burnt-Out Case." *The New Yorker* 50 (28 October 1974): 185–88.
———. *Language and Silence: Essays on Language, Literature, and the Inhuman.* New York: Athenaeum, 1967.

———. *Real Presences*. Chicago: University of Chicago Press, 1989.
Stephenson, Alan M. G. *Anglicanism and the Lambeth Conferences*. London: SPCK, 1978.
Stratford, Philip. *Faith and Fiction: Creative Process in Greene and Mauriac*. Notre Dame, Ind.: University of Notre Dame Press, 1964.
Sullivan, John, ed. *G. K. Chesterton: A Centenary Appraisal*. London: Paul Elek, 1974.
Tallett, Frank, and Nicholas Atkin, eds. *Catholicism in Britain and France Since 1789*. London: Hambledon Press, 1996.
Teachout, Terry. "Coming to Terms with Chesterton." *American Scholar* 58 (Winter 1989): 105–12.
Thineau-Dangin, Paul. *The English Catholic Revival in the Nineteenth Century*. 2 vols. London: Simpkin, Marshall, Hamilton, Kent, & Co., 1914.
Thornton, Francis B. *Return to Tradition: A Directive Anthology*. Milwaukee: Bruce Publishing Co., 1948.
Tonsor, Stephen J. "The Use and Abuse of Myth." *Intercollegiate Review* 15 (Spring 1980): 67–70.
Towers, Robert. "An Amiable Graham Greene." *New York Times Book Review* (19 September 1982): 1, 32.
Updike, John. "The Man Within." *The New Yorker* 71 (26 June and 3 July 1995): 182–87.
Veldman, Meredith. *Fantasy, the Bomb and the Greening of Britain: Romantic Protest 1945–1980*. Cambridge: Cambridge University Press, 1994.
Voegelin, Eric. *The New Science of Politics*. Chicago: University of Chicago Press, 1952.
Wade, Mason. "A Catholic Spengler." *The Commonweal* 22 (18 October 1935): 605–7.
Wald, Richard. "'I Don't Think I'm Modern.'" *New York Herald Tribune* (8 July 1962): 3, 11.
Walsh, Michael. "Ecumenism in War-Time Britain: The Sword of the Spirit and Religion and Life." Parts 1 and 2. *Heythrop Journal* 33 (July 1982): 243–58; (October 1982): 377–94.
———. *From Sword to Ploughshare: Sword of the Spirit to Catholic Institute for International Relations, 1940–1980*. London: Catholic Institute for International Relations, 1980.
Ward, Elizabeth. *David Jones: Mythmaker*. Manchester: University of Manchester Press, 1983.
Ward, Maisie. *Gilbert Keith Chesterton*. New York: Sheed & Ward, 1943.
———. *Unfinished Business*. London: Sheed & Ward, 1964.
Wassmer, Thomas. "Faith and Belief: A Footnote to Greene's 'Visit to Morin.'" *Renascence* 10 (Winter 1959): 84–88.
Watkin, E. I. "Christopher Dawson." *The Commonweal* 18 (27 October 1933): 607–9.
———. *Roman Catholicism in England from the Reformation to 1950*. Oxford: Oxford University Press, 1957.
———. "Tribute to Christopher Dawson." *The Tablet* (4 October 1969): 974.
Waugh, Evelyn. *The Diaries of Evelyn Waugh*. Ed. Michael Davie. Boston: Little, Brown & Co. 1978.
———. *The Essays, Articles and Reviews of Evelyn Waugh*. Ed. Donat Gallagher. Boston: Little, Brown & Co., 1984.

———. *The Letters of Evelyn Waugh*. Ed. Mark Amory. New Haven, Conn.: Ticknor & Fields, 1980.

———. *Monsignor Ronald Knox*. Boston: Little, Brown & Co., 1959.

Wells, Ronald. "Whatever Happened to Religion in Britain?" *Books & Culture* 4 (January–February 1998): 31–33.

Wendorf, Thomas. "Allegory in Postmodernity: Graham Greene's *The Captain and the Enemy*." *Christianity & Literature* 50 (Summer 2001): 657–77.

Wethersfield Institute, ed. *Christianity and Western Civilization*. San Francisco: Ignatius Press, 1995.

White, George Abbott, and Charles Newman, eds. *Literature in Revolution*. New York: Holt, Rinehart & Winston, 1972.

White, Hayden. "Religion, Culture, and Western Civilization in Christopher Dawson's Idea of History." *English Miscellany* 9 (1958): 247–87.

———. *Tropics of Discourse: Essays in Cultural Criticism*. Baltimore: Johns Hopkins University Press, 1978.

Whitehouse, J. C. "Grammars of Assent and Dissent in Graham Greene and Brian Moore." *Renascence* 41 (Spring 1990): 157–71.

———. *Vertical Man*. London: Saint Austin Press, 1999.

Wicker, Brian. *The Story-Shaped World*. Notre Dame, Ind.: University of Notre Dame Press, 1975.

Wiener, Martin. *English Culture and the Decline of the Industrial Spirit 1850–1980*. Cambridge: Cambridge University Press, 1981.

Wilcockson, Colin. "David Jones and 'The Break.'" *Agenda* 15, nos. 2–3 (1977): 126–31.

Williams, Charles. *Outlines of Romantic Theology*. Ed. Alice Mary Hadfield. Grand Rapids, Mich.: William B. Eerdmans Publishing Co., 1990.

Wills, Garry. "Catholic Faith and Fiction." *New York Times Book Review* (16 January 1972): 1–2, 14, 16, 20.

———. "A Chesterton for the Religious Right?" *Christian Century* 107 (16–23 May 1990): 532–33.

———. *Chesterton: Man and Mask*. New York: Sheed & Ward, 1961.

Wilson, A. N. *C. S. Lewis: A Biography*. New York: Fawcett Columbine, 1990.

Wolfe, Gregory. *Malcolm Muggeridge: A Biography*. London: Hodder & Stoughton, 1995.

Wolffe, John. *God and Greater Britain: Religion and National Life in Britain and Ireland, 1843–1945*. London: Routledge, 1994.

Wood, Michael. "Spies Together." *Saturday Review* (1 April 1978): 33–34.

Wood, Ralph. "An Instinct for Orthodoxy and an Appetite for Truth." *Books & Religion* 13 (November–December 1985): 6, 11.

Woodman, Thomas. *Faithful Fictions: The Catholic Novel in British Literature*. Philadelphia: Open University Press, 1991.

Woodruff, Douglas. "Obituary: Christopher Dawson." *The Tablet* (6 June 1970): 558–59.

Young, R. V. "Chesterton's Paradoxes and Thomist Ontology." *Renascence* 49 (Fall 1996): 67–77.

Special Collections

G. K. Chesterton Archives. Manuscripts Department, The British Library. London.
G. K. Chesterton Collection. John J. Burns Library. Boston College. Chestnut Hill, Mass.
G. K. Chesterton Correspondence and Prose Collection. G. K. Chesterton Study Center. Plater College. Oxford.
G. K. Chesterton Press Clippings and Archive and Biographical Archive, G-15, Reel 9—"From 'Buchman' to 'Clauberg.'" The Wiener Library. London.
Christopher Dawson Correspondence. University of St. Thomas. St. Paul, Minn.
Christopher Dawson-John J. Mulloy Correspondence. University of St. Thomas. St. Paul, Minn.
Christopher Dawson Manuscripts. University of St. Thomas. St. Paul, Minn.
Christopher Dawson Personal Library. University of St. Thomas. St. Paul, Minn.
Graham Greene Collection: Miscellaneous Correspondence. Georgetown University. Washington, D.C.
Graham Greene-Sir James Marjoribanks Collection. Georgetown University. Washington, D.C.
Graham Greene Papers. John J. Burns Library. Boston College. Chestnut Hill, Mass.
Graham Greene Personal Library. John J. Burns Library. Boston College. Chestnut Hill, Mass.
Harman Grisewood Papers. Georgetown University. Washington, D.C.
David Jones Collection. John J. Burns Library. Boston College. Chestnut Hill, Mass.
David Jones Collection. Department of Printed Books. The National Library of Wales. Aberystwyth.
David Jones 1985 Purchase Groups A, B, and C. Department of Manuscripts and Records. The National Library of Wales. Aberystwyth.
Alan Redway Papers. Georgetown University. Washington, D.C.
Marion E. Wade Collection and Oral History Project. Wheaton College. Wheaton, Ill.

Journals and Newsletters

The Chesterton Review. Ed. Ian Boyd. Published quarterly by the G. K. Chesterton Society, South Orange, N.J.
The Dawson Newsletter. Ed. John J. Mulloy. Published quarterly by the Wanderer Forum Foundation, Marshfield, Wis. Publication suspended in 1996.
Gilbert!: The Magazine of G. K. Chesterton. Ed. Sean Dailey. Published nine times annually by the Chesterton Institute, South Orange, N.J.
Midwest Chesterton News. Ed. John Peterson. Published monthly by the Midwest Chesterton Society, Barrington, Ill. (1988–97).

INDEX

Anglicanism, 19, 20–21, 25, 27, 28, 57, 59, 69, 71–73, 74, 75, 76n. 145, 77, 79–82, 83, 89, 91, 104, 108, 116, 142, 143, 147–48, 149, 152–53, 155, 155n. 181, 181, 200, 205, 208–9, 216–19, 220, 223, 229, 270, 272, 278, 283, 284, 291, 292, 296, 311, 316n. 128, 316–17, 318–19, 373, 379n. 7

Anglo-Catholicism, 1, 22, 32, 56, 57, 69, 71–72, 76n. 145, 77, 79–80, 81–82, 86–87, 89n. 192, 108, 139, 206, 208, 210, 212, 213, 214, 216–19, 220, 223, 226, 227, 228, 231, 232, 233, 237, 240, 243, 265, 266, 277, 282, 283, 290–91, 316

Arendt, Hannah, 11, 20, 22, 200
Auden, W. H., 14, 27, 202, 287, 353
Augustine of Hippo, Saint, 105, 106, 164, 179, 213, 222, 233, 238, 244–47, 248, 330, 339, 377

authority, 20–23, 65, 65n. 112, 68, 72, 207, 318–19, 380n. 10, 382; absent from secularism, Protestantism, and Anglo-Catholicism, 3, 16, 21, 76n. 145, 80, 86, 108, 147–49, 210, 217, 223, 232, 282, 284, 314–16; appeal of in Roman Catholicism, 3, 20–22, 71n. 129, 75, 76n. 145, 82–84, 102, 108, 147–49, 182n. 72, 185, 214, 215, 223–25, 226, 228, 232, 244, 284, 289, 314–16, 319, 373, 376–77; present in some secularist ideologies, 21–22, 148

Baring, Maurice, 70, 78, 79, 80, 82, 86n. 183, 89n. 192, 89–90, 91
Barth, Karl, 237, 240, 266
Bell, Clive, 306
Belloc, Hilaire, 70, 76, 89n. 193, 250, 263, 270, 381
Berkhamsted School, 112, 116–17, 118–32, 133, 134, 140, 141, 142, 143–44, 145, 152, 153, 154, 155n. 181, 162, 185, 199, 200–201
Bilton Grange (preparatory school), 208, 212
Bloomsbury Group, 150, 202, 367
Browning, Robert, 40–41, 113, 189

Camberwell Art School, 292
Camus, Albert, 23–24, 51, 131–32, 186n. 295
Carter, Lionel, 122–25, 122n. 54, 126n. 70, 127, 128, 132, 133, 144, 154, 161
Chesterton, Cecil, 32, 70, 75, 76, 77
Chesterton, Edward, 32, 64, 65, 77, 90
Chesterton, Frances (née Blogg), 56–57, 69–70, 75–76, 77, 79, 82, 89–91, 108–9, 139
Chesterton, G. K., 9, 13, 24, 28, 29, 30–109, 111n. 3, 112, 114, 120, 124, 127, 128, 129, 130n. 87, 135, 139, 141, 142, 144, 145, 147, 148, 151, 153, 157n. 186, 171, 179, 188–89, 198–99, 200, 201, 202, 204, 205, 207, 210, 212, 213, 216, 217, 219, 220, 224, 227, 229, 230, 234n. 116, 238, 239, 240, 241, 246, 246n. 169, 250, 251, 252, 261n. 239, 264,

411

Chesterton, G. K. (continued)
280, 281, 283, 289, 290, 292, 297, 298, 302–3, 312, 315, 316, 317, 318, 324, 325n. 162, 330, 334, 337, 338, 352, 355n. 287, 359, 360, 367, 369, 370, 372, 375, 376, 378, 381, 382, 383, 384; as "Catholic writer," 92–93; adolescent crisis of, 34–45; conversion to Roman Catholicism of, 89–92; courtship and marriage of, 56–58; debt to Newman of, 106–7; early attraction to Catholicism of, 69–75; *The Everlasting Man*, 94–100; family background of, 32–34; gratitude theme in, 32, 41–43, 44, 45, 49, 54, 55–56, 60, 65–66, 69, 85, 88, 101, 105, 106, 108; influence of Roman Catholicism on work of, 92–106; influence on Dawson of, 13, 213, 250; influence on Greene of, 13, 96n. 215, 97, 99n. 223, 108, 110–11, 199, 199n. 345; influence on Jones of, 13, 63n. 105, 303, 306; *The Man Who Was Thursday*, 46–55, 60, 68, 72, 73; *Orthodoxy*, 31, 59–69, 71, 72, 73, 78, 83, 86, 88, 94, 98, 99, 100, 102, 103, 107, 199n. 345, 303, 306; reaction to 1920 Lambeth conference of, 79–82; sanity theme in, 31, 32, 34–45, 47, 48–49, 49–50, 51n. 70, 54, 55, 59, 60, 61–62, 63, 69, 72, 73, 80, 84–85, 86–87, 88–89, 92, 102, 104, 104n. 244, 106, 108, 120; severe illness of (1914–15), 75–77; *St. Thomas Aquinas*, 101–6; theology of history of, 94–100; trip to Holy Land and Italy of (1919–20), 78–79

Chesterton, Marie, 32, 90, 91
Church of England. *See* Anglicanism
confession. *See* sacrament of penance
Copelston, Frederick, 2, 15

D'Arcy, Martin, 332n. 192, 344
Dawson, Christopher, 9, 13, 14, 27, 28, 29, 78, 92, 105, 145, 149n. 155, 193, 202–85, 287, 289, 290, 292, 293, 296, 312, 315, 316, 318, 319, 324, 330, 334, 335, 337, 352, 361, 363, 365, 366, 367, 370, 372, 375, 376, 378, 380, 381, 383; adolescent loss of faith of, 209–12; baroque in, 214, 217, 228, 237, 254, 262, 276; clashes with conservative Roman Catholics of, 272–73, 274, 276; conversion to Roman Catholicism of, 222, 228–29; courtship and marriage of, 219–21; critical reception of work of, 202–4, 258–59, 268–69; cultural studies by, 259–69; debt to Chesterton of, 13, 108, 213, 250; debt to Newman of, 215–19, 222, 228, 230n. 96, 282; dislike of liturgical changes of, 276–80; dislike of Roman Catholic parochialism of, 271–72, 273, 274, 284; dislike of schools of, 207–9, 212; family background of, 205–7, 229; historiography by, 247–59; idea of Christian culture in, 265–68; influence of Roman Catholicism on work of, 230–33; influence on Jones of, 231n. 100, 232nn. 102, 107, 241n. 148, 246nn. 172, 173, 247n. 178, 263n. 250, 269n. 286, 286–87, 312n. 115, 325, 330, 332nn. 192, 193, 370; relation between religion and culture in, 262–65, 269, 284; theology of history of, 233–44; trip to Rome of (1909), 213–16

Dawson, Henry, 206, 207, 209, 216, 220, 229, 230, 259, 283
Dawson, Mary (née Bevan), 205–6, 220, 229
Dawson, Valery (née Mills), 219–21, 229–30
Dawson, William, 208–9, 216, 220
De la Taille, Maurice, 300, 343–47
dualism, 15, 245n. 163; Chesterton and, 104–6, 360; Dawson and, 239, 246; Greene and, 134, 143, 162, 170, 191, 191n. 312; Jones and, 104–5, 324–31, 337, 358–59, 360, 373
Dublin Review, The, 273–74
ecumenism, 149n. 155, 205, 269–77, 284, 361

Index 413

Eliot, T. S., 1, 2, 6, 10n. 18, 14, 22–23, 27, 52, 111, 261–62, 287, 335n. 207, 338, 348, 349, 353, 354, 368, 383; debt to Chesterton of, 383; debt to Dawson of, 202, 260, 268, 275; influence on Greene of, 164–65, 168, 185n. 290; influence on Jones of, 287n. 5; praise for Jones of, 287

Forster, E. M., 150
Fry, Roger, 299, 306

Gill, Eric, 2, 14n. 34, 303–4, 306, 314, 316–17, 318, 320, 321, 324, 328, 331, 344, 362, 368, 369, 373, 376
Gnosticism. *See* dualism
Graves, Robert, 292, 293, 294n. 35, 319, 343
Greene, Charles, 115–16, 117, 118, 119–20, 121, 122, 124–25, 126n. 70, 132, 133, 142, 153, 155–56, 200
Greene, Graham, 9, 12n. 28, 13, 14, 24, 27, 28, 29, 36, 55, 67, 73, 78, 92, 92n. 199, 100, 110–201, 202, 204, 205, 207, 208, 209, 210, 211, 212, 214, 219, 229, 230, 231n. 96, 239, 240, 276, 277, 278, 279, 281, 283, 289, 290, 292, 293, 300n. 59, 315, 317, 318, 323, 330, 332, 333, 334, 336, 338n. 216, 339, 340, 342, 346, 361, 363, 364, 365, 366, 367, 368, 370, 371, 372, 375, 376, 378, 380, 381, 383, 384; adolescent breakdown at Berkhamsted School of, 119–25, 132; affair with Catherine Walston of, 138–39, 181–82; as "Catholic writer," 150–52; betrayal theme in, 123–24, 123n. 59, 154–55; *Brighton Rock*, 160–69, 175; conversion to Roman Catholicism of, 139–49; courtship and marriage of, 135–38, 139; criticism of Catholic officialdom of, 148–49, 175–76, 192–99; debt to Chesterton of, 13, 96n. 215, 97, 99n. 223, 108, 110–11, 199, 199n. 345; debt to Newman of, 145, 148n. 152, 153, 184n. 282, 187n. 298, 188n. 303, 199, 230n. 96; dislike of liturgical changes of, 192–96; disloyalty theme in, 130–31, 157, 158; distinction between "belief" and "faith" of, 176–83; distinction between Good and Evil and Right and Wrong of, 164–69, 170–71; distinction between pity and compassion of, 172–75; doubt theme in, 133, 145, 185–89; *The End of the Affair*, 136–37, 140n. 120, 141, 144, 156, 157, 176–78, 180, 182, 184nn. 280, 283; family background of, 115–18; *The Heart of the Matter*, 173–76; influence of Roman Catholicism on work of, 149–63, 165–72, 173–76; literature as purgative in, 113–15; *Monsignor Quixote*, 73, 176, 178, 184, 186–89, 194–95, 198; persistent Roman Catholicism of, 196–200; *The Power and the Glory*, 169–72; praise for Jones of, 287; self-excommunication of, 181–83, 197, 199, 201; sympathy for victims of, 131–32, 158–60, 172–75; theology of history of, 188–89
Greene, Marion, 115–16, 118, 124–25, 126n. 70, 132, 133, 142, 153, 155–56, 181, 200
Greene, Vivien (née Dayrell-Browning), 135–39, 140, 141, 143, 148, 160, 200, 221

Harnack, Adolf von, 225–26
Heaney, Seamus, 288, 372
Hell, 5, 36, 43n. 45, 51, 53n. 76, 118, 120–21, 122, 142, 143–44, 147, 152, 161–63, 166, 167, 176, 183–85, 193, 201

impressionism, 9, 34, 37, 38–39, 40, 40n. 28, 49, 50, 127
Inge, Dean, 104, 203
Italianate style of Roman Catholicism, 19–21, 27–28, 29, 70, 83, 215–16, 224, 376–77, 380, 380n. 10

James, William, 7, 78n. 152, 199n. 346, 319

Jerrold, Douglas, 126, 274
John XXIII, pope, 193, 194, 380, 381
John Paul II, pope, 382
Johnson, Paul, 13–14, 198, 382
Jones, Alice (née Bradshaw), 290–92, 316
Jones, David, 9, 12n. 28, 13, 14, 24, 27, 28, 29, 78, 92, 96, 104, 136, 145, 149n. 155, 193, 195, 204n. 2, 229, 250, 276, 277, 278, 283, 286–374, 375, 376, 378, 380, 381, 383, 384; as "Catholic writer," 366–67; conversion to Roman Catholicism of, 316–18; debt to Chesterton of, 13, 63n. 105, 108, 303, 306; debt to Dawson of, 23n. 100, 232nn. 102, 107, 241n. 148, 246nn. 172, 173, 247n. 178, 263n. 250, 269n. 286, 286–87, 312n. 115, 325, 330, 332nn. 192, 193, 370; dislike of liturgical changes of, 361–66; distinction between gratuity and utility of, 304–16; family background of, 290–92, 318–19; Great War service of, 292–96, 309, 310, 317–18, 319–20, 323n. 155, 326–27, 329, 331, 340–43, 347, 352–53; importance of Christ's Passion and Crucifixion to, 290, 335–37, 338, 339n. 218, 340–47, 348, 362, 372, 373; importance of Mass to, 290, 292, 294–95, 299–302, 307–8, 317–18, 321, 333, 343–48, 349, 352, 359, 361–66, 373; link between art and sacrament in, 292, 296–302; lives at Ditchling, 320, 331; myth in, 354–61; praised by Greene, 287; theology of history of, 331–47.
Jones, James, 291, 296, 305, 317n. 130, 318–19, 339

Knox, Ronald, 2, 14, 28, 30–31, 42, 61, 77, 80, 89–91, 93n. 204, 108, 196, 216, 217, 220, 279, 302

Last Romantics, 5, 351, 352
Lewis, C. S., 27, 52n. 74, 114, 169n. 225, 187, 237, 268, 270, 311, 356, 359

liberal Christianity, 6, 17, 18n. 44, 32, 33, 42, 70, 81–82, 112, 115–16, 127, 128, 133, 142–43, 155, 156, 167, 168, 169, 200, 208, 210, 216–18, 220, 223, 225, 233, 283
liberalism, 3, 4, 8, 22, 33, 39, 81–82, 107, 115, 118, 127, 128, 156, 165, 167, 169, 188, 195, 199–200, 216–18, 226–27, 228, 231, 231n. 96, 232, 233, 237, 261, 264, 266, 282–83, 375, 384
Lodge, David, 100, 190n. 309, 380n. 9, 381–82

Manicheanism. *See* dualism
Marcionism. *See* dualism
Maritain, Jacques, 302–3, 306, 320–23, 324, 327, 332n. 192, 346, 357–58, 370n. 355
McNabb, Vincent, 76, 344
Modernism: literary, 9, 103–4, 150, 161, 165, 201, 290, 367–69, 371, 374, 377; theological, 9, 33, 69, 71, 72, 79–82, 103–4, 105, 143, 168, 216, 217, 218, 228, 232, 266, 377
Moore, George, 38–39
Muggeridge, Malcolm, 2, 15
mysticism, 9, 42, 59, 62, 76, 102, 103, 170, 177, 179, 180–81, 187–88, 206, 209, 211, 211n. 26, 213, 214, 221, 228, 231, 245, 256, 276, 330, 332, 356, 377

Newman, John Henry, 2, 3–4, 6, 8, 13, 25, 66, 79, 108, 112, 177, 179, 199–200, 222n. 68, 225, 229, 248, 280, 293, 316, 372, 384; influence on Chesterton of, 106–7; influence on Dawson of, 215–19, 222, 228, 230n. 96, 282; influence on Greene of, 145, 148n. 152, 153, 184n. 282, 187n. 298, 188n. 303, 199, 230n. 96
Niebuhr, Reinhold, 259, 267, 268
Noel, Conrad, 57, 70

O'Connor, John, 70, 74, 75, 77n. 145, 89n. 192, 90–91, 302–3, 316–17, 318, 362, 373

Index 415

Order Group, 250, 270, 323n. 154, 331, 332n. 192, 343, 344
original sin, 22–23, 39, 66–68, 69, 105, 127, 142, 153–55, 156, 162–63, 171–72, 183, 184, 185, 193, 199–200, 201, 230–31, 233, 255, 333–34, 338
Orwell, George, 5–6, 11, 21, 93n. 204, 168–69, 282
Owen, Wilfrid, 342–43
Oxford Movement, 13, 71–72, 81–82, 200, 206, 209, 215n. 46, 216–19, 222, 226n. 81, 228, 250, 269–70, 282, 372
Oxford, University of, 9, 34, 134, 135, 143, 191, 210, 211, 212–13, 215, 216, 217, 219, 221, 222, 292

Patmore, Coventry, 2, 136, 137n. 109
Paul VI, pope, 193
Philby, Kim, 186
Pius X, pope, 8, 83n. 166, 213, 220
"post-Christian" thesis, 16–19, 143n. 136, 378, 382–83
postimpressionism, 292, 296, 298–99, 303, 305–6, 368, 373
Progressivism, 3, 4–5, 9, 22–23, 31, 33, 34, 35, 36, 59, 95, 96, 108, 116, 190–92, 230–31, 232–33, 233, 255, 264, 284, 337–40, 373, 375
prophet trope, 17–18, 25–26, 27, 29, 376, 377; in Chesterton, 31, 32, 33, 43, 59–61, 83, 93, 108; in Dawson, 203n. 2, 205, 218–19, 227, 228, 232, 280–82, 284, 285; in Greene, 152, 170; in Jones, 290, 369–71, 374; in Newman, 3–4, 218–19

radical conservatism, 25, 68, 88, 284–85, 377
rebel trope, 3, 23–26, 27, 29; in Chesterton, 31, 32, 33, 41, 43, 48–49, 50, 51–52, 54, 57, 61n. 102, 67–68, 69, 75n. 141, 87, 88, 98, 102–3, 199, 383; in Dawson, 205, 206–7, 226–27, 234, 236, 237, 243, 249n. 184, 261–62, 280, 281–82, 284, 285; in Greene, 14, 111, 112, 130, 155–58, 167–68, 180–81, 189, 198–99; in Jones, 289, 290, 312–13, 353, 371; in Newman, 3, 107, 199, 218, 384
Russell, Bertrand, 1, 5, 156

sacrament of penance, 71n. 129, 84–85, 91, 94, 144, 147, 167, 181–82
Sassoon, Sigfried, 287–88, 292, 319, 343
Sayers, Dorothy L., 27, 297, 305n. 85, 311, 368
Scholasticism. See Thomism
Schumacher, E. F., 2, 15
Shaw, George Bernard, 1, 5, 58, 74n. 135, 165, 202
Sitwell, Edith, 2, 135
Slade School of Art, 32, 34–46, 47, 54, 55, 59, 69, 85, 106, 108, 127, 128, 292
solipsism: in Chesterton, 37, 39, 43, 43n. 48, 53, 62, 83, 90, 101, 144; in Dawson, 210
Spark, Muriel, 382
Spengler, Oswald, 261, 262
Spiritualism, 5, 9, 36–37, 48, 50, 65, 80, 81, 87, 104, 132, 133, 166
Stevenson, Robert Louis, 40–41, 41n. 33, 48
Sword of the Spirit, The, 272–74

Teilhard de Chardin, Pierre, 190–92, 339–40, 373, 377
Thomas Aquinas, Saint, 92, 100–106, 178, 179, 222, 246–47, 325
Thomism, 41, 100–106, 109, 145, 177, 178–79, 246–47, 252, 268, 289, 302–3, 320–31, 332, 369, 373, 377
Tolkien, J. R. R., 100, 297, 297n. 50, 359
Toynbee, Arnold, 14, 203, 203n. 2, 235, 239, 258, 260, 261, 275
Tractarians. See Oxford Movement
tradition, 25–26, 68, 193, 207, 235, 290, 348–54, 368, 369; appeal of in Roman Catholicism, 3, 22–23, 24, 25, 27, 78, 83, 86, 87–88, 103, 172, 193–96, 225–26, 228, 232, 275, 278–80, 282–83, 284, 352, 362–63; disregard for in secularism, Protestantism, and Anglo-Catholicism, 3, 22–23, 27, 48, 86, 172, 208, 216, 217,

tradition (*Continued*)
    225–26, 229, 232, 255, 282–83, 284, 327, 343, 350–51, 368–69, 376, 378
Troeltsch, Ernst, 262, 264

Vatican Council, First, 224
Vatican Council, Second, 27–28, 112, 149n. 155, 192–96, 276–80, 361–66, 380, 381, 382

Wall, Frank, 302, 303, 318
Walston, Catherine, 138–39, 181–82
Ward, Barbara, 202, 272, 274
Ward, Wilfrid, 70, 216
Watkin, E. I., 12n. 26, 209–10, 213, 218, 219, 220, 221, 229, 234, 268, 277n. 317, 278
Waugh, Evelyn, 2, 14, 71, 89n. 193, 113, 150–51, 179, 229, 287, 330n. 187, 376

Wells, H. G., 1, 5, 58, 95–96
Westminster School of Art, 296, 299, 301, 302
Wheeler, A. H., 122–25, 126n. 70, 127, 132, 133, 154
Whig interpretation of history, 233–34, 339. *See also* Progressivism
White, Hayden, 26, 236, 245n. 163, 246n. 169, 249, 269
Whitman, Walt, 40–41, 41n. 34, 57, 62, 107
Williams, Charles, 27, 136–38, 177n. 251, 318, 346
Winchester (public school), 208, 209, 212
Wiseman, Nicholas, 19
Woodruff, Douglas, 280
Woolf, Virginia, 1, 5, 150

The Third Spring: G. K. Chesterton, Graham Greene, Christopher Dawson, and David Jones was designed and composed in Dante with Footlight display typography by Kachergis Book Design, Pittsboro, North Carolina.

www.ingramcontent.com/pod-product-compliance
Lightning Source LLC
Chambersburg PA
CBHW032023290426
44110CB00012B/641